Hancock's War

D1563434

Winfield Scott Hancock, stern, punctilious, and insistent on strict adherence to his directives, led the Expedition for the Plains westward in search of the Cheyennes. His inflexibility, lack of understanding of the Plains Indians or their culture, and subsequent unfortunate actions would precipitate what became known as Hancock's War. *Courtesy of Fort Larned National Historic Site.*

Hancock's War

Conflict on
the Southern Plains

by
William Y. Chalfant
Foreword by Jerome A. Greene

Hancock's War
Conflict on the Southern Plains
By William Y. Chalfant
$26.95s Paper · 978-0-8061-4459-7 · 296 pages

This first thorough scholarly history of the ill-conceived expedition offers an unequivocal evaluation of military strategies and a culturally sensitive interpretation of Indian motivations and reactions. Chalfant explores the vastly different ways of life that separated the Cheyennes and U.S. policymakers, and argues that neither side was willing or able to understand the needs of the other. He shows how Hancock's efforts were counterproductive, brought untold misery to Indians and whites alike, and led to the wars of 1868.

Cpl Michael Frysinger
512 E Wayne St
Celina, OH 45822

UNIVERSITY OF OKLAHOMA PRESS
Norman

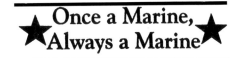

ALSO BY WILLIAM Y. CHALFANT

Cheyennes and Horse Soldiers: The 1857 Expedition and the Battle of Solomon's Fork
(Norman, 1989)
Without Quarter: The Wichita Expedition and the Fight on Crooked Creek
(Norman, 1991)
Dangerous Passage: The Santa Fe Trail and the Mexican War (Norman, 1994)
Cheyennes at Dark Water Creek: The Last Fight of the Red River War (Norman, 1997)

For

Martha

Library of Congress Cataloging-in-Publication Data
Chalfant, William Y. (William Young), 1928–
  Hancock's war : conflict on the southern plains / by William Y. Chalfant ; foreword
by Jerome A. Greene. — 1st ed.
    p. cm. — (Frontier military series ; 28)
  Includes bibliographical references and index.
  ISBN 978-0-87062-371-4 (cloth) — ISBN 978-0-8061-4459-7 (paper) 1. Indians of
North America—Wars—1866–1895. 2. Hancock, Winfield Scott, 1824–1886. 3. Indians
of North America—Wars—Kansas. 4. Cheyenne Indians—Wars—Kansas. 5. Chey-
enne Indians—History—19th century. 6. Indians of North America—Wars—Great
Plains. I. Title. II. Series.
  E83.866.C46 2009
  970.004'97—dc22

2008053610

The paper in this book meets the guidelines for permanence and durability
of the Committee on Production Guidelines for Book Longevity
of the Council on Library Resources, Inc. ∞

Copyright © 2010 by the University of Oklahoma Press, Norman,
Publishing Division of the University.
Paperback published 2014.
Manufactured in the U.S.A.

Contents

Maps and Illustrations

FOREWORD

Jerome A. Greene

In the summer of 1865, less than a year after the massacre by volunteer soldiers of a Cheyenne and Arapahoe village at Sand Creek in Colorado Territory, U.S. Indian agent Jesse Leavenworth wrote to Brig. Gen. John B. Sanborn about conditions on the plains frontier. The atrocity had so unnerved the tribesmen, wrote Leavenworth, that "an angel from Heaven would not convince them but what another 'Chivington Massacre' was intended." The tragedy had elicited an immediate consequence as retaliating Lakota, Cheyenne, and Arapahoe warriors swept the Platte River corridors, attacking settlements, killing newcomers, burning stage and telegraph stations, and closing emigrant roads and mail routes. For years to come, the specter of Sand Creek continued to alarm Native people, making interactions with whites, particularly those involving U.S. troops, tentative at best. The tribes of the plains remained angry, frightened, and uncertain in the wake of that carnage, and those feelings hardly ever subsided.

The federal government's reaction to the situation became known as Hancock's War—the subject of this book. With more bravado than reasoned purpose, a large army command under Maj. Gen. Winfield Scott Hancock took the field in the spring of 1867 intent on intimidating the tribes, mostly southern Cheyennes, Lakotas, southern Arapahoes, and Kiowas but others as well. With bullying tactics, Hancock outraged the Cheyennes and their allies by destroying their villages at Pawnee Fork, Kansas, an incident that set the tone for the balance of the campaign. Over several months, the tentacles of Hancock's columns spread across Kansas and into Nebraska and Colorado Territory, further inciting the Indians and inflaming passions on both sides. While the campaign provided entrée

into the West for Lt. Col. George A. Custer and his newly organized
Seventh Cavalry regiment, in the end Hancock's operations simply exacerbated existing tensions.

For its long-range impact on post–Civil War Indian relations, Hancock's ill-conceived and futile maneuver was without question one of the
most significant Indian campaigns in American history. In *Hancock's War*,
William Y. Chalfant offers the most comprehensive, well documented,
and accurate treatment of the so-called Expedition for the Plains to date.
Using techniques that have defined his other works about Indian-white
warfare on the plains, Chalfant employs Indian and non-Indian sources to
create a narrative reflecting multiple cultural perspectives. His treatment
is open-minded and just, thorough and wide-ranging, as he discusses
personalities and policies and analyzes issues of culture and belief, land
ownership, the environment, state and federal politics, and the sporadic
peace offensives and corrupt treaties that the government applied to the
tribes, all while formulating broad context and new conclusions about
Hancock's campaign. The inclusive operations of Custer—his various
pursuits of the Indians, his participation in events surrounding the controversial Kidder affair, and his well-known excesses culminating in his
court-martial, conviction, and suspension from the army—are chronicled
and evaluated. Significantly, Chalfant contends that Hancock's effort to
cow the tribes nurtured a continuum of warfare beyond the Medicine
Lodge councils and their fraudulent treaties that lasted through Custer's
Washita campaign well into 1869. It is a valid observation, one of many
to derive from this fine work that will stand as a literary cornerstone in
the history of the West.

Abbreviations

AAAG	Acting Assistant Adjutant General
AAG	Assistant Adjutant General
Aff'd.	Affidavit
AGO	Adjutant General's Office
Det.	Detached
HDQ	Headquarters
HQ	Headquarters
KHC	Kansas Historical Collections
KSHS	Kansas State Historical Society, Topeka
MNM	Museum of New Mexico
LC	Library of Congress
LR	Letters Received
LS	Letters Sent
NA	U.S. National Archives and Records Administration
OIA	Office of Indian Affairs
Rec.	Records

PROLOGUE

At 8:30 A.M. on Wednesday, March 27, 1867, a military expedition of approximately 1,300 men began their march west from Fort Riley, a post situated in the Flint Hills of east-central Kansas at the point where the Smoky Hill and Republican rivers join to form the Kansas River. The expedition consisted of four companies of the Seventh Cavalry, Battery B, Fourth U.S. Artillery; seven companies of the Thirty-seventh Infantry; a commissary train; a quartermaster train; and a train of pontoon bridges. Four additional companies of the Seventh Cavalry would join them en route. They were led by Maj. Gen. Winfield Scott Hancock, Union hero of Gettysburg, now commanding the Department of the Missouri. Their mission was to show the flag on the high plains of Kansas and to ensure peace by convincing the Cheyennes and their allies to refrain from molesting whites and to stay away from the great trails and advancing railroads—or, failing that, Hancock and his troops were to make war on the hostile tribes. The end result was not peace but a protracted conflict that became known in history as Hancock's War.

It was not a war like other wars. No grand armies faced one another across some intervening divide or no-man's-land. There were no positioning marches or countermarches, no spectacular charges, no booming artillery barrages, no desperate fusillades of small-arms fire, and no decisive attacks. It was a war in which there was no brilliant grand strategy, no masterful battlefield tactics, and no clearly defined objective. In the end it was counterproductive. In terms of casualties inflicted by and on either side—dead and wounded—it would register only marginally on any scale of measure. With few exceptions, as in most wars and battles, it was fought by the unknown and the forgotten. Today its memory survives only in various repositories of seldom used records maintained by succeeding generations of a largely unaware public and in a few articles, papers, and books.

Though many characteristics of war were absent, the misfortunes of war were not; they came in large doses to both sides. Aside from the continuing conflict that Hancock's expedition generated, misfortune was perhaps the only clear legacy of the entire campaign. Foremost was human misery, the one certain result of armed conflict and the one usually borne mainly by the innocent. Present also were other unfortunate characteristics of war—arrogance in the leadership, ignorance of the enemy, lack of understanding of the enemy culture, lack of compassion, blundering in planning and execution, self-serving decisions, and selfish motivations. And there was a gross want of concern for the misery, hardship, and death inflicted on the women, children, and old of a people who sought only to defend themselves, their homeland, and their way of life.

The protagonists in this war were the army of the United States on one hand and the southern bands of the Cheyenne Nation on the other. Unfortunately for the Cheyennes, they and their Arapahoe allies occupied that portion of the Great Plains lying between the Platte River on the north and the Arkansas on the south, or between the Oregon-California Trail and the Santa Fe Trail. It was territory coveted by the government for the location of transcontinental railroads already under construction, albeit without having first obtained any right-of-way or consent from the affected tribes. Moreover, the Cheyennes were the perfect symbol of what many whites, particularly western frontiersmen who wanted their lands, considered Native savagery, intransigence, and obstructionism against the inexorable march of Western civilization. Because of previous conflicts the tribe's name was familiar both on the western frontier and in the East. They were extraordinarily brave, incredible horsemen who were fierce and unyielding in battle, and, most important, unwilling to surrender their own country to the whites. So destiny chose them to become the subject of a harsh object lesson for all Plains Indians, a lesson to be delivered by military force.

The times were a factor as well. The Civil War had only recently ended, and now the eyes of an expanding white population were cast covetously on the undeveloped and, to their way of thinking, unclaimed lands of the West. That a different race of people lived there, observing a distinct and contrasting culture, was of little concern. The Native inhabitants were following a nomadic, hunting way of life, and though they claimed specific territories as their own, they had no system of individual land ownership as did Euro-Americans. This allowed whites to indulge in the pretext that Indians did not claim ownership of the land and merely roamed across it in search of game. Consequently these lands belonged to no one and, being subject to the sovereignty of the United States by dint of treaties with various European powers (who themselves had no legitimate claims) or by conquest, could be parceled out to white, "civilized," Christian settlers as a part of nation building. It was in truth a continuation of the great impulse of imperialism and expansionism that had begun in Europe some three centuries earlier: that which belonged to weaker, "uncivilized," non-Christian peoples could be appropriated to advance the interests and well-being of the more powerful, "civilized," Christian nation claiming it. It came with divine approval as "manifest destiny."

Despite the rationale of the American government and people, to the indigenous tribes their own country had defined boundaries, was provided for their exclusive use by the Creator, was held in community by their people, and was defended by war with encroaching peoples, be they Indian or European. As a gift from the Creator to his people, their land could neither be alienated nor sold. They had never knowingly granted sovereignty over their land and people to the United States or any other foreign power, and though the concept of "sovereignty" did not exist in their language or thought, it is clear they would never have submitted if they had understood.

Few white authorities had a realistic concept of tribal organization and government, choosing to treat with tribes as if they were organized and governed in the European tradition. But they were not. Whatever the impact on their societies of direct and indirect contact with whites (and they were many), nearly all Plains Indians maintained a pervasive individualism in how they dealt with one another, with neighboring tribes, and with the advancing white culture. There was commonly a strong tribal leadership, which was by the example of those who were the wisest, most capable, and most forceful personalities. Tribal members were free to follow or to disassociate themselves as they chose. There were strong moral, ethical, and spiritual beliefs, and for these conformity was enforced by shunning or banishment from tribal society—powerful tools indeed. The people lived what they saw as a sacred way of life, established by the Creator and ordered by the seasons and the land they inhabited. Dependent as they were on horses and the game on which they subsisted, they were mobile during the season of growth, which was when they raided, made war, hunted bison and other game, and held their great tribal ceremonies. During the season when the grasses were dormant and grazing was poor, they broke into small groups, usually based on family or kindred, and sought sheltered winter camps in areas where at least some small game might be had to supplement the jerked bison meat and pemmican they put aside from their summer and fall hunts.

With tradition and spiritual beliefs governing their life, leadership requirements were relatively simple. Civil leadership dealt with such things as determining when to move a village, selecting new village sites, deciding when and where to hunt, judging violations of tribal law and meting out punishment, overseeing relations with other Indian tribes or peoples, and making war. Once a war was decreed or thrust upon them, leadership in battle was generally in the hands of the military societies and their chiefs, although where, when, and even whether a warrior fought was a matter of individual choice. Rarely were there disciplined combat units such as whites used, and warriors normally attached themselves to or fought in the company of another prominent warrior they admired. Combat was individual and to a degree ritualistic, with each warrior's skill and success in battle measured more by the daring and bravery he exhibited (as in the counting of coup) than by the number of the enemy he killed. Predictably, when whites invaded their homeland, this form of warfare worked to the disadvantage of the Indians.

The entry of whites onto the Great Plains and into Cheyenne country was a gradual process. Aside from early parties of Spanish, English, French, or American explorers, it began with the desire for trade with New Mexico and Chihuahua, which resulted in establishment of the Santa Fe Trail in 1821. The route followed by early traders was surveyed in 1825, becoming the first great national highway and an international road of commerce. Later it was followed by the Oregon-California Trail to the north—the famed immigration route across the North American continent. At that time the plains were viewed as a desert, an obstacle to be overcome in the movement of people, animals, and goods. Only later would they be considered a place where white people might settle and practice agriculture.

As white Americans grew more familiar with western parts of the continent and as demand for furs grew, trappers, hunters, and traders began to pursue their occupations in the Rocky Mountains and on the plains. Eventually the admission of Texas into the Union, the acquisition of the northern Mexican provinces following the Mexican War, the gaining of Oregon Territory from Britain, and the discovery of gold in California and then in the Rocky Mountains resulted in a stampede of whites to the gold fields. This in turn caused the rapid peopling of the west coast and a demand for faster, safer, more economical means of transportation to bind the two coasts together. That brought the railroads, the end of the concept of a permanent Indian Territory fostered by Thomas Jefferson, and the settlement of the inland West.

The presence of whites in their country naturally angered the Native inhabitants. With total disregard for the needs of the Indians, whites slaughtered the game along the trails (often for the sport of killing alone), cut down the sparse stands of timber the tribes used as village sites, fouled and polluted the rivers and streams, and shot at even friendly Indians who approached them. Bison and other game animals were driven from the great rivers the trails followed and their numbers depleted, making hunting difficult for the Natives and causing hunger and hardship in their camps. In response Indians made war on whites, desperately trying to keep them out of their tribal domain in order to preserve their own way of life. As they did, attacks on wagon trains revealed that they carried many things useful to a people with few material possessions. Soon attacks on white travelers developed a dual purpose—to repel or expel them from Indian country and to acquire livestock and material goods.

The warfare that flared along the great trails sparked demands from many whites for protection from and removal of the Indians. In that day reports of hostilities with Native tribes were seldom characterized as "war" in the conventional sense. Instead Indian attacks were described in terms of murder, rape, and pillage committed by "savages" against innocent travelers or settlers—honest folk toiling to create homes and futures for themselves on lands given to them by a benevolent government. But the Native peoples had a totally different perspective. To them it was an invasion. Outsiders were entering their lands, slaughtering their game, destroying their grass and timber, bringing terrible diseases for which they had no natural immunity, and visiting upon them many other misfortunes. To the Indians the whites were seen as people who lied, cheated, and stole from them. And now it was their lands that the whites wanted. So the Indians did what courageous people have always done—they fought the invaders in the only way they knew, with whatever means they could find. And whites called it murder. The solution, the intruders said, should be removal or extermination of the tribes.

Despite these calls for drastic measures, as the flood of settlers moved westward across the continent, they faced a serious moral and legal dilemma. Though they believed they had the authority of the biblical command to "be fruitful, multiply, and replenish the earth, and subdue it," there was still the troublesome matter of the legality and morality of what they did to the original inhabitants. The United States claimed to be a nation of laws—laws providing equal protection to all people within its boundaries, not just whites. Both the colonial powers and the United States, as their successor in claiming sovereignty, had repeatedly acknowledged Indian title to the lands they occupied. Therefore it was necessary to extinguish that title, and the means of doing so was by treaty. Fortunately for the government, Chief Justice John Marshall had defined Indian tribes as "domestic dependent nations," which permitted treaties between the dominant nation and the dependent nations.

There followed a spate of treaties in which Native peoples who could neither read, write, speak, nor understand the English language were requested, cajoled, "slickered," forced, or induced by fraud to sign treaties with the United States. These written documents contained the highly sophisticated and imprecise phraseology of diplomacy that no Indian of the time could possibly comprehend. So by "touching the pen" and marking an "X," they surrendered all rights to their tribal homelands, though rarely did they have any realization of what that meant. As "compensation" for giving up their country, they were awarded a reservation, often in a remote place. Commonly the land set aside for the reservation was considered worthless by whites and thus suitable for the Indians. As additional compensation these treaties granted the tribes annuities of food and trade goods for a specified period. At the end of that time it was intended that they would have learned to live as white men. In terms of equivalency the value of what they received, if they ever received it, did not approach the value of what they had surrendered. And though these treaties salved the conscience of many government officials and white citizens, they were not voluntary bargains between equals but simply a taking by force, coercion, and fraud.

Seldom did white authorities make an effort to determine if those "signing" a treaty possessed authority under tribal law and custom to do so or to surrender their tribal country or even if they were in fact "chiefs." Nor did the authorities ensure that the signing parties or their fellow tribesmen understood the meaning of the document or what they were giving up. In fairness the meanings of words or intellectual concepts were elusive in translation, and there were few competent interpreters in the frontier West. Too often, to the Indians, the touching of the pen was thought to be only a method of obtaining peace with the whites, freeing them from harassment and incursions into their country by the white military and settlers. The receiving of gifts from the Great White Father in Washington was the means of confirming that peace and was within the tradition of Plains Indians for sealing a bargain. To them the annuities were just that, not payment for their homelands. Surrender of their country was almost never intended, and rarely was that facet of a treaty clearly explained or understood.

The story that follows is set near the end of the conflict with the Cheyennes of the southern plains. With the end of the Civil War came abhorrence of further bloodshed and of maintaining a large standing army. This forced the government to try its own variation of the carrot-and-stick approach. Treaties were to be attempted, whereby in exchange for peace the Indians would surrender their own country and remove to a secure home on a reservation. There they would be trained in the fruitful pursuits of a sedentary agricultural life, free from the bedevilment of greedy white men. They would receive the blessings of enlightenment through the teaching of the Christian religion and suppression of their own "heathen" beliefs, raising them from the depths of "savagery." The alternative to this form of peace, of course, was total war and extermination.

Not surprisingly, most of the Plains tribes, including the Cheyennes, had no interest in leaving their country and living as white men, or even in becoming Christians. They wanted to be left alone in their own land to pursue the sacred life they believed God had ordained for them. And they wanted the whites out. It was into this circumstance that Maj. Gen. Winfield Scott Hancock was to lead his troops in March 1867.

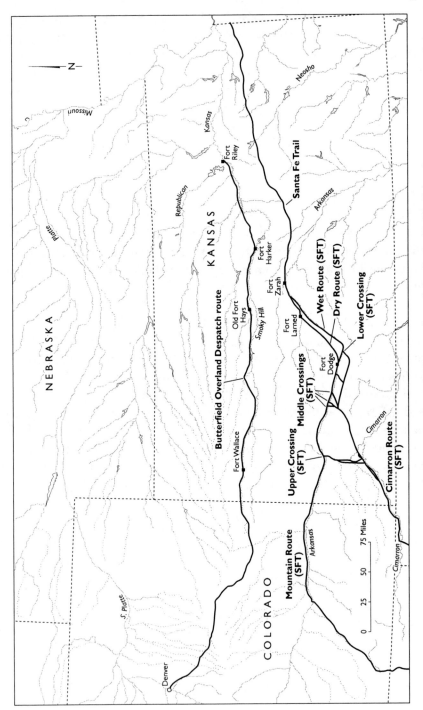

Routes of the Butterfield Overland Despatch and the Santa Fe Trail (SFT) through Kansas during March–August 1867. *Map by Bill Nelson.*

CHAPTER ONE

An Ill Wind Blows

The Cheyennes, or, as they called themselves, the Tsistsistas, meaning "the People," were in their free period an archetypical tribe of Plains Indians—honest and unpretentious, devoutly religious, family oriented, renowned as horsemen, hunters, and warriors, and fiercely protective of their own country. They were never governed by one preeminent leader as were the European and American whites but rather were led by a council of civil leaders the whites called "chiefs." About eight and a half of the ten principal bands of Cheyennes lived on the southern plains during the conflict with whites. The remainder, including the largest single band, the Óhméseheso (Eaters), lived on the northern plains, where they occupied a common country with their great friends and allies, the northern bands of Arapahoes and Lakotas. On the southern plains the Cheyennes shared lands between the Platte and Arkansas rivers with their fellow Algonquian relatives, the southern bands of Arapahoes, and were friends and allies of the Kiowas and Comanches, who occupied the area south of the Arkansas River. Though living apart, prior to the reservation era the various bands of Cheyennes never thought of themselves as other than one tribe, and their leadership reflected this.[1]

At the apex of Cheyenne civil authority or leadership was the Council of Forty-four, a body composed of four civil chiefs from each of the ten principal bands, plus four "old man chiefs," who were among the wisest and most experienced of the tribal elders. Presiding at the meetings of the council was the one designated as the Sweet Medicine chief, the most honored leader in the tribe and the titular successor to the legendary Sweet Medicine. Sweet Medicine was the spirit man who in the dim recesses of time taught the Cheyennes their sacred way of life and gave them the

---

[1] Berthrong, *Southern Cheyennes*, 3–4, 20–26; Grinnell, *Cheyenne Indians*, 1:1, 39–46, 88–101; Grinnell, *Fighting Cheyennes*, 3; Hoebel, *Cheyennes*, 1, 31–32; Powell, *People of the Sacred Mountain*, 1:xvii; Powell, *Sweet Medicine*, 1:18–22, 175.

sacred Medicine Arrows, provided for him by Mother Earth, to protect them from evil and adversity.[2]

The Council of Forty-four normally met only during those times of the year when the entire tribe came together for sacred ceremonies such as the annual Sun Dance, and for communal bison hunts and socializing. During the rest of the year the bands lived and hunted separately, unless kept together by the demands of war, and in the winter they were further broken down into small, far-flung encampments or villages within their own country. But they usually knew, generally if not specifically, where the other camps were in the event of need. During these periods of separation the four chiefs of each band exercised their authority over it by consensus. Most tribal members chose to follow the decisions of their leaders, but that was always a matter of individual choice, a trait that frequently frustrated white authorities. The American government, for its own purposes, wanted and needed a strong leader whose word could bind his whole people as law. Such a system facilitated treaty making and provided a basis for punishing an entire people for breaches of treaties. But in fact among the Cheyennes, and indeed among most of the Plains Indians, no such person existed—or ever had.[3]

Compounding the problem for a government seeking a monarch, prime minister, or president to deal with on behalf of his people, was the matter of religion. Religion was a pervasive and integral part of tribal organization and life, and no Cheyenne would have conceived of them separately. God, "Maheo" in their language, was invoked in nearly all things and for all important purposes and had decreed their sacred way of life. For the Tsistsistas, therefore, what should be already was. Priests, or holy men, performed religious rituals, made medicine (seeking divine blessing and assistance in an undertaking), and prayed with and for tribal members and the tribe itself. Most important of all were the two divine gifts to the tribe: the Maahótse, the four Medicine Arrows brought to them by Sweet Medicine, and Esevone, the Sacred Buffalo Hat, brought by their great prophet Erect Horns to the Sutaio (Suhtai) band when it was still a separate tribe. These holy objects represented divine power and blessing given the tribe for its protection and well-being, connecting them to Maheo.[4]

---

[2] Berthrong, *Southern Cheyennes*, 70–72; Grinnell, *Cheyenne Indians*, 1:336–58; Hoebel, *Cheyennes*, 37–48; Powell, *Sweet Medicine*, 1:92–93, 93n5.

[3] Berthrong, *Southern Cheyennes*, 31–32, 70–75; Grinnell, *Cheyenne Indians*, 1:336–58; Hoebel, *Cheyennes*, 31, 37–48, 58–59.

[4] Grinnell, *Cheyenne Indians*, 2:88–91; Hoebel, *Cheyennes*, 86; Powell, *Sweet Medicine*, 2:433–37, 442–43, 863–65.

The Medicine Arrows, two bison arrows and two man arrows, were, and still are, entrusted to the care of the Arrow Keeper, the direct spiritual successor to Sweet Medicine. So important and so sacred is this post that no important decision of the Council of Forty-four affecting the interests and fortunes of the entire tribe is binding on the tribe and all of its bands and people unless it is first approved and blessed by the Keeper of the Sacred Arrows. Therefore for any other people to enter into an agreement or treaty with the Cheyenne Nation, be it the government of the United States or another Indian nation, that treaty must first receive the approval of *all* members of the Council of Forty-four, along with the approval and blessing of the Arrow Keeper. Although the Cheyennes did have such agreements with some of their Indian neighbors, none was ever made with the United States.[5]

For the Cheyennes the first purported treaty with the United States was that signed at the mouth of the Teton River in present-day Montana on July 6, 1825. Brig. Gen. Henry Atkinson, accompanied by fifty mounted troopers and four hundred infantry, along with the new Indian agent, Maj. Benjamin O'Fallon, ascended the Missouri River during the summer of that year, charged with making peace treaties with the tribes inhabiting the regions through which the river flowed, as well as those of the northern plains. As they met with each tribe, Atkinson and his men provided a feast, a display of military drill and prowess, and the music of a military band. O'Fallon then addressed the Indians in an effort to explain his mission as one of peace and friendship, following which Atkinson presented the treaty as a means to bind both the tribe and the United States to those principles. After that a peace pipe was smoked and the Indians were invited to sign the treaty. The treaty document having been prepared in advance, there were no negotiations, and the whole affair was represented as being intended only to ensure peaceful intercourse and trade. Once the representatives of each tribe had signed, medals were presented to the signers, and additional presents were distributed.[6]

The Cheyennes and Lakotas had previously been informed, when invited to council, that the primary purpose of the treaty was to permit white travel through their lands and to accommodate peaceful and profitable trade. It was with this understanding that the council members present

---

[5] Hoebel, *Cheyennes*, 37–48; letters from Fr. Peter J. Powell to the author dated June 9, 2004, and July 11, 2005, citing and quoting John Stands in Timber, tribal historian (b. 1882), Jay Black Kettle (the Arrow Keeper), Henry Little Coyote (Keeper of Esevone—the Sacred Buffalo Hat), John Fire Wolf, council chief, and Ralph Whitetail (one of the four Sacred Arrow Priests).

[6] Berthrong, *Southern Cheyennes*, 22; Nichols, *General Henry Atkinson*, 90–100; Powell, *People of the Sacred Mountain*, 1:30–31.

in the north had authorized a treaty. However, Article I of the Cheyenne treaty stated that the tribe recognized that it resided within the territorial limits of the United States, acknowledged the supremacy of the U.S. government, claimed its protection, and admitted its right to regulate all trade and intercourse with the tribe—in effect acknowledging sovereignty over them. Article II provided that the government would receive the tribe under its protection and extend to its people "such benefits and acts of kindness as may be convenient, and seems just and proper to the President of the United States." History records how much protection was provided to the Cheyennes and how many benefits and acts of kindness were extended to them by that government. Other articles dealt with the regulation of trade and the relationship with white Americans, primarily the application of American law to Indians interfering with the persons or property of whites, including the right to punish them.[7]

The Indians, of course, had no conception of what the treaty meant, and had they known, they certainly would not have signed. It was to be only the first of a series of treaties made through fraudulent misrepresentation and intended to deprive the Native peoples of their lands, their freedom, their own culture, and their way of life. But as a treaty it suffered from a fatal deficiency that typified all of the treaties ever made with the Cheyenne Nation. It was considered only by those members of the Council of Forty-four then present on the Northern Plains, and it was signed by only four council members—namely, High Back Wolf (Wolf-with-the-High-Back. who was then the Sweet Medicine chief), Little Moon, Buffalo Head, and Leaving Bear (One-Who-Walks-against-the-Others). Nine warriors accompanying them were also asked to sign, and did, but were without any kind of right or power to do so or to represent the tribe. The treaty was never blessed by the Keeper of the Sacred Arrows nor approved by the entire body of the Council of Forty-four. Therefore, for the Cheyenne tribe as a whole the treaty was something of a nonevent, a simple agreement by the northern bands to be friends with the people of the Great Father, trade with them, and allow them passage across their lands—nothing further.[8]

More than twenty-six years would pass before the Cheyennes were again asked to enter into a treaty with the United States, the next being the one signed at Horse Creek, Wyoming, on September 17, 1851. Ostensibly the

---

[7] *U.S. Stat.* 255–57; Berthrong, *Southern Cheyennes*, 22; Nichols, *General Henry Atkinson*, 90–100; Powell, *People of the Sacred Mountain*, 1:30–31.

[8] Berthrong, *Southern Cheyennes*, 22; Nichols, *General Henry Atkinson*, 90–100; Powell, *People of the Sacred Mountain*, 1:30–31.

treaty's primary purpose, as envisioned by the federal government, was to secure peaceful relations between the signatory tribes and the United States, on one hand, and peace between warring tribes on the other. It was the culmination of the efforts of former mountain man and fur trader Thomas Fitzpatrick, called the "chief of the withered hand" or "Broken Hand" by the Indians, who had been appointed the first agent for the new Upper Platte and Arkansas Agency on December 1, 1846. After considerable procrastination, Congress finally passed the Deficiency Appropriations Act in February 1851, which included $100,000 for the expenses of holding treaty councils with the "wild tribes of the prairie."[9]

In June 1851 Fitzpatrick met with a vast throng of Cheyennes, Arapahoes, Kiowas, Comanches, and Plains Apaches then camped along both sides of the Arkansas River above and below Fort Atkinson, to invite them to the great council to be held at Fort Laramie the following September.[10] The entire region was in the grip of a terrible drought, and except for a few stagnant pools, no water covered the bed of the Arkansas above its Great North Bend. All of the tribes Fitzpatrick met with were greatly affected by the cholera epidemics of 1849 and 1850, adding to their deep distress over the continuing disappearance of game from the vicinity of the rivers because of the two great trails along them. Their impoverished and starving condition, in combination with promises that the Great Father in Washington was sending many presents to assist them in their hour of need, doubtless was key to securing the attendance of any of them. Even so, the Kiowas, Comanches, and Plains Apaches declined to attend on the grounds that it was too far and that they had too many horses and mules to risk on a journey to the country of "such notorious horse-thieves as the Sioux and the Crows."[11]

The great council, one of the most spectacular gatherings of the Indians of the plains and the mountains in the history of the West, was formally opened on Monday, September 8, 1851. Thomas Fitzpatrick and David D. Mitchell of St. Louis, superintendent of Indian affairs for the

[9] Missouri Republican, October 24, 26, and 29 and November 9, 21, 23, and 30, 1851; Berthrong, Southern Cheyennes, 115–16; Grinnell, Fighting Cheyennes, 100; Hafen, Broken Hand, 269–301; Hafen and Young, Fort Laramie, 177–96; Killoren, "Come, Blackrobe," 127–42; Nadeau, Fort Laramie and the Sioux, 66–68; Powell, People of the Sacred Mountain, 1:101–10; Washburn, American Indian, 4:2477.

[10] Fort Atkinson had been established during the preceding summer of 1850 at a point about three-fourths of a mile west of the ruins of Fort Mann, or about two and a half miles west of present Dodge City, Kansas, to protect the midregions of the Santa Fe Trail.

[11] Berthrong, Southern Cheyennes, 116–18; Hafen, Broken Hand, 280–81; Hafen and Young, Fort Laramie, 179; Killoren, "Come, Blackrobe," 144; Nadeau, Fort Laramie and the Sioux, 68; Powell, People of the Sacred Mountain, 1:101–102.

Central Superintendency, acted as treaty commissioners for the United States. After the ritual smoking of the pipe of peace, Mitchell opened the proceedings by making a general statement concerning the objectives of the council: "We are but the agents or representatives of your Great Father at Washington, and what we propose is merely what he desires you should do for your own happiness. We do not come to you as traders; we have nothing to sell you, and do not want to buy anything from you. We do not want your lands, horses, robes, nor anything you have; but we come to advise you, and make a treaty with you for your own good." Having said this, Mitchell proceeded to outline what it was that this mythic, benevolent Great Father in the East, so concerned with the welfare of his "red children," really did want.[12]

It was, Mitchell said, the desire of the Great Father to compensate his Indian peoples for the damages and losses resulting from the passage of white immigrants across their country. *But* he also wanted them to understand that white immigration and travel through their lands would be permanent and that there must be free passage of traffic along the two great east-west roads: the Oregon-California Trail in the north, the primary immigrant road; and the Santa Fe Trail in the south, essentially a road of trade and commerce. Moreover, there must be restitution for any damage or injuries inflicted on white travelers by the tribes through whose lands these roads passed. To ensure that neither side would harm the other, the Indians must acknowledge the right of the government to establish military and other posts to protect them. To assure that justice be done to each Indian nation and that peace be preserved between them, their tribal territories were to be defined. It was explained, however, that this definition was not intended to take any of their own country away from them or to destroy their right to hunt, fish, or travel across it as they had always done. Rather it was to assign responsibility for a designated area to a particular tribe or tribes, which would then be held accountable for any depredations within it. This would permit the Great Father to accomplish his primary objective, "to punish the guilty and reward the good." The Great Father would further undertake the task of driving out the bad white men from among them but would retain the exclusive right to determine which ones were bad and what their punishment should be. Lastly, the Great Father desired that each tribe designate a "Chief of the whole nation," who would

[12] Berthrong, *Southern Cheyennes*, 119–20; Hafen, *Broken Hand*, 289–94; Hafen and Young, *Fort Laramie*, 185–88; Killoren, *"Come, Blackrobe,"* 151–54; Nadeau, *Fort Laramie and the Sioux*, 73–75; Powell, *People of the Sacred Mountain*, 1:103–105.

be the representative of the authority of the government and would be supported and sustained by it "so long as he acts properly."[13]

As with the treaty of 1825, there were no negotiations at Horse Creek. The treaty documents had been prepared in advance and were merely presented for approval by the assembled tribes. There were debates, dissension, and disagreements within the tribal councils, but in the end, to receive the total compensation of $50,000 per year in presents over a period of fifty years (for the combined signatory tribes), they had to sign what was presented to them. The most contentious and divisive issue was that of assigned tribal territories, which caused a good deal of doubt and suspicion because the boundaries drawn by the whites did not coincide with the lands that each tribe claimed and occupied. On their face these boundaries separated tribal territories that in fact overlapped, with shared usage, and they shrank the claims of most, especially where the whites' roads or advancing settlements were concerned. But assurances that they were not surrendering anything, only restricting their responsibilities for hostilities, finally overcame the concerns of many. The concept of a paramount tribal chief, quite contrary to the leadership traditions of most of the tribes and their individual bands, caused surprisingly few problems, doubtless because this person was cast not in the guise of a supreme leader but more as a go-between with the tribal leadership and the representatives of the Great Father in Washington. The man selected to represent the Lakotas, for example, was picked by David Mitchell when their bands could not agree on one "head chief." He was Bear That Scatters, or Scattering Bear, a headman of the Sicangu (Brulé) Wazhazha band and not a chief. But he was a fine, honest, respected man and a great hunter and was accepted for purposes of the treaty.[14]

The treaties that were signed by the representatives of the government and of those tribes present on September 17, 1851, proclaimed lasting peace between the United States and each of the tribes, as well as among the tribes themselves. But it also recognized the right of the United States to establish roads and military and other posts within the tribal territories; committed the government to protect the Indian nations from "all depredations by the people of the said United States"; and obligated the Indians to make

[13] Berthrong, *Southern Cheyennes*, 119–20; Hafen, *Broken Hand*, 293–98; Hafen and Young, *Fort Laramie*, 187–88; Killoren, *"Come, Blackrobe,"* 154–55; Nadeau, *Fort Laramie and the Sioux*, 75–76; Powell, *People of the Sacred Mountain*, 1:103–105.

[14] Berthrong, *Southern Cheyennes*, 120; Killoren, *"Come, Blackrobe,"* 156–67; Nadeau, *Fort Laramie and the Sioux*, 76–80; Powell, *People of the Sacred Mountain*, 1:106–109.

restitution for any wrongs committed against Americans lawfully residing in or passing through their respective territories. It established specific boundaries for the territories for which each tribe was responsible and acknowledged that the selected principal or head chief of each would be the party "through whom all national business will hereafter be conducted."[15]

For the Cheyennes the treaty provided that their territory, in common with the Arapahoes, would be that "commencing at the Red Butte, or the place where the road leaves the north fork of the Platte River to its source; thence along the main range of the Rocky Mountains to the headwaters of the Arkansas River; thence down the Arkansas River to the crossing of the Santa Fe road; thence in a northwesterly direction to the forks of the Platte River; and thence up the Platte River to the place of beginning." This was subject, however, to the following proviso: "It is, however, understood that, in making this recognition and acknowledgment, the aforesaid Indian nations do not hereby abandon or prejudice any rights or claims they may have to other lands; and further, that they do not surrender the privilege of hunting, fishing, or passing over any of the tracts of country heretofore described." Though the Cheyennes made the selection themselves, the man they picked to be their principal in dealing with the United States was not a council chief and member of the Council of Forty-four. He was Stone Forehead, Keeper of the Sacred Arrows and a member of the Aorta band. High Back Wolf the younger, the Sweet Medicine chief who presided over the Council of Forty-four, announced Stone Forehead's selection to act as intermediary with the government. Because Stone Forehead was the holy man who sat in the seat of the Prophet, Sweet Medicine himself, it was right that he should speak for the People when the Great Father had business with them.[16]

Despite the language of the treaty and the assurances they were not giving up any of their lands, the definition of the tribal territories had an insidious purpose that the Indians could not possibly have known. By separating allied tribes that roamed across a common country, the government was engaging in a "divide and conquer" strategy. Each territory would have its own agency where the tribe was required to go for consultations with the agent, issuance of annuities, and similar matters. Had the

[15] Berthrong, *Southern Cheyennes*, 119–21; Hafen, *Broken Hand*, 298–99; Hafen and Young, *Fort Laramie*, 193–94; Killoren, *"Come, Blackrobe,"* 167–68; Nadeau, *Fort Laramie and the Sioux*, 80; Powell, *People of the Sacred Mountain*, 1:109–10.

[16] Berthrong, *Southern Cheyennes*, 119–22; Nadeau, *Fort Laramie and the Sioux*, 80; Powell, *People of the Sacred Mountain*, 1:105, 109–10.

tribes been unified in their dealings with the government, they might have been better able to resist the many demands of the Great Father. But once the tribes were separated and as bison and other game disappeared, the government intended that in time their dependency on the food issues would reduce them to impotence. And the designation of a "principal or head chief," the go-between for the tribe and the United States, would be the means of enforcing government edicts and treaty provisions that none of the Indian people had understood.[17]

At the time, the Cheyennes were truly desirous of peace and wanted desperately to keep whites from their country. The treaty seemed to many of them the only solution to this problem. But the territorial definitions remained a stumbling block to others. Under the treaty, most of the country of the northern Cheyenne bands was by definition the land of the Lakotas, with a portion assigned to their traditional enemies the Crows. A large portion of the country of the Masikota (Dog Soldier) and other bands that occupied the lands between the Pawnee Fork, the Smoky Hill, the Solomon, and the Republican rivers was omitted from the description, leading to a not unreasonable suspicion that whites might claim that it was not part of the Cheyenne domain. But it was, and for this reason many of the chiefs would not approve the treaty. In the end only four of the People's leaders signed: Stone Forehead (the Arrow Keeper and newly designated principal); White Face Bull, one of the four chiefs of the Scabby band; Bear Feather, a chief of the Southern Eaters; and White Antelope, one of the chiefs of the Ridge People. Not one chief of the Óhméséheso or Sutaio approved it, and not one Dog Soldier.[18]

The Horse Creek treaty had only a fleeting effect. Because the treaty did not surrender the rights of any of the tribes to their own country, it was quickly ignored by white settlers and ultimately by the government. When the government did little or nothing to enforce the terms benefiting the Indians, they too went back to their old ways, attacking white settlers moving into their lands, raiding white caravans, and making war on enemy tribes. Congress, thinking a term of fifty years for annuities of $50,000 per year for most of the Indians of the plains and the Rocky Mountains was far too liberal, cut the period to fifteen years, though the treaty did not per-

---

[17] Killoren, "Come, Blackrobe," 178–79.

[18] Berthrong, Southern Cheyennes, 121–22; Powell, People of the Sacred Mountain, 1:109–10. In 1849 the Dog Soldier military society was also transformed into a band when the members of the Masikota (Flexed Leg, or "Gray Hair") band joined with them. Thenceforth the Dog Soldiers assumed the place in the tribal circle held by the Masikota. Powell, People of the Sacred Mountain, 1:97–98.

mit any unilateral change. This caused considerable consternation in the Office of Indian Affairs, and Commissioner Luke Lea made a strong protest, noting that the treaty was a contract that could not be changed without the consent of all parties. In 1853 Thomas Fitzpatrick had the galling task of obtaining Indian consent to amendments reducing their entitlements under a treaty that was supposedly already settled. In this, surprisingly, he had some success even though the Indians received nothing in exchange for surrendering thirty-five years of annuities. In the long run it was of little moment. The Senate never completed ratification, and the treaty was never perfected. The government nevertheless held the signatory tribes to its terms, and annuities were paid for a fifteen-year period.[19]

The first treaty seeking removal of the Cheyennes from most of their own country and establishing a reservation for them was made at Fort Wise, Colorado, in 1861. Their old friend and trader William Bent, was named agent for the Upper Arkansas tribes in April 1860. During his brief tenure of less than five months he attempted to engineer a treaty placing the Cheyennes and Arapahoes on a reservation along the Arkansas River and centered, to no one's surprise, on Bent's New Fort. Only government employees and licensed traders would be allowed there, almost assuring a trade monopoly for Bent. The treaty was not concluded until August 1861, during the service of Bent's successor, Albert G. Boone. But this treaty, like those before and after, was fatally flawed. Just six of the forty-four council chiefs signed it, representing only Black Kettle's Southern Eaters band and part of the Ridge People band under White Antelope. Black Kettle, convinced the Cheyennes could not withstand the coming flood of white soldiers and settlers, signed every peace treaty ever presented to him, despite the lack of authority from his people. The Council of Forty-four, however, absolutely forbade the making of the treaty, the surrender of any of the Cheyenne country, and any change in the sacred manner in which they lived their lives, thereby rejecting reservation life. The federal government, disregarding the legalities, declared Black Kettle's treaty binding on the entire tribe and named five of the six signers the ruling chiefs of the Cheyenne Nation, though as council chiefs they represented only a small part of it, and the American government

[19] Berthrong, *Southern Cheyennes*, 123; Hafen, *Broken Hand*, 300–301, 312–14; Leckie, *Military Conquest*, 19; Nadeau, *Fort Laramie and the Sioux*, 83; Utley, *Frontiersmen in Blue*, 69.

[20] Berthrong, *Southern Cheyennes*, 148–51; Hoig, *Sand Creek Massacre*, 8–17, 32–33; Hyde, *Life of George Bent*, 114, 114n5, 118–19, 328; Leckie, *Military Conquest*, 19–20; Powell, *People of the Sacred Mountain*, 1:234–37; Utley, *Frontiersmen in Blue*, 283–84.

was without authority to designate anyone a chief. Except for those who signed it, the treaty was ignored by the Cheyennes.[20]

The period of the Civil War, the War between the White Men, was a difficult time for all Plains Indians, including the Cheyennes. The discovery of gold in the mountains of western Kansas Territory in 1857 resulted in a rush of smaller parties across the Cheyenne country to Cherry Creek in 1858 and a stampede in 1859. Even the coming of war between the states in 1861 and the subsequent creation of the state of Kansas and Colorado Territory did little to slow the influx of gold seekers. But it did result in the withdrawal of regular soldiers, as they marched away to fight for the North or the South, and in their replacement by volunteers from among the frontiersmen. These men had strong feelings against the Indian tribes that occupied the plains between the Missouri River and the foothills of the Rocky Mountains and adjacent to the roads and trails that connected them to white "civilization" in the East. Their preference was extermination, not peace, and the sooner the better. In 1864 this fanatical desire to rid Kansas and Colorado Territory of their Native inhabitants resulted in the atrocious massacre of the most peaceful Cheyennes, followers of the ever-trusting Black Kettle, by the Methodist minister turned volunteer soldier, John M. Chivington.[21]

Black Kettle, seeking safety for his band, reported to Fort Lyon as required of those Indians desiring peace, and was directed to remain in camp on Sand Creek to be out of harm's way. All Indians not reporting by a specified date were to be deemed hostile, an entirely unreasonable demand when one considers that most would not even hear of it until long after the deadline was passed. Nearly all hostilities, moreover, occurred when whites entered into the Cheyenne country without, as Cheyennes saw it, any right to be there. During the early morning hours of November 29, 1864, Colonel Chivington led some 700 troopers of the First and Third Regiments of Colorado Volunteers in a surprise attack on the sleeping camp of Black Kettle and his followers and friends. It became one of the most controversial actions ever taken against a band of Indians seeking peace and resulted in the death of 137 Cheyennes and Arapahoes, of whom about 30 were men and the rest women and children. Acts of barbarism far beyond even those so commonly attributed to the Native peoples were perpetrated by the undisciplined volunteers, and grisly trophies were soon on display in Denver,

[21] Leckie, *Military Conquest*, 20–24; Utley, *Frontiersmen in Blue*, 211–18, 282–86; Utley, *Indian Frontier*, 67–72, 86–93.

body parts cut from both the living and the dead. Not even babies were spared in response to Chivington's declaration that "nits make lice."[22]

Although Colonel Chivington's report claimed a glorious victory, allegedly resulting in the death of four chiefs, including Black Kettle, and 400 to 500 "warriors," stories soon began to filter back from soldiers who could not or would not conceal their shame and disgust over what had been done at Sand Creek. In time these stories reached the East, causing a great backlash against the terrible deeds perpetrated by Chivington and his men and against the "military solution" in general. Finally the pressure was sufficient that a board of inquiry was convened by the civil and military authorities to determine the truth of what happened at Sand Creek. Chivington himself, who in a later day would have been deemed guilty of war crimes, escaped punishment by the simple device of resigning his commission and being mustered out of the service, thus placing himself beyond the jurisdiction of a military court-martial. In the end the Sand Creek Massacre, as it came to be called, generated pressure for peace on the plains and a treaty with the Cheyennes.[23]

But even as revulsion against the actions of Chivington and his troops at Sand Creek was beginning to sweep the eastern states, the Cheyennes were planning their own form of revenge. The survivors from Black Kettle's camp made their way north and east to the Big Timbers of the Smoky Hill, where most of the other southern bands were wintering together for protection.[24] The Dog Soldier band was in winter camp farther northeast on the south fork of the Solomon, along with bands of southern Oglalas, southern Sicangu (Brulés), and northern Arapahoes. The available surviving members of the Council of Forty-four met, and the war pipe was sent to the Lakota and Arapahoe bands on the Solomon. They smoked it, pledging war with the whites to avenge the wrongs of Sand Creek, after which those Cheyennes on the Smoky Hill moved to the Solomon to participate in planning the coming conflict.[25]

[22] Berthrong, *Southern Cheyennes*, 214–23; Grinnell, *Fighting Cheyennes*, 165–80; Hoig, *John Simpson Smith*, 152–62; Hoig, *Sand Creek Massacre*, 145–62; Hyde, *Life of George Bent*, 146–63; Leckie, *Military Conquest*, 22–24; Powell, *People of the Sacred Mountain*, 1:299–310; Schultz, *Month of the Freezing Moon*, 125–42; Utley, *Frontiersmen in Blue*, 290–96; Utley, *Indian Frontier*, 91–93; Wynkoop, *Tall Chief*, 15–23.

[23] Hoig, *John Simpson Smith*, 164–67; Hoig, *Sand Creek Massacre*, 163–76; Leckie, *Military Conquest*, 24; Schultz, *Month of the Freezing Moon*, 143–74; Utley, *Frontiersmen in Blue*, 296–97; Utley, *Indian Frontier*, 92–93; Wynkoop, *Tall Chief*, 23–24.

[24] The Big Timbers of the Smoky Hill River, a grove of large cottonwood trees, was about a mile east of the Kansas-Colorado border on the river's south fork.

[25] Berthrong, *Southern Cheyennes*, 224–25; Grinnell, *Fighting Cheyennes*, 181; Hyde, *Life of George Bent*, 164–68; Leckie, *Military Conquest*, 24; Powell, *People of the Sacred Mountain*, 1:311; Schultz, *Month of the Freezing Moon*, 141–42, 146–47; Utley, *Frontiersmen in Blue*, 300–301.

It was not long before it was clear to everyone that Chivington's attack was bearing fruit, though not the kind anticipated or desired. On January 7, 1865, riding northwest from a new camp at the mouth of Cherry Creek where it flows into the South Fork of the Republican River, the combined war party of southern Lakotas, northern Arapahoes, and southern bands of Cheyennes, struck hard at the little town of Julesburg on the South Platte. They ambushed and killed fourteen soldiers, one recruit, and three civilians in their initial attack, sacked the town, besieged neighboring Fort Rankin, then burned nearby trading ranches and stage stations. After loading their packhorses with great quantities of booty, they returned to their Cherry Creek encampment to celebrate the great victory. A few days later, on January 27, they returned to the attack, ranging up and down the South Platte, destroying stage stations and trading ranches, ripping up telegraph lines, and attacking wagon trains and stage coaches. On February 2 they again attacked Julesburg, sacking and finally burning it in a futile attempt to make the small garrison at Fort Rankin come out and fight. After that the warriors and their families began a slow and deliberate migration northward to join their northern kinsmen.[26]

Still determined to avoid war with the whites, Black Kettle (who had escaped death at Sand Creek despite Chivington's claim) now led his surviving followers south to camp on Bluff Creek below the Arkansas with the Comanches, Kiowas, and southern bands of Arapahoes. Those moving north did have occasional fights with the military as they migrated, but nothing of great consequence, and no warriors were killed. By mid-February they reached the Black Hills, where the allied tribes parted company, the southern Sicangu (Brulés) moving east to join their northern brethren and hunt bison, and the eighty lodges of northern Arapahoes traveling northwest to rejoin their kinsmen. The southern bands of Cheyennes and the southern (Kiyuksa) Oglalas continued north, finally camping on Powder River west of the Black Hills with the northern bands of Cheyennes and the northern Oglalas of Old Man Afraid of His Horses.[27]

For a time the great camp of Cheyennes and Oglalas rested and hunted to replenish their food supply. Then, in late February, a large war party was organized to strike white installations along the North and South Platte

---

[26] Berthrong, *Southern Cheyennes*, 225–31; Grinnell, *Fighting Cheyennes*, 182–203; Hyde, *Life of George Bent*, 168–97; Powell, *People of the Sacred Mountain*, 1:311–26; Schultz, *Month of the Freezing Moon*, 151–53; Utley, *Frontiersmen in Blue*, 301–304; Williams, *Fort Sedgwick*, 9–28.

[27] Berthrong, *Southern Cheyennes*, 228–31; Grinnell, *Fighting Cheyennes*, 182–203; Hyde, *Life of George Bent*, 177–97; Powell, *People of the Sacred Mountain*, 1:316–26; Utley, *Frontiersmen in Blue*, 302–304.

rivers. The most notable of these attacks occurred at the old Platte River Bridge near present Casper, Wyoming, on July 25 and 26, 1865, resulting in the death of Lt. Casper Collins and six other men from the garrison, who were guarding the bridge, and twenty-two soldiers from a wagon train bringing supplies for the post. Other war parties struck along both rivers and their tributaries. Naturally all of this called forth the wrath of the military.[28]

Brig. Gen. John Pope, the pompous and verbose commander of the huge Military Department of the Missouri, which extended from the ninety-fifth meridian west to the Rocky Mountains, and from the Canadian border south to Texas, was a convinced believer in military force as the only effective solution to resistance against white encroachment on Indian lands. He sent columns under generals Sully, Connor, and Ford, about six thousand men in all, against the Plains Indians from Dakota Territory south to below the Arkansas River. Despite being encumbered with large, slow-moving supply trains, they marched hundreds of miles, but they were unable to find or bring to battle the mounted warriors of the plains when they chose not to fight. The enormous cost of such operations during the post–Civil War era, a time when the public demanded greatly decreased military expenditures, and the singular inability of the expeditions to either find or fight the Indians (or do much more than keep themselves alive and provisioned in difficult country and weather) resulted in almost complete failure and a return to base. For the military the campaign was a disaster—the victim of inhospitable country, weather, distance, logistical problems, low morale among volunteer troops wanting discharge from service, and poor planning.[29]

The combination of failure of the so-called military solution and revulsion against the Sand Creek Massacre prompted a strong move by some in Congress to try a peace policy. Delegations, including a few generals assigned to the task, visited tribes on both the northern and southern plains. On the southern plains, peace treaties were made (at least nominally) on the banks of the Little Arkansas River, near present-day Wichita, Kansas, with the Comanches, Kiowas, Plains Apaches, and southern bands of Cheyennes and Arapahoes. But once again the commissioners produced treaties that failed to deal with the Indian tribes in a realistic manner, the

[28] Berthrong, *Southern Cheyennes*, 245; Grinnell, *Fighting Cheyennes*, 216–29; Hyde, *Life of George Bent*, 197–222; Powell, *People of the Sacred Mountain*, 1:327–42; Utley, *Frontiersmen in Blue*, 319–22.

[29] Berthrong, *Southern Cheyennes*, 249–57; Hyde, *Life of George Bent*, 223–43; Powell, *People of the Sacred Mountain*, 1:375–88; Utley, *Frontiersmen in Blue*, 300–38; Utley, *Indian Frontier*, 86–98.

result of ineptness, lack of knowledge and understanding, and eagerness to produce a written peace document.[30]

The treaty with the Cheyennes and Arapahoes, ostensibly signed on October 14, 1865, called for perpetual peace between the United States and the Cheyenne and Arapahoe nations, surrendered to the United States all of the Cheyenne and Arapahoe country between the Arkansas and Platte rivers, subject to their right to remain and range at their pleasure on all of the unsettled portions, and established a reservation for them south of the Arkansas as soon as the ownership rights of the tribes holding title could be extinguished. The land south of the Arkansas and below that of the Cheyennes and Arapahoes was the country of the Comanches, Kiowas, and Plains Apaches, territory unfamiliar to most Cheyennes and a place where they did not want to live. The reservation the treaty created encompassed most of south-central Kansas and northwestern Oklahoma lying between the Arkansas and Cimarron rivers east from the mouth of Buffalo Creek, approximately longitude 99°15' west. Neither tribe understood where this reservation was located or what its purpose was. The language of the treaty, as explained to those Cheyennes and Arapahoes present, gave them to understand that whites were prohibited from settling in the remainder of their country, and therefore the Indians believed they could remain there indefinitely. Whites, of course, had no such intentions.[31]

Once again the treaty purportedly made with the Cheyennes was fatally flawed. Only four council chiefs and approximately eighty lodges remained on the southern plains, camping on Bluff Creek, and they were the now destitute surviving followers of Black Kettle. Most of the southern bands were still in the north, just then planning a return to their own country, and none had even heard of a proposed peace treaty. So it was that on October 14, 1865, after having repeatedly assured the commissioners that they had no authority to speak for or bind the rest of the tribe, Black Kettle, Seven Bulls, Little Robe, and Black White Man made their mark on the Treaty of the Little Arkansas. Four of forty-four were the only signatories, without consent or authority of any kind from the rest of the council chiefs or the Arrow Keeper. Two other Cheyennes, Minimic (Eagle's Head) and Bull That Hears, also made their mark, but they were

[30] Berthrong, *Southern Cheyennes*, 234–42; Hyde, *Life of George Bent*, 246–49; Leckie, *Military Conquest*, 24; Powell, *People of the Sacred Mountain*, 1:391–403; Utley, *Frontiersmen in Blue*, 336–37; Utley, *Indian Frontier*, 95–98.

[31] Berthrong, *Southern Cheyennes*, 242–44; Hyde, *Life of George Bent*, 248–50; Leckie, *Military Conquest*, 24–26; Powell, *People of the Sacred Mountain*, 1:395–403.

not council chiefs—though Minimic would later become one. Adding insult to injury, the Senate amended the treaty without referring it back to the tribes, although a provision to allow that had been struck as a precondition to the signing of the treaty by the only chiefs present. Among other things, the Senate amended the language describing the new reservation to eliminate that part within the boundaries of Kansas, which was more than half of its territory. That amendment, of course, could not be legally binding on the Indians unless accepted by them later, and then only if the original treaty was valid.[32]

The rest of the southern bands of Cheyennes, except the southern Sutaio, began their return south in early October 1865. Not until reaching the Platte River did even one of the bands hear of Black Kettle's peace treaty, but because they were attacked by soldiers soon after, they concluded there was either no truth to the story or that whites were not honoring it. When they reached the south fork of the Solomon, the Dog Soldiers halted, for now they were back in their own country. Stone Forehead, Keeper of the Sacred Arrows, remained with the Dog Soldiers, setting up the sacred lodge at its honored place in their camp circle. But the other bands continued southward, splitting up as they traveled so that each might return to its favored part of the Cheyenne country. A few chiefs and members of their bands, hearing that William Bent was once again trading with Black Kettle's people on Bluff Creek, continued south of the Arkansas and joined them there. It was then they first learned that Black Kettle and the other three had agreed to surrender the country the People had been fighting so hard to keep.[33]

Upon their return to the Smoky Hill country, the Dog Soldiers soon became aware that whites were once again intruding on their lands without consent. Beginning in June 1865, during their absence, first surveyors and then construction crews laid out a road for the Butterfield Overland Despatch, a stage and freight line running from Atchison, Kansas, on the Missouri River to Denver, following the Smoky Hill. Stations were established about ten to fifteen miles apart for changing horses and mules, and, depending on terrain and ease of travel, about every second or third station was a home station where meals were served. Although freight wagons were

[32] "Indian Peace Commission Report," 486–501; Berthrong, *Southern Cheyennes*, 243–45,256; Grinnell, *Fighting Cheyennes*, 245–46; Hyde, *Life of George Bent*, 248–50; Leckie, *Military Conquest*, 25; Powell, *People of the Sacred Mountain*, 1:401–403, 411; Washburn, *American Indian*, 1:145; Worcester, *Forked Tongues and Broken Treaties*, 136–41.

[33] Berthrong, *Southern Cheyennes*, 256; Hyde, *Life of George Bent*, 243, 250; Powell, *People of the Sacred Mountain*, 1:404–405.

using the Smoky Hill route almost in the wake of the construction crews, the first stagecoach began its run on September 11, reaching Denver on September 23. Most such runs, however, were a danger-filled trip of about fifteen days through inhospitable country inhabited by decidedly unhappy and hostile Indians. The presence of the new road, the stations, and the travelers and commerce on it predictably enraged the Dog Soldiers. Conflict began almost as soon as they returned to their homeland, with attacks up and down the line. These continued until cold weather put an end to travel and forced the Indians into their winter camps.[34]

The year 1865 ended on the southern plains almost as it had begun. The Cheyennes continued to be filled with anger for what white soldiers had done to Black Kettle's sleeping camp at Sand Creek and distrustful of any of the white men's promises or pledges. Whites, for their part, remained determined to keep the road along the Smoky Hill and to push a new railroad to completion along much the same route. The civil and military authorities alike concluded that this required the removal of the Cheyennes and Arapahoes from the area to avoid conflict with whites. The government's preference was to use peaceful means, through a valid treaty whereby the United States acquired title to the homeland of the two tribes in exchange for a secure reservation south of the state of Kansas, along with gifts of goods for a period of years. The alternative, of course, was war: a war that would result in the forced taking of the Indian lands and the extermination of the people.[35]

The Treaty of the Little Arkansas, while on its face accomplishing the government's objectives, was obviously imperfect because it was made with council chiefs representing only a small minority—less than one-tenth—of the Cheyenne Nation and lacked the approval and blessing of the Arrow Keeper. Much remained to be done before the Cheyennes could be removed and title to their country acquired for the American public. The problem facing the white authorities was that most Cheyennes were inalterably opposed to surrendering their country, and it appeared to many that war and an acquisition by conquest would be the only alternative. To most westerners and to some in the military, this was no doubt the preferred solution.

---

[34] Hyde, *Life of George Bent*, 243; Lee and Raynesford, *Trails of the Smoky Hill*, 52–85; Powell, *People of the Sacred Mountain*, 1:404–405.

[35] Athearn, *William Tecumseh Sherman*, 24–44; Berthrong, *Southern Cheyennes*, 256–58; Hyde, *Life of George Bent*, 249–54; Powell, *People of the Sacred Mountain*, 1:405; Utley, *Indian Frontier*, 96–97, 102, 108–109.

Edward W. Wynkoop, an officer in the First Colorado Volunteer Cavalry, became a special agent, then the agent for the Cheyennes, Arapahoes, and Plains Apaches in 1866. He strongly opposed Hancock's decision to march to the Cheyenne and Oglala villages and his subsequent burning of them. Wynkoop predicted that such actions would lead to war and was ultimately proven correct. This sketch by Theodore Davis depicts Wynkoop on the left and Dick Curtis, one of the post interpreters for Fort Larned, on the right. *Harper's Weekly*, May 11, 1867.

CHAPTER TWO

IN THE WAKE OF THE TREATY

Following the signing of the Treaty of the Little Arkansas, the treaty commissioners were concerned that it be accepted by those of the southern bands of Cheyennes and Arapahoes not present, which was the overwhelming majority of both tribes, because without their approval it would be of little worth. Eventually Maj. Edward W. Wynkoop of the First Regiment of Colorado Volunteers was designated as a special Indian agent, to serve with the Interior Department's Office of Indian Affairs on detached duty from the army. His assignment was to persuade the chiefs of the nonsignatory bands to accept the treaty provisions and remain at peace. Wynkoop, a former commander of Fort Lyon, had been relieved of command on November 2, 1864, prior to the Sand Creek Massacre, apparently because of his sympathetic views of the Indians, unauthorized peace councils, and distribution of food to them. While in command at the fort he had developed a great respect for the Cheyenne and Arapahoe tribes because of previous dealings with them and certain of their leaders, including Black Kettle. And though he, in common with most nineteenth-century Americans, viewed them as childlike, unenlightened savages, he was nonetheless held in high regard by them as one of the few fair, honest, and relatively impartial white officials they had dealt with since the time of "Broken Hand" Thomas Fitzpatrick. At the time of the Little Arkansas treaty, Black Kettle had requested that either Wynkoop, known to the Indians as Tall Chief, or their old friend and trader William Bent be sent to them as their agent to replace the current one, the perpetually intoxicated Dr. I. C. Taylor.[1]

Originally Wynkoop's council with the Cheyenne chiefs was to be held

---

[1] Berthrong, *Southern Cheyennes*, 257; Hyde, *Life of George Bent*, 251; Powell, *People of the Sacred Mountain*, 1:405; Wynkoop, *Tall Chief*, 15–23, 25–26.

at the agency headquarters at Fort Zarah, Kansas, but those camping on Bluff Creek were fearful of moving north of the Arkansas, primarily because the rest of the southern bands were still at war with the whites and it seemed too dangerous. Consequently Wynkoop went to the Bluff Creek camp of Black Kettle's followers, about twenty miles south of the Santa Fe Trail's old Lower Crossing at the south bend of the Arkansas River. There, on March 1, 1866, he met with a few of the surviving chiefs who had not been present at the Little Arkansas, including Old Little Wolf of the Ridge People, Sand Hill of the Aorta band, Old Whirlwind of the Hair Rope People, and Curly Hair of the Poor People. Also present were Black Kettle, Seven Bulls, and Black White Man, who had already signed the treaty; Stone Forehead of the Aorta band (the Keeper of the Sacred Arrows); and a small delegation of Dog Soldiers, led by Tangle Hair (also known as Big Head), a headman or war leader. For his part, Wynkoop believed he was meeting "the head men of the late hostile bands of the Arapahoe and Cheyenne tribes." But absent were the council chiefs of the Dog Soldiers and southern Sutaio, as well as most other members of the Council of Forty-four. Also absent was Little Robe, who had signed the treaty at the Little Arkansas and was now riding north to talk to the Dog Soldier chiefs in an effort to persuade them to meet with Major Wynkoop.[2]

The council was only moderately successful, despite Wynkoop's subsequent representations to the contrary. He explained the treaty and the advantages to the Indians of maintaining peace with the United States. But Tangle Hair, while expressing a desire for peace and a willingness to permit free travel by whites on the roads along the Arkansas and the Platte, expressed the firm opposition of his people to allowing any road through the Smoky Hill country and to giving up their traditional homelands between the Arkansas and Platte rivers. Disheartened, Wynkoop stated that he would report these views to the proper authorities, but that in the interim the southern bands should remain peaceably where they were. To this Tangle Hair agreed.[3]

Despite the expressed desires of the chiefs and others present, Wynkoop continued to press them to sign a written consent to abide by the terms of the treaty as signed at the Little Arkansas. A few of those present did

[2] E. W. Wynkoop to John Pope, March 12, 1866, LR, OIA, MC234-R879 (hereafter this collection is designated "MC234-R879"); G. M. Dodge to John Pope, March 15, 1866, MC234-R879; Berthrong, *Southern Cheyennes*, 257–258; Powell, *People of the Sacred Mountain*, 1:405–407.

[3] Wynkoop to Pope, March 12, 1866; Dodge to Pope, March 15, 1866; Berthrong, *Southern Cheyennes*, 258; Hyde, *Life of George Bent*, 250–51; Powell, *People of the Sacred Mountain*, 1:406–407.

place their mark on a paper intended to ratify the treaty, but their understanding of its contents and meaning is questionable. Wynkoop claimed
that all present had understood and consented, but George Bent, who
was present interpreting for the Cheyennes, stated that Stone Forehead
and Tangle Hair absolutely refused to sign, saying only that they intended
to keep their country and wanted neither roads nor railroads through it.
What does seem clear is that those who did sign thought it meant only a
cessation of hostilities and that they would be left alone, not that they
were giving up their homeland.[4]

Major Wynkoop and his escort left Bluff Creek on March 3, returning
first to Fort Dodge, then moving on to Fort Larned. There on March 5
he wrote to Commissioner of Indian Affairs D. N. Cooley, reporting his
success and transmitting the agreement. And on March 12 he wrote to
General Pope, who commanded the Department of the Missouri, reporting that he had met with all leaders of the formerly hostile bands of
Cheyennes and that each had signed an agreement to honor the treaty
provisions. Such a statement, of course, was untrue, for not one council
chief of the Dog Soldiers or the southern Sutaio was even present, nor
were most other formerly hostile bands represented by more than one
council chief. This undoubtedly reflects not dishonesty but ignorance on
the part of Wynkoop with respect to how civil matters were dealt with by
the Cheyennes. Most whites of that era, including those in the Office of
Indian Affairs and the military, had no concept of tribal organization and
tended to look for one overall chief or for those who seemed to wield the
most authority and influence. Hence headmen (war leaders), leaders of
the military societies, and great and respected warriors were all seen as
powerful chiefs.[5]

The misunderstanding was clearly borne out by a letter from Maj. Gen.
Grenville M. Dodge to General Pope on March 15, reporting on the coun-
cil at Bluff Creek. In addition to the seven council chiefs above men-
tioned, he enumerated the leaders of the hostile bands and Dog Soldiers
present as being "Medicine Arrows" (Stone Forehead, the Arrow Keeper),
Big Head (Tangle Hair), George Bent, Hairy Wolf, Bear Tongue, and
Red Iron, all allegedly representing some four thousand hostile Cheyennes.
None of those Dodge named was a council chief, and Stone Forehead

---

[4] Berthrong, *Southern Cheyennes*, 258; Grinnell, *Fighting Cheyennes*, 246; Hyde, *Life of George Bent*,
250–51; Powell, *People of the Sacred Mountain*, 1:406–407.
[5] Wynkoop to Pope, March 12, 1866; D. N. Cooley to E. W. Wynkoop, March 19, 1866, Wynkoop
Collection, MNM; Hyde, *Life of George Bent*, 210; Powell, *People of the Sacred Mountain*, 1:406–407.

was a member of the Aorta band, not a Dog Soldier. George Bent, son of William Bent, was a member of the Elkhorn Scraper (Crooked Lance) military society, and not a Dog Soldier, though General Dodge reported him to be the Dog Soldiers' leader. The confusion and lack of understanding on the part of the white authorities is illustrative of their persistent failure to learn anything about the culture and leadership of the tribes they dealt with.[6]

Early in March 1866 the Dog Soldier warriors, along with warriors of Black Shin's southern Sutaio band of about fifty lodges, now camping with them, prepared to resume their strikes along the Smoky Hill route. But before they could do so, Little Robe rode into their camp accompanied by Edmund Guerrier, the half French Canadian, half Cheyenne often used by federal authorities as an interpreter. Little Robe was a former Dog Soldier council chief but severed his ties with the band when he went south with Black Kettle, refusing to participate further in the war of revenge for Sand Creek. In time he was replaced as council chief by Tangle Hair. Still, he was a double Dog-Rope wearer, a man of undoubted bravery who was held in great respect. He persuaded the Dog Soldier and southern Sutaio council chiefs to at least listen to what "Tall Chief" Wynkoop had to say.[7]

In response to his plea, the Dog Soldier council chiefs and a number of the headmen rode south and on April 4 met with Wynkoop at a site on Wood Creek, about fifteen miles from Fort Larned.[8] Before they left, these chiefs made their mark on Wynkoop's paper, but with what understanding is disputed. Wynkoop contended that they agreed to abide by the terms of the Little Arkansas treaty, but the chiefs always asserted it was expressly agreed that they were permitted to retain the Smoky Hill country and their homeland between the Arkansas and Platte rivers. It was their opposition to use of the Arkansas and Platte roads they thought they were surrendering for peace. This disagreement may have been the result of a failure to properly translate the words of either Wynkoop or the Dog Soldier chiefs.[9]

Whatever the understanding on either side, the southern bands of Cheyennes and Arapahoes remained largely at peace throughout the spring and summer of 1866, in no small part due to the tireless efforts of Major

---

[6] Dodge to Pope, March 15, 1866; Hyde, *Life of George Bent*, 210; Powell, *People of the Sacred Mountain*, 1:406–407.

[7] Berthrong, *Southern Cheyennes*, 259; Powell, *People of the Sacred Mountain*, 1:408.

[8] There is today no stream known as Wood Creek within fifteen miles from Fort Larned; the stream was possibly Sawmill Creek or some other small tributary of the Pawnee Fork.

[9] E. W. Wynkoop to John Pope, April 5, 1866, MC234-R879; E. W. Wynkoop to D. N. Cooley, April 8, 1866, MC234-R879; Grinnell, *Fighting Cheyennes*, 246; Powell, *People of the Sacred Mountain*, 1:408.

Wynkoop. But it was to be an uneasy peace. As if to bear out the contentions of the Dog Soldiers and Sutaio about what transpired at Wood Creek, men returning from Santa Fe in early May reported to Thomas Murphy, superintendent of the Central Superintendency, that there was unrest along the Smoky Hill. They said that a trader returning from the Dog Soldier country told them the Dog Soldiers and Arapahoes would not accept their treaty annuity goods that summer. The Indians told the trader they had no intention of molesting white traffic and travelers along the Arkansas or on the Platte route to Denver, but along the Smoky Hill it would be war unless the new road was abandoned. This report raised questions concerning the validity of Wynkoop's treaties and was followed shortly by other expressions of skepticism, especially among the military.[10]

Adding further doubt as to the legitimacy of the Wynkoop agreements, in mid-May a party of Cheyennes, probably Dog Soldiers or Sutaio, forcibly evicted several white claim seekers from the area along the lower Solomon River. They informed the white men that the country belonged to them and that whites were not allowed there. Although the Cheyennes did them no harm, the whites were given to understand that if they returned, they would be killed. Such activities by the Indians were nearly always referred to by the white authorities as "insolence" and "outrages," but their persistence did raise concerns in the Office of Indian Affairs and elsewhere.[11]

The matter did not end there. W. H. Watson, an agent of the Interior Department, investigated the charges that Wynkoop had concealed the true nature of the treaty from the Cheyennes during his councils with them both at Bluff Creek and Wood Creek. Superintendent Thomas Murphy told Watson he was reliably informed that the Dog Soldiers agreed to abide by the terms of the Treaty of the Little Arkansas only upon the strict understanding that they not give up their country and that whites were to keep away from the Smoky Hill route. That was the reason, he said, that the Indians were reacting to white intrusions as they did. William Bent, Ed Guerrier, and John Smith, as well acquainted with the Cheyennes as anyone in that day, each expressed strong doubts that the Cheyennes, and particularly the Dog Soldiers, had any understand-

---

[10] Aff'd. Maj. William Davidson, May 16, 1866, MC234-R879; Thomas Murphy to D. N. Cooley, May 5 and July 6, 1866, MC234-R879; W. H. Watson to D. N. Cooley, June 26 and July 5, 1866, MC234-R879; Berthrong, *Southern Cheyennes*, 260; Powell, *People of the Sacred Mountain*, 1:408.
[11] Aff'd. S. A. Robbins and Joseph Fry, May 16, 1866, MC234-R879; Aff'd. Hiram Markham, James Jerod, and S. Williams, May 16, 1866, MC234-R879; Berthrong, *Southern Cheyennes*, 260.

ing of the provisions of the treaty requiring abandonment of their country and would never consent to abandon it or leave it voluntarily. Jesse Leavenworth, agent for the Comanches and Kiowas at Fort Larned, confirmed this view from reports he received from others who were there.[12]

By July, evidence was mounting that the Cheyennes, and especially the Dog Soldiers, would not leave the Smoky Hill country. On July 21 Agent I. C. Taylor distributed annuities to members of the southern bands who appeared at the agency at Fort Zarah for the occasion. Predictably these included the bands of Black Kettle, Old Little Wolf, and other chiefs who had already approved the treaty signed at the Little Arkansas. Absent, as they had vowed, were the chiefs of the Dog Soldiers, southern Sutaio, and others. After they received their annuities, Black Kettle asked Taylor for a permit allowing those present to travel to the Smoky Hill to hunt buffalo. There, he said, they would also offer the Sun Dance. Taylor granted the permit but sent John S. Smith along to watch for any evidence of hostile action. Before leaving Fort Zarah, Black Kettle told Taylor he would do his best to persuade the Dog Soldier chiefs to come in and council with the agent on the question of allowing right-of-way across the Smoky Hill country. Later Black Kettle did in fact meet with Tall Bull, Bull Bear, and White Horse, the three remaining Dog Soldier council chiefs, but their answer was the same: they would not surrender their country or allow whites to cross it.[13]

In an effort to prevent the uneasy peace from unraveling, Wynkoop next met with eight prominent Cheyennes at Fort Ellsworth on August 14, 1866.[14] He believed all eight to be important chiefs, when in fact the only council chiefs present were Black Kettle, Old Little Wolf, and Curly Hair (also known as Big Head). But for the first time at any of the councils held with the Cheyennes relating to the treaty on the Little Arkansas, the southern Sutaio were represented, not by a council chief but by Gray Beard, son-in-law of Black Shin, who was one of their council chiefs and the leader of fifty lodges. Attending with Gray Beard was his great friend Woqini, or Hooked Nose, known to whites as Roman Nose. A member of the Ôhméséheso band, the principal northern band and largest in the tribe,

[12] Watson to Cooley, June 26 and July 5, 1866; Murphy to Cooley, July 6, 1866; Berthrong, *Southern Cheyennes*, 260; Powell, *People of the Sacred Mountain*, 1:408–409.
[13] I. C. Taylor to D. N. Cooley, August 15, 1866, MC234-R879; Powell, *People of the Sacred Mountain*, 1:408–409.
[14] Fort Ellsworth, originally located along the Smoky Hill River at the junction of the Smoky Hill Trail and the road to Fort Zarah and Fort Larned, was later moved to a more elevated site about a mile to the northeast and renamed Fort Harker.

and a member of the Elkhorn Scraper military society, Roman Nose was
not a council chief nor even a headman of his society. But he was one of
the bravest and most famous warriors in the tribe, a man respected and listened to even by the council chiefs. He was also a great admirer of the Dog
Soldiers, with whom he had fought in many a battle. Wynkoop, with his
lack of understanding of Cheyenne tribal leadership, reported him to be
the "head chief of the northern band of Cheyennes." Rounding out the
eight prominent Cheyennes present were three men said by Wynkoop to
be the Man That Shot the Ree, Little Black Kettle, and Sitting Bear. Presumably, the result of faulty translation, the first two were Pushing Ahead,
who was also known as Shot by a Ree, and Gentle Horse, a younger brother
of Black Kettle who was sometimes called Little Black Kettle. The identity of Sitting Bear is unclear, but he was probably the prominent warrior
of that name.[15]

Wynkoop's meeting with the eight men resulted in no changes in position. The three council chiefs present, who were among those already
approving it, were concerned that the government was not fulfilling any
of its promises made in the treaty, had not returned the two children captured alive at Sand Creek, and had not provided promised annuities for
those who had signed. They spoke movingly of the difficulty they would
have in surrendering their country and leaving it and expressed their hope
the government would look after them, since they would be deprived of
their game and their traditional way of life. But for all of the professions
of good intentions by the three peace chiefs, those necessary for acceptance of the treaty and the Senate amendments were not present. Neither
the Dog Soldiers nor the southern Sutaio council chiefs had agreed to
remove from their country, nor had any of them knowingly signed anything saying they would. Nor would they. And there was anger in their
hearts as Gray Beard and Roman Nose rode away from Fort Ellsworth.[16]

Wynkoop's official report of the meeting focused particularly on the
desire of those Cheyennes present that peace be maintained between the
U.S. government and their tribe. Wynkoop claimed they promised to
punish those guilty of treaty infractions and (in his words) "if necessary
for an example, kill him." This could not be true, for the killing of a fellow member of the tribe was a great taboo, calling down the displeasure
of Maheo, bloodying the Sacred Arrows, and placing the very existence

---

[15] E. W. Wynkoop to D. N. Cooley, August 14, 1866, MC234-R879; Powell, *People of the Sacred Mountain*, 1:409–10.
[16] Wynkoop to Cooley, August 14, 1866; Powell, *People of the Sacred Mountain*, 1:410.

of the People in jeopardy. For the perpetrator it meant exile from family and tribe. For the tribe it required the solemn ceremony of Renewal of the Sacred Arrows, cleansing them and the tribe of the blight brought upon them by that great sin. For such a killing to be suggested by any Cheyenne, especially a council chief committed to peace, would be unthinkable. Most likely, Wynkoop's desire to cast the Cheyennes in the most favorable and conciliatory light agreeable to his superiors caused him to exaggerate and embellish his report. And ignorance of the Cheyenne culture and religion led him to report them as promising that which they could not and would not do—kill a fellow tribal member. But if Wynkoop embellished what was said, it seems he did so with the greater motivation of preserving a peace that was both fragile from the beginning, and grounded on misrepresentation and coercion.[17]

Underscoring the perception of the Cheyennes with respect to what they had agreed to at the council, parties of Cheyenne warriors, led by Spotted Horse and Roman Nose, began making visits during the latter part of August to the newly established Fort Wallace and the various stations of the stage and freight line along the Smoky Hill route, now owned by Ben Holladay.[18] The Cheyennes told the whites to abandon the fort and the stations and be out of the country within fifteen days, or they would burn all the stations and kill all the white people still there. The commander of Fort Wallace, Lt. Alfred E. Bates of the Second Cavalry, sent William (Medicine Bill) Comstock, the post's chief scout and guide, to learn the truth concerning reports of these threats. The Cheyennes informed Comstock that the soldier societies were resolved that if the road up the Smoky Hill was not abandoned by the time their "medicine lodge" ceremony was finished, they would close it.[19] The Indians did exercise restraint when the time came, but as a warning of the seriousness of their intentions, on September 19 a war party led by Spotted Horse raided the horse herd at Fort Wallace, running off fourteen horses and two mules.[20]

Reports persisted that the Dog Soldiers and other Cheyenne bands would

---

[17] Wynkoop to Cooley, August 14, 1866; Powell, *People of the Sacred Mountain*, 1:410.

[18] Holladay had purchased the line from the Butterfield company at a bargain price in March 1866, due to the great losses it suffered during the Indian troubles of 1865. Lee and Raynesford, *Trails of the Smoky Hill*, 87–88.

[19] This would not have been the annual Sun Dance, held at or near the summer solstice, but rather was probably a ceremony of the Dog Soldiers seeking divine assistance in protecting their country. Powell, *People of the Sacred Mountain* 1:410n28.

[20] Berthrong, *Southern Cheyennes*, 262–63; Oliva, *Fort Wallace*, 45; Powell, *People of the Sacred Mountain*, 1:410.

not ratify the Treaty of the Little Arkansas, and that those who had done so had been misled concerning its provisions. This, in combination with the Senate's amendments to the treaty during its conditional ratification in 1866, convinced the Interior Department and the Office of Indian Affairs that another council should be held with the Cheyennes and Arapahoes to clarify the issues and obtain the necessary consents. W. R. Irwin and Charles Bogy were appointed as special agents of the Indian bureau for this purpose, and Major Wynkoop, despite the skepticism about his councils and the results he reported, was directed to make necessary arrangements. The new council was to be held at Fort Zarah in mid-October, and Wynkoop, having supposedly obtained a list of the goods desired by the two tribes, set out for Washington to procure them, promising to return by a given date.[21] These goods, it was hoped, would place the Indians in the proper frame of mind to sign the treaty and ratify the Senate amendments to it—a bribe, as it were.[22]

Although the spring and summer of 1866 passed in relative peace, despite the refusal of the larger part of the Cheyenne tribe to sign the Treaty of the Little Arkansas and surrender their country, the onset of fall brought new violence. The Dog Soldiers and Sutaio had warned whites manning the military posts and stage stations to leave their country, but this had not happened. The raid on the Fort Wallace livestock on September 19 was but the first overt act to enforce their demand. On September 29, prior to commencement of the Fort Zarah council, a war party struck the Chalk Bluffs stage station, fifty-seven to fifty-eight miles east of Fort Wallace, killing one stock herder outright and mortally wounding another.[23] The wounded man died the following morning but not before stating that the war party was Cheyenne. The arrows that struck the men

---

[21] Fort Zarah was near the Walnut Creek crossing of the Santa Fe Trail, a short distance above that stream's confluence with the Arkansas River. Established in 1864 as an outpost of Fort Larned, it was abandoned by the military in 1866 but continued to serve as the agency for the Cheyennes and Arapahoes until December of that year. A stage station was located on the opposite (south) side of the creek. The fort was reoccupied by the military early in 1867.

[22] W. H. Harrison, AAAG, to E. W. Wynkoop, October 10, 1866, Wynkoop Collection, MNM; E. W. Wynkoop to J. W. Davidson, October 25, 1866, MC234-R879; E. W. Wynkoop to D. N. Cooley, November 3, 1866, MC234-R879; Berthrong, *Southern Cheyennes*, 263–64; Powell, *People of the Sacred Mountain*, 1:411.

[23] Lt. Robert E. Flood, then commanding the fort, stated that it was seventy miles to the east, but that was clearly his own estimate. The surveyors who laid out the route along the Smoky Hill measured sixty miles from Chalk Bluff Station to Pond Creek Station, which was about two and a half miles northwest of the fort. R. E. Flood to W. H. Harrison, September 30, 1866, MC234-R879; Lee and Raynesford, *Trails of the Smoky Hill*, 55.

were likewise identified as Cheyenne. Some three weeks later another war party of about forty men from Bull Bear's band of Dog Soldiers again struck Chalk Bluffs Station, this time burning it. Although it was the last significant act of war by the Dog Soldiers for the year 1866, and though that year was far more peaceful than 1865, letters flew between the headquarters of the Department of the Missouri, the District of the Upper Arkansas, and the various posts along the Smoky Hill, seeking the identity of the tribe guilty of the attacks. General Hancock, the new commander of the Department of the Missouri, wanted to fix responsibility and inflict punishment.[24]

---

[24] J. Hale to W. H. Harrison, September 30, 1866, MC234-R879; Flood to Harrison, September 30, 1866; Harrison to Wynkoop, October 25, 1866; W. S. Hancock to E. W. Wynkoop, October 30, 1866, Wynkoop Collection, MNM; M. W. Keogh to Henry E. Noyes, December 19 and 20, 1866, MC234-R879.

CHAPTER THREE

THE FORT ZARAH COUNCIL

Despite careful preparations, the council at Fort Zarah did not go well. It began on October 16, 1866, with Special Agent W. R. Irwin and Col. Jesse Leavenworth (agent for the Kiowas and Comanches) present to represent the government, and John S. Smith as their interpreter. Major Wynkoop had not yet arrived with the presents, though it was beyond his promised date of return, causing concern among the Indians. Eighty-five lodges of Cheyennes, with about 425 people, left the council grounds and moved north to the Smoky Hill, refusing to wait longer. Moreover, none of the council chiefs of the Dog Soldier or southern Sutaio bands were present. Those who did attend were, for the most part, the ones who had already signed or ratified the original treaty. There were present, however, warriors from the several military societies, including the Dog Soldiers, and because of their presence and obvious displeasure those chiefs who had signed, including Black Kettle and Little Robe, now withdrew their assent and refused to ratify the Senate amendments. Compounding Irwin's problems, whiskey was being supplied to the warriors, some by members of the Kanza tribe from their Council Grove reservation and some by traders at or near Fort Zarah. The fort had been temporarily abandoned as an outpost of Fort Larned and the site was not on an Indian reserve where federal law applied, so the traders were subject only to the laws of Kansas, which were nearly worthless because there was no way to enforce them. Charles Bent, the youngest son of William Bent, was also a disruptive influence, facilitating the flow of whiskey to the warriors and two or three times, while drunk, threatening to kill his father and his brother George.[1]

Once the council with the Cheyennes began, it quickly became clear to Special Agent Irwin that only a minority of the tribe, the eighty lodges

---

[1] W. R. Irwin to Lewis V. Bogy, November 3, 1866, MC234-R879; Wynkoop to Davidson, October 25, 1866; Berthrong, *Southern Cheyennes*, 263–64; Powell, *People of the Sacred Mountain*, 1:411.

whose chiefs were either present and signed the treaty at the Little Arkansas the previous year or subsequently ratified it, would recognize and carry out its provisions. The remainder of the southern bands, those returning from the northern plains after the treaty was signed, were a large majority and held the balance of power in the tribe. These bands and their chiefs strongly objected not just to the Senate amendments but to the treaty itself. "The majority of the Cheyennes," Irwin reported, "claim the country between the Arkansas and the Platte which is relinquished by the treaty and object to the railroad being run up the Smoky Hill Fork and the advance of white settlements into the country." It was his impression that Black Kettle and his followers "seemed disposed to do almost anything that was required," but that they were largely controlled by the rest of the tribe. And the feelings of the rest of the tribe, Irwin was assured by John Smith, the interpreter, and Indian agents Leavenworth and Taylor, were "bad." In his report, Irwin noted another thing of interest. The Indians were commenting on U.S. troops coming into their country, and stories were circulating among them that the government was contemplating another Sand Creek Massacre.[2]

More dissatisfaction became apparent when the Cheyenne and Arapahoe chiefs present learned the nature of the goods Major Wynkoop was bringing them. They stated that guns, powder, and other items were promised to them but were not on the purchase list. Because William Bent had a train containing a supply of such things not more than three days' travel from Fort Zarah, Irwin struck a bargain to buy them from him, subject to approval of the commissioner of Indian affairs. Irwin judged that if he could obtain them, nearly all Arapahoes and a minority of Cheyennes, those who consented to the treaty, would abide by its terms. Moreover, if he could get them promptly, these Cheyennes agreed to accept them in lieu of the ponies promised by the treaty to replace those stolen by Chivington's men at Sand Creek. The Indians gave Irwin a limited time to secure permission and conclude the purchase, as they were tired, out of provisions, and needed to hunt. The council was adjourned until this could be done, and Irwin hurried off to telegraph for the necessary authority.[3]

By October 20 Irwin was back at Junction City, outside of Fort Riley, and telegraphed a report to the commissioner of Indian affairs the same day. The little town was the new end of line of the Union Pacific Rail-

[2] Irwin to Bogy, November 3, 1866.
[3] Ibid.

road, Eastern Division (later renamed the Kansas Pacific Railroad), and was increasing in importance as the place where merchandise was transshipped by wagon to Santa Fe and Denver over the Santa Fe Trail and the Smoky Hill route. Neighboring Fort Riley, three miles to the northeast, was at that time also the headquarters of the District of the Upper Arkansas, a subdivision of the Department of the Missouri. Major Wynkoop, who had arrived at Junction City some days earlier with the goods he purchased for the Indians, was waiting there for Irwin. Wynkoop told Irwin that he intended to establish his agency at Fort Ellsworth on the Smoky Hill River and from there would issue the goods to his three tribes. Irwin and Wynkoop then wrote to William Bent and John Smith, both still at Fort Zarah, requesting that they ask the Indians to move to Fort Ellsworth to resume the council.[4]

On the morning of October 25 Major Wynkoop met with Maj. (Bvt. Maj. Gen.) John W. Davidson, who commanded the Second U.S. Cavalry and Fort Riley as well as the Military District of the Upper Arkansas and supervised the organization of the newly authorized Seventh U.S. Cavalry. They discussed the situation regarding the Indians of the Upper Arkansas Agency and the forthcoming issuance of annuities. General Davidson offered to send a column of troops with Wynkoop to Fort Ellsworth, Wynkoop's new agency headquarters, to serve as an escort and to protect the annuities.[5] Wynkoop politely declined on the very reasonable grounds that such a force would put the Indians in fear of another Sand Creek Massacre, and its mere approach would panic them and cause them to flee. He also related the current mission of Special Agent Irwin and reported that the Cheyennes were now refusing to accede to the amendments to the Little Arkansas treaty, largely, he thought, because of the objections of the Dog Soldiers.[6]

Wynkoop then proposed to Davidson that if the Cheyennes persisted in withholding their consent, the "good" Indians should be separated from the "evil disposed" ones. This, he said, "would in reality be placing the

---

[4] Ibid.; Dobak, *Fort Riley and Its Neighbors*, 40–41.

[5] Regular career officers reverted to their permanent peacetime rank as the army was downsized following the end of the Civil War, but many continued to be addressed by their brevet rank. Brevet ranks were honorary ranks awarded in recognition of distinguished service. The system was much abused, with many bestowed for meritorious staff service far from the battlefield. Herein an officer is referred to by his brevet rank only if he was serving in that rank. Thus Col. A. J. Smith, colonel and commander of the Seventh Cavalry, is referred to as "General Smith" because he was serving in that rank as commander of the District of the Upper Arkansas. Lt. Col. George A. Custer, as lieutenant colonel of the Seventh Cavalry, is referred to as "Colonel Custer" because he was serving in his regular rank with his regiment. See Utley, *Frontier Regulars*, 37n13.

[6] Wynkoop to J. W. Davidson, October 25, 1866; Davidson, *Black Jack Davidson*, 135–39.

Dog Soldiers in a situation of open hostility to the whites." In effect, they would either sign the agreement as dictated and give consent, or there would be war—a proposal somewhat short of voluntary treaty negotiations. Wynkoop suggested that the "well disposed Indians" be placed within certain safe boundaries in the neighborhood of Fort Ellsworth if those refusing to sign must be punished, thus avoiding the former mistakes of "punishing the innocent for the crimes of the guilty." The crimes referred to, of course, were the refusal to sign the treaty surrendering their homeland and resistance to white encroachment by attacking those who trespassed. What to whites were "crimes" and "outrages" were to the Cheyennes acts of resistance to the invasion of their country by the only means available to them. They had little choice, for they were always far too few to face a large, well-equipped body of troops in open combat. Wynkoop also pointed out to General Davidson that, despite General Hancock's orders to see that the Indians remained within the boundaries of their reservation, as yet they had no reservation and were by the treaty expressly permitted to roam at large.[7]

Wynkoop summarized his conversation with Davidson in a letter written to him the same day. Davidson doubtless forwarded this letter to General Hancock at his headquarters at Fort Leavenworth. Though it is unlikely the agent intended such a result, given his strong objections to the actions of the force that ultimately took the field under Hancock's command, it may be that his suggestion for punishment of the "guilty" was a factor in organizing that very expedition, or at least in making the Cheyennes its primary focus. If so, he must surely have later regretted placing it in a letter written to an army commander. Moreover, his observations about the effect on the Cheyennes of the approach of a large military force would ultimately seem prophetic. Wynkoop forwarded a copy of the letter to Commissioner Cooley, noting in his cover letter that though the majority of the Indians of his agency were "undoubtedly willing to subject themselves to any terms the Government of the United States may dictate," there were "some outlaws" among the tribes who should be punished. Wynkoop is generally considered to have been as fair and impartial an advocate as the Indians of his agency could have hoped for in that day, but it seems not to have occurred to him that the Indians had any rights to their own country or any choices in the making of a treaty that would surrender it.[8]

---

[7] Wynkoop to Davidson, October 25, 1866.

[8] Ibid.; E. W. Wynkoop to D. W. Cooley, October 26, 1866, MC234-R879.

This is the earliest-known photograph of Fort Riley, made in late 1866 or early 1867. The view is from the northwest, and the Flint Hills loom beyond. The Seventh Cavalry was organized there in 1866, and Elizabeth (Libbie) Custer waited there for her husband during much of his absence in the field in 1867. It was to Fort Riley and Libbie that Custer returned from Fort Wallace without leave or authorization in mid-July of 1867, leading to his court-martial. *Courtesy of the U.S. Cavalry Museum, Fort Riley, Kansas.*

Hopes for an early agreement with the Arapahoes and those Cheyennes who had signed the treaty were dashed when John Smith arrived in Junction City on Thursday, October 25. He informed Irwin and Wynkoop that the Indians had held a council and decided not to go to Fort Ellsworth. Smith was sent back to Fort Zarah the following day with instructions to again urge the remaining Arapahoes and Cheyennes to move to Fort Ellsworth, a distance of about forty-six miles, to receive their goods. Major Wynkoop also left at about the same time, taking the annuity goods to Fort Ellsworth for distribution. The next day, October 27, he reported to Commissioner Cooley from Fort Ellsworth, stating that he had "entered upon my duties as U.S. Indian Agent for the Arapahoe, Cheyenne and Apache Indians." This made it abundantly clear that the Indian bureau, painfully aware of Agent Taylor's shortcomings, had already effectively replaced Taylor without notifying him. In fact, Wynkoop signed his bonds for the office on September 26, while still in Washington. Later reports received from John Smith indicated that he failed to persuade the Indians to move to Fort

Ellsworth, and this compelled Major Wynkoop to leave that post for Fort Zarah on October 30 in an effort to salvage the council.[9]

Wynkoop's subsequent report from Fort Zarah likewise indicated no success. On the evening of November 2, Special Indian Agent Charles Bogy, brother of the commissioner of Indian affairs, arrived in Junction City from St. Louis. Irwin told him what had occurred at Fort Zarah and of the dissatisfaction of the friendly Cheyennes and Arapahoes with the goods purchased for them. Irwin wrote his report of the council for the commissioner on November 3, and Charles Bogy supplemented it with a letter of his own. He enclosed copies of the invoices listing the goods purchased for the Kiowas and Comanches by Colonel Leavenworth and those brought to the Cheyennes and Arapahoes by Major Wynkoop, noting that the only items of hardware included for the latter were needles. The omission was significant and the source of much distress to the friendly Cheyennes and Arapahoes. Because of the impasse, on the evening of November 3 Irwin and Bogy took the stagecoach to Fort Ellsworth. Though unaware of it, en route they passed Wynkoop, who was then returning to Junction City. Prior to leaving Fort Ellsworth, however, Wynkoop telegraphed the commissioner of Indian affairs, advising him that the Cheyennes and Arapahoes felt aggrieved at having received no arms and ammunition like those issued to the Kiowas and Comanches. If authorized to do so, he proposed exchanging the unsuitable goods previously sent for suitable arms and ammunition.[10]

On November 5 Charles Bogy telegraphed his brother Lewis from Fort Ellsworth, advising that Wynkoop, while at Fort Zarah, had provided a great feast for the remaining Arapahoes and Cheyennes, creating a better feeling among them. Though still unwilling to go to Fort Ellsworth, probably because it was on the Smoky Hill and in Dog Soldier country, those who moved back south of the Arkansas were now willing to return and hold a council on Walnut Creek near Fort Zarah. He emphasized the importance of the arms distribution in securing a resolution of the matter. But later the same day he again telegraphed the commissioner, this time advising that John Smith had returned to Fort Ellsworth and reported that things were about as they were when Irwin telegraphed his preliminary

---

[9] E. W. Wynkoop to D. W. Cooley, September 26 and October 27, 1866, MC234-R879; Irwin to Bogy, November 3, 1866.

[10] E. W. Wynkoop to Commissioner of Indian Affairs, November 3, 1866 (telegram), MC234-R879; Chas. Bogy to Lewis V. Bogy, November 3, 1866, MC234-R879; Irwin to Bogy, November 3, 1866, MC234-R879.

report of October 20. Because of the contradictory assessments of Smith and Wynkoop, Bogy stated he would have to investigate further, but that the Cheyennes were definitely not then at Walnut Creek.[11]

At Fort Ellsworth—a motley assortment of dugouts, tents, adobe buildings, a log blockhouse, a corral, and the stage station—Irwin and Bogy finally concluded that even the friendly Indians would not come to council there. Therefore they took the stage on to Fort Zarah, arriving on the evening of November 9. The annuity and treaty goods, which were with Wynkoop at Fort Ellsworth, were left there under army protection in the event no peaceable resolution was possible. On November 10 the two special agents held a council with the Arapahoe chiefs, nearly all reportedly being present (at least as the agents believed), and the chiefs apparently made their mark on a document ratifying the amendments to the treaty. A courier was sent to Fort Ellsworth, requesting Wynkoop to hurry the Arapahoe goods to Fort Zarah for distribution.[12]

In their report of November 12, Irwin and Bogy stated that few of the Cheyenne chiefs were present for the council, and of those that were, some expressed a willingness to approve the amendments and others objected. Couriers were sent out to request that the other chiefs come in, but it was not possible to predict the result. They also reported that on the evening prior to their arrival a Mexican herder employed by William Bent had been killed by a Cheyenne. This referred to a killing attributed to Fox Tail, a son of Stone Forehead. Fox Tail had been with his family in the largest of the various Cheyenne villages, then located south of the Arkansas River about four days' ride from Fort Zarah, probably on the Cimarron River or its Bluff Creek tributary. He apparently had an argument with his father concerning peace with the whites and left the village, riding north to Fort Zarah. Fox Tail arrived on November 8 and soon fell in with the white whiskey peddlers (perhaps including the agent himself) who infested the area of the Indian agency. By evening he was in a drunken state that led to the killing. Following an argument, Fox Tail shot the Mexican and then rode north and west to the Dog Soldier village, most likely located at the time on the south fork of the Solomon River.[13]

By November 13 a number of the Cheyenne chiefs arrived to council, and Irvin and Bogy met with them on that day and the next. All matters

[11] C. Bogy to L. V. Bogy, November 5, 1866 (two telegrams), MC234-R879.
[12] W. R. Irwin and C. Bogy to L. V. Bogy, November 12, 1866, MC234-R879; Oliva, *Fort Harker*, 25–30.
[13] Irwin and C. Bogy to L. V. Bogy, November 12, 1866; Berthrong, *Southern Cheyennes*, 264–65; Grinnell, *Fighting Cheyennes*, 246; Powell, *People of the Sacred Mountain*, 1:412.

of difference were discussed, and the chiefs present assented to the Senate amendments. But although in their report of November 15 Irwin and Bogy claimed that the "principal chiefs" of the Cheyennes were present, in fact they were the same ones that Irwin had met with in October, primarily Black Kettle and his fellow peace chiefs. Absent were all of the Dog Soldier council chiefs and those of the southern Sutaio, as well as most other members of the Council of Forty-four. No doubt a combination of weariness to conclude the matter and ignorance of Cheyenne tribal leadership resulted in their decision to wind up proceedings at Fort Zarah, for they must have been aware that the unyielding Dog Soldiers were not present. What they could say was that those who had signed the treaty in the first place or later ratified it had signed off on the amendments, and consequently the amended treaty was at least as valid as the original one.[14]

During their council, Irwin and Bogy discussed the killings and depredations the Cheyennes were accused of after the original treaty, and demanded of those chiefs present that the man (Fox Tail) who had killed the Mexican herder be surrendered. This demand was declined, the Indians noting that he was not in their camp and had not been seen since the event, and though they disapproved of his act, the entire tribe should not be held responsible for the actions of one foolish man. Besides, they said, it was white men who provided the whiskey and got him drunk, and they were as responsible as he was. They also pointed out that the United States had not performed its treaty promises in full either. To mitigate this complaint, the two special agents suggested that the office do all it could to locate the two Cheyenne children seized by Chivington's men at Sand Creek. Both were girls (and sisters as well), and at least one was reportedly being displayed at a circus sideshow, while the other was thought to be held in the vicinity of Denver.[15]

In a supplemental report of November 15, Irwin and Bogy advised they had certified three vouchers totaling $9,149.11, representing the cost of additional goods and provisions purchased to satisfy promises to the Arapahoes, Cheyennes, and Plains Apaches.[16] The largest single amount was

---

[14] W. R. Irwin and C. Bogy to L. V. Bogy, November 15, 1866, MC234-R879; Berthrong, *Southern Cheyennes*, 264; Grinnell, *Fighting Cheyennes*, 246; Powell, *People of the Sacred Mountain*, 1:411–13.

[15] Irwin and C. Bogy to L. V. Bogy, November 15, 1866; William Bent to John Pope, August 28, 1866, MC234-R879; Berthrong, *Southern Cheyennes*, 264–65; Grinnell, *Fighting Cheyennes*, 246; Powell, *People of the Sacred Mountain*, 1:412–13.

[16] The Plains Apaches, who ranged south of the Arkansas with the Kiowas and Comanches, wanted to remain in the vicinity of the Arkansas River and therefore, by treaty signed at the Little Arkansas on October 17, 1865, were confederated with the Cheyennes and Arapahoes for administrative purposes.

for fifty-one rifles and ninety-eight Navy pistols, plus holsters, belts, caps, powder, and lead, all purchased from David A. Butterfield, former owner of the Butterfield Overland Despatch, who had acquired the entire stock of William Bent. Bent, apparently concluding the council was a failure, had sold out to Butterfield and left the area. Irwin and Bogy suggested that this purchase was absolutely necessary to effect an amicable resolution to the council and that now the Indians were satisfied.[17]

Eight days later, on November 23, however, the two men again wrote the commissioner, reporting a further purchase of goods from Butterfield totaling $14,356.02. This represented the bulk of the remaining items Butterfield had bought from Bent—mostly blankets, bolts of cloth, items of clothing, saddles, and bridles, along with cooking gear, tin pans, plates, and cups. This purchase too was said to be absolutely necessary to alleviate the great dissatisfaction of the Indians with the other goods provided them and to comply with promises repeatedly made to them. This suggests either that the original goods delivered by Wynkoop were lacking in many items desired by the Indians or were of poor quality or insufficient quantity, as well as deficient in the matter of arms and ammunition, or that the council was not going as well as earlier reported, and an additional inducement was necessary. Irwin and Bogy indicated they hoped to finish what they could accomplish within a few days, and would then send a complete report. Clearly the objectives of the council had not been accomplished in full by November 23.[18]

On November 26 Agent Wynkoop reported to Commissioner Bogy that he had removed his agency to Fort Larned, Kansas. He advised that he had issued annuity goods to the Arapahoes and Plains Apaches and some of the Cheyennes, and that they seemed to be very well satisfied. He made further note that the visit of the two special commissioners, Irwin and Bogy, had been of the "utmost benefit." Wynkoop then asked the commissioner to obtain from the War Department an order that he was to be furnished with transportation, quarters, and storage by any army post in the region, particularly Fort Larned. That his agency's Indians remained in a nomadic state, he said, required him to maintain his headquarters on the plains "far removed from civilization," rendering him dependent on the military authorities. Wynkoop forwarded a similar report to Thomas Murphy, superintendent of the Central Superintendency, on December 2,

---

[17] Irwin and C. Bogy to L. V. Bogy, November 15, 1866; Berthrong, *Southern Cheyennes*, 264; Powell, *People of the Sacred Mountain*, 1:411.
[18] W. R. Irwin and C. Bogy to L. V. Bogy, November 23, 1866, MC234-R879.

in which he stated that the "Indians were never more quiet or peaceable than since my arrival among them." That would soon change.[19]

The council held with the Cheyennes and Arapahoes at Fort Zarah was the last one that attempted to persuade all of the bands of Cheyennes to agree to the terms of the Treaty of the Little Arkansas, as amended by the Senate. Though represented as a success by white authorities, it was in fact a failure. No known member of the Council of Forty-four made his mark at Fort Zarah who had not previously approved the treaty, and it was not sanctioned and blessed by the Arrow Keeper. The matter of the cession of the Cheyenne and Arapahoe lands between the Platte and the Arkansas remained exactly where it was before the treaty. The Indians, particularly those Cheyennes other than Black Kettle and his followers, continued to insist they still owned their country, and continued to roam across it as they had since first coming south. They also persisted in their version of what they had agreed to in the various councils, namely that whites could have free and unobstructed passage across their roads along the Arkansas and Platte rivers but could have no road or railroad along the Smoky Hill or make other incursions into their country. For its part the government simply ignored this view, asserting that the treaty and its amendments had been approved by all of the "leading chiefs" and therefore was binding on the entire tribe.[20]

The various bands of Cheyennes of the southern plains went into their several winter camps in late December, some along the Arkansas, some on the Cimarron, some on Bluff Creek. The Dog Soldiers and southern Sutaio apparently made their original winter camp somewhere on the south fork of the Solomon, since the presence of Forts Harker, Hays, and Wallace as well as the stage line and its stations now made many of their traditional campsites along the Smoky Hill untenable. Sometime during the winter, probably in late February or early March, they were joined by the Kiyuksa, or southern, band of Oglalas under Bad Wound, with Pawnee Killer as their headman.[21]

---

[19] E. W. Wynkoop to L. V. Bogy, November 26, 1866, MC234-R879; E. W. Wynkoop to Thomas Murphy, December 2, 1866, MC234-R879.

[20] Grinnell, *Fighting Cheyennes*, 246; Powell, *People of the Sacred Mountain*, 1:411–13.

[21] Henry Douglas to Henry E. Noyes, March 24, 1867, Fort Dodge, LS, NA, MC989-R1; Henry Douglas to C. McKeever, March 31, 1867, Fort Dodge, LS, NA, MC989-R1; *Junction City Weekly Union*, April 18, 1867; W. S. Hancock to W. T. Sherman, April 13, 1867, in "Difficulties with the Indian Tribes," 7:51; Berthrong, *Southern Cheyennes*, 273; Powell, *People of the Sacred Mountain*, 1:413, 462. Maj. Gen. Christopher C. Augur reported to General Hancock that the southern Oglalas were camping on Beaver Creek in northwest Kansas in February 1867. They apparently moved southeast to join the Dog Soldiers soon after, as they were with the Dog Soldiers when they moved to the Pawnee Fork in early March.

Soon after the arrival of the Kiyuksas, the Cheyenne and Oglala villages moved south, going into camp on the north, or Heth's, branch of the Pawnee Fork, about thirty-three miles northwest of Fort Larned. It was their intention, they reported to F. F. Jones, post interpreter at Fort Dodge, to "make medicine" with other bands of their tribe now camping south of the Arkansas. The southern Oglalas were said to be friendly and had come south to avoid the difficulties north of the Platte resulting from the recent Fetterman fight. Still camping to the northwest on a tributary of the Republican, probably Sappa Creek or Prairie Dog Creek, was a large village of Sicangu (Brulé, or Burnt Thigh) Lakotas under Spotted Tail, Two Strike, Swift Bear, and Big Mouth, with fifty lodges of the Óhmésėheso Cheyennes under Turkey Leg. Turkey Leg and his followers lived alternately in the south and the north, sometimes with the Dog Soldiers and southern Sutaio, sometimes with the southern Sicangu or the Kiyuksas, and sometimes with the other Óhmésėheso and the northern Oglalas in the Powder River country. This village was in constant contact with the village on the Pawnee Fork. From all appearances both were entirely peaceful.[22]

So ended 1866. E. W. Wynkoop was now officially the agent for the Cheyennes and Arapahoes, the drunken I. C. Taylor having resigned on November 28, 1866, after more than half a year without pay. Even before Wynkoop's appointment, however, it became apparent that a storm was brewing on the southern plains. On October 30, as Wynkoop was traveling from Fort Ellsworth to Fort Zarah in an effort to salvage the council between the Cheyennes and Special Agents Irwin and Bogy, General Hancock wrote to him these ominous words: "Let me know as soon as advised what Indians accept the terms of the treaty proscribed by the Senate. . . . It will be necessary to punish some of these Indians, and I will be very happy to have it understood who are not proper subjects for punishment before proceeding to extremities."[23]

---

[22] Douglas to Noyes, March 24, 1867; Douglas to McKeever, March 31, 1867; *Junction City Weekly Union*, April 18, 1867; Berthrong, *Southern Cheyennes*, 273; Hyde, *Life of George Bent*, 272–73; Powell, *People of the Sacred Mountain*, 1:413, 462.

[23] I. C. Taylor to D. N. Cooley, August 10, 1866, MC234-R879; E. W. Wynkoop to D. N. Cooley, November 26, 1866, MC234-R879; I. C. Taylor to L. V. Bogy, December 4, 1866, MC234-R879; Hancock to Wynkoop, October 30, 1866.

CHAPTER FOUR

A Storm Brewing

Though Special Agents Irwin and Bogy, along with Major Wynkoop, thought their efforts successful, with the Indians at peace and resigned to their fate, other forces were at work that would prove them wrong. The Dog Soldier and southern Sutaio Cheyennes believed not only that they had agreed with the U.S. government that they could retain their own country but also that whites were forbidden to enter it except on the roads along the Arkansas and Platte rivers. Moreover, the destruction of Capt. William J. Fetterman's entire command on the northern plains in late December 1866 effectively closed the Bozeman Trail. This apparent capitulation by the whites probably encouraged the Cheyennes to conclude that, with a little help from friends, they too might successfully prevent use of the Smoky Hill route if the government did not do it for them. Unfortunately for the Cheyennes, they had no way of knowing that federal authorities would not go to war over the Bozeman Trail, which would soon be unnecessary due to construction of the Central Pacific and Union Pacific railroads and development of alternate routes to the gold fields. The Smoky Hill, on the other hand, was precisely the route the Union Pacific Railroad, Eastern Division (E.D.), was to follow. To acquire the right-of-way for this, the American government would go to war if necessary.[1]

Though unrelated to the raids and attacks along the Smoky Hill, negotiations began in early October between Ben Holladay, now spread thin financially, and Wells Fargo to join forces. A new corporation was organized by Holladay bearing the name "Wells Fargo," and the stage lines of both parties were conveyed to it. Ostensibly Holladay was buying out the

---

[1] Powell, *People of the Sacred Mountain*, 1:413; Utley, *Frontier Regulars*, 104–107; Utley, *Indian Frontier*, 105.

other company, but Wells Fargo, with 40,000 shares, owned majority control. When the merger was completed on November 1, 1866, it was Wells Fargo that operated most of the significant stage lines west of the Missouri River.[2]

Within the military establishment, changes were also occurring that were to bode ill for the Indians. With the Civil War recently concluded and the army greatly reduced in size, in mid-1865 William Tecumseh Sherman ("Cump" to his family and friends) replaced John Pope as commander of the huge Military Division of the Mississippi. Pope in turn was given command of the Department of the Missouri, westernmost and largest of the three subdivisions within the division, stretching east to west from Missouri to Utah and north from the southern borders of Missouri, Kansas, New Mexico, and Utah to the Canadian border. Like nearly all military officers who assumed commands in the West after the Civil War ended, Sherman possessed limited knowledge of the physical environment of the plains and of the Native inhabitants, their culture, and their ways of war. Though he had served as a lieutenant in California following the Mexican War, worked briefly in San Francisco as a banker, and later tried his hand at the practice of law in Leavenworth, Kansas, on the Missouri River, he had no experience with the lands between. In early November 1865, while yet a novice, he suggested that as soon as the Indians were aware that regular cavalry were among them, "they will realize that we are in condition to punish them for any murders or robberies." Clearly Sherman had yet to grasp that he was dealing not with murder and robbery but with open warfare, which, from the perspective of the Indians, resulted from the ongoing white intrusion into their country without their consent, and the destruction of the timber, grass, and game on which their way of life depended. Nor did he seem to understand that American cavalry, with large, heavy, grain-fed horses, were unlikely to ever catch the mounted warriors of the plains in open combat. But unlike most officers new to the plains, Sherman did attempt to do something about his lack of knowledge. Until cavalry was available to protect white caravans, he followed the advice and example of Gen. John Pope and established a series of rendezvous points along the well-traveled immigrant and trade routes. At those places all overland parties were to be organized with at least twenty wagons and thirty armed men present for self-defense. Such arrangements were often ineffective against sudden and

---

[2] Lee and Raynesford, *Trails of the Smoky Hill*, 91.

unexpected Indian attack, but it was the best available solution at the time.[3]

Soon it became clear to Sherman that the Department of the Missouri was far too large and unwieldy, charged with protecting vital travel routes westward that were more than one commander could effectively deal with. At his recommendation the department was split in March 1866. That portion controlling Utah and the plains and Rocky Mountains north of the Platte River was designated as the Department of the Platte, while the Department of the Missouri retained responsibility for the lands of the old department south from the river. Over Sherman's objections, Gen. Ulysses S. Grant appointed Philip St. George Cooke to command the new department. Cooke, fifty-six years old, was a veteran campaigner in the West but, in Sherman's eyes, too old to be aggressive. "We need a young general who can travel and see with his own eyes, and if need be command both Whites and Indians to keep Peace," he told Grant. He suggested Winfield Scott Hancock, but Grant did not comply.[4]

The want of officers with knowledge and experience in Indian relations and warfare, and the lack of both understanding and a coherent Indian policy, ultimately caused the War Department and the army to turn to Brig. Gen. John Pope for advice. Pope was vain, verbose, and a self-appointed expert on Indian affairs, but his years on the western frontier nonetheless gave him greater understanding of the problems of Indian warfare than most of the ranking officers of the day. He was an outspoken critic of the treaty system, not from legal or philosophical considerations but rather from the pragmatic belief that the Indians would abide by treaties for only as long as it suited and profited them. Paradoxically, this was precisely what whites had done from the time they first began intruding on the Plains Indian country. For Pope the Indians' title to their own lands was not a consideration; a treaty was simply a matter of peace. In his view a treaty was to be grounded not on giving anything of value such as annuities, which he viewed as bribes, but on an exchange of promises of peace. If the Indians kept the peace, the army would as well; and if the Indians broke the peace, the army would make war on them. That

---

[3] W. T. Sherman to U. S. Grant, November 6, 1865, Grant Papers, ser. 5, 47, reel 21, LC; General Order No. 27, February 28, 1866, Senate Ex. Doc. 2, 40 Cong., 1 Sess., 2–4; Athearn, *William Tecumseh Sherman*, 3–17, 36–38; Wooster, *Military and United States Indian Policy*, 114.
[4] W. T. Sherman to U. S. Grant, March 10, 1866, Division of Mississippi, LS, 1865–1866; Athearn, *William Tecumseh Sherman*, 33–39; Jordan, *Winfield Scott Hancock*, 183.

breaches of the peace commonly resulted from the actions of whites was not relevant to his military logic.[5]

While General Pope was stern in his approach to the keeping of the peace, he was not entirely unsympathetic to the plight of the Indians. He believed that teachers should be sent among them to instruct them in Christianity and the methods of individual agriculture, thus settling them down, "civilizing" them, and allowing them to earn their own keep. Knowing this would entail a lengthy process, he also believed the Indians should be removed from their own country to a location where they could "never again be brought into contact with white emigration, nor obstruct the settlement and development of the new territories." The question of ownership of the "new territories" did not enter into the thinking of Pope or other military commanders; nearly all of them assumed that the treaties purporting to relinquish title were valid for that purpose, if otherwise worthless, regardless of whether the United States had fulfilled its part of the supposed agreements. A certain naïveté was also apparent in the assumption that a location might be found on which Indians could be placed and that whites would abstain from entering. Nevertheless, Pope was sincere in his belief that removal was the only way to prevent extermination of the tribes and reduce bloodshed. In time his theories did influence his superiors.[6]

General Sherman was impressed with Pope's concept of removal and recommended it to Grant. These views, of course, were hardly unique. Removal to reservations had long been practiced with the Woodland Indians of the eastern parts of the country, and the recent peace commissions had included them in the treaties signed at the Little Arkansas, Fort Sully, and Fort Laramie. But the military considered such treaties of little worth because, based on their experience, the Indians would not abide by them. There was truth in this, not because Indians lacked regard for solemn treaties and promises but rather because, as they saw it, no valid treaties had been signed, or if there had been, the Indians asserted that they were told the treaties said and meant something different from what appeared on the written page and that the whites were not living up to those promises. The Indians remained adamant in their refusal to surrender their country and their way of life.[7]

[5] J. Pope to W. T. Sherman, August 11, 1866, U.S. Department of War, *Annual Report of the Secretary of War, 1868*, 3:26–27; Utley, *Frontiersmen in Blue*, 309–10, 333; Wooster, *Military and United States Indian Policy*, 114–15.

[6] Pope to Sherman, August 11, 1866; Utley, *Frontiersmen in Blue*, 309–10, 333; Wooster, *Military and United States Indian Policy*, 114–15.

[7] Sherman to Grant, November 6, 1865; Wooster, *Military and United States Indian Policy*, 115.

The role of Sherman, as a military man, was not to make treaties or judge their validity but to enforce them. Moreover, he was to enforce the peace, and he set about to do just that. To learn about the vast military division he commanded and the Indian problems that the press and populace of the West constantly complained of, Sherman made two trips during the summer of 1866 to see for himself. These occurred even as the Interior Department and its Office of Indian Affairs were feverishly trying to get more chiefs to approve the treaties recently made. Sherman's first trip, in May, took him out across the plains of Kansas as far as Fort Riley, from there northwest along the Republican River more than one hundred miles, and then north to Fort Kearny on the Platte River. From Fort Kearny he headed east for Omaha by army ambulance, traveling the last seventy-five miles by rail on the new tracks of the Union Pacific. Leaving Omaha, Sherman next went north by riverboat on the Missouri River to Sioux City and then northeasterly across the prairie country of Iowa and Minnesota to Fort Snelling and St. Paul. He then returned to his headquarters in St. Louis to take care of business before embarking on his next trip west in mid-August.[8]

The stampede of whites to Montana for gold made it necessary to reshuffle the western commands. On August 6, 1866, prior to departure on his second journey, Sherman's division was renamed the Division of the Missouri, the Department of the Ohio was shifted to an eastern command, and the Department of the Platte was split. The portion including Minnesota, Dakota, and Montana now formed the Department of Dakota, with Gen. Alfred Terry commanding. At the same time, General Grant sent Maj. Gen. Winfield Scott Hancock to the Department of the Missouri, replacing John Pope, and sent Gen. E. O. C. Ord to the Department of Arkansas. Sherman was pleased with the changes, which he had recommended, and believed that these officers would keep things well in hand while he completed his tours of familiarization.[9]

General Sherman left on his second tour westward shortly after completion of the reorganization and by August 15 was at Fort Leavenworth. From there he traveled north by riverboat to Omaha, then west on the Union Pacific to Fort Kearny in the company of his brother John. After inspecting the fort, the Sherman brothers and their party traveled by army ambulance to Fort McPherson, Fort Sedgwick, and Fort Laramie. In accordance with his plans Sherman would head south from Fort Laramie to Denver,

---

[8] Athearn, *William Tecumseh Sherman*, 45–51.
[9] Ibid., 54–56.

Colorado City, and Pueblo, then on to Fort Garland in the San Luis Valley, where he would meet with Kit Carson. After that he would return across the plains of Colorado and Kansas to Fort Leavenworth and then on to St. Louis. During the course of his trip Sherman was impressed with the absence of widespread Indian troubles, despite the clear threat to their way of life and the many provocations of white settlers and travelers. He found the continual reports of a frontier aflame greatly exaggerated. From Fort McPherson he wrote, "As usual, I find the size of Indian stampedes and stories diminishes as I approach their location." Three days later he wrote that he had "met a few straggling parties of Indians who seem pure beggars, and poor devils, more to be pitied than feared." Nevertheless, he recognized the mistrust evident on both sides that could quickly explode into open hostilities. And it was the Indians he would have to punish, regardless of who was at fault in bringing on conflict. He was not yet ready to deal with that, and for 1866 he needed a period of calm. By the next year, he wrote, "We can have the new cavalry enlisted, equipped, and mounted, ready to go and visit these Indians where they live."[10]

When he reached Fort Laramie, Sherman received reports of several attacks in which a number of whites were killed, usually the result of their own foolish actions. But by the time he arrived at Denver and the new towns established all along the Front Range of the Rocky Mountains in Colorado Territory, he was impressed with both the development of population centers and flourishing farms and the apparent absence of an Indian threat. He personally experienced no troubles with Indians during his extended trip, although he was traveling with a very small and lightly protected party. The stories and rumors to the contrary he attributed to the fact that the western settlements "are resolved on trouble for the sake of profit resulting from military occupation." During his return trip along the Santa Fe Trail and a stop to inspect Fort Dodge, however, Sherman learned of the attack on the Box family of Montague County, Texas. James Box had been killed by a Kiowa raiding party, and his wife and daughters captured. Two of the daughters were later ransomed from Satanta by the commanding officer at Fort Dodge, but Sherman forbade the further ransom of persons as only encouraging the taking of captives.[11]

After concluding his tours, Cump Sherman sat down in his headquar-

[10] W. T. Sherman to J. A. Rawlins, August 21 and 24, 1866, U.S. House, "Protection across the Continent," 4:26, 6–8; Athearn, *William Tecumseh Sherman*, 56–64.

[11] W. T. Sherman to John Sherman, October 20, 1866, William T. Sherman Papers, vol. 19, LC; Athearn, *William Tecumseh Sherman*, 65–90; Oliva, *Fort Dodge*, 36–38.

ters in St. Louis and wrote a report of what he had found. Whereas the eastern reaches of his division—Minnesota, Iowa, Missouri, and Arkansas—were fertile and well adapted to settlement, to the west lay the Great Plains, a vast ocean of grass devoid of trees and likely even of valuable minerals. In his opinion this great semiarid stretch of country could never be successfully cultivated or populated and would be valuable only as an immense pasture for livestock. On the other hand, he thought, the mountains and territories beyond held great promise based on the possibilities of development of natural resources, such as minerals and timber, and of farming in the valleys.[12]

The plains lying between the mountains and the developed states to the east, themselves a natural impediment to travel and movement of goods, were the home of the nomadic Plains Indians, to Sherman the most dangerous barrier to the expansion of the nation. Although he realized the aggressive and expanding white population was the root cause of most of the conflict, he saw no solution other than removal of the Native peoples to reservations. To this end he proposed moving the Lakotas and other northern tribes to the territory north of the Platte River, west of the Missouri, and east of the Bozeman Trail. The tribes of the southern plains—the Cheyennes, Arapahoes, Comanches, Kiowas, and Plains Apaches—would be moved to the region south of the Arkansas River, west of the state of Arkansas, and east of Fort Union, New Mexico. "This," he said, "would leave for our people exclusively the use of the wide belt, east and west, between the Platte and the Arkansas, in which lie the two great railroads, and over which passes the bulk of travel to the mountain Territories."[13]

With his recommendations for a future course of action complete, Sherman directed the heads of the plains departments—Terry, Cooke, and Hancock—to prepare expeditions that would go among the Indians the following spring to show the flag and engage any hostiles. But before these plans were finalized, a large war party of Miniconjou and Oglala Lakotas and Ôhmésêheso Cheyennes on December 21, 1866, successfully decoyed Capt. William J. Fetterman and eighty other officers and men into an ambush along the Bozeman Trail just beyond Fort Phil Kearny in Wyoming, killing them all. Fetterman, who had allegedly boasted that

[12] Report of W. T. Sherman, November 5, 1866, *Annual Report of the Secretary of War, 1868*, 3:18–23; Athearn, *William Tecumseh Sherman*, 93–96; Berthrong, *Southern Cheyennes*, 267–68; Wooster, *Military and United States Indian Policy*, 116–17.
[13] Report of W. T. Sherman, November 5, 1866, 3:18–23; Athearn, *William Tecumseh Sherman*, 93–96; Berthrong, *Southern Cheyennes*, 267–68; Wooster, *Military and United States Indian Policy*, 116–17.

with eighty men he could ride through and defeat the entire Sioux Nation, was effectively proven wrong, if indeed he ever made that statement. Wherever the real fault lay, the disaster stunned and outraged the army, which called for immediate reprisal. Sherman's famous temper now got the best of him, and on December 28 he telegraphed Grant, "We must act with vindictive earnestness against the Sioux, even to their extermination, men, women, and children." Sherman certainly did not intend the literal result of his words and, unlike Chivington, would never have intentionally targeted women, children, or the old for annihilation. But though such actions were not government policy, and though the words were uttered in anger by a man well known for his fiery temper and would come back to haunt him, Sherman's statement was nevertheless symptomatic of a mind-set all too common within the army and the western states. It was the same mind-set that resulted in the Sand Creek Massacre.[14]

Following the Fetterman disaster, and apparently assigning a degree of responsibility to General Cooke, Grant replaced him with forty-five year-old Gen. Christopher C. Augur, a classmate of Grant's at West Point. Though Sherman found it difficult to understand how Cooke could be at fault for what happened to Fetterman, he was nonetheless pleased. With relatively young men now commanding the three western departments, Sherman had what he believed to be aggressive field commanders. Initially he was disappointed with the performance of Hancock, who seemed reluctant to move to the frontier and acquaint himself with his department and the problems it faced, as Sherman desired. Instead Hancock preferred to remain in St. Louis with his family. But finally he transferred his headquarters to Fort Leavenworth and began planning his spring operations.[15]

Sherman was a soldier's soldier, a believer in (and one of the early American practitioners of) total war against an entire enemy population—men, women, children, and the old. What he had practiced in Georgia and South Carolina he intended to apply to the Plains Indians if the appropriate occasion arose—the relentless pursuit and destruction of enemy property and personnel so complete as to reduce the opponent to abject poverty and an inability to wage war. Despite his early hesitance to move to the frontier, Hancock was an enthusiastic proponent of Sherman's philosophy of total war and heartily believed that force, firmly applied, would

[14] W. T. Sherman to U. S. Grant, December 28, 1866, U.S. Senate, "Fort Phil Kearny Massacre," 2:4; Athearn, *William Tecumseh Sherman*, 98–99; Berthrong, *Southern Cheyennes*, 268; Utley, *Frontier Regulars*, 104–107, 111; Wooster, *Military and United States Indian Policy*, 117–19.
[15] Athearn, *William Tecumseh Sherman*, 55, 99–100.

resolve the "Indian problem" once and for all. But he knew even less of the Plains Indians or their methods of warfare than did Sherman and other career officers reporting for duty on the western plains for the first time. Nor did he know their country, a land vastly different from that which he had recently fought over in the East.[16]

Plans for an early spring and summer campaign against the Plains Indians had been in process for some time. The Dog Soldier and southern Sutaio raids of September 1866 rankled General Hancock and his staff at Fort Leavenworth. In combination with Wynkoop's letter of October 25 to General Davidson, recommending punishment for "evil disposed" Indians, and Fox Tail's killing of the Mexican at Fort Zarah, the raids apparently focused Hancock's attention on the Cheyennes as the most appropriate tribe to "chastise." Although 1866 was much quieter on the southern plains than the preceding two years and Major Wynkoop had reported the Cheyennes far more peaceable than at any time since he arrived among them, by early December Hancock decided to make them one of the principal targets of his spring operations in the new year. It was true that there were several troublesome tribes in his department, but he subscribed to the view that punishment of any one tribe would likely dampen the raiding ardor of the rest. Consequently he suggested to division headquarters that the Cheyennes be his principal target, as they "appear to be as deserving of chastisement as any other." Later, in a letter to General Sherman dated January 14, 1867, he stated that the killing of the Mexican at Fort Zarah, the livestock theft at Fort Wallace, and the attacks on Chalk Bluffs Station were themselves sufficient reason for punishment of the tribe. He told Sherman he intended to demand that the Cheyennes either deliver the killer of the Mexican or, if he had "run away," deliver to the army, as hostages to guarantee his delivery, two chiefs "who behaved insolently on the Smoky Hill last summer." This, he assured Sherman, would no doubt "lead to war" with the Cheyennes. Then, revealing his true intentions, he said: "I think it would be to our advantage to have these Indians refuse the demands I intend to make, a war with the Cheyennes would answer our purposes, as some punishment seems to be necessary. This matter, I wish to dispose of in March or April, before the grass comes up."[17]

The army's resolve for early spring campaigns against the mounted tribes

[16] Ibid., 3–4, 100; Jordan, *Winfield Scott Hancock*, 182–86, 188; Utley, *Frontier Regulars*, 114.
[17] W. S. Hancock to W. S. Nichols, AAG, Division of the Missouri, December 2, 1866, Department of the Missouri, LS, NA; W. S. Hancock to W. T. Sherman, January 14, 1867, Department of the Missouri, LS, NA; Berthrong, *Southern Cheyennes*, 268–69; Powell, *People of the Sacred Mountain*, 1:463; Wooster, *Military and United States Indian Policy*, 120.

of the northern and southern plains was doubtless bolstered by the Fetterman fight. Writing to his brother John on December 30, 1866, only two days after his angry letter to Grant calling for the extermination of the Sioux, Sherman was clearly in a determined and reflective mood when he stated: "I expect to have two Indian wars on my hands. The Sioux and Cheyennes are now so circumscribed that I suppose they must be exterminated, for they cannot & will not settle down, and our people will force us to it." Rumors abounding on the plains that the tribes would unite for war against the whites when the grass greened, reinforced this view. That was particularly true of Hancock. Though he finally moved his headquarters from St. Louis to Fort Leavenworth, to Sherman's chagrin he made no tours of his department or its facilities, contenting himself with reports from his field commanders. He seemed to place credence in the swirling rumors and allegations of impending Indian troubles, despite the lack of any credible supporting evidence.[18]

The flurry of rumors of an imminent Indian war appear to have originated from several sources. One of these was Governor Samuel J. Crawford of Kansas, no friend of the Native peoples. Starting in the summer of 1866, Crawford sent a flood of letters to both Hancock and Sherman, asking for federal troops to protect the frontier. He felt certain that the large winter camps of Cheyennes, Arapahoes, and southern Lakotas along the Pawnee Fork, the Saline, the Solomon, and the tributaries of the Republican, presaged an all-out attack on the westernmost white settlements and the advancing railroads. Though Crawford had no firm evidence to support these allegations, Hancock was solicitous of the governor and seems to have accepted them as fact. Sherman, on the other hand, was far more skeptical.[19]

Crawford's true motives are speculative. Presumably submitting to pressure from traders, travelers, and settlers along the frontier in east-central Kansas, in 1866 he commissioned Maj. Gen. William Cloud of the Kansas Militia to raise a battalion to protect the white population in the absence of a strong federal presence. Some area newspapermen accused Crawford of fomenting fear of a general uprising of Plains Indians so that an entire regiment of state troops would be authorized at federal expense, thus sup-

[18] W. T. Sherman to John Sherman, December 30, 1866, William T. Sherman Papers, vol. 20, LC; Athearn, *William Tecumseh Sherman*, 100–101; Berthrong, *Southern Cheyennes*, 268; Jordan, *Winfield Scott Hancock*, 186; Powell, *People of the Sacred Mountain*, 1:463; Utley, *Frontier Regulars*, 114–15.

[19] Garfield, "Defense of the Kansas Frontier," 326–27; Athearn, *William Tecumseh Sherman*, 57; Crawford, *Kansas in the Sixties*, 251; Jordan, *Winfield Scott Hancock*, 196; Leckie, *Military Conquest*, 36–37.

plementing a struggling state economy and providing the appearance of strong protection. The militia he called up at state expense had a less than stellar record, spending more time hunting bison than Indians. But more central to Crawford's actions, in all likelihood, were the machinations of the railroads. All of those building west were anxious to have the Native peoples removed from the areas of their rights-of-way in order to stimulate settlement, the sale of adjacent lands given to them by patent from the government, and ultimately a population base that would use their services. Crawford was later charged with accepting a bribe from the Union Pacific Railroad, E.D., and though a legislative committee investigating the affair acquitted him, he did receive 640 acres as a gift from the railroad.[20]

Reports from the commanders of both Fort Dodge and Fort Larned also tended to confirm Hancock's belief. The most dubious of these were submitted by Maj. Henry Douglass, Third Infantry, commanding officer at Fort Dodge. On February 9, 1867, Fred F. Jones, a post interpreter, filed a complaint with the major, alleging that when he, post sutler John E. Tappan, and Maj. John H. Page had gone to Satanta's Kiowa camp nearby along the Arkansas River to trade, the Kiowas seized all of their goods and threatened to kill them.[21] Moreover, before they left the camp, a Kiowa war party allegedly returned with some two hundred horses stolen in Texas, along with the scalps of seventeen black soldiers and one white man. The records of the newly formed black units, just then beginning their service on the southern plains, do not show the loss of seventeen men during this period, and George Bent stated that neither the Cheyennes nor any other plains tribes took the scalps of black soldiers.[22] In addition to these false allegations, Jones also passed on threats reportedly made by Satanta in his presence. Page and Tappan both later appeared before Douglass and denounced Jones's claims as baseless. Though Douglass passed the Jones charges on to Hancock, inexplicably he failed to report the subsequent denunciations of the other two supposed witnesses.[23]

---

[20] *Junction City Weekly Union*, August 3, 1866, 2; Crawford, *Kansas in the Sixties*, 230–34; Leckie, *Military Conquest*, 36–37; Oliva, *Fort Dodge*, 41–42.

[21] Page then held the permanent rank of captain and was a major by brevet. He later (December 1867) became the post commander at Fort Dodge.

[22] The refusal to take the scalps of black soldiers was not because of racial bias but because most black males of that era wore their hair close cropped. Only long hair was suitable for a trophy scalp, and hence scalps were likewise not taken from whites who were bald or wore their hair cut short.

[23] H. Douglass to W. S. Mitchell, AAAG, District of the Upper Arkansas, February 24 and March 19, 1867, Fort Dodge, LS, NA, M989-R1; H. Asbury to W. S. Mitchell, AAAG, District of the Upper Arkansas, February 27 and March 6, 1867, Office of the Adjutant General, LR, NA; Berthrong, *Southern Cheyennes*, 271; Hyde, *Life of George Bent*, 254–55; Leckie, *Military Conquest*, 35–36; Oliva, *Soldiers on the Santa Fe Trail*, 184–85; Utley, *Frontier Regulars*, 115.

Major Douglass apparently convinced himself that an all-out Indian war was looming. As a result, he held a series of conferences with Satanta, Satank, Stumbling Bear, and some of their Kiowa followers. Since the death of the great Kiowa chief Dohásän (Little Mountain), the leadership of the Kiowa tribe was fractured. The successor to Dohásän was Lone Wolf, who was known not to favor peace with whites or surrender of tribal lands. But Lone Wolf lacked the moral authority of his predecessor, and the tribe became divided in its attitudes, opinions, and loyalties. Satanta, the tribe's greatest orator and second most influential chief, was also the most bellicose. Undeniably brave and even reckless in battle, he was equally reckless with the truth, when it served his purpose. It was Satanta who seems to have been behind many of the stories and rumors concerning a confederation of Plains tribes to make war on whites.[24]

During his meetings with the officers from Fort Dodge, Satanta warned that when spring came there would be a council between the tribes of the northern and southern plains, with war against the white intruders the likely result "as soon as the grass was one inch high." Whites had come to his country without invitation, he said, and had used its resources to the harm of his people. He wanted them out. He demanded that Fort Dodge and Fort Larned be abandoned forthwith and that the soldiers and other whites cease using the water, wood, grass, and game belonging to his people, for which no compensation was being paid. He wanted all military units removed to a location no farther west than the Council Grove, the Santa Fe Trail and other trails closed, and construction of railroads and telegraph lines across the southern plains halted. Satanta also humorously noted that the livestock at Fort Dodge appeared to be in poor condition and requested that they be given better care, as they would be his when he took the fort in the spring.[25]

Although many of the rumors floating around a nervous frontier had their roots in falsehoods originating with men like Jones and Satanta, there were some troublesome developments grounded in fact. Both Major Douglass at Fort Dodge and Capt. Henry Asbury at Fort Larned reported

---

[24] H. Douglass to W. S. Mitchell, AAAG, District of the Upper Arkansas, February 13 and 21, March 19 and 24, 1867, Fort Dodge, LS, NA, M989-R1; *Annual Report of the Commissioner of Indian Affairs, 1868*, 2:499; Leckie, *Military Conquest*, 36; Oliva, *Fort Dodge*, 43–44; Oliva, *Soldiers on the Santa Fe Trail*, 184; Strate, *Sentinel on the Cimarron*, 38–39; Utley, *Frontier Regulars*, 115.

[25] H. Douglass to W. S. Mitchell, AAAG, District of the Upper Arkansas, February 10, 1867, Fort Dodge, LS, NA, M989-R1, and in U.S. Senate, "Indian Hostilities," 102; Leckie, *Military Conquest*, 36; Oliva, *Fort Dodge*, 43–44; Oliva, *Soldiers on the Santa Fe Trail*, 184–85; Strate, *Sentinel on the Cimarron*, 38–39; Utley, *Frontier Regulars*, 115.

that large quantities of arms and ammunition were being sold to the southern Plains tribes by traders licensed by the Office of Indian Affairs. Moreover, whiskey was being provided to the warriors by these and other traders, resulting in unnecessary difficulties between Indians and travelers, as well as the military. Among those said to be responsible were David A. Butterfield, who supplied area traders through his license to provide firearms to Indians at peace with the United States, and Charley Rath, who had a trading house that shared a common location with Fort Zarah and was actually the older installation by several years.[26] When he received these reports, Hancock was furious. He passed the information on to General Sherman, who in turn wrote General Grant at army headquarters in Washington, D.C. Sherman asked that the army be granted the right to revoke the permits, whose issuance in the first instance he considered "monstrous." Grant agreed, and on January 26, 1867, upon the authority of Grant and Sherman, Hancock issued orders barring the sale of weapons and ammunition to the Indians in his department, except with the express approval of the commanding officers of Fort Dodge and Fort Larned. This resulted in a predictable outcry, first from the affected traders, who were making a profit of up to twenty times their actual cost, and finally from the Office of Indian Affairs.[27]

Feuding between the army and the Interior Department was nothing new. The Office of Indian Affairs had originated with the War Department in 1824 but was transferred in 1849 to the newly organized Interior Department. Once it was dominated by civilians, it quickly fell victim to graft and corruption as political hacks were appointed, by their friends and patrons in both the administration and Congress, to jobs for which they had no qualifications. The surprise is not that there were so many utterly incompetent and dishonest Indian agents but that there were those among them who did indeed have a genuine concern for the welfare of their charges. Their views, and the self-interest of the more corrupt agents, often brought them into bitter conflict with a military leadership that believed the army was best equipped to understand and deal with the "Indian problem."[28]

---

[26] Rath would later achieve added fame as a partner with Robert M. Wright in the operation of the well-known Wright and Rath store in Dodge City during the trail-driving era.

[27] General Order No. 2, HDQ, District of the Upper Arkansas, January 26, 1867, U.S. Senate, "Indian Hostilities," 7–11, 18–20; Athearn, *William Tecumseh Sherman*, 109; Berthrong, *Southern Cheyennes*, 269; Oliva, *Soldiers on the Santa Fe Trail*, 184; Powell, *People of the Sacred Mountain*, 1:463; Stanley, *My Early Travels*, 1:12–13; Utley, *Frontier Regulars*, 112.

[28] Athearn, *William Tecumseh Sherman*, 109–11; Berthrong, *Southern Cheyennes*, 269–70; Utley, *Frontier Regulars*, 112; Utley, *Indian Frontier*, 41–47.

The army's interference with the right of licensed traders to sell arms and ammunition to peaceful Indians for the presumed purpose of hunting brought a sharp outcry from both Secretary of the Interior Orville H. Browning and Commissioner of Indian Affairs Lewis V. Bogy, who held such actions illegal, unwarranted, "imperious," and certain to lead to war along the western frontier. Army officers and the western press and public believed such views, and those of the eastern peace advocates, were pure fantasy. In their opinion it was far better to end the division of authority between the military and the civilian agents by returning responsibility for Indian affairs to the War Department. This suggestion naturally horrified peace proponents, who firmly believed the army knew of no other solution to problems with the Indians than the use of force. For advocates of the army's position the upsurge in arms sales to the Plains Indians in the wake of the Fetterman disaster seemed ominous, making it a most opportune time to seek the change. On February 9, 1867, a bill drafted by Col. Ely S. Parker, General Grant's Seneca Indian aide, was introduced into the Senate to effect the transfer.[29]

Unfortunately for the army, the opponents of transfer had considerable political influence and were able to cite a large number of "Indian outbreaks" that could be traced directly to military blunders. Moreover, the recent release of the report of the special joint committee of Congress headed by Senator James R. Doolittle of Wisconsin, investigating the condition of the Indian tribes and their treatment by both civil authorities and the military, did much to undercut the army's position. Formed following the Chivington massacre of peaceful Cheyennes at Sand Creek, the committee amassed an enormous amount of reliable testimony pointing to the conclusion that the desperate plight of the Indians was the direct result of the incursions of whites into their country. Most Indian wars, it found, resulted from white aggression, and the best way to reduce the friction was by a policy of conciliation and moderation.[30]

The bill to transfer passed the House of Representatives but failed in the Senate, where General Sherman's unfortunate words about exterminating the Sioux with vindictive earnestness were quoted to prove the army untrustworthy in the administration of Indian affairs. Adding to Sherman's woes, Secretary Browning convinced President Johnson that it was better to try conciliation than to allow the army to impose a peace by force,

---

[29] Athearn, *William Tecumseh Sherman*, 110–11; Berthrong, *Southern Cheyennes*, 271; Utley, *Frontier Regulars*, 112–13.

[30] Athearn, *William Tecumseh Sherman*, 111; Utley, *Frontier Regulars*, 113.

the only solution it seemed to recognize. Accordingly, a peace commission was appointed to seek out the causes of the Fetterman debacle, determine the attitude of the Indians to settling on reservations, and find out if arms and ammunition were really necessary for the Indians to feed themselves. Four of the six commissioners were present or former military men, including the chairman, General Sully. But considering their charge as peace advocates, this was small comfort to General Sherman.[31]

The plans for early spring campaigns on both the northern and southern plains that Sherman set in motion in late 1866 were approaching completion by the beginning of March 1867. In the Department of Dakota, General Terry was busy reinforcing the posts along the Missouri River and adding new ones. His troops were also being readied to sally forth in pursuit of any Lakota war parties that might attempt to obstruct either river or overland travel. In the Department of the Platte, General Augur was preparing the Second Cavalry and a force of infantry gathered at Fort Laramie, about two thousand men in all, to march to the Powder River country. There they would make war on the Lakotas who had been raiding the Bozeman Trail, presumably the same who were responsible for the defeat and annihilation of Captain Fetterman and his troops. In the words of General Sherman, "No mercy should be shown these Indians for they grant no quarter, nor ask for it." The Powder River expedition would be under the immediate command of Col. John Gibbon. And on the southern plains General Hancock was to lead his expedition west to show the flag and engage any hostile Cheyennes or Kiowas he might encounter who were disposed to fight. Originally it was intended that he take the field by March 1, 1867, but heavy rain, high water in streams, and impassable roads forced a delay in Hancock's plans.[32]

Unhappily for General Sherman, the peace commission arrived in Omaha early in March 1867, preparing to travel west and north to hold talks with the Lakotas. A frustrated Sherman was compelled to order General Augur "to delay actual hostilities" until the commissioners were forced to admit they could not bring peace by "pacific measures." No such problem as the peace commission faced General Hancock in the south, and there military planning continued at a rapid pace. Sherman had whole-

---

[31] Athearn, *William Tecumseh Sherman*, 111–13; Utley, *Frontier Regulars*, 113.

[32] W. T. Sherman to K. Leet, AAG, March 13, 1867, HDQ Army, LR, U.S. Senate, "Expeditions against the Indians," 1–3; W. S. Hancock to W. S. Nichols, AAG, May 22, 1867, AGO, LR, NA, MC619-R563 (hereafter this collection is designated "MC619-R563"), and in U.S. House, "Difficulties with the Indian Tribes," 78; Athearn, *William Tecumseh Sherman*, 104–107; Utley, *Frontier Regulars*, 113–14.

heartedly supported Hancock's plans for an early spring campaign from the beginning. And he wanted that campaign commenced before the first growth of spring grass could restore the strength of the Indian horses, because, as he told Grant, "an Indian with a fat pony is very different from him with a starved one."[33]

With his plans complete, General Hancock traveled by rail to St. Louis and the Division of the Missouri headquarters, where he met with General Sherman on March 8 to review those plans. The two discussed the plans at length and finalized them, and Hancock returned to Fort Leavenworth to begin assembling his troops and gathering supplies. In a letter to army headquarters on March 13, Sherman explained that the object of the Hancock expedition was to reach the Indians and "confer with them to ascertain if they want to fight, in which case he will indulge them." The primary mission, he said, was to impress on them "the imprudence of assuming an insolent manner and tone when they visit our posts" and "that it is in their interest to keep their hunting parties and their young warriors off our main lines of travel, where their presence gives the occasion for the many rumors which so disturb our people." Obviously knowing the temperament of Hancock and his desires and concluding that a fight was probable, he added, "Our troops must get among them, and kill enough of them to inspire fear, and then must conduct the remainder to places where the Indian agents can and will reside among them, and be held responsible for their conduct."[34]

The following day Sherman wrote to Hancock, confirming in writing the oral instructions he gave at their meeting in St. Louis. First, carefully noting that congressional placement of management of Indian affairs with the Interior Department deprived the army of the legal right to control Indians or adopt preventive measures, Sherman pointed out that the military was compelled to respect Indian treaties as the law of the land and further to respect the authority of Indian commissioners or agents. Therefore, he said, Hancock need not make a demand on the Cheyennes for the "drunken fellow who killed the Mexican at Zara last fall," nor for those who killed the stock herders and ran off the livestock at Chalk Bluffs Station. "Leave these cases to the agents, and so notify them," he added,

---

[33] W. T. Sherman to U. S. Grant, February 18, 1867, HDQ Army, LR, U.S. Senate, "Expeditions against the Indians"; Sherman to Leet, March 13, 1867; Athearn, *William Tecumseh Sherman*, 106; Berthrong, *Southern Cheyennes*, 271; Powell, *People of the Sacred Mountain*, 1:463; Utley, *Frontier Regulars*, 114; Wooster, *Military and United States Indian Policy*, 119.

[34] Sherman to Leet, March 13, 1867; Athearn, *William Tecumseh Sherman*, 105; Berthrong, *Southern Cheyennes*, 271–72; Jordan, *Winfield Scott Hancock*, 187; Powell, *People of the Sacred Mountain*, 1:463–64.

almost as though he recognized that Hancock was spoiling for a fight and would use those events as an excuse to start one.

Continuing, Sherman observed that it was the army's duty to provide for the protection of lawful settlers "on surveyed land or other lands where it is lawful for them to make locations," mail routes established by law, and lines of travel through the Indian country "established by competent authority or to which a right has accrued by former implied consent," as well as military posts and personnel. Sherman then stated his understanding that the Cheyennes, Arapahoes, and Kiowas had on several occasions assembled near the army posts on the Smoky Hill and Arkansas "in numbers and strength manifestly beyond the control of their agents" and by manner and word threatened to disrupt use of the roads. "This cannot be tolerated for a moment," Sherman thundered. "If not a state of war, it is the next thing to it, and will result in war unless checked." To this end he authorized Hancock "to organize, out of your present command, a sufficient force to go among the Cheyennes, Arapahos, and Kiowas, or similar bands of Indians, and notify them that if they want war they can have it now; but if they decline the offer, then impress on them that they must stop their insolence and threats." So Hancock was now armed with written orders authorizing him to make war on the Indians of the southern plains for "insolence and threats" as well as actual acts of war. What was not clear was how he was to recognize lawful settlers or roads for which a right-of-way was granted by "former implied consent." The Indians had in fact repeatedly made it clear they wanted no roads through their country, had never knowingly consented to such by implication or otherwise, and would not. Nor was it clear just what degree of insolence was sufficient to bring on war and the killing of the offending parties, or even what should be considered "insolence." That would apparently be left to the not unbiased judgment of General Hancock, a man spoiling for a fight.[35]

Once back at Fort Leavenworth, and with the full support of General Sherman, Hancock began to assemble his troops and signal his intentions to the Indian agents. In similar letters of March 11, 1867, Hancock notified Major Wynkoop, agent for the Cheyennes, Arapahoes, and Plains Apaches, and Colonel Leavenworth, agent for the Kiowas and Comanches, that he intended to march into their country. The plan, he said, was "to convince the Indians within the limits of this department, that we are able to pun-

[35] W. T. Sherman to W. S. Hancock, March 14, 1867, U.S. Senate, "Difficulties with Indian Tribes," 7:98–99; Utley, *Frontier Regulars*, 115.

ish any of them who may molest travelers across the plains, or who may commit other hostilities against the whites." He requested that the agents notify the chiefs of each tribe of his impending arrival and stated that he would be glad to have interviews with them. The agents were also to tell them

> that I go fully prepared for peace or war, and that hereafter I will insist on their keeping off the main lines of travel where their presence is calculated to bring about collisions with the whites. If you prevail upon the Indians of your agency to abandon their habit of infesting the country traveled by our over-land routes, threatening, robbing, and intimidating travelers, we will defer this matter to you. If not, I would be pleased by your presence with me when I visit the locality of your tribes, to show that the officers of the government are acting in harmony.

It was apparent that Hancock disregarded that it was white lines of travel penetrating the Indian country, not Indians "infesting" those routes, that gave rise to the hostilities.[36]

Hancock intended to meet with the chiefs of all of the southern Plains tribes, but of course they were widely scattered across thousands of square miles and would not likely even hear of the proposed meeting until long after it had occurred. Most of the Comanches, Kiowas, and Plains Apaches were south of the Arkansas in their own country. Many of the southern bands of Arapahoes and some of the Cheyennes were likewise now south of the river, bent on staying out of harm's way. But the tribes had unknowingly fallen back into Hancock's jurisdiction. Early in March 1867 the state of Arkansas was removed from Sherman's Division of the Missouri and transferred to another. The balance of the former Department of Arkansas (present Oklahoma), the only surviving remnant of Jefferson's original Permanent Indian Territory, now became a part of Hancock's Department of the Missouri. As a result nearly all of the lands of the southern Plains tribes were placed within the expanded boundaries of Hancock's department and within his ability to pursue and "chastise."[37]

Hancock was a proud, ambitious, and vain man, as is not uncommon with those accustomed to the adulation of the public. Not wanting to overlook favorable publicity, on March 10, immediately after returning from

[36] W. S. Hancock to E. W. Wynkoop, and W. S. Hancock to J. H. Leavenworth, March 11, 1867, Department of the Missouri, LS, U.S. House, "Difficulties with the Indian Tribes," 7:16–17, 92–94; Leckie, *Military Conquest*, 38; Oliva, *Soldiers on the Santa Fe Trail*, 185; Powell, *People of the Sacred Mountain*, 1:465; Utley, *Frontier Regulars*, 115–16; Wooster, *Military and United States Indian Policy*, 120.

[37] Report of W. T. Sherman, October 1, 1867, in *Annual Report of the Secretary of War, 1867*, part 1, 3; Athearn, *William Tecumseh Sherman*, 105.

Henry M. Stanley was another newsman traveling with General Hancock, whom Stanley admired for his Civil War record. Greatly biased against the Indians, his reports and subsequent autobiographical writings nevertheless provided insights into events of the Indian wars otherwise not well reported. *Frank Leslie's Illustrated Newspaper*, 1867.

the St. Louis conference with General Sherman, he wrote a letter to Theodore R. Davis, an artist and reporter for *Harper's Weekly* in New York City. Hancock invited Davis to join the expedition at Fort Harker and accompany it during the approximately six weeks he expected to be in the field. The purpose of the expedition, he said, had originally been "to redress some outrages," but recent congressional action had compelled him to limit the objective to displaying such force as would show the Indians the army was ready for either peace or war. Then, on a more hopeful note, he wrote: "Our visit may prevent an outbreak. If one is intended, it may precipitate it. The Indians threaten to stop travel over the Overland and Pacific R.R. We will demand peaceful dispositions and also will punish aggressions or hostile acts coming under our notice." Hancock went on to say that they might meet a good many Indians and. if so, would talk to them. No hostilities were anticipated "unless arising from the omission to notice old outrages." Obviously the inability to properly "chastise" the Indians rankled Hancock, who noted that they would attribute the failure to do so to fear and would possibly be "insolent," giving grounds for action.[38]

---

[38] W. S. Hancock to T. R. Davis, March 10, 1867, Theodore R. Davis Collection, Manuscript Division, KSHS.

The *St. Louis Missouri Democrat*, probably learning of the expedition from Sherman's headquarters in that city or from Hancock himself, was also dispatching its own correspondent. He was a twenty-five-year-old immigrant from Britain who had the rare distinction of having served in the armies of both the Confederacy and the Union, and was now pursuing a career as a newspaper correspondent. His name was Henry M. Stanley, and not only would he follow and report on the Hancock expedition and its famous leader, whom he much admired, but one day would find Dr. David Livingston in the jungles of Africa.[39]

Now the planning and preparations were complete. The route of march had been determined, supplies and provisions laid up at Fort Riley and other posts on their itinerary, the participating units alerted, transient officers and those on leave recalled, and transportation arranged. The media were informed and would be present to provide coverage of this important operation and its commander.[40] It remained only for the Expedition for the Plains to begin its march into history.

---

[39] Powell, *People of the Sacred Mountain*, 1:464; Stanley, *My Early Travels*, 1:xiii.

[40] Hancock ran for the nomination as the presidential candidate of the Democratic Party in 1868, 1876, and 1880, was successful in 1880, but lost the general election to James A. Garfield. Therefore it seems probable that during his 1867 expedition to the plains he was quite conscious of the favorable publicity that might come his way if he won added glory fighting hostile Indians.

CHAPTER FIVE

The March Begins

The force constituting the Expedition for the Plains, to be com-posed of troops presently under Hancock's command, would by his order consist of seven companies of the Thirty-seventh U.S. Infantry, eight companies of the Seventh Cavalry, and Battery B of the Fourth U.S. Artillery. The artillery battery and six of the infantry com-panies were stationed at Fort Leavenworth and the seventh infantry com-pany (F) would be attached from Fort Riley, its assigned station. Four companies of the Seventh Cavalry (A, D, H, and M) were then at Fort Riley, where the regiment had been organized, and the remaining four companies would join the expedition at Fort Harker and Fort Larned. Accompanying them in support would be a commissary train, a quarter-master train, and the company wagons for each infantry and cavalry com-pany and the artillery battery. Also assigned to the expedition was a train of pontoon bridges for crossing rivers and streams, clearly reflecting Gen-eral Hancock's failure to familiarize himself with the environment and understand the difference between watercourses on the western plains and those in the eastern states where he had recently fought.[1]

Each of the wagon trains consisted of twenty-four wagons in the charge of a wagon master and an assistant wagon master, with a teamster for each wagon, a cook to prepare meals for the personnel, and a watchman to look after the teams and the camp at night. The government wagons, of stan-dard design, had six wagon bows and weighed about 1,800 pounds with extra parts and equipment, and, when fully loaded for a campaign, could carry approximately 6,800 pounds of military equipment and supplies.

[1] Hancock to Nichols, May 22, 1867; *Army and Navy Journal*, April 6, 1867, 4:418; Barnard, *Ten Years with Custer*, 22; Chandler, *Of GarryOwen in Glory*, 3; E. Custer, *Tenting on the Plains*, 484; G. Custer, *My Life on the Plains*, 31; Jordan, *Winfield Scott Hancock*, 187–88; Kennedy, *On the Plains*, 49; Leckie, *Military Conquest*, 38n18; Utley, *Frontier Regulars*, 116.

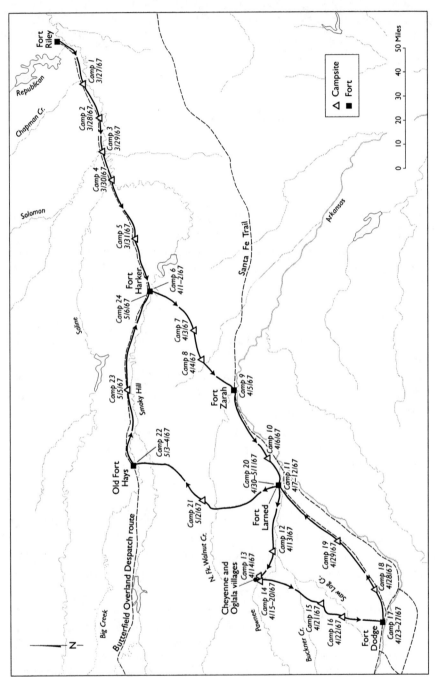

March of Hancock's Expedition for the Plains, March 27 to May 6, 1867. *Map by Bill Nelson.*

Each wagon was pulled by six mules, driven in pairs and guided by a jerk line. Where there was a road to travel on, the wagons usually moved single file. When a road was lacking or they were in Indian country, they might travel either two or four abreast, facilitating the circling of the wagons in times of danger. During travel outside of secure areas they would be escorted by troops, either infantry or cavalry, with an advance and rear guard, and flankers on both sides.[2]

The train of pontoon bridges accompanying the expedition was in the charge of a detachment from the U.S. Army Engineer Battalion, consisting of a sergeant, a corporal, and six privates, under the command of 1st Lt. Micah R. Brown, chief engineer of the Department of the Missouri. Their bridging equipment was made up of four hundred feet of canvas pontoon bridge (a series of canvas boats over which the wooden bridge segments were laid), carried in wagons driven by the usual crew of teamsters and wagon master. General Smith detailed Capt. R. W. Barnard and his Company F of the Thirty-seventh Infantry to escort the pontoon train and help with bridge building. Upon receiving his assignment to Hancock's staff on March 15, Brown telegraphed the army's chief engineer in Washington, D.C., requesting the necessary instruments for a thorough reconnaissance in the field. Their departure from Fort Leavenworth on March 25 was prior to receipt of the equipment, however, and Brown was limited to prismatic and common compasses, an odometer, and pocket levels available at Fort Riley as his equipment in making the more technical of his observations and measurements. He also had a thermometer for taking atmospheric temperature and devices for measuring the depth and rate of flow of streams crossed, which he did regularly.[3]

The expedition's mounted regiment, the Seventh Cavalry, was one of four new cavalry units authorized by the Army Act of July 28, 1866—the Seventh and Eighth, to be composed of white enlisted men and officers, and the Ninth and Tenth, to consist of black enlisted men and white officers. The organization of the Seventh was ordered on August 27, 1866, and the first steps for organization were taken on September 10. On November 2 the War Department issued General Order No. 92, assigning Col. (Bvt. Maj. Gen.) Andrew Jackson Smith as the colonel of the regiment, Capt. (Bvt. Maj. Gen.) George Armstrong Custer as the lieutenant colonel, and Maj. (Bvt. Maj. Gen.) Alfred Gibbs as the senior

[2] Barnard, *Ten Years with Custer*, 22–23.
[3] M. R. Brown to W. S. Mitchell, AAAG, May 30, 1867, MC619-R563.

major. By the end of September all twelve companies, A through M (there was no J), had been organized and had reached a total enlisted strength of 882 men. All were temporarily commanded by officers of the Second U.S. Cavalry, then stationed at Fort Riley, pending assignment and arrival of their own company officers.[4]

Major Gibbs arrived on October 6 but was immediately sent to appear before an examining board in Washington, D.C., to confirm his qualifications to hold his position and rank in the Seventh Cavalry. Lieutenant Colonel Custer reported on November 3 but was likewise sent to Washington on November 9 to appear before the same examining board, not returning until December 16. General Smith arrived on November 26, and at the end of December all companies had some or all of their own officers. By the end of November, only the regimental headquarters and Companies A, D, H, and M remained at Fort Riley, the others having been ordered to various posts in the Department of the Missouri. Companies B and C were at Fort Lyon, Colorado Territory; Company E at Fort Hays, Kansas; Companies F and G at Fort Harker, Kansas; Company I at Fort Wallace, Kansas; Company K at Fort Dodge, Kansas; and Company L at Fort Morgan, Colorado Territory. During December most of the remaining officers arrived, and by year's end the regiment had 15 officers and 963 enlisted men.[5]

The Seventh Cavalry had but one army surgeon assigned to it, Assistant Surgeon Henry Lippicott of the army's Medical Department, whose rank was the equivalent of a first lieutenant. As the men prepared for their march, it was deemed necessary to contract for an additional doctor to provide medical care for the men while in the field. Contracting for the services of a doctor for special extended operations was a common practice in that day. Newspapers in the East had learned of an intended expedition against the Indians of the southern plains, probably through Sherman's St. Louis headquarters or perhaps from Hancock himself. After reading this story early in March 1867, Isaac Coates, a trained surgeon from Chester, Pennsylvania, with a penchant for adventure and a cold, austere wife, wrote to the War Department, seeking an appointment. Coates had previously served as a surgeon with the U.S. Navy during the Civil War. Within three days he received his answer with the desired appointment and orders to report to the medical director of the Department of the Mis-

[4] Barnard, *Ten Years with Custer*, 17–18; Chandler, *Of GarryOwen in Glory*, 2–3.
[5] Chandler, *Of GarryOwen in Glory*, 3; Millbrook, "Custer's First Scout in the West," 76.

souri at Fort Leavenworth. There he received further orders to report to
Fort Riley for service as "Acting Assistant Surgeon" with the Seventh Cavalry on its upcoming expedition. Traveling by rail, he reached the post on
March 22 and met Custer and the regiment's other officers that evening
at a social gathering at Custer's quarters. Coates would serve admirably,
not only by performing his duties as a regimental surgeon but also by keeping a careful and insightful journal of his experiences.[6]

The train that carried Isaac Coates to Fort Riley on March 22 also
brought the men and equipment of Battery B, Fourth U.S. Artillery. On
Sunday, March 24, another train from Fort Leavenworth transported six
companies of the Thirty-seventh U.S. Infantry to the post, joining the
one company already there. The commanding general, Winfield Scott
Hancock, and Headquarters, Department of the Missouri in the Field,
arrived by special train from Leavenworth on the evening of March 25.
With them, at the order of General Sherman, came a young Indian boy
called Wilson Graham, captured by Chivington's men at Sand Creek and,
by the terms of the Treaty of the Little Arkansas, to be returned to his
tribe. The army assumed him to be Cheyenne and a member of Black
Kettle's band. Sometime during late March fifteen Indian scouts of the
Delaware tribe, recruited from their reservation southwest of Fort Leavenworth and led by Fall Leaf, one of their chiefs, also reported for duty
with the expedition, as did three white scouts—James Butler (Wild Bill)
Hickok, Jack Harvey, and Tom Atkins.[7]

Once all of the players—troops, scouts, livestock, equipment, and expedition headquarters—were assembled, last-minute preparations began and
a flurry of orders were issued. On Tuesday, March 26, the department's
adjutant directed the quartermaster at Fort Riley to issue no public stores
during the pendency of the expedition except by authorization of departmental headquarters. The department's quartermaster was instructed to
inform the railroad company that the cars carrying the Thirty-seventh
Infantry companies to Fort Riley were five hours late in arriving at the
Fort Leavenworth depot, and those for Hancock and his headquarters
staff were three hours late, and that it had not fulfilled its commitment
promptly. Such orders reflect General Hancock's rigid insistence on pre-

[6] Kennedy, *On the Plains*, 26, 35–36, 45–47; Reedstrom, *Custer's 7th Cavalry*, 21; Utley, *Life in Custer's Cavalry*, 288.

[7] Hancock to Nichols, May 22, 1867; Special Orders 29, Division of the Missouri, February 23, 1867, AGO, LR, NA, MC619-R562; G. Custer, *My Life on the Plains*, 35; Jordan, *Winfield Scott Hancock*, 188; Stanley, *My Early Travels*, 35.

cise punctuality and a strict adherence to orders from anyone he dealt with, a quality that would not serve him well in his forthcoming dealings with the Plains Indians.[8] The officer commanding the Fort Leavenworth Arsenal was then notified that ten Spencer rifles issued to the Indian scouts accompanying the expedition were not new, such as were shown to Fall Leaf, and that three were broken and unserviceable.[9]

With the various cautions and complaints attended to, the expedition's chief quartermaster was ordered to issue without delay fifteen days' forage for the command and five full cavalry companies, to be placed at Fort Larned in addition to the supply already sent there. The expedition's commissary officer was likewise directed to forward fifteen days' rations for 1,600 men to Fort Larned to supplement those previously ordered to that post. The next order of the day was directed to General Smith, commanding the District of the Upper Arkansas and the Seventh Cavalry, and provided for the length of each day's march and camping points en route to Fort Harker. It also directed Smith to instruct troop commanders to burn away dry grass surrounding campsites before making camp each day to prevent the possibility of fire spreading through a camp. Finally on March 26, in preparation for the march, General Hancock issued his General Field Orders 1: all troops would receive their orders from General Smith, commander of the District of the Upper Arkansas, in whose territory the expedition was to move; for unity and harmony, no one but the expedition commander was to have "interviews with the Indians"; straggling was prohibited, being too dangerous in Indian country; firing of weapons was permitted only with prior authority; hunting was restricted to authorized parties charged with procuring meat; and guards were to be maintained as if in a state of hostility.[10]

The most significant part of General Hancock's order, in terms of purpose and warlike intent, was included in paragraph 2, a portion of which read:

---

[8] Indians in general did not understood the whites' system of measuring time, nor did their culture attach a similar importance to punctuality.

[9] W. S. Mitchell, AAAG, to G. W. Bradley, March 26, 1867, MC535-R1354 (hereafter this collection is designated "MC535-R1354"); W. S. Mitchell, AAAG, to L. C. Easton, March 26, 1867, MC535-R1354; W. S. Mitchell, AAAG, to J. McNutt, March 26, 1867, MC535-R1354.

[10] Mitchell to Bradley, March 26, 1867; W. S. Mitchell, AAAG, to H. B. Sedgard, March 26, 1867, MC535-R1354; W. S. Mitchell, AAAG, to A. J. Smith, March 26, 1867, MC535-R1354; General Field Orders 1, HDQ, Department of the Missouri, March 26, 1867, in U.S. House, "Difficulties with Indian Tribes," 7:12–13, and in U.S. Senate, "Indian Hostilities," 83.

George Armstrong Custer, two years after his dashing exploits during the Civil War and now lieutenant colonel of the new Seventh Cavalry, was more concerned with having his wife, Elizabeth (Libbie), with him than in pursuing Cheyennes or other Indians during Hancock's expedition. *Courtesy of Fort Larned National Historic Site.*

It is uncertain whether war will be the result of the expedition or not; it will depend upon the temper and behavior of the Indians with whom we may come in contact. We go prepared for war, and will make it if a proper occasion presents. We shall have war if the Indians are not well disposed towards us. If they are for peace, and no sufficient ground is presented for chastisement, we are restricted from punishing them for past grievances which are recorded against them; these matters have been left to the Indian Department for adjustment. No insolence will be tolerated from any bands of Indians whom we may encounter. We wish to show them that the Government is ready and able to punish them if they are hostile, although it may not be disposed to invite war.

Though the government may not have been disposed to invite war, it is clear that General Hancock was not adverse, and the tenor of his order to the troops was far more bellicose in tone than were his letters to Indian agents Wynkoop and Leavenworth. It is difficult, moreover, to believe that the Indians would likely be "well disposed" to having a large body of troops prepared for war entering their country.[11]

---

[11] General Field Orders 1, in U.S. House, "Difficulties with Indian Tribes," 7:13, and in U.S. Senate, "Indian Hostilities," 83.

On Tuesday, March 26, 1867, and again at dawn on Wednesday, March 27, Fort Riley was the scene of feverish activity. Troops packed their necessary clothing, supplies, and equipment in company wagons, cavalrymen groomed, fed, and prepared their horses for the march, and artillerymen fastened their guns to their limbers and readied their horses. As the loading of the wagons was finished on Wednesday morning, the teamsters hitched up their teams and brought them into line with the others in an assigned order. By early morning preparations were complete for those who would be first to march. After consulting with General Hancock, at 8:30 A.M., General Smith gave the order to move out, and the march of the Expedition for the Plains began. It was a drawn-out affair, with the lead elements well beyond Junction City before the last crossed the Republican, a short distance above its confluence with the Smoky Hill to form the Kansas River. The crossing was made on a pontoon bridge constructed a few yards upstream from the railroad bridge, about three miles northeast of the town.[12]

Junction City was at the time a typical small western town, not much more than a village, with a significant presence of saloons, gambling halls, sporting houses of prostitutes, and other dens of vice aimed at satisfying the desires of the lonely soldiers, as well as separating them from their pay. The temptations there were of sufficient concern to General Hancock that he issued orders directing the commanding officer at Fort Riley to send a detachment to Junction City and arrest and return to the post any stragglers from the Seventh Cavalry or Thirty-seventh Infantry found there. Any personnel of either unit remaining in their barracks or around the post without proper authority following the departure of their regiments were also to be arrested. Those with written authorization to be in Junction City were permitted to rejoin their commands.[13]

The route the expedition followed was the Fort Riley–Fort Harker–Fort Larned military road, an extension of the Fort Leavenworth–Fort Riley road. By this time these military roads were also being used by civilians and formed a part of the Butterfield Overland Despatch (now Wells Fargo) route, as far as Fort Harker. From that post westward the Wells Fargo stage line paralleled the Smoky Hill River, more or less following the route

[12] *Journal of the March of Troops under command of Major General Hancock* (hereafter "*March Journal*"), March 27, 1867, accompanying M. R. Brown to W. S. Nichols, AAG, May 30, 1867, MC619-R563; Kennedy, *On the Plains*, 49.
[13] W. S. Mitchell, AAAG, to J. C. Craig, March 27, 1867, MC535-R1354.

of the old Smoky Hill Trail of Colorado gold rush days. The stage road in turn was now being used by the military to supply and communicate with Fort Hays and Fort Wallace. The older military road from Fort Riley ran southwesterly beyond Fort Harker to Fort Zarah at the Great North Bend of the Arkansas River, where it joined the Santa Fe Trail and continued on to Fort Larned, Fort Dodge, and eventually Fort Lyon on the Mountain Route to Santa Fe. The expedition would follow the latter route outbound and the former from Fort Hays on its return to Fort Riley.[14]

Only three established towns were to be found west of Fort Riley at that time: Junction City, the Davis County seat, was three miles west of the Republican River crossing;[15] Abilene, the Dickinson County seat, lay to the south of the road's crossing of Mud Creek (sometimes known as Abilene Creek); and Salina, the Saline County seat and the town (and county) farthest west on the Smoky Hill road. Though Junction City was relatively well developed as a town, the other two hardly deserved the title. Joseph G. McCoy, the entrepreneur who extended the Chisholm Trail north to Abilene later in 1867, starting that village on the road to fame as a cattle town, described it as consisting of about a dozen log huts scattered along a nondescript street, only one of which had a pitched, shingled roof. The rest had the usual crude roofs of frontier buildings, supported by poles or vigas, over which were laid canvas, branches, twigs, and grass, with sod and mud forming the upper layer. One of the huts was a hostelry and saloon, kept by a jovial old plainsman. Around it was a large prairie dog town, whose inhabitants the saloonkeeper fed and cultivated as pets. Salina, about thirty miles farther west, was older, having been started in 1859 near the trail with the erection of four log houses, a small log store, and a blacksmith shop. By 1867 it had grown little and was in appearance much the same as Abilene.[16]

Kansas in 1867 was sparsely settled, with most of its population living in the approximate eastern one-fourth. Before the Civil War this region was

---

[14] Hancock to Nichols, May 22, 1867; Lee and Raynesford, *Trails of the Smoky Hill*, 6, 20, 52–56.

[15] Davis County was named for Jefferson Davis by the Territorial Legislature prior to the War between the States. In 1889 it was renamed Geary County, in honor of former territorial governor John W. Geary. An effort to restore the name to "Davis County" was submitted to the voters in 1894 but failed by 65 of the 1,111 votes cast, suggesting an abiding southern sentiment in a county that had a large southern population bloc from its inception. See KHC 8:451, 469; KHC 13:405; and Pride, *History of Fort Riley*, 143–44.

[16] Brown, *March Journal*, March 27, 28, and 30, 1867; Mead, "Saline River Country in 1859," 9:11–12; Montgomery, "Fort Wallace," 17:190–99; Tisdale, "Travel by Stage," 462–63; Gard, *Chisholm Trail*, 64; McCoy, *Historic Sketches*, 44.

the scene of vicious fighting between pro-slavery and free-state settlers, giving the state the nickname "Bleeding Kansas." Successive slavery and free-state constitutions, each adopted with the aid of considerable fraud, were submitted to Congress and rejected for want of approval by the required two-thirds majority. Finally secession made it possible for the most recent of the free-state constitutions, adopted at the fraud-filled and malapportioned Wyandotte Convention in 1859 and previously rejected, to be resubmitted and approved by Congress, allowing the territory to be admitted as a free state. Though some pro-slavery settlers returned to their states of origin to fight with Confederate forces there or formed Kansas units within the armed forces of Confederate states (such as the South Kansas–Texas Mounted Volunteers of the Texas Third Cavalry), others joined guerrilla or partisan units that plagued the state throughout the war, both from within and without its borders. Most pro-slavery settlers, however, probably resigned themselves to the new circumstances and simply focused on building new lives. With the end of the war, internal strife subsided, but a few of the former partisans turned to a life of crime with the new gangs of bank and train robbers, like the James and Dalton gangs. Most of these, however, operated farther to the east, at least until the postwar western movement of population began in earnest. As 1867 dawned, though there was turmoil and a trickle of settlers trying to crowd into the eastern extremities of the Plains Indian country, the great rush for settlement of the plains had not yet begun. But it would not be long in coming.[17]

Fort Riley and Junction City lay about midway across the breadth of the Flint Hills. These hills, composed of Permian-age limestones containing numerous bands of flint, or chert, rise to the west of the Osage Cuestas of far eastern Kansas and roughly approximate the border with the Great Plains to the west. The military road from Fort Riley to Fort Harker and Fort Larned ran more or less parallel with the Smoky Hill River, clinging to the upper edge of its valley to be safely above the floodplain, and a little north of the roadbed of the Union Pacific Railroad, E.D. (Kansas Pacific), then under construction. Except for the hamlets of Abilene and Salina, and Council Grove to the south, there were no true towns to the west of Junction City. Only the military roads, stage roads and stations, the trails of commerce along the Arkansas and Smoky Hill rivers, a few trading and hunting ranches, and the scattering of military posts

[17] Kansas Constitutional Convention, *Proceedings*, 359, 518; Athearn, *William Tecumseh Sherman*, 93–94; Gaeddert, *Birth of Kansas*, 35, 39; Jordan, *Winfield Scott Hancock*, 184–85; Page, *Legislative Apportionment in Kansas*, 30–34; Walton, *Sentinel of the Plains*, 105–18.

gave evidence of the whites' presence. Trees were to be found solely along
a few of the larger streams, and previous white travelers, military and civilian, had significantly reduced the number of these in their relentless search
for firewood. As yet it remained Indian country, widely believed to be
uninhabitable by whites, and Hancock's troops were about to enter it.[18]

As the expedition moved ponderously westward, it first passed through
Junction City. Here the enlisted men doubtless winked, waved, and called
out to the gamblers, saloonkeepers, and young ladies of the sporting houses
watching them wistfully from their windows or porches. For them business would fall off sharply for the duration. The Indian scouts had probably left earlier, heading on down the trail to locate suitable camping and
hunting grounds. The usual order of march would see the commanding
officer of the District of the Upper Arkansas, General Smith, and his
headquarters party, at the head of the column. Following them would be
the infantry, marching by company in ranks with the company wagons
bringing up their rear, then the artillery battery and their wagons, the cavalry companies trailed by their company wagons, and finally the commissary and quartermaster trains, followed by the train of pontoon bridges.
The commissary train alone stretched out to nearly a half mile in length.
General Hancock and his headquarters staff traveled where he designated,
but were often to be found on the flanks of the column, traveling with
Custer and the Seventh Cavalry. Once the expedition was beyond the
well-traveled "safe" part of the road, probably beyond Salina, a guard would
be established at the head, rear, and flanks of the marching column, with
scouts well in advance. But for the moment that was unnecessary. As the
march continued and the day wore on, typically the infantry companies
would become strung out as the men tired. The same would be true with
the artillery battery, the various company wagons, and the wagon trains,
as the horses and mules tired. The cavalry companies, though starting
their march later each day, commonly passed the others during the march,
a look of pity on their faces as they did, and were first into camp.[19]

The first day's march was only as far as Chapman's Creek, a distance
of about fourteen miles. To the left of the column lay the winding course
of the Smoky Hill River. Beyond it to the south the land rose sharply as
the Flint Hills crowded the valley's edge. To their right the hills loomed

[18] Brown, *March Journal*, March 28 and 30, 1867; Buchanan, *Kansas Geology*, 19–20; Jordan, *Winfield
Scott Hancock*, 184–85; Merriam, *Geologic History of Kansas*, 161–65.
[19] Barnard, *Ten Years with Custer*, 21–25; E. Custer, *Tenting on the Plains*, 515–16; Kennedy, *On the Plains*,
49–50.

above them a short distance from the road, their relatively level tops protected by a flinty gravel that resisted erosion. According to the surgeon
Isaac Coates, the day was very cold, with chill winds. When night came,
the temperature dropped below freezing. And so it may have been. However, in terms of temperature it may not have been as cold as he thought,
for the average daily high temperature in the early spring in that region
is in the upper fifties to low sixties, and the average lows a few degrees
above freezing. What he and most of the other men present were not
accustomed to was the wind, for winds at the surface of the plains average fourteen to fifteen miles per hour during the entire year, and considerably higher during a frontal passage, with the strongest winds usually
occurring during early to middle spring. Although the prevailing winds
across the southern plains are from the south, occasional intrusions of cold
air masses from the north bring northerly winds and bitter cold. Measur-
able snow usually falls only three or four times a winter and rarely covers
the ground for more then a few days as the warm southerly winds return.
So it is quite possible that the discomfort Coates and the others experienced was more the wind chill factor, something not understood in that
day, rather than actual freezing temperatures. This seems borne out at
least to some extent by the very different reports of the temperatures from
other participants on the expedition.[20]

The troops went into camp on the west side of the stream, a short distance upstream from the road, the customary practice of most wagon trains
and military units. This allowed evaporation to dry the wagon sheets and
any equipment or cargo that might have become wet during the fording
of a stream. Bridges had been built across all continually flowing streams
as far west as the Saline to accommodate the stage coach traffic, but these
were apparently not used by any of the troops, livestock, or vehicles of the
expedition, possibly because their weight far exceeded what the bridges
were designed to carry. The country was relatively wet from the recent
rains, but the road thus far had been good. On the east bank of the stream
north of the road was a "ranch," most likely the one known as the Hay
Ricks, the establishment of a trader and whisky dealer who sold his wares
to hungry and thirsty travelers across the plains or otherwise met their
needs. Though Custer and his tentmates spent a warm and comfortable
night in his Sibley tent with its efficient stove, most junior officers and

---

[20] Brown, *March Journal*, March 27, 1867; Buchanan, *Kansas Geology*, 19; Kennedy, *On the Plains*, 49–50;
Kraenzel, *Great Plains in Transition*, 12–23.

enlisted men were cold and uncomfortable in unheated tents on hard ground in the ceaseless wind.[21]

March 28 saw the usual early morning departure from camp, the infantry and artillery leaving first, and the cavalry following at about 8:30 A.M. Five miles out on the road west the cavalry overtook the others and went into camp during the early afternoon after a march of a little over thirteen miles. This day the road moved closer to the railroad roadbed, with the hills retreating a thousand or more yards to the north. The Union Pacific Railroad, E.D., had laid rails to Lamb's Point, six miles beyond Chapman's Creek, before construction was halted for the winter the previous November. But work was begun again during the late winter, and by March 14 track had been laid to Mud Creek at Abilene, though no traffic other than work trains as yet moved west of Junction City. The road followed by the expedition continued to be relatively level and in good condition. The march ended after the troops passed the village of Abilene and went into camp along the west bank of Mud Creek.[22]

During the afternoon and evening of March 28 General Hancock issued two orders and a report, the orders directed to General Smith and the report to the assistant adjutant general of the Division of the Missouri at St. Louis, Bvt. Maj. Gen. W. A. Nichols. The former asked that General Smith (a) direct the post commander at Fort Hays to provide an escort of twenty-five infantrymen to George F. Wickes, chief engineer of the Union Pacific Railroad, E.D., to accompany Wickes and his party during their survey of right-of-way from Big Creek, near Fort Hays, to Denver, provided Fort Hays could spare the men; and (b) provide to the Headquarters of the Department of the Missouri in the Field copies of all of his orders relative to the movement of troops during the expedition. The latter informed General Sherman's headquarters that the two companies of the Seventh Cavalry at Fort Lyon (B and C) had been ordered to move down to Fort Dodge to meet the expedition, while the company at Fort Hays (E) had been directed to march to Fort Larned to join the others.[23]

Custer thought the camp on Mud Creek very pleasant, with good water, good ground, and sufficient wood to make everyone comfortable. How

---

[21] Brown, *March Journal*, March 27, 1867; E. Custer, *Tenting on the Plains*, 515–16; Kennedy, *On the Plains*, 50; Montgomery, "Fort Wallace," 17:191; Utley, *Life in Custer's Cavalry*, 18.

[22] Brown, *March Journal*, March 28, 1867; E. Custer, *Tenting on the Plains*, 516–18; Kennedy, *On the Plains*, 50–51; Snell and Richmond, "Union and Kansas Pacific," 335–36.

[23] Brown, *March Journal*, March 28, 1867; W. S. Hancock to W. S. Nichols, AAG, March 28, 1867, MC535-RI354; W. S. Mitchell, AAAG, to A. J. Smith, March 28, 1867 (two), MC535-RI354.

others viewed it was not recorded, but doubtless his commodious quarters and Sibley stove made him more generous in his assessment than some others might have been. He and a few of the married officers, moreover, had with them a large store of foodstuffs prepared by their wives or cooks, which, for so long as they lasted, kept them far better nourished and content than were those subsisting on simpler army fare. Custer also had five of his hunting dogs with him with which he daily made serious assaults on the Kansas jackrabbit population. During the night these same companions lay next to his bedroll, adding to his warmth and comfort.[24]

The bachelor officers fared far worse than most men with respect to meals. Whereas married officers like Custer had a large stock brought with them from their homes and enlisted men were provided meals by the army, the bachelor officers were responsible for their own meals, and frequently the larder was bare. They were sufficiently hungry at their camp on Mud Creek that three of them sought and received permission to return to Abilene, a short mile away, to partake of the limited fare offered at the local hostelry and saloon called the Pioneer Hotel, set in the midst of the prairie dog town. Whatever nourishment they found, they clearly needed, for most of the officers other than Custer complained of being awakened by intense cold sometime after 1:00 A.M.[25]

The column left the camp on Mud Creek on Friday morning, March 29, and continued in a generally west-southwest direction parallel with the Smoky Hill River. The day was significantly warmer, as the road was now soft in the low spots, with mud and mire in the dry arroyos it crossed. After a march of about eight miles the railroad curved northwestward, and the expedition crossed it before passing an incipient settlement of five log houses sporting the lofty title "Solomon City." A hundred yards beyond, the road passed through a low bottom in its approach to Solomon's Fork, an area underwater during the wet season and now marshy and difficult to negotiate. The troops were held up for more than half an hour at this point while the engineers and their infantry helpers threw a pontoon bridge across the river. The Solomon was no more than one hundred feet from bank to bank on the level prairie above, but its bed was cut deep into the surrounding country. The earlier cold snap had left thick ice on its surface, and the ensuing thaw then brought large quantities of

[24] Brown, *March Journal*, March 28, 1867; E. Custer, *Tenting on the Plains*, 516–19; Kennedy, *On the Plains*, 50.
[25] Brown, *March Journal*, March 28, 1867; E. Custer, *Tenting on the Plains*, 519–21.

water downstream from the uplands, raising its depth from two or three feet to eight and a half feet and breaking up the ice cover.[26]

Once the bridge was in place, the long column of troops, cavalry, artillery, and wagon trains began its crossing. All the troops and most of the wagons were safely across when suddenly a powerful freshet of ice and water came surging down the stream. Lieutenant Brown saw the danger, halted the crossing, and was in the process of swinging the bridge around from its far end to the shore for safety, when the ice and debris struck with great force, crushing and sinking several of the pontoon boats, and sweeping others on downstream into the Smoky Hill. After the ice and debris were past and the water level stabilized, the bridge was restored using additional pontoon boats, there being far more than needed to cross any river on the plains even in rare times of high water. The rest of the wagons then completed crossing safely. The great surge of water was probably caused by a blockage upstream, with driftwood and fallen trees becoming entangled along the banks, catching floating ice and other debris, and forming a dam that finally broke when the pressure became too great.[27]

The command was in camp on the west bank of the Solomon by noon on March 29, after marching some nine miles. The encampment was apparently pleasant, with a moderating temperature. The character of the country through which they were passing was undergoing subtle changes and had been since before Mud Creek, for they had left the Flint Hills midway between Chapman's Creek and Abilene. Now, the ranges of hills in the distance were lower, and the lowlands were crowded with sand dunes marking an ancient course of the Smoky Hill. They had passed beyond the Central Lowland Plains and entered the eastern fringes of the Great Plains. Thereafter a changing topography, different plant and animal life, and an ever-increasing altitude would mark their course as the plains began their dramatic but invisible rise to the foothills of the Rocky Mountains. The tallgrass prairies were behind them, and shortgrass country ahead. Now they would move slowly into the rolling, treeless land of bison, pronghorn antelope, elk, deer, and their predators, and, more importantly, the land of the Plains Indians.[28]

On Saturday, March 30, the troops were on the march by 6:45 A.M. The

---

[26] Brown, *March Journal*, March 29, 1867; Brown to Nichols, May 30, 1867; E. Custer, *Tenting on the Plains*, 519–20.

[27] Brown to Nichols, May 30, 1867; E. Custer, *Tenting on the Plains*, 520.

[28] Brown, *March Journal*, March 29, 1867; Buchanan, *Kansas Geology*, 8, 19–20, 23–27, 181–82; E. Custer, *Tenting on the Plains*, 519; Merriam, *Geological History of Kansas*, 161–65.

Look's Ranch on Spring Creek, originally known as Pritchard's Station or Pritchard's Ranch and later called Spring Creek Station, was built as a home station on the Butterfield Overland Despatch, the stage line to Denver that followed the course of the Smoky Hill River. Like the earlier stage stations in the Smoky Hills and Blue Hills, it was built mostly of adobe, but it did have a rare peaked roof. General Hancock's expeditionary force camped along Spring Creek about a half mile from the station on the afternoon of March 31, 1867. *Harper's Weekly*, June 15, 1867.

stage and military road lay well to the south of the railroad embankment, running through wet and marshy lowlands then known as Ten Mile Bottom. This took them to the Saline River, a quarter of a mile south of the railroad bridge then being built to take rails not yet laid. The stream was only about sixty feet wide bank to bank from the level plain but like the Solomon, it had a narrow, deep bed. The thaw and recent rain caused an increased volume of water to be discharged through its winding course, resulting in a great rise in the surface level (which now stood at nine feet) and making it entirely unfordable. This necessitated employment of the pontoon bridge once again. Large quantities of debris and ice were floating downstream on a current measured at four miles per hour, creating a hazardous situation similar to that faced on the Solomon. Despite the danger, however, the bridge remained intact until the entire command had passed safely over to the west bank, and only one pontoon was dam-

At a distance of about seven miles east of Fort Harker the expedition encountered the natural phenomenon now known as the Mushroom Rocks. These remarkable monuments were carved by water and wind erosion from the sandstone of the Dakota Formation, with the softer stone at the bottom eroding away from the harder concretions at the top, giving a mushroom appearance. This scene shows Pulpit Rock, with surveyors for the railroad at work in the area. It rather fancifully depicts two engineers hiding behind the rock from Indians apparently approaching on foot, a highly unlikely scenario for mounted Plains Indians in the vastness of their country. *Harper's Weekly*, June 15, 1867.

aged by having a hole punched in the canvass cover by floating ice. The experiences on the Solomon and the Saline convinced Lieutenant Brown that canvas pontoon boats were unsuitable for use on the plains, that wooden boats should be used when and where necessary, and that no more than seven would be required in any event.[29]

Once on the west side of the Saline, the column continued its march along the road for another mile and a half, going into camp on the north bank of the Smoky Hill River at 1:00 P.M. The little village of Salina lay just over two miles west of the camp along the banks of the Smoky Hill. There the course of the Smoky Hill turned sharply to the south, while the stage and military road continued westward, and the expedition would

[29] Brown, *March Journal*, March 30, 1867; Brown to Nichols, May 30, 1867; E. Custer, *Tenting on the Plains*, 521–22.

not encounter its waters again until reaching Fort Harker. Beyond this camp the streams they would encounter would be more typical of the High Plains, with few if any trees along their banks, a depth of water more often measured in inches than feet, and crossings mostly by fords with few bridges. There were no towns beyond Salina. Evidence of any white presence was limited to the roads, the bed graded and prepared for the advancing railroad, a scattering of trading and hunting ranches, the stage and mail stations, and the military posts. The troops were also now in the Smoky Hills, the easternmost region of the Dissected High Plains, an area eroded from Dakota sandstone and clay, marking the edge of the Cretaceous deposits underlying much of the western half of Kansas. The eastern edge of this region is beautifully rugged, marked by outlying hills and buttes rising sharply above the surrounding plains and capped by outcrops of dark reddish sandstone. The road they were following led almost due west into these hills.[30]

Sometime during the late afternoon or early evening the stagecoach from Junction City reached their camp, discharging a passenger whom General Hancock would find most welcome. It was Henry M. Stanley, special correspondent for the *Missouri Democrat* of St. Louis, on assignment to cover the expedition for his paper. A small man, about five feet five inches in height, he made his way to the general's tent with valise in hand. Finding that the famous man was asleep, Stanley took a stroll through the camp, observing the soldiers as they went about their various tasks of preparing for supper, currying their horses, cleaning their arms and accoutrements, arranging their tents and bedding, playing chess, cards, or dominoes, or standing around in knots discussing the likelihood of a fight with the Indians. It seems to have been a relaxed and pleasant scene, apparently with comfortable temperatures and subsiding winds.[31]

It was not until after lights-out at 9:00 P.M. that an orderly approached Stanley and said that the general wished to see him. On entering Hancock's tent, Stanley found the general to be "a hale, hearty, and tall gentleman, in the prime of life." After reading Stanley's credentials, Hancock welcomed him and, following a brief discussion, bade him goodnight. Once in his assigned quarters, Stanley wrote the first of the reports for his paper. The general told him the troops would proceed to the point

[30] Brown, *March Journal*, March 30, 1867; Buchanan, *Kansas Geology*, 24–27; E. Custer, *Tenting on the Plains*, 521.

[31] Jordan, *Winfield Scott Hancock*, 189–90; Knight, *Following the Indian Wars*, 57–59; Stanley, *My Early Travels*, vii, 1–2.

where he had arranged a meeting with "the chiefs of the different hostile Indian tribes." Stanley described Hancock's intentions in these words: "If they evince a disposition to be submissive and peaceable they will be allowed to depart in peace. If they are fractious, and prefer war, General Hancock will at once commence hostilities." Stanley also noted the presence of the little five-year-old Indian boy called Wilson Graham from the name of the circus that had exhibited him, referring to him as "a boy of extraordinary intelligence."[32]

Stanley, who became a great admirer of General Hancock, would stay with him throughout his own participation in the expedition, writing the most flattering and supportive stories of Hancock and his difficulties with the Indians that the general would receive. Stanley accepted at face value all secondhand stories and rumors of atrocities, as well as Hancock's personal assessment of the situation and most other stories he heard. He quickly developed a hearty dislike for the Indian agents he met during the expedition, apparently considering them as much the enemy as the Indians whose oversight they were charged with. As for the Indians themselves, he seems to have made no effort of any kind to acquaint himself with their culture or the difficulties they faced, regarding them merely as "savages" who were an obstacle to the march of Western civilization. This view of Native peoples stayed with him through his life and was clearly evident during his African expeditions of later years. He was nonetheless a lively and interested correspondent and writer, and his reporting, however biased, has provided insights into events not otherwise well recorded in the years immediately after the War between the States.[33]

The expedition decamped from the Smoky Hill early on the morning of Sunday, March 31, passing through Salina after a march of a little over two miles. Lieutenant Brown observed that it was a very small town with "very muddy streets." Beyond Salina the road wound through gently rolling prairie, the railbed a short distance to the north, and the Smoky Hills all around them. The troops halted at the crossing of Elm Creek to water the livestock, much wearied by the muddy condition of the road. There was a ranch and stage station on the east bank of Elm Creek, just north of the road, and some of the men likely sought a little food or drink there. Eight miles beyond Elm Creek the column camped on the north bank of Spring Creek. The Smoky Hills rose sharply just south of the stream, and

---

[32] Hyde, *Life of George Bent*, 256–57; Stanley, *My Early Travels*, 2–3.
[33] Knight, *Following the Indian Wars*, 64–68; Stanley, *My Early Travels*, v–xi.

on the north they moved closer to the road. About a half mile from the camp, north of the road and east of a small intermittent stream draining into Spring Creek, was an establishment known as Pritchard's Ranch or Pritchard's Station, a home station on the Butterfield Overland Despatch where horses could be changed. Also known as Look's Ranch, it was famous in the region for serving "square meals." Later it would be called Spring Creek Station.[34]

On Monday, April 1, the column marched through very hilly, rolling country on a winding road that was constantly going up steep inclines, then down on the equally steep reverse slopes. At the bottom of nearly every hill, the road crossed a small intermittent stream or dry arroyo draining the surrounding country. After a march of six miles the troops passed a mail station, and six miles beyond it they reached Clear Creek, a running stream with the first significant growth of timber along its banks since the Saline River. Six miles farther they arrived at Fort Harker and camped along the military road on the east side of Page Creek, about halfway between the new post and old Fort Ellsworth. The bed prepared to receive the rails of the Union Pacific Railroad, E.D., ended there, but crews would be back to continue the westward construction as soon as the ground dried. The march of more than eighty-three miles from Fort Riley had been tiring and enervating, but had brought the expedition into the country of the Cheyennes and Arapahoes and nearly halfway to its first meeting with representatives of the former tribe. But first there would be rest and reprovisioning and the addition of two more cavalry companies.[35]

---

[34] Brown, *March Journal*, March 31, 1867; W. S. Mitchell, AAAG, to A. J. Smith, March 30, 1867, MC535-R1354; *Harper's Weekly*, June 15, 1867; Montgomery, "Fort Wallace," 17:196.

[35] Brown, *March Journal*, April 1, 1867.

CHAPTER SIX

From Fort Harker
to Fort Larned

W hen General Hancock and his Expedition for the Plains reached Fort Harker early in the afternoon of April 1, 1867, they found a military post in transition. Established in early August 1864, it was situated near the north bank of the Smoky Hill River, north and a little west of the junction of the military road to Fort Larned and the stage road to Denver. It occupied the site of the stage station and trading ranch that preceded it, a place Maj. Gen. Samuel R. Curtis found suitable for a new military post intended to guard an important junction and crossing point for the military and stage roads. There the small garrison built a blockhouse and temporary quarters for the men. The fort's commissary storehouse was likely the former trading ranch and stage station.[1]

First named Fort Ellsworth, the post evolved slowly, consisting largely of the log blockhouse, the sod and adobe commissary storehouse and a few similar buildings, a sod and log corral, several dugouts, log cabins, and a number of tents. By early 1866 it was garrisoned by one company of infantry and one of cavalry, all housed in rapidly deteriorating quarters, and it was determined that new and suitable structures should be erected. Meanwhile, arrival of surveyors for the Union Pacific Railroad, E.D., and, later, construction crews grading the roadbed resulted in relocation of the post to a site on high ground about a mile to the northeast, placing it close to the railroad. Construction of the new buildings began in the late summer and early fall of 1866, and in November the name of the post was changed to Fort Harker in honor of Brig. Gen. Charles Garrison Harker, killed in the Battle of Kennesaw Mountain. Many of the

[1] Mead, *Trading and Hunting*, 117–18; Oliva, *Fort Harker*, 20–23; Tisdale, "Travel by Stage," 462.

Fort Harker was a remote military post deep in Plains Indian country when the Expedition for the Plains arrived on April 1, 1867. By the time of General Hancock's return on May 6 the Union Pacific, Eastern Division, had reached Spring Creek, eighteen miles to the east, and by late June arrived at Fort Harker. As the rails continued west, the fort's importance became more as a military supply depot than as an active combat post. This view of the expedition's encampment on April 2, from the northwest looking to the southeast, was sketched by Philip D. Fisher, a civil engineer working for the railroad. The buildings of Fort Harker can be seen on the hill in the center of the sketch. *Harper's Weekly*, April 27, 1867.

planned structures were completed and occupied, with the rest nearing completion, when Hancock's troops arrived on April 1.[2]

Two companies of the Seventh Cavalry, F and G, were already stationed at Fort Harker, having been posted there in November 1866. Company G (called Troop G to distinguish it from an infantry company) consisted of 91 men and horses and was commanded by Capt. Albert Barnitz, who arrived on March 22 to assume his duties. The horses were provided with good stables, and the men were quartered in a large wood-frame barrack. While Barnitz and the other officers were housed in floored tents with "board doors," he reported that the new officers' quarters were "progress-

[2] Oliva, *Fort Harker*, 24, 30–49.

ing finely," would be even more handsome, pleasant, and cozy than those at Fort Riley, and were "beautifully situated."[3]

Though Captain Barnitz was well pleased with the new Fort Harker, his assessment was by no means universal. Henry M. Stanley, after the expedition arrived on April 1, described it as having the appearance of "a great wart on the surface of the plain"—a reference to the dark sandstone used on some buildings and the lack of trees or vegetation other than bleached prairie grasses. While finding it with promise, General Hancock was less than satisfied with the new post. On the afternoon of April 3, 1867, he wrote General Sherman that he had had a thorough inspection made of the fort. He reported that though a good deal of work had been accomplished during the winter, the plan for the officers' quarters was very faulty. He said he had given instructions to Bvt. Brig. Gen. L. C. Easton, chief quartermaster of the Department of the Missouri, to prepare new and suitable plans for those buildings yet to be constructed, but preserving the general architectural appearance of those already built.[4]

The impending arrival of the expedition prompted Major Gibbs, now commanding Fort Harker as well as the squadron of the Seventh Cavalry stationed there, to issue orders on March 28 detailing preparations. Captain Barnitz wrote to his wife's sister Hattie that, in compliance with the order, he had turned in all of his troop's surplus property to the Ordnance and Quartermaster departments, and the command was held in readiness to march at one hour's notice. Barnitz said they had no idea where they were going; he supposed that secrecy was necessary lest the Indians become alarmed. Nor did he have any idea as to the real object of the expedition, but he thought that General Hancock wished to make a reconnaissance through his department, visit the Indian tribes and the Rocky Mountains, and have a buffalo hunt on a grand scale. Clearly, as an officer posted to a frontier fort, his view of the immediacy of any Indian danger was quite different from that held by his commander and others far removed from the Indian country.[5]

With the arrival of the Expedition for the Plains, Companies F and G of the Seventh Cavalry, the squadron stationed at Fort Harker, moved out of their quarters and went into camp along with the four companies arriving from Fort Riley. Among the senior officers present was Maj. (Bvt.

---

[3] Utley, *Life in Custer's Cavalry*, 18–21.
[4] W. S. Hancock to W. T. Sherman, April 3, 1867, AGO, LR, MC535-R1354; W. S. Mitchell to L. C. Easton, April 4, 1867, AGO, LR, MC535-R1354; Stanley, *My Early Travels*, 4.
[5] Oliva, *Fort Harker*, 66–67; Utley, *Life in Custer's Cavalry*, 21–22.

Maj. Gen.) John W. Davidson. Originally the commander of the Second
Cavalry, the District of the Upper Arkansas, and Fort Riley, Davidson
had been relieved of his command of Fort Riley and the District of the
Upper Arkansas and appointed as inspector general of the Department
of the Missouri, with station at Fort Leavenworth. He remained commander of the Second Cavalry on detached duty, however, a common
practice in the years following the Civil War. Davidson's presence with
the expedition was to perform inspections of the several military posts
they would encounter during the march. Command of Fort Riley and the
District of the Upper Arkansas was given to General Smith, commander
of the Seventh Cavalry.[6]

The expedition remained at Fort Harker through April 2, 1867, while
they replenished their supplies from the stores sent ahead from Fort Riley.
They also took advantage of the opportunity to rest both men and animals, much wearied by the march during a cold and blustery early spring.
Reflecting on the very changeable weather common on the southern plains
during this season, on April 2 Captain Barnitz wrote to his wife, Jennie,
that the "day is very pleasant—or rather unpleasantly warm!"[7]

Hancock's troops, now reinforced by the addition of two more companies of the Seventh Cavalry, left Fort Harker early on the morning of
April 3, 1867. Their next destination was Fort Larned and the anticipated
meeting with the chiefs of the "hostile Indian tribes." In contrast to the
excessive heat of the previous day, the morning was cold and overcast,
with a dull gray sky. They passed old Fort Ellsworth, still occupied by a
part of the infantry garrison, and forded the Smoky Hill River. Beyond
it the road wound across a rolling prairie, surrounded on both sides by the
Smoky Hills, leading them in a southwesterly direction. The road was
firm and the surrounding hills and valleys dry, prompting General Smith
to order Custer to drill the six cavalry companies that had been unable to
do so during the winter when they were preoccupied with such matters
as shelter and caring for the horses. The drilling went well, and Custer
reported to his wife, Libbie, that the companies were improving rapidly.[8]

The Fort Harker–Fort Zarah segment of the military road they followed, though in good condition, was actually nothing more than a trail
marked by the ruts and worn vegetation of previous traffic and the cuts

[6] Davidson, *Black Jack Davidson*, 25; Utley, *Life in Custer's Cavalry*, 25.
[7] Utley, *Life in Custer's Cavalry*, 25.
[8] Brown, *March Journal*, April 3, 1867; Hancock to Sherman, April 3, 1867; E. Custer, *Tenting on the Plains*, 524; Stanley, *My Early Travels*, 20.

made at stream crossings where steep banks were present. As the road pursued its southwesterly course, it crossed a series of arroyos and intermittent streams spaced at about a mile from each other that drained water from the surrounding Smoky Hills during times of precipitation. Normally dry, in March, April, and May—the wet season on the plains—they frequently held water from passing thunderstorms. The depth of these arroyos and streams varied from four to six inches as the expedition passed, much more typical of small watercourses in this semiarid region even in times when moisture was present. Their evening's destination, Plum Creek, was no more than one foot deep, but even it was dry much of the year. During the greater part of the travel season drinking water was available to humans and their livestock only at the springs behind the stage coach station near the west bank of the stream.[9]

The expedition camped in an oxbow on the west bank of Plum Creek early in the afternoon of April 3, after a march of about sixteen and a half miles. The day seemed unusually cold to most of the officers and men, probably because of a stiff breeze and the wind chill factor. Custer, if he is to be believed, was the exception. Major Gibbs, riding next to him during the march, was "nearly numb" and, when he found that Custer felt entirely comfortable, exclaimed, "Well, you are a warm-blooded cuss!" Once in camp, wood parties were dispatched to chop down trees from the scraggly growth along the creek's banks. They were told that little or no wood was to be found along the banks of Cow Creek, their next day's destination, and that a supply of firewood was needed for at least two nights.[10]

That afternoon Hancock wrote his report to General Sherman, recounting the march from Fort Harker to their present camp, the planned itinerary en route to Fort Larned, and his critical assessment following his inspection of Harker. He stated that their march would be more rapid except for considerations of water, since the available supply of potable water was limited. Of greater concern, to this point his expedition had suffered the loss of forty or more men by desertion, and he expressed his fear that regiments could not be kept at a good standard of combat readiness unless desertion was made a serious crime and punished accordingly. That he was still spoiling for a fight with the Indians was made clear in the closing line of his letter: "We get along well, and trust that the Indians will give us a proper cause for chastisement."[11]

[9] Brown, *March Journal*, April 3, 1867.
[10] Ibid.; E. Custer, *Tenting on the Plains*, 524.
[11] Hancock to Sherman, April 3, 1867.

The long column of infantry, artillery, cavalry, and wagon trains left the camp on Plum Creek early the following morning en route to their next camp on Cow Creek. There was fine weather for the march, with comfortable temperatures and a bright, clear blue sky. Rather than continuing on the Fort Harker–Fort Zarah segment of the military road, which ran in a south-southwesterly direction, General Smith elected to leave the trail and traverse the plains on a more west-southwesterly path. This would bring them to a point on Cow Creek about four miles above the usual crossing of that stream, where at least a small supply of timber might be found. The established crossing point had long been denuded of trees by the voracious needs of white travelers, both civilian and military. Since leaving Fort Harker, General Smith had formed the expedition into two principal columns for security, with the infantry and most of the wagon trains making up one column, and the artillery battery and its train the other. The cavalry, except for small details charged with keeping the columns compact and preventing straggling, generally moved in a close-knit body by squadron in columns of twos and far out on the flanks of the parallel columns of infantry and artillery. As they marched General Smith ordered Custer to put the cavalry through its paces, moving them from squadron column into columns of fours, or platoons, then forming into line at the gallop, with sabers drawn, guidons fluttering, and bugles blaring the signals. They made an impressive sight, particularly in the view of Henry Stanley, who thought they would surely strike terror in the hearts of any bands of Indians who might be watching. Perhaps that would have been a valid observation for an enemy fighting in the European style. But these tactics would be of little use against an enemy like the mounted warriors of the plains, who did not fight in that manner.[12]

Their route away from the military road took the troops through a number of prairie dog villages. Captain Barnitz observed that this required the troopers to remain vigilant lest their horses stumble in the holes and fall. Such a fall would be hazardous not only to the riders, who would at the least be thrown, but also to the horses, which might break a leg. Custer, on the other hand, was amused by the antics of the little animals that sat at the edge of their burrows and scolded the intruders. He was especially amused at the frustration experienced by his dogs, which would charge

---

[12] Brown, *March Journal*, April 4, 1867; W. S. Hancock to W. T. Sherman, April 4, 1867, AGO, LR, MC535-R1354; E. Custer, *Tenting on the Plains*, 524; Stanley, *My Early Travels*, 20; Utley, *Life in Custer's Cavalry*, 25–27.

The Expedition for the Plains marched south from Fort Harker to Plum Creek during the morning of April 3, 1867. The skies were overcast and the south wind they faced seemed cold to most of the men. When Custer told Major Gibbs that he felt comfortable, Gibbs remarked, "Well, you are a warm-blooded cuss!" This sketch of the scene was made by the famous western artist Frederick Remington to illustrate Elizabeth Custer's later book entitled *Tenting on the Plains.*

in, thinking to catch them, but were foiled when their quarry popped down into their holes at the last moment.[13]

The column reached the evening's campground on the left bank of Cow Creek about midday, after a march of a little less than thirteen miles. Camp was made on the left, or northeast, bank of the stream because a range of sand hills covered the opposite bank, rendering that side unsuitable as a campground. The location was apparently one of the better camping places in the area, for it had also been used as a hunting camp by a band of Plains Indians, probably Cheyennes, not more than a month earlier. The sites of their lodges were clearly visible, and at some a few of the lodge poles were left in place. The area where buffalo hides were dressed was nearby, and

---

[13] Brown, *March Journal*, April 4, 1867; E. Custer, *Tenting on the Plains*, 525; Utley, *Life in Custer's Cavalry*, 27.

the scrapings and remains of one buffalo were within fifteen yards of Custer's tent. During their march the troops had seen the skeletal remains and carcasses of a number of bison, leading them to conclude they would be seeing Indians at any time, now being deep within their country.[14]

The expedition left Cow Creek on the morning of April 5, its next destination Walnut Creek near Fort Zarah. It crossed the dunes onto the plains and moved south-southwest about four miles to a junction with the military road. Beyond Cow Creek the column left the Smoky Hills and entered into the Arkansas River Lowlands. Here the river valley was filled with sand and gravel eroded from the Rocky Mountains, with irregular hills and, along the river itself, ranges of sand hills. The road the expedition followed was originally known as the Fort Riley–Fort Larned Military Road but was now commonly called the Santa Fe Road, in part because it joined the famous old trail at Walnut Creek, and in part because a great deal of the freight for Santa Fe and beyond was now being carried by railroad to Junction City and from there over the military road to its intersection with the original trail. So the column's route now led nearly due southwest to the trail's crossing of the Walnut.[15]

Having traveled fourteen and a half miles, the troops reached Walnut Creek, camping in an oxbow on the left stream bank about three-fourths of a mile above Fort Zarah. The stream was wooded at that point, with a channel twenty-eight feet wide and steep banks but with a flow of water just ten feet wide and one foot deep. The Santa Fe Trail crossed the stream below them next to the fort at two places. The upper, original crossing was by ford, and the lower one was a diverted road leading to a toll bridge. Due to the unpredictability of watercourses on the plains during rainstorms and flash flooding, a bridge 340 feet long was required to safely span what was on most days a mere trickle of water. The fort itself was so called only by ample exercise of imagination. In his official report of May 22, 1867, General Hancock referred to finding "a small, badly constructed 'Round House,' loopholed for defense and capable of accommodating probably thirty (30) men, with no accommodations for officers." He observed that the commanding officer lived "several hundred yards" from the "Round House," implying the existence of another structure or structures.[16]

[14] Brown, *March Journal*, April 4, 1867; Hancock to Sherman, April 4, 1867; E. Custer, *Tenting on the Plains*, 524–25.

[15] Brown, *March Journal*, April 5, 1867; Buchanan, *Kansas Geology*, 8, 34–35.

[16] Brown, *March Journal*, April 5, 1867; M. R. Brown to AAAG, April 30, 1867, AGO, LR, MC619-R563; Hancock to Nichols, May 22, 1867; Stanley, *My Early Travels*, 12.

Fort Zarah was established in the summer of 1864 by Maj. Gen. Samuel R. Curtis shortly before he founded Fort Ellsworth. The site selected was the point at which the Santa Fe Trail crossed Walnut Creek a short distance above its junction with the Arkansas River. Nearby was a trading post founded in 1855 by William Allison and Francis Boothe and known variously as Allison and Boothe's Fort or Allison and Boothe's Ranch. Originally located about one hundred yards from the crossing of Walnut Creek on its east bank and north of the Santa Fe Trail, it dealt in merchandise and supplies suitable for trade with travelers on the Santa Fe Road and with the various tribes of Plains Indians inhabiting the country to the north and south of the Arkansas River.[17]

Boothe was murdered by a former employee in September 1857, and Allison subsequently died at Independence, Missouri, on April 19, 1859. He was succeeded by George H. Peacock, an experienced plainsman and Santa Fe trader, who ran the post until he was killed on September 9, 1860, by the Kiowa war leader Setangya (called Satank by whites) in revenge for a humiliating trick Peacock played on him. Within a matter of weeks Peacock was followed by trader Charles Rath, who continued the post's operation until the arrival of General Hancock's expedition on April 5, 1867. Sometime while the trading post was under the ownership of either Peacock or Rath, it was moved to a new location south of the trail. Rath was operating the post in the new building when Hancock and his men reached the Walnut.[18]

Hall and Porter, mail contractors for the Santa Fe route, built a mail station near the crossing on the west side of Walnut Creek sometime in 1858. This was burned by a party of outlaws in mid-July of 1860 but subsequently rebuilt as a mail station and stagecoach change station for the run to Santa Fe. Early in 1863 Charles Rath and four partners formed a bridge company and constructed the toll bridge across the Walnut a few hundred yards downstream from the usual trail crossing. During June and July 1864 the army built a stone fort (blockhouse) on the east bank of the Walnut that it named Fort Zarah in honor of General Curtis's son, Maj. Zarah Curtis, killed at Baxter Springs, Kansas, in an 1863 fight with Confederate guerillas under William Quantrill. In February 1865, troops of the Second Colorado Cavalry completed a new octagonal stone blockhouse equipped with a tin roof, as well as another building of sandstone

[17] Lowe, *Five Years a Dragoon*, 101–102; Oliva, *Fort Larned*, 7; Oliva, *Soldiers on the Santa Fe Trail*, 153.
[18] Barry, "Ranch at Walnut Creek Crossing," 121–23; Hunnius, sketches of Fort Zarah in 1867.

The Hancock expedition reached Walnut Creek and the Santa Fe Trail early on the afternoon of April 5, 1867, camping about three-fourths of a mile above Fort Zarah. The little fort was then an outpost of Fort Larned, providing escorts for travelers and wagon trains moving east or west along the trail. This crude sketch was made by Ado Hunnius, a soldier who passed by it on June 27, 1867. It is viewed looking west, with the little post on the left, or west, bank of Walnut Creek. Across the toll bridge on the right stream bank is the mail and stagecoach change station with its corral. *Courtesy of the Kansas State Historical Society, Topeka.*

and adobe bricks and a sod or mud roof, with a narrow boardwalk across it where a guard kept lookout.[19]

During 1865 and 1866, following separation of the agency for the Cheyennes, Arapahoes, and Plains Apaches from that of the Comanches and Kiowas, the agency for the former was moved to Fort Zarah by the new agent, Dr. I. C. Taylor. But, due to his ineptitude and drunkenness, Dr. Taylor's tenure was short, and his successor, Maj. E. W. Wynkoop, moved the agency back to Fort Larned following his entry into office in the fall of 1866. As the winter faded into early spring the little post on Walnut Creek held only a small garrison, plus the adjacent trading post of Charles Rath and the stage station on the west side of the stream. Fort

[19] Barry, "Ranch at Walnut Creek Crossing," 128, 138, 141; Hunnius, sketches of Fort Zarah in 1867; Oliva, *Fort Larned*, 22–23.

Zarah was an appendage or outpost of Fort Larned until 1868, and its garrison was drawn from troops stationed at the latter post, so the personnel probably varied from season to season according to need.[20]

Following their arrival in camp on Walnut Creek, a number of the officers, including generals Hancock and Davidson, along with Henry Stanley, rode downstream to inspect Fort Zarah. Col. Jesse H. Leavenworth, agent for the Kiowas and Comanches, was there to meet them, having moved his agency to Fort Zarah from Fort Larned. Hancock was clearly appalled at what he found at Zarah, and in his report of May 22, 1867, stated he was having plans prepared "for a blockhouse, or defensible barrack" to replace the round house. Of equal concern, apparently, was the presence of Charles Rath and his trading post. Hancock was well aware of the report of Maj. Henry Douglass, the Fort Dodge post commander, claiming that Rath had armed several bands of Kiowas with firearms and ammunition. Now complaints were leveled that he was selling whiskey to the Indians as well. In the April 5, 1867, report of his inspection, General Davidson stated: "Rath, the trader, I learn, sells whiskey to the Indians, in violation of military orders and Act of Congress and should be put off of the reservation." Henry Stanley called Rath "a notorious desperado" who had sold firearms and powder to the Indians and whiskey to both soldiers and Indians. Neither Davidson nor Stanley gave any source for the allegation. While Rath no doubt did sell firearms, powder, and other supplies to the Indians, which he did under license from the Interior Department, he was certainly no "notorious desperado," and the accusation of selling whiskey is likely untrue. He always claimed that he had not done so, on the advice of his friend William Bent, and that was his reputation. A letter appearing in the July 29, 186,3 issue of the *Council Grove Press* stated: "Mr. Charles Rath, Trader at Walnut Creek, sells large quantities of goods to the Kiowas, Arapahoes and Comanches, and takes in exchange furs, robes, &c.; and we are reliably informed that he has persistently refused to sell whiskey to the Indians." His predecessor, Peacock, had sold whiskey, however, as had former Indian agent I. C. Taylor, and it seems likely the prior reputation of the trading post and the Indian agency for selling whiskey was simply attributed to Rath, perhaps as a means for getting rid of an unlicensed civilian trading post at a military establishment.[21]

[20] Barry, "Ranch at Walnut Creek Crossing," 144–46; Hunnius, sketches of Fort Zarah in 1867; Oliva, *Fort Larned*, 23; Stanley, *My Early Travels*, 12.

[21] Hancock to Nichols, May 22, 1867; Barry, "Ranch at Walnut Creek Crossing," 139, 141–42, 145–46; Stanley, *My Early Travels*, 12–13.

Although the army was well aware that Rath claimed ownership of both his trading house and the nearby toll bridge, General Davidson nonetheless ordered him "off the reservation," presumably meaning the Fort Zarah military reservation. Stanley stated that General Davidson "warned him off the Indian Reserve." But while well within the Plains Indian country, the Walnut Creek trading post was never within the boundaries of any government-defined Indian reserve. Nor was there a military reservation for Fort Zarah until it became an independent post and the president ordered a reservation on September 30, 1868. Despite the lack of a legal basis to order him off, Charles Rath was apparently sufficiently concerned that he moved his trading operations. Possibly he moved it just across Walnut Creek to the stage station, for he seems to have continued trading with Indians and travelers in that vicinity for the remainder of the year.[22]

On April 6 the expedition began its march from Walnut Creek, heading southwest to a junction with the Santa Fe Trail about two miles distant. The morning was bright and clear but cold. As the temperatures rose, however, the prevailing south winds began to pick up velocity and dust began to blow. Hancock later complained to Sherman that the winds on the plains at that season were like a storm or hurricane at sea. Blowing dead against them, the winds made the march very hard for the infantry. At a distance of five miles from where the troops struck the old Santa Fe Trail, they met a party of Plains Apaches leaving on a buffalo hunt. Their village was to the east of the trail near the Arkansas River, and doubtless the sight of the long, strung-out line of soldiers and their wagon trains caused them considerable concern. But aside from curious stares, the soldiers paid them no heed and marched on. Several men from the village did ride up to the column, however, and were taken to General Hancock in accordance with his orders. One was wearing the regulation hat, cross sabers, and numbers of the Third Cavalry, with the shoulder straps of a first lieutenant. Hancock thought him a medicine man but gave no basis for his belief other than that he was wearing the uniform parts. The man was bearing a note from Col. E. W. Wynkoop, the agent for the Plains Apaches as well as the Cheyennes and Arapahoes, addressed to the chiefs of the three tribes and requesting that they meet with Hancock on April 10 at Fort Larned.[23]

[22] Barry, "Ranch at Walnut Creek Crossing," 141, 145; Oliva, *Fort Larned*, 22–23.

[23] Brown, *March Journal*, April 7, 1867; W. S. Hancock to W. T. Sherman, April 7, 1867, AGO, LR, 1867, MC535-R1354.

Within another six miles the expedition reached the famous Pawnee Rock, the first important rocky prominence serving as a marker for merchants and travelers following the Santa Fe Trail. It consisted of a massive outcrop of Dakota sandstone, which could be seen for miles across the plains in a time when there were few trees along the banks of the Arkansas River. The rock rose about sixty feet above the surrounding plains, making it an admirable spot from which to observe trail traffic coming from either direction and therefore a favorite lookout point for Plains Indians and one of the most dangerous places along the entire trail. It received its name when a party of Pawnees, on a horse-stealing expedition, came south from their village in the Platte River country and were chased by warriors of one of the southern Plains tribes, either Cheyennes or Comanches. The Pawnees took refuge on top of the rock and were besieged by their enemies. Finally, when it was clear there would be no escape and they had run out of food and water, they sang their death songs, dashed down from the summit, and were killed to the last man. From the earliest entry of Europeans into this country, travelers had inscribed their names in the soft sandstone face of the rock. Included were those of Spanish explorers and traders, such famous Americans as Kit Carson and Susan Magoffin, and many officers and soldiers of the Army of the West in 1846, bound for Santa Fe to wrest control of New Mexico from the Mexican government.[24] The rock was about one hundred yards west of the road, with the ruins of an old hunting or trading ranch at its base.[25]

The long column of troops and wagon trains continued until reaching Ash Creek, crossing to its south bank, and stopping at the trail campground after a march of a little over twenty-two miles. Shortly after the troops had made camp, four Oglala warriors from the Kiyuksa band arrived and held a discussion with General Hancock. They had with them a document signed by Col. Henry E. Maynadier, commanding at Fort Laramie, which authorized them to camp on Horse Creek, a tributary of the North Platte River and the scene of the famous 1850 treaty. They reported they were now encamped on the north branch of the Pawnee Fork about thirty miles northwest of Fort Larned, along with a band of Cheyennes, and had been sent south by the commander from the north to avoid involvement

[24] Nearly all of the early inscriptions were destroyed during the settlement of the country in the 1870s, because of the lack of historical consciousness by homesteaders quarrying rock for building materials and the Santa Fe Railroad in obtaining ballast for its tracks.
[25] Brown, *March Journal*, April 7, 1867; Inman, *Old Santa Fe Trail*, 404; Rydjord, *Indian Place Names*, 141–42; Wright, *Dodge City*, 25–26.

On April 6, 1867, the troops of the Hancock expedition passed the famous Pawnee Rock, the first high rocky prominence serving as a marker for travelers along the Santa Fe Trail. This photograph, circa 1889, was taken during the period of settlement, after new settlers and the Santa Fe Railroad had stripped away much of the upper layers of rock for building purposes and rail ballast. Nevertheless the photograph shows the abruptness with which the formation rose above the surrounding plains, its value to Plains Indians as a lookout point, and its usefulness in establishing location on the great trail across the trackless plains. *Courtesy of the Kansas State Historical Society, Topeka.*

in war. Though they would have stayed on tributaries of the Republican River, at the southern extremity of their usual hunting range, no buffalo were to be found there at that time, so they had moved south to camp and hunt with the Cheyennes.[26]

Later the same evening an old Cheyenne called Slim Face rode in, looking for the Indian boy known as Wilson Graham (said to be Cheyenne) in an effort to identify him and assure himself that the army did intend to return him as agreed. Hancock assumed the man to be a former chief on the "retired list," as the army called it, but still a man of considerable influence. Slim Face, or more properly "Lean Face," was at the time about

---

[26] Brown, *March Journal*, April 7, 1867; Hancock to Sherman, April 7, 1867.

Ado Hunnius, the same soldier who sketched Fort Zarah in June 1867, made this rendering of Pawnee Rock a short time later. Though primitive as artwork and not to scale, it does give an idea of how the Dakota sandstone rock appeared to travelers on the Santa Fe Trail. The ruins of an old adobe trading ranch are shown below it. *Courtesy of the Kansas State Historical Society, Topeka.*

seventy-nine years of age but in fact still an active council chief of one of the smaller bands currently south of the Arkansas River with Black Kettle's followers. It was an ironic meeting, with Custer in the camp, for the following year Custer would take Lean Face and two others captive by an act of deception after a supposed peace parley.[27]

The Expedition for the Plains left Ash Creek on the morning of April 7, 1867, continuing southerly along the Santa Fe Trail. About a mile beyond Ash Creek the trail split between the Wet Route, which continued close to the course of the Arkansas River, and the Dry Route. At that time the Dry Route led first to Fort Larned and then southwesterly in a more or less direct line across the dry, open plains to a point just below Fort Dodge, where it rejoined the Wet Route. After another three miles or so, the road forked again, the more westerly branch, which Lieutenant Brown called the "old road," leading to a wooden bridge built during 1859–60. But the

---

[27] Hancock to Sherman, April 7, 1867; Powell, *People of the Sacred Mountain*, 1:189, 2:714–19, 721.

bridge had been burned by a Kiowa war party in 1864 and never replaced. The expedition therefore took the more easterly alternative.[28]

The march from Fort Zarah gave the troops at least some relief from the monotony of the rolling plains, where land and sky seemed to merge into a far distant horizon. Here and there small herds of timid pronghorn antelope, frightened by the approach of the long column, bounded off into the screening hills. Large numbers of the gray wolf of the plains were seen prowling the flanks of the column, as if expecting to find some discarded food or some weakened, lagging animal of which to make a meal. They passed numerous prairie dog towns and also met their first live bison. For a time the great shaggy creatures stood and watched the marching soldiers approach, then suddenly turned and galloped away.[29]

Lieutenant Colonel Custer, although at least nominally leading the cavalry on their march, spent a significant part of each day engaging in sport with his hunting dogs, usually in chasing pronghorn antelope or jackrabbits. During the march on April 7 the hounds started a jack, and both the dogs and Custer, mounted on his horse, Phil Sheridan, took up the pursuit. Custer's saddle girth was not tight enough, and the saddle turned, taking Custer with it. He broke his stirrup trying to regain his seat and shortly found himself stretched full length on the ground, but he suffered neither scratch nor bruise. His horse's legs were considerably scratched by the saddle, but the stallion otherwise escaped serious injury. The rabbit got away. Back in the saddle later that day, Custer had his first experience with that peculiar western phenomenon known as a mirage. He saw what appeared to be a beautiful lake about five to ten miles distant, set against a background of trees. The appearance of the lake was so perfect that the reflection of the trees on it could be plainly seen. But when he and his troops reached the apparent site of the lake, there was nothing but dry ground and nothing to explain the strange vision.[30]

The eastern fork of the Dry Route taken by Hancock's troops led them over a high ridge and just to the west of a rock quarry of light sandstone. This was the quarry used to produce stone for the new buildings being constructed at Fort Larned, and the ridge was what was then known as Lookout Hill and later Jenkin's Hill. Beyond it they passed to the immediate

---

[28] Brown, *March Journal*, April 7, 1867; Clapsaddle, "Wet and Dry Routes," 111–15; Simmons and Jackson, *Following the Santa Fe Trail*, 121–24.

[29] E. Custer, *Tenting on the Plains*, 525; Kennedy, *On the Plains*, 52; Stanley, *My Early Travels*, 20–23; Utley, *Life in Custer's Cavalry*, 27.

[30] E. Custer, *Tenting on the Plains*, 529–30; Kennedy, *On the Plains*, 52.

east of a plateau about seventy feet high, at the southern base of which flowed the Pawnee Fork. This stream had its origin about one hundred miles to the southwest and was fed by three principal branches that converged to the west and southwest of the fort. The north, or Heth's, branch was the longest, followed by the middle, or Buckner's, branch, and the south, or Schaff's, branch, also known as Sawlog Creek because soldiers from Fort Atkinson and later from Fort Dodge cut wood along its banks. The Kiowas and most other southern Plains tribes originally called the stream Dark-Timber River, each in its own language. But after the Yamparika Comanche war leader Ikanosa (Red Sleeve) was killed in a fight with a Mexican wagon train near the crossing of the Santa Fe Trail's Wet Route on May 12, 1847, it was often referred to as Red Sleeve's Creek or, by the Cheyennes, Red Arm's Creek. The original Indian name was appropriate, for particularly in its lower reaches the stream had even more significant stands of timber than the thin cottonwood groves scattered along the Arkansas River into which it emptied. But even so, timber was sparse. Nevertheless, the Pawnee Fork provided favored camping places for the southern tribes, particularly the Comanches, Kiowas, Cheyennes, and Arapahoes, though since the establishment of Fort Larned they made their camps farther to the west along one of the branches.[31]

Once the troops were across the stream and back on the level plain, the flagstaff of Fort Larned could be seen due west. Marching directly toward the fort and parallel with the course of the Pawnee, they made their next camp along its banks about a mile and a half upstream from the crossing and slightly over a mile east of Fort Larned. Their march had been long and tiring, but it had brought them deep into the Plains Indian country and to the point where Hancock and his subordinates believed they were to meet the chiefs of most of the southern Plains tribes.[32]

[31] Brown, *March Journal*, April 7, 1867; Chalfant, *Dangerous Passage*, 72; Mooney, *Calendar History*, 286.
[32] Brown, *March Journal*, April 7, 1867; Hancock to Nichols, May 22, 1867.

The Hancock expedition reached Fort Larned on April 7, 1867. This scene, which was sketched by artist Theodore R. Davis to illustrate his report in the June 8, 1867, edition of *Harper's Weekly*, shows the fort as viewed from the southwest. All of the buildings to the left (north and west) of the flagpole are the original adobe structures built when the post was moved to this site in the summer of 1860. To the right of the flag are the two new stone buildings, a hexagonal blockhouse and a commissary storehouse, too distant to be seen well or identified. Some of the personnel, probably civilian construction workers, were clearly still living in dugouts along the Pawnee Fork, as depicted in the foreground.

CHAPTER SEVEN

In Camp at Fort Larned

A rrival of the expedition at its new camp on the Pawnee Fork was as usual a protracted affair. After consulting with the guides and officers, General Smith directed the location of the infantry, artillery, and cavalry encampments, as well as those for the quartermaster and commissary wagon trains and the train of pontoon bridges. As the baggage wagons for each rolled to their assigned areas, the men unloaded the tents and other necessary gear, while the officers' strikers were doing the same.[1] Meantime General Hancock, General Smith, and other senior officers rode upstream to Fort Larned to meet the garrison commander, Capt. (Bvt. Maj.) Henry Asbury, and the agent for the Cheyennes, Arapahoes, and Plains Apaches, Col. E. W. Wynkoop.[2] They were accompanied by Henry M. Stanley, the newspaper correspondent who was as always looking for his next story. At the fort, after being formally greeted by the post commandant and an honor guard, Hancock met briefly with Wynkoop. The agent advised that he had sent runners to each of the agency tribes, or at least to those bands in the vicinity, requesting that they come to the fort for a council with Hancock on April 10, and they had promised to do so. He asked that Hancock remain at the post until that time, to which the latter acceded, probably mostly because he wanted his men and animals to get a much needed rest and because he desired to make a thorough inspection of Fort Larned before leaving it.[3]

Fort Larned was one of the older posts on the Santa Fe Trail and the southern plains. Founded in 1859 as Camp on Pawnee Fork, the small gar-

---

[1] A striker was an enlisted man who accepted work from an officer for compensation, usually for caring for horses, cooking, setting up a tent, and similar services.

[2] Indian agents were addressed with the honorary title "Colonel," regardless of the rank they held in the military service.

[3] Brown, *March Journal*, April 7, 1867; Hancock to Sherman, April 7, 1867; Hancock to Nichols, May 22, 1867; Barnard, *Ten Years with Custer*, 24–25.

rison's primary duty was to protect the mail station at the crossing of the Pawnee and patrol about 140 miles of the Santa Fe Trail. The name of the post was changed to "Camp Alert" on February 1, 1860, because the troops there had to be constantly on the alert for Indians. In 1860 it was moved to a new site about two and a half miles upstream and renamed Fort Larned in honor of the army's paymaster general, Col. Benjamin Franklin Larned. Here a number of adobe buildings were constructed during the summer of that year. When completed, they formed an impressive complex but, because of the fragile nature of adobe, required constant repair to prevent them from deteriorating. The effects of the occasional rains during springtime, along with wind erosion, made it clear that if the post was to be permanent, a more resistant building material would be needed.[4]

With manpower and resources required at the scene of the great conflict in the East, during the Civil War no new construction was undertaken at Fort Larned. At the end of the war, regular troops returned to the post, but there was now escalating warfare with the Indians as great numbers of travelers and settlers moved west in search of the free lands promised them by the government—Indian lands. Because of the increased Indian resistance, it was concluded that more posts were required to protect Santa Fe Trail traffic and that they all needed adequate facilities to house, care for, and protect their troops. It was in this post–Civil War atmosphere that new construction began at Fort Larned.[5]

On July 17, 1864, the Kiowas raided Fort Larned, running off 172 horses. This prompted General Curtis to issue an order requiring all military posts in his department to provide protection for their livestock and troops. He particularly cited Fort Larned for its failure to have a stone blockhouse or a stockade for its animals. At the time there was only one stone building at the post—the sutler's store. In compliance with Curtis's order, a new hexagonal blockhouse was completed on February 20, 1865, followed by a commissary storehouse in 1866. Though planning for additional buildings was in process, these were the only two stone military buildings completed and in service when the Expedition for the Plains arrived on April 7, 1867.[6]

The reactions to the fort by Hancock and those accompanying him on his tour of inspection were varied. Henry M. Stanley was impressed with its location from the standpoint of aesthetics; viewing it from Lookout

---

[4] Hancock to Sherman, April 7, 1867; Oliva, *Fort Larned*, 7–16; Oliva, *Soldiers on the Santa Fe Trail*, 114–23.

[5] Oliva, *Fort Larned*, 17–24; Oliva, *Soldiers on the Santa Fe Trail*, 131–66.

[6] Oliva, *Fort Larned*, 25–28.

Hill during their approach, he said, had gladdened their eyes. He thought the fort's site to be "a green oasis in the Sahara of bleached grass." Once they reached the post, he climbed to the top of one of the adobe barracks, from which could be seen "a wide area, stretching away in all directions, the hills swelling into every variety of form, until the indistinct outline of their summits blends with the sky where it touches the horizon." Nearby was the trading camp of David Butterfield, who had acquired about three thousand fine buffalo robes by trade with the Indians.[7]

The military men who commented on the appearance of the fort were less focused on aesthetics and more on its facilities and defensibility. Captain Barnitz described it as consisting of "a couple of stone buildings, one of which is the Sutler's Store, and the other the Commissary building," a number of low adobe structures, plus several quarters and stables dug out of the riverbank and covered with poles, straw, and mud. For some reason Barnitz failed to notice the hexagonal blockhouse.[8]

General Hancock personally inspected the post and expressed his serious concerns about its current location in a letter to General Sherman. He opined that it was in the most dangerous site possible for a military post in Indian country. It was surrounded, he said, by the dry bed of a former channel of the Pawnee Fork on one side, capable of concealing "thousands of Indians," as he saw it, and by the stream channel on the other sides except one (the south), with very high banks that offered "every facility for a surprise." He observed there was an entrenchment that surrounded the post in part, presumably on the south side, which a thousand troops could not adequately man. He concluded that the fort should be moved immediately to a more secure site in the area before any more building was done. While noting that a storehouse (commissary) and guardhouse (blockhouse) would have to be taken down and removed to the new location, he found the rest of the buildings of no value, in a state of disrepair and decay, and believed they should be torn down and any usable materials preserved. Hancock thought a site on or near Lookout Hill would be appropriate and commented that it had been considered more than once. He appointed a "competent board" that would examine his proposed site as well as the current site on the following day. Their conclusions would be forwarded to General Sherman. He further noted that there had been no new construction at Fort Larned since Sherman visited it the previous year.[9]

[7] Stanley, *My Early Travels*, 27–29.
[8] Utley, *Life in Custer's Cavalry*, 27.
[9] Hancock to Sherman, April 7, 1867.

With his inspection completed, General Hancock and his staff, probably accompanied by Henry Stanley, returned to the expedition encampment along the Pawnee Fork a good mile to the east. Following their arrival they had been joined by two additional companies of the Seventh Cavalry—Company E, commanded by Capt. A. P. Morrow, stationed at Fort Hays, and Company K, commanded by Capt. R. M. West and stationed at Fort Dodge. Except for minor additions or subtractions caused by transfers or illness, the expedition had now reached full strength as provided by Hancock's orders. From this time until the projected council with the chiefs of the southern Plains tribes camping near Fort Larned, the men of Hancock's command would concentrate on rest, resupply, repair of equipment, and the tending of mounts and teams.[10]

On the evening of April 7, General Hancock sat down in his headquarters tent and penned his latest report to General Sherman. He described the march from Ash Creek, the encounters with the Plains Apaches and southern Oglalas en route, and the results of his inspection of Fort Larned. More importantly he reported that Colonel Wynkoop, as agent for the Cheyennes, Arapahoes, and Plains Apaches, had "invited his chiefs to meet me here tomorrow, or the next day, in order that we can discuss all matters of complaint against them." Wynkoop had actually scheduled the council for April 10, as Hancock himself reported to Sherman earlier in the same letter. It is clear from this that Hancock's entire focus was on complaints against the Indians, not on gaining insight or understanding as to the root causes for Indian dissatisfaction or violent reactions to white incursions into their country. In fairness to the general, however, he was a man trained only for military service and had no knowledge of either the Indians or their culture. Nor did he have any interest in learning about those matters. He assumed that the treaties the government claimed to have with the Indians were understood by them and were valid and binding, as did most whites, including the Indian agents.[11]

In his letter Hancock also reported receiving word of one or two recent depredations by the Indians. Both were the work of raiders belonging to Little Raven's band of Arapahoes. A raiding party had gone west to the Ute country in the Colorado mountains to raid but, upon returning from an unsuccessful effort, ran off the herd of livestock belonging to an American wagon train camped along the Santa Fe Trail at Pretty Encamp-

[10] Chandler, *Of GarryOwen in Glory*, 3; Utley, *Life in Custer's Cavalry*, 27.
[11] Hancock to Sherman, April 7, 1867.

ment.[12] The second incident was of similar character. Hancock's proposed solution was disarmingly simple: "We will make Little Raven return the animals, or will whip him if he can be found." Fortunately for Little Raven, Hancock did not find him until a council was held with him at Fort Dodge, when Little Raven promised their return. While discussing the matter of the boy known as William [Wilson] Graham, Hancock also gave his thoughts on the Cheyenne girl in Colorado. There were actually two young Cheyenne sisters in captivity, but the general was apparently aware of only one. He commented that Governor Cummings of Colorado was reluctant to return her unless absolutely necessary, because "she is well cared for by a family who are raising her in Christian ways and who do not wish to throw her back into a savage state." While Black Kettle had apparently indicated that might be arranged if her family was satisfied that it was the wish of the child, Hancock clearly disagreed. "It is," he wrote, "plain that she ought to be returned. It is an excuse for the Indians to keep captive white children. They suppose that their way of raising children is as good as ours. It would be better that every chicken return to its own nest until the mother lets it run."[13]

Hancock also related his plans to Sherman, stating that he had sent ten days' supplies to Fort Dodge for 1,600 men and 2,000 animals. He would take with him twelve days of supplies, which would permit him to march south from Dodge, possibly to the Washita River. When he returned, he would move back to Fort Larned before marching to Walnut Creek and the Smoky Hill. He intended to strike the Smoky Hill at about Downer Station on the stage route, as that was near where a band of Ôhméséheso Cheyennes, said to be followers of a chief known as Cut Nose, were thought to be camping. It was understood that Cut Nose had a little white girl in his possession.[14]

On the following day, April 8, the Expedition for the Plains remained in camp, resting, checking and repairing arms and accoutrements, and preparing for the anticipated council with the Cheyenne, Arapahoe, and Plains Apache chiefs. The weather appears to have been very pleasant and springlike, allowing for rest and relaxation. But nature is capable of cruel

---

[12] Pretty Encampment was one of the many campgrounds used by travelers along both the Cimarron and Mountain routes of the Santa Fe Trail and was adjacent to the Arkansas River near the mouth of East Bridge Creek, about five miles east of present-day Coolidge, Kansas. See Chalfant, "In Search of Pretty Encampment."

[13] Hancock to Sherman, April 7, 1867; Talk Held with "Little Raven," Head Chief of the Arapahoes, April 28, 1867, MC619-R563.

[14] Hancock to Sherman, April 7, 1867.

surprises on the plains, and one was in store for the men of Hancock's command. Western Kansas lies within the rain shadow of the Rocky Mountains, the area of limited moisture resulting from its loss in crossing those mountains from west to east. The moist Pacific air cools as it rises, then condenses and falls as rain or snow on the western slopes. By the time these air currents reach the plains of eastern Colorado and western Kansas, nearly all of the Pacific moisture has been lost from the airstream. The region also lies west of the normal flow of moisture-laden air from the Gulf of Mexico. But despite this, occasionally some weather event steers masses of moist Gulf air farther west, causing showers, heavy thunderstorms, or, if a cold front has dropped south, a snowstorm or blizzard that strikes the area where the two meet. Though the average high temperature in the Fort Larned vicinity is nearly seventy degrees in April, and the average low about forty-two degrees, a late-season cold front can confound the averages. So it was on April 9, 1867.[15]

The day apparently began quietly, though a great bank of clouds had moved in during the night. At Fort Harker, to the northeast on the Smoky Hill, the stagecoach from Junction City bound for Santa Fe with mail, public documents, the companies' special messenger, and one passenger, Theodore R. Davis of Harper and Brothers, had become stuck a little after dawn while crossing the river. It remained stuck, due to its burden of public documents, until a team could be obtained from the fort to help pull it out. The heavy clouds began to spit first sleet and then snow while the coach was still in the river, and when it was at last freed from the grip of the river bottom and resumed its journey, the snowstorm intensified. Back at Fort Larned the falling sleet greeted the soldiers just beginning their day at the fort and at the expedition's encampment to the east. Something had steered warm Gulf moisture farther to the west, where it collided across western Kansas with a cold front dropping down from Canada. Worse than the sleet and snow, however, was the wind that blew ever more fiercely from the northwest, then gradually shifted to the north, and finally to the northeast as the frontal system moved off to the east. The temperature doubtless dropped to freezing or below, but its effects were greatly exacerbated by the wind chill factor. The storm lasted from shortly after dawn until about 10:00 that evening.[16]

---

[15] Soil Survey of Pawnee County, Kans., 1978, USDA, 2–3, 60.

[16] E. Custer, *Tenting on the Plains*, 551; Davis, "Summer on the Plains," 292; Kennedy, *On the Plains*, 53; Utley, *Life in Custer's Cavalry*, 27.

At the expedition's encampment, what was to have been a day of rest and relaxation for the troops became a day of forced confinement. The high winds accompanying the storm shrieked and howled through the camp, pounding at the tents and causing the snow to drift around them. Most of the men wrapped themselves in their blankets and attempted to get some sleep, while on the picket line the horse tenders and guards were kept busy feeding the poor animals a double ration of corn to help them generate body heat and warmth, and using whips to keep them moving lest they freeze. The officers of the Seventh Cavalry were busy dressing and preparing themselves to answer an "officers call," which was to be sounded at 9:45 A.M. according to a regimental directive of the prior evening. They were to gather at the regimental adjutant's tent, then move as a body to the Headquarters of the Department of the Missouri in the Field, about three hundred paces from the cavalry camp, to pay their respects to General Hancock. But just as the appointed time was approaching, an orderly delivered to each officer a circular notification that, owing to the inclemency of the weather, the visit was to be postponed.[17]

With the visit delayed, a number of the officers went to Custer's tent, one of the few Sibley tents in the encampment, since the army had dropped them in favor of the wall tent. Sibley tents were conical, equipped with a heating stove, and designed to approximate the Plains Indian tepee. They were more commodious than wall tents and accommodated a larger number of men more comfortably. While at Fort Harker, General Hancock had ordered the doubling up of officers in order to save transport space, and Custer was now sharing his tent with Major Gibbs. Gibbs had been experiencing considerable difficulty with his eyes for several days, and though he claimed to be up to continuing the march, Custer did not deem it prudent. He reported the problem to both General Smith and General Hancock, and it was finally decided that Gibbs would return to Fort Riley to take command of that post, since it was in disarray in the absence of a senior field-grade officer. He would leave the expedition when it left Fort Larned.[18]

Those officers who met in Custer's tent at 10:00 A.M., including General Smith, Custer, Gibbs, Captain Barnitz, and a few others, had what

---

[17] Hancock to Nichols, May 22, 1867; Barnard, *Ten Years with Custer*, 26; E. Custer, *Tenting on the Plains*, 551; G. Custer, *My Life on the Plains*, 37; Kennedy, *On the Plains*, 53; Utley, *Life in Custer's Cavalry*, 27–28.

[18] E. Custer, *Tenting on the Plains*, 526, 551–52, 555; Utley, *Life in Custer's Cavalry*, 28.

Barnitz described as a "social talk" for half an hour or so. Then Smith excused himself and returned to the expedition headquarters. Major Gibbs retired to get some sleep and was tucked in under a half-dozen blankets. Custer began telling Barnitz and the others remaining of the currently projected plans. General Hancock, he said, intended to hold a council with the "head chiefs" of the Cheyenne and Kiowa tribes, whom he apparently expected to arrive the next day despite the storm. He intended to make a treaty with them to go south and remain at least one hundred miles south of the Smoky Hill road. If the Indians kept the treaty, the expedition would move to either Fort Harker or Fort Hays and remain there until May, when some companies would be sent to Pueblo, Colorado, and others to Fort Morgan, northeast of Denver.[19] Barnitz was clearly pleased with the prospect of being stationed in a mountainous area, with beautiful scenery and opportunities for hunting and fishing, and away from the hostile and warlike Plains Indians. His enthusiasm was shared by Custer, who would then command Fort Garland. But there was a proviso. If the Indians refused to accept the terms General Hancock offered, the expedition would initiate hostilities immediately and force them to do so—an early form of gunboat diplomacy. If they did agree to a treaty but then broke it, the Seventh Cavalry was to "ride about and 'expend' a few thousand of them!" Barnitz likely misunderstood the matter of a treaty, as neither Hancock, Custer, nor any other army officer acting in that capacity was authorized or empowered to engage in treaty making with the Indian nations. That authority resided with the Interior Department and the president. Neither Hancock nor Custer ever referred to treaty making in their own reports and writings on the subject, and doubtless what was intended was a council and orders to the Indians to move away from the white trails under threat of war.[20]

After Barnitz left Custer's tent, he retired to his own, wrote a letter to his wife, Jennie, and then got some sleep. Most of the officers and men were doing just that, and the only real activity was that of the guards and the horse tenders, who were trying to keep the animals from freezing. The guards had cut and gathered wood along the Pawnee Fork and built a roaring fire. Between patrols around the encampment they stood near the fire, trying to absorb a little of its warmth. Later in the morning or perhaps

---

[19] Barnitz apparently misunderstood Custer, as the southern post was to be Fort Garland, south and west of Pueblo. E. Custer, *Tenting on the Plains*, 527–28.

[20] Hancock to Nichols, May 22, 1867; E. Custer, *Tenting on the Plains*, 526–28, 551–52, 555; Utley, *Life in Custer's Cavalry*, 28–30.

early afternoon, Custer mounted one of his horses and rode to Fort Larned, "on duty," as he said, "through the thickest of the storm, and was not affected by it." He did not relate what duty took him out into the storm or why he was unaffected by blinding snow driven slantwise by the howling wind. In his headquarters tent, General Hancock was giving thought to the council scheduled for the next day, but apparently no thought to the possibility the storm might delay or prevent travel by the Indians. Sometime during the day he had his adjutant send a brief message to Agent Wynkoop, requesting that he advise the general when the Indians arrived for the council and how many rations they would need. These he would have issued to them from Fort Larned.[21]

While the men and animals of the expedition were confined to their camp by the storm, to the northeast the same storm was providing a harrowing experience for another important participant. The stagecoach in which Theodore R. Davis was riding, en route to catch up with the expedition, had progressed southwest along the Fort Riley–Fort Larned Military Road after being freed from the river bottom. As the coach continued, the snow came down faster and harder, clothing the undulating plains and nearby hills in a mantle of white. After enduring a poor but expensive meal at the stage station and ranch at Plum Creek, the party headed for their next stop, Cow Creek Station. But soon the coach and mules were covered with snow, blending them in with the plains, and the road was nearly obliterated from sight. After twelve miles of travel from Plum Creek, and apparently within two to three miles from their next stop, the coach became stuck in a large drift and could not be moved. The mules would freeze to death if left exposed to the storm, so after a hurried council it was decided that the driver would attempt to get them to the next station, while the company messenger and Davis stayed with the coach and guarded the mail and public documents. Davis thought the driver had about nine chances in ten of becoming lost and freezing to death, but there were no other options.[22]

The driver disappeared into a swirl of white, leading his team of mules and unleashing a series of potent bullwhacker oaths, while Davis and the messenger settled down to make the best of their plight. They lined the interior of the coach with blankets to keep out as much of the wind and snow as possible, then considered the matter of food and drink. There was

[21] W. G. Mitchell, AAAG, to E. W. Wynkoop, April 9, 1867, MC535-R1354; E. Custer, *Tenting on the Plains*, 551; Kennedy, *On the Plains*, 53; Utley, *Life in Custer's Cavalry*, 27.

[22] Davis, "Summer on the Plains," 292–93.

nothing in the coach except one bottle of corn whiskey and one tin of half-cooked corn. The contents of the can, along with water from a melted snowball, were heated over a candle and served as their dinner. That gone, they heated the whiskey in like fashion, calling it "warm punch." Then they passed the night talking, as sleep was made impossible by the roaring wind and the howling of the wolves that had gathered around them. The high winds continued through much of the night but by morning had dropped off sharply, and sunshine was now flooding the snow-covered land. The two men dug the drifts away from the coach, then contemplated their surroundings. The air was strangely clear, and the sky dotted with magnificent billowing clouds quickly moving off to the north and east. The snow-clad country around them seemed to dance and sparkle in the bright sunlight, but hunger made it difficult for them to appreciate the scene. Their distress was soon relieved, however, as men with teams appeared, rescued their coach from the drift, and had it on its way again. Their driver had beaten the odds against him. By the following morning they reached Fort Larned, and Davis joined General Hancock's expedition.[23]

The storm dissipated by about 10:00 that night, having deposited seven to eight inches of snow and sleet, much of which formed into drifts. The accompanying winds also blew themselves out during the night, and then came one of those marvels of the southern plains—a rapid thaw and melting. A foot of snow is the equivalent of approximately one inch of moisture and quickly disappears in the prevailing warm south winds as a cold front moves off to the east. So it was at Hancock's encampment, and on the day following the storm, April 10, Custer was able to write his wife that the temperatures had greatly moderated and were quite comfortable. The snow shrank rapidly and was mostly gone within a day or two. The debilitating effects of the blizzard that made it necessary to postpone the anticipated council with the various tribal chiefs on April 10 were gone, both in fact and, by Hancock's way of thinking, as an excuse for further delay by those chiefs in keeping their appointment with him. On the morning of April 11 Agent Wynkoop informed Hancock that, though the Cheyennes encamped on the Pawnee Fork had started for Fort Larned, they stopped to hunt when a herd of bison appeared near their village. Hancock believed this was suspicious and not sufficiently important to warrant a delay in their arrival to council with him. But the general had never had to depend on the hunting of wild game to feed himself and his

---

[23] Ibid., 293–94.

family nor spend an entire winter largely confined to camp with weakened horses and dependent on a shrinking supply of dried meats, wilding fruits, and vegetables for food.[24]

Despite his suspicions, Hancock decided to give the Cheyenne chiefs another day before resuming his march, this time to their village, following which he intended to move south to Fort Dodge. But this day too seemed to be passing with no sign of the chiefs. Hancock made up his mind to wait no longer and, during the afternoon, issued orders that the march up the Pawnee Fork would commence at 7:00 the following morning. The chief quartermaster of the expedition was directed to take along all hay and grain at Fort Larned when the command marched, leaving only a sufficient supply for the post until the next train arrived with forage. He also directed Captain Asbury, commanding at Fort Larned, to provide Colonel Wynkoop with a mule and equipment with which to send a messenger to the camps of the Cheyennes and Lakotas. Hancock told Asbury that he would be taking with him the post interpreter, Dick Curtis, and would require his services for ten or fifteen days. Lastly, he instructed Asbury to defer all negotiations for purchase of the sutler's store until it was determined if the fort's location would be changed, and told him that he would be leaving the Indian boy known as Wilson Graham, to be held until he could be delivered to his relatives. His mother was believed to be living and a member of Black Kettle's band.[25]

Late in the afternoon or early evening of April 12 a small entourage of Indians appeared, riding in from the west along the Pawnee Fork. When they reached the expedition encampment, General Hancock had a Sibley tent prepared for them and necessary rations issued. They proved to be the three chiefs of the Dog Soldier Cheyennes, Tall Bull, Bull Bear, and White Horse, along with White Hair of the Óhmésèheso band, and Lean Face from one of the smaller southern bands. They were accompanied by perhaps ten to twelve warriors, whom Hancock described as men of "less importance." Stanley assumed them to be "fifteen chiefs of the Cheyennes" but mentioned Tall Bull and White Horse as the "two principal chiefs." That was inaccurate, of course, since council chiefs were coequals in terms of authority. Like Hancock, the Seventh Cavalry regimental surgeon, Isaac

[24] E. Custer, *Tenting on the Plains*, 553; G. Custer, *My Life on the Plains*, 37–38; Kennedy, *On the Plains*, 53.

[25] Hancock to Nichols, May 22, 1867; W. G. Mitchell, AAAG, to H. Asbury, April 12, 1867, MC535-R1354; W. G. Mitchell, AAAG, to G. W. Bradley, April 12, 1867, MC535-R1354; G. Custer, *My Life on the Plains*, 38–39; Davis, "Summer on the Plains," 294.

White Horse, another of the Dog Soldier council chiefs, also attempted to persuade Hancock not to march to the Cheyenne and Oglala villages (GN 00222). *National Anthropological Archives, Smithsonian Institution.*

Coates, observed what he thought were ten to twelve Indian, and stated that, among the great chiefs present, "Tall Bull and White Horse were the spokesmen for this council." Custer recalled the Indians appearing for the council as "two chiefs of the Dog Soldiers," accompanied by a dozen warriors. Recounting the story forty years later, George Bent named the Dog Soldier chiefs present as Tall Bull, White Horse, Bull Bear, and Little Robe. But Bent was not present at the event and probably assembled the facts for his statement from interviews with older people who knew who the chiefs were at that time. In fact Little Robe had disassociated himself from the Dog Soldiers in 1865 and was now camping south of the Arkansas with some of his own followers and Black Kettle's people. Except Wynkoop, and later White Hair in his Medicine Lodge testimony, no one actually present ever mentioned any Cheyenne chief other than Tall Bull and White Horse. Why Bull Bear, White Hair, and Lean Face were not introduced to Hancock was never explained, but likely it was because Tall Bull and White Horse were designated to speak for them at the council. It is clear from Tall Bull's subsequent speech to Hancock that none of the Lakotas or Arapahoes were present, despite Bent's assertions to the contrary.[26]

Following the arrival of the Cheyennes, they retired to the Sibley tent erected for them not far from the general's own. Hancock ordered rations issued to them, and they ate and refreshed themselves. At the same time, on the general's orders, a huge log fire was prepared in front of the headquarters tent, with other logs arranged for the seating of the Indians and of the army officers and representatives of the press who would be present. Hancock, in his profound ignorance of the Indians and their culture, ordered the council to be held that night. But for the Plains Indians, and particularly the Cheyennes, councils of this sort were only to be held in the light of day, so that Sun, one of the Sacred Powers, could look down and cast light into each man's heart. This would ensure that only truth would be found there and that the Cheyenne council chiefs would be blessed and filled with wisdom to deal with the problems at hand. No one can say with certainty what those Cheyennes present thought of this, but it is likely they believed either that Hancock was a fool who knew nothing or that he intended to treat them and their beliefs with disrespect.

---

[26] Hancock to Nichols, May 22, 1867; G. Custer, *My Life on the Plains*, 38–39; Davis, "Summer on the Plains," 294; Hyde, *Life of George Bent*, 256; Kennedy, *On the Plains*, 53–54; Stanley, *My Early Travels*, 29–30; Stanley, "British Journalist," 301.

Certainly it would have enhanced the suspicions already held that whites were motivated by malice and that Hancock intended to perpetrate another massacre like the one at Sand Creek.[27]

Both Hancock and Custer claimed that the Cheyenne chiefs requested the council but had not said when they wanted it. It is clear the chiefs were present only because they had been summoned by Hancock and had no reason to request a council themselves. They had ridden nearly thirty-five miles to get there and were doubtless tired as well as hungry. Moreover, considering their religious convictions against councils at night, it is extremely doubtful they would have requested one under any circumstance. No participant or observer stated with certainty that Hancock was aware of the Cheyenne bias against night councils, but Wynkoop implied so in his September 14, 1867, letter to Thomas Murphy, superintendent of the Central Superintendency. It was, Wynkoop wrote, "hitherto unknown as holding a friendly converse with an assemblage of Indian chiefs after sunset," it being "against their medicine." Further, it seems likely that either Wynkoop or General Smith would have advised Hancock of this fact if asked or upon learning of his intentions. But the general repeatedly ignored their advice throughout the expedition.[28]

While Tall Bull, White Horse, and the accompanying chiefs and warriors were resting and eating, General Hancock ordered his officers to don their full dress uniforms, or at least the finest they had available, to impress the Indians with their importance and the power and might of the U.S. government. Hancock himself was wearing the full dress uniform of a major general in the U.S. Army, bedecked with gold epaulettes, brass buttons and buckles, gold medals, and colorful stripes on his trousers. Most successful in this effort were the artillery officers, whose dress uniforms included tall helmets surmounted with red horsehair plumes, and gold aiguillettes across their chests. All of the officers were to assemble at the council ground at 8:00, when the council would be convened.[29] Now

---

[27] Berthrong, *Southern Cheyennes*, 273; G. Custer, *My Life on the Plains*, 38–39; Davis, "Summer on the Plains," 294; Grinnell, *Fighting Cheyennes*, 248; Hyde, *Life of George Bent*, 256; Kennedy, *On the Plains*, 53–54; Powell, *People of the Sacred Mountain*, 1:465; Stanley, *My Early Travels*, 29.

[28] Hancock to Nichols, May 22, 1867; E. W. Wynkoop to T. Murphy, September 14, 1867, *Annual Report of the Commissioner of Indian Affairs, 1867*, 311; G. Custer, *My Life on the Plains*, 38.

[29] It may be that General Hancock intentionally scheduled the event for nighttime in the belief that the great log fire would illuminate the profusion of gold and color on the uniforms, in hopes of impressing or intimidating the Indians. There is also the fact that he intended to march to their villages the next day and had already scheduled departure for 7:00 A.M.

the stage was set for the first of the councils with chiefs of the southern Plains tribes. Although in his report of the expedition Hancock asserted that the Indians had requested a conference with him, to which he assented, in truth it was Hancock who had summoned them for reasons they did not fully understand. The one thing they did know with certainty was that they did not want him marching his troops to their villages, where their women, children, and old people would be vulnerable. The memory of Sand Creek was still fresh in the minds of all Cheyennes—indeed, of all of the Plains Indians.[30]

---

[30] Berthrong, *Southern Cheyennes*, 273; G. Custer, *My Life on the Plains*, 39; Kennedy, *On the Plains*, 53; Stanley, *My Early Travels*, 29.

CHAPTER EIGHT

THE FIRST COUNCIL

Dark came and the great log fire was lit and blazing by 8:00 P.M. on April 12, 1867. The officers, including General Hancock, General Smith, Custer, Gibbs, and Davidson, plus a score of others, took their places on one side of the fire, across from the seats arranged for the Indians. Soon after, the Cheyennes filed out of their Sibley tent accompanied by their agent, Colonel Wynkoop, and the interpreter, Edmund Guerrier. They were tall men, shrouded in buffalo robes and furs, and moved silently, the silver ornaments in their scalp locks swaying to and fro and glinting in the firelight as they walked. Their faces were painted in the ritual tradition of their people, to invoke the power and blessing of Maheo the Creator, the Sacred Persons who guarded the four sacred directions and the Sacred Powers. Once they had all emerged from the tent, they formed into line and moved abreast, not in file, with Wynkoop on their right and a few paces ahead, flanked by two of the Dog Soldier chiefs, Tall Bull and White Horse, and made their way to the log seats prepared for them at the right hand of General Hancock. There followed the shaking of hands and exchanges of salutations; then the Indians were seated. For approximately the next twenty minutes the proceedings, as intended by Hancock, were delayed while the Cheyenne chiefs and warriors smoked the pipe of peace, each offering it to the four sacred directions, to sky, and to earth, then taking four puffs and passing it on to the next man on his left. When their invocation of the sacred was complete, Tall Bull and White Horse were introduced to General Hancock. Hancock removed his greatcoat and stood forth in his dress uniform as a major general, the gold on it glittering in the flickering light of the fire. And then he began to speak.[1]

---

[1] Hancock to Nichols, May 22, 1867; *Frank Leslie's Illustrated Newspaper*, May 11, 1867, 115; E. Custer, *Tenting on the Plains*, 555; G. Custer, *My Life on the Plains*, 38–39; Davis, "Summer on the Plains," 294; Kennedy, *On the Plains*, 53–54; Stanley, *My Early Travels*, 29–30.

I told your agent some time ago that I was coming here to see you, and if any of you wanted to speak to me, they could do so. Your agent is your friend. I don't find many chiefs here; what is the reason? I have a great deal to say to the Indians, but I want to talk with them all together; I want to say it at once; but I am glad to see what chiefs are here. Tomorrow I am going to your camp. I have a boy, said to be a Cheyenne, whom the Cheyennes claim; we have made a promise in which we pledged ourselves, if possible, to find this boy and a girl, who were somewhere in the United States. We have found the boy, and here he is, ready to be delivered to his nearest relatives, who may call for him. I will leave him at Fort Larned with the commander; he will deliver him up to them. The girl is near Denver. We have written for her, and she will no doubt be sent here, either to your agent, or to the commander of Fort Larned, for delivery to her relatives. You see the boy has not been injured; the girl will be delivered by us also uninjured. Look out that any captives in your hands be restored to us equally uninjured. I tell you these things now, that you may keep your treaties.

Now, I have a great many soldiers, more than all the tribes put together. The Great Father has heard that some Indians have taken white men and women captives. He has heard also that a great many Indians are trying to get up war, to try to hunt the white man. That is the reason I come down here. I intend, not only to visit you here, but my troops will remain among you, to see that the peace and safety of the plains is preserved. I am going, also, to visit you in your camp. The innocent, and those who are truly our friends, we shall treat as brothers. If we find, hereafter, that any of you have lied to us, we will strike them. In case of war we shall punish whoever befriends our enemies. If there are any tribes among you who have captives, white or black, you must give them up safe and unharmed as they are now. I have collected all the evidence of all the outrages committed by you, so that your agent may examine into the matter and tell me who are guilty and who are innocent. When your agent informs me who the guilty are, I will punish them. When just demands are made, I will enforce them if they are not acceded to. I have heard that a great many Indians want to fight. Very well; we are here, and we come prepared for war. If you are for peace, you know the conditions; if you are for war, look out for its consequences. If we make war, it will be made against the tribe, who must be responsible for the acts of their young men. Your agent is your friend, but he knows his friendship will not save you from the anger of your Great Father, if we go to war. If we find any good Indians, and they come to us with clean hands, we will treat them as brothers, and we will separate them from the malcontents, and provide for them if necessary. This we will do, that the innocent may escape the war which will be waged against the guilty. The soldiers are going to stay in the country, and they will see that the white man keeps his treaty as well as the red man. We are building railroads, and building roads through the country. You must not let your young men stop them; you must keep your men off the roads. These roads will benefit the Indians as well as the white man, in bringing their goods to them cheaply and promptly. The steam car and wagon train must run, and it is of importance to the whites and Indians that the mails, goods and passengers carried on them shall be safe. You know very well, if you go to war with the white man you will lose. The Great Father has plenty more warriors. It is true, you might kill some soldiers and surprise some small detachments, but you will lose men, and you know that you have not a great many to lose. You cannot replace warriors lost; we can. It is to your interest, therefore, to have peace with the white man. Every tribe ought to have a great chief, one that can command his men. For any depredations committed by any one of his tribe, I shall hold the chief and his tribe responsible. Some Indians go down to Texas and kill women and children; I shall strike the tribe they belong to. If there are any good Indians, who don't want to go to war, I shall protect them. If there are any bad chiefs, I will help the good chiefs to put their heels on them. I have a great many chiefs with me that have commanded more men than you ever saw, and they have fought more great battles than you have fought fights. A great many Indians think they are better armed than they were formerly, but they must recollect that we are also. My chiefs cannot derive any distinction from fighting with your small numbers; they are not anxious for war against Indians, but are ready for a just war, and know how to fight and lead their men. Let the guilty, then, beware, I say to you, to show you the importance of keeping treaties made with us, and of letting the white man travel unmolested. Your Great Father is your friend as well as the friend of the white man. If a white man behaves badly, or does a wrong to you, he will be punished, if the evidence ascertained at the trial proves him guilty. We can redress your wrongs better than you can.

I have no more to say. I will await the end of this council, to see whether you want war or peace. I will put what I say in black and white, and send it to each post commander in the country I command; you can have it read to you when you please, and you can come back after a while and read it, and you will know whether we have lied to you or not.[2]

General Hancock's speech was translated for the Indians, sentence by sentence, by Edmund Guerrier, the half-Cheyenne interpreter for Colonel Wynkoop. From time to time his words were greeted by what appeared to be guttural expressions to the white men present but in the Cheyenne language were intended to express approval, skepticism, or downright disapproval. This was especially so when General Hancock suggested that whites would be punished for the wrongs they perpetrated against Indians and that the Great Father could and would rectify those wrongs better than they could. If anything had become clear during their years of increasing contact with whites, it was that bad white men were almost

[2] Hancock to Sherman, April 13, 1867, 7:54–56; Kennedy, *On the Plains*, 54–58; Stanley, *My Early Travels*, 30–33.

never punished for their misdeeds against Indians and that the government's actions usually accommodated and made them worse.[3]

Hancock's requirement that each tribe have one all-powerful chief who could "command his men" no doubt puzzled and perplexed Tall Bull, White Horse, Bull Bear, White Hair, Lean Face, and the other Cheyennes present. They had heard of this before, as at the Horse Creek treaty council, but only in the context of a person serving as an intermediary or contact between the Great Father and the People. Hancock would have one person responsible for the actions of all tribal members—one who would also be punished along with the tribe itself for any attacks on white intruders in their lands. White men did not deal with their own people in this fashion, and Indian tribes in general were not organized like whites. They were highly individualistic people, and their society was only loosely organized. The idea of an all-powerful chief must have struck the Cheyennes as both alien and foolish, and equally impossible. It also violated the tribal organization provided for them by their legendary prophet and culture hero, Sweet Medicine. Of equal or greater concern was the general's announcement that he intended to march to their village in the morning. When Hancock finally finished talking, and the last of his words were translated for them, the Cheyennes sat silently, taciturn, with serious and thoughtful expressions on their faces.[4]

For a time a deep silence prevailed on both sides of the council fire. It was probably during this lull in the talk that the expedition's officers had their first real opportunity to examine their Cheyenne guests carefully, illuminated by the light of the great log fire. They were dressed and adorned in various manners. Some were wearing buffalo robes to protect them from the chill of the night air, while others wore red-and-black trade blankets or the standard army overcoat, the latter probably acquired from traders or as a part of the annuities distributed to the tribes under the terms of the Horse Creek treaty. They wore buckskin shirts underneath, and their faces were painted in accordance with the "medicine" of the individual. Some had brass rings hung through slits in their ears, and most wore silver armlets, copper wristbands, and colorful bead necklaces. There were breast ornaments as well, some the antelope bone breastplate, and others silver shields or Johnson silver medals. To the scalp locks of a number of

---

[3] Davis, "Summer on the Plains," 294; Kennedy, On the Plains, 56; Stanley, My Early Travels, 33.

[4] Davis, "Summer on the Plains," 294; Dorsey, Cheyenne, 2–3; Kennedy, On the Plains, 56; Llewellyn and Hoebel, Cheyenne Way, 67–98; Powell, Sweet Medicine, 1:92–93; Stands in Timber and Liberty, Cheyenne Memories, 42–45; Stanley, My Early Travels, 33.

the warriors there was attached a long string of thin silver disks that swayed and bobbed as they walked. According to Stanley, there were "a great many noble faces among the Indians around the council fire." And then he made a remarkable admission for a man with such an ingrained bias against the Natives: "We were formerly under the impression that there were no noble-looking Indians, save in the fervid fancies of a Fenimore Cooper, but we must confess that they do exist,—and that we have seen them." For the officers and men of the expedition who were present at the council, most of whom had never before been in the West, much less seen a Plains Indian, it must have been a moment of fascination and wonder.[5]

After a period of silence, an Indian on the far right of the seated Cheyennes, probably Tall Bull, lit the sacred pipe. Offering it first to the Sacred Persons, guardians of the four sacred directions, to Maheo the Creator, and to Grandmother Earth, he took four puffs from the pipe, then handed it, stem and mouthpiece pointed skyward, to the man on his left. This sacred ritual was repeated with each warrior until it reached the far left end of the Cheyenne line and was smoked out. With the sacred and holy thus invoked, Tall Bull stood and, with his red and black blanket folded around him, extended his right arm and hand toward General Hancock, greeting him in the Cheyenne tongue. This he repeated to each of Hancock's officers, gravely shaking hands with them. He was a tall man, slender and wiry, who moved with great dignity. Custer described him as a "fine, warlike-looking chieftain," while to Isaac Coates he resembled the image he held of Shakespeare's Cassius, having "a lean and hungry look." He was probably the same one who reminded Stanley of Andrew Jackson, as depicted in the standard pictures of him. When he had finished his salutations, Tall Bull stepped to the center of the council circle and addressed General Hancock and his officers, speaking slowly and distinctly, though not loudly, and using gestures that were at once simple and extremely graceful.[6]

> You sent for us, we came here. We have made the treaty with our agent, Colonel Wynkoop. We never did the white man any harm. We don't intend to. Our agent told us to meet you here. Whenever you want to go on the Smoky Hill, you can go; you can go on any road. When we come on the road, your young men must not shoot us. We are willing to be friends with the white man.
> This boy you have here we have seen him, we don't recognize him; he must

[5] Kennedy, *On the Plains*, 53–56; Stanley, *My Early Travels*, 29, 35.
[6] *Frank Leslie's Illustrated Newspaper*, May 11, 1867, 115; G. Custer, *My Life on the Plains*, 40; Kennedy, *On the Plains*, 56; Powell, *Sweet Medicine*, 1:17; Stanley, *My Early Travels*, 33–35.

belong to some tribe south of the Arkansas. The buffalo are diminishing fast. The antelope, that were plenty a few years ago, they are now thin. When they shall all die away, we shall be hungry; we shall want something to eat, and will be compelled to come into the fort. Your young men must not fire on us. When they see us they fire, and we fire on them.

The Kiowas, Comanches, Apaches, and Arapahoes, send and get them here and talk with them. You say you are going to the village tomorrow. If you go, I shall have no more to say to you there than here. I have said all I want to say here.

At this point General Hancock interrupted Tall Bull, saying, "I am going, however, to your camp tomorrow." Tall Bull then continued, "I don't know whether the Sioux are coming here or not; they did not tell me they were coming. I have spoken."

His speech concluded, Tall Bull folded his blanket around him and resumed his seat. The sacred pipe was again lit, and the ceremony of the smoke repeated.[7]

When the Cheyenne ceremony was finished, General Hancock once more stood forth in the council circle and spoke, this time even more bluntly and bellicose.

I did not come here to see you alone; I came to see the Arapahoes, Comanches, Kiowas, and Apaches, when I learn where they are. I was told that some Indians were seeking for war. I want to see those who are friendly and those who are not, and wish war. You say that the soldiers and other white people fire on you when you go to the Smoky Hill. That was because your young men went there to molest the white people, and fired on them first. We know the buffalo are going away. But we cannot help it. The white men are becoming a great nation. You must keep your young men off the roads. Don't stop trains and travelers on the roads, and you will not be harmed. You ought to be friends to the white man. Soldiers expect to be killed when they are at war; their business is to fight; but as fast as our soldiers are killed we can get more to take their places. But you must keep off the great roads across the plains; for if you should ever stop one of our railroad trains, and kill the people in it, you would be exterminated. You must go to the white man to be taken care of hereafter, and you should cultivate his friendship. That is all I have to say.

Though none of the observers who wrote of the council made mention of it, it is probable that the Indians made their same expressions of approval or disapproval during the course of Hancock's second speech. It was filled with admonitions of what they must or must not do, without mention of

[7] Hancock to Sherman, April 13, 1867, 7:55; Kennedy, *On the Plains*, 57; Stanley, *My Early Travels*, 33–35.

their own terrible plight resulting from white actions, or what help they might expect from the Great Father for the way of life and the living they were being deprived of. They were painted by him as the wrongdoers, people who were somehow trespassers and transgressors in their own land and who should and would be dealt with harshly for their resistance. But if Hancock spoke bluntly, insensitively, and with bias, it was not only his voice delivering this bitter message. It was a reflection of the views held by a majority of whites of that day, particularly by the new settlers on what were or had been Indian lands. Humans have always found a means of justifying even their most questionable or wrongful actions against others, thereby salving an uneasy conscience. It is always, as has been well said, the victor who writes the history of every war and its battles. That was ever the way the whites dealt with the Indians until the conquest of the continental United States was complete.[8]

The council with the Cheyenne chiefs and their accompanying warriors lasted until about 10:00 that night. It must have broken up in a rather informal manner with General Hancock simply returning to his tent, and his officers following his example. Wynkoop and Edmund Guerrier may well have led the Indians back to their tent, then given them a few final encouraging words to comfort them. Tall Bull, White Horse, Bull Bear, and the others were mightily concerned about Hancock's determination to march to their village. They knew full well the panic this would cause among the women, children, and old people, fearing a repeat of the Chivington Massacre. At the time the only experience Cheyennes had ever had with American soldiers coming to their villages while filled with people was that at Sand Creek and its terrible aftermath. The chiefs pleaded with Wynkoop to do what he could to dissuade Hancock from going there. This he would attempt, but without success.[9]

The council impressed those present in different ways. Theodore Davis reported Hancock's speech as being a simple statement of the reason for his presence. Some Indian tribes were said to have bad hearts and desired war with whites. These he would fight. He would not permit the killing of whites or the impairment of travel on the great roads or trails but desired that all Indians be at peace and friendly to the whites, who would then be kind to them and take good care of them. Davis reported that though the Indians did not want railroads through their country, they did wish

[8] Hancock to Sherman, April 13, 1867, 7:55–56; Kennedy, *On the Plains*, 57–58.
[9] Wynkoop to Murphy, September 14, 1867, 311; E. Custer, *Tenting on the Plains*, 555; Kennedy, *On the Plains*, 53, 61.

for peace. He found their words good but thought something in their demeanor suggested they were just trying to gain time. To what end they needed this time he did not say. The other reporter present, Henry Stanley, gave a slightly abbreviated version of Hancock's first speech and Tall Bull's response and said nothing of Hancock's second speech, turning instead to a recounting of rumored or alleged Indian atrocities. He referred to "diabolical and cruel massacres" that called for "instant retaliation and severe punishment," apparently referring to the defeat of Captain Fetterman and his troops by the Miniconjou and Oglala Lakota and Óhmésèheso Cheyennes, known to whites as the Fetterman Massacre. Although admitting that the Indians of the southern plains were entirely innocent of participation in "the atrocities," he stated it was rumored "that, due to the success experienced in the north, the southern tribes intended to try the same game." Stanley expressed his opinion that the current Hancock expedition would "awe" the southern tribes into quiet.[10]

Regarding Hancock's speech, Custer wrote that "he particularly informed them that he was not there to make war, but to promote peace." Custer dismissed Tall Bull's speech as containing "nothing important, being made up of allusions to the growing scarcity of the buffaloes, his love for the white man, and the usual hint that a donation in the way of refreshments would be highly acceptable." Hancock himself, in his later official report of the expedition, was perhaps more candid than the reporters or Custer. He stated that he gave his views "quite freely" as to the course he intended to pursue toward the Indians and what was expected of them in the future.[11]

The observer who gave the most complete, careful, and thoughtful report of the council was Dr. Isaac Coates. He recorded the speeches in full, along with a brief summary of what happened before and after each party spoke. Of Tall Bull's speech he said: "The Indian warrior spoke like one who, feeling his weakness, was yet not afraid to speak the feelings of his heart at all hazards." Following his reporting of Hancock's closing remarks, he gave a candid and insightful commentary on the council as he saw it. He recorded it in full, he said, "because the knowledge of such proceedings . . . is very infrequent, because it particularly explains the causes of the war, and again to discover to the world how tyrannical, dictatorial and insolent this government is over Indians. It is the same old story of might makes right." He then added, "And how galling it must have been to those Indian warriors—

[10] Davis, "Summer on the Plains," 294–95; Stanley, *My Early Travels*, 35.
[11] Hancock to Nichols, May 22, 1867; G. Custer, *My Life on the Plains*, 39–40.

whose fearless hearts had braved a thousand dangers—to be talked to as if they were children. The 'musts' and 'wills' and 'shalls' were more wounding to them than steel-pointed arrows. General Hancock talked to those Indian warriors and orators as a cross schoolmaster would to his refractory scholars." But, he said, he found no fault with Hancock, who after all was a soldier whose tongue was not given to soft phrases and who had been sent to intimidate and, if necessary, make war on the Indians.[12]

Hancock, Custer, and the other officers and reporters present all contended the march to the village was necessary because so few of the Cheyenne chiefs or their people had come to Fort Larned for the council. Although the recent blizzard and the poor condition of the Indian horses at the end of the winter season should have been apparent as a valid reason, they managed to convince themselves the fault lay with the Indians. Hancock wanted and needed a large Indian audience to see the numbers and power of his troops to place them in "awe" of that power. Nearly all whites of the day who dealt with the Indians, including the agents themselves, were without any significant knowledge of the tribes they dealt with, their tribal organization and culture, their religion, their country, or their language. When they dealt with a band, or even part of a band, they often thought they were dealing with the entire tribe. Some, of course, didn't care and deemed any mark of a male Indian sufficient to bind the tribe to an agreement. Most knew there were multiple chiefs but had no idea how many there were, who they were, or what kind of authority was vested in them. Nor did they understand who in their tribe those chiefs could speak for or bind with a treaty.

There was clearly an awareness that the village on the north branch of the Pawnee Fork was that of the Dog Soldier and southern Sutaio Cheyennes, along with a village of visiting southern Oglala Lakota, the Kiyuksas. But Hancock appears to have believed he was meeting with those who could speak for the entire Cheyenne tribe or that at least the rest were at the village and had failed or refused to come to the fort as directed. He did not know that there were never more than four council chiefs of the Dog Soldier band and, due to the departure of Little Robe, presently only three. Camping with the Dog Soldiers were the people of Black Shin's southern Sutaio, a band that roamed much the same territory between the Pawnee Fork and the Republican River and centered on the Smoky Hill country. With them were Gray Beard, Black Shin's son-in-law and a former Dog Soldier, and Medicine Wolf, one of the head-

---

[12] Kennedy, *On the Plains*, 54–58.

men of a Cheyenne military society, neither of whom was then a council chief. Of the council chiefs present in the village, only the aged Black Shin was not present for the council at Fort Larned, and he sent Gray Beard to hear for him what the white soldier chief had to say. Also in this camp was White Hair, one of the council chiefs of the Ôhméséheso Cheyennes, down from the north country with his followers to hunt, visit, and winter with friends and relatives. Called Slim Face by whites, Lean Face, a council chief of one of the smaller southern bands camping south of the Arkansas, was likewise present in the village. He had come to help identify the boy Hancock was returning to the Cheyennes under the erroneous belief he was a member of Black Kettle's band of Southern Eaters. Both White Hair and Lean Face were present for the council at Fort Larned.[13]

The Kiyuksa band of Oglala Lakota were also in camp on the Pawnee Fork, but they had not been invited to the council, which is why Tall Bull mentioned to Hancock that he did not know their intentions. Neither Wynkoop nor Leavenworth was their agent, and no messenger had been sent to invite them. Except for the Dog Soldiers, the southern Sutaio, and White Hair's Ôhméséheso, the other southern bands of Cheyennes were either scattered across their country in winter villages or now camping below the Arkansas in search of safety, as were the Arapahoes, Kiowas, Comanches, and many of the Plains Apaches. No council with the Cheyennes would involve tribal members who were not council chiefs, and therefore, from the Cheyennes' perspective, the only chief from the village on the Pawnee Fork that Hancock had not seen or spoken to was Black Shin. In his ignorance of all this, Hancock faulted the Indians for not having turned out for him in large numbers as he expected and especially for not sending Roman Nose, the famous Ôhméséheso warrior he believed to be the principal chief and war leader of the Cheyenne Nation.

Both in his speech to the Cheyennes and in his report of the expedition, Hancock made much of the fact that, in accordance with the Treaty of the Little Arkansas, he was delivering to them the boy "Wilson Graham," captured by Chivington's men at Sand Creek two and a half years earlier. Although Hancock did not realize it, the boy was not Cheyenne. Of the two Cheyenne children known to have been captured, one girl had been taken in by a family in Denver, while her sister had somehow ended up in the same Wilson and Graham Circus sideshow as had the boy. The government ordered a search for them following the treaty with Black Kettle's followers at the Little Arkansas, and they were eventually located

[13] Powell, *People of the Sacred Mountain*, 1:464, 469; Stanley, "British Journalist," 301.

at the circus. One night, following the evening performance, the government agent and some local police officers charged in behind the scenes and secured the boy, but the girl was spirited away by showmen during the confusion and never found again. The boy was delivered to General Sherman, who sent him on to Hancock to be turned over to his family.[14]

When the expedition left Fort Larned the following morning, April 13, Hancock transferred Wilson Graham to the commanding officer, with instructions to deliver him to his family when they appeared to claim him. Hancock reported to Sherman that the Cheyennes who saw him believed him to be from Black Kettle's band, said to be then in Texas. Black Kettle's band was not in Texas, however, but in camp on the North Canadian River, nor did Tall Bull say the boy was of his band. Rather he said he must belong to some tribe then south of the Arkansas. In fact he was an Arapahoe, one of those at Sand Creek at the time of Chivington's attack. He was eventually recognized by Arapahoes visiting the fort at a later time and delivered to his family. Henry Stanley met him again at the Arapahoe village during the Medicine Lodge peace council. He grew up on the reservation in Oklahoma and was later known as Tom Whiteshirt. The Cheyenne girl held by the white family near Denver was apparently never produced nor handed over to her family. She and her sister disappeared into history, probably living out their lives in the Anglo world, but under what circumstances is a matter of conjecture.[15]

The council of the previous evening was the only one General Hancock would have with the Cheyennes. He had intended to threaten and intimidate the Indians by the presence of such a large military force. Instead he placed them in fear for the lives of their families. It is understandable, so soon after the Sand Creek Massacre, that they would conclude the only purpose the Americans could have in marching to their village was to attack it. The white soldier chief had, after all, already met and made his demands of the three Dog Soldier chiefs present in their village, along with two of the other three council chiefs present. There seemed little else he could intend by his march but to repeat the slaughter of the innocent—the women, children, and old people.[16]

---

[14] Hancock to Nichols, May 22, 1867; E. Custer, *Tenting on the Plains*, 555; G. Custer, *My Life on the Plains*, 38–39; Davis, "Summer on the Plains," 294; Kennedy, *On the Plains*, 53–54; Stanley, *My Early Travels*, 29–30.

[15] Hancock to Sherman, April 7, 1867; Hancock to Nichols, May 22, 1867; G. Custer, *My Life on the Plains*, 40–41; Hyde, *Life of George Bent*, 256–57, 268; Stanley, "British Journalist," 274–75.

[16] Hancock to Nichols, May 22, 1867; Wynkoop to Murphy, September 14, 1867, 311; Kennedy, *On the Plains*, 61.

CHAPTER NINE

THE MARCH RESUMES

Reveille sounded at 5:00 A.M. on Saturday, April 13, 1867. A stiff breeze was blowing from the south, the skies were overcast, and for a brief time there was a spattering of rain. This quickly passed to the northeast, and the skies cleared. The expedition broke camp at 7:00 A.M. and began its march westward along the Pawnee Fork. This was necessitated, said General Hancock, because the Cheyennes "had shown bad faith in their engagement to meet me at Fort Larned." Custer agreed with Hancock, as did Stanley, who noted that Hancock ordered a march to their village because the "principal chief of the Cheyennes did not intend to present himself." Davis observed that the Cheyennes did not want white soldiers near their village, while Isaac Coates said Colonel Wynkoop had protested that the Indians would be intimidated and run away, fearing another Sand Creek. None of the whites present appears to have understood that they had already met with five of the six council chiefs present and representing the Cheyenne bands camping on the Pawnee Fork. Nor did any seem to understand that there was no "principal chief" of the Cheyennes or that Roman Nose was not a chief at all. The failure to learn or understand anything of Cheyenne tribal organization or leadership, or to anticipate their concerns about having a very large body of American troops approach their villages, would dog Hancock throughout the expedition and beyond. Far from awing the tribe into submissiveness, he was about to stampede them into war.[1]

The route followed by the expedition was westward along the right, or south, bank of the Pawnee Fork, first following the Dry Route of the Santa Fe Trail to Fort Larned and then an old Indian trail. From time

---

[1] Brown, *March Journal*, April 13, 1867; Hancock to Nichols, May 22, 1867; E. Custer, *Tenting on the Plains*, 555; G. Custer, *My Life on the Plains*, 42; Davis, "Summer on the Plains," 295; Kennedy, *On the Plains*, 61; Stanley, *My Early Travels*, 37; Utley, *Life in Custer's Cavalry*, 31.

immemorial the rivers and streams of the plains had served as the highways for migrating bands, hunting parties, trading parties, and war parties of the Plains tribes. This was the line of travel followed by the Cheyenne chiefs and their party of warriors en route to Fort Larned for the council with Hancock, and now it was being followed by the soldiers on their way to the Cheyenne and Oglala villages.[2]

The westward march of the expedition took the troops away from the Arkansas River Lowlands and back into the Dissected High Plains—into the southern reaches of the Smoky Hills. But here the hills were more rounded and less dramatic as they inclined upward to their merger with the High Plains proper. The course of the Pawnee Fork was generally a little north of west until it reached the confluence of Heth's Branch (north fork) and Buckner's Branch (middle fork), some distance beyond which point the north fork would angle northwesterly. The trail they followed westerly ran parallel with the stream, which because of its erratic course was sometimes closer and sometimes farther to the north of them. By now the day was filled with sunshine, attended by the stiff southwesterly breeze so typical of spring on the southern plains.[3]

The expedition's march did not go unobserved. The farther the troops moved westward, the more they began to see small knots of Indians watching them from the hills in the distance. As the column drew closer, they would disappear, only to reappear on different, more distant hills. Others, sometimes a solitary man and sometimes two or three men, were seen at a distance all around them. To the officers and men of the expedition the Indians appeared to be moving toward their village, but in truth they were moving parallel with the column, keeping an eye on its progress and trying to discern the soldiers' intentions. Although most of these Indians were mounted, some were afoot, probably because their horses were in poor condition after the winter, when their only food source was the dried grasses of the plains and bark stripped from trees along the streams. But most Plains Indians were superb runners, and though they could not outrun a cavalry horse, they were masters of making themselves invisible in a land of few visible hiding places. Some drew close enough to the column to call out "How!" to the soldiers, and Isaac Coates claimed to have seen on a couple of occasions a woman mounted on a "poor miserable pony" and accompa-

---

[2] Hancock to Nichols, May 22, 1867; Clapsaddle, "Wet and Dry Routes," 112–15.

[3] Brown, *March Journal*, April 13, 1867; Buchanan and McCauley, *Roadside Kansas*, 96, 149, 209; Buchanan, *Kansas Geology*, 175; Merriam, *Geologic History of Kansas*, 51, 165; Kennedy, *On the Plains*, 62; Utley, *Life in Custer's Cavalry*, 31.

nied by two or three small children that he, like most whites of the day, referred to as "papooses."[4] It is impossible to say with certainty what Coates may have seen, but it is unlikely that women from either of the Cheyenne or Oglala villages would be out on the plains and near the soldiers with small children during a time of such fear and apprehension. What is clear is that the expedition's movements were being carefully monitored.[5]

Lieutenant Brown wrote that, for most of the route beyond Fort Larned, the banks of the Pawnee Fork had only "thinly scattered timber." But as the troops approached the forks of the stream, it became thicker. Halfway through their day's march the soldiers began to observe heavy smoke ahead to the west, and most assumed this marked the location of the tribal villages. In fact, as they later learned, the Cheyenne and Oglala warriors were firing the dry grasses of the plains in an effort to slow, if not discourage, the expedition's approach to their homes and families. About eighteen miles upstream from Fort Larned the course of the Pawnee Fork makes a sharp turn to the south for about a mile and a half, then turns once again to the west. To avoid the delay involved in a march along the south bank of the stream, where the burned grasses still smoldered, Smith and Hancock decided to cross to the opposite bank at this point. It was no problem for the cavalry, which simply splashed across the shallow waters, probably allowing their horses a drink as they did, then moved up the steep bank beyond at an angle. But for the infantry and artillery, and especially the wagon trains, the creek was a more difficult barrier. Though the flow of water was both narrow and shallow, the banks were quite steep. It was necessary to remove the trees on either bank where the crossing was intended, cut down the banks for a smooth approach, and use a few of the pontoons to effect an easy crossing by the infantry, the artillery pieces, and the many wagons. This took considerable time, so although the cavalry crossed at 3:00 in the afternoon, their wagons did not reach them until near dusk.[6]

Once across on the Pawnee Fork's north bank, the lead elements of the

---

[4] The word "papoose" is from the Narragansett language, that of a small Algonquin tribe living in the northeastern United States. Whites learned this term from them and assumed it meant "baby" in the Indian language of all tribes they met. It is still widely believed that all Indian babies were "papooses." In Cheyenne the word for "baby" is *mèèškevoto*.

[5] Hancock to Sherman, April 13, 1867; Hancock to Nichols, May 22, 1867; G. Custer, *My Life on the Plains*, 42–43; Kennedy, *On the Plains*, 61; Utley, *Life in Custer's Cavalry*, 31.

[6] Hancock to Sherman, April 13, 1867; Hancock to Nichols, May 22, 1867; Brown, *March Journal*, April 13, 1867; Kennedy, *On the Plains*, 61–62; Stanley, *My Early Travels*, 42–43; Utley, *Life in Custer's Cavalry*, 31–32.

column continued the march, having waited only long enough for the infantry and artillery to complete their crossing. After marching perhaps a mile they suddenly came upon the Kiyuksa war leader, Pawnee Killer, in company with four or five of his warriors. Speaking through an interpreter, he informed General Hancock that the Kiyuksas were encamped a few miles further on, along with the village of the Cheyenne Dog Soldiers and southern Sutaio, and would remain there until the expedition approached to have a "talk." Later the Dog Soldier chief White Horse rode up with several of his warriors. Clearly he, Tall Bull, and some of the other Cheyennes attending the Fort Larned council had returned to their village earlier that day or perhaps sometime during the night. He too conversed with Hancock through an interpreter, but the substance of their conversation was not recorded. What is known is that "it was arranged that they should remain" in the expedition camp during the night and that "all of the chiefs from the villages" were to come to Hancock's headquarters tent the next morning for a "conference." Though this arrangement was described by Custer as one in which the chiefs "should accept our hospitality," the Indians were not looking for hospitality but rather were intent on delaying the march and avoiding having the soldiers at their villages at all. For this reason they fired the grasses on the south side of the stream, and it was the reason they kept an anxious watch on the marching troops. But whether acceptance of Hancock's "hospitality" was voluntary or involuntary, the Indians remained the night.[7]

Following his discussions with Pawnee Killer and White Horse, Hancock decided to take his troops into camp along the north, or Heth's, branch of Pawnee Fork. The wagon trains were backed up, detained by the slow and laborious task of crossing the bridge thrown up by the engineers, and the lead elements of the column had now reached the forks of the stream. Close to 4:00 in the afternoon the expedition's march was halted, and the troops went into camp on Heth's branch about a mile above the forks. All of the men and animals were tired and hungry, having had nothing to eat since their morning departure. Tents were pitched as soon as the baggage wagons reached them, and meals prepared after arrival of the commissary train. The delay was hardest on the cavalrymen, who were accustomed to shorter days because of their mobility. But now, without the company wagons that carried their equipment, the cavalry horses had to be held on their leads until the wagons came up with the

---

[7] Hancock to Sherman, April 13, 1867; Hancock to Nichols, May 22, 1867; G. Custer, *My Life on the Plains*, 43; Kennedy, *On the Plains*, 62.

picket ropes at dusk. Both animals and men were exhausted, and the mules pulling the heavy wagons were especially spent. Not long after they reached their campsite, vivid and frequent flashes of lightning were seen to the west, and occasionally the booming of thunder could be heard. But the approaching spring storm evidently followed the southwest-to-northeast course customary on the southern plains and passed to the north of them.[8]

Although most of the Indians who came in to talk with Hancock during the afternoon spent the night at the expedition encampment, at least one did not. Captain Barnitz noted in his journal that an Indian, whom he assumed to be a Cheyenne, was sent to communicate with his tribe shortly before the column turned off to the left and went into camp. He believed the man to be an important chief because of the manner in which he was made up. He had twenty to thirty silver dollars, flattened out to the size of saucers, strung on a leather thong about a yard and a half long, one end of which was attached to his scalp lock while the other floated out behind him as he rode. The man wore moccasins embroidered with small beads, and his torso was enveloped in a dark blanket—quite likely a buffalo robe, since most traders' blankets were red or a red-and-black combination. He rode a "quite respectable looking" pony and set off at a canter, his train of silver disks trailing out behind him. He was seen for some time bobbing up and down as he headed west. The identity of the warrior is uncertain, for several of the warriors attending the council at Fort Larned were similarly adorned, but he may have been the Óhméséheso chief White Hair. In talks with the commissioners at the Medicine Lodge peace council, White Hair (called Gray Hair by whites) told them that on the second day he went ahead to tell Roman Nose and the warriors that the white chief was coming. Because the only chiefs or headmen known to have come to Hancock's column on April 13 were White Horse, White Hair, and Slim Face of the Cheyennes, and Pawnee Killer, the headman of the Kiyuksa band of Oglalas, the likelihood is that the man was either White Hair or a warrior of one tribe or the other. Whoever he was, he carried Hancock's message requesting that the other chiefs come to his camp for the meeting. White Horse, Slim Face, and Pawnee Killer remained the night, and Pawnee Killer left very early the following morning to bring in the other tribal chiefs, as he said, for their talk with Hancock.[9]

---

[8] Hancock to Sherman, April 13, 1867; Brown, *March Journal*, 4/13/67; Utley, *Life in Custer's Cavalry*, 31–32.

[9] Hancock to Nichols, May 22, 1867; E. Custer, *Tenting on the Plains*, 556–58; Stanley, "British Journalist," 301; Utley, *Life in Custer's Cavalry*, 31–32.

After the wagons finally arrived in camp, Hancock had another Sibley tent pitched in which to house his "guests." That night Custer, in violation of Hancock's express orders that no one but he was to have dealings with the Indians, went to the tent shortly after dark and remained there until after 10:00 P.M. He had not been invited, since the Indians spoke not a word of English, and he spoke neither Cheyenne nor Lakota. A sentry had been stationed outside to prevent anyone from approaching too closely, but he was apparently intimidated by Custer's rank and presence. No other officers or soldiers were present, though one of the guides and interpreters, probably Edmund Guerrier, was there part of the time as was Theodore Davis, the artist and reporter for *Harper's Weekly*. The Indians were preparing their own dinner and had built a fire in the middle of the tent, over which each man was roasting his own ration of meat—about two or three pounds per man. Custer's presence did not seem to disturb the Indians, who were seated in a circle around the fire on buffalo robes, so he made his way to an open space on one of the robes and seated himself. He spent his time observing them, while Davis used his in sketching the scene.[10]

Custer believed that a large village of Lakotas, Cheyennes, and Apaches was located within three miles of the expedition's encampment and that a number of their "principal chiefs" were now among the guests. But Custer was new to the plains and lacked knowledge of the Plains Indians. He believed there were perhaps a dozen of these chiefs in the tent, and he took his place between White Horse, whom he thought to be a "head chief" of the Cheyennes, and a man he believed to be an Apache chief. There were no Plains Apaches camping on Heth's branch, and if the sketch of the scene appearing in *Tenting on the Plains* is accurate, the Indian to Custer's right may well have been Pawnee Killer, dressed as he was later depicted in *Harper's Weekly*, with a white man's broad-brimmed hat with a feather. Custer described the ornaments worn by several of the warriors present, which included silver pendants in a half-moon shape and a string of silver disks attached to the scalp locks. He said there were forty or more of these disks, that closest to a warrior's head being as large as a saucer, with the others gradually diminishing in size until the last, which was about the size of the bottom of a cup. Because two of the warriors seemed to be assisting with the cooking of the meal and were stripped to the waist (likely because of the heat), Custer concluded they were acting as "strikers"

---

[10] E. Custer, *Tenting on the Plains*, 556–58.

for the others. But of course even prominent chiefs did not have servants, and most likely these men were just taking their turn at helping to prepare the meal.[11]

The expedition's camp was guarded that night by a mounted picket guard as well as the usual dismounted guard. When other pressing matters had been taken care of, General Hancock sat down at his desk in the headquarters tent and wrote another letter to General Sherman, reporting on the day's march and the important events that occurred during the course of it. He told Sherman that the "chiefs are all to come to my camp tomorrow morning," adding that "I will then hold talks with them, and move up to their village immediately after, and possibly encamp near it." It was clear from these words that the talk with "all of the chiefs," the alleged reason for going to the villages, was only one of Hancock's objectives; more important was his desire that the two tribes be intimidated by his army. He still seemed to be convinced that most of the chiefs of the Cheyenne Nation were in the camp and thus available for council with him. Hancock was also impressed with the country around him, stating: "This is a beautiful camp. I am not surprised that the Indians do not wish to give up this country and the heads of these streams. The Pawnee Fork for five miles back is well wooded for this country. The buffalo grass is a perfect carpet." He expressed uncertainty about how long he would remain near the Cheyenne and Oglala villages, saying that it would depend on developments but would be at least the next day and night. Lastly he reported having left the "Cheyenne" boy at Fort Larned to be turned over either to his family or to Black Kettle, whom he believed to be "the chief of his band."[12]

The night passed without incident, and the next morning, before dawn, Pawnee Killer left for the avowed purpose of bringing in the other chiefs. White Horse may well have left with him or soon after, for they met him again in the early afternoon. General Hancock had appointed 9:00 A.M. on April 14 as the time for the council. The Indians, who were neither conversant with the European system of measuring time nor valued precise punctuality in the same manner as did the general, tried to dissuade him from expecting an early arrival. Both Custer and Hancock seemed to think their present encampment was only a short distance from the Indian villages, perhaps no more than three miles or, at the most, six miles. The

---

[11] Ibid., 558–59.
[12] Hancock to Sherman, April 13, 1867, 7:50–54; Utley, *Life in Custer's Cavalry*, 32.

Indians tried to convey to him that they could not arrive much earlier than 10:00 or 11:00 in the morning, by pointing midway between the horizon and the zenith. But even the astute Dr. Coates thought they meant 9:00 by this. In his letter to General Sherman of Sunday, April 14, Hancock admitted that Pawnee Killer left word for him that the Indians could hardly arrive before 10:00 or 11:00. What Hancock did not understand was that the villages were at least two to three times as far from the encampment as the whites believed. When 9:00 A.M. arrived and the expected entourage of chiefs did not, the general waited only a short time before expressing his belief that the Indians felt guilty and would not come. Of what they felt guilty he did not say, but presumably he meant one or another of the "outrages" committed in his department within recent months by as yet unidentified Indians who had so far gone unchastised.[13]

At 9:30 A.M. Bull Bear, one of the Dog Soldier council chiefs, rode up to the camp, reporting that the others were on their way and would arrive soon. But General Hancock was already angered by the perceived delay and would wait no longer. He told Bull Bear that "if they could not come in at once, I would see them in the evening near their camp." Bull Bear left shortly after to deliver this message, since they met him again in the early afternoon in company with the other chiefs. Hancock also claimed that it was in all events too windy in their present camp to talk with the Indians at length as he desired, because it was "blowing a gale." Such winds are common in that region during the spring, even the norm, and tend to be at their strongest during the afternoon, subsiding when the sun goes down. Hancock gave no explanation as to how a talk in his tent near their village in the afternoon would be less affected by the winds than a talk in his tent at the expedition's camp near the forks, Camp 12, during the morning. Instead he ordered the camp broken and the march resumed.[14]

The journalists, Hancock, and Custer all concurred that the Indians had breached their "agreement" to come to Hancock's headquarters for a talk at 9:00 A.M. Custer referred to Bull Bear's report that the chiefs were on their way as "a mere artifice to secure delay." Dr. Coates, however, was more thoughtful and perceptive. Of this problem he wrote in his journal:

---

[13] Hancock to Sherman, April 14, 1867, MC535-R1354; Hancock to Nichols, May 22, 1867; *Annual Report of the Commissioner of Indian Affairs, 1867*, 311; Davis, "Summer on the Plains," 295; Kennedy, *On the Plains*, 62.

[14] Hancock to Sherman, April 14, 1867; Hancock to Nichols, May 22, 1867; G. Custer, *My Life on the Plains*, 43–44.

The General forgot (or did not care to recollect) that savages, counting their time by "moons" or "sleeps," were not accustomed to "keep time like a watch," to be "punctual as lovers to the moment sworn;" that they were strangers to the momentary exactment of appointments, like the white man, as they are strangers to the speed of the locomotive and the lightning of the telegraph. At 9:30 A.M., Bull Bear, a Cheyenne chief, came in and reported that the chiefs were on their way and would soon arrive. This want of punctuality on the part of the poor savages, the General treated with as much rigor as if the Indians had been white soldiers. The time had passed for the council at this camp and he would defer it until the next one, that evening, near their village.

From the beginning Hancock had insisted on going to the Cheyenne and Oglala villages, and in the supposed delay beyond the deadline he established, he found the excuse he desired. He wanted the entire population of the villages to see how potent his forces were and to be fearful of them. This, he thought, would make them submissive and unlikely to cause further problems for the advancing railroads, the increasing traffic along the great trails, and the land-hungry whites waiting to settle the Indian country. Hancock and others reported that Bull Bear assented to the expedition's advance to the villages, but no one who spoke Cheyenne ever confirmed that. It was of no consequence anyway, for he was going there with or without assent.[15]

---

[15] Hancock to Sherman, April 14, 1867; Hancock to Nichols, May 22, 1867; G. Custer, *My Life on the Plains*, 44; Davis, "Summer on the Plains," 295; Kennedy, *On the Plains*, 62.

Theodore R. Davis accompanied the Hancock expedition as
reporter and artist for *Harper's Weekly*. He sent back regular reports
and illustrations of events, many of which he did not witness but
sketched based on statements of participants. This self-portrait
appeared in the September 7, 1867, issue of *Harper's Weekly*.

CHAPTER TEN

CONFRONTATION

It took a good deal of time to break up a large military encampment, strike the tents, and pack them in the company wagons along with the other camp equipment. Then there was the matter of hooking up the teams, saddling the horses, and having all in readiness for the march. It was shortly after 9:30 A.M. when General Hancock ordered General Smith to have the camp struck and the march resumed, and 11:00 before the expedition was finally formed and prepared to move out. This day they formed themselves in the order of battle, the infantry in line, followed by the artillery battery, most of the cavalry in close column on the flanks, and the trains in three columns following in the center. One squadron of the Seventh Cavalry, under Captain Barnitz, acted as the rear guard. Generals Hancock and Smith rode at the head of the column along with their staffs. The scouts and guides moved out, following a course a little north of west and more or less parallel with the meandering course of the north branch of the Pawnee Fork. Hancock, Custer, Stanley, and Dr. Coates all reported a departure at 11:00 A.M., but the more exacting Lieutenant Brown, charged with keeping a precise record of movements, recorded it at 11:15 A.M. There was apparently some difficulty and delay in coordinating the movements of the column and its various components, for they had moved little more than a mile and a half within the next hour.[1]

Heth's branch of the Pawnee was angling to the northwest as they left camp but would shortly turn back westerly, then southwesterly, and then abruptly to the west-northwest. Ahead of them lay a low ridge that knifed out into the valley, obscuring the view of the river's course beyond. The route of march led directly up this ridge, and as they topped it, they beheld

---

[1] Hancock to Sherman, April 14, 1867; Hancock to Nichols, May 22, 1867; Brown, *March Journal*, April 14, 1867; G. Custer, *My Life on the Plains*, 44–46; Kennedy, *On the Plains*, 62; Stanley, *My Early Travels*, 37; Utley, *Life in Custer's Cavalry*, 44–46.

157

a sight that none had expected, because, said General Hancock, "it was not a part of the programme." Dead ahead, at a distance of about a mile, was a long column of Cheyenne and Oglala chiefs and warriors moving rapidly toward them. When they in turn saw the soldiers suddenly appear on the ridge, the Indians themselves "formed line" and, with a warrior on their left (subsequently identified as Roman Nose) bearing a white flag, began to advance toward the soldiers. General Hancock immediately halted the column and ordered it into line of battle, with the infantry on the left, the artillery in the right center, and the cavalry on the far right. Having been out on the right flank, the cavalry rode up at a gallop, and without waiting to carefully align the ranks, Custer gave the order to draw sabers. More than 500 burnished blades flashed brightly in the noonday sun as they emerged from their scabbards, and at the same time the infantry brought their weapons to the carry. According to Dr. Coates and others observing, the entire command presented "as formidable appearance and as warlike an aspect as anything of the kind during the late war."[2]

Once formed in line of battle, the troops advanced down the ridge and across the valley of the north branch of the Pawnee toward the Indians. The near mile that at first separated the two sides narrowed rapidly until, according to General Hancock, "when we were within a few hundred yards of each other, I halted the troops and directed the Indians to halt also." The two lines now faced each other across what Custer described as a level valley "favorable for an extended view, allowing the eye to sweep the plain for several miles," and where "not a bush or even the slightest irregularity of ground intervened between the two lines which now stood frowning and facing each other." On the expedition's side were about 1,400 men, infantry, artillery, and cavalry, along with support and supply trains. The officers and correspondents present gave varying estimates of how many Cheyenne and Oglala warriors faced them. General Hancock in his report of May 22, 1867, simply stated "several hundred in number." Captain Barnitz reported 300 to 400, a figure more or less agreed on by the others. Dr. Coates reported "several hundred Indian warriors," of whom 300 were mounted. Stanley gave the most precise number, 329 chiefs and warriors of the Cheyenne and Sioux nations, but it is improbable that he could have made so exact a count. As Coates noted, the mounted warriors were

---

[2] Hancock to Sherman, April 14, 1867; Hancock to Nichols, May 22, 1867; Wynkoop to Murphy, September 14, 1867, 311–12; G. Custer, *My Life on the Plains*, 46; Davis, "Summer on the Plains," 295; Dippie, *Nomad*, 21; Kennedy, *On the Plains*, 62–63; Stanley, *My Early Travels*, 37; Utley, *Life in Custer's Cavalry*, 32.

constantly in motion, a tactic that made them a much more difficult target should the enemy open fire. Under such circumstances it would have been extremely difficult to arrive at a reliable figure. Custer was more inclined to exaggeration, probably to inflate the danger, the likelihood of open combat, and the sense of excitement. To his wife, Libbie, he wrote on the afternoon of April 14 that they had been met by a "deputation of three hundred warriors and chiefs." Yet in his October 26, 1867, letter to the sportsman's journal, *Turf, Field, and Farm,* he reported 500 chiefs and warriors, while in his later book, *My Life on the Plains,* he described the Indian strength as several hundred in the line of battle, with many others in the rear apparently acting as reserves and couriers.[3]

However many Cheyenne and Oglala warriors may have been present (and clearly at best no more than a third of the strength of Hancock's forces), they presented a bold and spectacular sight. Theodore Davis described it as "one of the more picturesque arrays possible," while Dr. Coates said they "presented to us a splendid appearance." It was Custer, however, who gave the most complete and colorful descriptions. Writing to Libbie on that day he said:

> I wish you could have seen them as we approached. They were formed in line, with intervals, extending about a mile. The sun was shining brightly, and as we arrived the scene was the most picturesque and novel I ever witnessed. Many officers pronounced it the most beautiful sight they ever saw; but beauty is an improper name to apply to it, in my mind. What rendered the scene so striking and so magnificent were the gaudy colors of the dress and trappings of the chiefs and warriors. Added to this was a profuse intermingling of silver ornaments. The whole scene reminded me of descriptions I have read of Moorish or Oriental cavalcades.

In his later book, *My Life on the Plains,* composed of material first written by him in 1872, Custer described the scene as follows:

> At 11:00 A.M. we resumed the march, and had proceeded but a few miles when we witnessed one of the finest and most imposing military displays, prepared according to the Indian art of war, which it has ever been my lot to behold. It was nothing more nor less than an Indian line of battle drawn directly across our line of march; as if to say: thus far and no farther. Most of the Indians were mounted; all were bedecked in their brightest colors, their heads crowned with the brilliant war-bonnet, their lances bearing the crimson pennant, bows strung, and quivers full of barbed arrows.

---

[3] Hancock to Nichols, May 22, 1867; Wynkoop to Murphy, September 14, 1867, 311; E. Custer, *Tenting on the Plains,* 559; G. Custer, *My Life on the Plains,* 44–47; Dippie, *Nomad,* 21; Kennedy, *On the Plains,* 62–63; Stanley, *My Early Travels,* 37.

This was one of the few times in the history of the West where the Plains Indians were seen by whites so arrayed, drawn in line and resplendent in their warbonnets and paint. In the annals of Cheyenne warfare only one other such display is recorded by the white military—that at Solomon's Fork in 1857. For Custer it would be the one and only time, even including the Little Big Horn.[4]

Although it was a moment of high drama and spectacle, the line of warriors approaching Hancock's troops were not, as Custer and many of the others first thought, planning to fight. On the contrary, they would never have ridden so close to such a large, heavily armed force of American soldiers if it was war they intended. They came with a white flag desiring peaceful discussions if that was possible. Plains Indians rarely engaged in combat with a larger, better-armed force unless they were being attacked. And once familiar with the manner in which the soldiers fought and the weapons they used, they rarely made a frontal attack in a line as did the white man's armies of that day. What Hancock and his column saw were the Dog Soldier, Sutaio, and Oglala chiefs and their warriors riding and walking in column, responding to the soldier chief's summons to council with him at his camp near the forks of the Pawnee. The report Bull Bear had given him was true, the other chiefs and warriors were on their way and would be there soon. Their concept of "soon" and that of Hancock were, of course, quite different. Coming from a point two to three times as far distant as the soldiers believed their villages to be, riding weakened horses, and slowed by the pace of the dismounted warriors, they were in all events prevented from meeting the precise schedule Hancock demanded of them. But they had done their best, motivated by a strong fear of what the soldiers would do if they came to their villages. They wanted peace, but they were uncertain of the soldiers' intentions and wanted them to remain at a safe distance from their families. If necessary they were willing to fight to protect their families despite the great odds against them. Hence the strung bows and the quivers full of arrows. Still, combat with the much larger and more powerful white army would be only a last resort.[5]

The presence of a large number of dismounted warriors was noted and commented on by nearly all who recorded the affair. General Hancock reported the "Sioux principally dismounted" and "the Cheyennes generally

[4] E. Custer, *Tenting on the Plains*, 559–60; G. Custer, *My Life on the Plains*, 44; Davis, "Summer on the Plains," 292; Kennedy, *On the Plains*, 62.

[5] Grinnell, *Fighting Cheyennes*, 249–50; Hyde, *Life of George Bent*, 258; Powell, *People of the Sacred Mountain*, 1:468–69.

mounted." In his profound ignorance of the Plains tribes inhabiting his department, Hancock would not have known who were Lakota and who Cheyenne; but it is entirely possible, even likely, that he was told by one of the interpreters who would have known, most probably Ed Guerrier. Why most of the Oglalas were afoot was not explained by anyone, doubtless because they did not know. The Kiyuksas usually made their winter camps along the Platte or Republican rivers or one of their tributaries, but this year had come even farther south than usual when they joined the Dog Soldiers and southern Sutaio in late February or early March. Living farther north, perhaps their horses had undergone the rigors of a much harder winter than those of the Dog Soldiers or southern Sutaio and were not up to the journey. It is also possible the Oglalas had already decided that a northward flight was necessary for safety and left their horses in camp to keep them as fresh as possible, to be prepared for the march. Unlike the Cheyennes and other tribes of the southern plains, the Lakotas in general did not fight from horseback. Though fine riders, their usual practice, like that of the American cavalry, was to ride to the scene of battle and then dismount and fight on foot, availing themselves of cover. Since combat was not intended that day if it could be avoided, this may or may not have been a factor in their decision to leave their horses behind.[6]

Like Hancock, Custer knew nothing of the Indians and seemingly was unaware of any distinction or tribal differences between those who were mounted and those dismounted. He viewed the various bodies of dismounted men in the rear in terms of the military battle tactics that he was familiar with:

> In the line of battle before us there were several hundred Indians, while farther to the rear and at different distances were other organized bodies apparently acting as reserves. Still farther were small detachments who seemed to perform the duty of couriers, and were held in readiness to convey messages to the village. The ground beyond was favorable for an extended view, allowing the eye to sweep the plain for several miles. As far as the eye could reach small groups or individuals could be seen in the direction of the village; these were evidently parties of observation, whose sole object was to learn the result of our meeting with the main body and hasten with the news to the village.

Because nearly all of the mounted warriors were in the advancing line, those in the rear were undoubtedly the ones afoot. Custer was attributing to them a form of military organization and tactics that did not exist among

---

[6] Hancock to Sherman, April 14, 1867.

the Plains Indians in the manner he was accustomed to. Whether they were simply moving to the council site with the mounted men or had some particular purpose in being afoot, nearly all of the observers agreed that after coming in sight of the great body of troops they faltered, then gradually began to move back up Heth's branch toward the villages, rapidly or at a run. Likely they viewed the appearance of Hancock's strong force marching toward them as presaging an all-out attack on the villages, and they were anxious to return to their families and speed their departure from harm's way.[7]

Custer, probably to enhance the drama and element of danger to the heavily armed troops in his later writings, or perhaps simply to take a swipe at the Office of Indian Affairs and Interior Department, declared that each of the warriors was supplied with a late-model breech-loading rifle or a revolver. This, he claimed sarcastically, was done out of a sense of fair play and to even the odds between soldiers and Indians. But that was not the case. The only late-model weapons the Indians had must have been captured in battle, and these would have been few indeed. Neither the Indian bureau nor the Interior Department had issued weapons, and those that were supplied as annuity payments came from licensed traders such as David Butterfield and Charles Rath. Most of those, however, were old, outmoded, surplus weapons that they sold or bartered for many times the cost to them. While some of the warriors doubtless had firearms, for the most part they were not late models, and they had a relatively small amount of ammunition for those they did have. No other observer made mention of the Indians being in possession of large quantities of modern rifles, carbines, or pistols, and even Custer contradicted that statement in his earlier description and again three paragraphs later when he wrote: "Here in battle array, facing each other, were the representatives of civilized and barbarous warfare. The one, with but few modifications, stood clothed in the same rude style of dress, bearing the same patterned shield and weapon that his ancestors had borne centuries before; the other confronted him in the dress and supplied with the implements of war which the most advanced stage of civilization had pronounced the most perfect." The Cheyennes and Oglalas may have been armed mainly with bows and arrows, war lances, and war clubs, but they were masters in their use and at close range were often more deadly than a man with a rifle or pistol.[8]

---

[7] Ibid.; Hancock to Nichols, May 22, 1867; G. Custer, *My Life on the Plains*, 45–46; Kennedy, *On the Plains*, 63; Stanley, *My Early Travels*, 37.

[8] G. Custer, *My Life on the Plains*, 45,47; Grinnell, *Fighting Cheyennes*, 250.

General Hancock reported that after ordering his troops and the Indians to halt, he "invited the chiefs to an interview and rode forward to meet them between the lines." This was only partially true. Hancock had neither the power to order the Indians to halt nor the ability to personally communicate his wishes to them. What actually happened was that Colonel Wynkoop, who along with Colonel Leavenworth had accompanied the expedition from Fort Larned, became concerned about what the Indians might do and requested permission from Hancock to ride toward the Indian lines to reassure them. Permission being granted, Wynkoop rode to the center of their line. In his letter of September 14, 1867, to Thomas Murphy, superintendent of Indian affairs for the Central Superintendency, Wynkoop stated, "Apparently overjoyed when they recognized me, they surrounded my horse, expressing their delight in seeing me there, saying that now they knew everything was all right, and that they would not be harmed."

Seeing Roman Nose, whom he and the other whites believed to be one of the "principal chiefs," Wynkoop rode to him and instructed him to keep his people steady and restrain flight, and they would not be harmed. Wynkoop could no more converse with the Cheyennes or Oglalas than could Hancock, which means that he was accompanied by an interpreter, doubtless Edmund Guerrier. Through the interpreter he learned that the villages were at a considerably greater distance than they originally supposed and that the Indian column had started from their villages as soon as possible after receiving Hancock's message to meet with him. Neither Hancock nor Custer made any mention of Wynkoop's role in the ensuing talks or of his bravery in riding over to the Indian lines. There was probably no desire on their part to share any credit or acknowledge any important service by the Indian bureau or any of its agents. But that it happened cannot be doubted. Even Hancock's most ardent admirer, Henry Stanley, stated that the "Indians also stopped to await Major Wynkoop, their agent, who was coming towards them." And Dr. Coates, probably watching with the Seventh Cavalry staff, wrote in his journal: "Having permission of General Hancock, Colonel Wynkoop rode forward into the Indian lines and reassured them with his presence that no harm was imminent. It was plain to be seen how overjoyed they were to see their agent." For the moment the tension was broken and trouble was averted.[9]

---

[9] Hancock to Sherman, April 14, 1867; Hancock to Nichols, May 22, 1867; Wynkoop to Murphy, September 14, 1867, 312; Kennedy, *On the Plains*, 63; Stanley, *My Early Travels*, 37.

Once the Indians were reassured, Wynkoop conducted a few of the chiefs and more prominent headmen and warriors to a meeting with General Hancock about midway between the lines. For the Cheyennes these included the great warrior Roman Nose, bearing the white flag; Bull Bear and White Horse, council chiefs of the Dog Soldiers; Gray Beard and Medicine Wolf for the southern Sutaio; and White Head, a council chief of the Ȯhméséheso. For the Kiyuksa band of Oglalas there was Bad Wound, their chief; Pawnee Killer, their headman, or war leader; and Tall Bear, The Bear That Walks under the Ground, Left Hand, Little Bear, and Little Bull. General Hancock was accompanied by General Smith, Custer, and several of their staff officers. For a time after they arrived, following the introductions and shaking of hands and as Hancock's words were being translated by Edmund Guerrier, Roman Nose sat on his horse holding the white flag and looking directly into the eyes of General Hancock.[10]

Hancock first asked, quite sharply, if they were the Indians who were anxious to fight, stating that he was ready if that was the case. When this had been translated, Roman Nose responded, "We don't want war; if we did, we would not come so close to your big guns." Hancock seemed satisfied with this response and proceeded to introduce General Smith, commanding the Seventh Cavalry and the District of the Upper Arkansas, telling the Indians that he was his "big chief" who would remain in the country with his troops when he, Hancock, returned home. Then he addressed Roman Nose directly and, based on his ill-founded belief that the great warrior was the "head chief" of all of the Cheyennes, asked why he hadn't come to Fort Larned for the council as requested. Not being a council chief, Roman Nose was neither necessary nor entitled to represent the tribe (or even his band) at such occasions, and it must have puzzled him that Hancock would ask. Despite this he responded in a matter-of-fact manner: "My horses are poor, and every man that comes to me tells me a different tale about your intentions." Though Hancock made no mention of it in his reports, it appears that additional discussions with the Indian leaders followed, as Custer later wrote in his October 26, 1867, letter to *Turf, Field, and Farm*:

> The trouble was soon made apparent. The Indians desired to hold the council then and there, thus preventing our troops from approaching their village, and frightening their squaws and papooses, who, as the chiefs stated, feared another

---

[10] Hancock to Nichols, May 22, 1867; Wynkoop to Murphy, September 14, 1867, 312; G. Custer, *My Life on the Plains*, 47–48; Dippie, *Nomad*, 21–22; Grinnell, *Fighting Cheyennes*, 250; Kennedy, *On the Plains*, 63; Stanley, *My Early Travels*, 37.

massacre. To this request General Hancock would not listen, he desired particularly that as many Indians as possible should witness our numbers, and thus be impressed with the power of the Government to punish refractory subjects.

Whatever was said between them, Hancock made it clear that his troops were going to move on toward the villages and encamp near them, but that he would give orders that none of the soldiers were to enter them or molest their inhabitants in any manner. According to Colonel Wynkoop, General Hancock told the Indians it was too windy to talk at that point and that a council would be held at his camp near their villages after his tent was pitched. A strong wind was blowing at the time, but neither Hancock nor Custer, the only other two present at the meeting between the lines who wrote about it, mentioned the wind as a reason for marching on to the villages. Regardless of the reasons given by the white soldier chief, it was not for this that the Cheyennes and Oglalas had made the difficult trip from their villages, with their horses in such poor condition. Even the unsympathetic Hancock observed this reluctance, stating in his official report of May 22, 1867, "The chiefs appeared to be exceedingly nervous during the interview." And Custer remarked, "Very reluctantly the Indians faced toward their village, and set out in advance of us to return to it." Clearly Hancock was determined to go to the villages despite the willingness of the Indians to council where they were, notwithstanding their expressed concerns about the effect on their women and children or Wynkoop's warning.[11]

Though Roman Nose was not a council chief or a headman, the part he played in the meeting between the lines and his general appearance generated considerable comment by several of the white observers. Though neither Hancock nor Custer mentioned his dress or arms, the two reporters and Dr. Coates did. Stanley wrote, "Roman Nose himself drew up near the General's staff with a small company of chiefs and warriors. He had a fine pair of gold epaulettes, and was otherwise dressed magnificently." Theodore Davis's assessment was nearly identical to that of Coates, who wrote in his journal:

> Of all the chiefs, Roman Nose attracted the most attention. He is one of the finest specimens, physically, of his race. He is quite six feet in height, finely formed with large body and muscular limbs. His appearance decidedly mili-

[11] Hancock to Sherman, April 14, 1867; Hancock to Nichols, May 22, 1867; Wynkoop to Murphy, September 14, 1867, 312; G. Custer, *My Life on the Plains*, 48–49; Kennedy, *On the Plains*, 63; Stanley, *My Early Travels*, 37–38.

tary, and on this occasion, particularly so, since he wore the full uniform of a General of the Army. A seven-shooting Spencer carbine hung at the side of his saddle, four large Navy revolvers stuck in his belt, and a bow, already strung, with a dozen or more arrows, were grasped in his left hand. Thus armed, and mounted on a fine horse, he was a good representative of the God of War; and his manner showed plainly that he did not care much whether we talked or fought.

The meeting with the Indian leaders took place about midway between the lines that, according to Hancock, were halted several hundred yards apart. Roman Nose and the others were mounted on horses just beyond Hancock, Smith, Custer, and the staff officers and would have been at least partially screened by them from the view of the main body of troops. Davis and Stanley were probably riding with the headquarters staff at the head of the column but necessarily remained behind when Hancock and the others advanced to talk with the Cheyenne and Oglala leaders. Dr. Coates, as the Seventh Cavalry surgeon, likely rode with the regimental headquarters staff and would have been on the far right of the expedition line. How then did these men know this much about the appearance of Roman Nose, his weapons, or what transpired? What was said could easily have been related to them later by one or more of the officers, by Wynkoop, or by Ed Guerrier, and probably was. The same might be true of the dress and arms of Roman Nose, as described by Davis and Coates, but why then did neither Hancock nor Custer mention it? A renowned Cheyenne warrior with a widely publicized reputation for both fierceness and fearlessness, appearing in front of any army officers armed with a Spencer carbine, four Navy revolvers in his belt, and a strung bow with a dozen or so arrows in his left hand, would surely have made such an impression as to be worthy of comment, particularly by the loquacious Custer.[12]

The idea of having four large Navy revolvers thrust through a belt seems the least likely. Assuming the accuracy of the statement that they were Navy-model revolvers, there were two possibilities—the older Colt Model 1851 .36 caliber, or the later 1861 .44 caliber, both excellent and reliable weapons. But any large six-shooter pistol of that day was a bulky affair with a barrel approximately seven to eight inches long and weighing from two and a half to three pounds loaded. The cartridge, including bullet, was about an inch and a half long and, with six cylinders, required a cartridge

[12] Hancock to Sherman, April 14, 1867; Hancock to Nichols, May 22, 1867; E. Custer, *Tenting on the Plains*, 559–60; G. Custer, *My Life on the Plains*, 48–49; Davis, "Summer on the Plains," 295; Dippie, *Nomad*, 21–22; Kennedy, *On the Plains*, 64; Stanley, *My Early Travels*, 37.

box to carry a sufficient supply for even a brief action. Plains Indians in general did not use or like the kind of broad belts worn by whites. If Roman Nose was wearing the dress coat of a major-general, with epaulettes, and that is certainly possible, it likely had the conventional two rows of brass buttons, a wide belt, and tails. Worn belted and buttoned, this would be very uncomfortable and constricting to a warrior accustomed to loose-fitting buckskin garments and would have hampered him during the long ride from the village. He would not likely have worn the uniform trousers, if indeed he had any, for similar reasons of comfort and ease of movement. If he was wearing the coat, it was most likely open, with a buckskin tunic or shirt underneath, neither buttoned nor belted. He could have had a loose belt or sash around his midriff, but if so, any weapons thrust through them would have been difficult to see and, considering their bulk and supposed number, mostly hidden by the coat. Stanley mentioned the coat and epaulettes but no weapons. Dr. Coates's version was remarkably identical to that of Theodore Davis, and most likely the surgeon obtained his information from Davis either orally or by reading notes he had made, since Davis was the closer of the two to the scene. Even so, at a distance of two or three hundred yards and partially screened by Hancock's party, it would have been difficult if not impossible to make out with any certainty what weapons Roman Nose might have had thrust through a belt under the coat. He may have had a pistol, but not likely four. He probably did have a scalping knife and a war club, which from a distance could have appeared as something different to an untrained eye. But it is unlikely that Roman Nose owned, wanted, or carried four bulky six-shooter revolvers thrust through a belt.

Almost as baffling as the four revolvers allegedly in his belt is the picture of Roman Nose advancing, so dressed and armed, holding a strung bow and a dozen arrows in his left hand, the large white flag flapping in a strong south wind in his right hand, and apparently no means of controlling his horse with its bridle and reins. Plains Indians were remarkable horsemen and accomplished at controlling the movement of their horses with no more than pressure from their knees and thighs. This was often done in battle, when a warrior's hands were otherwise occupied in the use of his weapon. Even so, it would have been much more difficult to control a measured approach in line with other riders, bring the animal to a halt, then turn and ride away, all the while with a large white flag whipping wildly in the spring winds of the southern plains. Indeed, with the awkward bulk of four large pistols thrust through a belt, the tails of his general's coat flapping in harmony with the flag, and his left hand filled with bow and arrows, any rider would be hard-pressed to remain mounted before each blast of the wind. As with the pistols, no whites present other than Davis and Dr. Coates mentioned the bow and arrows held in the left hand. Those not carrying the flag could easily have done this, but it would be far more difficult and awkward for the flag bearer. A bow and a dozen or more arrows would also most likely be too much bulk to be held in one hand. Perhaps, noting others among the Indian leaders and their warriors armed in this way, Davis assumed that Roman Nose was also. Or perhaps, being a reporter looking for drama in a story, he may have used a little literary license to spice up the scene. Most likely Roman Nose would have carried his bow slung over his shoulder, and his arrows in their quiver across his back, leaving his left hand free to control his horse.

It has sometimes been suggested that Roman Nose was also wearing his magnificent warbonnet with the single horn in the front. None of the white observers present mentioned this, and it was of such impressive dimensions and appearance that had he been wearing it, they would undoubtedly have said so. Ice, or Hail, a great Óhméséheso holy man, fashioned it for Woqini (Hook Nose or Roman Nose) sometime during the spring of 1860. Nothing made by whites was used in it: no cloth, no iron or metal, and no glass beads. The crown and trails were made from the hide of a young buffalo bull, and at the center of the forehead was fastened a single buffalo horn. Directly behind the horn, on the crown of the bonnet, was the skin of a kingfisher tied to the buffalo hair. At the right side of the crown the skin of a hawk, while on the back, part way down on the crown of the bonnet, was the skin of a barn swallow. On the left side was the skin of a bat, Woqini's name as a youth. From the bonnet's crown two long trails of eagle feathers swept down to the earth, those on the right trail dyed red, and those on the left trail white. All of these objects represented mystical sacred beings, comprising the sacred bonnet seen by Ice in a vision in which Thunder, one of the Sacred Powers, appeared to him wearing it and commanding him to make one like it. To Roman Nose it brought the blessings and protection of Thunder and the other Sacred Powers. When he was mounted, the two trailers flowed back across his horse's flanks. It seems unlikely that any white man seeing such a war bonnet, with two trailers, would not have made note of it in his writings, probably at length. Roman Nose and the others were there for peaceful talks, not battle; therefore he had no reason to wear it. Had he done so, and were he dressed as Davis and Coates described, if nothing else dismounted him in the face of the gusty wind, surely the bonnet would have. In fact the great warrior appears to have worn only a single large red feather in his scalp lock, as noted by Custer in his letter to General Smith's adjutant on the afternoon of April 16.[13]

After Hancock concluded his discussions with the Dog Soldier, Sutaio, and Kiyuksa Oglala leaders, the chiefs, headmen, and others faced about and rejoined their mounted warriors. Those on foot, apparently mainly Oglalas, had previously begun moving rapidly west-northwest up the north branch of the Pawnee Fork, and now the mounted warriors too began a hasty migration back toward their villages. There is some question about how quickly Hancock's troops resumed their march, Hancock himself merely reporting that the "command followed in the direction the Indians had taken." Wynkoop said that the military column "took up the line of march in the same direction in a short time afterward." Stanley simply wrote that the troops "then moved on," but both Davis and Dr. Coates suggested a delay. Davis reported that "Hancock did not move forward for some time, as he expressed himself anxious that the Indians reach the village and inform the inhabitants of his peaceful intentions before the command came in sight of it." He then described a ritual smoke engaged in by the Indians who remained with the column, which included Bull Bear. Coates stated that after half an hour the Indians were out of sight, and the column moved on. Custer, as usual, was inconsistent. Though he wrote nothing of it to Libbie, in his October 26, 1867, letter to *Turf, Field, and Farm,* he wrote:

> When both parties set out for the village, the Indians were not more than a quarter of a mile in advance: the country was open prairie, yet, notwithstanding that the cavalry marched at its most rapid pace, there was not an Indian to be seen after marching five miles. They had all, both foot and mounted, so far outmarched us that we had lost sight of them; this, too, in a country where the eye could sweep the horizon for several miles. The anxiety of the Indians to reach their village in advance of us, had impelled them to such a rapid gait.

But in his book, *My Life on the Plains,* in material written five years later, Custer contradicted himself, saying that "the Indians moved off in the direction of their village, we following leisurely in the rear." That the impatient Hancock intentionally delayed the march to allow the Indians to reach the two villages well in advance of his troops seems doubtful, and he said noth-

---

[13] G. A. Custer to T. B. Weir, April 16, 1867, U.S. House, "Difficulties with Indian Tribes," 7:68; Kennedy, *On the Plains,* 75–76; Powell, *People of the Sacred Mountain,* 1:229–30.

ing to indicate this. He did not trust the Indians and would not have wanted to give them an opportunity to flee. Whatever his motives may have been, however, a delay of half an hour is not unlikely. The expedition was spread out in line of battle, and it would have taken some time to reorganize and get back into their marching formation before resuming the advance. Although making no comment on the time factor, Captain Barnitz appears to contradict Custer's earlier statement about the disappearance of all of the Indians. In a letter to his wife, Jennie, on the same day, April 14, he wrote: "Our force then advanced and the Indians disappeared, except small parties that were seen passing over the hills on our front, flanks and rear." But of course these may have passed out of sight after five miles.[14]

Several chiefs or other prominent Cheyennes remained behind to ride along with the column, probably hoping to persuade Hancock not to camp near their village. One of these was Bull Bear, who, during one of the halts taken to rest or water the horses and mules, implored Colonel Wynkoop, through Edmund Guerrier the interpreter, to again ask General Hancock not to march his troops close to the villages. As all the chiefs with whom he had previously conversed warned, to do so would frighten the women and children and they would likely flee in apprehension of another Sand Creek Massacre. Wynkoop complied with this request, but Hancock's only response to him was that "it was his intention to camp his troops in the immediate vicinity of said village." Dr. Coates observed that "the General's mind was made up" and that "not intending any harm to them, he did not pause to consider their just grounds for fear, and moved on." Theodore Davis suggested that Hancock had to march to a point less than a mile from the village because "every particle of grass had been burned off the country." But this does not appear to be the case. No one else, including Hancock and Custer, mentioned any burning after April 13, and none used this as an excuse for continuing the march. Certainly neither Bull Bear nor Wynkoop would have made a plea for an earlier encampment if it was rendered impossible by prior burning. The fact was, General Hancock had made up his mind to march to the village to display the might of the United States, and no argument, no matter how reasonable, was going to persuade him to do otherwise.[15]

[14] Hancock to Nichols, May 22, 1867; Wynkoop to Murphy, September 14, 1867, 312; G. Custer, *My Life on the Plains*, 49; Davis, "Summer on the Plains," 295; Dippie, *Nomad*, 22; Kennedy, *On the Plains*, 66; Stanley, *My Early Travels*, 38; Utley, *Life in Custer's Cavalry*, 32–33.

[15] Wynkoop to Murphy, September 14, 1867, 312; Davis, "Summer on the Plains," 295; Kennedy, *On the Plains*, 66.

CHAPTER ELEVEN

THE VILLAGE

When the march resumed, Hancock's troops followed the trail of the Indians, moving in a nearly straight line to their villages to the west-northwest. About four and a half miles from the meeting with the Indians, and six from Camp 12, the column came to a small pond, where they took their third rest and water stop of the day. By 3:00 P.M. they reached the banks of Heth's branch of the Pawnee Fork as it swung back to the northwest. Shortly after, they went into camp along the stream about a mile below the Cheyenne and Oglala villages, after a march of ten and a half miles. The villages were located in what General Hancock described as a "charming spot" in a loop of the stream and amid a grove of cottonwood and other trees. It was, said Custer, "a most romantic spot" with an abundant supply of wood, water, and grass. On the north and west were bluffs that during the winter and early spring helped shelter any encampment from cold and blustery winds. Dr. Coates reported that the buffalo grass, just then beginning to grow, "was soft as velvet to the feet." There were upwards of three hundred lodges in the two villages, "a small fraction over half" belonging to the Cheyennes and the balance to the Kiyuksa Oglalas, according to Custer.[1]

After the separate infantry, artillery, and cavalry campsites were established and the company wagons had arrived, tents were pitched and an infantry guard placed around the entire perimeter to prevent soldiers from wandering over to the Indian villages and causing trouble. As this was going on, a number of Indians could be seen standing outside their village, watching the soldiers establishing their camp a mile downstream. Some Indian horses found grazing near the encampment were gathered up and sent to

---

[1] Hancock to Sherman, April 14, 1867; Hancock to Nichols, May 22, 1867; Brown, *March Journal*, April 14, 1867; G. Custer, *My Life on the Plains*, 49–50; Davis, "Summer on the Plains," 295; Dippie, *Nomad*, 22; Hyde, *Life of George Bent*, 259; Kennedy, *On the Plains*, 66; Stanley, *My Early Travels*, 38.

the village, presumably as a means of reassuring the Indians that the soldiers' intentions were peaceful. It was probably with this small party that
Theodore Davis rode to the Indian camp and found that the women and
children had fled in fear of an attack, while the remaining male inhabitants were enjoying "a dog-feast." In this Davis partook, finding the meat
"not such bad eating," but the copious quantities each Indian host insisted
that he consume "discouraging in the extreme." While Davis was so occupied, four prominent Cheyenne chiefs and warriors rode downstream to
the military camp and had a talk with General Hancock. Included were
Roman Nose, Bull Bear, Gray Beard, and Medicine Wolf, and they
informed the general that, as they had been warning him in their previous
meetings, the women and children had fled upon approach of the troops,
being terrified of them and fearing another Chivington Massacre. Also,
they reported, some of their young men were hunting buffalo up on the
Smoky Hill and they could not say what those men would do. The Kiyuksa
Oglalas had nearly all left as well: men, women, and children.[2]

Despite the numerous warnings he was given about what would happen if he brought his troops close to their village, news of the flight of the
women and children and of the Oglalas seems to have both surprised and
infuriated Hancock. He was, after all, a general officer of the United States
Army, he had assured them he did not intend them harm, and he was not
accustomed to having his word doubted. He asked the four Indian leaders why the women and children had fled, and it was Roman Nose who
gave the response. He inquired of Hancock if the women and children of
the whites were not, in general, more timid and fearful than the men, who
were supposed to be warriors and unafraid. He said that he (Roman Nose)
and his comrades, who were warriors, were not afraid of the general and
his troops, but that their women and children were. And then he asked
if Hancock had never heard of the massacre at Sand Creek, where many
women and children were murdered by U.S. troops who came to a peaceful village in much the same manner as Hancock and his men now did,
and whether it was not natural under these circumstances that the women
and children would become panic-stricken. To these questions General
Hancock's only response was that he considered the flight of the women

---

[2] Hancock to Sherman, April 14, 1867; Hancock to Nichols, May 22, 1867; Wynkoop to Murphy, September 14, 1867, 312; Davis, "Summer on the Plains," 295; Grinnell, *Fighting Cheyennes*, 252, 295; Stanley, *My Early Travels*, 38.

and children an act of treachery and that he wanted them brought back immediately.[3]

At this point Roman Nose turned to Bull Bear and told him to ride back to the village with the others because he was now going to kill Hancock, and he and the others might then be killed by the soldiers. When Hancock and his troops first reached the site of the new military encampment, Roman Nose and other chiefs, headmen, and warriors were watching from their village. As the soldiers drew near, Roman Nose, very angry and with his usual fearlessness, announced to the others that they must prepare to fight, as he intended to ride up and kill Hancock at the head of his troops. "This officer is spoiling for a fight," he said. "I will kill him in front of his own men and give them something to fight about." The others immediately became alarmed that if he actually did so, the troops would kill all Cheyennes they could find, including the women, children, and old people who were traveling on horses that were in poor condition and could not move rapidly. Neither could the warriors protect them by fighting the soldiers with their own weakened mounts. So when the four men traveled to the army camp to report to Hancock that the women and children had fled, Bull Bear was one of them. Bull Bear, who was a Sun Dance priest and holy man as well as a council chief, had considerable influence over Roman Nose, who greatly respected him, and the others relied on him to prevent any such rash actions. When Roman Nose told Bull Bear and the others to leave, Bull Bear suddenly grabbed the bridle on his friend's horse and led him away. Though he did not know it, General Hancock had a very close brush with death that day. But Ed Guerrier knew it, and it was he who told George Bent the story later.[4]

It has been said that Roman Nose made his threat to kill Hancock during the confrontation between the troops and the Indians, rendering it an even more dramatic moment in western history. But the only known source for this story is George Bent, who had in turn heard it from his brother-in-law, Ed Guerrier, as well as others who were in the village and knew of Roman Nose's intentions. It was only after having inquired of Hancock if he had never heard of the Sand Creek Massacre and its aftermath, and then listening to the general ignore his questions and respond only that

[3] Hancock to Sherman, April 14, 1867; Hancock to Nichols, May 22, 1867; Wynkoop to Murphy, September 14, 1867, 312; G. Custer, *My Life on the Plains*, 50; Davis, "Summer on the Plains," 295; Grinnell, *Fighting Cheyennes*, 251; Kennedy, *On the Plains*, 66–67; Stanley, *My Early Travels*, 38.

[4] Hyde, *Life of George Bent*, 259–60.

the flight of the women and children constituted treachery and they must be returned, that Roman Nose determined to act. Hancock never knew of his close call, but ironically it finally did occur to him that the fear of a massacre was in fact the motivation for the flight of the Cheyenne families. Writing to General Sherman following his meeting with Roman Nose and the three others, Hancock said: "It may be true, and I think it is, that the women and children became frightened. They told me such would be the case if I came to their camp, recollecting the Chivington massacre still, as Roman Nose stated. Yet I am in that doubt about the Sioux, that if they do not return I shall feel inclined to think they have been doing something wrong, or were fearful of being punished for the acts of the northern Sioux." It is difficult to understand why the man was unable to grasp the terror he was inspiring in the Cheyenne women and children at an earlier time, especially considering the many warnings and pleas that he received long before reaching the villages. He was presumably a highly intelligent man, a graduate of West Point, a major general in the army, and the Union hero of Gettysburg. Perhaps the explanation lies in a variety of factors—an arrogance that comes with power, success, and adulation; the loss of a sense of humility and "the common touch"; an expectation of obedience to orders; an innate belief in the superiority of the Anglo-Saxon race; and a total lack of sympathy for those deemed uncivilized savages. But the times were surely a factor as well, for the anxiety of a burgeoning white population to acquire free lands in the West—Indian lands—had long relegated the interests and rights of the Native peoples to the rubbish heaps of history. High-ranking army officers were not immune to the perception that they represented the march of civilization against the opposing "barbarians." Whatever the factors that clouded his mind, Hancock clearly failed to comprehend what was plain to see.[5]

When General Hancock demanded the return of the women and children, the Cheyenne leaders told him that they were willing to try, but according to Wynkoop, they appeared doubtful of success. Hancock in his letter to General Sherman and his later report claimed the Indians stated they would have nearly all of them brought back that night, if not all. Under the circumstances this seems an unlikely claim or possible result, and in all probability General Hancock simply demanded that they be brought back and the Cheyennes agreed to make the effort. But before

---

[5] Hancock to Sherman, April 14, 1867; Hyde, *Life of George Bent*, 259–60.

they could do so, they said, they would need to borrow horses with which to pursue them, as their own were too weak to overtake them. General Hancock ordered that two horses be provided them, and two of the men started after the missing families.[6]

While the two horses were being secured, General Hancock informed the Cheyenne leaders that he was sending Ed Guerrier with them, with instructions that he remain the night and report to him every two hours whether there were any movements among the Indians and especially whether they were leaving their village. Hancock had previously asked him if he was afraid to go to the Indian camp and remain the night to watch for any such movements. When Guerrier affirmed his willingness to do so, the general told him, "If those Indians run away, I shall hold you responsible." With that Guerrier declined, stating that he could not keep them from running away but could merely report that they had done so. Hancock relented and told him to go to the camp anyway and just let him know if they left. The Cheyenne leaders assented to Guerrier's presence, and when the two horses were delivered, they all left the military camp. Two of them rode off in search of the women and children, while the other two and Guerrier returned to the Cheyenne village. According to Hancock, the Cheyennes agreed to have all of their missing women and children returned during the night and be present for a conference with him the next day, presumably in the morning. It was about 7:00 P.M. when the Indians departed the military camp. Then the soldiers settled into the routine of camp life, tending to their animals and preparing their meals. General Hancock composed his letter to General Sherman reporting the day's events. What he could not know at the time was that much more would occur before that night ended.[7]

Edmund Guerrier was not unwelcome at the Cheyenne village. After all, he was half Cheyenne, the son of William Guerrier, a French-Canadian trader, and a Cheyenne woman. Moreover he was married to Julia Bent, daughter of William Bent and Owl Woman, a full-blooded Cheyenne, and thus a brother-in-law to George Bent, Charlie Bent, and the other Bent children. A Cheyenne cousin was married to the great

---

[6] Hancock to Sherman, April 14, 1867; Hancock to Nichols, May 22, 1867; Wynkoop to Murphy, September 14, 1867, 312; G. Custer, *My Life on the Plains*, 50; Davis, "Summer on the Plains," 295; Grinnell, *Fighting Cheyennes*, 251; Kennedy, *On the Plains*, 66–67; Stanley, *My Early Travels*, 38.

[7] Hancock to Sherman, April 14, 1867; Hancock to Nichols, May 22, 1867; Grinnell, *Fighting Cheyennes*, 251–53.

Roman Nose and was living in the village until the flight of the women and children. Guerrier himself had from time to time lived with the Cheyennes. It would not be difficult to imagine that his sympathies were divided, but he seems to have always done a conscientious job as interpreter and guide as well as a peacemaker. When he went to the Cheyenne camp, Guerrier met with the chiefs and other important warriors, but they would say nothing definite as to their plans or intentions. They were clearly concerned and agitated, and finally they left their council lodge to consult among themselves, leaving Guerrier alone with the young men. When they returned, they told him they had decided not to stay but to leave and join their families. The two riders had returned, having failed to find the women and children, who had scattered in all directions and whose trails were impossible to follow in the dim twilight anyway. Having failed to return the women and children, they apparently concluded General Hancock would hold them responsible and attack them. They delivered the two soldier horses to Guerrier, who then returned to the expedition's camp, leading the horses. He reached Hancock's headquarters tent at about 9:30 P.M. and reported that the Cheyennes were mounting up and preparing to leave, intending not to return. It has been said that Guerrier delayed his return and report to allow the Cheyennes the needed time to escape, and it is likely true. But considering that only two and a half hours elapsed between his departure and return, which included the time spent in the council lodge with the Indians awaiting the return of the two riders, and the time required to ride the mile to and from the Indian village while leading the two riderless horses through the twilight during his return, it cannot be said the time factor was unreasonable.[8]

When he received the news the Cheyennes were leaving, General Hancock seems to have been torn between disbelief and towering anger. He had come to the Cheyenne country to intimidate them, to awe them with the power of the American government, and, if the opportunity arose, to chastise by force of arms any Indians daring to flout that power. His plans were now crumbling around him, with the quarry fleeing beyond his grasp and, along with them, his dreams of a national reputation as a great Indian fighter and pacifier—a plus in any future political campaign. What happened during the next two to three hours is unclear, depending on whose

[8] W. S. Hancock to W. T. Sherman, April 15, 1867, 12:30 A.M., MC535-RI354; Hancock to Nichols, May 22, 1867; Grinnell, *Fighting Cheyennes*, 251–53; Hyde, *Life of George Bent*, 83, 83n3, 260.

recounting of events is believed and how it is interpreted. Hancock, as would be expected, reported that he immediately directed General Smith to send Custer and a portion of the Seventh Cavalry "to surround their villages, and if practicable, to prevent their departure." Writing to his wife at 2:40 A.M. on April 15, Custer said: "One of the guides, a half-breed, reported this fact, or, rather, that they were saddling up to leave about sunset. General Hancock sent for me, and it was determined that I, with the Seventh Cavalry, should surround the village and keep the Indians from leaving. I advised against delay. I obeyed my orders, and completely surrounded the Indian encampment by 12 o'clock tonight." According to Custer's contemporary letter, then, there was about a two-and-a-half-hour gap between Guerrier's report that the Cheyennes were leaving and the completion of the surround. Moreover, it was General Hancock who gave the order directly, not General Smith.[9]

Writing to *Turf, Field, and Farm* on October 26, 1867, Custer stated:

> In a few hours after their departure from our camp one of the interpreters who had been visiting the village returned to General Hancock with the information that the entire population of the village was leaving as rapidly as possible. In other words, they were, according to their opinions, "fleeing from the wrath to come." They certainly intended to avoid another massacre. The commander of Uncle Sam's forces was enraged by this intelligence. Was his favorite plan to be thus thwarted? Were the laurels he was to reap from his Indian policy to prove a crown of thorns? For nearly two hours he could not believe the intelligence given him to be true. Convinced, finally, of its correctness, he assembled some of his principal sub-ordinates to consult as to the proper course to pursue. He finally decided that the cavalry should surround the village and detain by force, all Indians who had not taken their departure.

This letter was written after Custer faced a court-martial and been convicted on charges preferred against him on the order of General Hancock. It raises a valid question about whether there actually was an unreasonable delay. Dr. Coates said that the cavalry marched for the Indian village at about 10:00 P.M., which would certainly have indicated promptness on Hancock's part. But that would have meant that the decision was made, orders given, and all preparations completed within thirty minutes or less, which would have been extraordinarily efficient. Further, departure at 10:00 and completion of the envelopment of the Indian villages by midnight

[9] Hancock to Sherman, April 15, 1867; Hancock to Nicholls, May 22, 1867; E. Custer, *Tenting on the Plains*, 560–61.

would have meant a two-hour operation, which is much too long. It seems unlikely Custer would have mentioned the time delay if it was entirely false and could be easily disproved, exposing him to defamation or other charges. In his later book, *My Life on the Plains*, Custer confirmed Hancock's account that Guerrier returned at 9:30 P.M. to report that the male Cheyennes were leaving their camp. Assuming the accuracy of Custer's statement to his wife that the surround of the village was complete by midnight, and there is little reason to doubt it, two and a half hours in fact elapsed between the time Hancock received word the warriors were leaving and the time the Seventh Cavalry completed the surround. Since all observers present agreed that the troops moved out with alacrity, it seems likely the general was seized with doubt and indecision that would account for a delay of one to one and a half hours in issuing orders. For the next hour after orders were given, the time could be easily accounted for in giving orders, awakening the troops, issuing ammunition, and mounting them, then moving silently the one mile to the Indian camp and surrounding it. As Hancock reported to Sherman, "Being a bright moonlight night, General Custer was enabled to move very promptly."[10]

Whatever reason there may have been for the delay, orders were issued to Custer to mount his command and proceed as rapidly as possible to the Cheyenne village and prevent the departure of any remaining Indians. At the same time, the infantry and artillery were ordered to parade under arms in the event of resistance. The artillery battery was planted so as to command each side of the Indian camp, and all the soldiers remained under arms throughout the night. When the orders were issued, the entire command, except for the guard, the headquarters staff officers, and the commanders, was sleeping soundly. The operation was to be conducted noiselessly, to avoid alerting the Indians, and no bugle calls or loud voice commands were permitted. All orders were to be given by word of mouth. After receiving his own orders, Custer rode to the tents of each of his subordinate officers, first the adjutant and then the company commanders, awakening them quietly and whispering his orders to them. They were to mount their men as rapidly and silently as possible, provide each with one hundred rounds of ammunition (Captain Barnitz said forty-five rounds per man), and put the companies in column behind the lead

---

[10] Hancock to Sherman, April 15, 1867; G. Custer, *My Life on the Plains*, 51; Dippie, *Nomad*, 23; Kennedy, *On the Plains*, 69.

squadron. The company commanders awakened their first sergeants, who then roused the men. Soon the troopers had rolled out of their blankets, pulled on their boots, strapped on their sidearms, and were saddling their horses. When all was ready, the men were mounted and moved into line. Once all were in column, Custer gave the command to move out. The regimental tents were left standing in the charge of a small guard. None of the men knew the purpose of the movement, though all surmised that the Indians were in some way involved.[11]

The bright moonlit night allowed rapid movement of the column. The air was clear, mild, and pleasant, with only a light, soft breeze. According to Dr. Coates, the night was breathless and "more fit for whispering lovers' vows than for the terrible voice of Mars." Rumors abounded as to what they were doing, some claiming that a great force of Indians was about to attack them, while others declared the cavalry was going to surround the village and massacre the Indians. Their arms and equipment were so arranged as to prevent unnecessary sounds, and except for the muffled sounds of the horses' hooves, they moved almost noiselessly toward the Cheyenne village. Behind them they could still see their campfires, and at headquarters the light in General Hancock's tent shown brightly, serving as a guide point in the event that a cloud cover moved over, causing them to lose their bearings. Ahead and a little to their left lay the Cheyenne village, partially concealed by the cottonwood trees lining the banks of the north branch of the Pawnee. A number of lodges, showing white in the brilliant moonlight, could be plainly seen, and in a few they could glimpse the lodge fires through the openings. In a short time—a matter of a few minutes, according to Dr. Coates—the column reached a point within half a mile from the village. Except for the occasional barking and howling of the Indian dogs, they detected no signs of life to indicate that the Indians were still there.[12]

In an effort to prevent escape by the Indians, if any remained, Custer determined to throw a cordon around the village. This was done by moving the long line of companies in a circle with the village as the hub and a radius of about half a mile. An officer at the back of the column halted the rear files at intervals and faced them toward the center. There they

---

[11] Hancock to Nichols, May 22, 1867; G. Custer, *My Life on the Plains*, 51–53; Dippie, *Nomad*, 23; Kennedy, *On the Plains*, 68–69; Stanley, *My Early Travels*, 38–39; Utley, *Life in Custer's Cavalry*, 34.

[12] Hancock to Sherman, April 15, 1867; Hancock to Nichols, May 22, 1867; G. Custer, *My Life on the Plains*, 53–54; Dippie, *Nomad*, 23–24; Kennedy, *On the Plains*, 68.

stood—mounted, immobile, and as "silent as a statue." The surround was completed in a short time, and escape by the remaining Indians made difficult at best. To this point there had been nothing but what Custer called an "ominous silence" emanating from the Indian camps—silence some interpreted as suggesting the possibility of an ambush. It was a large encampment, estimated by most observers as containing about 300 lodges within both the Cheyenne and the Lakota villages, and a hazardous place to enter. When the later inventories were taken, by actual count there were 140 Oglala lodges found in place, and either 111 or 136 Cheyenne lodges still standing. About 25 lodges had been removed when the village was vacated. Although there was no mention about whether these were Cheyenne or Oglala lodges, the probability is that they were Cheyenne. As noted by Hancock, a great many of the Lakota lodges had huge pieces of the cover cut out to provide temporary shelters, and the lodges removed were doubtless taken by those having a sufficient number of animals to do so. The Oglalas were away from their own country, had to travel far, fast, and lightly encumbered, and seemed to have fewer horses. The Cheyennes were from all appearances the better-mounted and had the larger number of animals, though then in poor condition. They were in their own country and did not have nearly as far to travel to be safe. Between the Dog Soldiers, the southern Sutaio, and White Head's Óhméseheso, it is likely that the two tribes had about an equal number of lodges at the encampment, and the Cheyennes the most.[13]

Once the cordon around the Indian camp was complete, the troopers closed in on it, with carbines advanced, shrinking the radius until only a few hundred yards remained. At that point Custer ordered the entire line of troopers to halt and stay mounted with carbines at the ready, while a small party of half a dozen men reconnoitered the villages. This party, which included Ed Guerrier, Custer, Dr. Coates, and Lt. Miles Moylan, moved forward cautiously on horseback. When they reached the edge of the villages, which they found to be surrounded on three sides by a deep, dry ravine and on the other by the flowing stream, they paused for a moment to listen for sounds of activity. Hearing nothing except the dogs, Custer urged his horse down the steep embankment and up the other side, followed closely by Dr. Coates and the others. In only moments they

---

[13] Hancock to Sherman, April 15, 1867; Hancock to Nichols, May 22, 1867; U.S. House, "Difficulties with Indian Tribes," 7:71; E. Custer, *Tenting on the Plains*, 560; G. Custer, *My Life on the Plains*, 54–55; Dippie, *Nomad*, 24; Kennedy, *On the Plains*, 68–69; Utley, *Life in Custer's Cavalry*, 34.

Following what he considered a failed council due to lack of a greater number of Cheyenne chiefs, on April 14, 1867, Hancock marched his men up the
north branch of the Pawnee Fork to the Cheyenne and Oglala villages. He
became enraged when he found that the Cheyenne women, children, and elderly, as well as the Oglalas, had fled in fear of another Sand Creek Massacre.
Only the Cheyenne warriors remained, and when Edmund Guerrier brought
word that they too were leaving, Hancock sent Custer and his Seventh Cavalry troopers to surround the villages and prevent their escape. It was too late,
but Hancock did seize the villages and their contents, intent on their destruction if the Indians did not return. This view sketched by Theodore Davis shows
the Cheyenne village as it appeared on April 15 or 16, 1867, and was published
in the May 11, 1867, edition of *Harper's Weekly*.

were alongside the first of the lodges and could see a low fire inside. Custer
ordered one of the party to dismount and enter and for Guerrier at the
same time to call out loudly in Cheyenne that their presence was for peaceful purposes—a statement that might reasonably be met with some skepticism by any occupants. Only silence greeted his announcement. Then
the dismounted man ducked under the tepee flap and disappeared within,
while the others waited breathlessly. In a moment his voice, no doubt
with some relief, was heard to call out, "Gone, by Jupiter!" Dismounting,
Custer and the others went from lodge to lodge to verify that the village

was indeed abandoned and examine the many articles left behind. According to Coates, it was evident that the majority of their furnishings had been taken away by the fleeing Indians, yet the quantity remaining was nonetheless astonishing. Because of the large number of standing lodges to be searched, Custer ordered additional troops to enter the village and assist in the process, which was then accomplished in a short time.[14]

As soon as it was clear that the Cheyennes were gone, Custer dispatched a courier to General Hancock to inform him. Then they began a hurried examination of the villages. As might be expected of excited young men, a good deal of looting took place. Some of the lodges were protected by having brush or logs piled against the entrance, the owners hoping to preserve the contents until they could be retrieved after the soldiers were gone. Others, apparently mainly in the Oglala village, had huge pieces cut from their sides to serve as temporary shelters. In most lodges a fire still flickered or smoldered in the fire pit. However much of the interior furnishings may have been removed by their Indian owners, great quantities remained of every kind and description. "There were enough trophies and curiosities," said Custer, "to have filled all the museums and private cabinets of such articles in the country." There were buffalo robes, some finely ornamented, as well as head mats, parfleches with their contents undisturbed, doormats, paint bags, rawhide ropes, cooking equipment and eating utensils, and a myriad of other items for use in the lodge. There were saddles, war clubs, arrows, and other articles of horse equipment, combat and hunting gear, and camp equipment. As the men moved through the lodges, they picked up great quantities of souvenirs and mementos. Even Custer admitted in his October 26, 1867, letter to *Turf, Field, and Farm,* that "our party at once resolved itself into individual plundering committees." Dr. Coates, as well, stated, "We left the Indian village, after securing many curious articles."[15]

During the search of the two villages, more than merely lodge and camp equipment was found. Cooking kettles in many lodges had meat stewing for an evening meal the former occupants would never enjoy. Ed Guerrier began to sample one of these, declaring it "dog soup" and a "dish for

[14] Hancock to Sherman, April 15, 1867; Hancock to Nichols, May 22, 1867; Brown, *March Journal,* March 14–15, 1867; G. Custer, *My Life on the Plains,* 55–59, 61; Dippie, *Nomad,* 24–25; Kennedy, *On the Plains,* 69; Utley, *Life in Custer's Cavalry,* 34.

[15] G. Custer, *My Life on the Plains,* 59–62; Dippie, *Nomad,* 25; Kennedy, *On the Plains,* 22–23; Utley, *Life in Custer's Cavalry,* 34–35.

the gods." He urged Dr. Coates to try it, and the latter, finding the odor quite savory and "wishing to be ignorant of no dish," joined in the feast. He was quite pleased with its taste and said, "I found nothing whatever disgusting about this great Indian dish, as might be supposed." After hearing of this, Custer, either believing the good doctor to be the victim of a joke or merely wanting to report it that way, wrote to Libbie that Coates had partaken of the meat, thinking it was buffalo. When Guerrier pronounced it to be dog, he "took the laugh quite cooley, remarking, 'I don't care, its good, any how.'" By October 26, in his letter to *Turf, Field, and Farm*, Custer expanded on the story by saying that upon hearing the meat was dog, the doctor abruptly "concluded his repast," and a "hearty laugh" was enjoyed by all at his expense. This was yet further expanded upon in 1872, when Custer wrote the stories that became his autobiographical *My Life on the Plains*, stating: "I will not attempt to repeat the few but emphatic words uttered by the disgusted member of the medical fraternity as he rushed from the lodge." Such stories, as in most human experience, grow better with the telling, and Custer's tales were no exception.[16]

Entering another lodge, obviously in the Oglala village, Guerrier and Coates found "an old, crippled, sick Sioux who, being unable to travel, was abandoned by his tribe." The old man had a broken knee. Coates did not find this cruel or heartless, but military necessity, "no more cruel than military necessities are in civilized armies where, on the field of battle, or in a hasty retreat, the wounded are often abandoned, and the dying left with the dead." Hancock reported the discovery of the old man to Sherman the next morning, claiming to have found him during his personal inspection. In his report of the expedition made on May 22, 1867, he also told of the finding of an "old Sioux woman who was subsequently discovered near the Indian camp." Custer made no mention of the old man until writing *My Life on the Plains* some five years later, and Davis related the finding of the old man but not the woman. In a story appearing in the May 11, 1867, issue of *Harper's Weekly*, he wrote:

> In one of the lodges an old Sioux was found. Curtis the interpreter, learned from him that he had been left by his band, who told him that they would come back for him as soon as the troops left. The old man was extremely emaciated, and almost unable to move. He stated that the Cheyennes desired to

---

[16] E. Custer, *Tenting on the Plains*, 577–78; G. Custer, *My Life on the Plains*, 61; Dippie, *Nomad*, 25; Kennedy, *On the Plains*, 70.

fight; but the Sioux would not accede to the proposition and left. The Cheyennes soon after became frightened, and also left. This old Indian was placed under the kindly care of Colonel Edward Wynkoop, the Indian agent, who accompanies the expedition.

Stanley, doubtless employing a good deal of literary license, described the finding of "one old warrior and his squaw," the old man having allegedly been abandoned because he was "old, decrepit, and useless, and of no earthly use to the tribe," and therefore left to starve with his wife. The woman, he reported, "was found busily preparing a dog for supper." There is nothing in the official reports or other writings to suggest the woman was the wife of the old Oglala man, and from Hancock's report it would appear she was not found with or near him. So far removed in time, her identity and relationship to the old man must necessarily remain speculative.[17]

The only other person found in either village was a young girl about eight to ten years of age, who had been raped when found, perhaps more than once. It appears that she was found by Guerrier and Dr. Coates while visiting yet another lodge, this one in the Cheyenne village. Upon entering the lodge, they heard a suppressed moaning and, on removing a buffalo robe from where the sound originated, discovered her. She was in a pitiable condition, "perfectly naked, eyes mattering and swollen, hair matted and tangled into knots; and blood trickling down her legs." The girl was apparently soon removed to the military encampment, since Dr. Coates made an examination of the child and an official report of her condition on orders from Gen. A. J. Smith, who had not been present when the villages were surrounded and entered. Coates concluded the girl had been brutally raped and abandoned and was suffering all of the terrible consequences of the frightening experience. When this information was given to General Hancock, he seems to have altered the circumstances in his initial report so that he was the one who, during his personal inspection on the morning of April 15, found "in the Cheyenne camp a little girl, partly white, I believe, and not one of the tribe." According to Hancock, she had been "horribly outraged by the Indians, immediately previous to their deserting their camp." By the time of his May 22 report, however, he said the girl was found in the Cheyenne village by "some of our officers," was probably eight or nine years

[17] Hancock to Sherman, April 15, 1867; Hancock to Nichols, May 22, 1867; *Harper's Weekly*, May 11, 1867, 302; Davis, "Summer on the Plains," 296; Kennedy, *On the Plains*, 71; Stanley, *My Early Travels*, 44–45; Stanley, "British Journalist," 302.

of age, and "said to be partly white." He thereby backed off of his earlier claim of having personally found her or of having determined her to be partly white. His reports are interesting for another reason, since he stated he found her during his inspection of the Cheyenne camp and later that she was found in the Cheyenne camp. In the succeeding days he would claim not to be able to distinguish the Cheyenne village from that of the Oglalas.[18]

In reporting for their readers the rescue of the girl, Davis and Stanley also embellished the truth. Davis described her a "little half-breed child, of not more than nine years" who had "suffered a most abominable outrage from the Indians before they left." Stanley, as might be expected, made the story even more sensational. He called her a "little captive girl" who "seems to be eight years old, and is undoubtedly white." Moreover, he said, she "has been outraged by no less than six Indians." But more remarkable still is the story developed by Custer. He made no mention of her at all until he wrote to his wife on May 2, when he said: "I forgot, also, to tell you in a former letter about the only occupant of the Indian camp. It was a little half-breed girl. We found her half naked. She was perhaps eight or nine years old. It is all true that you have heard about the Indians' treatment of the little creature. I had the doctor make an examination and he found she was in a horrible condition. She was almost insensible when we discovered her, and after recovering sufficiently to talk she said 'the Indian men did her bad.'" While not directly stating that he was included with the "we" who found the girl, the implication is there. Even more surprising is the statement Custer attributed to the girl, for in the long run it was determined that she did not speak English. He did not mention the child in his "Nomad" letters to *Turf, Field, and Farm* but made a great deal of her in *My Life on the Plains*. There he claimed he entered the lodge where she was found in the company of Dr. Coates, but finding it almost entirely dark and his fagot having died out, he sent the doctor to get another lit one. While waiting in the darkness, he heard movement nearby, his hand brushed against a human foot, followed by a voice unmistakably speaking an Indian language, at which point he began to suspect an Indian warrior was crouching in the dark and waiting to spring upon him with war club and scalping knife. But soon the doctor returned with the light and, after being cautioned by Custer that an Indian was present and weapons might be needed, carefully entered the lodge

---

[18] Hancock to Sherman, April 15, 1867; Hancock to Nichols, May 22, 1867; Kennedy, *On the Plains*, 72.

with pistol drawn, when they found the little girl lying before them wrapped in a buffalo robe. She was, he said, a half-breed Indian girl, and after he called in Guerrier to interpret (she speaking no English), it was learned that she had been raped by "a few of the young men of the tribe" who apparently returned to the deserted village and lodge for just that purpose. Why he did not recognize the voice he heard in the dark clearly speaking in an Indian tongue as that of a female child, he did not say.[19]

The stories swirling around the little girl were typical of the sensationalism of news writers of the day and the willingness of both the white press and public to attribute to the Indians the basest and most savage character. That they would pillage and rape the women of an enemy is true, but they did so in the context of an act of war, just as did the whites. What they, and especially the Cheyennes—widely known as the "Puritans of the Plains"—would never do is sexually assault one of their own. It was a great taboo, against their religious beliefs, and warranted a most harsh punishment for the perpetrator. Colonel Wynkoop conveyed this to Hancock and the others, but his assertions appear to have had little influence. Dr. Coates, a cooler and more thoughtful head, never subscribed to what was reported by the others. Of the little girl he wrote:

> At first it was supposed that the Indians had committed the outrage, which called down vengeance on their village from General Hancock. The girl at first appeared to be white, or at least half-breed, and that on this account the Indians had committed the cruel deed. But subsequent investigation showed the child to be an Indian—and it was then a question whether our troops, and not the Indians, had not been guilty of the outrage. Colonel Wynkoop, who declared the girl was an Indian (and an idiot), said that there were no instances on record of Indians committing such an outrage on one of their own people.

The little girl, who was mentally retarded, had refused to go with the others and was left behind by her people in the haste of their flight. It is probable that she was of the Óhméséheso band, as White Head, the only Óhméséheso chief present in the village, later testified at the Medicine Lodge peace council that he had known her for her entire life, that he was the last to leave the village, and that she was then unharmed.[20]

George Custer significantly stretched the truth in other ways while writ-

---

[19] E. Custer, *Tenting on the Plains*, 578; G. Custer, *My Life on the Plains*, 62–64; Davis, "Summer on the Plains," 296; Stanley, *My Early Travels*, 39–40, 44–45.

[20] Grinnell, *Fighting Cheyennes*, 251; Hyde, *Life of George Bent*, 261; Kennedy, *On the Plains*, 72; Powell, *People of the Sacred Mountain*, 1:471–72; Stanley, "British Journalist," 302.

ing *My Life on the Plains*. Though all who wrote of it at the time, including Custer, described the night as clear and flooded with moonlight, in his
book he inserted clouds that broke only occasionally to permit a glimpse of
his command and the village ahead. When the surround was complete, the
clouds mysteriously parted, allowing the troopers to enter the village. This
not only added drama to the scene but also provided an explanation about
why it wasn't immediately apparent that the Indians were gone. Once at
the village, he had his party dismount and crawl in among the tepees on all
fours, and he became the one to enter the first lodge in the company of Dr.
Coates. While obviously providing an exciting and sensational aspect to the
story for readers of that day, much of what he later wrote about his personal
actions and conduct was clearly fictionalized for his own benefit.[21]

Along with a considerable number of dogs, several Indian horses were
also found in the villages, all in too weak and poor a condition to be taken
with their owners when they left. The horses of the plains, both wild herds
and those belonging to the Indians, subsisted during the winter by grazing on the dormant grasses and by eating the bark and branches of cottonwoods and other trees found growing along the banks of some of the
larger streams. Buffalo and grama grasses, even in a dormant state, contain a great deal of nutrition stored in their blades and top growth. They
cure well and provide excellent forage in winter and early spring. The men
of the expedition, not understanding the fauna and flora of the Great
Plains environment, were unaware of their nutritional value, or that they
were warm-season grasses that did not break dormancy until the soil temperature had risen sufficiently, generally in early to mid-May. This made
them think that it must have been an unusually hard winter to have thus
delayed the growth. Even so, the lack of a fresh and abundant growth did
make life hard for the Indian horses. While confined to their winter camps,
the large herds of horses belonging to a band or village were allowed to
graze out from the village center in concentric circles, under the watchful eye of young men and boys. Well before a winter ended, the grazing
in the vicinity became meager, and until new growth appeared in sufficient quantity, the animals remained in a much weakened condition. Dr.
Coates came across two of the poor beasts that were in such a starved state
that he pushed them over with only the momentum gained in two or three
steps. He noted in his journal, however, that they were said to regain their

---

[21] G. Custer, *My Life on the Plains*, 53–59.

strength and high spirits in a matter of days after the season of growth returned. In a few of the animals he observed a small hole between the ribs leading to the chest cavity, causing a whistling sound as they inhaled and exhaled. He speculated that some worm might have been the surgeon performing that operation.[22]

After the quick search of the Indian villages and a considerable amount of "souvenir" gathering, Custer started his command back to the expedition encampment. He left Captain Barnitz and his squadron from Fort Harker to take possession of the Indian camps and to hold them until daylight returned. Barnitz established sentry outposts to guard against any surprise visits from returning Indians, arranged for the picketing of the squadron's horses, and then took a party to look through the many lodges and inspect the camps. Like those entering the villages before him, he was "astonished at its magnitude and magnificence." He was surprised to find that the lodges were "all made of dressed buffalo hides—almost as white and soft as kid gloves." He found them filled with buffalo robes and a vast quantity of domestic camp equipment, "some of which," he wrote to his wife Jennie, "I took away with me." But Barnitz and his squadron were ordered back to the expedition camp well before dawn, bringing their inspection and artifact collecting to an abrupt end.[23]

When the other six companies of the Seventh Cavalry began their return to camp, Custer galloped ahead to report "the particulars" to General Hancock. Prior word by courier of the flight of the Cheyennes and receipt of the details seem to have once again put the general in a rage. Gone was his recently expressed belief that the flight of the Cheyenne women and children was caused by fear of another Sand Creek Massacre, as he had expressed in a letter to General Sherman only hours before. In its place was substituted an almost irrational conviction that the underlying motive for the Indian departure was guilt for past offenses, fear of retribution, and an intention to make war. "This looks like the commencement of war," he wrote to General Sherman at 12:30 A.M. that very night. "I feel quite satisfied that some of both Sioux and Cheyennes who were in this village were from the north, and had most likely been concerned in the recent outrages there; and this, no doubt, was the main reason why they feared to meet my troops, and the cause of the abandonment of their village." The Cheyenne Dog Sol-

---

[22] Dippie, *Nomad*, 24; *Prairie and Range Plants*, 19–21, 25; Kennedy, *On the Plains*, 72.
[23] G. Custer, *My Life on the Plains*, 65; Utley, *Life in Custer's Cavalry*, 34–35.

diers had not been in the north since 1865 and had nothing to do with the Fetterman affair or other troubles on the northern plains. Nor did the Kiyuksa Oglalas participate in them. Indeed, they came south of the Platte to stay away from any conflict in the north, with the express approval of General Augur. It is difficult to say whether Hancock actually believed that to be the case, though his written and oral statements certainly support that view. At the same time, however, he had seemingly hoped for conflict and a chance to redress old "outrages" and had strong motives to make a name for himself fighting Indians. But whatever his underlying reasons or beliefs, he saw their flight as a cause to begin hostilities against the Indians if they failed to return or engaged in any acts of war against whites.[24]

Following a hurried council with his officers, General Hancock ordered Custer and the Seventh Cavalry to pursue the fleeing Indians, both Cheyenne and Oglala, men, women, and children, as soon as daylight came. They were to overtake them and bring them back, if possible, to hold the elusive council with Hancock. If they refused to return and were disposed to fight, Custer was to accommodate them. Hancock ordered several companies of infantry to the deserted Indian villages to replace Captain Barnitz and his squadron of cavalry, with orders to protect the lodges and their contents until their final disposition could be determined. The fox, it seems, was now to guard the henhouse following its own raid. With the return of Barnitz and his men, the remainder of the night was spent in preparation for the forthcoming march. Each man inspected the shoes on his horse to ensure fit and tightness. Mess kits were "overhauled," and fresh supplies of foodstuffs and staples were laid in. Weapons were checked and ammunition replenished. Blankets were tightly rolled to minimize the space required to carry them. Only necessary items of clothing were to be taken, and all unnecessary baggage was left behind. Most of the company baggage wagons, three from each company, with the tents, company desks, and other unnecessary items, were placed in the charge of 2nd Lt. Henry Jackson, who remained behind with about eighty men and all of the extra replacement horses. All was in readiness for the march before dawn broke.[25]

With his course of action against the fleeing Indians determined,

---

[24] Hancock to Sherman, April 15, 1867; Hancock to Nichols, May 22, 1867; G. Custer, *My Life on the Plains*, 35.

[25] Hancock to Sherman, April 15, 1867; Hancock to Nichols, May 22, 1867; E. Custer, *Tenting on the Plains*, 560; G. Custer, *My Life on the Plains*, 65; Davis, "Summer on the Plains," 296; Utley, *Life in Custer's Cavalry*, 36.

Hancock stated his intended disposition of their villages and property as vengeance for what he deemed their treachery. To his officers and the agents and reporters present he expressed his resolve to burn the villages and their contents the next day. Colonel Wynkoop subsequently confirmed this statement, saying, "That night, in my presence, General Hancock expressed his determination of burning the village the next day." Stanley reported the same. This declaration by Hancock brought an immediate objection from Colonel Wynkoop and disagreement from General Smith and several other officers. By noon that day, April 15, possibly as a result of their disapproval and disagreement, Hancock modified his intentions in his report to General Sherman, stating: "I have now determined to burn their village, and destroy everything they have left behind, such as robes, camp-kettles, axes, &c., of which they have left a large quantity; they will be difficult to replace; but I shall wait to hear from General Custer before doing so. His operations may influence me."

As dawn on the morning of Monday, April 15, 1867, approached, General Hancock had already decided to destroy the Cheyenne and Oglala villages, provided Custer's operations did not bring some kind of result that might make him reconsider. He intended to maintain his headquarters near the two villages, with the infantry and artillery remaining with him, until he learned whether Custer had succeeded in catching up with the Indians and what had resulted from any encounter.[26]

---

[26] Hancock to Sherman, April 15, 1867; Wynkoop to Murphy, September 14, 1867, 312–13; Stanley, *My Early Travels*, 40.

CHAPTER TWELVE

PURSUIT

Breakfast was served to the officers and men of the Seventh Cavalry a little after 3:00 A.M. on Monday, April 15, 1867. By 5:00 A.M. they were mounted, and the order to move out was given. They were accompanied by Edmund Guerrier as guide and interpreter, Thomas Atkins, Thomas H. Kincaid, and James Butler (Wild Bill) Hickok as guides and couriers, and six Delaware scouts. The Delaware scouts were to locate the main trail of the fleeing Indians as quickly as possible. The cavalry companies rode directly to the Cheyenne and Oglala villages and waited for sufficient light to find a trail. When it came, the individual Delawares began to circle the two villages, looking for something meaningful. It was not easy. Hunting parties had come and gone from the camps each day, bringing back bison, elk, antelope, deer, and other game and leaving many diverse trails while doing so. When the Indians fled, first the women, children, and old people, along with the Oglalas, and finally the Cheyenne warriors, they did so in small groups. Each band moved in a different direction and left a separate trail, then eventually doubled back or changed direction to reunite with others of their tribe at some predetermined point. Adding to the difficulty, the multiple trails were now covered with dew, obscuring the signs that might otherwise have been visible.[1]

As the Delawares circled the camps, the cavalry waited and rested. But in a short time they signaled that a good trail had been discovered, and the march began. The order of march had the Delaware and white scouts well in advance of the troops, avoiding delays during the momentary halts of the scouts as they examined the trail. The cavalry, which usually marched

---

[1] Hancock to Sherman, April 15, 1867; G. A. Custer to T. B. Weir, AAAG, April 16, 1867, AGO, LR, NA, MC619-R562; Hancock to Nichols, May 22, 1867; *Harper's Weekly*, June 29, 1867, 406; G. Custer, *My Life on the Plains*, 67, 71; Davis, "Summer on the Plains," 296; Dippie, *Nomad*, 28–29; Kennedy, *On the Plains*, 74–75.

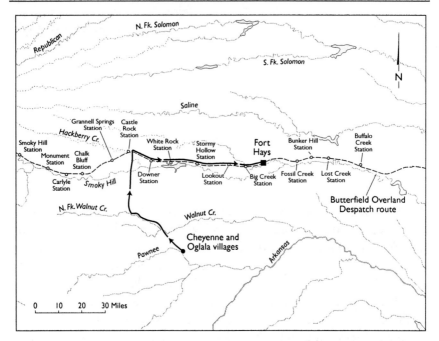

Seventh Cavalry march from Cheyenne and Oglala villages
to old Fort Hays, April 15–19, 1867. *Map by Bill Nelson.*

in one long column, was now divided into six smaller detachments. They
rode abreast of each other, with from one to five hundred yards separating a detachment from its neighbor to the left or right. Once a proper
trail was found, the companies moved steadily along and parallel to it at
a cavalry walk, a rate of about four and a half miles per hour. The trail led
up and across a high rolling plain in a generally northwesterly direction.
Neither Custer nor the men of his command could detect any percepti-
ble trace of hoofprints, dragging lodge poles, or moccasined feet, but the
leader of the Delawares assured him the signs were there. When they
reached the first small stream of water, the judgment of the Indian scouts
was vindicated. What would not make an imprint on the rock-hard surface of the upland plains showed clearly when even a small amount of
moisture was present in the sandy loams of the valley.[2]

---

[2] Custer to Weir, April 16, 1867; G. Custer, *My Life on the Plains,* 71–72; Dippie, *Nomad,* 29–30.

The northwesterly march of the Seventh Cavalry took them to Walnut Creek after a march of eleven and a half miles. The banks of the Walnut were very steep and abrupt at that point, making a crossing by the wagons impossible and that of the cavalry difficult as well. Except for a small number, even the Indians whose trail they were following moved farther upstream to cross. There was one encouraging find, however, for it appeared this body of Indians had stopped, built fires (which were still burning), and prepared a meal. According to the Delaware scouts, that occurred not more than four or five hours earlier. To Custer this meant that his command was rapidly gaining on their quarry, considering that at least some had a near twelve-hour start on them.[3]

Despite the early elation over apparently closing the gap, their mood was quickly dampened by further delay. To find a suitable crossing, they were forced to march westerly along the south bank of the stream. They found their passage impeded by a series of dry arroyos draining the plains to the south of the Walnut. Although these carried water only after a heavy rain, they were from twenty to one hundred feet wide, with steep banks, and difficult and tedious to cross. The scouts moved quickly upstream, looking for a suitable place to cross. But the cavalry, encumbered by their small wagon train, took a much longer time following their lead because of the formidable task of getting the wagons across each of the arroyos. After a labored march of two miles they came upon the waiting scouts, who had located the most promising crossing point in the area. It was by no means good, but the best they could find. The banks were steep, especially on the opposite side, and the distance between banks was about 250 feet. In order to make a crossing here it was necessary to double up the teams to pull the wagons to the far bank. It had taken an hour to find a place to cross, and now they experienced further delay.[4]

During their search for a suitable crossing, the Delaware scouts came upon several Indian pack animals, some tied to trees about 1,100 yards above the crossing point, and others loose and grazing nearby. In his first report to General Smith, Custer stated that these consisted of "several ponies and one mule, some of which were tied to trees and still bore their packs." There were likely at least three or four animals, and probably more, including the mule, and they must have been ridden or led quite recently

---

[3] Brown, *March Journal*, April 15, 1867; Custer to Weir, April 16, 1867; G. Custer, *My Life on the Plains*, 73; Dippie, *Nomad*, 30; Kennedy, *On the Plains*, 75.
[4] Brown, *March Journal*, April 15, 1867; Custer to Weir, April 16, 1867; G. Custer, *My Life on the Plains*, 73; Dippie, *Nomad*, 30; Kennedy, *On the Plains*, 75.

as all were still warm and "somewhat blown." They were too worn to be taken with the cavalry column and were left where they were.[5]

There was considerable speculation about why the Indians had left the horses and mule behind, although logically their worn condition would seem the cause. The owners could not have been gone long, it was reasoned, because of the exhausted state of the animals. Given the condition of the abandoned animals, it seems likely that they could not keep up and were left at a place above the crossing point where they could regain their wind, graze a little, and be concealed from the pursuers. One or more of the Indians might then return later to reclaim them, and possibly did, though without the packs and their contents.[6]

Of greater interest than the abandoned animals, at least to the Delawares, were the contents of the packs. A search of these revealed various garments and ornaments, and one appeared to belong to a warrior of distinction. It contained a scalp shirt along with feathers and other ornaments. The Delaware scout who found it insisted it belonged to none other than Roman Nose, containing, as he claimed, the large red feather the great warrior had worn at the confrontation on the Pawnee Fork. Custer observed that this was speculation. While certainly possible, it seems unlikely that Roman Nose would have kept the feathers or scalp shirt separate from his great warbonnet during a rapid departure, and the warbonnet was clearly with him.[7]

The crossing of the Walnut, made just below the confluence of the north and south forks, took some time. Once on the north side, and with clear evidence of the trail of the Indians as well as the telltale discovery of the horses, Custer pushed the pursuit with increased energy. He was convinced they were closing on their quarry and would soon be upon them. The earth turned up in the valley of the stream by the hooves of the Indian horses and by trailing lodge poles appeared as fresh as that turned up by the horses of the Seventh Cavalry. During the afternoon they saw smoke signals around them on several occasions and further evidence of the Indian trail. Neither Custer nor his troops actually saw any of the fleeing Indians, but their Delaware scouts, now staying a few miles in advance of the column, reported sighting small parties who were watching their progress from distant hills.

---

[5] Brown, *March Journal*, April 15, 1867; Custer to Weir, April 16, 1867; Hancock to Nichols, May 22, 1867; G. Custer, *My Life on the Plains*, 73–74; Dippie, *Nomad*, 30–31; Kennedy, *On the Plains*, 75.

[6] Custer to Weir, April 16, 1867; G. Custer, *My Life on the Plains*, 73–74; Dippie, *Nomad*, 31; Kennedy, *On the Plains*, 75–76.

[7] Brown, *March Journal*, April 15, 1867; Custer to Weir, April 16, 1867; Hancock to Nichols, May 22, 1867; G. Custer, *My Life on the Plains*, 73–74; Dippie, *Nomad*, 30–31; Kennedy, *On the Plains*, 75.

A number of times both officers and men thought they had seen Indians, having observed small moving bodies in the far distance. Those Delawares riding with the column, however, no doubt with some amusement, assured them that what they saw were bison and wild horses.[8]

After their first crossing of the Walnut, the cavalry column followed a trail west-northwesterly, parallel with the stream's north fork. A little over six miles beyond, they crossed back to the south side of the stream. The trees along the banks had thinned appreciably, until finally there were none. Though their course was now over rolling prairie, it was broken periodically by the ravines and dry arroyos that drained the uplands. Even so, the trail left by the Indians was broad and clear, and the pace quickened. From time to time they began to find cast-off lodge poles and other items of camp equipment that convinced Custer the Indians were lightening their load. They also began to come across abandoned Indian horses, too exhausted to continue their journey. Satisfied that they were rapidly gaining on the Indians, Custer decided to speed up the pursuit, which was slowed by the needs of the wagon train in getting across the breaks in the plains and crossing the streams. Leaving one squadron of the Seventh to escort the wagons, with orders to follow the trail of the others as rapidly as possible, he pushed on with the remaining three squadrons. By 3:00 P.M. he felt that he could accomplish the objective before nightfall.[9]

The best-laid plans, they say, ofttimes go astray, and so it was with Custer and the Seventh Cavalry. Though they kept their horses at the brisk cavalry walking pace of four and a half miles per hour, certain they were no more than half an hour to an hour behind the Indians, they never caught sight of them. The party whose trail they followed had scouts observing the progress of the pursuing cavalry from the beginning and, as they drew closer, again resorted to the same stratagem as when first leaving their camp. What had been to that point a broad and clear trail, once more dissolved into a great number of slight and faint ones as the Indians split into many small parties and fanned out across the plains. For the pursuers it created the problem of which trail to follow, all having now faded into near invisibility. After consulting with his officers, guides and scouts, Custer concluded that the Indians were headed northwesterly to

[8] Custer to Weir, April 16, 1867; G. Custer, *My Life on the Plains*, 74–75; Dippie, *Nomad*, 31; Kennedy, *On the Plains*, 76; Utley, *Life in Custer's Cavalry*, 36.

[9] Brown, *March Journal*, April 15, 1867; Custer to Weir, April 16, 1867; Hancock to Nichols, May 22, 1867; G. Custer, *My Life on the Plains*, 74–75; Dippie, *Nomad*, 31; Kennedy, *On the Plains*, 76; Utley, *Life in Custer's Cavalry*, 36.

the Smoky Hill River and, once across it, would likely strike for the head-waters of the Solomon or perhaps one of several important tributaries of the Republican such as Beaver Creek. The main trail appeared to follow the north fork of Walnut Creek, and Custer and his troopers stayed with it. He noticed, however, that most of the small bands leaving it seemed to bear to the right as if being directed to the Smoky Hill.[10]

The march along the south bank of the north fork of the Walnut continued until 5:00 P.M., following an increasingly faint trail but the one that seemed most promising. Since leaving the north branch of the Pawnee Fork that morning, they had not stopped except to cross streams and to water their horses, and both men and horses were nearing exhaustion. It was a very hot day, and they had traveled thirty-five miles during twelve hours of continuous marching. The white guides advised that beyond their present location they would find no water for some twenty miles, until striking the Smoky Hill. Nor could they follow the Indian trail at night. Though disheartened that they had not achieved their objective, Custer nevertheless felt that they had drawn close enough that they might still bring their quarry to bay. The Indian horses were half famished and the fleeing tribesmen were encumbered with their families and such property as they managed to take with them. The cavalry horses, on the other hand, were still in good condition. With this hopeful thought, Custer called a halt and put his men into camp.[11]

The horses were unsaddled, watered in the adjacent stream, curried and their hooves checked for defective shoes, then picketed to graze under the watchful eye of a guard. The eight company wagons, one for each company, arrived with the escort about two hours later, bringing with them the grain and forage needed for the horses, along with food staples the men required. With their horses tended to, the men gathered buffalo chips from the plentiful supply to be found on the surrounding plains and built bright, cheerful fires to prepare their evening meal. In a land of few if any trees, the chips were the only available fuel, and served the purpose very well indeed. For the protection of the camp, pickets were posted on all of the highest elevations in the vicinity, and the Delawares were sent to scout the surrounding country. They pronounced it clear, and after the evening meal was finished, most of the tired troopers turned in, using saddles and sad-

[10] Custer to Weir, April 16, 1867; Hancock to Nichols, May 22, 1867; G. Custer, *My Life on the Plains*, 76–77; Dippie, *Nomad*, 31; Kennedy, *On the Plains*, 76.

[11] Brown, *March Journal*, April 15, 1867; Custer to Weir, April 16, 1867; Hancock to Nichols, May 22, 1867; G. Custer, *My Life on the Plains*, 76–77; Dippie, *Nomad*, 31–32; Kennedy, *On the Plains*, 76.

dle blankets as their pillows and sleeping on the ground. Some, including Dr. Coates, stayed around the fires for a time, telling stories of Indians and Indian fights, though few had experienced either.[12]

When Custer put his weary command into camp, he also ordered the faithful Delawares to scout ahead about six miles along the Walnut's north fork to see if they could pick up a more favorable trail to follow in the morning. They were unable to continue with the present trail, which had become too faint to follow in the fading light, and were forced to return. They did observe smoke signals to the north, east, and west of them but none closer than about ten miles. The most impressive of these was per- haps fifteen miles to the northwest, which the Delawares thought might signal a large body of fleeing Cheyennes or Lakotas, and perhaps their camp. Custer had enormous respect for the abilities of his Delawares. Accompanying his command were several white scouts, guides, and couri- ers "who had been accustomed for years to Indian warfare." These included the famous Wild Bill Hickok, who only recently had received national attention for his "various exploits and hair-breadth escapes" on the plains. But in Custer's judgment, "neither he nor any of the frontiersmen, could compete with the Delawares in taking and following the trail."[13]

Though neither Custer nor his troopers had so much as seen a single Indian other than their Delawares during the day's march, and even the Delawares had caught only glimpses of small parties of scouts observing them from the far distance, Edmund Guerrier did. In later years he told his brother-in-law, George Bent, that Custer ordered him to ride ahead of the column and, if he met any Indians, tell them the soldiers meant them no harm and only wanted to hold a talk. Any Cheyenne or Oglala hearing this would likely be skeptical, and it seems that Guerrier was as well. He did not, after all, want any harm to befall his Cheyenne relatives. While riding three miles in advance of the scouts and soldiers, he saw a Cheyenne man who had rounded up a number of horses that wandered off from their herd the previous night and was returning with them. When Guerrier saw him, the man was in one of the dry arroyos draining into Walnut Creek. Guerrier signaled him in sign language: "Get away, sol- diers coming." The man then ran down to the Walnut, leading the horses. Guerrier rode in a different direction, and when the cavalry column

---

[12] Custer to Weir, April 16, 1867; W. S. Hancock to A. J. Smith, April 17, 1867, AGO, LR, NA, 619-R562; G. Custer, *My Life on the Plains*, 77–78; Dippie, *Nomad*, 31; Kennedy, *On the Plains*, 76–77; Utley, *Life in Custer's Cavalry*, 36–38.

[13] Custer to Weir, April 16, 1867; G. Custer, *My Life on the Plains*, 37–38; Dippie, *Nomad*, 31.

approached him, reported to Custer that the Indians had scattered and asked which trail to follow. Custer told him to keep moving north, presumably along the most favorable trail identified by the Delawares. Though Guerrier's actions may have saved the Cheyenne man and his horses, it did not serve to warn the Indians that Custer was hard on their trail, as is sometimes believed. Custer and his cavalry had been observed by the Indian scouts from the time they left the villages on Pawnee Fork, and the Indians were always aware of where the soldiers were.[14]

The night's rest was brief for the men of the Seventh Cavalry. Reveille was sounded at 2:00 A.M. on Tuesday, April 16. The men roused themselves and answered stable call. With currycomb and brush they groomed their horses, then fed them their ration of grain and put them out to graze. While this was being done, the cooks for each company and officers' mess were busy preparing breakfast over the many small fires burning across the camp, all made entirely of buffalo chips. After the meal was served and hurriedly eaten, "boots and saddles" was sounded, and in a brief time the horses were retrieved and saddled. Shortly came the call "to horse," and the men mounted. Immediately after, the order to advance was given, and the column resumed the march, with the Delaware scouts in front as usual. It was sometime between 3:00 and 4:00 A.M. when they left the camp on the north fork of the Walnut.[15]

For a time the cavalry column continued west-northwesterly along the north fork, but after three and a half miles it turned abruptly north and crossed the fork about three-quarters of a mile below the mouth of a small stream known as Cold Springs Branch. Once across they moved north, parallel with Cold Springs Branch, for about four miles. Then the stream turned westerly, while the column continued northwesterly, heading, as they believed, in the direction of the largest column of smoke seen the previous evening. But the slight trail they followed soon disappeared in the short grasses of the High Plains, and after moving another three and a half miles, they turned southwest, then west, hoping to intersect some kind of meaningful trail. They found nothing after another three miles' march, and by noon were well beyond any flowing water. Custer, when informed by the white guides that they were uncertain whether water could be found within a one day's march in any direction except that from which they had come, ordered a return to the nearest point where sufficient water could

[14] Hyde, *Life of George Bent*, 261–62.
[15] Brown, *March Journal*, April 16, 1867; Custer to Weir, April 16, 1867; Hancock to Nichols, May 22, 1867; G. Custer, *My Life on the Plains*, 78; Dippie, *Nomad*, 33–35.

be found for the needs of both men and horses. They retraced their steps and by 2:00 P.M. made a new camp along Cold Springs Branch three-quarters of a mile north of where it emptied into the north fork of the Walnut. They had traveled thirteen miles outbound from their first camp and about nine miles back to the second, making them lose valuable time.[16]

Although they found no Indians, the morning did prove interesting, at least for Custer. Soon after leaving camp, and probably after they left Cold Springs Branch, Custer rode out in advance of the column with Sergeant King, the chief bugler, and accompanied by his four English greyhounds. As they rode, he spotted several antelope grazing on a bluff to the left of the line of march. He wanted to test the speed of the greyhounds Lu and Sharp, so he galloped towards the animals. The dogs soon saw them and away they went. Pronghorn antelope are among the fastest animals on the North American continent, and after about a mile Sharp tired and fell away; but to Custer's surprise Lu outran him and continued the chase for about four miles. The other two greyhounds, Rover and Rattler, took the trail of another pronghorn and chased it for some distance, so that they were soon beyond Custer's sight and hearing. He called Lu and Sharp back at once, and Rover rejoined him three hours and several miles later. Rattler never reappeared, and Custer assumed a wolf had killed him. But now he found that he had outrun Sergeant King, who was riding an ordinary cavalry horse and had fallen so far behind as to be out of sight. Custer was mounted on Custis Lee, his wife's favorite riding horse and a noble, blooded steed. Instead of going back toward the column, he was now distracted by seeing a large bison about three-quarters of a mile in the distance.[17]

Custer had seen bison from afar during the march to Fort Larned and earlier had killed a buffalo calf, but this was the first large buffalo that he actually had an opportunity to hunt. It was more than he could resist, so throwing caution and a knowledge of his whereabouts to the winds, he gave chase. In a letter to Libbie written four days later he said that he galloped in pursuit, and the buffalo, on seeing him, took off at full speed across the plains. Though tired and winded, Custis Lee caught up with it after a chase of about three miles. It was an enormous bull bison, taller even than Custis Lee, or so Custer said, but he was now completely blown, his tongue lolling to one side of his mouth, and apparently unable to continue his race for life much longer. The animal suddenly stopped and

[16] Brown, *March Journal*, April 16, 1867; Custer to Weir, April 16, 1867; Hancock to Nichols, May 22, 1867; G. Custer, *My Life on the Plains*, 78; Kennedy, *On the Plains*, 77; Utley, *Life in Custer's Cavalry*, 36.
[17] E. Custer, *Tenting on the Plains*, 564–65; G. Custer, *My Life on the Plains*, 78–80.

turned to offer fight, while Custer, unable to stop so quickly, passed just beyond the great beast. The chase resumed, with Custer moving over to the left side of the buffalo and bringing his pistol up to fire a shot. But at that moment it turned to gore his horse, causing Custis Lee to veer sharply to the left. Custer instinctively brought his right hand with the pistol back to the reins to regain control, but as he did, he accidentally pressed the trigger, firing a bullet directly into the neck of Custis Lee near the top of his head and penetrating the brain. The horse, running full tilt, fell dead in the course of his stride, throwing Custer over his head.[18]

Miraculously Custer suffered neither cut nor bruise. But now he was alone on the plains without any transportation, without knowledge of what direction his command was from him, and in the heart of hostile Indian country. The buffalo he was chasing, seemingly surprised by this turn of events, looked Custer in the eyes for a few moments, then turned and galloped off, finally stopping about a half mile distant to regain his wind and cast a wary glance back at his adversary. Except for the buffalo and the dead Custis Lee, there was nothing in view—neither living creatures nor trees or other natural features—to mark Custer's position. He thought back on his chase of first the pronghorns and then the buffalo and concluded that he had started to the left of the column and ridden in a semi-circle around its head a distance of about five miles. That, he thought, would place him about two miles in advance and an equal distance to the right of the troopers' route. Using the carcass of Custis Lee as a marker, Custer started off in the supposed direction of the cavalry column and walked for about two miles. Just as doubt was beginning to fill his mind about the accuracy of his course, he caught a glimpse of canvas wagon tops moving through a ravine. They seemed to be about two miles distant and coming his way, so he sat down to wait for them. His officers were surprised when they reached him, alone on the barren plain without his horse. He gave a brief explanation, a party was ordered to retrieve his saddle, bridle, and coat, and he was "loaned" a horse by one of the command. There is a question about what explanation Custer gave. Dr. Coates, repeating his story, reported that the horse threw up his head just as Custer fired his pistol at the buffalo.[19]

During the ride back to Cold Springs Branch and a water source, Custer's luck held again. They sighted what they thought to be a second

[18] E. Custer, *Tenting on the Plains*, 565–66; G. Custer, *My Life on the Plains*, 80–82.

[19] E. Custer, *Tenting on the Plains*, 566–69; G. Custer, *My Life on the Plains*, 82–85; Kennedy, *On the Plains*, 79; Utley, *Life in Custer's Cavalry*, 36.

band of hostile Indians, and several officers who were riding in advance of the column came galloping back, claiming they were being chased by those same Indians. But the "Indians" turned out to be a small herd of bison. At about the same time, to their left, there appeared a band of migrating Indians, this party having ponies that were dragging lodge poles. Captain Benteen was dispatched in pursuit with his squadron, but these "Indians" he found to be a gang of elk. The sighting of the bison brought out the hunting instinct in some, however, and a number of the officers, including Custer and Dr. Coates, went racing off pell-mell in pursuit, yelling like demons. Two of the buffalo were killed. One was brought down by Lt. Owen Hale, and although no one else mentioned who killed the other, Custer took credit for it in a letter to Libbie. A wagon was sent with a few men to retrieve, butcher, and deliver the meat to the new camp on Cold Springs Branch. It had been a long, tiring march on a very hot day, and all of the members of the command were hungry. They spent the remainder of their time on Cold Springs Branch cooking and eating a feast of buffalo meat.[20]

When they arrived at their new camp, the men were told that they would march again at 6:00 in the afternoon. The horses were groomed, then picketed to graze, and as soon as the meat arrived, the cooking fires of buffalo chips were kindled, and the rest of their time was spent eating, resting, and napping until departure. Meantime Custer wrote a dispatch to General Smith and General Hancock, recounting the march to this point through increasingly high temperatures, the failure to find any Indians, and his present intention to march north to the stage road along the Smoky Hill, striking it in the vicinity of Downer Station. He discreetly omitted mention of his buffalo hunting expedition and the loss of Custis Lee. This episode, after all, could easily have resulted in his becoming lost or being killed, leaving the command without its commander in hostile country. It also could have raised a legitimate question about his judgment. He focused instead on his plan for future operations. If he failed to learn of the Indians' whereabouts at Downer Station, he would march south to Fort Dodge. If, on the other hand, there was news of their location, he would pursue them after resupply at Fort Hays. He added that the hasty flight of the Indians and the abandonment of their villages and property "convinces me that they are influenced by fear alone," and "that

---

[20] E. Custer, *Tenting on the Plains*, 570; Kennedy, *On the Plains*, 77–79; Utley, *Life in Custer's Cavalry*, 36.

no council can be held with them in the presence of a large military force."
The dispatch was sent back to expedition headquarters with two couriers
who traveled after dark, one of whom was Tom Kincaid.[21]

The Seventh Cavalry left Cold Springs Branch at 7:00 P.M., heading
due north. After dark, when they could no longer see the compass, they
used the North Star as their guide. At first they traversed a high rolling
plain, broken by intermittent streams and dry arroyos that carried their
occasional burden of rainfall northeasterly to the Smoky Hill. Closer to
the river they struck a dry streambed about 250 yards wide, probably Wild
Horse Creek, that was extremely rough and difficult to cross. Then the
land became very broken and rough, slowing their pace. The moon, only
occasionally obscured by a passing cloud, illuminated the way and made
possible a night march through hills, valleys, and arroyos otherwise impossible to negotiate in the dark. They traveled in this manner through a
good part of the night. The men were nervous and apprehensive at suddenly coming upon a war party of hostile Indians, but the only unnerv-
ing experiences were the sudden barking and howling of wolves, the clatter
of hooves as some frightened animal disappeared into the gloom, and the
cries of hunting night birds. They reached the Smoky Hill River at 1:30
A.M. It had a relatively gentle slope to the south bank, but on the north
side they faced abrupt chalky-limestone bluffs about thirty feet high.
Though the bed of the stream was broad with a level sand base, the flow
of water in it was narrow and only six inches deep. It was totally without
trees along its banks, lending an air of desolation. The scouts located a
ford mostly free of quicksand. They crossed, found a break in the bluffs,
and gained the north bank, going into camp there at 2:00 A.M. Except for
the men posted as pickets and one detail dispatched to the nearest stage
station to learn any news of the Indians, the remainder of Custer's command unsaddled and tended to their horses. After picketing them to graze,
they threw themselves on the ground to catch a few hours of sleep.[22]

It had been a long and arduous march for the Seventh Cavalry, lasting
from 3:00 A.M. on April 16 to 2:00 A.M. on April 17. They had been frustrated in their effort to overtake the fleeing Indians, they had traveled a
considerable distance without water, and it had been especially hot dur-

---

[21] Custer to Weir, April 16, 1867; Albert Barnitz to Jennie Platt Barnitz, April 20, 1867, in Western
Americana Collection, Beinecke Rare Book and Manuscript Collection, Yale University; Burkey,
Custer, Come at Once, 4; G. Custer, *My Life on the Plains*, 85–86; Utley, *Life in Custer's Cavalry*, 38.

[22] Brown, *March Journal*, April 16, 1867; G. Custer, *My Life on the Plains*, 85–86; Dippie, *Nomad*, 35–36;
Kennedy, *On the Plains*, 80; Utley, *Life in Custer's Cavalry*, 36.

ing the daylight hours. Despite this Custer was anxious to find any news he could concerning the whereabouts of the Cheyennes and Oglalas. He ordered twenty-two-year-old Capt. Louis M. Hamilton, with twenty men as escort, to ride to Downer Station on the Smoky Hill road, some eleven miles distant, and determine if there was any news of the fleeing Indians.[23] Hamilton had traveled the Smoky Hill stage route before and professed a familiarity with the plains that the others lacked. But about an hour after his departure an officer came to Custer's tent, reporting that a party of men a few miles away appeared to be Hamilton and his detail, returning. Custer and some of the other officers watched them for a time and determined that, after a couple of changes in direction, they were moving neither toward Downer Station nor toward the Seventh Cavalry camp. The officers were puzzled by the movements and finally concluded that Hamilton had discovered a party of Indians and was moving toward them. Hamilton and his escort soon passed out of sight, and they saw nothing more of them until they returned several hours later. Then it was learned that they had become lost, had traveled in circles during a part of the time, and when they again came within sight of the cavalry camp, where a few Sibley tents resembling Indian lodges had been pitched following their departure, thought they had found an Indian village. They were preparing to creep up on it to reconnoiter the numbers of Indians present when they discovered their error. This was at the same time that the officers in the camp were watching them from Custer's tent, trying to understand what they were doing. For Custer and the others it was an occasion for a few good laughs and a general topic of conversation to while away the hours on the march.[24]

Captain Hamilton and his escort succeeded in making it to Downer Station and discovered that large numbers of Indians had been crossing the Smoky Hill route, heading north. They reputedly had attacked and burned several stations to the east and run off the stock, and reports told of the destruction of Lookout Station and the killing of three men stationed there. High winds kept the command in camp during the morning, but upon the return of Hamilton and his men and learning of the raiding of the stage stations, Custer ordered the march resumed. They

---

[23] Hamilton was the grandson of Alexander Hamilton and died about a year and a half later while leading his company when Custer and the Seventh Cavalry attacked Black Kettle's camp of peaceful Cheyennes on the Washita.

[24] Brown, *March Journal*, April 16–17, 1867; E. Custer, *Tenting on the Plains*, 563–64; G. Custer, *My Life on the Plains*, 86–93; Dippie, *Nomad*, 35–38, 131.

left camp at 3:00 P.M., marching in a north-northwesterly direction until striking the Smoky Hill stage road at its intersection with Castle Rock Creek.[25] Then they followed the road easterly, the cavalry companies and the wagon train reaching Downer Station at 6:30 P.M. Custer and a small detachment moved ahead of the rest of the command and arrived at the station at 5:00 P.M. It was located on the west bank of Downer Creek, built of lumber, and at that time manned by only two men even though it was a home station for the changing of livestock and the serving of meals. The troopers crossed the little stream and made their fourth camp on its east bank opposite the station.[26]

Once in camp the men tended to their horses, giving them their ration of grain and picketing them to graze, and then set about collecting buffalo chips for the cooking fires. Custer and his staff officers, meanwhile, questioned the two frightened men on duty at Downer Station about what they knew of the whereabouts and activities of the Indians. They learned nothing useful beyond what Captain Hamilton had reported, so after the evening meal Custer wrote another report to General Smith and General Hancock. He related the march from Cold Springs Branch to the Smoky Hill and then to Downer Station, where he was told that small bands of Indians, thought to be Sioux and others unknown, had been crossing the stage road thirty to forty miles to the east since the previous morning, moving north. He reported the attack on Lookout Station and the death of its crew, the theft of livestock, and the loss of livestock from Stormy Hollow Station. Then Custer unfortunately added that there "is no doubt but that the depredations at Lookout were by . . . the same Indians who deserted their lodges on Pawnee fork and whose trail I followed until they broke up in small bands." The report was sent back to expedition headquarters with a corporal and five men, guided by one of the Delaware scouts. It arrived early the following morning after an all-night ride. Why Custer would make the assertions he did based on no more evidence than the statements of the two unnerved men is difficult to say. They had witnessed nothing themselves and knew only what they had been told by passing stagecoach drivers as to what they had seen at Lookout or had been told at White Rock and Stormy Hollow stations. And the Indians Custer's command followed, after all, had moved much farther west than

[25] Castle Rock Creek is now known as Hackberry Creek.
[26] G. A. Custer to T. B. Weir, AAAG, April 17, 1867, AGO, LR, 1867, NA, MC619-R563, and in U.S. House, "Difficulties with Indian Tribes," 7:67–70; Brown, *March Journal*, April 17, 1867; G. Custer, *My Life on the Plains*, 93; Dippie, *Nomad*, 38; Kennedy, *On the Plains*, 81; Utley, *Life in Custer's Cavalry*, 36.

Lookout Station, which was about five miles south and two miles west of present-day Hays, Kansas. But Custer's words would have consequences far beyond what he may have intended.[27]

By now the men of Custer's command were exhausted, having had only three or four hours of sleep the previous night and probably less the night before. By the time they looked after their horses, secured the necessary supply of buffalo chips for their fires, and prepared and ate their evening meal, it was likely after sundown before they could get a little sleep. Unhappily a prairie fire interrupted their night's rest, probably caused by some untended cooking fire. Reveille sounded early the following morning, April 18, and the column left camp at 5:00 A.M. Moving easterly along the stage road, they reached White Rock Station after marching ten miles. It was situated on the west bank of a small stream that emptied into the Smoky Hill River a mile to the south. Though not a home station, it was one of the more substantial along the route, being constructed of the native limestone with loopholes in the walls for defense, and a stone corral in the rear that was not yet completed. A small stable was located nearby. Custer reported that White Rock Station was abandoned when the Seventh Cavalry passed it, but this was not so.[28]

On the evening of April 19, after arrival at Fort Hays, Custer wrote a report of his march from Downer Station to Lookout Station. In it he made no mention of White Rock Station but described accounts supposedly given to him at Stormy Hollow Station and accounts of events occurring at the station to the east of it. But the station to the east of Stormy Hollow was Lookout Station, whose entire crew had been killed and could not have reported anything regarding their encounters with Indians. The march journal kept by the accompanying engineer, however, reported that Stormy Hollow Station "was deserted in consequence of threatening Indians." No such report was made of White Rock Station. Apparently Custer became confused when naming the station, and his first interview with stage company employees who had actual encounters with hostile Indians must have been with those at White Rock Station, one of the most defensible on the route. If this is correct, then it was within five hundred

[27] Custer to Weir, April 17, 1867; Burkey, *Custer, Come at Once*, 4; G. Custer, *My Life on the Plains*, 93–94; Dippie, *Nomad*, 38; Kennedy, *On the Plains*, 81; Millbrook, "Custer's First Scout," 90; Utley, *Life in Custer's Cavalry*, 36.

[28] Brown, *March Journal*, April 18, 1867; G. A. Custer to T. B. Weir, AAAG, April 19, 1867, AGO, LR, NA, MC619-R562; Hancock to Nichols, May 22, 1867; Burkey, *Custer, Come at Once*, 4; G. Custer, *My Life on the Plains*, 94–95; Dippie, *Nomad*, 36–37; Kennedy, *On the Plains*, 83; Utley, *Life in Custer's Cavalry*, 36–37.

yards of this station that a party of Indians, estimated by the nervous crew as eight hundred in number, crossed the stage road going due north on Monday, April 15. The warriors were stripped and painted, had their bows strung, and were prepared for a fight. There were women with the party, but no mention was made of children or old people. They stopped near the station for two to three hours and tried to gain admittance but were denied. Failing that, they ran off four mules that were left outside the stable or corral, shooting and killing one when it tried to run back to the station. After this incident, and firing a few shots at the station building, the entire body resumed its march northward. According to the station employees, these Indians represented themselves as Sioux, Cheyennes, and Pawnees. This was clearly wrong, for the Pawnees were mortal enemies of both Lakotas and Cheyennes and were never in league with them. Moreover, the Cheyennes were traveling separately with their own families, not as a mixed war party, and their men had left the village on the north branch of Pawnee Fork several hours after the Oglalas departed. The stage company employees on duty at these stations almost certainly spoke none of the languages of the principal tribes of Plains Indians and probably had no knowledge of differences in dress, language, or any other indicator of tribal affiliation. From what is known, the likelihood is that this was a large party of Lakotas.[29]

Custer's report also said that the next station to the east, meaning Stormy Hollow Station, was visited by a party of about seventy-five Indians on their way north, apparently also on April 15, but the time and day were not stated. Only the chiefs were allowed to come close to the station, though it is doubtful any livestock herder, cook, or other employee of the stage line could tell a chief from a warrior. Of the ones who came forth, four were believed to be Sioux on the basis of having papers signed at Fort Laramie the previous fall that attested that they were "good Indians." The four men identified as chiefs were White Clay, Turkey Egg, Bull Knife, and Big Horse. These men told the station keepers that they had been down to the Arkansas and had made a treaty with General Hancock. They added that they were now good friends with the soldiers. Admittance was denied and the Indians continued north. Since the station was deserted

---

[29] Brown, *March Journal*, 4/18/67; Custer to Weir, April 19, 1867; Hancock to Nichols, May 22, 1867; Berthrong, *Southern Cheyennes*, 278; Burkey, *Custer, Come at Once*, 4; G. Custer, *My Life on the Plains*, 94–95; Dippie, *Nomad*, 36–37; Grinnell, *Fighting Cheyennes*, 253–54; Hyde, *Life of George Bent*, 261; Kennedy, *On the Plains*, 83–84; Powell, *People of the Sacred Mountain*, 1:473; Utley, *Life in Custer's Cavalry*, 36–37.

when the Seventh Cavalry passed it, Custer must have met these men at either White Rock Station or Big Creek Station to the east of Lookout Station, where they might have taken refuge in fear of the Indians. Or perhaps they told their story while passing these stations looking for safety.[30]

Following its pause at White Rock Station, the march resumed for another eleven miles before reaching Stormy Hollow Station, now deserted. It was a relatively new structure and of the same wooden construction as Downer Station. None of the stage company employees were present, having left for safer climes and presumably taken their livestock with them. The station itself was undamaged. During the march from White Rock Station the troops began to see the carcasses of large numbers of wolves lying near the road, apparently poisoned by white "wolfers" for their skins. And sometime before reaching Stormy Hollow Station they were also visited by high winds and rain caused by a spring frontal passage that continued off and on through the rest of the day's march. Between Stormy Hollow and Lookout Station they were struck by rain, hail, and winds so powerful that the wagons were nearly overturned. Beyond Stormy Hollow they traveled another fourteen or so miles until reaching Lookout Station at 3:00 P.M. They went into camp a half mile south of the stage road in a loop in the little stream that provided water for the station and its livestock, ending a day's march of thirty-five miles. The stage station was located west of the stream and north of the road and built of lumber like most of the others. The stables were located across a small ravine, however, and no tunnels connected the two structures, as was the case with many stations. This may in part account for the disaster that overtook it, for being caught in the open between the buildings, or trapped in one away from the others, would have rendered defense difficult at best.[31]

Custer had hoped to march farther, perhaps all the way to Fort Hays but, wanting to obtain evidence about which Indians were responsible for the destruction of the station and the killing of its crew, decided to encamp there. He reported that he was the first to reach the site, although no doubt he was accompanied by at least a small detachment of men. He found the station house, stables, and haystack reduced to ashes, with a few pieces of timber still burning. The bodies of the three men stationed

[30] Custer to Weir, April 19, 1867; Hancock to Nichols, May 22, 1867; Burkey, *Custer, Come at Once*, 4; Kennedy, *On the Plains*, 85; Millbrook, "Custer's First Scout," 91–92.

[31] Brown, *March Journal*, April 18, 1867; Custer to Weir, April 19, 1867; Lee and Raynesford, *Trails of the Smoky Hill*, 62; Utley, *Life in Custer's Cavalry*, 36–37.

there were lying near the ruins, covered with a number of charred poles to protect their bodies until they could be properly buried. Later it was determined that the attack on Lookout Station had taken place during the late afternoon or early evening of Monday, April 15, as employees at Big Creek Station, the next station nine miles to the east, could see the flames and smoke rising from it. Two men from that station, Captain Barron, a driver for the stage line, and John H. Betts, the trader operating nearby, traveled west to investigate and found that the station and barn had been burned. One side of the barn was heavily charred but still standing, and to this the bodies of the stock tender and the cook had been nailed. They were badly burned. All of the stock had been driven off. Barron and Betts removed the nails and placed the bodies on the ground nearby but then returned to Big Creek Station. They had no tools with which to bury the dead men and doubtless feared that Indians were still in the vicinity and might attack them. The following morning Nate Swan, supervisor of eight to ten stock tenders at Big Creek, took several of his men and rode west to check the damage and do what they could to protect the bodies until they could either be removed or buried. Even before they reached it, however, two Denver-bound stagecoaches passed Lookout Station, and a number of soldiers from Fort Hays visited the site as well. Though they observed the ruins and bodies, neither the stage drivers and passengers, nor even the soldiers, did anything toward burying the remains, likely for want of implements. When Swan and his men reached the site, the three dead men were lying on the road, and they "attempted to bury them." It was doubtless Swan and his party who covered the bodies with charred poles from the ruins, for they were not given a burial.[32]

With the arrival of Custer and the Seventh Cavalry, more appropriate action was taken. In his report Custer stated: "I caused them to be buried near the Station with as much care as the circumstances would permit." He stated that the party from Big Creek Station had attempted to bury them but, either for want of implements or fear of the Indians, had merely covered them with some poles. He said that the bodies were horribly burned, the hair singed from their heads, and their intestines bulging from

[32] Custer to Weir, April 19, 1867; Deposition of John H. Betts, August 27, 1867, *Wells Fargo and Co. v. United States, et al.*, U.S. Court of Claims, 30–31; Deposition of Nate Swan, September 7, 1867, *Wells Fargo and Co. v. United States et al.*, U.S. Court of Claims, 10; Burkey, *Custer, Come at Once*, 6; Lee and Raynesford, *Trails of the Smoky Hill*, 62, 98.

the abdomen. Their legs protruded sufficiently from under the poles that the wolves had eaten a considerable part of the flesh from them. He directed Dr. Coates to perform an examination of the bodies before their interment. They could, he said, scarcely be recognized. Once their burial had been attended to and the scene examined for evidence of the Indians who did it, the officers and men involved returned to their camp and went about their normal routine.[33]

Meanwhile the first stagecoach runs to reach Denver delivered the news of what happened at Lookout Station. The April 20 issue of the *Rocky Mountain News* carried the story and attributed the attack to Cut Nose's band of Óhméséheso Cheyennes, an error given that there was no council chief or leader of a band named Cut Nose, though there was a prominent Arapahoe of that name. Moreover, the Óhméséheso were not raiding along the Smoky Hill at that time, and even the military had no real idea who was responsible. The three victims were named Robert Anderson, John Reynolds, and Frank Carter. The story continued, "It is supposed that General Hancock is fighting or has obtained a victory over the hostile bands in the south and hence this attack." The report was hedged a bit with the observation that "it may be that the Indians are just starting on the spring raid that they threatened some months ago," referring to the rumors originating with Satanta, F. F. Jones, and others in late 1866 and early 1867. Included with the article was another version that was apparently provided by W. H. Cottrill, superintendent of the Denver division of the United States Express Company.[34]

The "news" obtained from Cottrill indicated that General Hancock had marched from Salina to Fort Zarah and had attempted to bring the Indians to a council, but they had refused. Then he surrounded their village but, before ordering an attack, again sent them a message proposing a treaty, at which time it was found that the village was deserted and most of the Indian property abandoned. In the village, the story went on, "was found a little white girl, eight or ten years of age, who had been the victim of the most atrocious outrages and was almost dead." The story reported that the Indians fled north, and it identified them as the same who destroyed Lookout Station, numbering "800 to 1,000 warriors," thereby converting

[33] Custer to Weir, April 19, 1867; Burkey, *Custer, Come at Once*, 6; E. Custer, *Tenting on the Plains*, 570; G. Custer, *My Life on the Plains*, 94–95; Dippie, *Nomad*, 38; Kennedy, *On the Plains*, 83; Powell, *People of the Sacred Mountain*, 2:830–31; Utley, *Life in Custer's Cavalry*, 37.
[34] *Rocky Mountain News*, April 20, 1867; Burkey, *Custer, Come at Once*, 6.

the women, children, and the aged into warriors. They "passed in sight of Downer's Station, but made no attack." Troops, the story concluded, were immediately sent for. Two days later another story appeared, based on information obtained from passengers arriving on the second coach passing Lookout Station. This one reported that one of the men was killed outright, while the other two, or so the passengers thought, "were roasted to death, with attending circumstances of fiendish atrocity." All three, according to the article, were found lying on their faces side-by-side in front of the station ruins, which was evidently where Barron and Betts had placed them. One was said to have been shot in the breast, and the other two stabbed in the ribs with knives. Only one of them had been scalped, probably the one whose body was not burned. Such stories, based on partial truths, total falsehoods, rumors, speculation, and bias, naturally inflamed the passions and prejudices of westerners, particularly those living on the frontier or whose lines of communication with the East passed through the troubled areas. The fact is that the Indians were fleeing from Hancock's forces out of fear that he intended to attack and annihilate them in a repeat of the Sand Creek Massacre. While the destruction of two small wooden buildings and the killing of the three men at Lookout Station was a tragedy, it was the predictable result of entering the Indian country without their consent and against their wishes and then sending a large force of troops to intimidate them. Despite the many rumors of several stage stations in flames and multiple atrocities, in truth only Lookout Station was burned and its three-man crew killed. Eight horses and four mules were run off from that station and four mules from White Rock Station, and no other station, employee, or property suffered harm. But this would prove sufficient for General Hancock to take steps that would quickly explode into an Indian war across the southern plains.[35]

The men of the Seventh Cavalry left camp below Lookout Station on the morning of Friday, April 19, 1867. Moving east on the stage road, they reached Big Creek Station about eight and a half miles beyond. This station was on the west side of the south fork of Big Creek and north of the stage road. On the south side of the road was the trading ranch operated by John H. Betts. The station house and barn were constructed of wood, like many along the route, and the stables and pasture were to the north of the bend in the creek. There was only a meager flow of water in the

---

[35] Hancock to Nichols, May 22, 1867; *Rocky Mountain News*, April 20, 1867; *Junction City Weekly Union*, May 2, 1867; Burkey, *Custer, Come at Once*, 6.

stream, but here, for the first time since leaving the forks of Walnut Creek, they began to see a thin scattering of cottonwoods and scrub trees along the banks. Big Creek Station, one of the most important on the Smoky Hill route, was a home station for the stage line, serving meals to passengers and maintaining a large herd of horses and mules. Because it was approximately halfway between Atchison and Denver, stage drivers changed at Big Creek, and in consequence a number of them boarded there while waiting their turn to drive a coach. Eight to ten stock tenders worked at the station under their supervisor, Nate Swan, and it was headquarters for the resident division agent of the stage line from Big Creek west to Denver. A. C. Pyle ran a blacksmith shop at the facility. Because of its importance, Custer and his command doubtless halted for a time to question Barron, Betts, Swan, and others who might have had any knowledge concerning the destruction of Lookout Station. With that done, they continued east another eight miles to (old) Fort Hays, going into camp on the west bank of the south fork of Big Creek about a half mile south of the stage road and a similar distance southwest of the forks of Big Creek.[36]

The unexpected arrival of Custer's command in the vicinity of Fort Hays caused quite a stir in the garrison. Two clerks from the sutler's store were out hunting buffalo about five miles to the west of the post. They caught sight of the long column of mounted men approaching from the west and immediately assumed they were an "overwhelming force of Indians bent on capturing the fort." They galloped back to the post and sounded the alarm. The long roll of drums was beaten and the men called to arms. The canon was loaded, and all preparations made for a desperate resistance by the small garrison. Custer wrote to Libbie, "No doubt a second edition of the Phil Kearney massacre was anticipated." But when the column drew close enough to see the wagons, guidons, and flags, "their fears and doubts were dispelled." An officer of the garrison rode out to greet the Seventh Cavalry, and they went into their camp. Their appearance had been the cause of considerable excitement, and now it became the source of many good jokes and laughs.[37]

At that time Fort Hays was located immediately next to the stage road in an oxbow on the south side of the north fork of Big Creek, a few hundred yards above the forks and about three-fourths of a mile north of the newly established cavalry camp. Upon their arrival in the new camp Custer

---

[36] Brown, *March Journal*, April 19, 1867; Lee and Raynesford, *Trails of the Smoky Hill*, 60–62.
[37] Burkey, *Custer, Come at Once*, 6; E. Custer, *Tenting on the Plains*, 562–63; Utley, *Life in Custer's Cavalry*, 38.

hastened to the fort to make arrangements for a supply of forage and grain for his horses, since the supply carried from Fort Larned was now exhausted. There was meant to be a twenty-day supply for three thousand horses on hand at the post for the use of the Expedition for the Plains, and the quartermaster had assured General Hancock it would be there. Instead Custer found nothing for the expedition, and only a one-day supply intended for the horses already at the post. This placed Custer in a great quandary. He had learned en route of the many small parties of Indians heading north into the country between the Smoky Hill and the Platte, probably to the branches of the Solomon or to one of the major southern tributaries of the Republican such as Prairie Dog, Sappa, or Beaver creek. He had himself, on April 18 or 19, seen two heavy Indian trails leading north that were two days old. And at Fort Hays he learned that a party of twenty warriors had crossed to the north a few miles east of the post on April 18, running off stock belonging to a construction crew building the railroad roadbed as they did. Custer's original intention was to go to Fort Hays, leave the wagons and worn-out horses there, and march that night with the serviceable part of his command, carrying the forage and rations on their saddles. They would march through the next morning to the forks of the Solomon, about forty-five miles distant, where they hoped to surprise any Indians who might be there, as Ed Guerrier supposed them to be. Now a different course of action was indicated.[38]

Faced with this new dilemma, Custer ordered Wild Bill Hickok to ride to Fort Harker on a fresh mule and deliver a dispatch to the commanding officer. The letter requested the commander to forward to him, with all possible haste, four days' forage for his command, using the Fort Harker post train to transport it. He expected Wild Bill to reach Harker the next morning and, allowing for the loading of supplies to take until noon the next day, anticipated that the train would reach Fort Hays by 4:00 P.M. the day after. If so, Custer's intention was to march south to the point on the north branch of the Pawnee Fork from which he had departed en route to the Smoky Hill and, if the rest of the expedition was no longer there, to follow their trail until he met them. Wild Bill left for Fort Harker at dusk, armed with two revolvers and a carbine lent to him by Captain Barnitz and declaring that he was "good for a dozen Indians in all events." As he rode away, he called out, "Good by! Boys! I'll take my breakfast at

---

[38] Brown, *March Journal*, April 19, 1867; Custer to Weir, April 19, 1867; Hancock to Nichols, May 22, 1867; Kennedy, *On the Plains*, 85, 86–87; Utley, *Life in Custer's Cavalry*, 37.

Harker's!" With Hickok's departure Custer turned to writing a further report to General Smith and General Hancock. In it he told of his march from Downer Station to Lookout Station, and from there to Fort Hays, what he found en route, his original intention to march north, and his revised plan, necessitated by the lack of forage. Before he finished, the courier Tom Kincaid arrived in camp, carrying only the cover letter enclosing dispatches in the possession of Lieutenant Sheldon of the Fourth Artillery. Sheldon had become too fatigued to continue and remained at Downer Station to recover. The two of them had been pursued by Indians nearly the entire way, fired on repeatedly, and once driven back across the Smoky Hill, and they had shot one Indian and one Indian horse. Kincaid had been sent by Custer from their Smoky Hill camp with dispatches for General Smith, and then back with orders for Custer, and had been riding continuously for about seventy-two hours. Although he was nearing total exhaustion and could barely talk, he reported that Sheldon intended to come to Fort Hays on the next stage. But there had been no stage through from the west for four days, though three were then at Monument Station and expected to come through at any time. Sheldon had retained the dispatches, believing it his duty to deliver them personally rather than entrust them to Kincaid, even though it was Kincaid who had been delivering them all along. A frustrated Custer thus found himself unable to determine what his superiors now expected him to do.[39]

Custer's report stated that no evidence could be found at Lookout Station concerning the tribe responsible for the attack on it. Several years later, however, in *My Life on the Plains*, he wrote that employees of the stage line, presumably at White Rock Station, claimed to have recognized them as Cheyennes and Lakotas from the villages on Pawnee Fork. How these men, who would have had little or no prior contact with those Indians, could possibly have recognized them he did not say. After expressing his frustration at being unable to pursue the Indians who perpetrated the attack or to find out what was now expected of him, Custer added a postscript that, for General Hancock, would prove something of a bombshell. In it he stated: "Lookout Station was burned out and the men massacred on Monday the 15th, which clears those Indians, who were at Pawnee Fork the day of our arrival, from the charge of being present at the murder. I am confident, however, that the act was committed with their knowledge and approval,

---

[39] Custer to Weir, April 19, 1867; Hancock to Nichols, May 22, 1867; Kennedy, *On the Plains*, 86–87; Utley, *Life in Custer's Cavalry*, 37–38.

which accounts for their hasty flight." How Indians who commenced their flight late in the day on April 14 could have prior knowledge of events that would cause them to flee, but that did not occur until the following day, Custer did not explain. Nor did he suggest how they could have known what other Indians were doing many miles and hours ahead of them.[40]

In his report Custer suggested that in light of the current difficulties with Indians being experienced by the couriers, General Smith should send future orders and dispatches with eight or ten men in the company of two or more Delawares because they knew how to avoid hostile Indians. Then he immediately ignored his own advice, allowing Thomas Kincaid only four hours of sleep before sending him back to the expedition headquarters with the new report. After completing his letter, Custer undoubtedly reflected on his own unhappy circumstance. He wanted to pursue the Indians but was prevented by a lack of forage for his worn-out horses. He knew that new orders for him were with Lieutenant Sheldon at Downer Station, but he had no idea what he would be expected to do. And if he did know, the probability was that he could not do it for the lack of forage. He had already given up any idea of pursuing the Indians even after the supply of forage arrived from Fort Harker, since he was convinced they were by then too far ahead of him and their horses were able to keep going on nothing but the grazing provided by the native grasses. The cavalry horses, by contrast, required the grain and forage that must be carried on slow, cumbersome wagon trains. "I feel that if we cannot overtake them now," he wrote in his letter to Smith, "in the present famished condition of their ponies, it will be a hopeless task to undertake it, after the grass has strengthened them." He wanted action and wanted to move beyond Fort Hays. But his frustration with inaction would continue, and he would remain at Fort Hays for another forty-two days.[41]

---

[40] Custer to Weir, April 19, 1867; Hancock to Nichols, May 22, 1867; G. Custer, *My Life on the Plains*, 95.
[41] Custer to Weir, April 19, 1867; Burkey, *Custer, Come at Once*, 7; Utley, *Life in Custer's Cavalry*, 37–38.

CHAPTER THIRTEEN

THE WRATH OF HANCOCK

When Custer and the eight companies of the Seventh Cavalry rode north on the morning of Monday, April 15, 1867, pursuing the fleeing Cheyennes and Oglalas, General Hancock turned to matters near at hand. He wanted the expedition's camp moved closer to the abandoned villages to keep them under surveillance in case the Indians returned. Because he intended to march for Fort Dodge after hearing from Custer about his success in catching the Indians, he wanted the new camp to be on the south bank of Heth's branch. To accomplish this, he directed the engineers to construct a bridge across the stream, a task they set about at once. It was needed to move the heavy wagons, livestock, and infantry across the stream's deep ravine to the south bank. Its location was about a quarter of a mile south of their first camp, Camp 13, probably because it was easier to bridge the channel at that point. The bridge was built of logs, using trees growing along the banks, and must have been completed by midmorning because the camp was moved before noon. The new Camp 14 was located one mile and 752 yards northwest of the site of Camp 13.[1]

During the morning, while the bridge was under construction, General Hancock rode to the Indian villages with General Smith and other staff officers to inspect them. It was there, he said, that he found an old Sioux man, sick and unable to travel, and in the Cheyenne camp a little girl about eight years of age, partly white, he believed, and not one of the tribe. Fall Leaf, Hancock claimed, said she was neither Cheyenne nor Lakota, had marks indicating she was a captive, and had some white blood. How Fall Leaf could tell this was not stated, and it is doubtful he actually said that or that his words were properly understood. Dr. Coates, who examined her, found clear evidence of rape, but nothing to suggest she was a

---

[1] Brown, *March Journal*, April 15, 1867.

captive or had white blood. The girl spoke only Cheyenne and could not communicate with anyone other than a Cheyenne interpreter, and none was available, pending the return of Ed Guerrier. Dr. Coates wrote that she was a full-blood Cheyenne, and eventually Hancock himself would refer to her as a "little Cheyenne girl." Later that year, at the Medicine Lodge peace council, her identity was confirmed by the Óhméséheso Cheyenne chief White Head, who was the last to leave the village on the evening of April 14.[2]

Fall Leaf also told Hancock, according to the latter, that the "sign" in the camp indicated hostile intentions that were demonstrated by the cutting of the lodges in the camp of the Oglalas. However, that had been done to provide temporary shelter during their flight and in itself had nothing to do with any intentions they might have had to go to war. It seems unlikely that Fall Leaf would attribute hostile motives to the Oglalas based on this alone. It is equally unlikely that a band of Indians would be heading to war minus their lodges and camp equipage, including much of their weaponry. One or the other of the two tribes, and perhaps both, had dug "very large excavations" in the dry ravine surrounding the village sites to conceal their property but lacked the time to complete them. Hancock told Sherman one of his reasons for concluding that Pawnee Killer was present for "mischief" was that he had told Pawnee Killer he would like to have a talk after the council to show there were no hostile intentions toward the Oglalas. Apparently Pawnee Killer's failure to remain and have this talk convinced Hancock the Oglalas were intending war. That the Indians might fear or mistrust the army evidently did not occur to him. Given the many times during the near fifty years of contact with whites in which American officers and officials had duped them, lied to them, misled them, and attacked them, they could not be blamed for a lack of trust, but Hancock did not consider their viewpoint.[3]

General Hancock instructed his adjutant to write the commanding officer at Fort Larned, Maj. Henry Asbury, telling him what had happened and warning him to be on guard against hostilities. It told Asbury to send a copy of the letter to his counterparts at Forts Harker, Hays, Wallace, Lyon, and Dodge and directed them to permit no travel between posts without proper guards. In addition, Hancock notified the mail compa-

---

[2] Hancock to Sherman, April 15, 1867; Hancock to Nichols, May 22, 1867; Stanley, "British Journalist," 302; Kennedy, *On the Plains*, 87.
[3] Hancock to Sherman, April 15, 1867.

nies handling the runs to and from Santa Fe and Denver to watch for trouble with the Cheyennes and Lakotas. Two companies of the Seventh Cavalry stationed at Fort Lyon, Companies B and C, were at Fort Dodge, and Hancock directed them to remain there pending his arrival. At noon he wrote another report to General Sherman, updating him on events that had transpired since his letter of eleven hours earlier. He told of his inspection of the villages and his "discoveries" there, of Custer's pursuit of the Indians, and of his intention to burn the villages if Custer had nothing favorable to report. He expressed his opinion that he had faced nearly all of the fighting men of the Cheyennes the previous day and that there were probably five hundred Cheyenne and Lakota warriors in front of him. This estimate enlarged on the numbers given by most other witnesses but was still within the "several hundred" in his original report. He clearly had no idea how many bands of Cheyennes there were, how many bands he and his officers had met with, or how many warriors and chiefs there were in the tribe. But then neither did most other officers or even the Indian agents.[4]

The letter to Asbury was probably sent by courier that morning and would have arrived later in the day. It ordered Asbury not to allow any Cheyennes or Sioux to come near the post, as the army was now in a state approaching hostilities with both tribes. In the letter, Hancock said this was the result of their refusal to hold a council and their flight from their villages, abandoning their lodges and property. "We now have the camp in our possession," he stated, "and will destroy it, unless further developments should make it seem unwise to do so." In the letter, Hancock also related Custer's pursuit of the fleeing Indians. "All Sioux and Cheyenne men, women, and children shall be arrested and held in custody whenever it is practicable to do so," he continued. He expressed his belief that some of the Cheyennes and Lakotas in the camps had been involved in the Fetterman Massacre, the "recent troubles in the north," and that the reason for abandoning their villages was "that they feared being called to account for their proceedings." Asbury was told that the Cheyennes would likely cross the Arkansas west of Fort Dodge and that the cavalry companies then at Dodge should be prepared to intercept them. Instructions were also given for the protection of supply trains and travelers on the Santa Fe Trail. Then Asbury was told that the Indians had "left a white child" in their village, "a girl whom they have brutally outraged." And

---

[4] Ibid.

Hancock added, "I shall therefore burn their encampment and destroy everything in it unless I see good reason to change my opinion."[5]

After the various post commanders had received Hancock's instructions, the commanding officer at Fort Dodge took immediate action. On April 17, 1867, he ordered Maj. Wyckliffe Cooper, commanding the squadron of the Seventh Cavalry from Fort Lyon that was then at Fort Dodge, to proceed to a point at or near the Cimarron Crossing of the Arkansas River and encamp there.[6] He advised Cooper that the crossing of the river known as the Pawnee Forts, about twenty-two miles above the Cimarron Crossing, was considered a favorite crossing by the Cheyennes and Arapahoes.[7] He recommended that a strong detachment be sent there and that the Santa Fe road be patrolled westward from Fort Dodge to the Pawnee Forts crossing, eastward from the post about sixteen miles, and northward as far as the south branch of the Pawnee Fork (Shaff's branch, or Saw Log Creek). The Cheyennes and the Sioux, he said, were in a state approaching hostilities with troops under General Hancock, and it was their duty to make prisoners of all members of those tribes they might encounter, men, women, and children, and if they refused to surrender, to "fight them without hesitation." Any prisoners taken were to be sent to Fort Dodge.[8]

At the time, General Hancock's headquarters had received nothing from Custer indicating that the Cheyennes or Oglalas had any hostile intentions or were doing anything other than fleeing from him. But his orders to take prisoner or fight any members of the two tribes found along the Arkansas had already gone out, and results were not long in coming. Cooper and his squadron were hardly in camp next to the Cimarron Crossing and the adjacent trading ranch and stage station (known as Anthony's Stage Station) when they discovered six young Cheyenne men whom they described as "skulking about."[9] Their names where Plenty of Horses,

---

[5] W. S. Mitchell, AAAG, to H. Asbury, April 15, 1867, MC619-R563.

[6] There were three principal crossings of the Arkansas on the Santa Fe Trail, known respectively from east to west as the Lower Crossing, the Middle Crossing, and the Upper Crossing, the last being that surveyed by the government in 1825. There were several variations in the Middle Crossing, and it was the one in use after 1853 that later, in the 1860s, became known as the Cimarron Crossing. See Barry, "Ranch at Cimarron Crossing," 345–66.

[7] The "Pawnee Forts," and the crossing of the Arkansas at that point, received the name as the result of a crude stockade erected in a grove of trees on an island in the river during pre-trail times by a party of Pawnees (traveling south from their villages on the Platte River or its branches on a horse-stealing expedition), apparently as an unsuccessful defense against the unforgiving enemy that discovered their presence, reputedly the Cheyennes. See Chalfant, *Dangerous Passage*, 15–16.

[8] G. C. Wallace, Post Adjutant, to W. Cooper, April 17, 1867, MC619-R563.

[9] The Anthony who operated the stage station was a cousin of the famed temperance advocate, Susan B. Anthony, who deplored the fact that her cousin dispensed whiskey to all comers at his establishment. Hyde, *Life of George Bent*, 265.

Pawnee Man, Eagle's Nest, Wolf Walks in the Middle, Big Wolf (or Burnt All Over), and Lone Bear (or One Bear). They were members of Black Kettle's band of Southern Eaters, survivors of the Sand Creek Massacre, and had traveled on foot from their village south of the Arkansas to visit friends in the Dog Soldier and southern Sutaio village on Pawnee Fork before the Hancock expedition arrived. Following abandonment of the village, they began their return to Black Kettle's village, at the time located on the Cimarron River about seventy-two miles southwest of the Cimarron Crossing of the Arkansas. On the morning of April 19 they reached a hill overlooking the trail crossing and Anthony's Stage Station. The station had replacement horses and mules for the stage run to Santa Fe, and they considered stealing a few to ride to their village. Before they could do so, however, they were observed by one of the sentries in Cooper's camp. Soon a party of soldiers was sent out after them, and they were forced to find a safe hiding place. Being on foot and without arms other than their bows and arrows, a couple of old pistols, and a rifle, the six decided to make for a hollow at the head of a ravine and hide there from the soldiers.[10]

The six young men had no more than started for the ravine when they saw another party of soldiers coming toward them from the opposite direction. Cut off from the ravine, they made a run for the river, intending to cross some distance above the stage station and hide in the tall grasses and brush on the opposite bank. When they reached the river, with the soldiers following, two of them, Pawnee Man and Wolf Walks in the Middle, ran upstream a short distance and hid in the tall grasses growing along the bank. The other four continued, running through the river's shallow waters to a small island, where they concealed themselves behind sandbanks and brush. The soldiers concentrated on the four men on the island and did not search for the two, whose separation from the others they may not have seen. The soldiers did, however, tether their horses to some of the scrub trees growing along the riverbank near where the two lay hidden, leading Pawnee Man to suggest that they steal two of them and attempt a mounted escape. Wolf Walks in the Middle wisely pointed out that they knew nothing of those horses and could easily pick the slowest and then be overtaken and caught. They remained concealed until nightfall, then waded the river and made good their escape.[11]

Meantime the four young Cheyennes on the island were keeping as low

[10] Hancock to Nichols, May 22, 1867; Grinnell, *Fighting Cheyennes*, 254–58; Hyde, *Life of George Bent*, 263–65.

[11] Grinnell, *Fighting Cheyennes*, 254–55; Hyde, *Life of George Bent*, 263–64.

a profile as possible, because the soldiers were maintaining a constant fire at their positions. Finally Lone Bear told the others that the firing was too intense and they must get to the far bank as quickly as possible or they would all be shot. They made a sudden dash across the river's channel, but just as they reached the south bank, Lone Bear was shot and killed. The other three retreated from the soldiers, who were now wading the river and firing wildly. Eagle's Nest suddenly began to run toward some sand dunes about a mile south of the river. Plenty of Horses called for him to stay with the others, but he either did not hear or chose not to return. Several of the soldiers, upon reaching the south bank, pursued and killed Eagle's Nest just as he reached the sand hills. The two who survived the dash from the island, Plenty of Horses and Big Wolf, made their way along the south bank of the Arkansas amid a hail of bullets and hid in the brush and high grass. Unable to see them, the soldiers were afraid to charge and contented themselves with laying down a heavy fire in the area where they thought they were hiding. Big Wolf was struck and injured in the shoulder, but Plenty of Horses stayed with him, and when darkness came, the soldiers withdrew and the two men reached the sand hills. They were later joined by Pawnee Man and Wolf Walks in the Middle, and the four eventually made it back to Black Kettle's village on the Cimarron.[12]

When the four young men reached Black Kettle's camp, they told their story to the people, including George Bent, who was visiting and trading with them. Major Cooper's report of the skirmish, as might be expected, told a rather different story. He stated that when the Indians were first observed, he sent 1st Lt. Matthew Berry and twenty troopers of C Company to demand their surrender, at which time the Indians opened fire. In the fight that followed, the Indians, who he conceded were on foot, "fought until death," and all six who were seen were killed. One soldier was wounded and one horse killed, according to Cooper's report. Examination of the bodies, he said, proved the dead Indians to be "Cheyenne and Sioux on the warpath. Probably spies." The property captured consisted of "one rifle, one pistol, two bows and quivers, three blankets, one pair of moccasins, one belt, and one powder flask, and one chief's headdress." The headdress, presumably a warbonnet, was likely that of Lone Bear, a courageous warrior but not a chief. The Sioux had all moved north to the Republican, however, so none were among the six, and neither were the young men spies, nor was there anything at the trail crossing to spy

---

[12] Grinnell, *Fighting Cheyennes*, 255–58; Hyde, *Life of George Bent*, 264–65.

on, other than the troops sent to block Cheyennes from crossing the river. And if the weapons captured from six men included no more than one rifle, one pistol, and two bows and quivers, it would hardly justify the conclusion that they were "on the warpath."[13]

How Major Cooper came to report all six of the young men killed is speculative. The troopers who pursued them, having killed two, were likely fearful of charging the positions of the four men they believed to be concealed in the scrub brush and tall grasses along the river, and contented themselves with shooting randomly into the area where they thought they were. When darkness fell, their task no doubt appeared hopeless. Wishing to return to camp for both their evening meal and safety, they may well have simply reported that they killed all six. It is also possible that Major Cooper, not wanting to admit that two companies of well-armed mounted soldiers failed to capture or kill six Cheyenne warriors on foot and lightly armed, exaggerated his report. But whatever the truth of the matter, Cooper's report was mild by comparison with Henry M. Stanley's newspaper account. Writing from Fort Dodge on April 25, following the arrival of General Hancock's expeditionary force, he reported on what he called a "spirited and exciting little affair." According to his story, an Indian shot at a cavalryman who was grazing his horse. The soldier raced back to camp and gave the alarm, after which Major Cooper sent out a scouting party that was soon fired on from an island in the Arkansas River. A few return volleys made the island untenable, and the Indians fled, throwing their rifles into the river. Stanley continued: "The soldiers crossed over after them and commenced an exciting chase of ten miles right into the heart of the Indian country, which seemed to be alive with the red men; and not until six Indians had been killed did they cease the pursuit. On inspection of the bodies there was found in the girdle of one of them the scalp of a woman with long auburn hair attached to it, which so angered the soldiers that they refused to bury the dead." The six dead men, according to Stanley, were part of an advance party of the main body of Cheyennes and were painted for war and stripped to the "buff." Moreover, he claimed that when their scouts failed to return, the main body crossed farther upriver, but a raiding party returned on the night of April 24 and robbed the stage station of eleven mules.[14]

Stanley's story was largely fanciful. The main body of Dog Soldiers and

---

[13] W. Cooper to H. Douglass, April 19, 1867, Fort Dodge, MC619-R563; H. Douglass to W. S. Mitchell, AAAG, April 19, 1867, MC619-R563; Chandler, *Of GarryOwen in Glory*, 3; Heitman, *Historical Register and Dictionary*, 214; Hyde, *Life of George Bent*, 265, 265n19.
[14] Stanley, *My Early Travels*, 50–51.

southern Sutaio was headed northwest beyond the Smoky Hill, not south of the Arkansas. There was no chase "into the heart of the Indian country," and, so far as is known, no woman's scalp was recovered. About the only accurate part of the story was that six male Indians had been seen, and the rest was fiction. Like Stanley, General Hancock did not learn of the encounter until after his arrival at Fort Dodge. His report in the main followed that of Major Cooper, except that he had the Indians "skulking" about the Seventh Cavalry bivouac near the cattle herd, apparently intent on running off the cattle. That would be an unlikely target for six men on foot, and it is possible that the horse and mule herd of the stage station, their real objective, was nearby and the soldiers simply mistook their purpose. Hancock also thought the six young men to be "runners" for their people and carefully reported that it was an interpreter who demanded their surrender. The response, he said, was that the Cheyennes opened fire on the troopers, precipitating the ensuing fight. Cooper made no mention of an interpreter (though there was a guide), and it is unlikely that one would have been available for Lieutenant Berry and his twenty men. This facet of the report was probably crafted to deflect criticism from the eastern press and populace.[15]

When Hancock's order was given to Major Asbury and other post commanders on June 15, 1867, the encounter with the six young men at the Cimarron Crossing was still in the future. Back at the expedition camp on the north branch of Pawnee Fork, meanwhile, there was a great deal of activity. The infantry companies, artillery battery, cavalry detachment, company wagons, and wagon trains all were involved in striking camp and moving across the newly completed bridge to the new Camp 14, opposite the Indian villages. The Cheyenne and Oglala villages were now under the guard of the infantry companies that replaced Captain Barnitz's cavalry squadron, with orders that nothing be disturbed or removed. These orders were likely a matter of creating a written record to protect the expedition and its commander from criticism by eastern newspapers and humanitarian groups. Custer and his men had already engaged in large-scale looting, as had Barnitz and his two cavalry companies while actively "guarding" the villages. And now the infantry companies appear to have done likewise, or at least made no effort to stop the plundering. As Henry Stanley reported:

> Detachments of infantry guard the camps to prevent spoliation by the troops. But in spite of the strict guard kept, the "boys in blue" are continually carry-

---

[15] Hancock to Nichols, May 22, 1867.

ing away momentoes of their bloodless victory, such as stiff buffalo robes, dog skins, calumets, tomahawks, war clubs, beadwork, moccasins, and we saw one officer of the artillery carrying off a picininny Indian pup which looked very forlorn. Arrows and knives are picked up by the dozen, and also little dolls, which have been the gratification of the papooses.

Though many of the larger items, such as buffalo hides, were quickly discarded as too cumbersome to keep, little attention seems to have been paid to General Hancock's orders, and the "strict guard."[16]

Relations between the military and the Office of Indian Affairs were often strained, and most high-ranking officers regarded the bureau and its officials with open contempt. There had been an uneasy truce between Hancock and the two agents accompanying the expedition, Jesse Leavenworth and Edward W. Wynkoop. The agents had tried to act in harmony and advise Hancock to this time, but following the announcement of his intention to burn the villages, this spirit of cooperation evaporated. Colonel Leavenworth wrote a letter to Indian Commissioner N. G. Taylor, reporting the expedition's encounters with the Indians to date, including Hancock's insistence on going to the villages against all advice. And sometime later that day, Colonel Wynkoop wrote a letter to General Hancock, strongly urging him not to burn the two camps. Hancock gave as his reason for wanting to destroy them his belief that the Indians had fled from him from a sense of guilt over past offenses, a fear of retribution for them, and an intention to make war. He believed that destruction of the villages was the appropriate vengeance for their "treachery." In his letter Wynkoop referred to his lengthy study of the Indian character and, based on it, concluded their flight was "caused by fear alone." So far as he could judge, "they met us at first with a determination to have a peaceful talk, at such a distance from their village as would make their women and children satisfied that no danger need be apprehended by them." But, he wrote, the movement of troops toward the villages terrified those women and children, causing them to flee with "such movable property as they could gather." Wynkoop respectfully requested that the villages not be destroyed, and expressed his belief that to do so would cause an Indian outbreak of the most serious nature and that there was no evidence that these Cheyennes deserved such a severe punishment.[17]

---

[16] Stanley, *My Early Travels*, 39.

[17] Hancock to Sherman, April 15, 1867; Leavenworth to Taylor, April 15, 1867, U.S. House, "Difficulties with Indian Tribes," 7:13–14; E. W. Wynkoop to W. S. Hancock, April 15, 1867, AGO, LR, 1867, NA, MC619-R562; Wynkoop to Murphy, September 14, 1867, 312–13.

Hancock had not requested an opinion from the Indian agents, especially one that ran counter to his own judgment and desires. But General Smith and several of the other officers also opposed destruction of the villages, and on substantially the same grounds. Adding to Hancock's quandary, Tom Kincaid and his companion arrived at Camp 14 on the morning of April 17. Kincaid was bearing Custer's letter of April 16 that reported no known Indian hostilities and expressed his opinion that the Indians' flight was due to fear alone. For a time Hancock seemed to waiver and lose his resolve. Whereas at noon on April 15 he told General Sherman that he had "determined to burn their village, and destroy everything they have left behind," in his next report on Wednesday, April 17, he stated:

> We have evidently frightened these Indians badly. We have as yet heard of no hostilities by them, either on the Arkansas or Smoky Hill. I shall remain here two days, or until the 19th, possibly the 20th, to hear again from the Arkansas mail route and the Smoky Hill, to learn whether they have commenced hostilities or not, holding in the meantime their camp in my hands. The Sioux and Cheyenne camps being together on the same ground, it would hardly be practicable, with our information, to destroy one without destroying the other. The question is really, whether we shall destroy both, or either, or which. Considering the uncertainty as to the truth, I think it is better to wait; for if I destroy their camps without its being clearly understood by the Indians generally that it was for sufficient cause, I shall inspire alarm among the Indians, and may not be able to see them. I think we have provocation sufficient to destroy the camp: still we may not have, and by burning it we will certainly inaugurate a war which might otherwise have been avoided. General Smith is averse to burning the camp. I have concluded not to do so unless I hear of hostile acts in my vicinity before I leave. It may be that we may regret not having destroyed this camp, but it is better to be on the safe side.

Hancock added that "the little Cheyenne girl" stated she was "outraged" by a young Indian, probably the last to leave the camp. He would learn all about that, he said, when "Gunier" (Guerrier), the Cheyenne interpreter, returned with Custer. Since the girl appeared to be mentally impaired and spoke only Cheyenne, in the absence of a Cheyenne interpreter it seems improbable that she could have been the source of the information that an Indian perpetrated the deed. And as it was later determined, the last Indian to leave the Cheyenne village was the venerable White Head, one of the older council chiefs of the Óhméséheso band of Cheyennes, who reported that at that time the girl was unhurt.[18]

---

[18] Hancock to Sherman, April 15, 1867; W. S. Hancock to W. T. Sherman, April 17, 1867, AGO, LR, NA, MC619-R562, and in U.S. House, "Difficulties with Indian Tribes," 7:65; Stanley, "British Journalist," 302.

Hancock's letter of April 17 shows clearly that the protests of the Indian agents, and especially the advice of General Smith and Custer's report, were undermining his determination to destroy the villages. As a combat commander he had proven his ability to stand fast in the face of imminent peril at Gettysburg. But now he faced an adversary he did not understand. He had made no effort to study their culture, character, or art of war, despite the obvious need for such by the commander of a department inhabited by warlike Plains Indians. He vacillated between thinking the Indians hostile and intending war on one hand and frightened and fleeing from him on the other. He believed they had given him provocation sufficient to destroy the villages by reason of their flight and failure to meet with him, but then admitted doubt. One thing he did understand, it seems, was the distinction between the Cheyenne and Oglala villages, which were organized in separate camp circles. And he was aware that to destroy them without good reason would probably cause the other tribes to flee in fear, making further councils unlikely. More important, he knew it could bring on a war that might otherwise be avoided. For the moment he was beset with doubt and indecision. This indecision convinced Colonel Leavenworth that Hancock would not destroy the village, and he reported such to Commissioner Taylor on April 17.[19]

That same morning, April 17, Hancock wrote a letter of instructions to General Smith, relating his desires of Custer and the Seventh Cavalry, a copy of which he included with his report to Sherman along with Wynkoop's letter of protest. He wanted Smith to order Custer south to Fort Dodge "as soon as practicable," because he intended to go south of the Arkansas for ten days, and if all of the forage and subsistence was consumed while waiting for Custer, this plan would be rendered impossible for lack of timely resupply. Hancock believed the expedition could remain at Camp 14 for another two days, possibly three, but after that would have no forage for Custer's horses when he rejoined them. He then expressed his belief that the Cheyennes had gone south while the Sioux had gone north to the Republican out of fear. Smith was to inform Custer that there was "such doubt about the propriety of destroying" the Indian camps, based on their existing information, that if he came that way and found them intact, he was to leave them untouched unless he had met resistance. In that case he was to burn them, "lodge poles and all." Hancock said that he could hardly determine whether or not abandonment of the villages was caused by panic until he had heard of hostilities by them, in

---

[19] Leavenworth to Taylor, April 17, 1867, U.S. House, "Difficulties with Indian Tribes," 7:14.

which event he would regret not destroying them. The agent for the Cheyennes, he stated, earnestly urged him not to burn them, believing that would have a bad effect on them and cause other tribes he desired to meet with to flee from him. Custer was to report immediately where he was, what news there was, whether he had heard of hostilities, which way he intended to go, and what he would do. It was most likely Smith's orders to Custer, based on these instructions, that were carried by Thomas Kincaid and Lieutenant Sheldon and, to Custer's frustration, held at Downer Station by the exhausted Sheldon.[20]

Following the move to Camp 14, the expedition's encampment on Heth's branch of the Pawnee Fork settled into the daily routine typical of any military installation on the plains in that day. Hunters went out to secure fresh meat daily, and soldiers policed their camp, observed the daily sequence of bugle calls directing their activities, drilled, and no doubt were bored. There must have been continuing speculation as to the whereabouts and intentions of the Indians and the Seventh Cavalry and what the soldiers would be called upon to do next. Then, on the morning of April 18, the speculation came to an end. Into the expedition's camp rode a corporal and five men led by a Delaware scout, bearing Custer's report of the previous evening. It detailed what was learned from the stage company employees at Downer Station—the burning of Lookout Station and the killing of the three men serving there, the running off of eight horses and four mules, and the taking of livestock from Stormy Hollow Station. More importantly for Hancock, it ascribed these actions to "the same Indians who deserted their lodges on Pawnee Fork." It was what he was looking for and, in his view, all that was needed to take action against the Cheyenne and Oglala villages.[21]

Within hours of receiving Custer's dispatch, Hancock issued a special field order for the destruction of the Cheyenne and Oglala villages.[22] It

---

[20] Hancock to Smith, April 17, 1867, and in U.S. House, "Difficulties with Indian Tribes," 7:65–66.

[21] Custer to Weir, April 17, 1867; Hyde, *Life of George Bent*, 262n15.

[22] There is mystery concerning this special field order (SFO). The copy in the records of the Department of the Missouri is dated April 18, 1867, and designated SFO No. 13 from Camp 15. That forwarded to the Division of the Missouri and on to Army Headquarters was dated April 17 and designated SFO No. 12 from Camp 14 (the correct camp). These numbers were altered in 1870 by order of the secretary of the army to conform to the records of the Department of the Missouri. It may be that the date of the former was changed to make it appear it was issued after receipt of Custer's dispatch blaming the attack on Lookout Station on the Indians from the Pawnee Fork villages, and the SFO and camp numbers were mistakenly advanced as well. Special Field Order No. 13, Department of the Missouri in the Field, April 18, 1867, MC619-R563; Special Field Order No. 12, Department of the Missouri in the Field, April 17, 1867, AGO, LR, NA, MC619-R562.

recited that it was to be done as punishment for the bad faith shown by the peoples occupying the camps, a reference to their flight and failure to return, and as a chastisement for the murders and depredations committed by the two tribes since his command arrived at that point. Presumably this referred to the burning of the Lookout stage station, the killing of the crew, and the running off of livestock. The order directed that the villages themselves would "be utterly destroyed" but that all property within the village, "such as tools, camp equipage, etc., will be preserved and taken up as captured property." General Davidson was ordered to make "an accurate inventory of all species of property within the village previous to its destruction," while General Smith was charged with implementation of the order. Hancock, who had been frustrated to this point by the flight of the Indians, would now vent his anger on their lodges and property.[23]

The actual burning of the villages was deferred until the morning of April 19, probably because of the time required to complete the "accurate inventory" the special field order called for. General Davidson and his assigned soldiers would have been busy most of the afternoon going through each lodge in the two villages. Agent Wynkoop was likewise making a careful inventory. Hancock's adjutant issued orders to the officer of the guard on April 17 to allow Wynkoop to examine the lodges and the property remaining in them and also to provide him "all facilities and assistance you can" to compel return of looted property and to see that all property was properly inventoried. It is doubtful that much, if any, of the looted materials were actually returned, since the Seventh Cavalry officers and men would have carefully packed away the items they desired to keep prior to their departure. For the most part, looting would have been limited to articles handcrafted by Cheyennes and Oglalas and of interest to Anglos: probably those with beadwork or quillwork, such as parfleches, and items small enough to be comfortably retained. Indian saddles and bridles might well have been coveted but were too large to be retained and carried away with the troops, except for a few of the officers.[24]

General Davidson and his assistants made two separate inventories, both based on the April 18 count. One, signed by General Davidson and certified as the official copy by Capt. W. G. Mitchell, acting assistant adjutant general of the expedition, was undated and made no mention of the camp. The other had Davidson's imprimatur but was not certified.

---

[23] Special Field Order No. 13.
[24] Mitchell to Officer of the Guard, April 17, 1867, MC535-R1354.

Upon receiving Custer's dispatch of April 17, 1867, advising that Indians, believed to be Sioux and others unknown, had burned Lookout Station on the stage line, run off the livestock, and killed the three-man crew, Hancock ordered the Cheyenne and Oglala villages destroyed. This was done on the morning of April 19, after inventories of the contents had been completed. Three companies of the Thirty-seventh Infantry dismantled the lodges, placing them in six large piles that were then set ablaze. The fire spread across the grasslands to the north, propelled by a stiff south wind. This sketch of the event was made by Theodore R. Davis to illustrate his story appearing in the June 8, 1867, issue of *Harper's Weekly*.

Stating that it originated at the expedition's headquarters in the field, it was dated April 18, 1867, signed by Hancock, and provided for the "Lieutenant General commanding the Division of the Missouri" (General Sherman). Although organized in a somewhat different manner, the two do not vary concerning their major points. There is some disparity in the remarks, that certified by Mitchell reciting that six ponies were found running loose near the village, while Hancock's stated that four ponies "were found loose in the camp" and added that about twenty-five lodges had been removed when the village was abandoned.[25]

Colonel Wynkoop also prepared an inventory, which contained some surprising discrepancies with those prepared by General Davidson.

---

[25] U.S. House. "Difficulties with Indian Tribes," 7:71, 95.

Wynkoop's inventory listed 132 lodges in the Cheyenne village, instead of the 111 shown on those of the military, and gave significantly different numbers for many of the lesser items. Wynkoop also listed fifteen sets of lodge poles standing but uncovered (without lodge covers) in the Cheyenne camp and five sets in the Oglala camp, indicating that the owners of those lodges had taken the covers with them. These may represent the approximate twenty-five lodges removed, but more likely are additional. Custer saw the deep imprint of lodge poles at stream crossings during his pursuit of the Cheyennes, and those probably represented the twenty-five missing lodges. No one can say with certainty why the military lists omitted the standing sets of lodge poles, but the probability is that Wynkoop, as an Indian agent with much more knowledge and experience with Indians than Hancock and his men, attached a different significance to them than did the soldiers. Dr. Coates used the Wynkoop inventory while recording the camps' destruction in his diary of the expedition. But regardless of the accuracy of the several inventories, it is clear that Hancock either confiscated or destroyed a considerable quantity of very valuable Indian property.[26]

Destruction of the two villages took place on the morning of April 19. Three companies of the Thirty-seventh Infantry pulled down the lodges and made six large piles of the poles and covers. Onto these were thrown the buffalo hides, saddles, furs, and other combustible items found in the lodges or around the camps that had not already been taken as souvenirs or confiscated as enemy property by General Hancock's order. Forty lodges, undoubtedly from those not subjected to the cutting and therefore most likely from the Cheyenne camp, were retained at Hancock's direction.[27] He intended to recruit Indian scouts during his projected council with Comanche, Kiowa, Arapahoe, and Plains Apache chiefs at Fort Dodge, and the lodges would be provided for their use. It seems not to have occurred to him that his actions in destroying the Cheyenne and Lakota villages would convince the Comanches and Plains Apaches that they should avoid councils with him altogether, and would make the Kiowas and Arapahoes so nervous and apprehensive that they would be reluctant to cooperate with him. In addition to the forty lodges, all "of the serviceable axes, camp ket-

---

[26] Wynkoop to Taylor, April 24, 1867, U.S. House, "Difficulties with Indian Tribes," 7:29; Kennedy, *On the Plains*, 88.

[27] Stanley later wrote that forty-five lodges were kept and subsequently stored at Fort Dodge after failure to enlist any Indian scouts there. But General Hancock ordered forty retained and reported such, so forty is probably the correct number. See Stanley, "British Journalist," 303.

tles, hatchets, crowbars, etc., etc., of which there were a great number, were ordered to be taken up by the Quartermaster Department as captured property." According to Theodore Davis, a number of items found in the villages had been taken from the bodies of soldiers killed in the Fetterman fight near Fort Phil Kearney. That was probably either repetition of a rumor heard from soldiers or an attempt at sensationalism for the benefit of the reading public. None of the inventories reflected this, nor did General Hancock or any of the other officers indicate anything of the kind in their official reports, aside from Hancock's speculation that some of the Indians must have been there and felt guilty, causing them to flee. The Dog Soldiers, the southern Sutaio, White Head's Ôhméséheso band, and the Kiyuksas were not in the north at that time, so it is clearly a fiction.[28]

The burning lodge poles, lodge covers, hides, and other items made a spectacular fire, filling the sky with great columns of black smoke and haze. Rising high above the surrounding plains and moving rapidly northward, propelled by the prevailing south wind, the smoke was seen by Indian scouts who carried the news to their people. Sparks from the roaring flames were spread by the wind, setting fire to the grasses north of the village sites. With no firebreaks of any kind, the wildfire raced northward, probably not stopping until encountering a river or stream too broad to jump, most likely the Smoky Hill. In Stanley's flowery language, "Every green thing, and every dead thing that reared its head above the earth, was consumed, while the buffalo, the antelope, and the wolf fled in dismay from the destructive agent."[29]

The destroyed and confiscated Cheyenne and Oglala lodges and camp equipage, said General Hancock, "will be almost impossible for them to replace, at least for a long time." Stanley, probably taking his cue from Hancock, was even more specific: "The loss of these articles will be severely felt by the Indian tribes—Cheyennes and Sioux. It will require 3,000 buffaloes to be killed to procure enough hides to make their 'wigwams.' The whole outfit of an entire wigwam costs, on the average, one hundred dollars." Though placing a dollar value on a lodge and all of the items with which a family might equip it would be almost impossible, particularly concerning the labor-intensive components such as lodge covers, parfleches, and decorated furnishings and clothing, Stanley was not far

[28] Hancock to Nichols, May 22, 1867; *Harper's Weekly*, June 8, 1867, 57; Davis, "Summer on the Plains," 296; Leckie, *Military Conquest*, 45; Stanley, *My Early Travels*, 46; Utley, *Frontier Regulars*, 118.

[29] *Harper's Weekly*, June 8, 1867, 57; Stanley, *My Early Travels*, 46.

off the mark as to the number of animals required to provide the needed hides for the lodges. On average, most lodges required ten to twelve tanned and carefully worked buffalo hides. Davis was less certain than either Hancock or Stanley about how great a blow had been struck against the two tribes: "I have heard some estimates of the value of this property that were ludicrously large. The loss inflicted upon the Indians could easily be made good by them in a single summer." That would be asking a lot of a warrior's wife, already burdened with the other duties of raising a family, hunting wilding fruits and vegetables, preparing meals, making and maintaining clothing, as well as making and decorating the lodges and their furnishings. The truth is probably somewhere between the opposing views, but without question the loss to the Indians was severe.[30]

General Hancock wrote to General Sherman on the evening of April 18, prior to destruction of the villages, giving his thoughts on the current situation and how the Indians should be dealt with. Among other things he expressed his frustration with and dislike of the two Indian agents. On one hand, he bemoaned that the agents had not forced the Indians to make restitution for any depredations committed against whites entering their country, and on the other he stoutly assailed any thought of restoring the property he was about to destroy or making restitution to the Indians who suffered the loss. Later, in his formal report of the expedition, he related Wynkoop's reaction to the burning of the villages: "Colonel E. W. Wynkoop, U.S. Indian Agent was in my camp (he had accompanied me from Fort Larned) at the time of the burning of the village. I had explained to him my reasons for destroying them. They failed however to convince him of the propriety of doing so." The reasons Hancock gave to Wynkoop were probably those he gave to Sherman: that the Indians committed treachery by running away from him and not returning, that some must have been at the Fetterman fight and feared punishment, and that they had burned Lookout Station, killed its crew, and run off livestock. Other than Custer's speculation that the Indians from the Pawnee Fork villages had done it, Hancock at this time had no clear evidence of which tribe was responsible. However, it was well within the thinking of Civil War officers to destroy property and stores of enemies as a means of eliminating their will and ability to wage war.[31]

[30] Hancock to Nichols, May 22, 1867; Davis, "Summer on the Plains," 296; Stanley, *My Early Travels*, 46.
[31] W. S. Hancock to W. T. Sherman, April 18, 1867, AGO, LR, NA, MC619-R562; Hancock to Nichols, May 22, 1867

The villages on the Pawnee Fork were destroyed prior to the receipt of Custer's additional report of April 19, stating that the people from those villages could not have reached the Smoky Hill in time to perpetrate the attack on Lookout Station. The question of whether they did or did not make the attack (or, if not, who did) has plagued historians since that time. Custer made the startling statement that though those who were at Pawnee Fork on the day the expedition arrived on April 14 could not have done it, since it occurred on the next day, nevertheless "the act was committed with their knowledge and approval, which accounts for their hasty flight." This is nonsense. The Indians at the villages would have had no way of knowing who was in the vicinity of Lookout Station at that time or of communicating with them if they had. It is true that Cheyenne hunting parties were out searching for bison and other game near the Smoky Hill, but they would have no timely knowledge of Hancock's actions or of what their own people were doing. Communication with them would have taken longer than the time frame available, and the Indians were not intentionally looking for a fight with the army anyway. The Oglala men, women, and children left their village on the Pawnee Fork at the same time as the Cheyenne women and children and headed straight north, trying to reach the Republican River country. Their route would have taken them to crossings of the Smoky Hill and the stage road in the vicinity of Lookout and adjacent stations, and likely the "two heavy trails" observed by Custer and his men represented the bulk of those people. The Cheyennes, on the other hand, headed northwest, first along the Walnut, then the Smoky Hill, and finally the Saline and Solomon rivers. The men did not leave their village until dusk on April 14 and, after leaving diverse misleading trails, proceeded to the point on the Walnut where their women had been told to gather and await them. Then they would either return to the Pawnee Fork village if Hancock's force departed peacefully or, if not, move to the Solomon or to Beaver Creek in far northwestern Kansas to find safety and begin the laborious task of replacing their losses. It was this trail of the fleeing Cheyennes that Custer and the Seventh Cavalry followed, then lost, as they moved northwesterly far beyond and to the west of Downer Station.[32]

The Cheyennes' route took them well away from the site of the attack on Lookout Station, and Custer was close enough to see their signal fires and perhaps even the fires at their main camp about fifteen miles to his

---

[32] Custer to Weir, April 19, 1867.

northwest on the evening of April 15. Therefore they could not have had anything to do with attacks far to their east. On the other hand, the Kiyuksa Oglalas passed within easy striking distance of Lookout Station and those adjacent to it. In his "Nomad" letter of December 15, 1867, Custer claimed it was known that the attack on Lookout Station took place "before the Indians had deserted their village" and that, "as the two were hundreds of miles apart," it was not possible for them to have been the perpetrators. But this vindictive letter was written after Custer's court-martial at the insistence of General Hancock. Later, in *My Life on the Plains*, Custer reversed course and attributed the attack to the Indians fleeing from Pawnee Fork. And it is possible for the Kiyuksas to have done so. Far from being "hundreds of miles apart," the Lookout stage station on the Smoky Hill road was more nearly fifty miles to the northeast of the villages on the Pawnee. However, it is unlikely that most of the Kiyuksas would have been involved. They were fleeing northward with their women, children, and the old, burdened with what personal possessions they could carry, and with horses greatly weakened by the winter. The two heavy trails observed by Custer were probably those left by the main body of Lakotas, and they would not have wanted any kind of confrontation that might endanger their families. But this would not be true of hotheaded young warriors forming war parties to avenge their people for the actions of Hancock and his soldiers. They could have and probably did perpetrate some of the raids or attacks in the vicinity of their route to the north.[33]

While some of the raiding may have been the work of young Kiyuksa Oglala warriors, there is reason to believe they were not alone. The 140 or so Lakota lodges would have housed approximately 700 to 1,000 people, of whom well over half would have been women due to the high mortality rate among warrior-hunters. Of the 300 to 400 males likely present, perhaps a fourth would have been children or teenagers too young to fight, and a similar number too old to be active warriors. There were probably no more than 150 to 200 men in their camp capable of aggressive physical combat, and most of these would have remained with the main columns of their people to protect their families. Of course it did not take a large number of warriors to inflict a great deal of damage on small stage stations or similar white installations. The report at Downer Station was that small parties of Indians, believed to be Sioux, had been crossing the Smoky

---

[33] G. Custer, *My Life on the Plains*, 96–99; Dippie, *Nomad*, 38–39.

Hill road thirty to forty miles to the east during the day on April 16, heading north. Thirty to forty miles to the east of Downer would have been a corridor ten miles wide flanking Lookout Station, five miles on either side. It was apparently in that vicinity that Custer observed the two heavy trails, as he made no mention of them until his dispatch of April 19, after passing White Rock and Stormy Hollow stations and encamping at Lookout Station. These reports would also have the larger part of the Oglalas crossing the road the second day following their flight from the Pawnee Fork, and while Custer was pursuing the Cheyennes more than forty miles to the west.

Although some of the raiding along the Smoky Hill route at this time may well have been the work of Kiyuksa warriors, could others have been involved? Here the answer seems to be yes. A large war party of northern Oglalas, having heard of the new road the white men had pushed through along the Smoky Hill and flushed with their success in effectively closing the Bozeman Trail in Montana Territory to all but military traffic, reputedly came down from the northern plains to help clear the Smoky Hill country of whites. It is held among the Cheyennes that these Lakotas were the ones responsible for the attack on Lookout Station and others, and that is certainly possible. The report of a large war party of 800 passing White Rock station could well have been the northern Oglalas. Even allowing for the customary white exaggeration of Indian numbers, it was too large a party to have been Kiyuksas if the bulk of them crossed the Smoky Hill road in the vicinity of Lookout Station the following day. Although women were in the party, no mention was made of children or the elderly, and large war parties commonly had women with them to attend to the camping and cooking chores. It now seems unlikely that a definitive answer will ever be found to the question of who actually perpetrated the attack on Lookout Station on April 15, 1867. But one thing is clear. It was not the Cheyennes.[34]

As the smoke began to clear from the remains of the Cheyenne and Oglala lodges burned at the village site on Pawnee Fork that fateful day of April 19, 1867, General Hancock sat down and penned a brief note to General Sherman. "I have the honor," he began, "to inform you that we utterly destroyed the Sioux and Cheyenne village this morning. What property could not be burned—such as tools &c—we carried off." He

---

[34] Powell, *People of the Sacred Mountain*, 1:473.

enclosed a copy of General Davidson's inventory and reported that the old Sioux man and woman left behind, and the young girl found in the Cheyenne camp, would be taken to Fort Dodge. And, he advised, "I shall leave here for that post in the morning." With these few words General Hancock, evidently satisfied that he had inflicted well-deserved punishment on the two tribes for their "treachery," turned his attention from those Indians to the four other tribes whose leaders he intended to council with at Fort Dodge. The expedition would leave Camp 14 the following morning, marching south to the next intended council. During that march, in camp on April 21, Hancock would write a rambling letter of observations and instructions to General Smith. In it he concluded: "It is war against the Cheyennes and Sioux between the Arkansas and Platte, save some few small bands on the headwaters of the Republican."

This time Hancock spoke truth. It was to be war. Not because the Dog Soldiers, southern Sutaio, or Kiyuksa Oglalas sought it but because he had forced it on them. Just as the short grasses of the high plains were being scoured by the wildfire sparked by the burning Indian lodges, so would the Smoky Hill road, and all of the lands between the Platte and the Arkansas, now be swept by the winds of war.[35]

---

[35] W. S. Hancock to W. T. Sherman, April 19, 1867, AGO, LR, NA, MC619-R562; Hancock to Smith, April 21, 1867, at 1:00 A.M., AGO, LR, NA, MC619-R562.

On the morning of April 20, 1867, General Hancock marched the Expedition for the Plains, minus its Seventh Cavalry component, south to Fort Dodge for councils with Kiowa and Arapahoe chiefs. They reached it at 11:00 A.M. on April 22, going into camp along the Arkansas River where the Wet and Dry routes of the Santa Fe Trail joined, a half mile to the east of the post. Though Henry Stanley described it in glowing terms as a fortress surrounded by a moat, it was hardly that. This sketch by Theodore R. Davis shows its then appearance as a work in progress, with the old adobe buildings being replaced by new ones of native sandstone. The encampment of the Hancock expedition can be seen to the immediate right of center, just below the horizon. *Harper's Weekly,* May 25, 1867.

CHAPTER FOURTEEN

THE KIOWA AND ARAPAHOE COUNCILS

The expedition broke camp on the north branch of Pawnee Fork early on the morning of April 20, 1867, and began the march south to Fort Dodge. The long column of infantry, artillery, and the detachment of Seventh Cavalry troopers, each followed by their respective wagon trains, led the way, with the commissary train, quartermaster train, and train of pontoon bridges traveling in their wake. The expedition headquarters and the Headquarters of the Department of the Missouri in the Field were at the head of the column, and infantry detachments acted as the lead, flanking, and rear guards. The remaining Delawares and the white scouts rode well in advance, keeping a wary eye out for any possible attack by Indians, bearing in mind the anger no doubt generated by the destruction of the Cheyenne and Oglala camps. Angling a little west of south, they marched ten and a half miles before crossing the Middle, or Buckner's, Branch of the Pawnee Fork. From there they marched south-southwest across the rolling plains for nine miles to a point where they made their next camp, Camp 15, at the base of a low ridge.[1]

Near midnight on April 20 Tom Kincaid arrived in camp, bearing the latest dispatch from Custer. Kincaid, though exhausted when he arrived at Custer's camp on Big Creek, rode another twenty hours to bring the report to General Smith. Smith immediately relayed a copy to General Hancock, who was clearly disturbed by the information it contained, exonerating the occupants of the Pawnee Fork villages from responsibility for the attack on Lookout Station. Within an hour Hancock wrote a letter to Smith in which he gave his thoughts on the future course of action for Custer, his exasperation with the quartermaster, how to deal with lack of

---

[1] Brown, *March Journal*, April 20, 1867; Hancock to Nichols, May 22, 1867.

forage for Custer's animals and subsistence for his troops, and his continuing belief in the guilt of the Cheyennes and Oglalas. Disregarding Custer's report that the attack on Lookout Station took place on the April 15, he placed it on the sixteenth and attributed it to "advanced parties" (the young men who were off hunting buffalo) who "could therefore readily have been on the Smoky Hill at the time of the massacre." Possibly recognizing that this was a flimsy basis for a decision to destroy the villages and go to war, he added: "But at any rate there was sufficient time for them to have reached the Smoky Hill from the Indian village after we arrived there, in season to have committed the murders and burning at Lookout Station, as we *know* that the main body of them evacuated the village at least 12 hours previous to General Custer's leaving." This ignored the fact that it was the Cheyenne women, children, old, and infirm that left first and constituted the "main body" of their tribe. It also overlooked Custer's report that he was hard on the heels of the fleeing Cheyennes until they were well to the west of Downer Station and thus nowhere near Lookout Station.[2]

Hancock's letter to Smith was likely in part a pulling together of his ideas on how to explain this situation to General Sherman. But it also had a more thoughtful side in developing a plan for Custer's future operations. He approved of Custer's decision not to rejoin the rest of the expedition and suggested that he focus on pursuing the Indians northward from the Smoky Hill and ensuring the safety of the coach runs along the Smoky Hill road. This, he said, could be done by placing infantrymen in the coaches. He recommended that Custer coordinate with Capt. Myles W. Keogh, commanding at Fort Wallace, to ensure the safety of the mail run to Denver. Hancock also stated his intention either to meet the Comanches and Kiowas at Fort Dodge, if they were there, or to go south of the Arkansas if necessary in order to form a coalition with them against the Cheyennes and Oglalas. Then he said he expected to march to Fort Hays via Fort Larned and to reach the former post in about ten days. After voicing his displeasure with Lieutenant Sheldon for failing to send the earlier orders to Custer with Kincaid, he suggested that Smith send his orders to Custer the following morning by one or two messengers, two of the Delawares, and four to six dragoons (cavalrymen), bearing in mind Custer's recommendation.[3]

---

[2] Hancock to Smith, April 21, 1867.
[3] Ibid.; Hancock to Nichols, May 22, 1867

General Smith sent his orders to Custer as directed during the morning of Sunday, April 21. The order was much more succinct than Hancock's rambling letter but covered all of the important points:

> By General Field Order No. 12 you are temporarily assigned to command from Harker west on the Smoky Hill Route. This Order is not to be construed as confining you to that line. You are to act as you deem best from the information in your possession. If not otherwise employed, give such assistance as you may be able, in re-establishing the stage line. For this purpose, infantry may perhaps be used to advantage inside the coaches. Direct the Commanding Officers of Posts as to the part they are to perform in this matter.

After listing the provisions made for Custer's resupply, Smith added: "War is to be waged against the Sioux and Cheyenne Indians between the Arkansas and Platte, except some small bands near the headwaters of the Republican, concerning which further developments are to be awaited."[4]

The expedition troops departed Camp 15 during the morning of April 21 and were promptly misled by their white guides, who professed to know the country but were themselves apparently quite lost. They wasted several hours as they were led first northwest, then south-southwest, then west, then east, followed by south, until at last they struck a trail that led them westerly toward the stone quarries used for construction of the permanent buildings at Fort Dodge. They went into camp in an oxbow on the north bank of the South, or Shaff's, Branch of Pawnee Fork. Their new camp, Camp 16, was later found to be only twelve miles northeast of Fort Dodge.[5]

Following establishment of Camp 16, General Hancock sat down to pen a new report to Sherman. It began cautiously, relating the lack of forage Custer encountered at Fort Hays, the failures of the Quartermaster Department, and the freshets, or flash flooding of streams, from spring rains that he claimed were thwarting pursuit of the Indians. He told of his decision to keep Custer in the Smoky Hill region to protect the mail and stagecoach runs, the possible present whereabouts of the Cheyennes and Oglalas, the current state of growth of the native grasses, and his plans to visit the Comanches and Kiowas to forge a coalition. Finally he addressed the question of the attack on Lookout Station. Clearly he had given the matter considerable thought since his letter to General Smith and took a somewhat broader approach in the letter to Sherman:

----

[4] A. J. Smith to G. A. Custer, April 21, 1867, AGO, LR, NA, MC619-R562; W. S. Hancock to W. T. Sherman, April 21, 1867, AGO, LR, NA, MC 619-R562.
[5] Brown, *March Journal*, April 22, 1867; Hancock to Nichols, May 22, 1867.

General Custer thinks that the Indians who committed the outrages on the Smoky Hill are not those who remained in the village when we arrived at it. He left on Monday morning, the 15th, at 5:00 A.M.—the last Indians to leave the village started at 10 or 11 the night before, and all had gone but a rear guard of warriors at 3 P.M. of the day when we encamped near it, and it is very probable that a good many left the previous night. The depredation occurred on the 15th. It is, from the Indian village to Downer's Station—by the direct route about forty two miles—from the same point in a direct line to Lookout Station, where the outrage was committed, is about 50 miles, so that it is possible that even the latest to leave the village might have been of the party who were at Lookout Station, although it does not seem to me to be of much importance, for I am satisfied that the Indian village was a nest of conspirators.

This letter is puzzling. Here Hancock had many of the Indian warriors leaving their camps the day prior to his arrival there. But earlier, on April 15, he reported to Sherman that he had met what he thought to be nearly all of the fighting men of the Cheyennes on the afternoon of April 14, the day of his arrival, and that there were probably 500 Cheyenne and Lakota warriors in front of him. While the Oglala warriors left with their women and children that afternoon, the Cheyenne warriors remained in their camp, and it was their reported departure at nightfall that enraged Hancock and caused him to send Custer and the Seventh Cavalry to surround the village. If Sherman noted this obvious disparity in Hancock's reporting of the Indian flight, and he probably did, he made no mention of it in his later communications with either Hancock or army headquarters.[6]

In his letter to Sherman, Hancock painted the Indians, not as a village of people fearing his approach and the possibility of another Sand Creek Massacre, but rather as a "nest of conspirators." He made no mention about what the conspiracy was and had no reliable information, but it was his belief they intended to make war on whites entering their country. They had been doing this anyway, in a doomed effort to keep the intruders out and retain their homeland. Hancock also suggested taking custody of the "Sioux and Cheyennes reported friendly near the Platte," placing them near military posts, and holding them hostage for the actions of their relatives. Such an act would have been a clear violation of the treaties the government claimed to have with the Indians, to say nothing of the morality of it. Then, changing the subject abruptly, he reported that he had failed to reach Fort Dodge that day because high wind and dust made it difficult for the infantry, that the courier Kincaid had reported

---

[6] Hancock to Sherman, April 21, 1867.

being chased and fired on by Indians on April 18 and 19, and that the quarrymen from Fort Dodge had been fired on by Indians a week earlier. He offered to meet with Sherman at Fort Harker on May 10 if he intended to be there. Enclosed with the letter was a copy of Custer's April 19 report, along with General Smith's April 21 instructions to Custer.[7]

On April 22 the expedition broke camp in the early morning and, angling southwest and following the quarrymen's and woodcutters' trail, reached Fort Dodge at 11:00 A.M., making their new camp, Camp 17, a half mile east of the post along the banks of the Arkansas River. The fort, established on April 10, 1865, was a half mile to the west of the western junction of the Wet and Dry routes of the Santa Fe Trail and occupied the former camping grounds at that point used by those traveling the trail. A stage station, Adkins Ranch, built on the site in 1863, was destroyed by hostile Comanches and Kiowas in 1864 as a part of their continuing effort to prevent whites from maintaining any kind of permanent presence in the region. This led to a decision by Maj. Gen. Grenville M. Dodge, then commanding the Department of the Missouri, to expand the military presence on the Santa Fe Trail. On March 23, 1865, he suggested to Col. James H. Ford, commander of the District of the Upper Arkansas, that a new post be established in the area of old Fort Atkinson. The site selected was occupied on April 10, 1865, and named Fort Dodge to honor the general.[8]

At first the new fort consisted of tents, dugouts, and sod buildings, all of which proved highly inadequate due to the high winds on the plains, the spring rains, annual flooding of the Arkansas River, and other climatic factors. One year after its founding, in April 1866, the post commandant reported the quarters and other structures inadequate and requested permission to begin construction of new barracks, stables, and other buildings. Permission was granted, provided that construction be accomplished with materials available in the area, and necessary labor performed by the troops. A stone quarry was discovered in the area, and departmental headquarters granted permission to hire stonemasons. During the summer and fall of 1866 a new quartermaster's storehouse and a bakery were completed, and a hospital and barracks begun. Work on two new barracks, along with other buildings, commenced the following spring, and when the Expedition for the Plains arrived, the post was a beehive of construction activity but still very much a work in progress. Most of the

---

[7] Ibid.

[8] Brown, *March Journal*, April 22, 1867; Hancock to Nichols, May 22, 1867; Oliva, *Fort Dodge*, 17–19.

soldiers and civilian workers still lived in dugouts, sod and adobe structures, and tents. Nevertheless, for reasons that defy understanding, Stanley wrote admiringly of it: "The old fort in which the garrison resides is surrounded by embankments with sallyports, moat, and wooden drawbridges. Some former commander evidently bestowed great care on it, and it has been planned with an amount of skill that was unexpected in the middle of the plains, and the fort is kept as neat as possible. The approaches to it are commanded by a battery of four howitzers." This mysterious bit of journalistic hyperbole must have been intended to stimulate the imaginations of eastern readers, for it possessed little of the truth.[9]

Though hardly impressive as a military post, arrival of the expedition did bring out the best Fort Dodge then had to offer a visiting major general. Hancock was greeted with a fifteen-gun salute while the garrison, turned out in their best uniforms, presented arms as the general inspected them. "Hancock," wrote Stanley, "seemed pleased with the manner of his reception, and paid great attention to the soldierly appearance of the men." After the formalities, General Hancock met with Major Douglass at post headquarters and received the report of the alleged killing of six Cheyenne warriors at the Cimarron Crossing of the Arkansas three days earlier. While he was meeting with Douglass, the troops of the expedition moved off to the east, following the Santa Fe Trail, and went into camp along the river a half mile from the fort. The rest of the day was spent in organizing the camp, tending to the horses, and resting the troops; the infantry especially were fatigued by the long march and by facing the incessant south wind. That night a little snow fell, but being too warm at ground level, it melted on contact with the earth. The snow quickly turned to a light rain that continued through the remainder of the night.[10]

The purpose of the march south to Fort Dodge was to meet with the chiefs of the Comanches, Kiowas, Plains Apaches, and southern bands of Arapahoes. Earlier their agents, Jesse Leavenworth and Edward Wynkoop, had sent messages requesting that they appear for a council with General Hancock. In anticipation of this, on April 21 Major Douglass sent orders to Maj. Wyckliffe Cooper, directing that he return to Fort Dodge with Company B of his squadron, since large numbers of Arapahoes and Kiowas were expected. He was to leave Lieutenant Berry and Company C at the Cimarron Crossing to continue watching for

[9] Oliva, *Fort Dodge*, 21–25; Oliva, *Soldiers on the Santa Fe Trail*, 171–75; Stanley, *My Early Travels*, 48.
[10] W. S. Hancock to W. T. Sherman, April 24, 1867, MC619-R563; Hancock to Nichols, May 22, 1867;
    Stanley, *My Early Travels*, 47–48.

While at Fort Dodge, Theodore R. Davis sketched this scene in the sutler's store. Such stores were operated by civilians under contract with the army and were in fact trading posts dealing in everything from food and drink to supplies needed by soldiers, civilian trappers, hunters, guides, and travelers along the trails. As illustrated here, they also traded with the Indians. They were the precursors to the later post exchanges. *Harper's Weekly*, May 25, 1867.

Cheyennes trying to move south of the Arkansas. Both Cooper and Berry were cautioned to use care in distinguishing between the Cheyennes and Sioux on one hand, and the "friendly" Indians on the other. The latter were not to be molested, but Berry and his men were to make prisoners of any Cheyennes or Sioux they might encounter, using only the minimum force necessary. Unfortunately the burning of the Dog Soldier and southern Sutaio Cheyenne and Kiyuksa Oglala villages alarmed all the other southern Plains tribes to such an extent that they fled far south of the Arkansas—some to Bluff Creek, some to the Cimarron, and possibly some to the Canadian or the Washita. But the followers of the Kiowa chiefs Kicking Bird and Stumbling Bear remained on the Arkansas, and Major Douglass told Hancock of their willingness to come in and council with him. Moreover, the Arapahoe chief Little Raven had been camping near Fort Dodge waiting for Hancock and his troops to appear. But

At Fort Dodge, General Hancock held a council with three Kiowa chiefs who had come in as requested. Sketched by Theodore R. Davis, they are, from left to right, Atalie (the Man That Moves), Set-imkia (Stumbling Bear or Pushing Bear), and Tené-Angópte (Eagle That Strikes with Talons, called Kicking Bird by whites). *Harper's Weekly*, May 25, 1867.

he moved south a few days earlier, probably after receiving word of the happenings on the Pawnee Fork. The Comanche bands that roamed the country between the Arkansas and Red rivers, and the Plains Apaches, had all fled in haste after hearing what befell the Cheyennes and were now well to the southeast on the Salt Plains. Under these circumstances the best Major Douglass could do was arrange a council with Kicking Bird and Stumbling Bear to take place the following morning.[11]

The council was held at Fort Dodge on April 23 in a Sibley tent and was attended by Tené-Angópte (Eagle That Strikes with Talons, or Kicking Bird, as he was called by whites), Set-imkia (Stumbling Bear or Pushing Bear), Atalie (the Man That Moves), half brother of the late chief Dohásän (Little Bluff or Little Mountain), and several warriors. At the time there were six principal Kiowa subtribes or divisions, the Kata, or Biters (the

---

[11] Hancock to Sherman, April 24, 1867; Hancock to Nichols, May 22, 1867; Wallace to Cooper, April 21, 1867, MC619-R563; *Harper's Weekly*, May 25, 1867, 328–29; Stanley, *My Early Travels*, 51.

largest division); the Kogui, or Elks' the Kiagwu, or Kiowa proper; the Kingep, or Big Shields; the Senett, or Thieves (the Kiowa-Apache); and the Kongtalyùi, or Children of Sinda, the great mythical hero of the Kiowas. Each of these divisions held a recognized place in the tribal camping circle.[12] The divisions, in turn, were broken down into a total of ten to twenty bands, some very small, usually based on kinship, but fluid in character and much influenced by economic and political factors. Each of the bands roamed over its own favorite territory but in general ranged either along the Arkansas River (the T'o-k'inabyup, or Men of the North) or through the Staked Plains in association with the Kwahadi Comanches (the Gwa-halego, or southerners). But even this was fluid. The total population of the tribe was between 1,600 and 1,800 people. Unlike most of the tribes of the Great Plains, the Kiowas did have a 'head chief' who was elected by the division or band chiefs and was held in great respect. At an earlier time head chiefs were said to have held almost despotic powers, but in later times they led more by force of personality, bravery, sagacity, and wisdom. As with other tribes, the individual warrior did as he was inclined, and followed his chief or band leader, if he chose to, by reason of respect. The last great head chief of the Kiowas was the much respected Dohásän, who died in 1866. Although he was nominally succeeded by Gui-pah-go (Lone Wolf), there was never again a principal chief who commanded the respect and following of the entire tribe. The tribe was now divided in its loyalties between Lone Wolf, Set-tainte (White Bear, called Satanta by whites), and Kicking Bird. Lone Wolf and Satanta in general favored war to keep whites out of their country, while Kicking Bird was a prominent leader among those favoring peace with whites. It was a power struggle in which no clear winner would emerge.[13]

Hancock's meeting of April 23, 1867, with Kicking Bird and Stumbling Bear was with two men who were strong proponents of peace with whites, though Hancock seemed unaware of that. Kicking Bird, moreover, was one of the most intelligent, thoughtful, and respected of the tribal leaders, even though his position on overall peace was costing him loyalty and

---

[12] The Kiowa-Apaches were a small Athapascan tribe that became associated with and were incorporated into the Kiowa tribal circle while they were still living far to the north. Called Gattackas by the French, they called themselves "Naichan" and were probably originally a part of the Lipan Apaches. They are one of several Apache peoples known as Plains Apaches but are most commonly identified with the Kiowas. See Terrell, *Plains Apaches*, 15–23.

[13] Hancock to Sherman, April 24, 1867; Hancock to Nichols, May 22, 1867; *Harper's Weekly*, May 25, 1867, 328; Mayhall, *Kiowas*, 112, 116, 124.

influence. The meeting began, as usual, with a speech by General Hancock, and as with the Cheyennes, it sent a mixed message. Claiming that the soldiers did not come to make war on Indians, he then said they did come to fight those wanting war. He gave his version of the council he had with the Cheyennes, the march up the Pawnee Fork and the meeting with the Cheyenne and Oglala chiefs, the confrontation with the warriors, and the subsequent flight of the Indians and the burning of their villages. He said the burning was done because the two tribes had attacked the Smoky Hill stage stations and killed three men. Hancock said they kept a number of lodges, including those of Bull Bear and Roman Nose, and would give them to Kiowas and Comanches who would enlist as army scouts. He also mentioned the six Cheyennes allegedly killed at the Cimarron Crossing, claiming they tried to shoot the soldiers. It was another rambling and confusing speech, blaming the Indians for all of the problems on the plains but still trying to enlist help from the Kiowas and Comanches.

At the conclusion of Hancock's remarks, the Man That Moves made a brief comment indicating his belief in what Hancock said, and admonishing the young men present to do the same. Then it was Kicking Bird's turn to respond. He referred to the recent death of the great Kiowa chief Dohásän and his advice to be friends with the whites. And he said the Kiowas and Comanches claimed the country south of the Arkansas, where they wanted no war. A further exchange followed, during which General Hancock asked for an answer to his request for scouts. Kicking Bird replied that they could not give an answer to that until the other chiefs were consulted. With this the council with Kicking Bird and Stumbling Bear concluded.[14]

Before Kicking Bird left, General Hancock arranged for him to follow the Arapahoe chief Little Raven and request his return to council with him. Kicking Bird promised to do so and to have him back within two days, indicating his belief that Little Raven and his people were still in the vicinity and probably camping on a stream not too far away. Accompanying Kicking Bird was a white scout known as Apache Bill, dispatched by Hancock to bring back word about whether or not Little Raven had been found and would return. Hancock then returned to his headquarters and the following day wrote a brief report to General Sherman. He described the interview with Kicking Bird and Stumbling Bear, enclos-

14 Transcript of Talk Held with Kiowa Chiefs Kicking Bird and Stumbling Bear, April 23, 1867, AGO, LR, NA, MC 619-R563.

ing a transcript recorded by his adjutant, and stated that he expected Little Raven and his Arapahoes, and possibly others, to return to Fort Dodge
shortly. It was raining as he wrote the letter, and perhaps the gentle sounds
of the drops pelting his tent made him more reflective, for he reported
that the Indians of his department had generally "gone far south—fearing complications which might involve their families." He continued,
"There are all kinds of influences bearing upon the subject, and the Indians are bewildered in consequence." After commenting on Little Raven's
willingness to return a number of horses and mules taken by some of his
young men from a white caravan on the Santa Fe Trail, even though eight
white men had stolen twelve horses from his people, he advised Sherman
of his change in plans about going south of the Arkansas.

> I have thought it best not to go farther south at present—in order not to
> complicate matters, and I cannot go far enough to have it prove advantageous,
> as I can see more of the principal men at Dodge and Larned, by being at those
> posts—than I would be likely to do in a march south of the number of days
> which my forage would warrant.
>
> My Cavalry being absent, I do not appear so formidable as I did a short time
> since, and the effect would not therefore be valuable. The Agent had sent for
> their Chiefs to come in at Larned, by the 30th, and I will be there then. At
> Hays by the 2nd or 3rd and at Harker about the 7th prox.[15]

His report completed, Hancock turned to his future course of action.
He still had the council with Little Raven and his Arapahoes ahead of
him, and another with more Kiowa chiefs at Fort Larned. It seemed clear
that he would not see any of the chiefs of the Comanches or Plains
Apaches, all having put considerable distance between themselves and his
expeditionary force after the events on Pawnee Fork. Beyond the upcoming councils and the continuing operations of Custer and the Seventh Cavalry, it seemed that the expedition could accomplish little more. Hancock
also appears to have concluded, belatedly, that there was nothing to be
gained by marching infantry across the plains in pursuit of mounted Indians and that the artillery battery had even less use in this kind of offensive
operation. Accordingly he issued orders to post three companies of the
Thirty-seventh Infantry at Forts Larned, Lyon, and Dodge, to provide
escorts for stagecoaches on the Santa Fe road. Of the two companies of
the Seventh Cavalry, presently at or near Fort Dodge, C was ordered to
return to Fort Lyon and B to remain at Dodge, and one company of the

---

[15] Hancock to Sherman, April 24, 1867; Stanley, *My Early Travels*, 60.

new Tenth Cavalry was ordered to Fort Larned. These three companies were to patrol the Santa Fe road and keep it free of hostile Indians. Maj. Henry Douglass, commanding at Fort Dodge, was given the added duty of overseeing protection of the Santa Fe mail route between Fort Zarah and Fort Lyon and. to that end, was authorized to call on the commanding officers of Fort Larned and Fort Lyon to provide details from the infantry companies stationed at their posts.[16]

The theft of eleven mules from the stage station at the Cimarron Crossing on April 23, which Stanley attributed to the Cheyennes, was also reported to Hancock. Although it was assumed that the thieves were Indians, the general admitted in his report of May 22, 1867, that there was no evidence to support the charge. The agent at the station who reported their loss admitted under questioning that no guards were watching over them and that all the station employees were asleep at the time. From what Hancock could learn, neglect to guard livestock was common along the entire mail and stage route to Santa Fe and along the Smoky Hill as well. If the employees at the stations were vigilant, he opined, "kept up proper guards and had their arms in readiness, it is believed that they would repel the attacks which are usually made upon the stations by the Indians, who are generally in small parties on such occasions."[17]

When the Expedition for the Plains marched south from Camp 14, it took along the old Oglala man and woman, as well as the little Cheyenne girl. At Fort Dodge they were delivered into the care of Major Douglass and his garrison. Presumably the girl, at least, was placed in the post hospital. When Hancock and his troops left for Fort Larned, the three remained behind. Their subsequent fate is a puzzle. The old Sioux man died at the post on June 23, 1867, allegedly of "old age." The young Cheyenne girl lived a month and a day longer, dying on July 24, 1867. No cause was given, but probably her death was due to the trauma and injuries sustained as a result of her rape. Surprisingly, the old Sioux woman managed to escape on July 1, 1867, and was never found by the troops. Unless she followed the Arkansas or some other stream to a friendly Indian village that took her in and cared for her, she likely died of exposure alone on the plains, a victim of age, lack of adequate clothing and food, and the heat and harsh conditions of summer.[18]

---

[16] Hancock to Nichols, May 22, 1867; Stanley, *My Early Travels*, 85–86.

[17] Hancock to Nichols, May 22, 1867; Stanley, *My Early Travels*, 51.

[18] Kennedy, *On the Plains*, 72; Oliva, *Fort Dodge*, 46; Reedstrom, *Custer's 7th Cavalry*, 30.

On the night of April 27, Apache Bill, the white guide who left with Kicking Bird to search for Little Raven and his Arapahoes, returned to Fort Dodge and reported they had been found and would arrive the following morning. Hancock had already given orders to march for Fort Larned the morning of April 28 but, on receiving this news, suspended his order until it could be determined if the Arapahoes would in fact appear. At 2:00 the next afternoon Little Raven, accompanied by Cut Nose, Beardy, Big Belly, and several other warriors, arrived for the council. Another Arapahoe chief, Yellow Bear, was also encamped near the fort with his people and in attendance. In his report Hancock, as was his usual practice, claimed that the Arapahoes arrived and requested an interview with him. In truth he had sent for them and they responded to his summons.[19]

According to Hancock, the council was held immediately following the arrival of Little Raven and the other chiefs. As was the case with the Kiowa chiefs Kicking Bird and Stumbling Bear, these Arapahoes represented those most keenly committed to the cause of peace. At that time there were four principal bands of Arapahoes, the names of which varied depending on who recorded it. These were most commonly known as the Antelope, the Quick-to-Anger or Spunky Men, the Greasy Face or Ugly Face Men, and the Beaver or Funny Men. The Ugly Face band was so called because many of its people were badly pockmarked from smallpox, and the Funny Men's name came from their smaller stature, caused by the incorporation of other peoples through intermarriage or captivity. Sometime during the early nineteenth century the bands separated, the Greasy Face and Beaver bands moving permanently south to the Arkansas River and the Antelope band and the Spunky Men remaining in the north along the North Platte River. Like all Plains Indians, they were true nomads and bison hunters, ranging over a wide area with the respective rivers constituting their heartland. Each band had its own favorite territory for hunting and for winter camps, and each had its own chief, chiefs of kindreds or subbands, and headmen or war leaders. Although the tribe did not have a "head chief" in the sense the U.S. government intended (with absolute governing authority), one of the band chiefs was recognized as the tribe's "principal chief," being the chief of the band that had gained prestige by having produced the previous principal chief, usually the Antelope band. When the most exalted chief died, was no longer able to serve, or lost the following of his band members, another popular leader

---

[19] Hancock to Nichols, May 22, 1867; Stanley, *My Early Travels*, 64.

was chosen as his successor. Even so, his authority was symbolic, and he had no more power or authority over the tribe than the other chiefs, all of whom led by prestige and example. Subsequently there were further divisions within the regional bands, resulting in four divisions among the Southern Arapahoes, each with its own chief. In 1867 the four principal chiefs in the south were Little Raven, Spotted Wolf, Yellow Bear, and Powder Face. Little Raven, one of the southern chiefs about to council with General Hancock, had been designated as the Arapahoe "head chief" by government authorities, although he was not. He was, however, happy to be considered as such.[20]

When the council began, it was Little Raven who spoke first. His speech, as translated by the government interpreters and recorded by the adjutant, was relatively brief: they had come to the council as fast as they could despite what had been done at the Cheyenne and Oglala villages; whites were free to use the trails along the Arkansas and Smoky Hill; they had kept the peace made at the Little Arkansas; they did not oppose the railroad; they would stay south of the Arkansas until the Cheyennes and Oglalas had moved north of the Platte; they were falsely blamed by others for depredations the others had committed, but admitted to taking forty horses on the Santa Fe road; and like matters. In response Hancock acknowledged Little Raven as "head chief" of the Arapahoes, a role he said whites liked because they could talk to "one responsible man," making it easier to hold the whole tribe responsible for its actions. He then launched into a detailed account of the council with the Cheyennes and the subsequent dealings with the Cheyennes and Oglalas in which, he asserted, their actions showed they wanted war. His speech was alternately threatening and conciliatory, as with the Cheyennes and Kiowas before them, and included a request for scouts to assist in the war against the hostile tribes.

Little Raven must have been confused after listening to this long and rambling talk. Although Hancock professed that he was pleased to see Little Raven, his message was both stark and clear. As with the Kiowas there was an additional interchange in which Little Raven declared firmly for peace and agreed to the return of stolen livestock. Hancock impressed on him the need to keep the road along the Arkansas clear of hostiles.

With that the council ended, and General Hancock returned to his headquarters to prepare for the march to Fort Larned. Before departure he turned the forty Cheyenne lodges over to Major Douglass for storage. Perhaps he

[20] Bass, *Arapaho Way*, 18–19; Trenholm, *Arapahoes*, 3–5, 52–53.

still held hopes that some Indians would sign on as scouts, or perhaps he simply wanted to unburden his wagon train of them. He told Kicking Bird that he had the lodges of Bull Bear and Roman Nose, though he would later tell Satanta they were Sioux lodges. It is unlikely that Hancock had any idea whose lodges were among those confiscated by his troops.[21]

In his lengthy speeches, Hancock revealed that he had at last realized, however belatedly, that marching a large force of troops near an Indian village would frighten the women and children and cause them to flee. However, he seems not to have considered that this was the real reason for the flight of the Cheyennes and Sioux or that they should not be forced into war because of his previous actions. Aside from this concession to Little Raven, he continued to use threats of harsh action to intimidate the Indian peoples he was dealing with into surrendering their country. His promises to give "redress" for the wrongs done to Indians by whites must have rung as hollow with Little Raven as they had with the Cheyennes. And he may have found a sort of sardonic humor in them, for Little Raven was a man known for a lively wit. At the time of the Medicine Lodge Peace Treaty later in 1867, it is said that N. G. Taylor, the pious commissioner of the Indians, talked with Little Raven about the Christian religion, presumably to persuade him to adopt it. Taylor explained that there was a heaven above, where all good people of all races go after they die, and a hell where evildoers go. Those who would lie, cheat, steal, and break their promises would not be permitted in heaven, he said. At that Little Raven began to laugh heartily, until he was nearly out of breath. That was a good thing to know, Little Raven allowed. Recalling all of the many broken promises and lies of whites, all of the cheating of Indians and the stealing of their country by force or deception, and all of the greed and cruelty whites demonstrated in their dealings with the Indian peoples, he declared that heaven must be a place where Indians would finally have little trouble from white men, for he knew of few he would expect to see there.[22]

General Hancock and his troops and supply trains left Camp 17 east of Fort Dodge the same afternoon, April 28, after the council with Little Raven and set a course for Fort Larned. They followed the Wet Route of the Santa Fe Trail for about a mile and a half, then moved up to the Dry Route and followed it the rest of the way to Fort Larned. After a march

[21] Talk Held with "Little Raven," April 28, 1867; Hancock to Nichols, May 22, 1867; Stanley, "British Journalist," 303.

[22] Talk Held with "Little Raven," April 28, 1867; Bass, *Arapaho Way*, 19–20.

of a little more than six additional miles they went into camp (Camp 18) along Coon Creek.[23]

The shortness of the day's march was partly due to the late afternoon start but was also no doubt influenced by the weather. During the morning, thunderheads rose above the horizon to the south-southwest, and by mid-day they were rolling northeastward and obliterating the sun. By the time the long column of infantry, artillery, and wagon trains moved out of Camp 17, dark clouds were hanging menacingly over the country, churning and scudding across the skies. To the surprise of those unfamiliar with the plains the normally persistent south wind suddenly dropped, and not a blade of grass stirred, so still was the calm. And just as suddenly, the winds returned with gale force, and the foreboding clouds came alive with lightning that streaked across the sky, accompanied by booming thunder. The wind swept the land, roaring through the draws and arroyos, picking up sand and grit from the earth's surface, then flinging it into the faces of man and beast. Stanley, a novice about the fickle and dangerous spring weather on the plains, thought it had the force of a hurricane. The great swirling clouds of dust made it impossible to see more than twenty yards, and the men and their animals were forced to grope their way along the barely visible trail, obscured from the view of all but a few to their front and rear. Soon their blue uniforms, the hides of the animals, and the canvas on the wagons were converted into a dingy gray-brown, and friend could not recognize friend. Thirst became a problem. They struggled on to their new campsite at Coon Creek and were grateful when a halt was called and orders issued to make camp.[24]

The gale did not subside as they pitched their tents, which flapped and groaned and wobbled before its powerful blows. And when they were erected, the dust sifted inside, choking the men. At last it began to rain, slowly at first, with large drops pelting the canvas. Gradually the rain increased in intensity, and as it did, the dust was settled and the wind subsided. Finally the rain stopped abruptly, the spring storm moved off to the northeast, and the skies cleared. Everyone's first task was to rid themselves of dirt and grime and to don clean clothing. After that the camp settled into its customary routine, with the livestock attended to, cooking fires lit,

---

[23] Brown, *March Journal*, April 28, 1867; Hancock to Nichols, May 22, 1867. Lieutenant Brown noted this stream as Little Coon Creek, but today that branch lies roughly eight miles to the north of the principal stream, flowing east-northeasterly to the junction of the two. In 1867, however, the modern Coon Creek was known as Little Coon Creek.

[24] Stanley, *My Early Travels*, 57–58.

During his second visit to Fort Larned on May 1, 1867, Hancock held a separate council with the wily Kiowa chief Satanta. Considered one of the most skilled Indian orators on the plains, Satanta mightily impressed the expedition commander, who rewarded him with a major general's coat and hat with a plume. General Davidson added a sash, which can be seen in this sketch by Theodore Davis. Satanta later wore the coat and hat while running off the horse herd at Fort Dodge. *Harper's Weekly*, June 8, 1867.

and humor returning to the face of each man. It was a weary band of soldiers that turned in for a night's sleep when taps was sounded.[25]

They left Camp 18 early the following morning, crossed Coon Creek and marched rapidly northeast for eighteen and a half miles, then made camp (Camp 19) on the south bank of what today is known as Little Coon Creek. This day there was no inclement weather to impede the march, and it was uneventful. The next morning after the troops were breakfasted and the animals attended to, the camp was in the process of being struck when in rode the Kiowa chief Satanta in the company of several of his warriors. As was his custom, Hancock claimed that Satanta requested a "talk" with him. The truth was that Satanta, along with the other Kiowa chiefs, had been summoned to a council with General Hancock to be held at Fort Dodge. However, he arrived at that post too late, and Major Douglass sent him on up the trail to Fort Larned to overtake Hancock and his troops. As they were in the process of striking camp, Hancock invited Satanta to accompany him to Fort Larned to hold the talks there. Satanta did accompany the troops to that post, a march of about twenty-six and a half miles, where

---

[25] Ibid., 58–59.

the expedition made its Camp 20 at 2:00 P.M. on the northwest side of the Pawnee Fork, directly to the west and northwest of the fort.[26]

The council with Satanta did not take place until the following morning, May 1, and was held at Hancock's headquarters. To Hancock's way of thinking, it was to be the most important of his several councils with the Indian leaders, because he considered Satanta to be "the Head Chief of the Kiowa tribe of Indians in Kansas." Satanta was assuredly one of the most important chiefs in the tribe, but not the "head chief," despite his own assertions. He was brave, boastful, brash, and well known for his penchant to overlook the truth when it served his purpose. The official interpreter hired for the occasion was Frederick F. Jones, the post interpreter at Fort Dodge. He and Satanta were responsible for much of the misinformation that had earlier been passed on to General Hancock by way of the commanders at Fort Dodge and Fort Larned and that in part had motivated him to organize the current expedition. According to Stanley, the two Indian agents, Leavenworth and Wynkoop, and all of the officers of the command were present in the tent, which must have been the Sibley tent used at Fort Dodge, along with "a small and select body of lesser chiefs" of the Kiowa tribe. No other Kiowa chiefs were known to be present, and likely Stanley assumed that anyone in the company of an important chief was also a chief. They were probably some of Satanta's leading warriors—important men in the tribe but not chiefs.[27]

Stanley claimed that before the proceedings began, confessions were received from Frederick Jones, John A. Atkin (not Thomas Adkins, the courier), and Thomas H. Kincaid, all of whom he referred to as "Indian interpreters" by profession. Jones and Atkin were employed, at least when the occasion arose, as interpreters at Fort Dodge and seem to have interpreted for the military with the Comanche and Kiowa leaders. Kincaid, on the other hand, was commonly employed in the region as a guide and courier and, according to Theodore Davis, acted in that capacity for the expedition. He had arrived in Hancock's camp at midnight on April 20 and may well have remained to rest and await another assignment. But nothing in the record indicates that he was ever qualified as an interpreter or that he spoke any of the several Indian languages prevalent on the southern plains. According to Stanley, the three men all confessed to having assisted in defrauding the Indians, in complicity with Jesse Leavenworth,

[26] Brown, *March Journal*, April 29–30, 1867; Hancock to Nichols, May 22, 1867.

[27] Hancock to Nichols, May 22, 1867; Proceedings of Council Held May 1, 1867, at Fort Larned, Kans., MC619-R563; Stanley, *My Early Travels*, 61–62.

by trading their own annuity goods to them in exchange for buffalo hides, furs, and lariats. Leavenworth would then, according to the alleged confessions, sell the hides, furs, and lariats to a trader in Leavenworth City named Durfy. Further, the three men allegedly claimed to have personal knowledge that Leavenworth had buried several bales of annuity goods with the intention of concealing and later profiting from their sale. It seems unlikely that three men hoping to retain their employment with the government, then and in the future, would gratuitously confess to criminal acts that would expose them to both loss of that employment and prosecution. Neither Hancock's report nor the transcript of the council proceedings indicate any of these confessions. Jones did level accusations at Leavenworth during the council, but none that involved himself in illegal activities. He had already established himself as a liar, but nothing more. Stanley admittedly disliked the Indian agents, considering them as somehow in league with the Indians against the government. The probability is that he fabricated the confessions after hearing the charges leveled against Leavenworth by Jones and Satanta, in an effort to discredit Leavenworth, the Office of Indian Affairs, and Indian agents in general.[28]

Satanta, the redoubtable Kiowa chief, entered the council tent sufficiently adorned to attract the attention of his audience. He wore the regulation coat of an army captain, complete with epaulettes, and elk-skin leggings that were gaudy and trimmed with small brass bells. His face was painted with vermilion. A large and muscular man, he had made a reputation for himself as brave, daring, and reckless in war and on raids, and as a notorious braggart and liar. Now he was prepared to match wits and oratorical skills with those of General Hancock. The proceedings began with an accusation by Jones that Leavenworth had told Satanta not to talk much during the council but to go to Fort Zarah the following day and he would "make it all right." Leavenworth quickly denied making any such statements. With that, Hancock invited Satanta to proceed. The Kiowa leader, a renowned orator in his tribe, did so with both verve and remarkable verbosity.[29]

Viewed as a whole, Satanta's speeches were long and rambling, filled with contradictions and more than a few lies. He professed to have always worked for peace on one hand, then by implication admitted his participation in the Texas raids. He claimed to be brothers with the Comanches,

[28] Hancock to Nichols, May 22, 1867; Proceedings of Council Held May 1, 1867; *Harper's Weekly*, June 29, 1867, 406; Stanley, *My Early Travels*, 63.

[29] Proceedings of Council Held May 1, 1867; *Harper's Weekly*, June 29, 1867, 357–58; Kennedy, *On the Plains*, 96–101; Stanley, *My Early Travels*, 61–82.

Cheyennes, Arapahoes, and Sioux, all of whom were poor and wanted only peace, yet talked about his efforts, present and future, to induce them to preserve peace. He objected to a railroad along the Arkansas River and the route of the Santa Fe Trail but magnanimously consented to one along the Smoky Hill, a generous concession indeed, considering that the Smoky Hill ran in the country of the Dog Soldier and southern Sutaio Cheyennes, not of the Kiowas. And he disparaged his brother Kiowa chiefs, suggesting that their following was tiny relative to his large one and that they came in for talks with white officials only to get something to eat. Satanta castigated Colonel Leavenworth not for stealing but for withholding his share of the annuity goods while delivering them to other chiefs and their bands who he suggested were less worthy, and some of whom had been on the same raids he had. Leavenworth explained that he had strict orders not to distribute to Satanta and others who participated in those raids until they had returned all captives without ransom and had given assurances that they would refrain from future raiding. Those receiving their goods had done so, and Satanta had not. A copy of Leavenworth's orders to that effect were filed with the transcript of proceedings of the council. To Satanta's credit, he did have the nerve to tell General Hancock to his face that he thought it a very bad thing to have burned the Cheyenne and Lakota villages, that they did not intend war, and that most of the bands from the southern tribes had not appeared to council with him out of fear of his intentions.

General Hancock's speech was no less verbose, rambling, and disjointed than that of Satanta, jumping from one subject to another, alternately threatening, cajoling, and conciliatory, and making assertions for which he had no hard evidence. He excoriated the Cheyennes and Oglalas for beginning a war by the attack on Lookout Station, although he had no real knowledge of those responsible for it. He suggested that the Cheyennes assented to his march to their village and making camp nearby, when he knew full well that they and their agent had repeatedly pleaded with him not to do so. And he accused the Cheyennes of lying to him by agreeing to bring back their women and children and have a council with him the following morning, when in fact the Cheyenne chiefs had expressed doubt that they could successfully accomplish that. At one point he sought to assure Satanta that the denuding of the streams of trees by whites was no great loss, since coal would replace it as soon as it was discovered in that country by whites. How he imagined nomadic bison hunters could come by a supply of coal that could be carried with them in quantity defies imagination. Satanta would not have understood a reference to coal, a substance he had neither seen nor heard of, and probably placed no faith in such an assertion. He likely also totally rejected, at least in his own mind, Hancock's claim that the soldiers had come to protect the Indians as well as the whites and that they would do a better job of seeing that justice was done for the Indians than they could do for themselves.[30]

The council was adjourned and the parties left. Not, however, before General Hancock, who was much impressed with Satanta's oratory, presented him with a major general's coat, with full insignia, and a plumed dress hat. General Davidson contributed a yellow sash to run across Satanta's chest, and all of this was supplemented by a blue army blanket that was worn around his loins.[31]

From his remarks at the council and in later statements, it would seem that Hancock was well aware of Satanta's complicity in the abduction of the Box family and the killing of the husband and baby, as well as other raiding. In all likelihood the gifts of the major general's coat and other articles were intended to make Satanta feel proud and important as a valued ally of the Great Father and to keep him at peace. Hancock seems to have been inordinately impressed with the chief's words, given their content and the fact that others such as Kicking Bird and Little Raven had been far more forthcoming and friendly and yet apparently received no similar rewards for their exemplary behavior.

In reporting on the council with Satanta, Stanley was much impressed with the Kiowa chief's oratorical skills and with his charges against Colonel Leavenworth: "Had General Hancock encouraged Satanta we have no doubt that he would have disclosed other dark deeds of Indian agents; but he did not feel himself licensed to play the inquisitor. These speeches reveal many true facts about Indian matters. The speakers appear to be on their honor to tell the truth; and between the Indian chief and the great General we get a good deal of it." Theodore Davis, witnessing the same proceedings, had quite a different perspective. He reported that when Satanta left the Fort Larned council, he boasted that "he had out-talked the big white chief, and the white chief had the first talk too." Davis

---

[30] Proceedings of Council Held May 1, 1867; *Harper's Weekly*, June 29, 1867, 357–58; Kennedy, *On the Plains*, 96–101; Stanley, *My Early Travels*, 61–82.

[31] *Harper's Weekly*, June 29, 1867, 357–58; Kennedy, *On the Plains*, 96–101; Stanley, *My Early Travels*, 61–82.

believed that Hancock was too disposed to think well of Satanta. He reported that on June 1 Satanta, wearing the major general's coat and hat given him by Hancock, stampeded away nearly all of the livestock at Fort Dodge: "He had the politeness, however, to raise his plumed hat to the garrison of the fort, though he discourteously shook his coat-tails at them as he rode away with the captured stock." Dr. Coates, nearly always an astute observer, this time seemed too much taken with what he thought the eloquence of Satanta's oration and too accepting of his assertions. Referring to the report of Satanta's theft of the Fort Dodge stock, he said that he had never heard confirmation of the event. Because soldiers and plainsmen were "such abominable falsifiers" when speaking of the Indians, Coates claimed that it was difficult to believe anything they said, so he gave Satanta the benefit of the doubt.[32]

The council was now over, each participant had formed his own opinion, the other chiefs summoned by Colonel Leavenworth had failed to appear, and General Hancock was ready to move on to Fort Hays. There he would assess the situation with the Seventh Cavalry, give Custer his orders for continuing operations, and retire from the field. The expedition to this point had not given him the important victory over the Indians that he desired; indeed it had been a humiliation from his perspective. Instead of holding the great general and his forces in awe, these small bands of people had refused to obey his orders, had fled from him, and with their poor starved horses had managed to elude even his vaunted cavalry led by the famous "boy general." Except for tracking them down and administering appropriate "chastisement," there was really nothing left for him to do. It must have been a disheartened Winfield Scott Hancock who ordered the march to Fort Hays to begin the following morning.

---

[32] Davis, "Summer on the Plains," 297–98; Kennedy, *On the Plains*, 102; Stanley, *My Early Travels*, 82–83.

CHAPTER FIFTEEN

FORT HAYS, FORT HARKER,
AND RETURN

G eneral Hancock spent the late afternoon of May 1 writing a report to General Sherman, summarizing the results of the three coun- cils held at Forts Dodge and Larned and the current status of the expedition. He complained that high water and bad roads were impeding the delivery of supplies and reported that though Custer was presently plagued by a lack of fodder and grain for his horses, when things "were a little more straightened out," he would be "an exceedingly valuable offi- cer to pursue the Indians." His greatest complaint was against the Indian agents, who he believed hampered his efforts. He claimed to listen to them when their views of the public interest coincided with his own, but in his opinion that was seldom. And he stated, "I have laid the evidence of out- rages and depredations before some of them but as yet I have in no instance been called on to make energetic efforts for restitution or redress from the Indians." The two agents he was referring to, Wynkoop and Leavenworth, parted company with Hancock at Fort Larned, Wynkoop remaining there because it was the seat of his agency, while Leavenworth proceeded to Fort Zarah, the agency for the Kiowas and Comanches. Neither the agents nor General Hancock regretted their parting.[1]

The expedition left Camp 20 early on the morning of May 2, 1867. In the absence of the Seventh Cavalry the combat troops were now just four companies of the Thirty-seventh Infantry, the artillery battery, and the detachment of eighty troopers caring for the cavalry horses left behind. There were also the commissary and quartermaster trains, the train of pontoon bridges, the remaining Delaware scouts, the white couriers and

---

[1] W. S. Hancock to W. T. Sherman, May 1, 1867, U.S. House, "Difficulties with Indian Tribes," 7:105–10.

guides, and Headquarters of the Department of the Missouri in the Field.[2] They first moved north-northwesterly for nine miles, then crossed the upper reaches of Ash Creek (nearly dry at that point), and continued on a little west of north for thirteen miles. They reached Walnut Creek and made their Camp 21 on the south bank. For part of the time, they followed a trail made by a company of the Seventh Cavalry and one of the Tenth, both having recently marched from Fort Hays to Fort Larned. The former was doubtless Company E, the one that joined the expedition at Fort Larned, and the latter probably the one ordered to Fort Larned by General Hancock while at Fort Dodge.[3]

The camp on Walnut Creek was relatively pleasant, with good water and some wood along the stream banks. Beyond it the intermittent streams and arroyos would be devoid of water, except for a few small pools, until they reached the Smoky Hill. When they broke camp the following morning, May 3, they crossed the Walnut, continued north for a mile and a half, then turned nearly due east for a little over a mile. They changed their line of march to the north-northeast for the next ten miles, then altered their course to due north until they reached the Smoky Hill River. The stream was flanked by high bluffs and the bed of the river was broad and sandy, but with almost no water or wood. General Hancock proclaimed the crossing "excellent" in his report, and once across the dry bed, his troops climbed up through the bluffs to the rolling hills of the Dissected High Plains above. An additional march of six miles brought them to Big Creek during the midafternoon, at a point about half a mile below the forks and three-quarters of a mile east of old Fort Hays. They made Camp 22 there on the south bank of the stream, next to a modest stand of cottonwood and a few scrub trees.[4]

On the evening of May 2, while General Hancock and the remainder of his force were in camp on Walnut Creek, Custer notified his cavalry companies at Fort Hays that on Saturday, May 4, they would be having a footrace between the fastest men of each company. The distance was to be three hundred yards, and the company fielding the winning contestant would be excused from guard and fatigue duty for one week, while the winner himself would be excused that duty for twenty days. The competition generated considerable enthusiasm among the men, and they immediately set about holding company races to determine their fastest man. Custer

[2] Stanley, "British Journalist," 303.
[3] Brown, *March Journal*, May 2, 1867; Hancock to Nichols, May 22, 1867.
[4] Brown, *March Journal*, May 3, 1867; Hancock to Nichols, May 22, 1867.

told his wife that he did this "to give the men exercise, innocent amusement, and something to do to keep them out of mischief." That was no
doubt true, but it likely had the added benefit of boosting morale at a time
when the desertion rate in the Seventh Cavalry was high. And Custer probably hoped it would impress and entertain General Hancock during his
brief stay.[5]

On the morning of May 3, prior to the expected arrival of General Hancock, Custer issued orders to his company commanders to see that the lines
of tents were straightened and uniformly spaced, and the entire encampment thoroughly policed before 10:00 A.M. the next day. Then, turning to
the matter of deteriorating discipline in the Seventh Cavalry camp, he issued
orders for the suppression of the use of profanity and vulgarity by both officers and men under pain of arrest and punishment. Hancock's well-known
insistence on tight discipline and soldierly bearing was perhaps partly
responsible for these orders, but Custer probably also recognized that nearly
two weeks of forced inaction was taking a toll on the fighting effectiveness
of his men and would come back to haunt him once in the field.[6]

With Hancock and his troops came 2nd Lt. Henry Jackson of G Company and eighty men, two-thirds of the remaining company wagons, and
the extra horses of the Seventh Cavalry. At the beginning of the expedition each company had four wagons to carry the company records and
equipment, tents, the extra clothing and personal belongings of the men,
and similar gear. But when the cavalry was ordered north in pursuit of the
fleeing Indians, each company was allowed only one wagon, and that was
to carry the bare minimum of tents, blankets, and (in the absence of commissary and quartermaster trains) grain and forage for the horses and provisions for the troopers. To the dismay of the officers and men, only two
of the missing three wagons of each company appeared at the Big Creek
encampment. A disease had broken out among the "led," or extra, horses
of the regiment, and about twenty-eight of them had died. The lack of
sufficient animals in proper condition likely resulted in the decision to leave
eight wagons behind, presumably at either Fort Dodge or Fort Larned,
though it is not clear that the draft animals were among those affected.
Some in the regiment believed the disease to be "glandis" (glanders), but
General Smith pronounced it "lung fever" (pneumonia).[7]

---

[5] E. Custer, *Tenting on the Plains*, 578–81; Utley, *Life in Custer's Cavalry*, 45.
[6] HQ Seventh U.S. Cavalry, circulars 12 and 13, Camp near Fort Hays, May 3, 1867, Rec. U.S. Army
    Mobile Units, Seventh U.S. Cavalry, Circulars Issued, NA, RG 391; Burkey, *Custer, Come at Once*, 10–11.
[7] Boniface, *Cavalry Horse and His Pack*, 496–99; Utley, *Life in Custer's Cavalry*, 36, 38, 45.

The Fort Hays that Hancock and his troops rode into was the first to bear that name and was located in an oxbow on the south bank of the north fork of Big Creek, a few hundred yards above the confluence of the north and south forks and about three-fourths of a mile north of the Seventh Cavalry camp. It first appeared that this site would be permanent, and construction of a series of log and adobe buildings was begun. Company B of the Thirty-seventh Infantry later took post and built two long, low stone quarters. Col. Elmer Otis, First Cavalry, acting as a special inspector for the Department of the Missouri, arrived at the post in mid-January of 1867, finding in addition to the quarters a low stone building with a canvas roof built as a commissary storehouse, and two log and mud-chinked officers' quarters, plus a dugout used as a bakehouse. Tents served as the post hospital and guardhouse. But in the interim the surveyed route for the new railroad had been placed about five miles to the north, and the question of relocation of the post was in part what brought Colonel Otis on his tour of inspection. After a careful review of the installation and its present location, he wrote to General Davidson, inspector general of the department, recommending its removal to a site where the proposed railroad would cross the south or main fork of Big Creek, approximately fifteen miles to the northwest. As a result no more permanent buildings were constructed at the site of the first Fort Hays, and its appearance remained much the same at the time of the arrival of the Seventh Cavalry on April 20 and of Hancock and the rest of the expedition on May 3.[8]

General Hancock and General Davidson were well aware of Colonel Otis's recommendation. One of the first things they undertook during their brief stay was an inspection of the post. In his later report of the expedition Hancock wrote that the garrison was then quartered in "rude log and adobe huts" and that the fort would likely be moved to a location near the point where the Union Pacific E.D. would cross Big Creek. Though on detached duty with the expedition, Capt. Albert P. Morrow, commanding Company E of the Seventh Cavalry, was also commander of Fort Hays when Custer and later General Hancock arrived. In June, Morrow was replaced by Maj. Alfred Gibbs, who returned to the field from Fort Riley. Gibbs, as the new commanding officer, selected the final site for the new post and ordered the garrison removed to it.[9]

By 10:00 A.M. on May 4 the company areas had all been policed and

---

[8] E. Otis to J. W. Davidson, January 18, 1867, Department of the Missouri, LR, NA, RG 393; Burkey, *Custer, Come at Once,* 16–17; Oliva, *Fort Hays,* 1–19.

prepared for inspection. It was something more than a mere walk-through: the entire regiment, dressed in their best available uniforms, were mounted and passed in review for inspection by General Hancock and his staff. Then in the evening, with Generals Hancock, Smith, and Davidson and Colonel Custer present, the footrace was held. Eight men, one from each cavalry company, competed, wearing only their shirts, drawers, and stockings. The race was won by a man from Capt. Louis M. Hamilton's A Company, with the entry from Captain Barnitz's G Company a close second. The footrace was followed by a horse race on a quarter-mile course between a horse from Capt. Frederick Benteen's H Company and one from Fort Hays. The horse from the post had never been beaten, and the infantrymen stationed there felt certain of success. But, as Custer phrased it, "as fortune favors the brave, the cavalry horse won handsomely."[9]

Following conclusion of the afternoon and evening activities, Custer joined Generals Hancock and Smith at Hancock's tent, probably to discuss the prospects for the Seventh Cavalry's early movement against the Dog Soldier Cheyennes and the Kiyuksa Oglalas, and the requirements to accomplish it. The problem of resupply must have been foremost in everyone's mind, along with the condition of the horses. The Seventh was now receiving sufficient hay in addition to the grain, but provisions for the men were adequate for only a few days without being replenished. Custer also raised the subject of bringing his wife to Fort Hays. How General Hancock reacted is unknown, but General Smith, who was always fond of Custer and his wife, was delighted, or so Custer told Libbie. Smith was planning on returning to Fort Hays after tending to business at Fort Leavenworth and Fort Riley and expressed a willingness to provide her with an ambulance and the wagons she might need for her comfortable transport. For Hancock, however, movement against the Indians was foremost in his thoughts.[10]

From the moment he first learned of it, General Hancock was greatly distressed by the inability of Custer and the Seventh Cavalry to pursue the fleeing Cheyennes and Kiyuksa Oglalas. The whole purpose of the expedition was to demonstrate the capacity of the army to pursue hostile tribes and punish any infractions of what the government considered treaty obligations binding upon them. To date he was successfully demonstrating quite the opposite. The Indians who were the chosen recipients of his

[9] Hancock to Nichols, May 22, 1867; Oliva, *Fort Hays*, 19–20, 23.
[10] E. Custer, *Tenting on the Plains*, 580; Utley, *Life in Custer's Cavalry*, 45.

object lesson and chastisement were far beyond his reach, and his cavalry remained immobile in their camp for want of forage, grain, and provisions. To what degree he held Custer, as cavalry field commander, responsible for his failure to move is speculative, but from his writings it would seem he did not. Nevertheless, on May 4, and probably at the meeting with Smith and Custer, he had General Smith formally request detailed reasons from Custer about why he had made no movement with his command. Custer provided those reasons in a responsive letter the same day.[11]

In his answer Custer stated that despite an expectation of finding forage and subsistence stores on hand when he reached the fort, there were none. By depriving the post of its own supply of forage, he obtained enough for a day and a half for his horses alone but made it last for three. Except for a small amount of "very indifferent hay," he was without forage until the arrival of a train of five wagons loaded with grain from Fort Harker, "sufficient but for one day and a half." This was no doubt the train sent following receipt of Custer's request delivered by Wild Bill Hickok. The reason given for the small amount was that there were only five wagons remaining at Fort Harker, the remainder having been sent loaded with supplies for Fort Larned, presumably for both the garrison and for Hancock's troops when they arrived there. Another train with a full supply of grain arrived on April 27, but by that time the cavalry horses were so weakened by several days without forage and dependant entirely on the dry native grasses, that they required feeding and grooming for an extended period to prevent further deterioration of their condition. Nor could he move west from Fort Hays by relying on supplies at Fort Wallace, since that post had forage and grain sufficient for only fourteen days for its own animals, which would have lasted Custer's command only three days. The quantity of subsistence stores reaching Fort Hays had been small and inadequate, and only a two-day supply was then on hand.[12]

Another reason Custer gave for his inability to march was that he had been devoting his attention to reestablishing the stage route and for this had materially weakened the garrisons at both Fort Hays and Fort Wallace. "I now have every station guarded by five men each from this post, to the distance of two hundred miles West," he wrote. The Indians, he asserted, had made no serious attacks along the road since his arrival, and the stages, without guards, were now able to make their regular runs with

---

[11] Burkey, *Custer, Come at Once*, 11; E. Custer, *Tenting on the Plains*, 580; Utley, *Life in Custer's Cavalry*, 45.

[12] G. A. Custer to T. B. Weir, AAAG, May 14, 1867, MC619-R563.

no interference. He further reported sending scouts in different directions "almost daily," to detect the presence of any bands of Indians, but without success, even though some scouts had traveled nearly a hundred miles from the fort. How Hancock viewed Custer's response was not recorded.[13]

Prior to leaving Fort Hays, General Hancock ordered one company of the Thirty-seventh Infantry to Downer Station to protect the stage route. Three companies of that regiment, along with their regimental headquarters, were to remain at Fort Hays pending final orders to proceed to New Mexico once Hancock had determined their distribution between the military posts there. He expected to have those orders to them by May 25. Inasmuch as three of the seven infantry companies from the expedition had already been posted at Forts Larned, Dodge, and Lyon, and one would accompany him back to Harker, it is probable that the company sent to Downer Station was one of the three that would ultimately be sent to New Mexico.[14]

Generals Hancock, Smith, and Davidson and their small remaining force, a mere remnant of the once formidable Expedition for the Plains, left their camp on Big Creek early on the morning of May 5. They crossed to the north side of the stream and, a little more than half a mile beyond, struck the stage road, which they followed east to Fort Harker. In addition to Headquarters, Department of the Missouri in the Field, commanded by General Hancock, and Headquarters of the Expedition for the Plains, commanded by General Smith, the column included the one remaining company of the Thirty-seventh Infantry, Battery B, Fourth U.S. Artillery; the commissary and quartermaster trains; and the party of engineers under 1st Lt. Micah R. Brown with their train of pontoon bridges. Though the measurements, observations, and reports of Lieutenant Brown and his men would have great value, it must surely have finally occurred to General Hancock that dragging pontoon bridges across the dry and dusty plains was a waste of time, money, and effort. Likewise the foolishness of marching infantry for hundreds of miles in pursuit of mounted Indians should have impressed itself upon him. All of this was a clear indicator of his profound ignorance of the environment he led his men into and of the quarry he pursued across it in March and April 1867.[15]

A march of four miles brought Hancock's troops to Walker's Creek, where they passed a mail station north of the road and west of the stream,

---

[13] Ibid.
[14] Hancock to Nichols, May 22, 1867.
[15] Brown, *March Journal*, May 5, 1867; Hancock to Nichols, May 22, 1867.

and a trading ranch on the east side. As a watercourse it was only a typical small rift in the rolling High Plains, but it was the only flowing water crossing the road between old Fort Hays and Fossil Creek Station, ten miles to the east. The stage station at Fossil Creek was on the west side of the stream, and a trading ranch on the east side, both north of the road. The creek was larger than most of those farther to the west, with a pebbled bottom and good water. The column continued east, crossing a few small streams, and in another ten miles reached the Bunker Hill Stage Station, on the north side of the road. There was no stream here, but the station had a well with good water, and the troops probably stopped for a drink. About a mile and a half beyond, the expedition left the stage road, moved southeast two miles, and made Camp 23 at the neck of an oxbow on the Smoky Hill River. There was a stand of timber there and plenty of good water, but the north bank was very steep, causing some difficulty in getting the horses and mules to water.[16]

During the day's march a courier arrived with a dispatch from Governor Crawford of Kansas to the commanding officer of Fort Riley, forwarded to Hancock by Major Gibbs. It stated that six white settlers had recently been killed by Indians at "White Rock" on the Republican River near "Lake Sibley" and requested that troops be sent there at once. There was no mention of the tribe responsible, nor when the attack took place. The location of the alleged killings was also unclear. White Rock was a tiny hamlet, hardly more than a sawmill and a saloon, situated on the banks of White Rock Creek at the western boundary of present Republic County in north-central Kansas, about eight miles south of the Nebraska border. The stream originated to the west in Smith County and flowed in a generally west-to-east direction until emptying into the Republican in Republic County. Lake Sibley, in Cloud County to the south (named for Maj. George C. Sibley and long since disappeared), was a semicircular body of water about three miles in length, occupying an old bed of the Republican River that was cut off during some change of course long before white settlement. The distance between White Rock and Lake Sibley was a little more than twenty-five miles as the crow flies, and so the two were not really near one another. There were few settlers in the area and no other settlements to make reference to, so this may have been as much information as Governor Crawford could provide to pinpoint the area involved.[17]

---

[16] Brown, *March Journal*, May 5, 1867.

[17] Hancock to Nichols, May 22, 1867; KHC 9:34; Hollibaugh, *Biographical History of Cloud County*, 37–44; Rydjord, *Kansas Place Names*, 79, 412.

Whether Crawford's report of the killings was accurate is doubtful and at best speculative. The Cheyennes were certainly attacking whites trying to enter or settle in their country and had killed six buffalo hunters on Little Cheyenne Creek, a tributary of Buffalo Creek, in late May of 1866. They also killed three people at the White Rock settlement in April 1867, but no other killings of white settlers in the immediate area were reported during the remainder of that year. Governor Crawford, on the other hand, was constantly exaggerating claimed attacks on whites in an effort to get the army to drive the Plains Indians out of what whites thought of as Kansas, and he may well have cited the prior year's killings in order to magnify the scope of the problem. Before starting on the expedition, Hancock had issued orders that, as soon as the grass was up, a company of infantry from Fort Harker and a company of cavalry from Fort Leavenworth should march to Buffalo Creek in that vicinity.[18] He now found, contrary to his expectation, that neither had moved, and he issued immediate orders for them to do so. Why he was surprised or irritated at the failure of the two companies to move to Buffalo Creek is baffling, since in his own report he claimed the grass was not yet up.[19]

Hancock's troops left camp early on the morning of May 6 and marched north-northeast about a mile to the stage road. A little more than a mile to the east they passed another trading ranch. An additional five and a half miles brought them to the Wilson Creek Stage Station on the west bank of that stream. The creek had little water where it intersected the road, but the station's well provided good water from which the thirsty men no doubt drank. The march eastward continued and finally, after marching about twenty-six and a half miles, they crossed Page Creek and made their Camp 24 on the same site at Fort Harker where they had camped while outbound on April 2. During the day General Hancock had received word that Black Kettle had sent a message to the commanding officer at Fort Larned, advising him that he was going to that post and wanted to meet Hancock there. Once at Fort Harker the general dispatched John S. Smith, then acting as an interpreter at that post, to Fort Larned to see if Black Kettle was in fact there and, if so, to bring him to Harker for a talk. Smith had only recently left Black Kettle's camp south of the Arkansas and was on good terms with the chief and his followers. He returned, apparently on the afternoon of May 7, stating that Black

---

[18] This Buffalo Creek flows into the Republican River a short distance west of present Concordia, Kansas.

[19] Hancock to Nichols, May 22, 1867; Hollibaugh, *Biographical History of Cloud County*, 37–44.

Kettle was not at Fort Larned but probably would be there as soon as the grass was grown sufficiently to allow him to travel.[20]

General Hancock was still angered by Custer's continuing inability to find, pursue, and bring to battle the fleeing Cheyennes and Oglalas. This failure was rapidly dooming his expensive and much touted expedition. Hancock's anger was probably directed at everyone up and down the chain of command who he deemed might bear any responsibility, including the expedition quartermaster and commissary officers, the officers responsible for transport, and Custer himself to some degree. Once at Fort Harker, he had his subordinates check the status of the supplies intended for the expedition, since it was serving as the depot for them. On May 7 he had his adjutant write a letter to General Smith, as commander of the District of the Upper Arkansas, that was in part advisory and in part directive. It reported that 45,000 rations intended for Fort Hays were then at Harker, and that they, along with the remaining supply of forage at Harker sufficient for the cavalry horses through the first of June, would be sent to Fort Hays the following morning. This, the letter said, should eliminate further difficulty or delay in moving troops against the Indians. Then General Hancock expressed his wishes that operations be commenced "at the earliest possible day with the cavalry at Fort Hays, or with that portion of it which may be in a condition to move" against all Cheyennes and southern Oglalas between the Arkansas and Platte rivers. "It is particularly desirable," the letter stated, "that the movement herein directed against the Sioux and Cheyennes should be made before their horses, which are now poor, are fattened on the new grass." Subsequent movements against the Indians, Hancock wrote, would be at Smith's discretion. As it turned out, this would be only partly true, because Hancock later, under directive from General Sherman, ordered Smith to guard the country as far north and west as Fort Sedgwick and to send the Seventh Cavalry to Fort McPherson on the Platte, thence to Fort Sedgwick, and from there to return to Fort Hays.[21]

General Hancock and the remaining troops accompanying him, minus the company of the Thirty-seventh Infantry to be posted at Fort Harker, started eastward from Harker on the evening of May 7. They marched through the night a distance of about twenty-five miles to Spring Creek. There Hancock and his staff, constituting the Headquarters of the Depart-

---

[20] Brown, *March Journal*, May 6, 1867; Hancock to Nichols, May 22, 1867.
[21] W. S. Mitchell, AAAG, to A. J. Smith, May 7, 1867, AGO, LR, NA, MC619-R563; Hancock to Nichols, May 22, 1867.

ment of the Missouri in the Field, along with General Smith, embarked on the cars of the Union Pacific E.D. on the morning of May 8 and proceeded east to his headquarters at Fort Leavenworth. Since the expedition had first reached Spring Creek at the beginning of April, the rails of the Union Pacific E.D. had been completed to Salina on April 20 and continued westward at the rate of about a mile and a half a day. At that rate the tracks would have reached Spring Creek on or about May 3. Passenger service west from Junction City began on Tuesday evening, May 6, so it is apparent that General Hancock was met at Spring Creek by the very first passenger train to run that far west on the new line. It is probable that meeting the train west of Salina, the westernmost population center at the time, was prearranged by Hancock with a telegraphed request, because he rode eastward in the private car of the railroad contractors, Shoemaker, Miller, and Company. It was a small hotel on wheels, with kitchen, dining room, sitting room, and an apartment of sleeping facilities, all done in the plush decor of the day. As the general rode eastward in relative comfort, Battery B, along with the wagon trains, continued east on the military road to Fort Riley, where the artillery battery was to take post temporarily. The wagon trains were to be reloaded there and then return to the several posts along the Arkansas and Smoky Hill with provisions and supplies, including forage and provisions to support the Seventh Cavalry in field operations.[22]

Arrival of the railroad at Spring Creek and its steady progress westward shortened the route of the stagecoach lines, which ran only from the most western rail terminal to points of final destination, and also served to push forward settlement of the plains. When the expedition reached Fort Harker in early April, it was in an Indian country with no white presence aside from the two roads to Santa Fe and Denver, the stage stations along them, and the military posts established to guard them. Much to the surprise of the expedition troops, Fort Harker now had a new neighbor—an incipient town named Ellsworth. Henry Stanley, about to return east, was both fascinated and amused by the budding settlement. Attributing this advance of "civilization" to the locomotive, he wrote: "At the time of my visit there were four houses already completed, and three of them were lager beer saloons, while one, a log shanty, bore the euphonious title of Kingsbury Hotel. The locomotive will pass through the town in less than

[22] Hancock to Nichols, May 22, 1867; E. Custer, *Tenting on the Plains*, 546; Snell and Richmond, *Union and Kansas Pacific*, 334, 336–37, 342; Stanley, *My Early Travels*, 86.

eight weeks from the date of this letter." According to Stanley, the town's population was estimated at forty men, four women, eight boys, and seven girls. In addition, there were fourteen horses, "about twenty-nine and one half dogs," and plenty of rattlesnakes, copperheads, gophers, owls, mice, and prairie dogs within the town limits, but no cow, hog, cat, or chicken. As a progressive town, he said, "no sooner has the fifth house begun to erect its stately front above the green earth, than the population is gathered in the three saloons to gravely discuss the propriety of making the new town a city and electing a mayor." Later, as he traveled east to Junction City, Stanley commented on the growth of both Salina and Junction City. He also noted that the southern division of the Union Pacific would soon intersect at the latter with the eastern division.[23] General Sherman was expected at Junction City on the evening of May 9, en route to Fort Harker for a tour of inspection.[24]

With the departure of General Hancock, operations against the Cheyennes and Oglalas were left in the hands of General Smith as commander of the District of the Upper Arkansas, and for that only the Seventh Cavalry would be employed. Five companies of the Thirty-seventh Infantry were now posted at the several forts along the Santa Fe and Smoky Hill roads through the Indian country, where they could be useful. The artillery battery was at Fort Riley awaiting further assignment. The two newsmen who accompanied the expedition, Davis and Stanley, parted company at Fort Hays; Davis remained to cover subsequent operations of the Seventh Cavalry, and Stanley returned to St. Joseph, Missouri. From there he would take a steamboat up the Missouri River to Omaha, Nebraska, and join General Augur for his projected northern expedition against the Lakotas. Because Augur's expedition was drawing all of his mobile forces north from the Platte, Sherman would order the Seventh Cavalry away from the Smoky Hill and up to the Platte River valley. Once there they would protect the Union Pacific Railroad, the Oregon-California Trail,

[23] It was originally intended that the Union Pacific E.D. would be built northwest from Junction City up the Republican River valley to the Platte at or near Fort Kearney, there to join the central division at the 100th meridian. When the Union Pacific, building west from Omaha, beat them to the 100th meridian, the destination was changed to Denver, following the line of the Smoky Hill, and the name later changed to the Kansas Pacific Railroad. A Union Pacific southern division was to connect Junction City with Emporia via the Neosho River valley, then run on south. It was later renamed the Missouri-Kansas-Texas Railroad. See Snell and Richmond, "Union and Kansas Pacific," 161–86; Shortridge, "'Missing' Railroad Towns," 188; Lee and Raynesford, *Trails of the Smoky Hill*, 147–54; Stanley, *My Early Travels*, 92.

[24] Stanley, *My Early Travels*, 88–93.

Beyond Salina, the last town on the Smoky Hill road to Denver, the route of the railroad led through the Smoky Hills to Fort Harker. This sketch of an engineers' camp in the valley of Spring Creek appeared in the June 15, 1867, edition of *Harper's Weekly*.

and the travelers and settlers in lands south of the river. Hancock would soon cross the plains to Denver, inspecting the military posts and the fortified stage stations en route, but aside from his general supervision from departmental headquarters at Fort Leavenworth, his active participation in operations against the Cheyennes and Oglalas was now at an end.[25]

When the passenger train bearing Hancock and his staff reached Fort Riley, about ninety miles east of Fort Harker and sixty-five miles from their Spring Creek point of embarkation, there was a moment of irony. The train was the first to travel out to Spring Creek, then the end of the line. The general enjoyed accommodations in the private car of the contractors who were inspecting the new part of the line to verify completion and collect the government subsidies. On such runs the train usually traveled at about twenty-five miles per hour, faster than the prescribed eight-

[25] E. Custer, *Tenting on the Plains*, 610; Stanley, *My Early Travels*, 88–104.

een miles per hour for scheduled passenger trains. At that rate, and including stops at both Salina and Abilene, it would have reached Junction City and Fort Riley in about three hours, or sometime in the late morning. Boarding there was Elizabeth (Libbie) Custer, who was traveling to Leavenworth for the avowed purpose of securing "supplies" for the "General" and herself when they were moved to their anticipated new post, Fort Garland.[26] Hancock met her in her car and informed her that her husband was off on a fifteen-day scout looking for Indians, but that upon his return there would be no objection to his going to Fort Riley to meet her and return with her to Fort Hays. Hancock gave Custer high praise, saying that the Seventh Cavalry would be doing all of the fighting, marching, and scouting and that he didn't know what he would do without him. Hancock added that he didn't know whether there would be an Indian war or not (though he had already declared war against the Cheyennes and the Kiyuksa Oglalas) and said that if there was none, Custer could go to Fort Garland in August, but if there was war, the Seventh would be roaming and wintering at Fort Harker, Hays, or Riley. That, of course, was not what Libbie wanted to hear.[27]

Mrs. Custer remained at Leavenworth until Saturday evening, May 11, when she took the night train back to Fort Riley. Also aboard the train was General Sherman, en route to Junction City and beyond to Fort Harker, where he would make his inspection and where he had originally intended to meet with Hancock. Sherman was obviously running behind schedule, since he had been expected at Junction City on May 9. In all probability his delay is explained by his desire to meet with Generals Hancock and Smith at Fort Leavenworth and hear their report and assessment of operations against the Cheyennes and Oglalas. It is likely that Smith too was on the train, returning to his headquarters for the District of the Upper Arkansas at Fort Harker and moving on to Fort Hays to give Custer his orders, since Libbie Custer and her party would accompany Smith and his escort on her subsequent trip to Fort Hays.[28]

Now the pot was boiling. With the military's declaration of war on the Cheyennes and the Kiyuksa Oglalas, other forces were entering the mix.

---

[26] Although Custer never held a permanent rank higher than lieutenant colonel of the Seventh Cavalry, Libbie Custer always insisted on calling him "General," his volunteer and brevet rank from the Civil War.

[27] E. Custer, *Tenting on the Plains*, 546–47; Lee and Raynesford, *Trails of the Smoky Hill*, 160, 166; Snell and Richmond, *Union and Kansas Pacific*, 342.

[28] E. Custer, *Tenting on the Plains*, 547; Stanley, *My Early Travels*, 92–93.

To the north the peace commission led by General Sully, commonly referred to as the Phil Kearney Commission, had engaged in peace talks with several bands of Sicangus (Brulés) and Oglalas, leading to an agreement. Though these talks were only with friendly bands and had no effect on those deemed defiant and hostile, General Sherman could not afford to unleash General Augur's expedition while the commission was in the vicinity and still trying to bring peace. But he was not to be totally silenced about the effect of their agreements. One of the provisions authorized the Sicangus and Oglalas signing the agreement to roam and hunt south of the Platte to within ten miles of the Smoky Hill, in an area defined east to west by Plum Creek and Lodge Pole Creek. When he learned of it, Sherman fired off a telegram on April 27, 1867, from his headquarters in St. Louis to General Grant at army headquarters in Washington, D.C. It stated his opinion that if any Indians were located between the Platte and Smoky Hill as proposed, the railroad and stage lines would make constant demands for troops to protect their stations. General Hancock learned of the agreement by a dispatch he received from General Sully at Fort Harker on May 6, 1867. In a report on May 22 Hancock suggested that such an arrangement would cause great confusion and make it necessary to terminate operations against hostile Indians because troops could not distinguish between those that were friendly and those on whom the army was making war. While the two generals were lamenting what they perceived as obstacles to the pursuit of hostile Indians, the two Indian agents who had accompanied Hancock were writing to their superiors in an entirely different mode.[29]

Two days after the burning of the Indian villages, Colonel Wynkoop wrote to Commissioner of Indian Affairs N. G. Taylor, stating: "I know of no overt act that the Cheyennes had committed to cause them to be thus punished not even since their flight." His most critical analysis he reserved for future reports. Colonel Leavenworth, writing from Fort Zarah on May 2 after the council with Satanta at Fort Larned, opined to Taylor that it would have been better if Hancock had never set foot in the Indian country, a statement echoed by his superior, Thomas Murphy, superintendent of the Central Superintendency. Writing to Taylor from his office in Atchison, Kansas, on May 13, following a conference with Leavenworth "relative to Indian affairs and military operations in the South West," Murphy stated:

---

[29] W. T. Sherman to U. S. Grant (telegram), April 27, 1867, MC619-R563; Hancock to Nichols, May 22, 1867; Utley, *Frontier Regulars*, 120–21.

General Hancock's expedition, I regret to say, has resulted in no good, but on the contrary has been productive of much evil. It would have been far better for the interest of all concerned had he never entered the Indian Country with his soldiers. Indians who at the time he got into their Country were peaceable and well disposed toward the whites, are now fleeing with their women and children. No one knows where to and what the final result will be is doubtful.

These letters were only the first of the rumblings that were to take place across the country as newspapers, congressmen, government officials, humanitarians, and others learned of events on the western plains. It was as if they were repeating the conclusions of the Senate's Doolittle Committee:

While it is true many agents, teachers, and employees of the government are inefficient, faithless, and even guilty of peculations and fraudulent practices upon the government and upon the Indians, it is equally true that military posts among the Indians have frequently become centers of demoralization and destruction to the Indian tribes, while the blunders and want of discretion of inexperienced officers in command have brought on long and expensive wars, the cost of which, being included in the expenditures of the army, are never seen and realized by the people of the country.

Those words would prove not only analytical but also prophetic.[30]

---

[30] Wynkoop to Taylor, April 22, "1867," U.S. House, "Difficulties with Indian Tribes," 7:28; Leavenworth to Taylor, May 2, 1867, U.S. House, "Difficulties with Indian Tribes," 7:14; Murphy to Taylor, May 13, 1867, U.S. House, "Difficulties with Indian Tribes," 7:29; U.S. Senate, "Condition of the Indian Tribes," 3–8.

CHAPTER SIXTEEN

FLIGHT

T he talk with Hancock during the confrontation on Pawnee Fork had ended with the Indians moving rapidly back to their villages. According to Lieutenant Brown, it was about 12:45 in the afternoon when the soldiers first sighted the oncoming Cheyennes and Oglalas. Considering the time it took to close the distance and form in line of battle, it was probably about 1:15 P.M. when the talk took place. It must have been at least 1:30 P.M., and perhaps later, when it ended. The Indians left immediately, and the expeditionary force resumed its march half an hour later. The soldiers reached the site of their new Camp 13 on Heth's branch at 3:00 in the afternoon. Although the Cheyenne warriors remained in their village, Cheyenne women and children and all of the Kiyuksa Oglalas had left hurriedly, fleeing northward in fear of another Chivington-style massacre. In the hour and a half it took the soldiers to reorganize and travel the approximate eight miles from the place of the talk to Camp 13, the Indians had returned to their villages, where the Lakota men joined their families in flight, taking their herd of weakened horses with them.[1]

In the Cheyenne village about twenty-five lodges were apparently removed in their entirety, and the lodge covers of another fifteen were taken, leaving most of the lodge poles standing. Plains Indian women were extremely adept and efficient in erecting and removing their family lodges and could take one down and fold the lodge cover in a matter of minutes—a skill honed by necessity. The removal of essential family possessions, gathering of the horse herd, and loading of the pack animals, including those with travois, would have taken longer. Likely the families that took

---

[1] Brown, *March Journal*, April 14, 1867; Hancock to Nichols, May 22, 1867; Wynkoop to Murphy, September 14, 1867, 312; G. Custer, *My Life on the Plains*, 49; Davis, "Summer on the Plains," 295; Dippie, *Nomad*, 22; Kennedy, *On the Plains*, 66; Stanley, *My Early Travels*, 38; Utley, *Life in Custer's Cavalry*, 32–33.

their lodges or lodge covers began the process even as their menfolk were heading south to meet General Hancock and his troops. They were the farsighted and fortunate ones, concluding that Hancock would not be dissuaded from coming to their village and massacring them. Others arrived at the same conclusion later, but too late to allow for packing more than basic needs and a meager food supply. For them. leaving meant the loss of their lodges and many of their household possessions. One can imagine the rising panic that must have seized the women of the villages, particularly after the first warriors returned. The men would have shouted the news that the soldiers were coming, and pandemonium would have ensued. Nevertheless, they managed to try to block entrance into those lodges left behind before they departed, and when the soldiers arrived, the Cheyenne families were nowhere to be seen.[2]

According to the old Oglala man found in the Kiyuksa village, the Cheyennes wanted to stand and fight whereas the Oglalas were bent on leaving. It was a very different matter for the two peoples. The Cheyennes were in their own country and were outraged by this invasion and the apparent threat to their families, whereas the Oglalas believed it wiser to escape back to their own homelands to the north. Considering the relative numbers of fighting men on the two sides and the differences in arms, discretion clearly called for withdrawal and protection of the women, children, and old people. Their possessions, after all, could be replaced, but their families could not. And so, after standing fast to screen and protect the flight of their people, even the fierce Dog Soldiers—pride of the "Fighting Cheyennes," as they were widely known by other tribes—were forced into a grudging exodus. They had no way of knowing, based on previous experience with whites, that General Hancock intended only a show of force to awe them with the power of the government—unless, of course, they were inclined to be insolent or belligerent and thus properly subject to chastisement.[3]

The departure of the frightened women, children, and elderly of both tribes was clearly a chaotic event. Some family members became separated from one another and in a few instances left behind. Such was the case of the little Cheyenne girl who suffered from some form of mental disability. She refused to leave with the others and, possibly hiding during the flurry of excitement surrounding the tumultuous flight, was lost

---

[2] Hancock to Sherman, April 15, 1867; Hancock to Nichols, May 22, 1867; U.S. House, "Difficulties with Indian Tribes," 7:29, 71, 95.

[3] *Harper's Weekly*, May 11, 1867, 302.

to her family. Another abandonment involved the aged mother of White Horse, one of the Dog Soldier council chiefs. She was said to be deaf and dumb and "partly demented." Lack of knowledgeable medical analysis of the woman's condition permits no more than speculation, but at one time she certainly enjoyed sound health, as she was a wife and mother. During her later years she may have suffered a stroke or some similar cerebral accident that left her speech impaired, or perhaps she had some form of senile dementia. Whatever her condition was, she was left behind during the panic-driven flight of the village inhabitants. Unlike the old Lakota man and woman and the Cheyenne girl, however, she was not found by the American troops. After the expedition burned the village and departed, a number of Cheyenne warriors returned to the site, looking for loose horses that had been missed during their roundup. When they first realized the old lady had been left, they assumed the soldiers would kill her, just as Chivington's men had killed women in Black Kettle's camp. Now, to their surprise, they found her alive and apparently unharmed. She had obviously hidden while the soldiers were there, or perhaps some tribal members, seeing her plight and not having time to take her with them, found a suitable hiding place and left her with sufficient food, possibly in one of the excavations prepared near the stream. It has been suggested that some kindly American soldier found her, pitied her, and concealed her so she would be found later by her people, but this is unlikely. None of the soldiers knew that the Cheyennes would be back. Moreover, Hancock had no intention of harming these captives, and the other three were turned over to Wynkoop and taken to Fort Dodge for care, so why not her? Her discovery could not have been easily concealed from other soldiers, and there can be little doubt that, if found, she would have been taken with them. However she escaped detection, eventually the warriors found her and returned to her family.[4]

The Kiyuksa Oglalas fled due north, heading for the Republican River. The Dog Soldier and southern Sutaio Cheyennes, along with White Head's Óhmésèheso Cheyennes and a few Oglalas, moved northwest, leaving the trail that Custer followed. Employing their age-old subterfuge, the women and their families left the camp in small parties, scattering in different directions but primarily heading to the north and west. There was probably at least one larger party that left an obvious trail in the event

[4] Hyde, *Life of George Bent*, 261, 263; Stanley, "British Journalist," 302; Powell, *People of the Sacred Mountain*, 1:471–72, 474.

the soldiers pursued them, but this trail would also soon split into smaller ones. Eventually they all came together at some predetermined point either to wait until the soldiers left and they could return or, if necessary, to move on in search of a safer haven. Unlike the soldiers and even their white scouts, the Cheyennes knew the country intimately and could conceal themselves in places that whites would never be aware of. From what Custer and his troopers observed, the small parties of Cheyennes apparently came together again on Walnut Creek and then moved northwest as one body along its north fork. The warriors, after leaving the village, followed the same route, eventually catching up with their families at some point along the way. However, rapid pursuit by the Seventh Cavalry forced them to keep moving, so once again they broke into small parties to foil the soldiers. They continued westward, with some evidence that family groups leaving the main body were headed toward the Smoky Hill, where they came together again. Sometime on April 16 or 17 they were likely joined by the hunting party, with a supply of freshly killed game and hides. A rider was probably dispatched to inform them of the happenings on Pawnee Fork and to summon them to join the others at a specified place.[5]

It is not possible to say with certainty when Custer and his troops came close to catching the main body of fleeing Cheyennes, but it was likely late on April 15 or 16. Old White Head, the only Óhméséheso chief present at the time, later told the peace commissioners at Medicine Lodge that his people were in camp resting when they received word that the soldiers were coming. This caused panic among the women and young, who were certain the white men would kill them. But Roman Nose and his young warriors quirted them into silence, lest the soldiers hear them. Then Roman Nose ordered them all to rush to where the Oglalas were resting and throw themselves on the ground to avoid being seen. This must have occurred during daylight hours when Custer was in hard pursuit, because it was just before he turned north, leading his men toward the Smoky Hill. To the west and south of Cold Springs Branch, lying between it and the north fork of Walnut Creek, there is very broken country that would allow concealment of a large body of people if the searchers did not accidentally stumble upon them. If this was the location, then it occurred during the morning of April 16, the very morning when Custer had his first encounter with an adult bison and killed his horse in the process. Smoke signals were seen all around the cavalry column the previous evening, and the troops were mov-

---

[5] G. A. Custer to T. B. Weir, April 16, 1867, AGO, LR, NA, MC619-R562; Kennedy, *On the Plains*, 75–76.

ing in the direction of the largest column of smoke they observed. White Head's testimony would suggest that the small band of Oglalas accompanying them were staying together, a natural result of the language differences, and were perhaps located at that time just under the breaks in the plains. Moving to the same place and pressing oneself against the lower side of the bluffs would provide the best concealment from the passing column of troops. Neither the soldiers nor their scouts ever saw the Indians, and it was after this that the cavalry column moved north to the Smoky Hill.[6]

When Custer led his men northward, the Cheyennes turned away, likely headed west far enough to be safe before again moving north toward the Smoky Hill. For the Cheyennes and all the Plains Indians, their highways were the ladder of rivers and small streams that drained their country. When they turned away from Custer's line of march (north from Cold Springs Branch), they probably continued along the north fork of Walnut Creek farther to the northwest, then followed either the line of Wild Horse Creek or the north fork to the divide between the watershed of the Smoky Hill and Walnut Creek.[7] From there they would have taken either one of several very long and deep, dry arroyos, or perhaps Cheyenne Creek, north to the Smoky Hill. Once across the river, which at that time and place probably had no surface flow, they would have followed one of several small streams, possibly Indian Creek or Plum Creek, north to Hackberry Creek. Then they would have continued north to the Saline and beyond to the Solomon. Ed Guerrier advised Custer that the Cheyennes would probably head for either the Solomon or Beaver Creek, the latter a tributary of the Republican River flowing from the south. The Solomon's south fork is the more likely, primarily because it was well north of the stage road along the Smoky Hill, and well south of the great highway along the Platte. It was also the larger stream and had more sizable groves of cottonwoods and other plains trees. Buffalo herds were in the vicinity, whereas on the Republican there were none, the reason the Kiyuksas had come south. The Solomon was close to the heart of the Dog Soldiers' country and a favored place for their camps and those of the southern Sutaio. And it was a place where they could find relative safety and the opportunity to hunt and begin replacing their losses.[8]

[6] Stanley, "British Journalist," 302; Powell, *People of the Sacred Mountain*, 1:472–73.

[7] This Wild Horse Creek was one of several small streams by that name in the region, and not the one Custer crossed that night, which emptied into the Smoky Hill.

[8] USGA 1:100,000 Scale Metric Topographic Map, 30 × 60 Minute Quadrangle, "Healy, Kansas"; G. A. Custer to T. B. Weir, AAAG, April 19, 1867, AGO, LR, NA, MC619-R562; Kennedy, *On the Plains*, 85.

The night following their close brush with the Seventh Cavalry the chiefs and warriors gathered in solemn council. There was considerable discussion about the intentions of the Soldier Chief in sending his horse soldiers after them. The conclusion was that the White Chief and his soldiers had come to make war. Roman Nose, as one of the bravest and most renowned warriors in the tribe, was invited to speak, and he agreed that the soldiers must have come to make war on the Cheyennes and Oglalas. He expressed his opinion that because of this the Cheyennes should go to war with the whites. But the chiefs, perhaps hoping that peace might yet be possible, withheld their decision about what to do. Then, three nights later, probably after they had gone into camp on the south fork of the Solomon or some neighboring stream, a Cheyenne scout arrived.[9] With him came terrible news—the Soldier Chief had burned their village on Red Arm's Creek along with everything in it! The chiefs had been patient and thoughtful up to this time, but now deep anger and resentment replaced their earlier thoughts and hopes for peace. And a thirst for revenge seized the young men. It would be war.[10]

Immediate strikes at white installations were not yet possible. A great deal of weaponry—knives, arrows, war clubs, and lances—had been left at their village and was now seized or destroyed. Moreover, their lodges and food supply were mostly gone and must be replaced. This meant that the first order of business was to hunt and obtain a sufficient supply of meat for their people during the coming spring and summer, enough buffalo hides to replace the lodges and enough deer, elk, and other skins to replace lost parfleches, clothing, and other necessities. The owners of the twenty-five lodges taken from the village on Red Arm's Creek erected them at the new village site, and the families who had salvaged their lodge covers probably did the same. Plains Indians were known to maintain caches of extra lodge poles near favored camping grounds, of which there were many along the three main branches of the Solomon and the nearby Saline. Therefore it was probably only a short time before there were forty or so lodges standing in the new camp, and here all of the women and their families would have taken refuge until those tepees that were lost could be replaced. There were also hunting lodges belonging to the party that was searching for game along the Smoky Hill when Hancock

---

[9] White Head is reported as saying that it was two nights later, but Custer moved north to the Smoky Hill on the afternoon of April 16, crossing it and going into camp early on April 17. The village was burned on the morning of April 19, so there was at least a three-day lapse after the council.

[10] Powell, *People of the Sacred Mountain*, 1:473; Stanley, "British Journalist," 302.

destroyed the village on Pawnee Fork. Moreover, the hunting party probably brought with it a meat supply and a number of hides, the quantity depending on their success. So as the men began the difficult and arduous task of finding and killing a large number of bison and other game animals, the women were no doubt busily engaged in drying and curing the meat they did have and in scraping and preparing the buffalo hides for making the new lodges. It would have been an intensive communal effort.

The great horse herds belonging to the two villages were taken with them as the people of the two tribes headed off in their separate directions. But the hurried nature of their departure, the forced pace of their flight, and the rapid pursuit by the soldiers made it inevitable that some were left behind, some wandered off, and some dropped behind, exhausted from their weakened condition. To prepare for their hunt and simply to recover lost animals, parties were sent back to search for them. One of these parties found White Horse's mother hidden at or near the destroyed village and returned her. No doubt they roamed the country on both sides of their line of flight, rounding up those animals they could find and returning them to the new village. Some would be those trained for the pursuit of game, primarily bison, some would be warhorses, and the remainder would be riding horses and pack animals. When they were sufficiently recovered by grazing on the new grass, the hunt would begin. April waned and faded into May, the "moon when horses grow fat," bringing with it an abundant growth of the native grasses and success in the hunt. By its end, both horses and men would be ready, and then the war would begin.

CHAPTER SEVENTEEN

CUSTER FOILED AND FRUSTRATED

The Seventh Cavalry's arrival at old Fort Hays on the afternoon of April 19, 1867, was the beginning of a prolonged period of frustration for Custer. The grain and forage that was to be there had not arrived, nor were there sufficient rations to sustain the men during a scout of any length. The post commissary had little more than canned fruit, and the bakery could not provide fresh bread in quantities equal to the need. The wagon train of supplies Wild Bill Hickok had been sent for was expected to arrive on the evening of April 22, but when it did arrive, on April 25, it consisted of only five wagons. Earlier Custer had appropriated the supply of forage on hand for the horses of the Fort Hays garrison. For the Seventh Cavalry mounts this was the equivalent of a one-day supply, but by careful rationing they made it last for three. From April 22 until April 25, however, their horses had neither grain nor forage, and nothing but the grazing of native grasses. Then came disappointment, for the five wagons from Fort Harker provided the several hundred horses in Custer's command with forage for only a day and a half. Finally, on April 27 a train arrived from Harker with an adequate supply of grain. But meantime the horses had fallen so far out of condition that an extended period of feeding, grooming, and exercise would be required to bring them back into proper shape for a campaign. Nor were there other supplies in sufficient quantities to allow for any protracted movement.[1]

Adding to Custer's dilemma was the weather. It was very warm at the time of his arrival on April 19 and again the next day. But on April 21 a low-pressure system moved in, bringing with it spring thunderstorms and cooler weather. Pending the arrival of General Hancock and the balance

---

[1] G. A. Custer to T. B. Weir, AAAG, May 4, 1867, MC619-R563; Burkey, *Custer, Come at Once*, 7–12; E. Custer, *Tenting on the Plains*, 571; Utley, *Life in Custer's Cavalry*, 39.

of the expedition with the rest of their tents, for the next three days the men spent miserable afternoons and evenings in pelting rain, protected only by hats and ponchos and unable to build warming campfires. The lack of nourishing food, particularly fresh fruits and vegetables, began to take a toll on the troops. Once again desertion became a problem, and within a week Captain Barnitz reported to his wife that it was a nightly occurrence. On one night ten noncommissioned officers and privates left with both horses and arms. A detail of one sergeant and three privates, sent to shoot bison, failed to return. In April alone sixty-five men deserted from the eight companies of the Seventh Cavalry camped on Big Creek.[2]

With the horses in no condition to move and the command without adequate forage and rations, Custer had already given up hope of catching either Cheyennes or Oglalas. Then, on the evening of April 21, word reached him that General Hancock wanted the Seventh to march south and join him at Fort Dodge. This was undoubtedly the order of April 17 sent with Lieutenant Sheldon and must have added to his frustration, since he was in no more of a position to move south than to march north against the Indians. April 22 brought two messengers, escorted by two Delawares and several cavalrymen, with new instructions that put Custer in a better frame of mind. He had been given temporary command of a new "Smoky Hill sub-district," with instructions to protect the Smoky Hill stage route west from Fort Harker to Denver and to assist in reestablishing the stage line. He was not confined to the immediate area of the Smoky Hill but could move to the north or south as far as necessary to perform his duties, at least within the limits of the department. On April 25 Custer held a meeting with the superintendent and division agent of the stage line, intended to develop a plan for protecting the route through Custer's sub-district. Though the company wanted a cavalry escort for its coaches during the period of danger, the Seventh's animals were in no condition to provide this. Custer did agree to furnish an infantry guard on the coaches as necessary, however, and to provide well-armed guards in numbers matching those provided by the stage line at many of the stations west from Fort Hays to Cheyenne Wells.[3]

Following receipt of his new orders, on April 23 Custer sent a detachment of twelve men to Lookout Station to protect the reconstruction work

----

[2] Burkey, *Custer, Come at Once,* 8, 23; Utley, *Life in Custer's Cavalry,* 44.

[3] A. J. Smith to G. A. Custer, April 21, 1867, AGO, LR, NA, MC619-R562; G. A. Custer to G. W. H. Stouch, April 25, 1867, Rec. U.S. Army Mobile Units, Seventh Cavalry, Det. 1867–68, LS, NA; Burkey, *Custer, Come at Once,* 8–9; E. Custer, *Tenting on the Plains,* 570–72.

there. Subsequent to his meeting with the stage line agents he also sent five-man details from Fort Hays to Stormy Hollow, White Rock, Downer, and Castle Rock stations. At the same time, he sent orders to Capt. Myles W. Keogh, commanding at Fort Wallace, to place similar details at all stations from Grannell Springs west to Cheyenne Wells. He instructed the details sent from Fort Hays to allow no Indians within one thousand yards of the stations and to have no communications with them whatsoever. If the Indians disregarded this order, whether claiming to be friendly or not, the troops were to fire on them. How the Indians were expected to understand an order delivered in English or what one thousand yards meant was not explained. The latter part of this order was omitted from the one sent to Captain Keogh, but his instructions did include two additional matters. First, he was to send William A. (Medicine Bill) Comstock, the Fort Wallace scout, to Fort Hays immediately to join Custer's cavalry force as a scout. Second, he was to keep the cavalry company at Fort Wallace ready to cooperate in operations Custer was planning against the Cheyennes and Oglalas. On the same day, Custer sent 1st Lt. Oliver Phelps (of the Thirty-seventh Infantry garrison at Fort Hays) back to Fort Harker to arrange for a twenty-day supply of rations and forage for Fort Hays, including the eight companies of the Seventh Cavalry.[4]

On April 26 Custer addressed the problem of maintaining the Seventh Cavalry horses. Following their daily periods of grazing, six of the eight company commanders had been allowing their troopers to straggle back to their camp in a disorganized fashion. To remedy this, Custer ordered morning and afternoon grazing periods, with the noncommissioned officer in charge of each company to put his men in company formation when recall was sounded and to return to camp in an orderly manner. Company commanders were ordered to administer severe punishment to any man who abused or neglected his horse. But the fact that the horses were being taken out for grazing does suggest some significant growth of new grass, and that is not surprising. The area of Fort Hays experiences its last spring frost by about April 27 and has a freeze-free growing period that extends approximately to October 15 each year. The average annual rainfall is 22.9 inches per year, of which 2.22 inches falls in April and 3.46 inches in May, one of the wettest months of the year. By May the daily high temperature

---

[4]Custer to C.O., Fort Hays, April 23, 1867, Rec. U.S. Army Mobile Units, Seventh Cavalry, Det. 1867–68, LS, NA; Custer to Stouch, April 25, 1867; G. A. Custer to M. W. Keogh, April 25, 1867, Rec. U.S. Army Mobile Units, Seventh Cavalry, Det. 1867–68, LS, NA; G. A. Custer to Phelps, April 25, 1867, Rec. U.S. Army Mobile Units, Seventh Cavalry, Det. 1867–68, LS, NA; Burkey, *Custer, Come at Once*, 9.

averages about 75 degrees and the low about 49 degrees, the optimum growing conditions for the region before the intense heat of summer arrives.
Henry Stanley was commenting on the new spring growth by the time the
expedition reached Fort Larned, and Isaac Coates mentioned the new buffalo grass at the time they reached the Cheyenne and Oglala villages on
Pawnee Fork. Captain Barnitz wrote to his wife, Jennie, on May 6 that
"our horses are beginning to look very well again," and that "grass is coming up finely—-also the flowers." Only Custer and Hancock appear to have
complained bitterly about the lack of new-growth grass, and they may have
had other motives for their complaints. Hancock was likely hard-pressed
for excuses to explain the failure of the expedition to catch and properly
"chastise" the Indians he claimed were militant, treacherous, and deserving of punishment. Custer's motives were more personal, because of his
plans to bring his wife to Fort Hays. Pursuit of the Cheyennes or Oglalas
could thwart those desires. The fact remains, however, that the heavy American cavalry horses could not survive by grazing the native grasses of the
plains unless they had supplemental nourishment.[5]

Compounding Custer's problems was a constant flow of misinformation, rumors, false or ill-founded reports, and blatant lies concerning the
danger of Indian attacks, originating with the stage line employees, operators of hunting or trading ranches, and even soldiers from the Fort Hays
garrison or the Seventh Cavalry. On the evening of April 24 an Irishman
came running into the cavalry camp on Big Creek "minus everything but
half a pair of trousers," reporting that thousands of Indians were all around
his ranch four miles distant, that the plains were black with them, and
that he had barely escaped with his scalp and his life. A party led by Captain Hamilton was ordered to make a reconnaissance but found neither
Indians nor any evidence that they had been in the vicinity. Reports of
this kind persisted through the early days of May. On the afternoon of
May 13 a man galloped into Custer's camp, reporting that more than two
hundred Indians had assembled around Lookout Station. He claimed that
a wagon proceeding on to Downer Station with a five-man escort had
barely escaped capture by them, and he had himself gone out to verify the
number and the tribe they belonged to. He was satisfied they were
Cheyennes and numbered four to five hundred beyond any doubt, because

[5] HQ Seventh U.S. Cavalry, Circular 11, April 26, 1867, Rec. U.S. Army Mobile Units, Seventh U.S.
Cavalry, Circulars Issued, RG 391, NA; Soil Survey of Ellis County, Kans., August 1975, USDA; Burkey,
Custer, Come at Once, 9; Kennedy, *On the Plains*, 66; Stanley, *My Early Travels*, 27–28; Utley, *Life in
Custer's Cavalry*, 45.

he had been within sixty yards of them and barely escaped capture himself. Davis reported that after sunset Custer led a column of three hundred troopers in pursuit of these Indians, planning a night attack on them. It is possible, however, that he actually meant to show his men the consequences of pursuing every wild report and to put an end to the constant rumors concerning Indians.[6]

Whatever the motivation behind the march of the Seventh Cavalry to Lookout Station, it was both exhausting and frustrating for the troopers. The entire command (with the exception of the sick and a guard detail) was ordered out, leaving their tents in place. They carried three days' rations in their haversacks, forty rounds of ammunition, and one day's forage for the animals. With them was one company of the Thirty-seventh Infantry from Fort Hays, and additional supplies were carried in their wagons. The distance from the camp on Big Creek to Lookout Station was eighteen miles, and they traveled this in the dark without a halt, leaving at 6:00 P.M. and arriving about midnight. To Custer's chagrin and irritation, the small garrison assigned to protect the stage station crew and the contractor's employees, though on the alert, knew nothing of any Indians in the vicinity. Inquiry of the civilians, then busily engaged in a game of draw poker, elicited no additional information. One player, in response to Custer's question, simply stated, "Dang me ef I know. I'm a rar hos ef I kere." The search for witnesses continued, and, according to Theodore Davis, the troops eventually came upon a man who claimed to have seen what he believed were Indians. Finally they found another who had been with the wagon that supposedly had a narrow escape. Examination of the area where the Indians were allegedly seen revealed that it had recently been crossed by a bison herd. The march had been of no use.[7]

Upon arrival at Lookout Station and discovery of the false report, the men were ordered to lie down in line, hold their horses by the reins, and get what sleep they could. Toward morning reveille sounded early, and fires were built near the little creek to brew their coffee. They marched shortly before sunup, first toward the cliffs west of Lookout Station (the bluffs of the Smoky Hill Valley), then south a mile or so, where they halted. Here they gathered buffalo chips, built fires, and apparently had a quick breakfast. Finally the march began again, this time eastward toward

---

[6] Burkey, *Custer, Come at Once*, 9, 14; Davis, "Summer on the Plains," 298; Utley, *Life in Custer's Cavalry*, 43.

[7] Burkey, *Custer, Come at Once*, 14; Davis, "Summer on the Plains," 298; Utley, *Life in Custer's Cavalry*, 49.

Lookout Station, then back to the camp at Fort Hays, all without a halt except for a brief two-minute break at Big Creek Station. The day was exceedingly hot, and tempers were frazzled. Custer was so incensed by the false report that on May 15 he issued a general order to all military units stationed along the Smoky Hill:

> The frequency with which fake and startling reports of the presence and move-ments of bodies of hostile Indians, are made by enlisted men and citizen employees of the Government, employed along the Smoky Hill route, and the importance of keeping the troops always on the alert, without at the same time unnecessarily exhausting their energies, demands that in future all persons whether civilians or soldiers who are guilty of bringing in false information, or who through fear, imagination or maliciousness originate reports, which are unfounded or greatly exaggerated regarding the presence of hostile Indi-ans, and which are calculated to produce unnecessary alarm, shall be consid-ered stampeders and at once subjected to summary punishment in the presence of the command to which the alarm is brought. Commanding officers will punish such persons with the utmost severity.

Custer added that subsequent investigations had shown every one of the reports of the previous weeks to be unfounded, and some based on the presence of buffalo. It was the duty of all officers and men, he said, to ver-ify positively that what they saw were Indians before reporting it to higher authority.[8]

The forced march to Lookout Station and the equally forced march back were hard on both the troopers and their horses. Writing in his jour-nal on May 14, Albert Barnitz said of the march, "Thus does General Custer expend his cavalry." Barnitz had become increasingly disgusted with Custer (to whom he contemptuously referred in his journal and let-ters as "the Brevet Major General Commanding"), and now he was given further reason to be critical. The troopers were hardly back in camp when, with no real investigation, Custer ordered Barnitz confined to quarters under arrest for failing to feed his squadron's horses that morning and abandoning government forage intended for them. Actually Barnitz had been the first to feed his horses and used all of his forage, but he chose to remain in confinement for four days rather than explain himself to Custer. He expressed his disgust with Custer in a letter to his wife, calling him the "most complete example of a petty tyrant" and indicating that this

---

[8] General Order No. 3, Smoky Hill Sub-District, May 15, 1867, Rec. U.S. Army Mobile Units, Sev-enth U.S. Cavalry, Circulars Issued, RG 391, NA; Burkey, *Custer, Come at Once,* 14; Utley, *Life in Custer's Cavalry,* 49.

opinion was widely held by the officers of the regiment. While he was holding Barnitz in confinement, Custer also disciplined six enlisted men on charges of leaving the cavalry camp and going over to Fort Hays without a pass. Their infraction: they had just received their pay and went to the post to purchase canned fruit to help ward off scurvy, which was widespread among the men of the Seventh Cavalry. They were gone only a brief time and missed no duty. For their punishment Custer ordered the officer of the day to have someone shave half of each man's head of hair, then parade them through the company streets before placing them in close confinement.[9]

Custer's ill humor, the cause of so much distress and disaffection among his officers and men, began shortly after the arrival of Smith and Hancock on May 3. On May 5, the day Hancock and Smith departed Fort Hays, he gave his officers a stern rebuke for failure to attend stable calls. The following day he was even more irritable for no discernible reason. Captain Barnitz speculated that there were two possible causes. One might be traced to the arrival of a copy of the March 23, 1867, issue of the *Toledo Blade*, which carried an editorial expressly citing Custer as an example of an opportunist who could easily abandon President Johnson during his period of unpopularity if it served his purpose and gained him favor with others. The second possibility Barnitz considered was that Custer had incurred the displeasure of either Hancock or someone else and had been severely berated. Neither Hancock nor Smith would likely be pleased by the lengthy delay in pursuing the Indians or making any significant moves beyond Fort Hays, despite Custer's several excuses. Whatever the cause, Custer's moodiness worsened during the following days, leading to a sharp drop in morale among officers and men and a decided decrease in the cooperation between commander and troops.[10]

Adding to the equation was the presence of scurvy, a disease caused by a deficiency of vitamin C (ascorbic acid) and characterized by weakness, muscle degeneration, bruising, joint pain, anemia, spongy gums, loss of teeth, and bleeding from the mucous membranes. Captain Barnitz wrote that by mid-May at least seventy-five cases had been reported in the Seventh Cavalry camp, and the men were craving canned fruit or fresh vegetables. Scurvy develops over a protracted period of time, usually two to three months before serious symptoms are present, and is preceded by an

---

[9] Burkey, *Custer, Come at Once*, 14–15; Utley, *Life in Custer's Cavalry*, 49–51.
[10] Burkey, *Custer, Come at Once*, 11–12; Utley, *Life in Custer's Cavalry*, 46–53.

interval of ill health characterized by a sallow complexion. For the men of the Seventh Cavalry this likely means it could be traced back to a poor diet during the winter at Fort Riley, followed by an even poorer diet in the field. General Hancock noted the presence of scurvy in both the fort garrison and the men of the Seventh Cavalry while he was in camp at Big Creek on May 4. He directed that antiscorbutics in the form of potatoes and onions be sent as soon as possible. Upon returning from Fort Leavenworth two weeks later, General Smith found they had not yet arrived and that scurvy was "rapidly on the increase." Nearly two weeks later he reported that no antiscorbutics had to date been received and that there were forty cases of scurvy in the cavalry camp alone. This was immediately before the departure of Custer and six of the eight cavalry companies on their next major operation and suggests that rations during the trip northwest to Fort McPherson were equally deficient in ascorbic acid.[11]

Desertion proved a continuing problem. No doubt the low morale among the men, induced by the stringent and often unfair discipline and punishment Custer meted out, was a major factor. Another must have been the lack of fresh fruits and vegetables in the soldiers' diet, resulting in rampant scurvy. In Custer's regiment alone desertions totaled ninety men during the encampment on Big Creek, and some reports said more. A letter to the *Junction City Weekly Union*, appearing in the June 1, 1867, issue, reported that over thirty men left in one night. Libbie Custer, following her arrival at old Fort Hays, claimed that forty men deserted in one night, "taking arms, ammunition, horses, and quantities of food." She also said that a full third of the regiment planned to desert at one time and that, had their plans not been discovered, the whole area of Fort Hays and the cavalry camp would have been at the mercy of the Indians, who "lay in wait constantly." The *Rocky Mountain News* in Denver ran a story based on the report of a passenger recently traveling the Smoky Hill route, claiming that three hundred men had deserted from Custer's and Smith's commands in a two-week period, taking their horses and gear. That seems an improbable number but the commands did encompass all troops operating in the District of the Upper Arkansas, including its forts.[12]

---

[11] G. E. Brewer to W. S. Mitchell, AAAG, May 11, 1867, MC619-R563; Hancock to Nichols, May 22, 1867; A. J. Smith to C. McKeever, May 16, 1867, Department of the Missouri, LR, RG 393, NA; A. J. Smith to W. S. Hancock, May 29, 1867, Department of the Missouri, LR, RG 393, NA; Burkey, *Custer, Come at Once*, 14–15; Millbrook, "West Breaks In General Custer," 119; Thomas, *Taber's Cyclopedic Medical Dictionary*, 1650; Utley, *Life in Custer's Cavalry*, 51.

[12] *Junction City Weekly Union*, June 1, 1867; Burkey, *Custer, Come at Once*, 23; E. Custer, *Tenting on the Plains*, 695; Millbrook, "West Breaks In General Custer," 119.

Theodore Davis stated that the desertion rate from the Seventh Cavalry was about fifty per month, which seems to comport closely with official records. But Davis attributed different reasons for the ongoing attrition of personnel:

> There seems but one way of accounting for this persistent desertion. Many of the men had enlisted under assumed names, and gone out on the Plains just to see the country, purposing, no doubt, to take advantage of any chance that might appear to afford them a bettering of condition. They were perfectly aware that the extent of the punishment which could be inflicted, in the event of capture, would be six months in the guardhouse, and in all probability not even that.
>
> In less than one year the Seventh Cavalry has lost by desertion nearly eight hundred men. Some of these men were killed by Indians, a number escaped south to Council Grove, where they joined the bands of desperados which infest that region; others are now among the mines of Colorado; and a few are busy among the breaks of the Platte, cutting ties for the Union Pacific Railroad.

Custer himself laid most of the blame for the high rate of desertion on the miserable quality of the food furnished for the troops. He claimed that bread baked as far back as 1860 was being issued to his men and that in some food packages stones were found that weighed as much as twenty-five pounds. Such fraud was indeed perpetrated on the government during the Civil War, but no similar reports concerning provisions were made at this time by other military units operating within the Department of the Missouri, nor from the garrisons of its various posts. All of these received their subsistence stores from the same commissary warehouses at Fort Leavenworth and Fort Riley. Captain Barnitz mentioned seventeen desertions within a week of the regiment's arrival at Fort Hays, but no more until the day after the "Brevet Major General Commanding" had the heads of the six men shaved. Fourteen men deserted from Companies E, H, and M on May 18, with an additional thirteen following over the next four days. Barnitz wrote to his wife that if Custer remained in command, recruiting would have to be significantly increased.[13]

A few of the happenings at the camp on Big Creek were of a more positive sort. Custer's letter to Captain Keogh resulted in the arrival of Will Comstock at Big Creek within the next five days. On April 30 Custer wrote a letter to Libbie, reporting that Comstock was then occupying an 'A Tent' directly in the rear of his own. And two days later he again wrote her:

[13] Burkey, *Custer, Come at Once*, 23–24; G. Custer, *My Life on the Plains*, 110; Davis, "Summer on the Plains," 298; Millbrook, "West Breaks In General Custer," 118–19, 144; Utley, *Life in Custer's Cavalry*, 53.

General Hancock had a number of white scouts and couriers with his expedition. Four of them, sketched by Theodore R. Davis, were, from left to right,
Will Comstock, Thomas Atkins, Thomas Kinkade, and Ed Guerrier. Given
that Comstock joined the expedition well after Custer and the Seventh Cavalry
arrived at Fort Hays, this sketch was probably made after the rest of the expeditionary force reached Fort Hays on May 3, 1867. *Harper's Weekly*, June 29, 1867.

"Comstock messes with me. I like to have him with me, for many reasons.
He is a worthy man, and I am constantly obtaining valuable information
from him regarding the Indians, their habits, etc."

William A. (Will, or Medicine Bill) Comstock was indeed a most valuable addition to Custer's stable of scouts. Aside from Ed Guerrier, he was
probably the most knowledgeable about the Indians among those on the
expedition. Theodore Davis wrote of him:

Will Comstock, the chief, has lived in the Far West for many years, his qualifications as an interpreter and scout are said, by those best qualified to judge,
to be unsurpassed by any white man on the plains. He is, moreover, a man of
tried bravery and a first-rate shot. Comstock is a rather reticent person, and
seldom talks of his exploits. . . . The Indians call him "Medicine Bill." The reason for this, Comstock says, is the fact of his having cut off a man's finger after
it had been bitten by a rattlesnake. The amputation saved the man's life and
gained Comstock a great amount of respect and a title from the Arapahoes.

Born in Michigan and a great-nephew of James Fenimore Cooper, Comstock left home and moved west at age fifteen. By 1867 he had achieved a reputation across the southern plains that was little short of legendary. Keogh had written to Custer about him as early as January 21, 1867, as the expedition was being organized. He was, Keogh said, "an eccentric genius and ardent admirer of everything reckless and daring." Whether reticent or reckless, Comstock was certainly one of the most capable scouts serving with Custer. The other famous Bill accompanying the expedition, Wild Bill Hickok, was no longer acting as a courier for Custer but, following a brief sojourn to Junction City, had apparently returned to Hancock's headquarters.[14]

Probably arriving with Comstock on or about April 30 were two letters from Captain Keogh that were not calculated to raise Custer's ill temper from the doldrums. The small garrison at Fort Wallace was stretched dangerously thin by Custer's order to provide five guards for the stage stations from Grannell Station west to Cheyenne Wells. Keogh called the order "ridiculous" and asked what the guard details were to do if the Indians did come closer than one thousand yards, since that instruction was omitted from Custer's April 25 letter to Keogh. Irritated, Custer had his adjutant give Keogh a mild dressing-down for the disrespectful language addressed to a superior officer. But then Custer went on to give further instructions that were outside the scope of his own orders, unconscionable and unreasonably brutal, and far beyond what was allowable under the moral and legal principles of the country and its army: "You will without regard to age, sex or condition kill all Indians you may encounter, belonging to either the Sioux or Cheyennes, except you are convinced they belong to certain bands of friendly (?) Indians, reported to be encamped on the Headwaters of the Republican."

Clearly Custer was now convinced that there were no friendly Indians anywhere in the vicinity. There was no mention of how these "friendly" Indians were to be identified or what to do if the friendly Indians were camping elsewhere. Custer went on to say that Keogh should not burden the command with prisoners—apparently a thinly veiled order to kill rather than take prisoners. As to the existing prisoners, Keogh was to wait until Custer had discussed the matter with the department commander. Then, in a stroke of irony, Custer added: "As to your pursuing Indians, while it

---

[14] *Harper's Weekly*, June 29, 1867, 11:406; Burkey, *Custer, Come at Once*, 20–21, 21n12; E. Custer, *Tenting on the Plains*, 575, 579; Gray, "Will Comstock, Scout," 2–15.

is not strictly forbidden, in doing so, you must exercise the greatest pre-caution against stratagem and surprise, remembering that it is the Indian's 'ruse de guerre' to decoy small garrisons away from their positions of defense." In time, at Little Big Horn, Custer's words to Keogh must have come back to haunt him.[15]

If there were few high points during the forty-two days of April and May 1867 that the Seventh Cavalry spent at the Big Creek encampment, the officer's buffalo hunt had to be one of them. In his May 2 letter to Libbie, Custer mentioned the plans for it: "It is also proposed that the officers of the Seventh and those of the post united, divide into two par-ties, and each go buffalo hunting, the party that kills the smallest num-ber of buffalo to pay the expenses of a supper for the entire number." The hunt was first scheduled for May 5, but because of Custer's bad mood fol-lowing the departure of General Hancock, it was postponed until May 7. The officers were divided into two parties, one headed by Maj. Wyckliffe Cooper and the other by Maj. A. P. Morrow. Seven officers were chosen as the hunters for each team by the leaders. Cooper's party was to go out on the first day and Morrow's on the second, and the hunt was limited to the hours between sunrise and sunset. They were not required to use all of their time, but they could not leave camp until after sunrise and had to be back in camp by sunset. No shot could be fired while an officer was dismounted. To provide evidence of their kills, the tongues of the downed bison were to be retrieved and hidden until time for the tally. According to Theodore Davis, the parties had to ride from fifteen to twenty miles to find any buffalo, which was not surprising since bison had long since been wary of coming close to human encampments.[16]

Custer went hunting with the Cooper party but apparently had no luck in shooting any bison, since no one, not even he, mentioned it. He did, however, manage to accidentally shoot another exhausted horse as he was dismounting. Doubtless this did not help his already sour disposition. Major Cooper's party ultimately proved to be victorious, having killed twelve buffalo while Major Morrow's party killed eleven. Individually Capt. Louis Hamilton was the champion, having killed four of the beasts him-self. Reward for their efforts came in the form of a dinner hosted by the losers on the evening of May 23. It was supposed to be a "right good feed,"

[15] G. A. Custer to M. W. Keogh, May 3, 1867, Rec. U.S. Army Mobile Units, Seventh Cavalry, Det. 1867–68, LS, NA; Burkey, *Custer, Come at Once*, 10.

[16] *Harper's Weekly*, July 6, 1867, 11:426; Burkey, *Custer, Come at Once*, 12; E. Custer, *Tenting on the Plains*, 579, 581.

and, wrote Davis, "The supper was certainly an excellent one." Despite the convivial atmosphere, Custer's irritability and moodiness continued, as did strained relations with his officers and men.[17]

The final part of the equation relating to Custer's ill temper, and by no means the least, was his wife, or more accurately her absence. Elizabeth Bacon Custer, Libbie, was a petite, slender, dark-haired woman. She was attractive, well educated, energetic, capable, and above all completely devoted to her husband. She went where he went, even to his camps in Virginia during the Civil War, and afterward to the frontier forts of Kansas and later the Dakotas. From the time of their parting at Fort Riley on March 27, 1867, they had carried on almost daily correspondence, much of it devoted to plans to be together at one or another of the department's military posts sometime that summer. Custer went so far as to establish a line of six courier stations between Fort Hays and Fort Harker to ensure that the mail would reach him at least three times a week. Fort Harker was a mail station, but Fort Hays was not. Ostensibly this was done for military purposes, for the army commonly used its own couriers to carry dispatches and orders, and not the U.S. mail. General Smith's observation to General Hancock, while en route to Fort Leavenworth, was that the courier stations they had seen between Forts Hays and Harker must be there so Custer could write to his wife. His eagerness to have her with him increased with the departure of Hancock and Smith on May 5. The day before they left he wrote her that his camp was "most beautiful" and "not only beautiful but clean." He told her of the Sibley tent General Smith was giving him for their use and said that a large hospital tent might also be found for their home on the plains. On May 6, the day after Hancock and Smith left, he wrote Libbie of his impatience for her arrival, and the following day he advised her, "Do not let the grass grow under your feet."[18]

For Libbie Custer a trip to Fort Hays was complicated in that she had a houseguest, twenty-one-year-old Anna Darrah from Monroe, Michigan, one of her bridesmaids. Anna, whom Libbie called Diana, was spending the summer with her hostess in the Custer quarters at Fort Riley. Anna was perfectly willing to go and even looking forward to it, so Custer and Libbie did not let her presence stand in the way of their reunion. He urged his wife to come to him at the earliest possible moment, and she

[17] *Harper's Weekly*, July 6, 1867, 11:426; Burkey, *Custer, Come at Once*, 12; E. Custer, *Tenting on the Plains*, 581, 612–13.

[18] Burkey, *Custer, Come at Once*, 8–11, 17; E. Custer, *Tenting on the Plains*, 546–47, 581; Utley, *Life in Custer's Cavalry*, 254–55.

took him at his word. Libbie had returned to Fort Riley from Leavenworth on the May 11 night train and so would have been back in their quarters on Sunday, May 12. General Sherman, who took the same train, invited her to ride the train with him en route to inspect Fort Harker. She packed only a small trunk and a roll of bedding so as to travel in "light marching order." Sherman had business at Fort Riley and Junction City, so their departure was on either Tuesday, May 14, or the morning of Wednesday, May 15. They must have arrived sometime on May 15, because Major Gibbs, now commanding temporarily at Fort Harker, refused to allow Libbie and Anna to continue to Fort Hays that night. The road was dangerous, with the possibility of an Indian attack ever present, and it would have required a special guard to protect the wife of the Seventh Cavalry's field commander, her guest, Anna, and her maid, Eliza. Custer would not have hesitated to use his troops in this manner but, much to Libbie's distress, Gibbs was less inclined to provide a special military escort for two adventuresome ladies. Therefore they left the following day, May 16, accompanying General Smith and his escort en route to Fort Hays, where he would oversee further operations against the Cheyennes and Oglalas. It was a monotonous eighty-mile trip, and they arrived on the morning of May 17.[19]

The delighted Custer had prepared well for his wife's arrival. He erected a series of tents, including a large hospital tent, about two to three hundred yards behind the cavalry camp at a pleasant point along Big Creek. Captain Barnitz claimed that Custer had "bowers and screens of evergreens erected, and triumphal arches." At first Libbie and Anna were excited and well pleased with their new, though temporary home. There were interesting things to see, people to meet, and stories to hear. They met frontier scouts and couriers that they had read or heard about, such as Will Comstock and Ed Guerrier. They saw the menagerie that had been developed at Fort Hays, including wolves, coyotes, raccoons, porcupines, badgers, wildcats, jackrabbits, prairie dogs, rattlesnakes, eagles, hawks, owls, buffalo calves, young antelope, elk and deer, and other curious denizens of the plains. Custer himself had a young beaver as a pet, apparently captured somewhere along Big Creek. At least until Libbie's arrival it was accustomed to sleeping with her husband and being hand-fed by him.[20]

[19] Burkey, *Custer, Come at Once*, 10, 17; E. Custer, *Tenting on the Plains*, 547, 600–609; Utley, *Life in Custer's Cavalry*, 52.

[20] Burkey, *Custer, Come at Once*, 19–21; E. Custer, *Tenting on the Plains*, 576; Utley, *Life in Custer's Cavalry*, 52–53.

Libbie's main pleasure was being reunited with her husband. But she and her friend Anna had arrived at an unfortunate time. Within the first week of their arrival the peace was disturbed on three different nights as deserters left en masse amid a hail of bullets fired both at them and by them. Then, on May 25 and 26, the two young women were exposed to the terrifying experience of a spring thunderstorm on the plains. High winds, booming thunder, and constant wild and brilliant streaks of lightning filled the skies, while soaking rain was hurled slantwise against the tents. So fierce was the wind that despite the frantic efforts of Custer and his guard the tent eventually blew over, and the women were forced to find shelter in a nearby Sibley tent. Designed after the tepees of the Plains Indians, it was circular and had no corners to catch the wind. There they spent the night with other refugees from the storm. As frightening as these experiences were, Libbie was willing to endure them all for the happiness and excitement she found in her husband's company. Within days he would be gone, leading a Seventh Cavalry scout northward to the Platte River.[21]

Plans for a scout had been discussed since General Hancock's arrival at Fort Hays. In fact, upon reaching that post, General Smith had issued Special Field Order No. 34, dated May 3, 1867, directing Custer to march the following day with six companies of the Seventh Cavalry, taking fifteen days of rations and five days of grain with them. Their destination was Fort McPherson, Nebraska, where further orders and added supplies would await them. Presumably the only reason Custer did not leave as ordered was the lack of rations. Hancock's instructions to General Smith on May 7 indicated that sufficient rations for the troops and enough forage for their livestock would be en route to Fort Hays the following morning, as well as his desire that operations be commenced by the cavalry "at the earliest possible day." Once back at Fort Leavenworth he again wrote to General Smith (then en route to Fort Hays), directing an early movement north to Fort McPherson. Before leaving Fort Harker for Fort Hays, Smith sent a letter to Hancock promising to "organize the available cavalry in compliance with your letter of the 7th inst., as soon as possible." On arrival at Fort Hays the next morning, one of his first acts was the dissolution of the subdistrict of the Smoky Hill and the return of Custer to his field command of the Seventh Cavalry as his sole duty. Smith intended to use Fort Hays as the temporary headquarters for the District of the

---

[21] Burkey, *Custer, Come at Once*, 21; E. Custer, *Tenting on the Plains*, 614–18; Utley, *Life in Custer's Cavalry*, 52–53.

Upper Arkansas in order to exercise the closest possible supervision over operations against the Indians.[22]

Despite his several orders, Custer was, for some reason, not ready or unwilling to move. He did place his troops on twenty-four-hour alert on May 20 but did nothing further. The following day General Smith had his adjutant again write orders to Custer, directing him to "proceed as indicated in SFO No. 34 . . . in a northerly direction to the Platte, and thence to McPherson, at which point you will find a large supply of rations and forage." From Fort McPherson he was to proceed up the south fork of the Platte to Fort Sedgwick and then on to Fort Morgan. If all was quiet in the vicinity of those posts, he was to move south to Fort Wallace, where further instructions would await him. Custer's response to these orders was to ask his officers on May 22 to report by the following morning what would be required for their companies to be ready to march. Still nothing happened, and on May 23 General Smith wrote to General Hancock that the delay was because of unusually cold weather that inhibited growth of the grasses and "some of the most terrific storms" he had ever experienced on the plains. This seems to be an excuse contrived to protect Custer from Hancock's wrath. Even if the weather was cooler than average, by late May it was well above what citizens of northern and eastern states were accustomed to, and there were no overnight freezes or frosts. Captain Barnitz maintained that the grass was growing well by early May, at least some of the days had been extremely hot, and the officers had been enjoying ice cream for a treat. The horses were in better condition, and in fact the entire command, except the sick and the guard, had been turned out to search for Indians on May 13 and 14. According to Custer, the matter of forage and grain for the command's horses had been resolved in late April, and if Hancock's letter of May 7 is correct, ample rations for the scout should have reached Fort Hays at least by May 9 or 10. There had been desertions and cases of scurvy, but these did not impair the command structure or unduly restrict the fighting effectiveness of the cavalry companies. Although the true reasons for Custer's delay are speculative, it is not difficult to imagine that a significant underlying reason was his strong desire to remain as long as possible with his newly arrived wife. Neither Smith nor Custer mentioned desertions or scurvy as a cause for the delay. The closest to any reliable information concerning the loss of personnel as an

[22]W. S. Mitchell, AAAG, to A. J. Smith, May 7, 1867, MC619-R563; A. J. Smith to C. McKeever, AAAG, May 16, 1867, Department of the Missouri, LR, RG 393, NA; Burkey, *Custer, Come at Once*, 23; Frost, *Court-martial*, 124; Millbrook, "West Breaks In General Custer," 121.

underlying motive is a letter dated May 22 that appeared in the June 1, 1867, issue of the *Junction City Weekly Union*: "The expedition de Hancock, or the remains of it, is still at Fort Hays, and is considerably reduced by desertion."[23]

Custer remained at the Big Creek camp through the end of May, and on May 29 General Smith was forced to write Hancock once again, promising that Custer would leave when the shelter tents arrived. This reflected the "terrific storms" he had earlier referred to as a cause, but presumably all of the rest of the company tents had arrived with Lieutenant Jackson on May 3. Violent storms are the norm on the plains during the springtime and are most frequent in May. They would not likely be a long-term cause for the delay in departure. At any rate, the tents must have arrived soon after, because on May 31 General Smith once again issued orders to Custer. He was to leave the following day with six companies of the Seventh Cavalry, twenty supply wagons, and fifteen days' rations for the men: "The object of the expedition is to hunt out and chastise the Cheyennes and that portion of the Sioux who are their allies, between the Smoky Hill and the Platte. It is reported that all friendly Sioux have gone north of the Platte and may be in the vicinity of Forts McPherson or Sedgwick. You will as soon as possible, inform yourself of the whereabouts of these friendly bands and avoid collision with them."

After receiving these orders, Custer issued his own. The six companies, A, D, E, H, K, and M, with a total of 357 men, along with the twenty supply wagons, were to be ready to march on two hours' notice. Every trooper was to carry two days' rations and forty-two rounds of ammunition in his haversack and cartridge case, with a shelter tent behind his saddle. After forty-two days of frustration, kept in camp by a combination of disparate factors, including Custer's longing for his wife, the Seventh would at last begin its march in search of the elusive Cheyennes.[24]

---

[23] A. J. Smith to W. S. Hancock, May 23, 1867, Department of the Missouri, LR, RG 393, NA; *Junction City Weekly Union*, June 1, 1867; Burkey, *Custer, Come at Once*, 23; Frost, *Court-martial*, 125; Millbrook, "West Breaks In General Custer," 121; Utley, *Life in Custer's Cavalry*, 45–49.

[24] Smith to Hancock, May 29, 1867; T. B. Weir, AAAG, to G. A. Custer, May 31, 1867, Department of the Missouri, LR, RG 393, NA; Circular 20, Seventh U.S. Cavalry, May 30, 1867, Rec. U.S. Army Mobile Units, Seventh Cavalry, Circulars Issued, RG 391, NA; Burkey, *Custer, Come at Once*, 23–25; Millbrook, "West Breaks In General Custer," 121–22.

CHAPTER EIGHTEEN

WAR BEGINS

Neither the Cheyennes nor the Oglalas were in a position to avenge the burning of their villages until they had first replaced the lost lodges and furnishings and replenished their food supply. But Plains Indians were great horsemen and hunters, and their most critical needs were satisfied in a remarkably short time. According to Henry Stanley, a party of Cheyenne men was sent to the Rocky Mountains, where they "hewed down eight thousand tall saplings," while hunters on the plains "killed over a thousand buffalo, skinned them, and converted their hides into lodges." He added that they now had four hundred new lodges and a surplus of buffalo robes to trade.[1] Then, as soon as their warhorses regained their stamina, small parties of young Cheyenne warriors rode off to raid and harass the whites' unwelcome roads and the stage stations along them. The valley of the Smoky Hill and all of the lands between the Pawnee Fork and the Republican were considered the prime hunting grounds for bison and other large game animals within the Cheyenne country and were the heartland of the Dog Soldier and southern Sutaio bands. To allow the stage and freighting road to remain and to permit construction of a railroad would mean the end of hunting as the game was either killed by whites or moved away. And it would mean the end of their way of life and their nomadic hunting culture. From the Cheyennes' perspective, they had no choice but to go to war—a war forced on them by the continuing intrusions into their country by whites and, more immediately, by the burning of the Dog Soldier and southern Sutaio village on the Pawnee Fork.[2]

When the war came, it began slowly. But as the strength of the Indians' horses returned and their losses were replaced, it increased in intensity.

---

[1] This is unlikely, given that it took ten to twelve buffalo hides to make a single lodge.
[2] Stanley, "Medicine Lodge Peace Councils," 304.

There had been one or two raids early in the year, prior to the Hancock expedition, primarily intended to stop the stage and freight traffic along the Smoky Hill route, as the Cheyennes had warned the previous year. The first was on March 26, 1867, against Goose Creek Station, about twelve miles west of Fort Wallace at the mouth of Goose Creek; it resulted in Company I of the Seventh Cavalry, under Captain Keogh, and twenty infantry from the fort going in pursuit. The raiders disappeared long before the soldiers arrived at the scene. But subsequent to the burning of the Cheyenne and Oglala villages, the attacks increased dramatically. By April 22, stagecoach passengers reported Indians swarming along the stage route, a gross exaggeration but indicative of increased hostile activity. The first major recorded attack took place on April 30, again at Goose Creek Station. The raiders swept away the livestock and killed three mules. The following day they burned the station. On May 4 there was an attack on Monument Station, between Forts Hays and Wallace, while another war party tried to burn Chalk Bluffs Station. Big Timbers Station, about a mile east of the Kansas-Colorado border, was attacked four times in one month, on May 6, 11, 23, and 24. It was built at the edge of a large grove of plains cottonwoods that had been one of the favorite winter campsites of the Cheyennes (particularly the Dog Soldiers and southern Sutaio) and also a sacred burial ground for their dead. The white presence there was bitterly resented and the cause of added fury among the tribe.[3]

Pond Creek Station, about two miles west of Fort Wallace and a home station for the stage line, suffered its share of attacks during May. Fortunately for the crew, the station and the stable were built in proximity for defense. Though the station building and the barn were constructed of lumber freighted in, the corral and the storage enclosure for hay were built of the native sandstone. Underground tunnels (really covered ditches about three feet wide and five feet deep) ran from the station to the barn and from both buildings to three rifle pits arranged around the site. The pits were large enough for two men to stand in them comfortably and were covered by large slabs of stone held above ground level by short posts set in the earth. This provided the defenders with excellent visibility for shooting and at the same time an almost complete barrier against Indian arrows or bullets. The station was armed, as were most stations, with several Spencer seven-shot repeating rifles and Henry breech-loading rifles, the latter being

[3] *Junction City Weekly Union*, April 27, 1867; Bell, *New Tracks*, 35; Lee and Raynesford, *Trails of the Smoky Hill*, 100–101; Oliva, *Fort Wallace*, 47.

eighteen-shot repeaters. Despite the well-designed protective fortifications, however, neither Pond Creek Station nor any of the others were immune to recurring attacks. At Pond Creek the Cheyennes struck on May 11 and tried unsuccessfully to burn it. Cavalry pursuit by Captain Keogh and Company I from Fort Wallace failed to find the raiding party. A discouraged Keogh wrote to Myles Moylan, the Seventh Cavalry adjutant at Fort Hays, on the same day, "I have never before appreciated the difficulty of finding Indians, and have concluded that without knowing exactly when to surprise their camp, or having a guide who can track them at a run—it is a waste of horseflesh and time to endeavor to come up with them."

On May 12 the Cheyennes struck again at Willow Creek Station (also called Fitch's Meadow Station), the next one west of Goose Creek Station, and ran off the livestock. Five days later, on May 17, they stole the supply of rations for the troops guarding Monument Station, and on May 18 they raided the Smoky Hill Station, eleven to twelve miles northwest of Monument Station. A stagecoach was attacked on May 26, and that night they once again raided Pond Creek Station, this time driving off a cattle herd. Pursuit of the raiders by the cavalry from Fort Wallace resulted in the recovery of all but five head of cattle that the Indians had killed for meat. This was the troops' only success against the raiders during the entire month.[4]

The series of attacks on the stage stations during the month of May occurred at a time when Custer was responsible for defense of the route either as commander of the Smoky Hill subdistrict or, after its dissolution on May 17, as field commander of the Seventh Cavalry companies at posts along the Smoky Hill. He must have been aware of these raids from Captain Keogh at Fort Wallace or from his adjutant, Myles Moylan. Yet he seems to have neither reported them nor commented on them, other than his general comments on the rumors concerning the presence of Indians. Far from having removed from the Smoky Hill to the Platte, the Cheyennes were busily restoring their losses and raiding the Smoky Hill route when the opportunity arose. Raiding along the Platte was primarily the work of Kiyuksa Oglala warriors led by Pawnee Killer, eventually aided by some from Turkey Leg's Óhméseheso band of Cheyennes. On May 30, shortly before the six cavalry companies departed on their march to Fort McPherson, General Smith ordered more soldiers to Downer Station and

---

[4] M. W. Keogh to M. Moylan, May 13, 1867, Fort Wallace, Kans., original in Ayers Collection (no. 228/843), Newberry Library, Chicago; Bell, *New Tracks*, 35; Burkey, *Custer, Come at Once*, 11n28; Lee and Raynesford, *Trails of the Smoky Hill*, 68–69, 100–101; Oliva, *Fort Wallace*, 47–48.

established a fort there to be known as Fort Downer. Nevertheless the attacks, which to that point had resulted only in the loss of livestock, property, and buildings, continued unabated. On June 3 two members of the Pond Creek Station crew, named Favor and Thompson, were killed and scalped between Pond Creek and Goose Creek. The raiders hacked off the skull of one to the eye level. The following day a war party attempted to run off the horse herd at Fort Wallace but failed. Two men riding their horses east from Denver, identity unknown, were killed on June 6 at nearly the same place Favor and Thompson were killed between Pond Creek and Goose Creek three days earlier; they were buried in the Fort Wallace Post Cemetery. And raiders, probably Cheyennes, killed three German farmers attempting to settle in the Solomon River valley twenty-five miles northwest of Salina.[5]

The station at Goose Creek was attacked again on June 8. On June 11 the stagecoach eastbound from Denver, accompanied by Lt. James M. Bell as a passenger and three soldiers as escorts, was attacked by a war party of twenty-five to thirty Cheyenne warriors west of Big Timbers Station. Lieutenant Bell and the mail guard dismounted and fought on foot, while the three soldiers fought from the top of the coach until they reached Big Timbers Station, after five miles and two hours of fighting. A soldier named Miller of E Company, Third Infantry, was killed in the fight. On June 15 two stagecoaches, one with mail and passengers and the other carrying the infantry guard, were attacked between Big Timbers Station and Goose Creek Station. Privates Edward McNally and Joseph Waldson of E Company, Third Infantry, and one passenger were killed in the ensuing fight with what was claimed to be a war party of more than one hundred Cheyennes. That is very likely the usual exaggeration of numbers, since the Indians seldom used war parties of that size and were otherwise engaged in hunting bison and collecting lodge poles. If there had been a hundred warriors, the small party of guards and all passengers and crew would probably have been wiped out. The survivors were unable to recover the bodies of the dead.[6]

About the same time in mid-June the Cheyennes struck at Big Creek Station, eight miles west of old Fort Hays, driving off fifty-six stagecoach horses and six government mules when the herder went in for a drink. Pursuit by the station crew and nineteen soldiers from the fort was to no

[5] Bell, *New Tracks*, 35–36; Lee and Raynesford, *Trails of the Smoky Hill*, 101–102, 105; Montgomery, "Fort Wallace," 206; Oliva, *Fort Wallace*, 48.
[6] Lee and Raynesford, *Trails of the Smoky Hill*, 108–109; Montgomery, "Fort Wallace," 197, 206–207.

avail. General Hancock and his cavalry escort from Fort Hays, commanded by Sgt. William H. Dummell, G Company, Seventh Cavalry, arrived at Fort Wallace the following day, June 16. Hancock was making a personal inspection of the posts along the Smoky Hill route and investigating the reports of Indian attacks on the stage stations as well. He was en route to Denver to determine their impact on the towns and cities of Colorado that depended on the stage and freight lines crossing the plains. After his arrival at the fort, he wrote to General Sherman, reporting that every stage station along the Smoky Hill road from ninety-five miles east of that post to seventy-five miles west of it had been attacked an average of four times. Then, on June 21, following Hancock's departure, a large Cheyenne war party attacked Pond Creek Station, running off much of the stock. Although there was immediate pursuit, no animals were recovered. This was an attack that was to presage a far more dangerous turn of events at Fort Wallace and the immediate environs.[7]

The attacks on traffic along the Smoky Hill was primarily the work of the Cheyenne Dog Soldiers and southern Sutaio. But the burning of the villages on Pawnee Fork had inflamed the other Cheyenne bands who learned of it, and indeed all of the tribes of the southern plains—particularly the Kiowas. At the time the Kiowas and Plains Apaches were camping on Bluff Creek, and Black Kettle's Cheyennes were on the Cimarron. To avoid trouble, Black Kettle's Southern Eaters moved south to the north fork of the Canadian, deep in Kiowa and Comanche country, where they camped near a Comanche village. Later they moved to the south fork of the Canadian, and while they were there, two runners, Iron Shirt and Riding on the Cloud, brought the news that General Hancock had burned the villages on Pawnee Fork. That alarming report caused them to move still farther south to the Washita in search of safety. They remained there about three weeks but then were compelled to hunt and moved west to the headwaters of the Washita. There they were joined by other Cheyenne bands, and together they made up war parties to exact revenge for what Hancock had done.[8]

One of the first war parties leaving the combined Cheyenne village on the Washita was a very large one, possibly having as many as one hundred warriors under the leadership of a man named Lean Bear. They headed north to the Arkansas in mid-May, probably reaching it in the

---

[7] W. S. Hancock to W. T. Sherman, June 16, 1867, AGO, LR, U.S. House, "Difficulties with Indian Tribes," 7:60; Utley, *Life in Custer's Cavalry*, 63.

[8] Hyde, *Life of George Bent*, 267–70.

vicinity of the Cimarron Crossing of the Santa Fe Trail. They then followed the trail to its north bend, always keeping far enough from the road
and the river to avoid travelers or patrolling soldiers. The portion of the
road from the Little Arkansas River Crossing westward to at least Cold
Springs on the Santa Fe Trail's Cimarron Route was considered the most
dangerous part of the trail in terms of Indian attacks. To counter this danger, the army had established Forts Zarah, Larned, and Dodge and at various times had temporarily stationed soldiers at a few of the important
stream crossings thought to be the most vulnerable. Because of heavy
attacks on trail traffic in 1864 and again in 1865, following the Sand Creek
Massacre, soldiers were sent to "Station Little Arkansas" during the summer of 1865. These included volunteer cavalry and troops of the Second
U.S. Volunteer Infantry (Galvanized Yankees). In 1867 the temporary post
was reestablished and manned by Company C, Tenth U.S. Cavalry, from
June through November 10. The Ranch at Cow Creek Crossing, farther
west, had likewise been established as a temporary post in the summer of
1865 and was also manned by volunteer cavalry and Company F, Second
U.S. Volunteer Infantry. Apparently it was not manned in 1867. Because
the more difficult stream crossings were the favorite ambush locations for
Indian raiders, the troops stationed at these summer encampments were
assigned to patrol and thwart any attacks. But unless a patrol came upon
an attack in process, it was extremely difficult to catch the raiders, and
the attacks continued.[9]

Lean Bear's warriors operated in the area of the trail about sixty miles
east of Fort Larned. This would have been in the vicinity of the trading
ranch at Cow Creek Crossing, but their operations undoubtedly extended
some distance to the east and west of that location. There they captured
and destroyed two wagon trains, looted their cargo, and ran off all of their
horses and mules. It was probably warriors from this party who came upon
and fought with six deserters from the Seventh Cavalry, then at Fort Hays,
who were obviously returning east. When the Indians came upon them,
they were busy hunting buffalo, and in the ensuing attack all were killed
but one man whose scalp was cut around but not taken. The survivor was
delivered to the trading ranch at the Little Arkansas Crossing by an eastbound wagon train and claimed that he and the others had "encountered
twenty odd Kiowas and Cheyennes." While possible, it is unlikely it was

---

[9] Barry, "Ranch at Little Arkansas Crossing," 201–202; Barry, "Ranch at Cow Creek Crossing," 439–41;
   Hyde, *Life of George Bent*, 271–72.

a mixed war party. The deserter, whoever he was, probably could not identify members of different tribes that he had not had significant contact with. While the Cheyennes were allied with the Kiowas, theirs had always been an uneasy alliance, dating back to the days of open warfare between them. Moreover, neither understood the other's language, and communication was limited to the universal sign language of the plains, a disabling factor for a small war party or even a large one. In all probability it was a party of warriors from Lean Bear's followers who, seeing a panic-driven stampede of buffalo, investigated and then attacked when the hunters were seen to be white men.[10]

Unfortunately for Lean Bear, the second of the wagon trains captured contained a large cargo of whiskey. As the war party started south with the captured cargo and livestock, they camped the first night in the sand hills on the south side of the Arkansas River. There a great many of the older men began sampling the whiskey and getting drunk. Lean Bear became very concerned about their condition and the fact that they were becoming careless and leaving a plain trail as they departed the next morning. He ordered members of the Bowstring Society to stop drinking and to get everyone packed up and moving. Some men were still drinking and were so drunk they had to be tied to their horses. In this condition their trail could easily be seen and followed. Lean Bear was greatly alarmed, fearing a patrol of soldiers might track them and attack while they were still too drunk to defend themselves. The younger warriors, who had not been drinking, looked after the captured horses and mules during their return. Despite their vulnerable condition, they were not followed and made it back to their village safely.[11]

A second large war party coming from the Cheyenne village on the Washita consisted of about seventy-five warriors, including George Bent. They were led by a medicine man named Lame Bull and moved north to the Middle Crossing (Cimarron Crossing) of the Santa Fe Trail. That was the principal crossing then in use by westbound trains, where the trail divided between the Cimarron Route (the original surveyed trail) and the Mountain Route. There was a large campground at the crossing, making it a prime location for raiding unwary trail travelers whose animals were being grazed or watered. When the war party reached the area of the crossing, the men found on the riverbank the skeletal remains of Lone Bear,

---

[10] Barry, "Ranch at Little Arkansas Crossing," 293; Barry, "Ranch at Cow Creek Crossing," 439; Hyde, *Life of George Bent*, 271–72.

[11] Hyde, *Life of George Bent*, 271–72.

which they reverently gathered and packed for return to his family. A careful search turned up no trace of Eagle's Nest in the extensive range of sand hills where he had been killed. That evening a mule train arrived, heading west, and the raiding party managed to run off fifty mules. The next morning the party headed southwest along the Cimarron Route. After traveling across the dreaded Jornada, or Water Scrape, where no water was to be found, they came to a large spring, probably the Lower Cimarron Spring near the breaks of the Cimarron River. It was in Comanche and Kiowa country, and it may have been at or near that spring that the famed frontiersman and mountain man Jedediah Smith was killed by Comanches in 1831.[12]

Shortly after the war party reached the spring, a mule train heading east was seen in the distance, so the raiders hid in a nearby arroyo draining into the Cimarron and awaited its arrival. The Cheyennes knew that wagon trains always stopped at any watering place in this arid country to allow their animals to drink and graze. The spring was the last water until reaching the Cimarron Crossing of the Arkansas River, some sixty miles to the northeast, and therefore especially important. Their plan was to wait until the mules had been turned loose to drink and then dash in and run them off. But, as frequently happened, excitable and inexperienced young warriors could not wait for the right moment, left their cover, and charged toward the herd. The white bell mare, seeing them coming, turned away and galloped back toward the camp, with the mules following. The main body of the raiding party, still in the arroyo, saw what was happening and rushed for the herd. The men of the wagon train opened fire on them, but the Indians nonetheless managed to cut off twenty-two mules and four horses. Howling Wolf, one of the warriors, charged toward the bell mare in an attempt to turn her but was shot in the thigh and gave up the pursuit. Following this, Lame Bull decided they should return with their captured stock to the Cheyenne village, by now located on the north fork of Red River deep in Kwahadi Comanche country and the farthest south Cheyennes had ever camped.[13]

The roads to Santa Fe and Denver were not the only focus of Cheyenne attacks. If anything, the railroad posed a greater threat to their culture, their way of life, and their homeland then did the great trails that wound through them. Railroads could transport far more people and goods faster

---

[12] Ibid., 270–71.
[13] Ibid.

and more economically than the plodding wagon trains, were less vulnerable, caused devastating wildfires that swept the grasses of the plains, and
frightened away the game that the Plains Indians depended upon. Track
had been laid as far west as Salina by Saturday evening, April 20, the day
following Hancock's destruction of the Dog Soldier and Oglala villages.
But work was being done well in advance of the track-laying crews. Far
to the west were the surveyors, marking the route to be followed. Behind
them a considerable distance were the grading crews, preparing the
roadbed that would elevate the rails above the surrounding plains, and the
adjacent ditches intended to carry run-off from the infrequent rains to the
arroyos, ravines, and watercourses. They were followed by those building
bridges, setting ties, and laying rails and finally by those spreading ballast
to hold the tracks firm. By mid-May the survey crew, under Col. W. H.
Greenwood, was working far out on the High Plains near the newly designated station of Monument, about two-thirds of the distance from Fort
Hays to Fort Wallace. On May 18 at 9:30 in the morning the crew was
struck by a war party of Cheyennes. There followed a fight that lasted
four and a half hours. In the end the Indians withdrew after capturing
thirteen mules but failing to take the camp. The surveyors claimed they
killed two warriors but could not verify that without having the bodies.
Then the party prudently returned to the main surveying camp to await
a military escort before again venturing out to continue their work.[14]

Robert M. Shoemaker, one of the principals of Shoemaker, Miller, and
Company, contractors for construction of the Union Pacific, E.D., and
the one who had recently delivered General Hancock to Fort Leavenworth in style and comfort, reported the affair to Gov. Samuel Crawford
of Kansas by telegram. Crawford, ever striving for the removal of all Indians from Kansas, had been in Washington in April, besieging Gen. U. S.
Grant and the secretary of the interior with demands that the government
refrain from providing food, clothing, arms and ammunition, or other
treaty annuities to the Indians. He claimed that the plains of Kansas were
"swarming with bloodthirsty Indians," that they had in early spring begun
"to concentrate their forces for the purpose of a general war against the
whites" and to prevent construction of the railroads, and that General
Hancock was even then "in the field endeavoring to hold them back."
According to Crawford, the Indians had broken through Hancock's lines

---

[14] Lee and Raynesford, *Trails of the Smoky Hill*, 158; Snell and Richmond, *Union and Kansas Pacific*,
    336–38.

and were in the valleys of the Smoky Hill, Solomon, and Republican rivers, where they "committed atrocities and outrages most brutal and barbaric." The fact that it was their country and where they lived seems not to have clouded his thinking. Returning to Kansas, he began to barrage General Hancock and General Sherman with demands that the army patrol all of the major river valleys to protect the advancing settlements. Many of these were farther west in the central part of the state than was safe, and no valid treaty existed transferring title to the government. General Sherman made a trip to Fort Harker to find out for himself the state of affairs on the frontier and, on his return to St. Louis, commented that "we can have an Indian war or not, as we choose." He went on to say that "certain parties in Kansas desire war, but don't think they will be gratified." This was not, of course, the response that Governor Crawford was looking for, and he continued to press the military for troops to protect settlers in Republic, Cloud, Ottawa, Marion, Butler, and Greenwood counties. Sherman, convinced that the real problem for the stage lines and railroad construction was heavy rains and high water in early June and low profitability, not Indians, continued to decline his requests.[15]

The drumbeat for military action was not limited to Kansas. Governors of nearly all of the western states and territories were demanding troops for real or fancied threats from the Indians. The post–Civil War army was far too small to provide protection for every small frontier village and the roads that were their lifelines to the East, and their leaders knew it. Yet the loud outcry continued, and in time the governors began to demand authorization to call up state volunteer troops at federal expense. Initially Sherman managed to thwart these requests by telling the governors he would authorize the volunteer troops, but that there was no authority to pay them from the treasury of the general government, and each state would have to pay its volunteers from its own resources, something the states would not do. Sherman was well aware of the problems generated when undisciplined volunteers were sent out in search of Indians, and he was adamantly opposed to such a solution. "I think I comprehend the motives of some of the Governors, whom I would not entrust with a picket post of fifty men, much less with the discretionary power to call out troops at national expense," he said to Grant. But the pressure was great and growing, and ultimately he was forced to give in to Crawford's demands.[16]

---

[15] Athearn, *William Tecumseh Sherman*, 149–52; Crawford, *Kansas in the Sixties*, 250–54; Snell and Richmond, *Union and Kansas Pacific*, 338.

[16] Athearn, *William Tecumseh Sherman*, 144–48, 155–58, 163–66; Utley, *Frontier Regulars*, 119–20.

CHAPTER NINETEEN

CUSTER MOVES NORTH

T he six companies of the Seventh Cavalry began their march northward from old Fort Hays to Fort McPherson at 7:45 A.M. on June
1, 1867. They were accompanied by the *Harper's Weekly* artist and
correspondent Theodore R. Davis. The first day's march was under the
command of Maj. (Bvt. Col.) Wyckliffe Cooper, the Seventh's second
major, and followed a northwesterly course parallel with the west bank of
the north fork of Big Creek. The first six miles were over low, level prairie,
followed by seven miles of rolling prairie, and finally by two miles of very
hilly and broken country, until the troops reached the crossing of the north
fork at the point where it turned westerly. They crossed the stream and
went into camp on the north side. As was the custom, it was a short first
day's march, allowing the men to adjust from camp life to life in the saddle and on campaign. In an ironic twist of fate, on the same day the Seventh Cavalry pushed north in search of hostile Indians, Satanta, the
redoubtable Kiowa chief, led a raiding party (while garbed in his major
general's coat) and ran off a large part of the Fort Dodge livestock.[1]

At Fort Hays, George Custer watched the six companies march off to
the northwest, then turned to the task of moving his wife, Libbie, and
her friend Anna to a safer location. The Seventh Cavalry camp had been
about three-quarters of a mile to the southwest of old Fort Hays, but with
the departure of six of its eight companies to the north, and F Company
sent to Monument Station, the remaining G Company was left exposed
to the danger of an Indian attack that might easily overwhelm it. It was
necessary to move the camp closer to the post for security. General Smith

---

[1] 2nd Lt. Henry Jackson, Itinerary of the March of the Seventh United States Cavalry, June 10 to July
13, 1867, Department of the Missouri, LR, RG 393, part 1, entry 260, NA (hereafter "March Itinerary"),
June 1, 1867; Burkey, *Custer, Come at Once*, 25; G. Custer, *My Life on the Plains*, 111–14; Davis, "Summer on the Plains," 298.

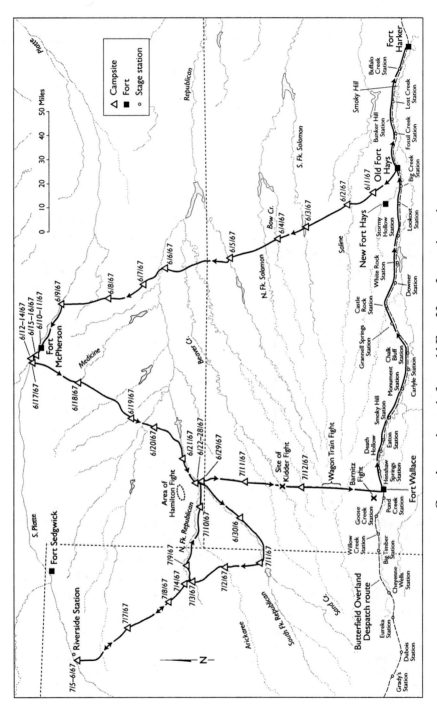

Custer's march north from old Fort Hays, June 1 through
July 19, 1867, with locations of related combat. *Map by Bill Nelson.*

and Major Gibbs were camping in an open area along the left bank of the north fork of Big Creek, while the G Company camp was relocated near the bluffs along Big Creek below the forks. Custer moved Libbie and Anna to a new site on a small knoll about five to six hundred feet east of the forks on the creek's north bank, a short distance above G Company. The nearby stream bank was thirty-six feet above the usual high-water mark of the creek, and the knoll on which Libby's tent complex was erected was three to four feet higher than the surrounding valley. It would prove to be a fortunate choice.[2]

After Custer was satisfied with the location and placement of Libbie's tent home, he posted a few of his Seventh Cavalry troopers a short distance upstream as a guard and prepared to join his troops. When the six companies left that morning, he kept with him two troopers, four Delawares as scouts and trailers, and Medicine Bill Comstock as scout and guide. Following a cup of army coffee and good-byes, Custer and his small escort set out shortly after midnight to overtake the rest of the command. For the most part they rode in silence, moving steadily along the course taken earlier by Major Cooper and the Seventh. From time to time they startled small herds of antelope or bison. The moon had set, and they were left with only starlight to illuminate their descent into the valley of the north fork of Big Creek and the first night's camp. The horses seemed to sense their approach, quickening their pace, and, as if to confirm it, reveille sounded, guiding them to their destination.[3]

Custer's arrival at the encampment of his six companies must have been about 4:00 A.M., for it generally took an hour and a half to two hours from reveille to complete the feeding and grooming of the horses, breakfast for the men, and the striking of camp. Care of the horses alone took an hour on average. At 6:00 A.M. the order "Advance!" was given, and the companies moved out in a column of fours. They first marched northwesterly, parallel with the north fork, then turned more northerly where the creek turned west. They traveled nine miles across the rolling plains. At first their route was marshy, and then they moved due north across a broken ridge flanked by two dry arroyos with a few water holes in them, until finally reaching the Saline River. The stream had low banks and a sandy bed that allowed an easy crossing. With good grass in the valley and clear water in the stream, Custer ordered camp made at a point about five hundred yards

---

[2] Burkey, *Custer, Come at Once,* 25; G. Custer, *Wild Life on the Plains,* 70–71; Utley, *Life in Custer's Cavalry,* 55.

[3] G. Custer, *My Life on the Plains,* 112–16.

On June 1, 1867, Custer and six companies of the Seventh Cavalry began their march north to Fort McPherson from Fort Hays. On the afternoon of June 2, in camp on the Saline River, Custer and his men observed a scaffold burial on a knoll in the valley about two miles from camp. He took a few men, including Medicine Bill Comstock and Theodore Davis, and rode to the site, removed the body from its resting place atop the scaffold, and uncovered it to satisfy their curiosity. It was the body of a young boy believed to be the child of a prominent family, along with his burial goods. *Harper's New Monthly Magazine*, February 1868, 299.

west of the crossing. A scattering of cottonwoods along the riverbanks provided them with fuel for their evening meal. The valley was about a half mile wide on the south side west of the crossing, but half a mile to the east the bluffs moved to the edge of the river.[4]

The troopers discovered a recently occupied Indian village site near the cavalry camp and next to the stream. A large number of elk bones found in the immediate area led Theodore Davis to conclude that the Indians "had done little else than kill and eat elk during their sojourn in that place." Actually it was probably a hunting camp where, after the tracking and killing of a large number of the animals, they were butchered and the meat dried and packed for use by their people. Though speculative, it is possible that this was one of the several camps of the hunting party sent out

---

[4]Jackson, "March Itinerary," June 2, 1867; G. Custer, *My Life on the Plains*, 116–18.

from the Dog Soldier and southern Sutaio village on Pawnee Fork. It was not likely a campsite of the fleeing Kiyuksa Oglalas, because they were moving north rapidly in their flight from Hancock's troops and not hunting. Moreover, they passed farther to the west on a line north from Lookout Station. Nearly two miles from the cavalry camp and situated on a rise in the valley, the soldiers could see a scaffold that Custer thought looked like a military lookout post in the late war. Overcome by curiosity, he took Comstock and a few soldiers and rode to the site. They were accompanied by Theodore Davis, who wanted to learn about the burial practices of the Plains Indians. When they reached it, they found that the scaffold was constructed of small saplings and about twenty feet in height. The body of the deceased had been placed on the elevated platform at the top.[5]

But the curiosity of Custer's party was not satisfied, so they removed the body from the scaffold and uncovered it. This was not an uncommon practice of whites of that day, who either were trying to discover what tribe was in the area and whether the deceased was an important leader or warrior or were simply interested in the burial practices of another culture. Some, of course, wanted to loot the scaffold of its burial goods to sell or keep as curios. Understandably, this infuriated the Indians, just as whites would have been infuriated by the exhumation of their dead. In this case the deceased was a young boy, apparently from a prominent family. To Custer this meant the "son of some important chief." Wrapped with him or fastened to the scaffold for use in the afterlife were a bow; a quiver filled with steel-pointed arrows, a war club, and a scalping knife; and a red clay pipe, with a small bag of tobacco. There was also a small supply of food, arms and ammunition, clothing, a "handsome parflèche," a number of carefully braided lariats, and part of a scalp. Both Custer and Davis claimed the scalp to be that of a white woman, but this is not likely. Few Plains Indians scalped women. The practice was reserved for an enemy warrior or fighter and usually represented a welcome reduction in the strength of the opposing enemy and nothing more. Indian enemies wore long hair, often braided, and this may account for the mistaken identity, along with cultural bias and a desire to inflame white sensibilities against the alleged savagery of the Indians. There was no report about the disposition of this young boy's body, but often soldiers and frontiersmen looted what they wanted of the burial goods, leaving the body where it lay.[6]

---

[5] G. Custer, *My Life on the Plains*, 118–19; Davis, "Summer on the Plains," 299.
[6] G. Custer, *My Life on the Plains*, 119–21; Davis, "Summer on the Plains," 299; Grinnell, *Cheyenne Indians*, 2:29–30, 36–37.

Most fights during the first year of Hancock's War were small hit-and-run raids on remote outposts and stage stations, but there were a few larger engagements with the Seventh Cavalry and other military units. One involving Company F of the Tenth Cavalry took place in the Saline River valley north of Fort Hays and became known as the Battle of the Saline. The Cheyennes rode the bluffs overlooking the valley and descended into it through the canyons and arroyos leading down from the High Plains above. *Photograph by the author.*

Custer's command continued its march northwest on the morning of June 3, moving parallel with the river, then turning north-northwest and marching over a rough and broken plain. After five miles, they crossed what Lieutenant Jackson called the south fork of the north fork of the Saline River. What they knew as the north fork of the Saline is now known as Sand Creek—one of many streams by that name to be found across the plains. Beyond the crossing, made difficult by quicksand, they moved northwesterly, parallel with the north fork of Sand Creek over a high rolling plain. The land once again became rough and broken, with rocky bluffs on both sides of their route. Finally they descended into the valley of the south fork of the Solomon River and reached their crossing point after a march of more than twenty-five miles. The banks of the stream were twenty feet high, but they found a ravine leading down to the river and used it for the crossing. The river itself was narrow and shallow. The north bank was low, but to their chagrin they found no grass on that side

This view of the High Plains overlooking the Saline River illustrates the breaks and canyons that led the Indians down into the valley for the Battle of the Saline. This area of the river and its valley is also near the location of Custer's camp as he moved north to Fort McPherson. It was in the Saline valley where he saw and desecrated the burial scaffold of a young Cheyenne boy. The bluffs on the south side of the river can be seen in the far distance. *Photograph by the author.*

and were forced to return to the south bank, west of their original crossing point. They camped on the north side of a "bad slue," with only fair grazing for the animals. The command was suffering the usual problems caused by the lack of accurate maps, and Lieutenant Jackson believed their location to be six to eight miles east of the forks of the Solomon. In fact they were more than seventy miles west of the forks.[7]

The following morning, June 4, the troopers marched northwest, parallel with the east bank of "Shell Creek"—probably modern Slate Creek or another nearby intermittent stream.[8] Limestone bluffs marked the edge of the stream's valley for the first eight miles. Then the valley widened into a high rolling plain that rose before them. They crossed a high ridge

---

[7] Jackson, "March Itinerary," June 3, 1867.

[8] Lieutenant Jackson, who was keeping the march journal, stated that the march was along the right bank of the stream. That is incorrect. The right or left banks are determined by facing downstream, and Jackson's map clearly shows the march to be northwesterly along the east bank, which would be the left bank.

and descended into the valley of Bow Creek to camp on the south bank, having marched eighteen miles. There was a relatively good stand of timber, mostly cottonwoods, along the creek banks. The little stream, the middle fork of the Solomon, was only about ten yards across, bank to bank, with a water flow six inches deep. But the banks were of soft sand and steep, making a crossing difficult for the wagons. To avoid this problem, in the afternoon they built a bridge across the stream. Meantime the horses enjoyed ample grazing on "good grass."[9]

On the morning of June 5 Custer's command crossed the stream on the bridge, then proceeding north-northwest over a broken divide. After a seven-mile march, the troops struck the north fork of the Solomon, which they thought was Prairie Dog Creek. The lack of accurate maps would plague Custer's command in identifying the streams and their own whereabouts from this point until they reached the Republican, and even beyond. Fortunately for them, the north fork was narrow and had low banks and a hard, sandy bed, and a shallow flow of water that allowed an easy crossing. Once on the north bank, they found excellent grass, persuading Custer to halt the column and graze the horses for three hours. During their stop a rainstorm struck, the first since leaving Fort Hays. It didn't last long, and when it ended, the march resumed, this time northwesterly to an intersection with an old wagon road coming from the east. This they believed to be the track left by Fremont's Expedition in 1843, the ruts still scarring the virgin sod. They followed the trail northwesterly to what they thought was Beaver Creek but was actually Prairie Dog Creek. They had traveled a little more than twenty-two miles over a hard rolling plain covered with cactus and very broken by dry arroyos and ravines.[10]

Prairie Dog Creek, at the place they reached it, had steep banks about twenty-two feet apart, a hard sand bed, and a water flow two feet deep. The column crossed to the north bank and made camp at 3:00 P.M. There was good grass nearby, and the horses grazed while the troopers set up their tents and prepared supper. The banks of the stream were heavily timbered, and beaver dams and felled trees were seen in the area. Comstock told Custer that if they waited until near sundown, there would be a chance of killing a few beavers. Custer the hunter accepted the offer. He stationed himself along the bank in the area above the camp that Comstock suggested, with a few of the other officers placed at intervals along

---

[9] Jackson, "March Itinerary," June 4, 1867.
[10] Ibid., June 5, 1867.

the banks. There they waited with rifles at the ready for an unwary beaver to appear. Custer was on the stream bank about twenty feet below the plain above, and on a path made by wild animals moving along it under the cover of the trees, brush, and tall grasses. Sundown came and went, and darkness grew, but no beavers were seen. They could not tell whether the animals were frightened away by the sounds of the nearby camp or by the noises of hunting parties coming and going. Just as he was about to conclude that the wait was in vain, Custer heard the rustling of grasses along the animal trail. He expected to see a beaver appear, but instead it was "an immense wildcat" that stepped into view a few feet from him. The animal was as surprised as Custer, who took hasty aim and fired. He heard a splash in the water below and assumed that he either killed or wounded the cat, whose body he believed was carried away by the stream and could not be found. Perhaps it was an "immense wildcat" or possibly a small mountain lion, a species also native to the area.[11]

The column left camp the following morning, June 6, marching northerly more than eight miles to "Stealing Horse Creek." This name is the English translation of that used by the Cheyennes and Arapahoes to designate the south fork and main branch of Sappa Creek. The stream was in fact the Sappa, the first major watercourse north of the Prairie Dog. Both streams flow northeasterly and empty into the Republican. The Sappa ran "very swiftly between high banks," was heavily timbered, and had good grass. They had traveled a little over fourteen miles from their camp on the Prairie Dog, so with good grass at hand Custer called a halt while the animals were grazed along the south bank. About four miles before reaching the Sappa they had crossed one of those invisible lines across the land by which white men marked boundaries of their political subdivisions, leaving Kansas and entering southern Nebraska.[12]

When they saddled up and moved out, the column had to travel half a mile to the east to find a passable crossing point. Even there the banks of the stream were very steep and of soft sand. The creek bed itself was of hard sand with water three feet deep, and the crossing thirty feet bank to bank. Once on the north side they continued on a course north-north-west by north over a high rolling prairie. They traveled more than six miles to an intersection with Beaver Creek. Lieutenant Jackson called it White Rock Creek, but the latter rises more than fifty miles to the southeast of

[11] Ibid.; G. Custer, *My Life on the Plains*, 122–23.
[12] Jackson, "March Itinerary," June 6, 1867.

their crossing of the Beaver. The banks of the creek were thirty feet apart, low, and muddy, while the bed was firm. There were stone bluffs on the south side below the crossing, but more important was the trail of ten to fifteen mounted Indians traveling northeasterly, parallel with the stream. Since the trail was about four days old, they believed that it would be futile to follow and so made their crossing and continued.[13]

Beyond Beaver Creek the cavalry companies marched on a northerly course over broken country for another ten miles until reaching a deep arroyo with steep banks. They crossed this with difficulty and went into camp a little more than a mile beyond, at the junction of two small streams with standing water and heavily timbered banks but poor grass. They were then only about two miles south of the Republican River, but the two streams had such soft mudbanks they decided not to continue farther, having already traveled over thirty-four miles that day. The next morning, June 7, they had to cut the banks down and corduroy the crossing of the stream to their north so the animals and wagons could pass. Once on the other side, they moved north to the Republican, then turned west for a mile to a good crossing point. The bottomland on both sides of the river was quite marshy. There were cottonwood trees along the banks, but poor grass because of the sandy soil. However, the banks were low and the bed firm, providing an easy crossing.[14]

When they reached the north bank, the column proceeded north-northwest for three miles to the hills formed by the rolling plains above. Here they came in view of a party of mounted warriors two miles to their west along what was probably Deer Creek. The Indians, on seeing the long column of cavalry, fled westward without, as Custer phrased it, "waiting for a parley of any kind." He immediately detached Capt. Edward Myers and companies E and H from the column and ordered them to pursue the Indians. Custer later estimated the party to be about one hundred strong. Theodore Davis, riding with the column, reported their number at thirty to forty. Myers and his troopers were unable to overtake them and rejoined the command a few miles to the northwest. According to Custer, examination of the hoofprints showed that the Indian horses had been stolen from the stage line and hence were much superior to those used by the cavalry. This was probably an excuse designed to explain why the Indians weren't caught. Davis wrote that the troopers and their horses had trouble getting up the steep banks of Deer Creek. According to him

[13] Ibid.; G. Custer, *My Life on the Plains*, 121; Davis, "Summer on the Plains," 300.
[14] Jackson, "March Itinerary," June 6–7, 1867.

many of the men and their horses fell back into the stream, and by the time they reached the other side the Indians had long since disappeared. This was the only time the column caught sight of Indians during its march northward to the Platte.[15]

Following departure of Myers and the two companies pursuing the Indians, the column altered its course in a more westerly direction for four miles, then turned nearly due north until striking what the men thought was Medicine Lake Creek, where they made camp on the south bank. They had marched nearly seventeen miles. An old cavalry campsite was nearby, with the picket posts still in the ground. Once again the lack of reliable maps caused confusion about their location. Today there is no Medicine Lake Creek, but there is a Medicine Creek that flows into the Platte west of Fort McPherson. Based on the mileages and direction of the line of march, and the fact they reached the Platte at a point about twenty-seven miles east of Fort McPherson, the stream they were following and camping on that night was probably Muddy Creek.[16]

While Custer's command was resting in camp that evening, June 7, events were unfolding far to the south that would have made Custer anxious for his wife's safety had he known of them. Four days after the troopers left old Fort Hays and were working their way to the northwest, Libbie and her friend Anna wanted to take a walk away from camp during the evening and persuaded Lt. Thomas B. Weir, General Smith's adjutant, to accompany them as escort. When they had not returned by 10:00 P.M., the alarm was given, weapons were fired in the air, and bugles sounded. Although the firing and sounding of bugles were meant to guide the walkers back to the camp, some of the sentries apparently thought it indicated an imminent Indian attack; they fired into the dark in the direction of the three walkers. Weir found a depression in the plains and put the ladies there for safety, instructing them to keep their heads down, while he crawled back to camp and stopped the indiscriminate shooting. Libbie believed there were bullets whizzing around their heads, narrowly missing them.[17]

One day later a violent thunderstorm struck the area of old Fort Hays, with the high winds, wild thunder and lightning, and torrential rain typical of storms during spring on the plains. This one was more violent and serious than most, saturating the area west and northwest of the fort—the

[15] Ibid., June 7, 1867; G. Custer, *My Life on the Plains*, 121; Davis, "Summer on the Plains," 300–301.
[16] Jackson, "March Itinerary," June 7, 1867.
[17] Burkey, *Custer, Come at Once*, 31; E. Custer, *Tenting on the Plains*, 619–22; Utley, *Life in Custer's Cavalry*, 56.

watershed of Big Creek and its branches. The surface of the Great Plains, scoured and beaten rock-hard by hundreds of years of rain, hail, wind, and the merciless sun, did not absorb most of the moisture. Instead it quickly ran off into the numerous dry arroyos, ravines, gullies, and watercourses that scarred its surface and fed into larger streams. Soon these streams were transformed from barely a trickle into raging torrents. As the rain fell in the drainage areas of the north and south forks of Big Creek, the custom-ary flow of one to two feet suddenly became a wall of water, a flash flood, as it raced down the channels toward the fort. Despite the heavy rainfall the soldiers endured, the seriousness of the situation did not become evi-dent until about 3:00 A.M., after the rains had slackened. Then the stream rose more than thirty-five feet in only a few hours. Men and horses were trapped on a projection of land where they were camping that suddenly became inundated. Libbie, Anna, and Eliza found themselves surrounded by water and their knoll transformed into an island, with water swirling wildly all around them. They saw six men drown and saved another by using Eliza's clothesline as a lifeline. It was a terrifying night for everyone, but with dawn the water receded as rapidly as it had risen. The danger seemed past and order was being restored when the rains came again that evening with even greater violence, and the night of terror was repeated.[18]

On the morning of June 8, as Libbie Custer's travails at old Fort Hays were coming to an end, the six companies led by Custer left their camp on Muddy Creek and marched northwest. According to Lieutenant Jack-son, it was a dark and misty morning. Six miles from camp they reached a small creek with standing water in holes. It was a difficult crossing, due to very steep and miry banks, and they were forced to build a bridge across it, though it was only ten feet from one side to the other. Then they turned north and traversed a rolling prairie until they again reached Muddy Creek. The banks showed evidence that the water had been at least six feet higher no more than a day or two before, and the crossing was so bad that the cavalry horses sank into soft mud up to their flanks. To get the wagons across, the men were forced to corduroy the bed, and then it took four horses to cross each of the twenty wagons, and fifty men to work on get-ting them over—all this even though the banks were only ten feet apart and the water only six inches deep. They camped on the north bank in thick timber, with poor grass, following a march of about seventeen miles.[19]

---

[18] Burkey, *Custer, Come at Once*, 31; E. Custer, *Tenting on the Plains*, 632–46, 649–52; Utley, *Life in Custer's Cavalry*, 56–57.
[19] Jackson, "March Itinerary," June 8, 1867.

While in camp that evening of June 8, tragedy struck the Seventh Cavalry. Maj. Wyckliffe Cooper—the most senior major in the three squadrons of cavalry present, and second major of the Seventh—committed suicide in his tent just as the other officers were finishing their evening meal. Cooper was a thirty-five-year-old officer born in Lexington, Kentucky, with a distinguished record in the Union army during the Civil War, including brevets up to colonel. He had easily won an appointment to the Seventh Cavalry as its second major and would likely have had a brilliant career except for his bouts with alcoholism. He was reputedly "a handsome manly fellow" but brought with him on the campaign a keg of whiskey, in which he indulged regularly. He apparently ran through his supply and in a fit of drunken despair shot himself. George and Tom Custer, along with Theodore Davis, were discussing Cooper's alcoholism when they heard a shot coming from the direction of the major's tent. Tom Custer was sent to investigate and returned to report the suicide. Cooper was found on his knees and face, his right hand still holding his revolver, the ground beneath him saturated with blood. Summoning the other officers to the major's tent, Custer said, "Gentlemen this is not the death of a soldier—it is unnecessary standing as we do in the presence of such an example that I should say more." To Libbie he later wrote: "May the example not be lost on them. But for intemperance Colonel Cooper would have been a useful and accomplished officer, a brilliant and most companionable gentleman. He leaves a young wife, shortly to become a mother." Cooper's body was taken to Fort McPherson by ambulance for burial.[20]

It must have been a somber command that left camp on the morning of June 9, given the events of the previous evening. The troops marched north over increasingly rough terrain as they cleared the divide between the watersheds of the Republican and Platte river valleys. Seven miles beyond their last camp they came to a small stream they thought was Deer Creek but must have been Plum Creek. They continued marching due north until reaching what the Indians called the Bad Lands. This very broken country lay beyond the divide between the waters flowing south to the Republican and those flowing north to the Platte. The terrain was a succession of ridges flanked by deep ravines and canyons, many of them at least fifty feet deep. Since it appeared to be impossible to get loaded wagons down them any other way, they were forced to cut a wagon road down some of the ridges. On one of them two wagons rolled over and crashed down the

---

[20] Davis, "With Generals"; Frost, *Court-martial*, 42; Merington, *Custer Story*, 205; Utley, *Life in Custer's Cavalry*, 253–54.

side into the ravine below. Two miles beyond they crossed the highest ridge and gradually worked their way downward to the Platte. In five more miles they reached a canyon (probably Hiles Canyon) that Medicine Bill Comstock said would lead to the river. Custer claimed that it was only through "Comstock's superior knowledge of the country that we found an easy exit from the deep cañons and rough defiles which we encountered." Perhaps so, but it is unlikely Comstock would know all of the canyons and defiles leading to the Platte in that area, which was well to the northeast of his usual territory. More likely, being familiar with the general topography of the plains, he made a shrewd guess—after all, every canyon north of the divide would lead to the Platte. After following the canyon for three and a half miles, they emerged into the great valley of the Platte River, at that point about two and a half miles wide, and made camp next to its waters after a day's march of twenty-four miles.[21]

The valley of the Platte was, according to Lieutenant Jackson, "one immense marsh." Paralleling the riverbanks was the famed Oregon-California Trail, also known in that region as the Great Platte River Road. This was the legendary trail followed by thousands of immigrants, gold seekers, adventurers, freighters, and others, and the longest national highway in the West. As Custer and his command emerged from the canyon, a large train of wagons on the trail suddenly circled for defense. They evidently concluded that the horsemen coming from the canyon's mouth were Indians and were preparing to fend off an attack. No doubt to their relief the riders turned out to be American cavalry, passing them en route to the new camp. Probably due to the marshy character of the soil, the grass in the Platte River valley was extraordinarily poor, forcing the troopers to rely primarily on the forage they had brought with them to feed the horses. But since they were no more than a day's march east of Fort McPherson and resupply, there was no concern.[22]

The march from old Fort Hays to their June 9 camp on the Platte was often monotonous and tedious, but not without interest. As Theodore Davis described it, "The country is broken into bluffs and cañons, never flat and uninteresting, as seems to be the general supposition of persons not familiar with the physical geography of that particular section of our country. . . . Game was abundant and furnished a continual and much-needed supply of meat for the command." Hunting to the south in Kansas

---

[21] Jackson, "March Itinerary," June 9, 1867; G. Custer, *My Life on the Plains*, 124.
[22] Jackson, "March Itinerary," June 9, 1867; Davis, "Summer on the Plains," 301.

had been primarily for bison and elk, but Davis reported that between the Republican and Platte rivers a large number of pronghorn antelope were killed. Presumably this was north of the Republican and south of the Bad Lands, since an antelope hunt in the latter would have been nearly impossible. During these hunts a number of young antelope were captured and quickly tamed, becoming favorite pets around the camp. One of these, named Little Bill, was a particular delight to Custer, who bestowed great affection on the animal and received it in return.[23]

At some camp between the Saline River and Fort McPherson, Theodore Davis reported that their tents were set up on grounds found to be infested with a large number of rattlesnakes. It is impossible to determine which camp this was, but clearly it was north of the Saline and probably no farther north than the Prairie Dog, because all of the camps beyond that stream were wet and miry, conditions in which rattlesnakes would be unlikely to den or congregate. Wherever it was, it provided both an unusual evening's entertainment and a variation in their diet. The tents had just been pitched when the snakes appeared. Soon officers and men alike were busily killing them with sabers and sticks. The cook for the officer's mess that Davis ate with (that of Maj. Joel N. Elliott) was a German immigrant from Schleswig-Holstein who spoke minimal English and was deathly afraid of snakes, particularly rattlers. He fled the vicinity of the snake killing but on his return found five or six dead rattlers laid out lengthwise on the mess chest. He refused to have anything to do with them, and so their mess was the only one that did not enjoy broiled or fried rattlesnake for dinner. Later that night the cook was heard yelling in German and pointing inside the mess tent. There a large and badly frightened rattlesnake was found rattling away. From what they could understand, it had crawled on or over the cook and tried to curl up next to his body for warmth. The rattler was killed and broiled for breakfast, and on tasting the meat, the cook declared it "so tam goot as de eel." From then on, he became an avid snake hunter.[24]

On the morning of June 10, Custer's command left camp and marched west along the south bank of the Platte River. During their march the troops passed six trading ranches. The first two had been destroyed and the next two abandoned, but the last two were still in operation. These ranches, like those on the Smoky Hill and Santa Fe roads to the south,

---

[23] Davis, "Summer on the Plains," 299, 301; Davis, "With Generals," 8.
[24] Davis, "Summer on the Plains," 299–300.

maintained a supply of foodstuffs and necessities for the passing wagon trains and also did a brisk business in trading sound livestock for broken-down or lame animals. Those received in trade they nursed back to health and then again traded or sold to later trail traffic. The destruction of two ranches and abandonment of two more was evidence of attacks by angry Lakotas and Óhméséheso Cheyennes. The troopers also passed a number of graves as they rode westward along the Platte. Some had a head-board stating, "Unknown Man killed by Indians," and a date. More often the graves were marked by a simple mound of earth. The column completed its march to Fort McPherson at 3:00 in the afternoon and went into camp on the banks of the Platte about a half mile north of the post. The grass at the new camp was described as "bad." The men had traveled 27 miles from their camp of June 9 and a total of more than 215 miles since leaving old Fort Hays ten days earlier.[25]

---

[25] Jackson, "March Itinerary," June 10, 1867; Davis, "Summer on the Plains," 301.

CHAPTER TWENTY

To the Forks of the Republican

A rrival at Fort McPherson gave Custer and his men the first oppor-
tunity to take a break from the hardships of the march since leav-
ing old Fort Hays. The post was on the south side of the Platte
River eighteen miles east of North Platte City and across from the Union
Pacific Railroad, which ran along the north side of the Platte and South
Platte rivers. The "Forks of the Platte" (the confluence of the North and
South Platte rivers) were about twelve miles to the west above Brady Island.
The site of the post, originally known as Cottonwood Springs, had been
an Overland Stage Company station along the Oregon-California Trail.
Because of conflict with the Indians, troops were sent to the area on Sep-
tember 27, 1863, naming their encampment "Cantonment McKean." The
name was changed to Fort Cottonwood on May 18, 1864, and to Fort
McPherson on March 11, 1866. When Custer and his men arrived, the
post's garrison consisted of three companies of the Eighteenth Infantry;
Company C, Third Artillery; and Company B, Second Cavalry.[1]

Although government wagon trains still delivered all supplies to the forts
of the southern plains (except Fort Riley), the Union Pacific Railroad had
reached the area of Fort McPherson in the fall of 1866, providing fast and
economical resupply from quartermaster and commissary stores at Omaha.
Custer's command devoted June 10 and 11 to replenishing supplies, rations,
and forage from the stores placed at the fort in advance for their use. Meanwhile Custer reported his arrival to General Sherman by telegraph. Sherman was at Fort Sedgwick, eighty-six miles to the west-southwest on the
South Platte River, just across the border in Colorado Territory. Sherman's
telegraphed response did not materially change the orders, but he did direct

---

[1] U.S. Department of War, Surgeon General's Office, Circular 4, Report on Barracks and Hospitals
(hereafter "Report on Barracks and Hospitals"), 334–36.

While Custer and his Seventh Cavalry troopers were in camp west of Fort McPherson near the Forks of the Platte, the Kiyuksa Oglala war leader Pawnee Killer and a few of his warriors, along with the Óhmésèheso Cheyenne chief Turkey Leg, appeared and held a council with him. This sketch of Pawnee Killer and two of his men was made by Theodore R. Davis to illustrate his story in the August 17, 1867, issue of *Harper's Weekly*. Custer believed he had made peace with Pawnee Killer but was subsequently disabused of that idea when Pawnee Killer's warriors were involved in several fights with his troops.

Custer to remain near Fort McPherson pending his arrival in a few days. Therefore Custer decided to move the Seventh Cavalry camp west to a site near the Forks of the Platte that had better grass for the horses.[2]

The Seventh left camp at 8:00 A.M. on June 12, marching a little over ten miles to the west along the river and going into camp near the Forks of the Platte on good grass. They were about seven to eight miles east of North Platte City, a small railroad town on the Union Pacific inhabited mainly by railroad workers and small traders. Later that day Pawnee Killer and seven other Indians appeared at the encampment. One of them, Turkey Leg, was a council chief of the Óhmésèheso band of Cheyennes; the rest were warriors of the Kiyuksa band of Oglala Lakotas. Their people were camped together on a small stream to the south that drained into

---

[2] Report on Barracks and Hospitals, 335, 338; G. Custer, *My Life on the Plains*, 124.

the Republican River—possibly Beaver Creek. Custer thought the Kiyuk-sas represented the Lakota tribe and had come to "sue for peace." He wished to talk with them to keep them at peace and away from the Cheyennes, apparently unaware of Turkey Leg's presence, since no mention was made of him. Following a brief discussion Pawnee Killer, Turkey Leg, and the other warriors left, promising to return for talks. After they left, Custer sent a dispatch to Sherman reporting the meeting, then penned a hurried letter to Libbie, filled with hope for an early reunion based on prospects for peace with the Oglalas. The rest of that day and the next, June 13, the troops remained in camp, grazing the horses and resting. On June 13 Sherman telegraphed a dispatch to Custer, instructing him to tell Pawnee Killer that there were men "out to exterminate him" and that he should report to Fort McPherson at once to answer charges relating to recent killings at O'Fallon's Bluff and Plum Creek. By then the Oglalas were long gone, but had they been there to receive the message, it seems unlikely Pawnee Killer would have been enthusiastic about submitting himself to white justice.[3]

Pawnee Killer, Turkey Leg, and four other warriors rode into the Seventh Cavalry camp on June 14 for the promised council. This was held in Custer's tent and lasted most of the afternoon. Custer's purpose was to induce the Kiyuksa band, and any others who might join them, to move their lodges near Fort McPherson and remain there at peace with the whites. They would be fed by the military and thus avoid any involvement in the burgeoning war on the plains. Pawnee Killer and the others present spoke strongly in favor of maintaining peaceful relations with whites, but no promises were made. The Oglala leaders, and especially Pawnee Killer, repeatedly asked where the soldiers were going and when they would resume their march, obviously concerned for the safety of their village and people, just as they had been at Pawnee Fork. Custer considered this to be an effort "to spy out and discover, if possible, our future plans and movements." He made no response to their inquiries, but to ensure their goodwill and a friendly attitude, he provided them with liberal gifts of sugar, coffee, and hard bread—at least as much as six mounted men could conveniently carry. Both Custer and Theodore Davis reported that the Oglalas left with expressions of their desire to live in peace and promised to bring their people in to the fort and remain there until the

[3] Jackson, "March Itinerary," June 12–13, 1867; G. Custer, *My Life on the Plains*, 124; Frost, *Court-martial*, 45–46; Hyde, *Life of George Bent*, 272–73.

troubles with the Cheyennes had ended. This seems at odds with Custer's own later statement that the council reached "no positive conclusions." Moreover, no interpreters qualified to translate the Lakota language were present, and communication was likely only through sign language. Professions of peaceful intentions were probably made, but it seems more plausible that the Oglalas indicated a willingness to report the request to their people rather than to make promises. Pawnee Killer, though a powerful and important war leader, was after all not a chief. Turkey Leg, wanting no trouble and concluding that war would likely continue between the Platte and the Arkansas for the rest of the summer, led his people north of the Platte after his return.[4]

During the council, the proceedings were interrupted by Custer's pet antelope, Little Bill. According to Theodore Davis, he "bounded into the tent" and, anxious for a little affection from his master, stuck his nose into Custer's "flaxen locks with insistency for sociable treatment." That was irresistible to Custer, who took him in his arms and caressed him. This satisfied Little Bill and surprised the Indians, who likely had never seen a tame antelope. Little Bill then divided his time between drinking from a bucket of water placed in the center of the tent to refresh the thirsty men and carefully investigating the beadwork on the clothing of the Indians—much to their delight. But the antic that most surprised and pleased their guests came when a dog entered the tent and sniffed his legs, at which point Little Bill attacked the dog and chased it away. This astonished the Indians, who complimented him with "a succession of how-how-hows!"[5]

After the Indians left, Custer telegraphed the results to Sherman. The following morning, June 15, the command broke camp and marched east along the south bank of the river, going back into camp two and a half miles west of the fort. Once again the grass was "very poor." Sometime during the day Custer received a response from General Sherman, stating that the Cheyennes were believed to be on the upper Republican. That may indeed have been where Turkey Leg's band was camping with the Kiyuksas at the time. Capt. John Mix and forty men of Company M, Second Cavalry, from Fort Sedgwick had left to scout the area of the upper Republican, and if they found the Cheyennes, Custer was to be ready to start after them "at the drop of a hat." Sherman added that he was leaving for North Platte City that day and would see Custer in his camp on

---

[4] G. Custer, *My Life on the Plains*, 124–25; Davis, "Summer on the Plains," 301; Frost, *Court-martial*, 46–48; Hyde, *Life of George Bent*, 272–73.

[5] Davis, "Summer on the Plains," 301; Davis, "With Generals."

the next. Mix and his men, however, would complete their scout without seeing any sign of Indians.[6]

June 16 dawned with gray, overcast skies, and it rained heavily for most of the day. Preparing for possible orders to move south and attack the Cheyennes, the six companies of the Seventh Cavalry spent the day at the fort, shoeing their horses. During the late morning General Sherman rode in from North Platte City to talk with Custer. Sherman had come to the plains to see for himself if there was any truth to the constant stream of complaints about Indian attacks on the trails, roads, and railroads. He believed that the scope of the ongoing guerrilla war was greatly exaggerated. Nevertheless he was under heavy pressure from the newspapers and from the governors of the western plains states and territories, most particularly those of Kansas, Colorado, and Montana. They wanted him to authorize the calling up of state volunteer troops to fight (and expel) the Indians at federal expense. Although Sherman, as commander of the military division, could authorize the use of volunteers, only Congress could appropriate funds to pay them. He used this fact cagily, since he knew no governor would call up troops and none would volunteer without assurance of compensation. To test the truth of their complaints, he journeyed to Omaha and met with General Augur, then traveled across the plains on the Union Pacific to Fort Sedgwick. At the same time, he sent General Hancock to survey the situation along the Smoky Hill road and its impact on Colorado, where Governor A. C. Hunt was making vociferous complaints and demands.[7]

Sherman's trip along the Union Pacific did not go as planned. Arriving in Omaha, he found a party of senators awaiting him, eager to have him host their trip of inspection to the end of track. Forced to put aside his concerns for the moment, Sherman played the part of a genial host, explaining what the railroad would mean to the development of the country (particularly the West), how it was changing life, and what it would do for the military by moving supplies and equipment. Traveling at the unheard-of speed of twenty-five miles per hour, they arrived at North Platte City on June 3 after only twelve hours. Sherman commented to his guests that it would have taken an ox train thirty days to travel the distance they had just

[6] Jackson, "March Itinerary," June 15, 1867; Frost, *Court-martial*, 48–49; Voight, "Death of Lyman S. Kidder," 4, 8.

[7] Jackson, "March Itinerary," June 16, 1867; Sherman to Grant, May 28, 1867, Telegrams Received, 1866–67, Office of the Secretary of War, NA; Athearn, *William Tecumseh Sherman*, 152–57; Frost, *Court-martial*, 49.

completed in half a day. The train continued to the end of track in another three hours, and there Sherman happily left the politicians, but not before enduring the usual ceremonies, including speeches about progress and destiny. That behind him, he and his small staff rode off along the South Platte bound for Fort Sedgwick, twenty-two and a half miles distant.[8]

At Fort Sedgwick, Sherman again found himself distracted from his intended duties. Governor Hunt of Colorado directed a constant barrage of telegrams to him, complaining about Cheyenne attacks along the Smoky Hill route. He requested authority to raise three hundred volunteer troops to scour the Smoky Hill and Platte river valleys for Indian villages—and to fight them. Sherman responded patiently, stating that the culprits were probably Cheyennes fleeing from Hancock, and the attacks mostly made by small bands of young men out to steal horses and make a reputation. Custer was already in the field looking for them and, if he came across them, would no doubt engage them. As for the call-up of volunteers, he would authorize it if they were necessary for the territory's safety and if the governor would get them out immediately and send them to the upper Republican, where they would serve the army for two months. They would be paid when and if Congress appropriated the money. If the governor was agreeable to these stipulations, it was fine with Sherman but must be done at once. Ultimately the plan fell through because the governor could not buy three hundred horses and Sherman had no authority to do so at federal expense. Nor would volunteers serve without the certainty of compensation. This generated howls of protest in Colorado, particularly from newspapermen, who excoriated Sherman. Ultimately the mayor of Denver apologized for the journalistic excesses, explaining that the trouble along the Smoky Hill had so reduced the flow of supplies from the East that prices had soared, immigration ceased, and business conditions stagnated.[9]

The governors' demands did not deter Sherman from analyzing the Indian problem, as he saw it, and issuing orders to both Hancock and Custer. On June 11 he expressed a dispatch to Hancock, then at Fort Hays en route to Fort Wallace and beyond to Denver: "I hear that Custer is arriving at McPherson. After a very short rest, I will have him to scour the Republican to its source to kill and destroy as many Indians as possible. He will then come into the Platte here or above for orders. Look out on your line in case they run that way. You may reduce to submission all Indians between

[8] Athearn, *William Tecumseh Sherman*, 152–55.
[9] Ibid., 155–57.

the Arkansas and Platte or kill them. All are hostile or in complicity. Keep our people as active as possible." Sherman had concluded that there could be no more waiting and it was time to remove the Cheyennes and their allies from their homelands between the Arkansas and the Platte. That same day he wrote to General Grant in Washington, stating that the war between whites and Indians would continue "till the Indians are all killed or taken to a country where they can be watched." This echoed the sentiments he expressed in a letter to Grant the day before: "The only course is for us to destroy the hostile, and to segregate the peaceful and maintain them." As far as Sherman was concerned, no more treaties were necessary; instead the Indian lands would be conquered. Now, following receipt of Custer's reports from Fort McPherson, he was ready to convert those plans into action.[10]

On his arrival at the Seventh Cavalry camp on June 16, Sherman held a lengthy conference with Custer. Sherman did not agree with how his subordinate had dealt with the Oglalas, and he had no confidence in their expressions of friendship. His first instinct was to send a party after Pawnee Killer and his Kiyuksa warriors and bring back some of the more promi-nent chiefs as hostages to ensure fulfillment of their alleged agreement. However, after discussion and further reflection, the two officers agreed that this was impractical—the Oglalas had too much of a head start to be overtaken. In accordance with the original plan and based on their best information about the present location of the Cheyennes, Sherman ver-bally ordered Custer to proceed southwesterly to the forks of the Repub-lican and search for the Oglala village and that of the Dog Soldier and southern Sutaio bands of Cheyennes. It was believed that neither the Cheyennes nor the Oglalas had crossed the Platte and moved north since fleeing their villages on Pawnee Fork, and it was supposed they were some-where near the forks of the Republican. After thoroughly scouting the region, Custer was to move northwest to Fort Sedgwick for supplies and further orders. If circumstances arose requiring a departure from these orders, Custer was to use his own judgment and pursue any fresh trail of the Indians, secure in the knowledge that no objection would be made if he marched his horses to death in the pursuit.[11]

Because of the rough character of the Bad Lands to the south of the post,

---

[10] W. T. Sherman to U. S. Grant, June 10 and 11, 1867, LR, 1865–69, Office of the Secretary of War, NA; W. T. Sherman to W. S. Hancock, June 11, 1867, LS, Division of the Missouri, NA; Millbrook, "West Breaks In General Custer," 123.

[11] U.S. Department of War, *Annual Report of the Secretary of War, 1867*, 35; G. Custer, *My Life on the Plains*, 125–26; Frost, *Court-martial*, 49, 191–93; Millbrook, "West Breaks In General Custer," 123.

they decided to march the command back to the vicinity of the Forks of the Platte and then strike south the following day through what was known as Jack Morrow's Cañon. They didn't leave their camp until 2:00 P.M. on June 17. While Sherman was meeting with Custer that morning, he received Hancock's message from Fort Wallace, repeating Captain Keogh's report that every stage station east from that fort for ninety-five miles and west for seventy-five had been attacked an average of four times. In response Sherman sent a dispatch to Secretary of War Stanton, in which he stated: "If fifty Indians are allowed to remain between the Arkansas and the Platte, we will have to guard every stage station, every train, and all railroad working parties. In other words, fifty hostile Indians will checkmate three thousand soldiers. Rather get them out as soon as possible and it makes little difference whether they be coaxed out by Indian Commissioners or killed." Sherman's well-known lack of patience and quick temper seemed to be getting the better of him. The dispatch sent, he rejoined Custer and his Seventh Cavalry troops for the westward march along the Platte. This day's march was nine miles, with their new camp near the Forks of the Platte about a mile and a half southwest of their June 12–14 campsite. Custer later wrote that there General Sherman commended "the Cheyennes and Sioux to us in his expressive manner" and bade farewell. He forded the Platte and rode to the Union Pacific station at North Platte City to begin the long trip back to St. Louis and his headquarters.[12]

Before leaving Fort McPherson, Custer again wrote a plaintive letter to Libbie, filled with thoughts about her joining him in the field, even though he was in the middle of an Indian campaign and on the move. He told her that Sherman had said he might not be returned to the Smoky Hill route until it was nearly winter, but that she could come to Fort McPherson to be with him. Sherman was going to direct the quartermaster at Omaha to arrange passes for her, but Custer told her not to wait for them if they were not immediately available, since money was no consideration. If General Smith sent a company on a scout to Fort McPherson, she could accompany them. Or if she had a chance to get to Fort Wallace, he would send a squadron there to meet her. It appears that sending a sizable military force on a hard and dangerous journey to escort his wife to him did not trouble Custer nor seem out of the ordinary. He suggested that she encourage Hancock to "make a fuss" about getting the Seventh returned to the Smoky Hill or that she give Hancock and Smith no peace until they sent

---

[12] Jackson, "March Itinerary," June 17, 1867; Athearn, *William Tecumseh Sherman*, 162–63; G. Custer, *My Life on the Plains*, 126–27; Frost, *Court-martial*, 49.

her to Fort Wallace. Clearly Custer's longing to be with his wife was impairing his judgment and subordinating the needs and mission of the military. What Custer was unaware of as he penned his letter was that on the previous night all of the women at old Fort Hays were removed to Fort Harker, and from there to Fort Riley, for their protection. Reports had reached General Smith that a large body of Indians (probably Lean Bear's war party) had passed Fort Larned and were headed toward old Fort Hays. Smith quickly concluded that the women should be removed to safety and that his headquarters should be removed to Harker as well, for convenience of commanding his district from a post close to the railhead. Fort Hays was then in the process of being moved fourteen miles up the south fork of Big Creek to a site near where the railroad was to cross.[13]

Though Lean Bear's war party did not go to Fort Hays, there was nevertheless considerable trouble in the area. On June 18 about twenty-five warriors, believed to be Oglalas, attacked a survey party eighteen miles north of old Fort Hays, driving off their livestock and reportedly killing their herder. Major Gibbs, commanding at Fort Hays, was informed of the attack by some of the surveyors but was unable to act on their request for help. At the time he was busily engaged in moving his garrison to its new location. More importantly, he had no cavalry available, since Captain Barnitz and Company G of the Seventh were away from the fort, escorting Gen. W. W. Wright's railroad survey party to Fort Wallace and beyond to Fort Lyon on the Arkansas. In his report to General Smith he sagely observed that "pursuit by Infantry of mounted Sioux would be too ridiculous to entertain for a moment." By then Smith was at Fort Harker and had taken the women with him. Libbie Custer, Jennie Barnitz, and the others remained at that post until June 21, when they left for Fort Riley by rail. General Sherman sent word to Libbie that she "had best remain quietly at Riley," as her husband would be on the march all summer. She did so, until her husband made an ill-conceived ride to see her.[14]

Custer led his Seventh Cavalry troopers south at 5:00 A.M. on June 18. The day before, Custer had hired two new interpreters who understood the Lakota dialect of the Siouan language. Both were white men married to Lakota wives and probably lived in or around nearby North Platte City. He still had Ed Guerrier with him to translate with any Cheyennes he

[13] Burkey, *Custer, Come at Once*, 26–27; E. Custer, *Tenting on the Plains*, 548, 581–82; Utley, *Cavalier in Buckskin*, 56; Utley, *Life in Custer's Cavalry*, 58–59.

[14] A. Gibbs to T. B. Weir, AAAG, June 19, 1867, Fort Hays, LS, T713-R1, NA; Burkey, *Custer, Come at Once*, 26–27, 32; E. Custer, *Tenting on the Plains*, 547–48; Utley, *Life in Custer's Cavalry*, 58–59.

might encounter. After marching southerly about one and a half miles, they passed Jack Morrow's (or Morrell's) ranch near the entrance of Jack Morrow's Cañon. At the time, Morrow was operating a trading ranch along the Oregon-California Trail south of the Forks of the Platte. The canyon that then bore his name (and likely the one known later as Moran's Canyon) was a defile between the high bluffs facing the Platte. From time immemorial it had been a principal route used by bison and Indians for movement to the north or south. The command emerged from it four miles from camp and continued southward over a succession of ridges and hills interspersed with valleys one to four miles wide.[15]

After marching about fourteen miles (their odometer was inoperative that day and mileages were estimated by time marched), the troops passed "a sheet of water" probably caused by the heavy rains that struck the region on June 16. Five miles beyond they encountered a very high ridge that they were forced to cross, and in another six miles reached the north bank of Medicine Lake Creek (the Medicine Creek of later geography), about a mile above its confluence with Little Medicine Creek. The column crossed it and camped on good grass on the south bank, after a march estimated at twenty-six miles.[16]

On June 19 they left camp and crossed the Little Medicine a half mile above where it emptied into Medicine Creek. The march continued up the valley of the Little Medicine for a mile, but where the stream turned west, the column continued southerly through a small canyon until emerging onto a level prairie. Then they maintained a generally south-southwesterly course. After marching seventeen and a half miles, they entered a canyon nearly a mile long, leading to Red Willow Creek, and followed that stream northwesterly half a mile to a crossing point. The creek was narrow and shallow, but the crossing was miry, and they had to corduroy the bottom to get the wagons across. Once on the west side the column turned upstream a half mile, then resumed its march to the south-southwest for eight miles, striking a dry creek bed the men called Stinking Water Creek (Little Blackwood Creek). They continued on the same course for another four miles and crossed Blackwood Creek, going into camp on its north bank after a day's march of thirty and a half miles.[17]

---

[15] Jackson, "March Itinerary," June 18, 1867; Report on Barracks and Hospitals, 334; Carrington, *Absaraka*, 62–63; G. Custer, *My Life on the Plains*, 126–29; Frost, *Court-martial*, 45; Hyde, *Life of George Bent*, 272–73.

[16] Jackson, "March Itinerary," June 18–19, 1867; G. Custer, *My Life on the Plains*, 128–29.

[17] Jackson, "March Itinerary," June 19, 1867.

The morning of June 20 dawned with heavy mist and fog that reduced visibility to less than one hundred yards in any direction. The troops left camp and marched on a generally southerly course for nearly six miles. The fog made an extended view of the surrounding country impossible, and when at last the sun rose high enough to dispel it, they discovered that they had reached an impassable ravine. This forced them to turn to the northwest for four miles, then go around the head of the ravine for a mile before they could return to their southerly course. They reached Whiteman's Fork of the Republican River (now Frenchman's Creek) fifteen miles from their last camp and half a mile below its junction with Stinking Water Creek. Though the banks were low and the water shallow, the creek was wide, with a strong current, making a difficult crossing. Once on the south bank, they continued south along the east bank of "Paladee Creek" (Bobtail Creek). They camped four miles south of its confluence with Frenchman's Creek, where the stream curved west. They had traveled more than nineteen miles and were happy to camp on good grass with "excellent water."[18]

On June 21 Custer's command struck a course southwest. In a little more than eighteen miles they reached Feast Creek (Muddy Creek), a mile above its confluence with the Republican. The creek was narrow and shallow, but the south bank was ten to twelve feet high and soft, the bed miry, and the flow of water swift, and crossing was difficult. They then turned westerly, parallel with the Republican, and after a march of nearly eight miles crossed what they called Red Willow Creek (now Indian Creek). A muddy bed made for a bad crossing of the small stream, but the grass on the west side was good, so they went into camp after traveling twenty-six miles. The next morning they continued westerly along the north bank of the Republican, going back into camp midmorning on the west bank of Forwood's Spring Creek (now Spring Creek). The stream had miry banks and a muddy bottom, but the water and grass were good. It flowed into the north fork of the Republican a mile to the south, just above the confluence of the north and south forks.[19]

The new camp was where General Sherman had ordered Custer to scout the surrounding country for Cheyennes and Oglalas. With suitable water, wood, grass, and a defensible position, Custer decided to use this camp as his base of operations. It was about three miles north of the Kansas border and, according to his scouts, seventy-five miles southeast of Fort Sedgwick

---

[18] Ibid., June 20, 1867; G. Custer, *My Life on the Plains*, 129.
[19] Jackson, "March Itinerary," June 21–22, 1867.

and the same distance northeast of Fort Wallace. His instructions from Sherman were to thoroughly scout the country between and along the north and south forks of the Republican, then march his command to Fort Sedgwick for further orders from him. Custer now claimed that circumstances favored a modification of that plan, one that would involve a "continuous march, which might be prolonged twenty days or more." He did not indicate what those circumstances were. His troops had seen no sign of Indians since the meeting with Pawnee Killer on the Platte, and his establishment of a camp as his base for scouting the area did not suggest continuous marching. The real reason is most likely contained in a letter he wrote to Libbie on June 22, soon after arriving at Spring Creek:

> You cannot imagine my anxiety regarding your whereabouts, for the reason that, if you are now at Wallace, you can join me in about six days, and we can be together all summer. I wrote twice from McPherson, telling you how to reach me by way of Wallace. I am expected to keep the Indians quiet on the Platte route to Denver. They are pretty well scared. I have already made peace with "Pawnee Killer" and his band of Sioux—the same that owned the lodges that were destroyed. It was intended that I should draw my supplies from Fort Sedgwick, but I am now equidistant from there and Wallace, and Comstock reports the road from here to Sedgwick almost impassable for trains, owing to the scarcity of water, while that to Wallace is good. I therefore send to Wallace. Mr. Cook will set out this evening at sunset, with twelve wagons and a company of cavalry as escort, a second company going half-way and there awaiting his return. Mr. Cook will return in six days, so you see what a splendid opportunity this is to join me. I hear that General Hancock is at Wallace. If so, General Smith is doubtless with him, and has taken you along. I never was so anxious in my life. I will remain here until Mr. Cook returns with the rations—and you, I hope. Now, to prepare for emergencies, you may still be at Hays. I hope not, but, thinking you might, I will act accordingly. I want Comstock to see General Smith, and will send him to Hays. If you are still there, Comstock will take this letter to you and bring your reply.
>
> Tell me when you can be at Wallace, and I will send a squadron there for you. Our marching will not be hard for you; although we sometimes make thirty-five miles a day, it is not usual.

From his letter it seems clear that Custer was obsessed with having his wife with him, whatever the danger and hardship for her or her escort. And he was operating under the assumption that she either had or would contrive a means for getting herself to Fort Wallace.[20]

As justification for sending a squadron of cavalry south toward Fort

---

[20] E. Custer, *Tenting on the Plains*, 582–83; G. Custer, *My Life on the Plains*, 129–31.

Wallace, Custer asserted that to sustain a prolonged march "additional supplies were necessary," despite having resupplied at Fort McPherson five days earlier. He said the guides told him the country between the forks of the Republican and Fort Sedgwick was nearly impassable to heavily laden supply trains because there was no water for fifty-five miles. That was not true. Sending a supply train up to and west along Frenchman's Creek would provide a surface flow of water to within twenty-five to thirty miles of Fort Sedgwick and at the same time avoid the extensive range of sand hills north of the Republican's north fork. Beyond that point lay the beds of at least five intermittent streams where water could be found by digging in the sand, the means used during Custer's later march to the South Platte. When writing *My Life on the Plains* several years later, Custer gave the reason as rough and impassable terrain between the Republican and Fort Sedgwick, whereas the country south toward Fort Wallace was supposedly level and unbroken. Neither statement was entirely true, and in that respect one route was hardly superior to the other. Moreover Fort Sedgwick was across the river from Julesburg, close to the end of track on the Union Pacific Railroad, facilitating relatively easy resupply from Omaha. Fort Wallace, on the other hand, was still supplied by wagon trains lumbering slowly from a distant end of track and susceptible to Indian attack. The fact is that Custer wanted Libbie with him, and according to his best information, that meant sending troops to Fort Wallace to escort her back. At the time he was unaware that the women had been removed from Fort Hays and sent back to Fort Riley and that she had not received his previous letters.[21]

At sunset on June 22 a squadron composed of companies D and K, under the command of Capt. Robert M. West, began the march south-southwesterly toward Fort Wallace with twelve of the command's wagons (Theodore Davis reported sixteen). The wagon train, commanded by Lt. William W. Cooke and escorted by Lt. Samuel M. Robbins and Company D, was to proceed to Fort Wallace for the added supplies. Captain West and Company K were to march only as far south as Beaver Creek, nearly midway to Fort Wallace, and from there to scout up and down that stream, pending return of the wagon train. If they found Pawnee Killer and the Kiyuksa Oglalas on the Beaver, they were to escort them back to Custer's camp. The two companies constituted a full squadron—the size

[21] G. A. Custer to C. C. Augur, June 22, 1867, LR, Department of the Platte, RG 393, part 1, entry 731; G. Custer, *My Life on the Plains*, 131–33.

of the escort Custer told Libbie he would send for her. At 3:00 A.M. the next day Maj. Joel H. Elliot left for Fort Sedgwick with a letter from Custer to General Augur at Omaha, advising him of Custer's whereabouts and present plan of operation. Elliot was to telegraph the letter to Augur from Sedgwick, await a response, then return with it and any new orders from Sherman. Elliot chose to travel light and fast, thus avoiding Indian war parties, and for this reason limited his escort to ten chosen men and one guide. The route they took was a line northwest to an intersection with Frenchman's Creek, then following it westerly to a point nearly due south of Fort Sedgwick, and then north to the fort. Elliot and his men took nearly the same route on their return. They left in the early morning hours of June 23 to avoid detection by any Indian scouts who might be watching the camp.[22]

Away from the Republican the situation with the Indians had been steadily deteriorating. On the very day Custer arrived at the forks of the Republican, Indians attacked crews preparing the roadbed for the Union Pacific, E.D., for up to thirty miles east of Fort Hays. Some of the Indians reportedly said they were Pawnees. This is unlikely, for the Pawnees had been on their own reservation north of the Platte River for a number of years, were no longer deemed hostile, and had long been forbidden by treaty to hunt or travel south of the Platte. In any event they would not have lightly intruded into the country of their mortal enemies the Cheyennes. It is also implausible that an attacking Indian war party would stop and identify themselves to their enemy or, if they did stop, give an accurate answer. Newspapers at the time gave various tribal identifications, some saying Sioux or Kiowas but most simply referring to "Indians." In fact the raiders were most likely those Indians inhabiting the area between the Platte and the Arkansas and suffering from the intrusions of whites into it—namely, the southern Oglalas, Cheyennes, and Arapahoes. Whoever they were, the attacks of June 22 were part of the ongoing warfare directed at white wagon roads, railroads, and advancing settlements. On June 19 General Smith had written to General Sherman from his headquarters at Fort Harker, urgently requesting the return of Custer and his six companies of the Seventh Cavalry to the Smoky Hill. He said the Cheyennes were now raiding on that river and many were

---

[22] Jackson, "March Itinerary," June 22, 1867; Custer to Augur, June 22, 1867; E. Custer, *Tenting on the Plains*, 582–83; G. Custer, *My Life on the Plains*, 130–33; Davis, "Summer on the Plains," 302; Millbrook, "West Breaks In General Custer," 123–25.

going south to the Arkansas. Satanta and his Kiowas were said to be "on the warpath," presumably because of their raid on the Fort Dodge livestock. Smith believed there was about to be "a grand combination on and south of the Arkansas." The previous day he had telegraphed Custer, probably at Fort McPherson, stating that the "Cheyennes are already on the Smoky from Harker to Wallace and beyond in small parties and have committed depredations." He reported that he had asked Sherman to send Custer back, since he was needed on the Smoky Hill "very much."[23]

After returning to St. Louis, Sherman received word that Custer was now at the forks of the Republican and had sent a wagon train to Fort Wallace for supplies. This clearly surprised him, and on June 27 he sent a message to General Augur's headquarters in Omaha to deliver new orders to Custer: "I don't understand about General Custer being on the Republican awaiting provisions from Fort Wallace. If this is so, and all the Indians be gone south, convey to him my orders that he proceed with all his command in search of the Indians towards Fort Wallace, and report to General Hancock, who will leave Denver for same place today." Lt. Henry G. Litchfield, Augur's chief of staff, forwarded the orders to Lt. Col. (Bvt. Brig. Gen.) Joseph H. Potter, commanding at Fort Sedgwick, with instructions to deliver them to Custer. The effort to do so would have unforeseen consequences.[24]

[23] Gibbs to T. B. Weir, AAAG, June 23, 1867, Fort Hays, LS, T713-R1, NA; A. J. Smith to W. T. Sherman, June 19, 1867, U.S. House, "Difficulties with Indian Tribes," 7:61; Burkey, *Custer, Come at Once*, 27; Frost, *Court-martial*, 51; White, *Hostiles and Horse Soldiers*, 50.
[24] W. T. Sherman to C. C. Augur, June 27, 1867, in *Report of the Secretary of War, 1867*, 35; Frost, *Court-martial*, 53, 200.

CHAPTER TWENTY-ONE

The Blooding of
the Seventh Cavalry

ollowing Major Elliot's departure during the early morning hours
of June 23, the four companies remaining at the forks of the Republican laid in camp, resting and enjoying the monotony of idleness.
As afternoon faded into evening, the horses and mules were allowed to
graze on the surrounding hills under the guards' watchful eyes. Then as
darkness began to gather, they were brought in and securely tethered near
the tents. Stable guards for each troop were assigned their stations and
pickets were posted. At 8:30 P.M., taps sounded, lights were doused, and
the camp settled in for a quiet night's rest. Only the moonlight reflecting
on the white tents revealed their presence. And so slumber prevailed and
the night passed peacefully for Custer and his men.[1]

At 5:00 A.M. on June 24, "that uncertain period between darkness and
daylight" as Custer described it, the peace of the camp was shattered by
the sharp report of a carbine fired on the picket line. In an instant sleepy
men stumbled from their tents with weapons in hand and prepared to
defend themselves. The officer of the day, 1st Lt. (Bvt. Capt.) Tom Custer,
went running by his brother's tent, stuck his head through the flap, and
yelled, "They are here!" Custer was already reaching for the Spencer rifle
he kept at his side, prepared to join the others. Before he could, there
came the sounds of a brisk fusillade, the alarm "Indians!" and war whoops,
leaving no doubt about the identity of their attackers. Custer burst through
his tent flap, wearing his crimson dressing gown and nothing on his head
or feet. By this time the morning light was sufficient to see their enemy
and be seen in turn. Custer later wrote that there were "hundreds" of Indians all around their camp and that a party of fifty of their best mounted

[1] Jackson, "March Itinerary," June 23, 1867; G. Custer, *My Life on the Plains*, 134–35.

343

warriors had approached through a ravine, intending to stampede the horse herd. Both numbers are probably gross exaggerations, since hundreds of warriors would have quickly overrun an encampment of only four sleeping cavalry companies. No more than ten to fifteen men would be required to stampede the horse herd, and any more than that in a ravine would have created congestion and too much noise. However many there were, an alert sentry and his warning shot clearly foiled the effort to achieve surprise and stampede the horses beyond the camp.[2]

The raiding party charging from the ravine shot the sentry and galloped over him. If not for the heavy fire directed at them from the camp, they probably would have scalped him. But they did manage to carry off his carbine and ammunition. Then they turned and galloped out of range while some of the sentry's comrades dashed out and brought him back to the safety of the camp. He was seriously though not mortally wounded by a bullet through his body and was cared for by Dr. Coates. Meanwhile the Indians, having missed the opportunity to surprise the soldiers and stampede the horses, withdrew to "a prominent knoll" about half a mile south of the north fork of the Republican and a mile south of the cavalry camp. The main body gathered there and began to flash signal mirrors for other small parties, who later joined them. To Custer it appeared that they were holding a council to determine what they should do next. He believed that they had intended to stampede the horses away from the camp and then finish off the soldiers at their leisure. This is possible but speculative. The Indians were far too canny and careful to attack a sizable party of well-armed soldiers, afoot or mounted, when they were on the alert. But they were opportunists. If the stampede attempt had been successful and if the soldiers were entirely surprised and disorganized, they might well have attempted a sudden charge through the camp. Failing to surprise and confuse the troopers, however, they probably would have been quite content to escape with the horse herd, thereby neutralizing their enemy and ensuring the safety of their families in their village to the south. There would also have been the added bonus of a few hundred fine cavalry horses. As it was, they obtained only the sentry's carbine and ammunition for their trouble but did escape without casualties.[3]

Custer was not concerned about further attacks by the Indians that day, for they had lost the element of surprise and now faced a large force of

---

[2] Jackson, "March Itinerary," June 24, 1867; G. Custer, *My Life on the Plains*, 135–37.
[3] G. Custer, *My Life on the Plains*, 137–38; Davis, "Summer on the Plains," 302.

heavily armed soldiers with superior weapons. But he did want to learn which tribe his enemy belonged to and, for this reason, proposed a parley. He sent one of his interpreters to invite the Indians to a council. Custer did not mention the identity of the interpreter, but Theodore Davis said he was named Gay. This may have been Ed Guerrier, whose surname usually eluded pronunciation by frontiersmen and soldiers, or it may have been one of the white Lakota interpreters he hired on the Platte. Whoever it was, he was conversant with Indian signs and rode his horse toward the assembled warriors in a zigzag fashion (symbolizing peace), periodically riding in a circle (meaning "council"), and repeated this several times. The Indians responded, and a small party detached themselves from the main body and rode toward the interpreter. When within speaking or signing distance, the party halted and proceeded to communicate with the interpreter. There was an agreement to hold a council in which Custer and six of his officers would advance to the banks of the Republican's north fork and converse with an equal number of "the leading chiefs." In all probability those present were not chiefs but headmen of the military societies.[4]

Suspicious of treachery, Custer placed most of his command under arms and instructed the officer left in command to charge at the sound of a bugle. Then he and six of his officers, accompanied by a bugler and an interpreter (probably the same man who had arranged the council), mounted their horses and rode a half mile to the designated meeting place. There they dismounted, leaving the horses with the bugler, and headed down to the riverbank. The bugler was instructed to watch for signs of violence or treachery by the Indians and, if he observed any, to quickly sound "Advance" on his bugle. Each of the officers removed his pistol from its holster and thrust it loosely through his belt. At the meeting point on the north side of the river, the bank was level, with an abundance of green grass, while the south bank was broken and covered with willows and tall grass. The river itself was so low that it was nothing but a small stream. Soon after Custer and his officers arrived, the seven "chiefs" appeared, removed their leggings, and waded across to where the officers waited. One of them was Pawnee Killer, the man with whom Custer had recently held friendly talks and given gifts while on the Platte. Custer claimed surprise that, after the cordiality and hospitality he believed he had extended, Pawnee Killer would return "to attack and murder us" without provocation. Why he should be surprised is a puzzle, since he was

[4] G. Custer, *My Life on the Plains*, 138–39; Davis, "Summer on the Plains," 302.

intentionally moving to the place he believed the Kiyuksa village was located, and he intended to return the band to the vicinity of Fort McPherson by first taking several of the "chiefs" hostage. Clearly Custer did not consider the matter from the perspective of the Indians, who only two months earlier had their lodges and possessions burned by General Hancock. Now they found themselves pursued by a sizable military force from the same expedition whose intentions they were quite naturally suspicious of. Their recent attacks on white trading ranches and travelers in their effort to expel them from their country also made it seem likely that the soldiers were sent to fight them.[5]

The conversations that followed were inconclusive. When they reached the north bank, Pawnee Killer and his warriors extended their hands in greeting and gave a "how." Suspicious of them, Custer kept one hand on his revolver during the entire meeting. Although Davis later said that Pawnee Killer refused to give any reason for his attack on the cavalry camp, Custer reported that he himself "avoided all reference to what had occurred." He did try to learn the location of the Oglala camp and where they would be moving next, but Pawnee Killer "skillfully parried" all such questions. Pawnee Killer asked why the soldiers had left the Platte and where they were going. He was no doubt fearful for the safety of his village and its families. This time Custer declined to answer. If the Kiyuksas, when fleeing their village on Pawnee Fork, left a scout behind to watch and find out the soldiers' intentions (and they likely did), they would have been quite aware of Custer's surround and subsequent entry into the village during the night. This would obviously make them as suspicious of Custer's intentions as he was of theirs following their early morning attempt to stampede the cavalry horses. Though they talked for some time, neither side was willing to reveal its future plans to the other.[6]

Toward the end of their talk a young warrior fully armed with bow and arrows, war club, and scalping knife appeared on the south bank and waded the river, greeting the officers as the others had done. They thought nothing about this until another warrior also crossed over, then another and another, until four additional men had joined the original seven. Custer called Pawnee Killer's attention to the agreement that only an equal number were to be present for both sides. To this the Oglala war leader responded that his men were "well disposed" toward the white officers and

---

[5] G. Custer, *My Life on the Plains*, 139–40; Davis, "Summer on the Plains," 302.

[6] G. Custer, *My Life on the Plains*, 140; Davis, "Summer on the Plains," 302.

simply wanted to meet them and shake their hands. Custer told him that no more must come over, and then the conference resumed. Soon another group of warriors could be seen preparing to wade the river. Already suspicious of the intentions of the Indians based on their earlier conduct, Custer now felt they had a preconceived plan to attack the officers as soon as their numbers were sufficient. Once again he reminded Pawnee Killer of their agreement and told him that not one more man should cross the river. Should they do so his bugler would, on his sign, sound the signal for all of his troops to charge to his side. This convinced Pawnee Killer that any further attempt to bring more men to the north side of the river would result in an all-out attack on his party, so he signaled them to stay where they were.[7]

Custer was extremely eager to detain the Kiyuksas and lead them back to Fort McPherson, or at least move their village nearer the cavalry camp, but this was an unrealistic hope at best. Pawnee Killer firmly resisted all such requests, and finally Custer announced that he would follow the Indians back to their camp. This was not agreeable to Pawnee Killer, who clearly recalled the recent experience with soldiers wanting to come to his peoples' village. Seeing that nothing further was to be gained, Custer was about to break off the meeting, when the Indians requested a gift of coffee, sugar, and ammunition. Bearing in mind their recent attack, Custer declined, and the two sides parted, with the officers returning to their horses and heading back to camp. Meanwhile the Oglalas crossed over the river, mounted their horses, and galloped back to their warriors, who were then about two miles away.[8]

When Custer and his officers reached the cavalry camp a half mile to the north, he had the "general" sounded by the bugler. Though the talks with Pawnee Killer were abortive, he intended to pursue the Kiyuksas to their village in hopes of forcing them to return to the Platte, but he also had concerns for the absent detachments, especially Major Elliot's small band, which could not withstand the assault of a large war party. According to Davis, the troopers were all mounted and prepared to march within twenty minutes. What is puzzling is that the brief attack on the camp commenced at 5:00 A.M., and the meeting on the riverbank took place soon after. Lieutenant Jackson, however, reported that they struck camp and marched in pursuit of the Indians at noon, meaning that seven hours elapsed

---

[7] G. Custer, *My Life on the Plains*, 140–42; Davis, "Summer on the Plains," 302.
[8] G. Custer, *My Life on the Plains*, 142–44; Davis, "Summer on the Plains," 302–303.

between the stampede attempt and the pursuit. This would not suggest a prompt departure unless the effort to get the Indians to council and the council itself took an extraordinarily long time. But whether they were ready to go in twenty minutes or lingered a few hours, at noon they did ride out and proceeded south across the north fork of the Republican to the south fork. This they followed southwesterly for about seven miles until, realizing that they could not overtake the Indians, they turned north-northwest for two miles, then northeast by east as they headed back to camp. According to Custer, the moment the Indians became aware that they were being followed, they set off at top speed, following the Republican's south fork, and were soon lost to sight. "We followed as rapidly as our heavier horses could travel," he said, "but the speed of the Indian pony on that occasion, as on many others, was too great for that of our horses." Discouraged, the four companies slowly returned to camp after a march of sixteen miles. When they arrived, probably around 3:30 or 4:00 P.M., they discovered that Indians had been at their campsite during their absence.[9]

Half an hour later, a small party of Indians—Custer said a half dozen and Davis ten to fifteen—appeared on a ridge northwest of the camp. Custer ordered Capt. Louis Hamilton to take A Company and "learn something of their intentions." How that could be achieved, especially by soldiers who could not communicate with Indians, he did not say. Once mounted, Hamilton led his men up the hill where the Indians were seen, but on reaching its crest, he found that they had fallen back to a ridge beyond. Hamilton's men followed with the same result, and this was repeated several times. This often-used "decoy" ruse was working. Finally, when the troops were several miles from their camp, the Indians divided into two small parties going in different directions. Hamilton also divided his troops into two detachments, one with twenty-five men under his command following one party, and the other, under Tom Custer, following the second. When they were a sufficient distance apart to be of no support to one another, Hamilton's detachment was charged by forty-three mounted warriors concealed in a ravine, each shouting his war cry. They circled the beleaguered troopers, hanging from the sides of their horses and sending arrows and bullets raining down on their quarry. Hamilton coolly halted, dismounted his men, and formed them in a circle, where they took steady aim and fired as their foes dashed by. The

[9] Jackson, "March Itinerary," June 24, 1867; G. Custer, *My Life on the Plains*, 144; Davis, "Summer on the Plains," 303.

On the morning of June 24, 1867, Pawnee Killer's Oglala warriors unsuccessfully attempted to stampede the horses of the Seventh Cavalry from its camp on Spring Creek above the forks of the Republican River. A subsequent parley and then pursuit of the Indians likewise met no success, but after the troops returned to camp, a party of Oglalas was seen and pursued by Capt. Louis Hamilton and his A Company. Drawing the soldiers farther from their camp and dividing them, the warriors suddenly turned and charged Hamilton's men. The soldiers formed a hollow square, with the horses in the center, and managed to successfully defend themselves. This sketch of the scene was made by Theodore Davis, who was not present but interviewed the troopers on their return. From *Harper's Weekly*, August 17, 1867.

Indians displayed great daring and courage, but their aim was poor because of the difficulty of firing accurately at a gallop.[10]

When Hamilton divided his men into two detachments, Dr. Coates, who had accompanied them to provide treatment for the wounded, attached himself to the one led by Tom Custer. Somehow, in the confusion of the chase, he became separated from them and found himself alone. Then came the sounds of firing in the direction Hamilton and his men had gone, so he rode to the sounds of the guns. He came within sight of them at about a half mile away. Fortunately he was to their south and nearest to the cavalry camp, for just as he saw the Indians attacking Hamilton's detachment, the Indians saw him. Immediately six warriors left the attack party and charged toward Coates. He put the spurs to his horse and began a life-or-death race for the safety of the camp. At the time he was

---

[10] Jackson, "March Itinerary," June 20, 1867; G. Custer, *My Life on the Plains*, 144–46; Davis, "Summer on the Plains," 303.

four or more miles from his destination, and his horse was tired from the morning's ride and the recent pursuit of the decoy party. The Indian horses, with their greater stamina and relative freshness, were faster and more likely than not to overtake Coates as their race began. However, the cavalry horses, unless accustomed to their presence, had as much fear of the Indians as they did a large predator. This, along with the frightening sounds of the Indian yells and war whoops gave the doctor's horse the needed incentive to keep up the race. Though the Indians were gaining on him and nearly within range to shoot arrows, Dr. Coates cleared a ridge and saw the camp a short mile ahead. When the Indians saw the encampment, they fired a final but futile volley of bullets and arrows at their target, then stopped their pursuit and disappeared in the direction from which they had come. Their own horses were by now too winded to risk a ride closer and find themselves pursued by soldiers on fresh horses.[11]

Coates galloped into the cavalry camp, both man and horse nearly spent, and he slid from his saddle and collapsed on the ground. He was too exhausted and excited to speak for a time. Officers and men gathered around him, aware that something extraordinary must have happened to put him in such a state. As soon as he had sufficiently recovered his breath and his composure, Coates told them of the plight of Captain Hamilton and his men, when last seen surrounded and under attack by a superior force of Indians. That was enough for Custer to mount his troops and head north at a brisk trot. They knew from Dr. Coates that the scene of the fight was at least five miles away, and they dared not move faster lest their own mounts become too exhausted to carry their riders into combat. After riding for about two miles, they saw Captain Hamilton and his troopers, probably including Tom Custer and his men, riding toward them in a leisurely fashion and heading back to camp. The Indians had broken off their attack and left. Whether they did so because they feared that the rest of the soldiers would soon be coming or because they found that they would pay too high a price for success is unknown. Custer preferred to believe that they had been driven off by the resolute fire from Hamilton and his men and claimed they had killed two warriors and wounded several more, while they themselves suffered only the wounding of one horse. Davis would later report that three Indians were killed and several wounded and that the attack was made by nearly three hundred warriors rather than

[11] G. Custer, *My Life on the Plains*, 146–48; Frost, *Court-martial*, 58; Kennedy, *On the Plains*, 119–20; Millbrook, "West Breaks In General Custer," 126.

the forty-three related by Custer. In truth it was difficult if not impossible to know the actual casualties among the Indians, because they nearly always carried away their dead and wounded.[12]

The day's events, beginning with the stampede attempt and ending in the fight with Hamilton's detachment, greatly disturbed Custer. He professed great concern for Major Elliot and his small escort because they had left for Fort Sedgwick in the same direction that Hamilton's men had their fight. He was convinced that all Indians between the Arkansas and the Platte were now set on war and would take revenge on any party they might come upon. That this could come about because General Hancock had burned their villages and declared war on them does not seem to have entered his mind. But his principal concern was for the wagon train that he had sent to Fort Wallace for supplies and to bring back his wife. A wagon train could hardly avoid detection by the Indians, especially in the region they were believed to be. Custer concluded they would allow the train to proceed to the fort unmolested but would attack on its return to capture the supplies. The Indians, he was certain, would be well aware that half of the escort had halted at Beaver Creek and that from there to Fort Wallace and back would be guarded by only the forty-eight men of Company D, led by Lt. Sam Robbins. An attack would be most likely between those two points during the train's return trip. Now panic for his wife's safety, if she were with the train, seemed to take over:

> Looking at these probable events, I not only felt impelled to act promptly to secure the safety of the train and its escort, but a deeper and stronger motive-stirred me to leave nothing undone to circumvent the Indians. My wife, who, in answer to my letters, I believed was then at Fort Wallace, would place herself under the protection of the escort of the train and attempt to rejoin me in camp. The mere thought of the danger to which she might be exposed spurred me to decisive action.

Another factor no doubt driving Custer's concern was that he had given Lieutenant Cooke verbal instructions that, should Indians attack the train, he was to shoot Libbie to prevent her being taken captive.[13]

To thwart the perceived danger to his wife, Custer later said that on the same day of the Hamilton fight he dispatched Capt. (Bvt. Lt. Col.) Edward Meyers with one full squadron, "well mounted and armed," in the direc-

[12] G. Custer, *My Life on the Plains*, 148–50; Davis, "Summer on the Plains," 303; Frost, *Court-martial*, 58; Millbrook, "West Breaks In General Custer," 126.

[13] E. Custer, *Tenting on the Plains*, 628–29; G. Custer, *My Life on the Plains*, 150–52; Frost, *Court-martial*, 58–59; Millbrook, "West Breaks In General Custer," 126–27.

tion of Fort Wallace. His orders were to move as rapidly as possible, following the wagon train's trail. Captain West was to join Meyers at Beaver Creek and, with West in command as senior officer, press on toward Fort Wallace until they met the returning train and its escort, then bring it back to the cavalry camp at the forks of the Republican. However, according to Lieutenant Jackson, Captain Meyers did not leave until the next morning and took only his E Company with him. Joining Captain West and his K Company would make a full squadron, and a full one-half of Custer's command would then be committed to escorting the wagon train and Libbie Custer. Meyers and his troopers did move out with alacrity on the morning of June 25 and marched without halting, except to water and graze the horses and feed the men, until they reached Beaver Creek, a distance of about thirty-seven miles. From there the combined force proceeded south toward Fort Wallace.[14]

The wagon train that Captain Meyers was sent to protect had left the forks of the Republican at sunset on June 22, escorted by Companies D and K. They traveled steadily through the night, stopping only to water and graze the horses and mules and provide a little rest for the men. The pace of march was restricted because of the slower speed of the wagon train, which moved at a walk even though the wagons were empty and making their best time. After crossing the north and south forks of the Republican, they moved on a bearing a little west of south, staying to the east of Big Timber Creek, a small stream that wound north until emptying into the Republican. A little over thirty miles from camp they crossed the headwaters of Little Beaver Creek. In its upper reaches it was an intermittent stream with a surface flow only after rain. Almost seven miles beyond, during the late afternoon of June 23 they struck Beaver Creek. There Captain West detached his company and went into camp. They would scout along the stream in small parties until the return of the wagon train, which was expected in two days.[15]

The wagon train and Company D continued south early on the morning of June 24. Beyond the breaks of Beaver Creek the land again flattened out into the rolling High Plains until they approached the north fork of the Smoky Hill (then also known as Black Butte Creek). Then the country became increasingly broken and rough, the hills interspersed with large draws, dry arroyos, and occasional streams, but few if any trees.

---

[14] Jackson, "March Itinerary," June 25, 1867; G. Custer, *My Life on the Plains*, 152–54; Davis, "Summer on the Plains," 303; Millbrook, "West Breaks In General Custer," 126.

[15] Jackson, "March Itinerary," June 22, 1867; G. Custer, *My Life on the Plains*, 132–33, 154–55.

As they approached this stream, according to Custer, the scout Medicine Bill Comstock told Lieutenants Robbins and Cooke, riding at the head of the column, that the most likely place for an Indian attack on them would be in that vicinity during their return journey. The valley on both sides of the stream was about a mile wide with good grass, so they probably laid over there for two or three hours to allow the livestock to graze and drink. The stream was only about two feet deep at the crossing point, but the water was very clear with a swift current. After a rest they continued over the rolling plains, crossed the dry bed of Lake Creek, and finally reached Fort Wallace in the late evening without incident. Lieutenant Cooke learned that Libbie Custer was not there to be escorted back to her husband. No time was lost in loading the wagons with the needed supplies, picking up the mail for the command, and preparing for departure the following day.[16]

The wagons left Fort Wallace on the evening of June 25, probably well before dusk. They retraced their route and by the following morning had crossed Black Butte Creek and moved back up onto the High Plains. As they continued, Comstock thought he observed something on the hills far away to their right (northeast). Using his field glasses, he confirmed that Indians were watching them from the reverse slope of the hills, and Robbins and Cooke both verified it with their own field glasses. It was some time before the Indians realized they had been observed, but when they did, they rode boldly to the crest of the hill and sat in plain sight, observing the oncoming train. Others soon joined their party and before long an estimated 100 warriors were in view. They were painted for war. Many wore feathers or brilliant warbonnets, carrying lances and brightly painted and ornamented buffalo hide shields as well as bows and arrows and a few firearms. Custer, who was not there, said they were nearly all armed with carbines and at least two pistols each—an unlikely claim. The Cheyennes were never this well armed in their entire history. They did not have such weaponry at the confrontation on Pawnee Fork, and they certainly had not had the opportunity to acquire them since. Although they probably had a few carbines, pistols, and other older firearms, for the most part they would only have had their traditional weapons. Custer also claimed their numbers continued to grow until there were 600 to 700 warriors (Davis reported 700 to 800). This also is highly unlikely. At that

---

[16] Jackson, "March Itinerary," July 13, 1867; G. Custer, *My Life on the Plains*, 154–56; Utley, *Life in Custer's Cavalry*, 64.

During the morning of June 26 Custer's wagon train, returning north to his camp at the forks of the Republican with supplies obtained from Fort Wallace, was attacked by a mixed war party of Kiyuksa Oglalas and Dog Soldier Cheyennes. Lieutenants Cooke and Robbins placed their men around the advancing wagon train, with every fourth man from D Company leading four horses between the two columns of supply wagons. This stylized depiction of the event was sketched by Theodore Davis to illustrate his story appearing in the August 17, 1867, issue of *Harper's Weekly*. The view is to the south, with the hill the Indians descended from shown to the left, or east.

time no other hostile Indians were known to be between the Pawnee Fork and the Platte, apart from the Dog Soldier and southern Sutaio Cheyennes and the Kiyuksa Oglalas. The southern Sicangu (Brulé) Lakotas had moved north of the Platte for safety, as had Turkey Leg's band of Óhméseheso Cheyennes. A few Arapahoes may have been with them but not in any numbers. At most these combined bands could not field more than 350 to 400 fighting men, and a large proportion of them were engaged that very morning in an attack on soldiers at Fort Wallace. In all likelihood the warriors about to attack the wagon train and its escort totaled no more that 100 to 150, and perhaps fewer.[17]

Lieutenants Robbins and Cooke prepared their defense, circling the wagons and putting the mounted men of Company D around them. Soon, however, Cooke reorganized the wagon train so that they could continue on toward Beaver Creek and have the assistance of Captain West and his

[17] J. Hale to T. B. Weir, AAAG, June 27, 1867, LS, Fort Wallace, RG 393, NA; *Harper's Weekly*, August 17, 1867, 513–14; G. Custer, *My Life on the Plains*, 157–59; Davis, "Summer on the Plains," 303; Hyde, *Life of George Bent*, 275, 278.

Company K. They placed the wagons in two parallel columns of equal numbers, leaving a wide space between in which to lead the cavalry horses. As was the standard practice, every fourth man of Company D was detailed to lead four horses. This left about thirty-six men to form a line of skirmishers surrounding the train as it lumbered forward. Having traveled about twenty-five miles, they were already more than halfway to Beaver Creek, leaving them some fifteen miles short of help. The Indians had been watching all of these preparations with interest as they began to file slowly down the hill to meet the advancing train. The wagon master instructed his teamsters to keep moving at a steady pace and to keep the wagons closed up, with little space between them. Lieutenant Cooke took command of one flank and Lieutenant Robbins the other. Both remained mounted so they could move quickly to any point where there was a need. Bill Comstock also stayed on his horse and dashed around to wherever he could be of the most help.[18]

Once down from the hill, the Indians slowly formed a line facing the moving wagon train but did not attack it immediately. In *My Life on the Plains* Custer said that suddenly "the entire band of warriors bore down upon the train and its little party of defenders." They were shouting war cries and evidently intended to stampede the horses and draft animals, then wipe out the soldiers and teamsters in the excitement and confusion that followed. The first charge was made on the flank commanded by Lieutenant Cooke, on the right side of the column. The Indians dashed in to overrun the line of skirmishers, but the cavalrymen stood fast, holding their fire until the Indians were within short rifle range, then took deliberate aim and fired a deadly volley into the oncoming warriors. According to Custer, several Indians reeled in their saddles, and a number of their horses were either killed or wounded. The heavy fire forced the warriors to wheel away to the right and then withdraw out of range of the military carbines to hold a council among themselves. Flushed with their apparent success, the men of Company D "sent up a cheer of exultation." Comstock, less certain of the outcome, commented that the Indians were not likely to let fifty men keep them from getting the coffee, sugar, and other useful items in the wagons and take a few scalps in the process.[19]

While they waited for a fresh attack, the two officers rode along the skir-

---

[18] *Harper's Weekly*, August 17, 1867, 513–14; G. Custer, *My Life on the Plains*, 157–61; Davis, "Summer on the Plains," 303.

[19] *Harper's Weekly*, August 17, 1867, 513–14; G. Custer, *My Life on the Plains*, 160–64; Davis, "Summer on the Plains," 303.

mish line and cautioned the men against wasting ammunition. Finally the Indians, apparently concluding they could not stampede the animals without taking unnecessary casualties, formed a circle, riding around the moving train and its escort but keeping at a greater distance and moving with caution. Instead of an attack by the entire body of warriors at one time, it became a matter of individual warriors choosing their own time and method of charging the wagon train and the line of soldiers surrounding it. After a while they began moving faster, gradually contracting their circle so that they could fire on the soldiers as they rode within range. Single file they presented a much more difficult target than during their earlier massed charge. And using their remarkable riding skills, they now dropped on the opposite side of their horses and fired their weapons either over or under the necks of the animals, protected by their mounts. In this manner they continued their attack on the wagon train as it moved slowly northward. They were never able to force it to halt, however, and the train maintained a steady advance toward help. The presence of the wagons, Custer observed, doubtless made it impossible for the warriors to charge through and over the soldiers, stampeding the horses and dividing the men. According to Custer, the march and the fight continued for about three hours. From time to time the "fourth trooper" holding the led horses was changed with tired men on the skirmish line. Finally, as ammunition began to run low, there was concern among the officers, troopers, and teamsters. Suddenly an Indian scout rode down the hill and communicated something to the war leaders. Word passed among them, and a final shower of arrows and shots was fired. After that the Indians turned and disappeared over the hills, much to the surprise and relief of the troopers. The fight was over.[20]

What the soldiers were unaware of was that sharp-eyed Indian scouts on the hill had detected a column of cavalry moving in from the north at a brisk pace. They were still nearly two hours away, but their horses would be relatively fresh in contrast to those of the Indians. To avoid the risk of pursuit by the cavalry under unfavorable circumstances, and seeing no immediate prospect of breaking through the train's defenses, the headmen decided to break off the engagement. The soldiers thought they had beaten back the attack, and while their wounded were tended, they began to congratulate themselves on their victory and exchange memories of the fight. But this was no victory; the Indians had made a strategic withdrawal to avoid unnecessary losses in a larger fight. Were it not for the approach

---

[20] G. Custer, *My Life on the Plains*, 164–70.

of the two cavalry companies, the men of Company D might soon have run out of ammunition and been overwhelmed. At best it was a standoff for Robbins and his men, but one for which they could be justifiably proud. They had, after all, survived and saved their train of supplies. They spent the next hour relaxing, swapping stories, and breathing a sigh of relief. Then someone noticed another body of horsemen approaching from the north, and their anxiety returned because they were now very low on ammunition. But the officer's field glasses revealed that it was Captain West, Captain Meyers, and their relief force. Soon Lieutenant Cooke, Comstock, and a few of the troopers galloped ahead to meet them. West's column had arrived none too soon.[21]

As often happened, there were differences between Custer's recollection of events and the reporting of Theodore Davis. There were inconsistencies as well between Davis's initial reporting for *Harper's Weekly* and his later summation of the Hancock expedition for the magazine. In his story in the August 17, 1867, issue Davis reported that the wagon train left Fort Wallace on the evening of June 25, was attacked the following morning near the Black Butte by "several hundred" Sioux and Cheyennes, and fought them for ten miles until reaching the Company K camp on Beaver Creek. He also declared that the Indians charged only in small parties that quickly broke before the concentrated fire of the troopers. His later article claimed there were "seven or eight hundred" Sioux and Cheyennes (more than even Custer's eventual number) and that the fight covered fifteen instead of ten miles and continued until reaching the relief column instead of Beaver Creek. In that day such inaccuracies and inconsistencies were common. Neither man was present, neither knew more than he was told or read, and both often exaggerated. The train did start back on the evening of June 25 as reliably reported by Captain Barnitz, who was then at Fort Wallace, and by Lt. Joseph Hale, Third Infantry, temporarily commanding the post. The north fork of the Smoky Hill (Black Butte Creek) is approximately halfway between the fort and Beaver Creek on the route followed, so the heavily laden wagons probably started in the early evening in order to cover the twenty miles or so to the place where they first sighted the Indians. The fight likely did encompass about three hours and ten miles, considering the slow movement of the wagons and the relatively fast pace of the relief column advancing toward them from Beaver Creek. Custer, who received his information directly from the two

---

[21] Ibid., 167–71.

officers involved, was probably the more reliable source. However, he was well known for exaggerating almost everything. Who first attributed hundreds of Indians to the affair is unknown, but that was clearly far more than there could have been.[22]

Once united, the three companies of cavalry and the wagons moved back north and camped on Beaver Creek that night, allowing the exhausted men and animals involved in the fight to recover. The next morning they resumed the march north to the forks of the Republican, moving steadily and without any interference from the Indians. Though Custer reported their return on the morning of June 28, Lieutenant Jackson noted it on June 27, undoubtedly after dark that night. The men of D Company regaled the others with stories of the fight, reporting that they had killed at least five Indians and wounded nine or ten others. That was speculative, of course, since they could not know whether a warrior struck by a bullet was dead, unconscious, or only slightly wounded. Two Crows and Yellow Nose, Dog Soldiers who were in the fight, later told George Bent that two or three of their horses were shot but no warriors were killed. Then, on June 28, Major Elliot and his men returned safely, completing a mission that took them some 150 miles round-trip (Custer and Elliot both called it about 200 miles). They had traveled mainly at night and concealed themselves in ravines by day. In writing of their return, Custer also reversed the arrival dates, reporting that Elliot and his party reached camp on June 27 and the wagon train and three companies of cavalry on June 28. This permitted him to claim his anxiety for Elliot and his men was dispelled and therefore he could focus his concern on the train—the one he believed might be bringing his wife to him. Happily for him both missions were completed without loss of life and with their objectives accomplished. Now Custer's command, or at least Companies A and D, had experienced their first combat. They were unaware that Captain Barnitz and his Company G had engaged in a ferocious fight of their own on the same morning as had D Company.[23]

---

[22] *Harper's Weekly*, August 17, 1867, 513–14; G. Custer, *My Life on the Plains*, 154–71; Davis, "Summer on the Plains," 303; Utley, *Life in Custer's Cavalry*, 64.

[23] Jackson, "March Itinerary," June 27–28, 1867; G. Custer, *My Life on the Plains*, 150–51, 172; Hyde, *Life of George Bent*, 273.

CHAPTER TWENTY-TWO

FORT WALLACE BESIEGED

O f the eight companies of the Seventh Cavalry that Custer led in the field during the earlier phases of the Hancock expedition, F and G had been left behind when he began his march north to the Platte. Company F had been sent to man Fort Monument and protect the surveyors and the workers who would follow to grade the railroad bed. Company G, commanded by Capt. Albert Barnitz, was left to protect Fort Hays and the railroad workers in its vicinity. But it did not remain there long. General Hancock, on his trip west to assess the Indian threat to the stage line and construction of the railroad to Denver, arrived at Fort Hays from Fort Harker with members of his staff shortly after the floods of June 6 and 7 receded. After a brief stay and conference with General Smith, he continued on to Fort Wallace on June 12, inspecting the stage stations en route. Accompanying him as escort was a detachment of troopers from Company G under the command of Sgt. William H. Dummell. They left old Fort Hays early in the morning and, after an uneventful four days of travel, arrived at Fort Wallace on the morning of June 16. That same day Hancock sent a dispatch to General Sherman, quoting Captain Keogh's report concerning attacks on every stage station ninety-five miles to the east and seventy-five miles to the west of Wallace. He must have sent it by courier to Fort Harker, where it could be forwarded to Sherman by telegraph, for Sherman received the dispatch while meeting with Custer near Fort McPherson on the morning of June 17. After listening to reports from Captain Keogh and other officers at the post, Hancock continued his journey to Denver on the morning of June 18. He left behind his G Company escort and instead took with him Captain Keogh and most of I Company—about forty men total. This all but stripped the post of cavalry, leaving it garrisoned by fewer than fifty soldiers, including the small

number of cavalry troopers remaining there. About an equal number of
civilian workers were present, constructing the fort's permanent buildings.[1]

Captain Keogh's I Company had achieved little success in thwarting
the Cheyenne and Oglala attacks to the east and west of Fort Wallace.
Recovery of most of the cattle stampeded from Pond Creek Station on
May 26 was the single small triumph they could claim. Now, with the
departure of Keogh and most of his company, there was little chance of
any successful operations against the Indians. Instead the question became
one of survival of the fort itself. On the positive side Col. W. H. Greenwood and his survey party of twenty men had arrived a few days previously, escorted by twenty-five black soldiers from the Thirty-eighth
Infantry. They had completed the survey of the railroad right-of-way to
a point about ten miles northeast of the post and intended to continue
northwest to make a preliminary survey of a branch line to Denver. At
the time the Union Pacific, E.D., contemplated completing a main line
southwesterly to the Pacific coast through New Mexico and Arizona, following nearly the same route eventually used by the Santa Fe Railroad.
Constant harassment by the Cheyennes and southern Oglalas, culminating in the running off of thirteen mules, forced Greenwood's survey party
to go to the fort to refit after completing their survey and, if possible, to
obtain a stronger escort. When Hancock arrived, they were engaged in
surveying the Fort Wallace military reservation for the government. Their
presence would add about forty-six more men to the defense of the fort.[2]

On the day of Hancock's departure and for the next two days things
were quiet in the vicinity of Fort Wallace. However, elsewhere along the
Smoky Hill route and the new railroad that would parallel it, attacks were
taking place up and down the line. Then, on the morning of June 21, a
Cheyenne raiding party struck at Pond Creek Station about two miles to
the west. They stampeded some of the horses and mules and began driving them north toward Beaver Creek. The short distance between the
stage station and the fort made it possible to see this activity through the
clear atmosphere of the High Plains. A small detachment of cavalry from
the fort rode toward them, hoping to recover the livestock, but a larger
party of Cheyenne warriors appeared from beyond the hills, forcing them

---

[1] W. S. Hancock to W. T. Sherman, June 16, 1867, AGO, LR, U.S. House, "Difficulties with Indian
   Tribes," 7:60; Bell, *New Tracks*, 37, 51–52; Burkey, *Custer, Come at Once*, 33n26; E. Custer, *Tenting
   on the Plains*, 653–54; Millbrook, "West Breaks In General Custer," 130; Nye, *Plains Indian Raiders*,
   86; Oliva, *Fort Wallace*, 53–54; Utley, *Life in Custer's Cavalry*, 63.
[2] Bell, *New Tracks*, 52–53; Burkey, *Custer, Come at Once*, 27; Millbrook, "West Breaks in General Custer,"
   130; Nye, *Plains Indian Raiders*, 86; Oliva, *Fort Wallace*, 54.

to retreat. The warriors continued heading toward the post, seemingly to run off the livestock grazing nearby. Maj. A. J. Calhoun, a Civil War soldier and now a newspaper correspondent, was present at the fort and witnessed the events as they unfolded. He had accompanied General Hancock as far as Wallace and remained there, perhaps hoping to get a story about the conflict with the Cheyennes and Oglalas who bitterly opposed the use of any kind of road along the Smoky Hill. That morning he rode out with Lt. Fred Beecher and four cavalry troopers to see Colonel Greenwood and his surveyors at work establishing the boundaries for the Fort Wallace reservation. On their return Calhoun and his five companions had just reached the top of a hill overlooking the post when they observed frantic activity below. Men were "rushing across the plain," presumably toward the fort, with great excitement. Beyond them a party of mounted warriors were dashing back and forth, harassing the men from the fort. The rattle of rifle and carbine fire and the cry "Indians!" could be heard.[3]

Lieutenant Beecher immediately set out for the fort at a gallop, with the others following. When they reached it, they began helping with the defense. Calhoun had been mounted on Lieutenant Bell's fine, blooded horse for his morning ride, apparently not having a suitable one of his own. When he reached the post, Bell was waiting for him, and as he dismounted, Bell vaulted into the saddle and galloped directly to the front, where twelve cavalry troopers, probably a mixture of men from G and I companies, were firing at the Indians. Calhoun borrowed a horse belonging to a wounded man and, "anxious to see how the 'noble red-men' fought," rode to the front. There he found an irregular line of infantry and civilian workers on foot, along with a number of wounded men. According to Beecher, there were in all about 125 "infantry, unhorsed cavalry, and citizens," the latter being civilian workers constructing the post's permanent buildings. Bell and the mounted troops were out in front of them, skirmishing with the Indians. To the left, or south, end of the little battle line, a party of about fifty warriors began to charge forward in a flanking movement. Just at that moment Sgt. William H. Dummell of G Company appeared over the hill with ten men, galloping straight toward the Indians. He shouted encouragement to his men and plunged directly into the approaching line of warriors. But at the last minute Sgt. William Hamlin of I Company suddenly turned away and retreated back toward the fort, followed by several men from his company. Probably unaware of Hamlin's defection, Dummell,

[3] J. Hale to T. B. Weir, AAAG, June 22, 1867, Fort Wallace, LS, NA; Bell, *New Tracks*, 53; Lee and Raynesford, *Trails of the Smoky Hill*, 110; Montgomery, "Fort Wallace," 17:207.

three troopers, and one finely mounted civilian continued in among the charging Indians. For a brief time Calhoun could hear the yells of the Indians and troopers, the encouraging shouts of Dummell, and the firing of Spencers. But the fight was over quickly, before help could reach Dummell's band. As the troopers were knocked from their saddles, they were shot or lanced to death. But for the arrival of Lieutenant Bell and his men with carbines blazing, they would have been scalped. As it was, the warriors returned to their own line with the soldiers' horses, weapons, ammunition, and equipment. The only survivor among Dummell's party was the civilian, who managed to escape on his fast horse.[4]

After the Indians left, Bell and his men recovered the bodies of the four dead men and returned them to the fort in an ambulance. Meanwhile Lieutenant Hale, the post adjutant commanding in the absence of Captain Keogh, recalled all of the men on foot in anticipation of a direct attack on the fort, posting them at strategic locations around it. The Indians were formed in a long line on a ridge overlooking the fort, and many of them were dismounted, watching the proceedings in the valley below them to the southeast. From time to time a small band of ten to twenty would dash forward, brandishing lances and shouting war cries, then wheel their horses and fire at the white cavalrymen before returning to their own line. They displayed courage and some semblance of discipline during the entire engagement. Finally Lieutenant Bell, desiring to determine the strength of his enemy and being well mounted on a fast horse, rode close to the Indian line and then parallel to it. As he did so, a warrior on a white horse galloped forward alone, evidently inviting individual combat. But Bell ignored him, continuing along the Indian line just out of range of their weapons. The warrior jerked his horse to a halt, fired a shot at Bell, then galloped back to his line. He subsequently led the final charge of the Cheyenne warriors. Some of the soldiers believed him to be Charlie Bent, the half-Cheyenne son of William Bent, who was about nineteen or twenty years old at that time and disowned by his father. He had vowed to shoot his father if given the opportunity and to wear his scalp in his belt. Others thought the man on the white horse was Roman Nose, the great Óhmésèheso warrior.[5]

While the main body of Dog Soldier and Sutaio warriors were threatening the fort, a detached party made a dash toward the stone quarries about three miles to the southeast of the post, at the foot of a long range

[4] Hale to Weir, June 22, 1867; Bell, *New Tracks*, 53–54; Millbrook, "West Breaks in General Custer," 130; Nye, *Plains Indian Raiders*, 87; Utley, *Life in Custer's Cavalry*, 63–64.
[5] Hale to Weir, June 22, 1867; Bell, *New Tracks*, 64; Nye, *Plains Indian Raiders*, 87–88.

of hills. From a distance they had the appearance of a huge cliff. About thirty men quarried and shaped the stone there, and six teams hauled it to the fort, where the masons would dress and lay it. The men working at the quarries lived there in tents and huts. When the Cheyenne war party attacked, two of the wagons and their teams were nearby, either hauling or returning for more stone. Both headed for the safety of the quarries, but only one team made it. The other one was overtaken and its driver, Patrick McCarty, killed. Those watching from the fort were amazed at the efficiency, dexterity, and speed with which the Indians cut loose the mules and ran them off. Then they upset the wagon, but because of the rapid and continuous fire kept up by the nearby quarry workmen, the warriors were forced to leave without scalping McCarty. Someone at the fort noticed that the quarry workers were preparing to make a run for the fort. A small body of horsemen left the post to protect them succeeded in doing so. Within ten minutes of their departure from the quarries, the Indians had entered and set fire to the stoneworks, the huts, and the tents.[6]

The fight with the Cheyennes on June 21 lasted nearly two hours, and when it ended, the Indians disappeared. With them went the livestock from Pond Creek Station, the horses belonging to Sergeant Dummell and the three cavalrymen killed with him, and the six mules from Patrick McCarty's team. The wounded were treated, and the four dead men prepared for burial, which took place at the post cemetery on Sunday, June 23. Meantime the garrison, the soldiers temporarily attached, the civilian workers, Colonel Greenwood, and his engineering party and escort all huddled in the fort in a state of high alert, with no one managing much sleep. The two stagecoaches that had been attacked while westbound for Denver on June 15, then forced back to Fort Wallace, attempted to return east from the fort on June 21 but were again driven back by the presence of Indians. They tried once more on June 23 and this time succeeded in escaping the confines of the post. They moved east along the stage road. At about 7:00 in the evening, as they approached the forks of the Smoky Hill River some fourteen miles east of Fort Wallace, the infantry guards on the coaches and the small cavalry escort thought they saw Indian scouts along the bluffs. They fired two or three shots at the supposed enemy and took one in response. But shortly they came in view of the great campground at the forks of the river, commonly known as Death Hollow because of the great number of trains and travelers attacked there by the Indians.

[6] Hale to Weir, June 22, 1867; Bell, *New Tracks*, 55–56; Nye, *Plains Indian Raiders*, 86–87; Oliva, *Fort Wallace*, 54–55; Utley, *Life in Custer's Cavalry*, 64.

Here they found not an enemy but Gen. W. W. Wright's survey party and its escort, Company G, Seventh Cavalry, commanded by Capt. Albert Barnitz. Each had mistaken the other for Indians, and both were sufficiently embarrassed by their error that little more was said of the incident.[7]

General Wright had managed railroad operations in Georgia for General Sherman during the Civil War and was now the superintendent of the Union Pacific, E.D. (Kansas Pacific). Presently he was engaged in the first phase of a survey to locate a suitable southern route to the Pacific coast through Kansas, Colorado, New Mexico, and Arizona. Company officers at the time held high hopes of spanning the West from the Missouri River to the ocean. The route to Denver would, under this scenario, be a branch line. Wright's party first came together at Salina, having traveled there by rail, and on June 7 their train of twenty wagons, headed by three ambulances, began moving west toward Fort Harker. They reached the post on June 10, experiencing en route the same severe spring storms as had Libbie Custer and those at Fort Hays, and left the following day. Three miles beyond Harker they passed through Ellsworth, only a month old but already experiencing remarkable growth. From the four or five "houses" there when Henry Stanley saw it in early May, it had now grown to seven or eight stores, two hotels, and about fifty houses occupied by nearly a thousand persons. Only weeks earlier a soldier had been killed and scalped where the schoolhouse now stood. By June 14 Wright's train was nearing Fort Hays, where it met the stagecoach from Denver that Lieutenant Bell had accompanied to Fort Wallace and that had been attacked on June 11 near Big Timbers Station.[8]

Wright's party spent June 15 at Fort Hays. There they left the twenty-four troopers from the Tenth Cavalry who had served as their escort beyond Fort Harker, and received as their new escort about fifty troopers from Company G, Seventh Cavalry, commanded by Captain Barnitz. The next morning, June 16, they left Fort Hays, their column now expanded from twenty to forty-seven wagons and the cavalry escort. By the afternoon of June 23 they reached Death Hollow and went into camp. Their travel to that point, aside from the heat of day, the desolation of the High Plains, and various disagreeable creatures such as rattlesnakes and wolves, had been largely uneventful. The only exception was that they found moccasin tracks of Indians around their camp each morning and, on going into camp at Death

[7] Bell, *New Tracks*, 48–49; Nye, *Plains Indian Raiders*, 88; Utley, *Life in Custer's Cavalry*, 63.
[8] Bell, *New Tracks*, ix–xx, 21, 27–30.

Hollow, found the remains of campfires, bark peeled and gnawed from the smaller cottonwood trees, and other signs that a large body of Indians had been there only a few hours before. That evening they had their encounter with the two stagecoaches, each mistaking the other for Indians.[9]

The guards and the passengers aboard the two stagecoaches told Barnitz of the fight at Fort Wallace two days earlier and of the death of Sergeant Dummell and the others. They also reported attacks on several stage stations in the vicinity. The Indians had attempted to burn them, using a kind of torpedo-arrow. These were made by placing percussion caps on the arrow blades and encasing them with a small cotton sack of gunpowder. This news, along with the howling of wolves and coyotes, caused everyone to spend an uneasy night on the alert for Indian attack. But none came, and they left the campground early the next morning, the two stagecoaches continuing east and the Wright party moving west to Fort Wallace. Wright's train and its escort reached the fort the following afternoon, June 24, and camped nearby. The men at the post had seen their column of dust at some distance to the east over the hills and, fearing the Indians were returning, stood to arms. The column of dust continued its slow approach, but finally a long line of horsemen and wagons came over a hill about four miles away. The sun reflected on the white wagon covers, and the gun barrels and scabbards of the cavalry glittered in its light. The adjutant, Lieutenant Hale, called out from the "look-out" on the roof of the sutler's store that the approaching column was General Wright's survey party with a cavalry escort. This of course greatly cheered those at the post. Wright and his men were hardly in camp, their tents pitched and their animals led to graze, when there was a second pleasant surprise. In from the east came two mail coaches, and soon bags of mail for the garrison and for the survey parties were carried to the post mailroom and emptied on the floor. Men sorted through the piles, and most found letters addressed to them.[10]

Early the same evening Lieutenants Cooke and Robbins arrived from the Republican River with Custer's wagon train. While the wagons were being loaded that evening and the next day with supplies for Custer's command, the officers and men caught up with the news that each had to provide. Although the men of Cooke's wagon train were unaware of the skirmishing with the Oglalas on the Republican after their departure, they were able to tell of Custer's present whereabouts and what his orders and

---

[9] Ibid., 36–37, 48; Utley, *Life in Custer's Cavalry*, 58, 63.
[10] Bell, *New Tracks*, 49–50, 56–58; Nye, *Plains Indian Raiders*, 88–89; Utley, *Life in Custer's Cavalry*, 63–64.

current plans called for. They also reported that Captain West and his company were scouting along Beaver Creek where some of the Indian villages were supposed to be. Barnitz could have (and probably did) inform Cooke and Robbins that neither Libbie Custer nor General Smith were at Fort Hays but had gone east to Fort Harker. And no doubt the details of the Cheyenne raids on the livestock of the nearby stage stations and the fort were discussed at length. On the evening of June 25 Cooke and Robbins left with the wagon train and its escort—northbound for the forks of the Republican. Neither the troopers leaving nor those remaining could imagine what awaited them the following morning.[11]

After his arrival at Fort Wallace, and with the state of high alert, Captain Barnitz kept his company horses on a picket line or lariated near his camp under a strong guard during the late evening and night. In the morning after breakfast they were sent downstream about two miles, where there was good grass for grazing in the valley of the south fork of the Smoky Hill. They were accompanied by a mounted guard some twenty men strong, and scouts were placed on the high ground a mile or so on either side of the valley. If the scouts observed any danger, Barnitz believed that the guards would be able to round up the horses and get them back to the post before the Indians could get among them. About 6:00 A.M. on June 26, as the men were breakfasting and attending to the first chores of the day, the peace was broken by the sounds of galloping horses and whooping Indians. A stagecoach had just arrived at Pond Creek Station two miles to the west when a raiding party attacked and ran off four of its horses. Those horses ran east on the Smoky Hill road, directly toward the fort, with a small party of raiders in hot pursuit. The stage horses ran two and two in exactly the same order as they were driven, and as they approached the fort, one was seen to be bleeding from a wound on a hind leg and another had been shot in the neck.[12]

The commotion caused great alarm at Fort Wallace and the nearby camps of the survey parties and their escorts. Men ran to get their weapons and prepared themselves for a fight. Captain Barnitz, who was just starting to breakfast, immediately ordered his men to arms and the horses brought in from the picket line. Within a minute the horses were coming in and being saddled. When his horse was ready, Barnitz mounted, then ordered his first sergeant, Francis S. Gordon, to form the troop,

[11] Bell, *New Tracks*, 58; Burkey, *Custer, Come at Once*, 32; Utley, *Life in Custer's Cavalry*, 64.
[12] Hale to Weir, June 22, 1867; Bell, *New Tracks*, 58; Nye, *Plains Indian Raiders*, 90; Utley, *Life in Custer's Cavalry*, 68–69.

mount, and follow him. Taking Edward Botzer, one of his buglers, Barnitz rode out a half mile northwest of the post to scout. From the high ground he could see small parties of Indians on the ridges along the horizon to the west and north, and a cloud of dust rising in the direction of Pond Creek Station. About the same time he could see his cavalry company approaching at a gallop and a small party of cavalry from the post coming to join him as well. When they reached him, he ordered Sergeant Gordon to take the First Platoon and deploy as skirmishers to the northwest at a steady gallop, bearing toward a party of Indians that included one mounted on a white horse. When close enough, they were to charge as foragers, but swinging to the left to head off another party of Indians that Barnitz thought were trying to escape from the stage station. He ordered the small detachment from Company I at the post to support Sergeant Gordon and his skirmishers, while the Second Platoon, under Sgt. Josiah Haines, was to follow the First Platoon in reserve and two hundred yards to the rear.[13]

Captain Barnitz organized his formation while at the gallop toward the enemy. But just as he completed it and they were moving forward in good order, Sergeant Gordon's horse, a fine animal, stepped into a prairie dog hole and threw its rider, who was badly bruised as a result. The horse continued toward the Indians, and to prevent it from falling into their hands, Barnitz pursued it. After repeated efforts he caught the animal's bridle and brought it to a halt, then sent it back to Gordon, who was by then far in the rear. Meanwhile, seeing that the Cheyenne raiding party from Pond Creek Station might get beyond the line of skirmishers and escape with the livestock they had stampeded, Barnitz ordered his bugler to ride to Sergeant Haines with directions to bear more to the right and head them off. By this time the Second Platoon had come abreast of the First, though separated from it, and Barnitz and a few other dispersed men moved into the center. In Sergeant Gordon's absence, Sgt. William Hamlin of I Company (the same whose retreat a few days earlier had resulted in the deaths of Sergeant Dummell and his comrades) was now the senior noncommissioned officer with the line of skirmishers.[14]

The Cheyenne raiders in front of them were being closely pressed by the men of G Company and seemed to be retiring beyond a ridge about three miles from the fort. However, they had slowed their movement and were from time to time riding their horses in small individual circles. When used

---

[13] Bell, *New Tracks*, 58–60; Utley, *Life in Custer's Cavalry*, 69–70.
[14] Bell, *New Tracks*, 58–60; Utley, *Life in Custer's Cavalry*, 69–71.

by Indian scouts (known as "wolves"), this signified "Enemy sighted" if there were no other accompanying symbolic actions. Suddenly the Indians were reinforced by another and larger party coming around a point of the ridge. As they did, the first party turned and came sailing back against the First Platoon on the left, each warrior crying out the distinctive "Hi!-Hi!-Hi!" followed by a war whoop. The First Platoon, on the left of the line of skirmishers along with the men from I Company supporting them, slowed and halted its advance at this unexpected Indian onslaught and began to waiver. Concerned that they might turn in flight and become vulnerable as the pursued, Barnitz shouted at the others to follow him to their aid. Cpl. Prentice G. Harris later told Barnitz that as he was moving to the left to support the skirmishers, he saw an Indian he thought was a chief holding a pole with a lot of feathers attached (probably a coup stick). The man waved it around his head five or six times, then pointed it at the captain. As he did so about six Indians started for Barnitz, firing their weapons. Fortunately for Barnitz, they all missed and he was unharmed.[15]

Barnitz was too late to stop the flight of his men completely. Sergeant Hamlin was already calling out for the rest of the skirmishers to retreat, even as he and some of his men turned and headed rapidly toward the fort. Those remaining, none of whom had ever been in an Indian fight, were now having difficulty controlling their plunging horses, frightened by the sounds of combat and the yells of the warriors. For a few critical moments it appeared there could be panic and a route, with the cavalrymen being wiped out by their foe. As it was, chaos reigned as the Indians came flying against them, and Sergeant Wyllyams and four others were cut off from the rest. They fought desperately, but one by one they fell from their saddles. Wyllyams's horse was killed, and after it went down, the Indians quickly dispatched its rider. A young bugler, Charles Clarke, was shot from his horse, and when he fell, a powerful warrior named Big Moccasin scooped him up, stripped him of clothing, smashed his head with a war club, and flung him to the ground. As this was happening, Barnitz was doing all he could to stabilize his line, calling out to those who were now retreating in confusion to face about and fire at the oncoming Indians. Eventually, by singling out individuals and with the help of Sergeant Gordon, who had finally reached them, he was able to halt the flight and restore a semblance of order. With enough men from the First and Second platoons concentrated, he dismounted a part of them and began to fire volleys from the

---

[15] Bell, *New Tracks*, 58–60; Utley, *Life in Custer's Cavalry*, 69–73.

Spencers into the Indian ranks. The Indians wavered for a moment, then slowly retired to the summit of the ridge beyond.[16]

While his men were reorganizing after the Indians disengaged, Captain Barnitz rode to the top of the ridge his troop was on and observed the Indians through his field glasses. They were drawn up in good order on the crest of the next ridge and appeared to be reloading their weapons and preparing to renew the combat. Barnitz was impressed by "the barbaric magnificence of their display, as they sat with their plumed lances, their bows, and shields, and their gleaming weapons." Since they made no effort to move toward the soldier lines, he returned to his command and waited for the arrival of an ambulance from the fort to retrieve the wounded and dead. He placed Sergeant Hamlin under arrest and ordered him back to the post. Next he advanced a dismounted skirmish line to the north and west to cover and protect the horses and wounded troopers. When at last the ambulance arrived, the dead and wounded were returned to the fort. That done, Barnitz took the rest of the mounted troopers and moved forward toward the next ridgeline, where he had last seen the Indians. None were visible now, so he continued on an additional mile to another ridge with the same result. Not so much as a single pony track could be detected on the hot, dry ground, and after scouting out a distance of about five miles, Barnitz halted his men and remained in place, watching for any signs of the enemy for another two hours. But the Indians had broken into small parties and disappeared in different directions. Finally Barnitz and his party joined the other troopers guarding the injured horses and slowly returned to the fort. The dead were buried with full martial honors soon after.[17]

Those at the fort were unable to witness the fight since it took place well beyond the ridgeline and hills to the northwest. Nor did they know anything of the results until the rider dispatched by Captain Barnitz to secure an ambulance reached the post. The story pieced itself together gradually as the various participants told of their own experiences and what they had seen of the combat. The Indians, it was clear from all who were there, had fought bravely and fiercely. They had apparently used a sophisticated system of signaling from one party to another, one employing not only the riding of their horses in circles and other modes but also using mirrors or reflecting metal. They did this during the early phases of the engagement, probably indicating to the raiding party coming from

---

[16] Bell, *New Tracks*, 59–61; Hyde, *Life of George Bent*, 276; Utley, *Life in Custer's Cavalry*, 71–75, 93.
[17] Bell, *New Tracks*, 59–61; Hyde, *Life of George Bent*, 276; Utley, *Life in Custer's Cavalry*, 71–75, 93.

Pond Creek Station where to lead their pursuers so that they would become the pursued. They also managed to direct the focus of combat to different points. A tall, splendid-looking warrior mounted on a white horse and carrying a long lance, who appeared to be their leader and who shouted directions, galloped along their front and ordered a charge. He seems to be the same man identified as Charlie Bent during the earlier fight: tall, riding a white horse, and daring. But no further mention was made of Charlie Bent, and that warrior may well have been the one who on this occasion was identified as the Cheyenne warrior Roman Nose. The writings of Captain Barnitz and Dr. William Bell are unclear about this, and there may have been more than one warrior described as powerful, tall, and fancifully dressed who rode either a white or gray horse along the line of warriors, shouting encouragement.[18]

Casualties among the forty-nine Seventh Cavalry participants were disproportionately large. Five men were killed outright, while another, Cpl. James Douglass of G Company, a Scot, died of his wounds the next day. Six others were wounded, four severely and two slightly. Of these Cpl. James K. Ludlow of G Company had been shot in the abdomen with a "revenge arrow," and it was thought that he would not recover. Despite repeated searches, the body of Pvt. John Welch of E Company was never found, having been carried off by the Indians after he fell. The cavalry also lost five horses—two killed and three run off by the Indians after their riders were killed. Four other horses were wounded but expected to fully recover. Of the men killed, the body of the bugler Charles Clarke had been pierced by five arrows and stripped naked, and his skull smashed. Pvt. Nathan Trial was shot four times, pierced by three arrows, stripped of clothing, and scalped, with his skull smashed. Pvt. Franklin Reahme's body was riddled with bullets and arrows and stripped, but not scalped. Corporal Douglass, who lived into the following day, had been felled with several arrows and his left arm badly hacked with a Cheyenne war club.[19]

The worst mutilation of all was the fate of Sgt. Frederick Wyllyams. A member of a prominent English family and a graduate of Eton, Wyllyams had been disowned by his family after a youthful indiscretion. He came to the United States and enlisted in the Seventh Cavalry, hoping to win a commission and thus regain his family's favor. Noted as gentlemanly, he had befriended Dr. Bell, a fellow Englishman, when G Company was escort-

[18] Bell, New Tracks, 59–61; Utley, Life in Custer's Cavalry, 71–72, 74–78.
[19] Bell, New Tracks, 60–62; Utley, Life in Custer's Cavalry, 72, 75–78.

ing the Wright survey party to Fort Wallace. Now Dr. Bell wrote that he had been shot through the head and scalped; "a blow from the tomahawk had laid his brain open above his left eye; the nose was slit up, and his throat was cut from ear to ear; seven arrows were standing in various parts of his naked body; the breast was laid open, so as to expose the heart"; his right arm was open to the bone in several places; and his legs were gashed from hip to knee, with the flesh from knee to foot terribly cut. He had promised that very day to help Dr. Bell, a physician then serving as the Wright party photographer, print copies of photos Bell had taken. Now Bell had to take a picture of him as he lay naked and mutilated. It would become one of the most famous photographs of a victim of Indian warfare ever made.[20]

The wounds inflicted on Sergeant Wyllyams and others were not entirely random. As Dr. Bell noted, in the Indian sign language the symbol for the Cheyennes was a slashing motion across the right arm, indicating "Cut-Arm People." For the Arapahoes the sign was seizing the nose with the thumb and forefinger, indicating the "Smeller People"; and for the Lakota, the "Cut-Throat People," it was a drawing of the hand across the throat. Thus the cutting of the right arm of the bodies of dead soldiers indicated the presence of Cheyennes in the war party; the slitting of the nose, the presence of Arapahoes; and the cutting of the throat, the participation of Oglala Lakotas. Most of these symbolic wounds would have been inflicted postmortem. Similarly the feathering and coloring of arrow shafts reflected the tribe, with many shot into the body after death to demonstrate the presence of warriors of that tribe in the battle.[21]

Indian casualties were mostly unknown because, as Captain Barnitz observed in his official report of the engagement, "they succeeded in carrying off their dead and wounded." He believed that they had suffered as severely as had the soldiers and in all probability much more so. The only one specifically mentioned was Roman Nose, who most agreed had been killed in the fight. Pvt. Patrick Hardyman, who had emptied his carbine and lost his saber, had been unhorsed and thrown to the ground. Cpl. Prentice G. Harris of G Company was nearby at the time, and seeing the warrior about to plunge his lance into Hardyman, struck him with his saber, in his left hand. The warrior turned on him, and as he did, Harris placed his carbine against his opponent's stomach and fired. The man fell forward onto the neck of his horse, but at that moment two other warriors who were riding up on either side of him took his arms and led both horse and rider to the safety of their lines. The soldiers believed his wound

[20] Bell, *New Tracks*, 62–65.   [21] Ibid., 63–64.

While Custer's supply train was under attack twenty-five miles to the north on the morning of June 26, another mixed war party of Dog Soldier Cheyennes, Kiyuksa Oglalas, and a few Arapahoes engaged Captain Barnitz's G Company and other soldiers from the post about two miles northwest of Fort Wallace. Six troopers lost their lives in the fight and another six were wounded, while Indian casualties were unknown. Referred to as a battle, it received considerable press in the East as the largest Indian engagement in the West since the Fetterman fight. This fanciful sketch of the affair, apparently by Theodore Davis, appeared with the story in the July 27, 1867, issue of *Harper's Weekly*.

to be mortal. He was described as the tall warrior with the white horse (Dr. Bell said gray) who led the charge against the cavalry and whose courage and daring served as an example for his fellow warriors. Tall and brave he may have been, but he was not Roman Nose. Woqini, or Hook Nose, was then in the Dog Soldier and Sutaio village on Beaver Creek. The man who was shot by Corporal Harris was in fact an Oglala. Because of the great fame of Roman Nose as a warrior, whites persisted in identifying him as present in most of the fights that took place during this period, but that was generally not true. Custer reported that Roman Nose was leading the Cheyenne and Oglala attack on his wagon train that same morning, which was also false.[22]

The number of warriors actually present at the fight is necessarily speculative. Those at the fort never saw most of the war party, and the members of the pursuing cavalry force were in no position to count their enemy even if so inclined. Moreover, the Indians were scattered along or con-

[22] G. A. Custer to W. T. Sherman, July 6, 1867, AGO, LR, NA; Bell, *New Tracks*, 61; Berthrong, *Southern Cheyennes*, 286; Hyde, *Life of George Bent*, 275–76; Utley, *Life in Custer's Cavalry*, 71, 76–78.

Fort Wallace, like most army posts on the western plains, was in the process of constructing permanent stone buildings when Captain Barnitz and his men fought with Indians nearby on June 26, 1867, and when Custer and the six companies of the Seventh Cavalry arrived at the fort on July 13. This view was sketched in part based on a photograph taken by Dr. William A. Bell, photographer for General Wright's railroad survey team, and appeared in the July 27, 1867, issue of *Harper's Weekly*.

cealed behind ridges and made a sudden appearance during a charge. Only when gathered on a far ridge at the end of the combat did most of them seem to have been together. After that, they split up and went in different directions, in part to foil any attempted pursuit and in part because members of different tribes were probably located at different villages. As was their custom, the warriors were in constant motion to avoid offering a stationary target. Considering that the Cheyennes and Oglalas at the Pawnee Fork villages could field only some 300 to 350 warriors in total when together, it seems clear that there would have been far fewer when in separate villages. Captain Barnitz estimated 200 warriors at a minimum, and probably many more. Certainly a milling and charging body of Indians would have seemed a large force, but his estimate likely far exceeds the number that could have been present, even adding in a few Arapahoes.[23]

The fight near Fort Wallace took place on the same morning as the attack on the Custer supply train more than twenty-five miles to the north, and the attacking force there (variously estimated by Custer and Theodore Davis at 600 to 800 warriors) probably had in excess of 100 of the available

[23] Utley, *Life in Custer's Cavalry*, 75.

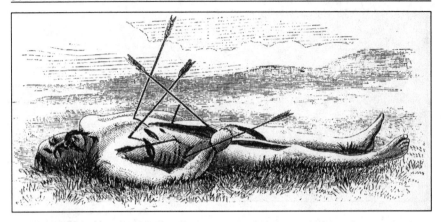

This sketch of the body of Sgt. Frederick Wyllyams, G Company, Seventh Cavalry, was made from the photograph taken by Wyllyams' fellow Englishman Dr. William A. Bell. To assuage the sensibilities of eastern readers, the pose, the wounds, and the view of Wyllyams' naked body were appropriately modified. The photograph became one of the most famous ever taken of a victim of Indian warfare. *Harper's Weekly*, July 27, 1867.

Cheyenne and Oglala warriors. It is likely that about the same number took part in the fight near the fort. Though it has been suggested that those in the latter fight rode north afterward to attack the supply train, that is most unlikely. The wagon train and its escort left the previous evening and traveled through the night. They were more than twenty-five miles from Fort Wallace when Bill Comstock first detected the Indians, and nearly thirty miles beyond when the fight began. Both fights began in the morning and both lasted for approximately three hours, so that timely movement from one site to the other would have been impossible. It would also have been nearly impossible for a large force of Indians to engage in spirited combat at Fort Wallace for that length of time, then ride north beyond the wagon train so as to be in position four or five miles north of it when it arrived. And even that journey would have called for fresh horses that were not already spent by prior fighting.

The G Company engagement near Fort Wallace drew considerable attention from the press, both in the East and in the West. It was referred to as a battle, and the biggest on the plains since Captain Fetterman's ill-fated ride onto the pages of history. That it was the biggest is questionable, since the wagon train fight that morning thirty miles to the north involved about the same number of fighting men on both sides if one does not count the infantry and dismounted civilians guarding Fort Wallace. By some it was considered a victory over the Indians—also questionable. If by victory it is meant that the soldiers were not overwhelmed and most survived, then it may be so. But if "victory" is given its standard definition of conquering and subduing an enemy, it was hardly that. Captain Barnitz stated in his official report that he and his men succeeded in repulsing the Indians and "driving them from the field," of which he retained possession. In the sense of repelling the Indian assault that statement would be true, but not much more. Company G, after its initial charge across the plains, was at all times on the defensive and came close to being overwhelmed. No one knows with certainty what the Indian objectives were. They may have merely wanted to drive off the livestock and put the whites afoot. Or perhaps it was their intention from the beginning to entice the white troopers out for a fight. They made no effort to attack the fort itself and never cared about taking and holding a battlefield as did the whites. Their primary interest was in luring small bodies of troops out where the Indians could fight them on more or less even terms, pitting their highly superior horses, riding skills, and accuracy with their weapons against the greater fire power of their adversary. Their long-term strategy was a desperate hope to discourage the invaders and force them to take their roads and people away from their country. The fights at Fort Wallace and with the wagon train would be models for others to come.[24]

In the days following the engagement at Fort Wallace, the soldiers and civilians alike remained nervous and on high alert. Sentries fired on anything that moved in the night—wolves, coyotes, antelope, or other creatures that they mistook for Indians. But attacks on the post itself were not renewed. Then, on June 30, a train of supplies for the stage line was ambushed about fifteen to twenty miles east of the fort, and a civilian scout riding a few hundred yards in advance was shot and scalped, losing his Henry rifle, revolver, and clothing. The same day, an ox train headed west was attacked a few miles west of Wallace and lost one man killed and another wounded before limping back to the post. On July 1 two stagecoaches from Denver arrived, their cavalry and infantry escort exhausted after fighting Indians all the way from Big Timber Station to a few miles beyond Goose Creek. One of the soldiers had been wounded. As they approached Goose Creek Station, they were fired on from the buildings.

---

[24] Ibid.

Realizing the station was in the hands of the Indians, they moved on by it at a gallop. Two miles east of Goose Creek they came upon the ox train, skirmishing with the Indians at long distance. The fight continued for two hours, after which the Indians tired of it and left, while the coaches and the train moved east to the fort. Though those at the post did not realize it at the time, this would be the last of the major Indian attacks in the immediate vicinity for the remainder of the year. The war was not over, but the action now moved farther east. Tracks of the Union Pacific, E.D., had arrived at Fort Harker in June, and on July 1 the first passenger train rolled into its new station. As the grading and track laying moved westward, the Indians were forced to turn their attention to the greater threat.[25]

Though the Indians were no longer a constant threat at Fort Wallace, the heat of summer had arrived in full force. To the soldiers, who had never experienced a summer on the plains, it had seemed intensely hot for some time. But on July 1 it was 102 degrees in the shade, as Captain Barnitz wrote to his wife, Jennie, and higher temperatures were in the offing. General Wright lingered at the post, ostensibly because he thought it unwise to leave it with so few troops to guard it, but actually because he was hoping for a larger escort for his survey party when General Hancock returned from Denver. Because the members of the party were already well armed with plenty of ammunition and had Captain Barnitz and his G Company to escort them, Wright's delay was unpopular with the others. On the afternoon of July 3 General Hancock and his party arrived and camped near the post. Because he had left so many members of his escort at various stage stations during his return, he had no troops to spare as an added escort for General Wright's party. Wright was on the verge of returning east with his men when Colonel Greenwood offered to accompany them the rest of the way through what was considered unsafe country to Fort Lyon. On the morning of July 8 the Wright and Greenwood parties, with their respective escorts, headed southwesterly toward the Arkansas River, running their survey lines as they did. They reached Fort Lyon on July 15. There G Company was replaced as escort by a company of the Third Cavalry and on July 20 began its return to Fort Wallace, reaching it on July 25. It remained there until August 12, 1867, when six of the eight companies of the Seventh Cavalry then encamped at the post, now rested and refitted, embarked on their next scout in search of Indians.[26]

[25] J. Hale to T. B. Weir, July 2, 1867, Fort Wallace, LS, 1867, NA; Nye, *Plains Indian Raiders*, 93; Snell and Richmond, *Union and Kansas Pacific*, 341; Utley, *Life in Custer's Cavalry*, 80–81.

[26] Bell, *New Tracks*, 65–67; Utley, *Life in Custer's Cavalry*, 81, 85, 95.

CHAPTER TWENTY-THREE

CUSTER, THE KIDDER FACTOR, AND THE MARCH FOR FORT WALLACE

O n the evening his command reached the forks of the Republican, Custer wrote a dispatch for General Augur telling of his arrival at the point, the probable time required to march to Fort Sedgwick, and his proposed operational plan. Major Elliott carried this dispatch to Fort Sedgwick to be telegraphed to Augur. He was to await Augur's reply and also to see if there were later orders from Sherman. Elliott returned on June 28, bringing with him a telegram from Augur but no new orders from Sherman. Augur said that while he thought General Sherman would order Custer back to the Smoky Hill route, until then Custer should complete his present scout and then report to Fort Sedgwick for further orders. Augur also said that General Myers was purchasing 150 new horses for Custer's men, as Sherman had promised, and expressed his hope that Custer could get Pawnee Killer and his band (who he thought desired friendly relations with whites) out of the Republican River country. Custer was to pitch into any Cheyenne villages he found. This was not what Custer wanted to hear. He knew that Libbie was not at Fort Wallace, and he probably knew that she was not at Fort Hays either. But he clearly hoped to be returned to one of the posts along the Smoky Hill in the Indian country, where he believed he could be reunited with her. Sherman's last orders for him while on the Platte had been to thoroughly scout the area around the forks of the Republican, then go to Fort Sedgwick for resupply and further orders. Custer had already obtained his supplies from Fort Wallace and was anticipating orders back to the Smoky Hill. Since those had not been forthcoming, as Generals Smith and Augur suggested they might, his only recourse was to follow the original orders and scout the upper Republican along and between the forks.

When last seen, Pawnee Killer and his warriors were headed up the left bank of the south fork, possibly toward their village, so that seemed the best starting point for a scout. Moreover, Custer believed the Cheyennes to be located on a tributary of the south fork and had told Augur he might make a strike for their village while scouting the Republican.[1]

Custer and his men broke camp on Spring Creek at 2:00 P.M. on June 29, the day following Major Elliott's return. The delay was probably to rest the men and animals involved in the trips of Major Elliott's party and the wagon train, graze the horses and mules, check the equipment, and load the wagons. After crossing the north fork of the Republican about a mile above the forks, they traversed a ridge, crossed the south fork, and went into camp on the southeast bank. This camp was just above where Big Timber Creek flows into the south fork, and about a mile north of the invisible border between Kansas and Nebraska, the fortieth parallel of latitude. The next morning, they left camp and marched southwesterly along the southeast bank of the south fork, making their new camp after a march of twenty and a half miles.[2]

The march southwesterly along the south fork of the Republican continued on the morning of July 1. They crossed Crosby Creek and Battle Creek, both dry, before crossing the mouth of "Whetstone Creek" (Bonny Creek) just across the border with Colorado Territory after a twenty-mile march. It was quite dry, though from its springs to about ten miles above its mouth it reputedly had flowing water. More importantly they crossed an Indian trail leading up the streambed. No mention was made of whether it was an old trail or a recent one, or whether it represented a large or small party of Indians. Though it might have led to a village, Custer chose to ignore it and continued on. The troops marched an additional four miles to a good crossing point, then forded the south fork and camped after a day's march of twenty-four miles.[3]

When they left camp the next morning, they angled west-northwest for a mile, then moved ten degrees west of north for a little more than ten miles over a hard, level prairie. This brought them to the head of several deep draws leading down into the valley of Bob Tail Deer Creek (Arickaree River), the middle fork of the Republican. They descended into the valley, crossed the stream, and camped on the north bank after marching

[1] Custer to Augur, June 22, 1867; Frost, *Court-martial*, 209, 220; Millbrook, "West Breaks In General Custer," 128.

[2] Jackson, "March Itinerary," June 29 and 30, 1867.

[3] Ibid., July 1, 1867.

fourteen and a quarter miles. The valley was about a mile wide on each side of the stream, with good grass for the animals. This campsite must have been a mile or so from where, in another year and seventy-seven days, the fight known as the Battle of the Arickaree (Beecher's Island) would take place. The following morning, July 3, they moved north-north-east three miles over very rough and broken ground as they climbed up through a deep ravine that pierced the bluffs to the north. Once above the valley they angled twenty degrees west of north until striking a hard, level prairie that they followed northerly for ten miles to Black Tail Deer Creek. This stream, also known as Rock Creek, merged with Chief Creek a few miles downstream to form the north fork of the Republican. Finding the ravines in front of them impassable, Custer's men turned east a mile and a half until they reached a break in the bluffs, then descended and moved northerly, crossing the creek in another two miles. They continued east along the north bank for another three and a half miles and made camp after a march of twenty-one and a half miles.[4]

The bluffs opposite the July 3 camp were of stone rising thirty to fifty feet straight up from the valley floor. To the north was a range of low sand hills that came down almost to the creek, leaving only a narrow space for the command to pitch tents. This probably compounded their problems when a hailstorm struck in the afternoon, with high winds that blew down most of the tents. The next day was Independence Day. Although they left camp at their usual hour of 5:00 A.M., they did not march a long distance. They moved northwesterly across the sand hills for two miles to the valley of Chief Creek, then westerly parallel to it for another three miles to a suitable crossing. Along this stream they saw the trail of a large column of men moving parallel to it, which they believed was the trail of Col. E. V. Sumner's expedition against the Cheyennes in 1857. Crossing Chief Creek, they went into camp on the north bank after a march of a little more than five miles. As on Rock Creek the soil was sandy, and low sand hills lay beyond the valley. But the grass was good, and nearby they discovered a "magnificent spring." Whether the early camp was made in recognition of Independence Day or the fact that a hard march lay ahead is unknown.[5]

Though the men may have been refreshed by the brief morning's march, there was doubtless considerable grumbling when their journey resumed at midnight. The sand hills were low, but the soft sand made their movement

[4] Ibid., July 2 and 3, 1867.
[5] Ibid., July 3 and 4, 1867.

tedious and difficult. Marching northwest, they skirted the dunes where possible and crossed them when necessary. After four hours they had traveled only nine miles, and both men and animals were fatigued. They stopped in place for two hours of rest, then resumed the march at 6:00 A.M. Three miles beyond, they emerged from the sand hills onto a hard, level prairie. From this point westward for the next fifteen miles they found the land covered with a thick carpet of prickly pear cactus, causing problems for men and animals alike. But they now moved more rapidly, and after eleven and a half miles reached a large water hole. Here they stopped to water the livestock and refresh the men. Thus far they had traveled nearly twenty-four miles, an average day's march. They resumed the march northwesterly, and in a little more than four miles passed through what they called Pawnee Gap, a defile through a ridge seventy-five feet high and about forty yards wide. But this was not the actual Pawnee Gap, which was on the Pawnee Creek that flows into the South Platte from the northwest.[6]

Beyond the gap they continued northwesterly and, after five miles, turned to the west-northwest. Within another mile they reached an arroyo that contained standing water in pools. By digging in the sand, they found they could reach good potable water, so they stayed to refill their canteens and water the horses and mules. By this time they had traveled a little more than thirty-four miles from Chief Creek. And now the sun was high and the summer heat of the plains weighed heavily on them, adding to the discomfort and misery of the weary men and livestock. When the watering was complete, the march resumed, and in another ten and a half miles they encountered a high ridge. They crossed it and descended onto a rolling prairie that they traversed until reaching the entrance of a small canyon two miles beyond. Here they turned north through the canyon and after two more miles emerged at the edge of the sand hills on the south side of the South Platte River. By now it was late afternoon and the heat was at its peak. It was probably here that Custer, accompanied by his adjutant, 1st Lt. Myles Moylan, as well as Dr. Coates and an enlisted orderly, left the command and pressed ahead, ostensibly to find a suitable campground along the river.[7]

The cavalry column and company wagons, temporarily under the command of their senior major, Joel Elliott, continued the march northeasterly after Custer's departure. Progress was slowed once they entered the

---

[6] Ibid., July 5, 1867.
[7] Ibid.; G. Custer, *My Life on the Plains*, 173–74.

sand hills, but by 8:00 P.M. on July 5 they reached the South Platte and went into camp about a mile southwest of Riverside Station and approximately forty-five miles southwest of Fort Sedgwick.[8] The tedious crossing of the sand hills was itself nine miles, and they had traveled a little more than fifty-nine miles from Chief Creek in that one day. Why Custer chose to make such a long and difficult march in twenty hours, exhausting both his men and animals, has long been a topic of speculation. In his own later writings he claimed the "march was necessarily effected in one day," without explaining why. He also claimed that it "was a painful journey under a burning July sun of sixty-five miles" and that it was "without a drop of water for our horses or draft animals." That sitting a saddle for the distance traveled made for a painful journey cannot be doubted, and the July sun on the southern plains is nearly always burning. But aside from that his assertions are untrue. It was not necessary to complete the march in one day. On their return trip they took about two and a half days to reach the old camp on Chief Creek. Measurement by odometer revealed it to be slightly more than fifty-nine miles to the South Platte on their route, not the sixty-five miles claimed by Custer, and existing maps of the area, however imperfectly, gave a good idea of the distances involved. Nor was water entirely absent, for after leaving the "magnificent spring" on Chief Creek, they stopped and watered their animals at least twice. The most probable reason for the rapid march is that Custer was anxious to receive orders back to the Smoky Hill and Libbie.[9]

When Custer and his three companions left the rest of the his command on June 5, he claimed that the sun was down, they were still many miles from the South Platte, and their way was lit only by a full moon. They allegedly traveled the "nearly fifteen miles" at a brisk rate, reaching the river at "about eleven o'clock." According to the march journal, however, the distance through the sand hills was only about nine miles, and the command reached the river by 8:00 P.M., though the wagon train and stragglers may have arrived up to four or more hours later. Their long journey occurred only fourteen days after the summer solstice, the longest day of the year, and there would have been strong sunlight well beyond 8:00 P.M. The disparity between the official journal and Custer's reminiscences written some years later suggest both faulty memory and embellishments calculated to make for a more interesting story. It also suggests

---

[8] Not as the crow flies but via the winding stagecoach road that hugged the river.

[9] Jackson, "March Itinerary," July 5, 1867; G. Custer, *My Life on the Plains*, 172–73; Millbrook, "West Breaks In General Custer," 128–29.

self-justification and an effort to explain actions subsequently sharply criticized by his own officers and others.[10]

Custer's orders had been to thoroughly scout the upper Republican, then go to Fort Sedgwick for resupply and further orders. Instead he made a march of only forty-four miles along the south fork of the Republican, perhaps no more than half the length of that stream's surface flow along which Indian villages might be found. He scouted none of its flowing tributaries, the most likely location for villages, did no more than cross the middle and north forks of the river without scouting along them, and did not scout at all east of the forks. Aside from Captain West's two days on that stream awaiting return of the wagon train, Custer ignored Beaver Creek even though it was where Ed Guerrier and Bill Comstock thought the Cheyennes would be camping. Instead, after his perfunctory scout along the south fork of the Republican, he began a purposeful march north and west to the South Platte, not to Fort Sedgwick but to Riverside Station. There he hoped to inquire by telegraph for orders sending him back to the Smoky Hill. This was well to the west and south of where his orders instructed him to be, and he could in all events have sent a much smaller detachment to send the telegram and avoid the grueling march.

Whatever motives Custer may have had for that difficult march, according to him his small party reached the South Platte at about 11:00 P.M. on July 5, which would have been three hours later than the main command. Totally exhausted by their rigorous journey and assuming that the rest of the men would not reach the river until the next morning, they threw themselves on the ground to sleep instead of locating a suitable campground as intended. They tethered their horses to the hilts of their sabers driven deep into the ground. Then using their saddles for pillows and saddle blankets and ponchos for covers, they quickly fell asleep. Custer said that it rained in the night, but they were so tired that they just pulled the ponchos over their heads without any awareness of raindrops. The following morning, by using their field glasses when the light was sufficient, they located the six cavalry companies downriver about three miles. A brisk gallop took them to the camp. There Custer found that the column could not follow his party in the dark and made their way directly to the river to camp, some not arriving until the morning of July 6—or so Custer claimed.[11]

After breakfast that morning, Custer sent a party to Riverside Station

[10] Jackson, "March Itinerary," July 5, 1867; G. Custer, *My Life on the Plains*, 174.
[11] G. Custer, *My Life on the Plains*, 174–76.

to transmit a telegraphic dispatch to Fort Sedgwick, asking if further orders had been received from General Sherman. Riverside Station was one of a series of stations on the south side of the South Platte River, serving the Overland Stage line from Denver to Julesburg near the end of track on the Union Pacific Railroad. Telegraph lines had been strung the entire distance, allowing rapid communication with a far headquarters. The officer entrusted with Custer's dispatch sent it from Riverside Station to the commanding officer at Fort Sedgwick. The reply from Sedgwick stated that new orders were received the day after Major Elliott's departure and had been given to 2nd Lt. Lyman S. Kidder, Second Cavalry, for delivery to Custer. Kidder's instructions were to proceed to Custer's camp near the forks of the Republican, following Elliott's trail, and deliver the new orders. If Custer and his troops were not there, he was to rapidly follow his trail until he overtook them. Kidder had an escort of ten troopers from Company M of the Second Cavalry stationed at Fort Sedgwick and an older Lakota guide named Red Bead. They left on their mission at 11:00 A.M. on June 29, heading for Custer's last known location.[12]

When Custer received this information, he immediately responded "that nothing had been seen or heard of Lieutenant Kidder's detachment" and requested that a copy of the orders be sent to him by telegraph. What he received was a copy of Sherman's message of June 27 sent to General Augur's headquarters and forwarded to Fort Sedgwick. It was just what Custer had been hoping for: orders to move south to Fort Wallace and report to General Hancock. Sherman said that Hancock was leaving Denver on June 27, eastbound on the Smoky Hill road. Custer would probably have left for Fort Wallace that very day, but given the long and difficult march they had just completed, his command was in no condition to move without rest. They needed more than one day for that, but Custer stated that supplies were low (despite receiving twenty days of new supplies on June 28) and he was determined to set out for Fort Wallace at first light the next morning. This decision was evidently the trigger for a mass desertion, since during the early morning hours of July 7 thirty-five men left camp and moved off in one direction or another along the stage road. Custer mainly attributed this to poor and insufficient rations, casting the blame on "persons connected with the supply departments of the army." He also acknowledged that being on the main route of travel to the gold mining country, with its prospects of high wages and possibly even great

---

[12] Ibid., 178; Johnson and Allan, *Find Custer!* 26; Voight, "Death of Lyman S. Kidder," 4–5, 11, 17.

wealth, was probably a contributing factor. It is likely that the long, hard marches and arbitrary discipline the men endured were also factors. There was no time to pursue the deserters, and at 5:00 A.M. the command moved out, retracing its route inbound.[13]

The failure of Kidder and his detachment to overtake Custer's command in something over a week caused considerable concern and speculation among the officers. Custer later claimed that anxiety over the fate of Kidder and his men was one of the reasons he started for Fort Wallace so soon after arrival on the South Platte. However, in a letter written on August 23, 1867, to Judge J. P. Kidder, the lieutenant's father, he stated:

> In returning from my scout I marched to Ft. Wallace, striking the trail referred to above [Lieutenant Cooke's wagon train trail] but a few miles south of the point at which I had left it, I at once discovered the trail of Lt. Kidder and party going towards Wallace, and knowing the dangerous country through which he must pass and the probabilities of his encountering an overwhelming force of savages, I became at once solicitous of his fate.

Whether or not his anxiety over Kidder's fate was a factor prompting an early departure, Custer and his command did begin the march southeast to Fort Wallace early on the morning of July 7. By noon they had marched about thirteen miles, taking them to the high ridge they encountered just east of the sand hills along the South Platte. Here they stopped for an hour to graze and rest their horses and mules. Some of the men, evidently concluding this was to be their evening camp, hatched a plot whereby up to one-third of the effective strength of the command would desert in the night and escape to the mountains with their horses and weapons. This would have seriously compromised the remainder of the force, rendering them all but ineffective for combat with hostile Indians. The plan was thwarted when Custer ordered the march resumed.[14]

The order to mount up, though foiling the plans for a nighttime desertion, convinced some of the would-be deserters that this would be their last, best chance to escape. Thirteen men with haversacks of provisions, most with carbines and seven of them mounted, began a deliberate movement northwesterly back to the South Platte in broad daylight and in full view of the command. Such a brazen act of desertion was unheard of.

[13] Jackson, "March Itinerary," July 6 and 7, 1867; G. Custer, *My Life on the Plains*, 179, 182–83; Davis, "Summer on the Plains," 306; Frost, *Court-martial*, 174–75.

[14] Jackson, "March Itinerary," July 7, 1867; G. Custer, *My Life on the Plains*, 172, 183; Davis, "Summer on the Plains," 306; Frost, *Court-martial*, 185; Voight, "Death of Lyman S. Kidder," 14.

Fearing further desertions if these went unchallenged, Custer immediately ordered Lieutenant Jackson, the officer of the day, to take the guard and pursue them. When the deserters were overtaken, he was ordered to shoot them "and not bring one back alive." Jackson went to the guard station, but only two or three members of the guard were present, the others having already returned to their own companies for the march. When he reported this, Custer ordered him to take what men he did have and move out in pursuit. By this time the deserters were from a mile to a mile and a half from the column but still within sight. Meanwhile due to the delay with the guard, Custer ordered three of his officers who were near him, Maj. Joel Elliott, Lt. Tom Custer, and Lt. William Cooke, to pursue the deserters and shoot them down. These three officers had either volunteered or asked if they should go in pursuit and were then directed to do so. They immediately mounted their horses and set out, with Lieutenant Jackson and three members of the guard following shortly after. The three officers were the first to reach the six deserters who were on foot, shooting three and capturing all six. Of the three wounded men, two had flesh wounds while the third, Pvt. Charles Johnson, had been shot in the head, the bullet entering near his temple and exiting under his jaw. Unlike the others, who had dropped their weapons on command, he apparently raised his carbine as if to fire at Major Elliott, and Lieutenant Cooke shot him. The seven mounted deserters, riding fast horses, had too much of a head start to be overtaken and escaped.[15]

The three wounded men were placed in a regular army six-mule quartermaster wagon and returned to the column. Upon its arrival, Dr. Coates stepped forward to render medical attention, but Custer loudly ordered him to stay where he was and not go near the wounded men at that time. Later, and about two hours after they were shot, Coates climbed into the wagon during the march, examined the wounds, and administered opiates to ease their pain. The injuries to Bugler Barney Tolliver, Company K, and Private Allburger, Company D, were flesh wounds only and, though painful, not serious. The injury to Private Johnson, who was quite conscious and talking though covered with blood, would prove fatal. According to Coates, Custer had privately authorized him to render medical aid, though not in the presence of the rest of the command. It was the doctor's opinion that Custer's original order was given to impress the

---

[15] Custer, *My Life on the Plains*, 183–86; Davis, "Summer on the Plains," 306; Frost, *Court-martial*, 102, 151–55, 159–63, 167, 175–76, 178–79, 185–86, 263.

men that desertion would be dealt with in a most severe and harsh manner and thus discourage it. While the wagon was being brought into line at the back of the column, Custer gave the order to move out, and the march resumed. They traveled another ten or eleven miles, then went into camp on a dry creek bed with water holes to the west of what they had called Pawnee Gap. They were now a little over twenty-four miles from their camp on the South Platte. Though they had to dig for reasonably clear potable water, when found it was good.[16]

During the march on the afternoon of July 7 a loyal sergeant reported that a large body of malcontents were planning to desert that night before they were too far from the South Platte. Custer believed the summary treatment given the deserters at the last halt would intimidate most men who might be contemplating desertion. He was also convinced that one more day of marching would bring them close enough to the dangerous hostile Indian country that only a very large body would dare attempt to desert. To secure the camp that night, he placed all officers on guard and under arms, ordered them to patrol the company areas, and ordered the men to remain in their tents after taps under pain of being shot. The night passed without incident, and they left camp at 5:00 the next morning. They continued along their old trail to the South Platte, marching twenty-five miles and camping in the sand hills about nine miles from their July 4 camp on Chief Creek. During the march they once again entered the prickly pear cactus region they had previously encountered. It was now a gorgeous tapestry of brilliant crimson and yellow because the cacti had come into bloom. Besides prickly pear, the plains in that day were dotted with cholla, or walking-stick cactus; Spanish bayonet (yucca); and in many areas sand sage, or big sage. The cactus thicket continued until they reached the sand hills abutting Chief Creek.[17]

The march resumed at first light (4:00 A.M.) on July 9, following their old trail until about a mile and a half from their July 4 camp, then angling left and striking Chief Creek about three-fourths of a mile below it. They crossed the stream, then halted for six hours to rest, refill their canteens, and water the livestock. When "boots and saddles" sounded again, the column reformed and the march continued along the creek's south bank for another seven miles. Then they turned southeasterly and crossed Rock

---

[16] Jackson, "March Itinerary," July 7, 1867; Frost, *Court-martial*, 101–102, 166–69, 173.

[17] Jackson, "March Itinerary," July 7 and 8, 1867; G. Custer, *My Life on the Plains*, 186–87; Davis, "Summer on the Plains," 306.

Creek two hundred yards above its confluence with Chief Creek. Their route to the crossing of Rock Creek was either on or parallel to the Sumner trail of 1857, but the latter crossed back to the north bank just above the confluence and continued along the north bank of the Republican's north fork. Custer's column continued east along the south bank until reaching Ironwood Springs Creek, where they camped after traveling about twenty-one and a half miles.[18]

The next morning, they crossed the creek and moved parallel with the river's south bank until reaching the Arickaree River near its confluence with the north fork, where they halted for dinner. Afterward the column crossed the Arickaree about three-quarters of a mile above its mouth and continued along the south bank of the north fork of the Republican. They made camp along the river's south bank after a march of a little more than twenty-six miles.[19]

During the course of their march from the South Platte, Medicine Bill Comstock had on a number of occasions been asked his opinion about where Lieutenant Kidder might be. His vast experience on the plains gave him insights into the probabilities of a favorable outcome that others in the command did not have. Being a cautious man and not wanting to lend encouragement to their speculations, he would simply shake his head and avoid a direct answer. But in camp on the north fork of the Republican on the evening of July 10, the officers and Comstock were gathered near Custer's headquarters tent, where they discussed the whereabouts of Kidder and his men. Comstock was quietly listening to the various theories and speculation about their present location and their chances of avoiding harm at the hands of the Indians. One theory, favored by most, including Custer, was that the Kidder party had traveled at night after reaching the dangerous county south of the forks of the Republican. Following the wagon train trail southward in the dark, they had probably missed the tracks of Custer's column as it left that trail.[20]

Finally Comstock was pressed hard to give his opinion on the subject. He thoughtfully observed that if he knew Kidder and what kind of man he was, he might be able to give a better analysis of the prospects for him and his men. He expressed confidence in the ability of Red Bead to guide them well and safely—*if* Kidder was disposed to follow his advice. Comstock

---

[18] Jackson, "March Itinerary," July 9, 1867.
[19] Ibid., July 9 and 10, 1867.
[20] G. Custer, *My Life on the Plains*, 180–81, 188–89.

commented that his previous experience with new young lieutenants, especially those from West Point, who were confident that they knew all about warfare and combat from their schooling, suggested that they did not easily take the advice of those who did know from experience. Comstock and other scouts and plainsmen of the era had a low opinion of the knowledge and leadership abilities of most frontier army officers, at least until they developed considerable experience with both the country and the Native peoples. What Comstock, Custer, and the others had no way of knowing was that Lyman Kidder was neither a West Point graduate nor without experience in Indian warfare. Comstock said he was told that Kidder was a new lieutenant and that this was his first mission. If that was true, he thought the matter very uncertain—Kidder and his men would be lucky to make it through safely. He added that on the following day, when they struck the trail to Fort Wallace, he would soon be able to tell if Kidder had passed that way. It seemed anything but an encouraging opinion.[21]

Custer's command broke camp and resumed its eastward march on the morning of July 11. After traveling two miles along the banks of the Republican's north fork, the troops turned south-southeast and left the river about ten miles above its junction with the south fork. For the next two and a half miles they crossed some rough and broken hills before emerging on a rolling plain, and in another four miles they reached the south fork of the Republican. Once on the south bank and re-formed, the column continued southeasterly over a shallow range of sand hills, then over a succession of ridges and ravines—some very deep and difficult to cross. Deep, dry arroyos coursed through the valleys, and here and there they found a few scattered trees. Then the topography changed abruptly into a hard, rolling plain that gradually descended into the valley of Big Timber Creek, which they reached a little more than fourteen and a half miles from their last camp.[22]

The men were very impressed with Big Timber Creek, believing it the finest stream they had found since leaving Fort Hays. The creek flowed northward to its junction with the south fork of the Republican between rolling hills, and the valley was covered with "magnificent grass." The banks were heavily timbered by High Plains standards, and in places trees were found in "large patches." The water in the little stream was "very clear and sweet." Custer halted the column here for four hours to rest and water the

---

[21] Ibid., 180–90; Johnson and Allan, *Find Custer!* 10–18.
[22] Jackson, "March Itinerary," July 11, 1867.

horses and mules and refresh the men. When they resumed the march, they crossed the creek and continued southeasterly for three miles over a rolling plain, skirting a deep ravine until striking the Cooke wagon train trail, which ran south to Fort Wallace from their old camp near the forks of the Republican. They had marched a little more than nineteen and a half miles to that point. They followed the trail south for another seven and a half miles before making a dry camp on the open plain after a day's march of more than twenty-seven miles. From the time they left Big Timber Creek, they once again found themselves on a plain thickly covered with prickly pear cactus, intriguing to look at but difficult to negotiate through.[23]

After leaving Big Timber Creek, Comstock and the Delaware scouts galloped ahead to examine the ruts of the wagon train trail made by Lieutenants Cooke and Robbins during their trip to Fort Wallace and back, looking for evidence of the Kidder party's passage. When Custer and the head of the column reached them, they were completing their examination. Reporting to Custer, Comstock stated: "They've gone toward Fort Wallace, sure." He said they found the tracks of shod horses moving at a walk and going in the direction of the fort. There was no sign of unshod pony tracks following them, as would be the case if Indians had discovered them. But Comstock added that it would be astonishing if Kidder and his men managed to reach the fort without a fight—so much so that it would make him lose his "confidence in Injuns" if it was true. Considering the known presence of Cheyennes, Arapahoes, and Kiyuksa Oglalas in the area of Beaver Creek and Fort Wallace and the recent fights in that region, Custer and his officers were of the same opinion. They were now within a two-day march from the fort, which meant that the mystery of the missing Kidder party must soon be resolved.[24]

---

[23] Ibid.
[24] G. Custer, *My Life on the Plains*, 191–92.

CHAPTER TWENTY-FOUR

A MYSTERY SOLVED

At the time he was ordered to deliver a dispatch to Custer on June 29, 1867, Lyman Stockwell Kidder was twenty-five years of age. Born in Braintree, Vermont, he was reared and educated there until his family moved to St. Paul, Minnesota in 1858. His father, Jefferson Kidder, was a prominent lawyer and the lieutenant governor of Vermont before moving to St. Paul, where he again became involved in politics. In 1859 he was elected as a delegate to Congress from "that portion of the Territory of Minnesota not included within the limits of the State of Minnesota, now by common consent called Dakota." His bid for that position was not recognized in Washington, and he was ultimately elected to a two-year term in the Minnesota House of Representatives. Meantime Lyman was completing his education, apparently at a boarding school.[1]

In 1861, the year the Civil War began, Lyman Kidder was nineteen. He was handsome, with dark hair and hazel eyes, and tall by the standards of the age. When the call came for volunteer troops from Minnesota, he enlisted, being enrolled at Fort Snelling, Minnesota, on November 1, 1861, as a corporal in Company K, Brackett's Cavalry Battalion of the Fifth Iowa Cavalry. He was sent to Camp Benton, Missouri, where he trained until ordered to Fort Henry, Tennessee, in April of 1862. He was involved in several fights with Confederate guerrillas in the country between Fort Henry, Fort Donelson, Tennessee, and Fort Heiman, Kentucky. On May 18, 1863, he was discharged by reason of appointment as a first lieutenant in the First Regiment of Minnesota Mounted Rangers.[2]

The Minnesota Rangers were organized to help quell the outbreak of the Santee, or Dakota, Sioux. These normally peaceful eastern Sioux had finally

---

[1] Johnson and Allan, *Find Custer!* 5–11.
[2] Ibid.

HANCOCK'S WAR

rebelled against the loss of most of their tribal lands to white settlement, delays in delivery of annuities promised as compensation, fraud by unscrupulous traders, and mismanagement by their agent. Resentment and frustration exploded in an orgy of violence on August 18, 1862, resulting in the deaths of some eight hundred settlers and the destruction of farms and towns. Brig. Gen. Henry H. Sibley, the first governor of Minnesota, was appointed as leader of its militia and on September 23, 1862, defeated Santee leader Little Crow at the Battle of Wood Lake in southwestern Minnesota and captured about two thousand Sioux. The remaining hostiles fled into eastern Dakota and dispersed but, along with some of the Sisseton and Yanktonai Nakotas and Teton Lakotas, vowed to resist any further incursions into their country by the whites. Maj. Gen. John Pope, commanding the newly established Department of the Northwest, devised a plan to break up any combination of these tribes. It called for General Sibley to move upstream along the Minnesota River to Devil's Lake in present North Dakota, while General Sully would ascend the Missouri with his troops and turn northeast to catch the hostiles in a pincher movement.[3]

Sibley's brigade numbered nearly three thousand officers and men of the Sixth, Seventh, and Tenth Minnesota Infantry, the Third Minnesota Battery, and the First Minnesota Mounted Rangers. Included with the latter was 1st Lt. Lyman Kidder. On July 24, 1863, Sibley overtook the Indians, who were out hunting buffalo near Big Mound, northeast of present Bismarck, and defeated them after a fierce fight. Sibley pursued the fleeing Indians and fought with them at Dead Buffalo Lake on July 26 and Stony Lake on July 27. Kidder participated in all three of these engagements and was singled out for gallantry at Dead Buffalo Lake. Afterward the main column of the Rangers, including Kidder's company, was ordered back to Fort Abercrombie. From there the Rangers participated in a treaty expedition to the Red Lake River in northwestern Minnesota. This resulted in the "Old Crossing Treaty" of October 2, 1863, whereby the Chippewas ceded to the United States most of the remainder of their lands in Minnesota. With the expedition concluded, Kidder was mustered out of the Rangers at Fort Snelling, Minnesota, on November 28.[4]

Kidder seems to have then worked as a clerk for about nine months. But as the Civil War in the East was entering its final phases, he once

---

[3] Carley, *Dakota War of 1862*, 1–6, 10–24, 59–62; Johnson and Allan, *Find Custer!* 12–17; Utley, *Frontiersmen in Blue*, 261–73.

[4] Carley, *Dakota War of 1862*, 87–92; Johnson and Allan, *Find Custer!* 12–17; Utley, *Frontiersmen in Blue*, 261–73.

again signed up as a volunteer soldier, this time as a private in Company
E of Hatch's Independent Cavalry Battalion, a contingent intended to
supplement General Pope's Indian fighting force. Within one week Kidder was promoted to first sergeant of the company, which was destined
for no more than patrol and garrison duty. The battalion was mustered
out of service during April, May, and June 1866, with Kidder's discharge
coming on May 1, 1866. Meantime his father, Jefferson Kidder, had
switched political parties, becoming a Republican. In early 1865 President
Lincoln appointed him as an associate justice of the Supreme Court of
Dakota Territory. He moved his family to Vermillion, in the southeast
corner of present South Dakota. Following his release from the volunteer
service, Lyman joined his family there and homesteaded on land where
the state university would later be established.[5]

Apparently his experience had given Kidder a taste for the military life,
and by October 1, 1866, he was working hard to secure appointment as a
lieutenant in one of the cavalry regiments of the reorganized regular army.
His father's political connections helped, and on February 8, 1867, Secretary of War Edwin Stanton notified him of his appointment as a second
lieutenant in the Second U.S. Cavalry—provided that he accepted
promptly and successfully passed the examinations required by law. He
did accept and passed his physical examination but failed the written test
on his first attempt due to lack of knowledge of world geography. He was
allowed to retake it and passed. Kidder was appointed a second lieutenant
to rank from February 8 and took his oath of office on May 18. By June
11 he had started for Fort Laramie, the headquarters of his regiment.[6]

Kidder was originally assigned to Company F, Second Cavalry, stationed at Fort Laramie. But on June 16, while en route to Laramie on the
Union Pacific Railroad from Omaha, he stopped at Fort Sedgwick, then
located across the river south three miles from the Julesburg station, near
the end of track. He intended to leave by stagecoach for Fort Laramie at
9:00 the following morning, but something delayed him and he was temporarily attached to Company M, Second Cavalry, stationed at Sedgwick.
Forty men from that company, commanded by Capt. John Mix, had left
on a reconnaissance of the upper Republican River on June 14 and returned
on June 22, having seen neither Indians nor any tracks indicating their
presence in the region. Company M had lost its second lieutenant, George
A. Armes, in February when he was promoted to captain of Company F

---

[5] Johnson and Allan, *Find Custer!* 17–21.
[6] Ibid.

of the new Tenth Cavalry. When Mix returned from his scout and met Lyman, he evidently found him a likable and competent young officer. Kidder had also met other officers at the post with whom he had much in common, particularly Maj. A. B. Cain, a twenty-seven-year-old Civil War veteran with whom he roomed and messed, and the post surgeon, Hiram Latham, both originally from Vermont. He also became a good friend of 2nd Lt. E. L. Bailey, Fourth Infantry, a member of the fort's garrison. On the return of Captain Mix, Dr. Latham urged him to telegraph the regimental headquarters at Fort Laramie and ask that Kidder be assigned to his company. Mix did so, and the request was granted— at least temporarily. Kidder wrote his father to this effect on June 28, adding that he was much pleased with the post because it was at the terminus of the railroad and that he found the other officers very agreeable.[7]

The Fort Sedgwick that Lyman Kidder was so pleased with was at the end of line on the Union Pacific, which reached Julesburg on June 25, 1867, just nine days after he did. By the standards of the day its presence provided rapid mail service and transport to and from the outside world. To the troops it brought not only military supplies but also fresh foods lacking at more remote posts. For a time Fort Sedgwick became an important supply depot. Aside from that, it had little to recommend it, and most men in its garrison were less enthusiastic about it than was Kidder. It was situated in the valley on the south side of the South Platte River about three miles south of the newest incarnation of Julesburg. The town, the third of that name in the vicinity, was moved north of the river to be adjacent to the railroad when it arrived. Surrounded by sand, cactus, and the rank valley grasses, the post was subjected to high temperatures in the summer and intense cold in the winter.[8]

Though the first buildings at Fort Rankin, as Fort Sedgwick was originally named, were constructed of sod, by 1866 the cavalry stable, the hospital, three barracks, the bakery, the post commander's quarters, and two officer's quarters were all built of adobe. Later buildings were either adobe or wood frame. In the summer of 1867 the post had a garrison consisting of four companies of the Fourth Infantry, two companies of the Thirtieth, a small squad of artillerymen, and Company M of the Second Cavalry.[9]

---

[7] Ibid., 23–24, 43; Stanley, *My Early Travels*, 109; Voight, "Death of Lyman S. Kidder," 2–3; Williams, *Fort Sedgwick*, 61–74, 105.

[8] Johnson and Allan, *Find Custer!* 24; Williams, *Fort Sedgwick*, 49, 121–26.

[9] Johnson and Allan, *Find Custer!* 24; Stanley, *My Early Travels*, 109; Williams, *Fort Sedgwick*, 49, 121–26.

Lyman Kidder's first important duty at the post was to sit as a member of a court-martial board considering the case of a sergeant major of the Fourth Infantry. Although Captain Mix and his men were called out frequently to chase down reports of theft of livestock by Indians (some real and some fraudulent), in general there had been no major Indian troubles in the vicinity of the post for some time. However, the garrison was well aware of the operations of Custer and the Seventh Cavalry a hundred miles or so to the south, and of the fighting along the Smoky Hill. Kidder mentioned some of these things in the letter to his father on June 28. Before he could send that letter, new orders for Custer arrived by telegraph from Omaha. It was believed at General Augur's headquarters that Custer and his command either had arrived at Fort Sedgwick for further orders or soon would.[10]

On the afternoon of June 28, Kidder was notified by Lt. Col. J. H. Potter of the Thirtieth Infantry, post commander, that he was to carry dispatches to Custer at the forks of the Republican. An apparently well-pleased Kidder added a postscript to his letter to his father: "I start for the forks of the Republican tomorrow with ten men. I am to carry dispatches to General Custer, to be absent 7 days." On the morning of June 29 Colonel Potter issued his written orders to Kidder to depart immediately and deliver the new orders to Custer:

> You will proceed at once with an escort of ten (10) men of Company "M" 2nd U.S. Cavalry to the forks of the Republican River, where you will deliver to General Custar the dispatches with which you will be entrusted; should General Custar have left that point you will take his trail and overtake him! After delivering your dispatches return to this post. Until you reach General Custar you will travel as rapidly as possible.

Although not contained in the written orders, it was understood that Kidder and his men were to follow the trail of Major Elliott and his ten men, who had just returned to the forks of the Republican two days earlier without any difficulties. But Kidder was obviously aware of the possibility of danger since he asked his new friend Lieutenant Bailey to write his father with the facts in the event an accident befell him.[11]

Kidder and his detachment left Fort Sedgwick at 11:00 A.M. on June 29, the same day Custer left the forks of the Republican. Kidder's men prob-

---

[10] Johnson and Allan, *Find Custer!* 26–27; Voight, "Death of Lyman S. Kidder," 2–5, 8; Williams, *Fort Sedgwick*, 74.

[11] Johnson and Allan, *Find Custer!* 26–27; Voight, "Death of Lyman S. Kidder," 2–5, 8; Williams, *Fort Sedgwick*, 74.

ably moved westerly along the banks of the South Platte for two or three miles as had Major Elliott on his return journey, then followed his tracks south-southeasterly to Frenchman's Creek and beyond to the forks of the Republican. Kidder's detachment included one sergeant, Oscar Close, a twenty-three-year-old native of Prussia; one corporal, twenty-three-year-old Charles H. Haynes from Popshen, Maine; and eight privates, one from Prussia, three from Ireland, and the rest native-born Americans. With the exception of Pvt. Charles Teltow from Prussia, who at thirty-six was the oldest man on the mission, they ranged in age from nineteen to twenty-three. All were considered strong young men, most were of short stature by modern standards, and each had seen more than one year of military service. Aside from Kidder, who had just been assigned to the company, all of the men had recently completed two fairly extensive scouts across much the same country with Captain Mix.[12]

The troopers in Kidder's detachment were equipped with Spencer carbines, and several carried pistols. They were provided with one hundred rounds of ammunition each for their carbines, six days of rations (the mission was not expected to take longer), and two extra horses to carry the load. Their guide was an older Oglala man named Red Bead. He and his family had lived among whites for many years, and he raised livestock for a living. Indians had stolen much of his stock that same summer, which may have compelled him to seek work with the army to bolster his income. As a guide Red Bead was considered faithful and sagacious. Neither Kidder nor the men of his escort detachment were without training or experience with military operations in the field, as has sometimes been suggested, and all had at least some familiarity with Indian warfare.[13]

When Lt. Col. George Armstrong Custer and his six companies of the Seventh Cavalry broke camp on the morning of July 12, they continued south, following the plain and heavy trail made by Lieutenant Cooke's wagon train and its escort. The route was now over a hard, level plain covered with prickly pear cactus and yucca as well as buffalo and grama grass, the short-grasses of the plains. It was not an established or regularly traveled trail they were following, for there were none north from Fort Wallace. Instead it was the trail and ruts left by passage of Custer's wagon train on its outbound and return trips along with the three cavalry companies providing its pro-

---

[12] Davis, "Summer on the Plains," 306; Johnson and Allan, *Find Custer!* 27–29, 31, 43–45; Voight, "Death of Lyman S. Kidder," 3–11.
[13] Davis, "Summer on the Plains," 306; Johnson and Allan, *Find Custer!* 27–29, 31, 43–45; Voight, "Death of Lyman S. Kidder," 3–11.

tection. According to Custer, they had left the larger and heavier track, probably because they had crossed the same ground twice, with wagons fully loaded on the return. Custer instructed Comstock and the Delaware scouts to keep a close eye on the trail of the Kidder party to ensure they did not lose it. It had rained the day before Kidder and his men passed that way, making their trail fresher and easy to follow. Bill Comstock was able to determine that fourteen shod horses had recently moved along it.[14]

After traveling a little over nine miles, they struck what Lieutenant Jackson called a ravine but was probably the dry bed of Little Beaver Creek. They had now reached the edge of the more broken and rolling country leading to the Beaver Creek valley. Here they altered their course to south-southwest by south, passing over a rolling prairie until reaching the stream in another six miles. They crossed the creek to the south side, the banks being low, the bed of the stream firm and about fifteen feet wide, and the water three feet deep. Although the bottomland along the creek was narrow, the grass was good, so they halted there for four hours to rest and graze the livestock.[15]

During the approach to Beaver Creek and at a distance of perhaps two miles beyond Little Beaver Creek, a large, strange-looking object was seen lying on the trail about a mile in front of them. Comstock and two or three of the Delawares rode ahead to investigate. Even before reaching it, however, the identity of the object was clear: it was the carcass of a white horse that had been killed recently. Custer was riding at the head of the cavalry column, and when they reached the vicinity of the dead horse, they halted so that Comstock and the Delawares could carefully examine the surrounding ground. The horse bore the brand "M.2.C.," indicating that it belonged to M Company, Second Cavalry. It had no saddle, bridle, or other equipment, those apparently having been removed and carried away, but by whom could not be determined. Major Elliott recalled that during his trip to Fort Sedgwick he had seen a cavalry company mounted on white horses, which convinced them that this was one of the horses from the Kidder party. There was no evidence about who killed the horse, though many thought it the work of Indians. Neverthe-

---

[14] Jackson, "March Itinerary," July 12, 1867; G. A. Custer to T. B. Weir, AAAG, August 7, 1867, in Johnson and Allan, *Find Custer!* 61–63, and in Voight, "Death of Lyman S. Kidder," 21–24; G. A. Custer to J. P. Kidder, August 23, 1867, in Johnson and Allan, *Find Custer!* 51, and in Voight, "Death of Lyman S. Kidder," 14–16; G. Custer, *My Life on the Plains*, 192.

[15] Jackson, "March Itinerary," July 12, 1867; Custer to Weir, August 7, 1867; Custer to Kidder, August 23, 1867; G. Custer, *My Life on the Plains*, 192.

HANCOCK'S WAR

less it was still believed possible that Kidder and his men had killed it after it became ill or lame and could not keep up, thereby preventing it from falling into the hands of Indians. This was a common practice while on the march in Indian country. The scouts could shed no additional light on the subject, so the march continued.[16]

Beyond the carcass, Bill Comstock noticed that the tracks of the Kidder party had changed. Instead of moving in a regular column as before, only two or three remained on the beaten trail, while the rest were in the grass on either side of it. This would indicate they were now riding abreast, or at least in a cluster, some on the tracks and some on the left and right flanks. Between a mile and a half and two miles farther along the trail Custer's column came upon the carcass of a second horse. It too had been shot in the head and all of its equipment removed. There was nothing to suggest who killed the horse or why, but uneasiness and concern were rising. Then Comstock detected the tracks of unshod horses, indicating that Indians had discovered the presence of Kidder and his men and that they were being followed. Soon it was clear that the tracks of the shod horses were leaving the wagon train trail and moving left at full speed, with the unshod horses pursuing.[17]

Within a mile from the second dead horse the cavalry column reached the rough country abutting the valley of Beaver Creek, leaving the rolling plain they had been traversing. The broken area around the stream extended out about two miles on either side of the valley, and now they began a gradual descent southwesterly to the creek. When within a mile of it the men of the command observed numerous vultures soaring lazily in circles to the left of the trail. At the same time they noticed a strong, terrible smell of decaying flesh, the stench of death so familiar to Civil War veterans following battles. Custer ordered the Delaware scouts to examine the country surrounding the trail and creek for evidence of the fight that must have taken place there and of the fate of Lieutenant Kidder and his men.[18]

Only a small amount of contemporary written information and documentary evidence from actual witnesses about what was found in the Beaver Creek valley on July 12, 1867, is known to have survived: the march journal

---

[16] Custer to Weir, August 7, 1867; Custer to Kidder, August 23, 1867; G. Custer, *My Life on the Plains*, 192–93.

[17] Jackson, "March Itinerary," July 12, 1867; Custer to Weir, August 7, 1867; Custer to Kidder, August 23, 1867; G. Custer, *My Life on the Plains*, 194.

[18] Jackson, "March Itinerary," July 12, 1867; Custer to Weir, August 7, 1867; Custer to Kidder, August 23, 1867; G. Custer, *My Life on the Plains*, 194.

of Lt. Henry Jackson; letters written by Jackson to Yankton Sioux agent W. A. Burleigh on September 29, 1867, and to Judge J. P. Kidder, Lyman Kidder's father, on November 5, 1867; the articles and illustrations by Theodore Davis appearing in the August 17, 1867, issue of *Harper's Weekly*, and the issue of *Harper's New Monthly Magazine* in volume 36; the official report of the finding of the Kidder party rendered by Lt. Col. (Bvt. Maj. Gen.) G. A. Custer on August 7, 1867; letters written by Custer to Judge Kidder on August 23 and 25, October 8, and November 2, 1867; and Custer's 1874 book, *My Life on the Plains*. Lapse of time and memory, and Custer's penchant for modification and exaggeration to enhance his own image or achieve dramatic effect, make the more contemporary documents, and especially his written report, by far the more reliable sources for any factual account. These reveal that Custer led his command across Beaver Creek and was in the process of preparing to rest and graze the animals. Before he had completed his dispositions for the halt, one of the Delaware scouts returned to report that they had found the bodies of a number of white men within a half mile from the camp. Taking his medical officer, Dr. Coates, and a small party of officers with him, Custer rode to the site to examine the bodies. Included in the party going with him were Lieutenant Jackson, Theodore Davis, the Delaware scout who found the bodies, and probably Bill Comstock. Eventually a burial detail was sent for.[19]

When they reached the bodies, Custer and the others examined them and the surroundings. Later, in *My Life on the Plains*, Custer would write that they were so brutally hacked and disfigured as to be beyond recognition; that the sinews of the arms and legs had been cut away, the nose of every man hacked off, and the features so defaced as to be unrecognizable. Further he said that "some of the bodies were lying on beds of ashes, with partly burned fragments of wood near them, showing that the savages had put some of them to death by the terrible tortures of fire." But this was quite a different story from that in his official report and early letters to Judge Kidder and probably represents pandering to the tastes of the reading public of that day, eager for any thrilling tales of terrible, bloodthirsty acts by the Indian foe. In his letter to Judge Kidder of August 25, 1867, Custer stated: "All of the bodies found had been scalped and pierced with numerous arrows. As several days had elapsed since the massacre, and as the wolves had disfigured the remains very much it was impossible to determine whether any indignities or barbarities other than scalping had been

---

[19] Custer to Weir, August 7, 1867; Custer to Kidder, August 23, 1867.

perpetrated by the Indians." This has more the ring of truth and was confirmed by Lieutenant Jackson in his letter to Judge Kidder on November 5, 1867.[20]

After the fight ended and the Indians were gone, the forces of nature would have taken over at once. The bodies had likely been in the ravine where they were found for at least ten days, the intense sunlight and heat of July on the High Plains bearing down on them. Captain Barnitz had written to his wife on July 1 that it was 102 degrees in the shade at Fort Wallace, only forty-five miles to the south, and such heat would have hastened decomposition. The actions of maggots and other insects, rodents, coyotes, and wolf packs would have quickly disfigured the features of faces and limbs. The circling vultures had doubtless descended and torn at the remaining flesh. Even had any Indians placed the mark of their tribe on the bodies, as they did with Sergeant Wyllyams, the evidence of it would have been quickly erased.[21]

According to Custer's official report, the bodies were found near each other in a ravine "about thirty yards in length and two to four deep." The crests of the ravine "were all bristling with arrows," which the Indians had used "very freely." The report states that hundreds of arrows were picked up and carried away by Custer's men and that a large number of exploded metallic cartridge casings lay near the bodies, indicating that the Kidder party had put up a stout and heroic resistance. Theodore Davis arrived at the opposite conclusion, writing in his article "A Summer on the Plains" that it was evident they had been killed almost without a fight, that few shots had been fired from their carbines, and that not more than ten to a dozen cartridge shells were to be found. Davis was unlikely to make such a claim if he thought it false, however barbarous he may have wanted to paint the Indians. But perhaps he merely failed to observe them. Custer, on the other hand, may have been motivated to portray a heroic struggle for the benefit of the cavalry's reputation and the lost men's grieving families. Still, it is unlikely that men fearing for their lives would not have fought desperately to their last breath. The truth of the matter will forever remain conjecture. But if Custer's report of the presence of a large num-

---

[20] Custer to Weir, August 7, 1867; Custer to J. P. Kidder, August 25, 1867, in Johnson and Allan, *Find Custer!* 54, and in Voight, "Death of Lyman S. Kidder," 15–16; Jackson to J. P. Kidder, November 5, 1867, in Johnson and Allan, *Find Custer!* 65–66, and in Voight, "Death of Lyman S. Kidder," 25; G. Custer, *My Life on the Plains*, 198; Utley, *Life in Custer's Cavalry*, 81.

[21] Custer to Weir, August 7, 1867; Custer to Kidder, August 25, 1867; Jackson to Kidder, November 5, 1867; G. Custer, *My Life on the Plains*, 198; Utley, *Life in Custer's Cavalry*, 81.

In early July 1867 Custer led his troopers on a grueling march from the forks of the Republican to the South Platte River, then back to the Republican, and finally south to Fort Wallace. His purpose was supposedly to scout the region and obtain new orders. Those orders had been sent to him with 2nd Lt. Lyman Kidder, ten enlisted men from M Company, Second Cavalry, and an Oglala scout named Red Bead. Kidder's party ran into a hunting camp of southern Oglalas and Dog Soldier Cheyennes near Beaver Creek and were killed to the last man. This sketch by Theodore Davis purports to show the bodies as Custer and his men found them. They were depicted as skeletons to avoid frightening or offending the sensibilities of eastern whites, particularly women. *Harper's Weekly*, August 17, 1867.

ber of arrows embedded on the crests of the ravine is accurate, and there is no evidence to contradict it, the ravine in which the bodies were found must have been the scene of their last fight. The bodies themselves were pierced with numerous arrows, and three or four dead cavalry horses lay nearby, suggesting that the climactic moments occurred there. While the Indians may well have fired some of the arrows into the bodies postmortem as a mark of their tribe, they would have killed the horses only to bring down a trooper or to prevent escape. They would have much preferred to capture them alive and unharmed for their own use.[22]

Though at the time it seemed of little significance in their efforts to identify bodies, Custer noted in his report that while the men of Kidder's party "had been stripped of nearly all of their clothing, a few still retained their drawers or shirts." He added: "One of the bodies had on a woolen shirt, white with black stripes, running in each direction. In the pocket of another was found a Sutlers check. Another had a round metallic baggage check." These last two items, Custer stated, were in the possession of Lt. Myles Moylan, the regimental adjutant. The presence of the shirt would in time prove the key to identifying the body of Lyman Kidder, and the recovery of his remains for burial in the family plot in a St. Paul, Minnesota, cemetery. As for the others, their bodies, unidentified, would ultimately be consigned to a common grave first at the Fort Wallace cemetery and, after its abandonment, in the National Cemetery at Fort Leavenworth, Kansas. But for the moment all of the bodies, including that of Lieutenant Kidder, were buried in a common grave, really a trench, dug by a burial party under the leadership of Sgt. James Connolly of D Company, Seventh Cavalry. Lieutenant Jackson wrote Judge Kidder that it was on a small ridge on the north side of Beaver Creek about seven hundred yards downstream from the trail's crossing, and about thirty to forty yards from the creek. In his march journal he said it was "on the hill side, north of creek and about 1/2 mile east of our crossing place." Custer said that the grave was near the point where the bodies were found.[23]

It was clear that all members of the Kidder party had met death at the hands of the Indians they encountered and that each had been scalped and his skull smashed with a war club—probably postmortem. The body of Red Bead, the Lakota scout, was the least mutilated, having been scalped but the scalp left next to him. According to Bill Comstock. this was because Indians would not keep the scalp of a fellow tribesman even when killed fighting on the side of the enemy. His body had been pierced by many arrows, but his skull had evidently not been smashed as were the others. Because of the condition of the bodies, it was not possible to determine more. The Indians had taken all of the troopers' arms and equipment, along with the surviving horses. While Custer would later claim that sev-

---

[22] Custer to Weir, August 7, 1867; Custer to Kidder, August 23, 1867; G. Custer, *My Life on the Plains*, 197–200; Davis, "Summer on the Plains," 306.

[23] Custer to Kidder, August 23, 1867; Jackson to Kidder, November 5, 1867.

eral in the Kidder party were put to death by fire, this seems grossly exaggerated. In his official report he made no mention of that, as he surely
would have if there were significant evidence. Theodore Davis reported
that "one or more" of the men were tortured to death, while Lieutenant
Jackson wrote that one had been "burnt." Though the presence of fire may
have been detected, given the decayed and ravaged condition of the bodies it would have been nearly impossible to make a certain determination
that it was a cause of death or even inflicted on a living man. Captain
West's company had camped in the area for two days awaiting return of
the wagon train, and the remains of their campfires were probably all over
the valley near the crossing. And the fact that the bodies had been dragged
around by the wolves would have compounded the problem. According
to Custer, all of the bodies were pierced by a multitude of arrows, making it unlikely, though possible, that anyone would have survived long
enough to meet such a fate. Like so many other facets of the fight on
Beaver Creek in July 1867, that question will defy certain resolution.[24]

For a time after finding the remains of the Kidder party, Custer vacillated about which tribe he believed responsible for their deaths. In his official report of August 7, 1867, he said it was the "band of Sioux and
Cheyennes that attacked Lt. Robbins and party on the 26 June, numbering over five hundred warriors." In his letter to Judge Kidder of August 23
he stated that it "is satisfactorily believed that the party attacking your son
was 'Roman Nose' and his tribe of Cheyenne warriors, numbering over
five hundred warriors." Later, in *My Life on the Plains*, he asserted that they
"could be none other than the Sioux, led in all probability by Pawnee Killer."
There was a modicum of truth in each of these assertions. George Bent
eventually told the story to George Hyde. A hunting camp of Kiyuksa
Oglala Lakotas, followers of Pawnee Killer and Bear Raising Mischief,
were camped on Beaver Creek. Near their camp were a few lodges of Dog
Soldier Cheyennes, numbering twelve warriors in all under the leadership
of Howling Wolf, Tobacco, and Big Head, who were also hunting buffalo. Included were two warriors named Good Bear and Two Crows, who
would become Bent's informants some years later. Buffalo were plentiful,
and they had enjoyed success. One day most of the Oglalas were off hunting, and the Cheyenne men were relaxing in camp in the shade of their
lodges. The women were gossiping and sewing or cooking. Suddenly sev-

---

[24] Jackson, "March Itinerary," October 12, 1867; Custer to Weir, August 7, 1867; G. Custer, *My Life on the Plains*, 198–200; Davis, "Summer on the Plains," 306.

eral Oglala hunters came riding in fast, calling out, "Hurry and gather your horses, all you Cheyenne men. Soldiers with pack mules are coming." The Cheyenne horses were picketed close to their lodges, so the Cheyennes were the first to get mounted. They rode out from their camp next to Beaver Creek and soon were able to see the oncoming soldiers.[25]

According to the story related by Good Bear and Two Crows, when Kidder and his men saw the Cheyenne warriors coming, they "took alarm and dismounted, taking refuge in a little grassy hollow near the creek." This suggests a race for shelter in the creek valley. Probably at or near the place where Custer and his men found the first dead horse, Kidder's detachment caught sight of the warriors galloping toward them. To that time they had been moving in column and at the "cavalry walk." Initially the odds were at least even—twelve men on each side, and the soldiers with their seven-shot carbines and their pistols stood an excellent chance of successfully defending themselves. But with the dust cloud they would have kicked up, they likely could not tell how many warriors there were or, if they could, correctly concluded that more would be coming.[26]

The two extra horses, probably bearing heavy packs with food and ammunition, were being led and were tired from the heat and the rigors of a fast march. Frightened by the sounds of the Indian war whoops and the sudden tugging at their leads, first one resisted being forced into following at a trot or gallop, then the other. When they would not willingly follow, the troopers probably shot them rather then allow them to fall into the hands of the Indians. Neither the Cheyennes nor the Oglalas seem to have made much if any use of firearms in the fight. After that the soldiers, probably seeing the Indians coming fast from the west, veered sharply to the east and away from the wagon trail and made for any defensible place they could find in the creek valley. It is possible they halted one or more times in the course of their flight to fire a volley at the Indians, then continued on. Whatever they did, it is clear they ended up in the ravine, Good Bear's "grassy hollow." Here the Cheyennes rushed up and circled around them, riding fast and shooting arrows as they did. It was not a good place for a defense, with the Indians on the high ground shooting down at them.[27]

---

[25] Custer to Weir, August 7, 1867; Custer to Kidder, August 23, 1867; Berthrong, *Southern Cheyennes*, 286–87; G. Custer, *My Life on the Plains*, 198; Grinnell, *Fighting Cheyennes*, 260–62; Hyde, *Life of George Bent*, 274–75.

[26] Berthrong, *Southern Cheyennes*, 286–87; Grinnell, *Fighting Cheyennes*, 260–62; Hyde, *Life of George Bent*, 274–75.

[27] Berthrong, *Southern Cheyennes*, 286–87; Grinnell, *Fighting Cheyennes*, 260–62; Hyde, *Life of George Bent*, 274–75.

Shortly after the initial Cheyenne attack, a number of Oglala warriors arrived, dismounting from their horses since they usually preferred to fight on foot, and then crawling toward the ravine from all sides. Their horses were probably left out of sight of the soldiers, who would have seen the Oglalas closing in on them only with difficulty. In the meantime the twelve Cheyennes continued circling and shooting arrows into the soldiers' refuge, forcing them to keep their heads down. As the Oglalas closed the distance, they too began shooting arrows into the ravine, which would account for the crests bristling with them, and the bodies being pierced by so many. The troopers were firing back, but Good Bear said they shot wildly, likely because they feared raising their heads to look for a target. None of the Cheyennes were hurt, probably because they presented difficult, rapidly moving targets, but two of the Oglalas were killed. One of these, a man named Yellow Horse, had been made a chief only a short time before. During the fight Red Bead, the guide for the Kidder party, kept calling out that he was a Lakota and asking the warriors to let him out. He was badly frightened, but the Oglalas only taunted him for being with the soldiers and refused to show him mercy. According to Good Bear and Two Crows, the fight did not last long before all of the soldiers and Red Bead were dead.[28]

Although Custer wrote in his report and letters of five hundred warriors in the attacking party and of "hundreds of red-visaged demons" in *My Life on the Plains*, there were probably fewer than one hundred, perhaps no more than fifty to sixty. This was not a war party Kidder encountered but a hunting camp of Oglalas, away from their main village. They were out hunting buffalo at the time and probably widely dispersed in smaller parties as was their custom. Only twelve Cheyenne warriors were present, but it would not have taken an overwhelming force to kill Kidder and his men, particularly once they were dismounted and in the shallow ravine. Custer variously attributed leadership of the Indians to Roman Nose of the Cheyennes and to Pawnee Killer of the Oglalas. It is certain that Roman Nose was not present, being then in the main Dog Soldier and Sutaio village on Beaver Creek, probably farther to the east. Whether or not Pawnee Killer was with his Kiyuksas is speculative. Good Bear and Two Crows said only that the Oglala hunting camp was "under Pawnee Killer and Bear Raising Mischief," not that either was present at the Kid-

[28] Berthrong, *Southern Cheyennes*, 286–87; Grinnell, *Fighting Cheyennes*, 260–62; Hyde, *Life of George Bent*, 274–75.

der fight. The likelihood is that if they were, their presence would have been mentioned, but there will be no definitive answer to that question. The death of Lieutenant Kidder and his men would come to be known as the Kidder Massacre. If by that it is meant that there were no survivors, it would be correct. But if it is intended to imply that there was killing with atrocity or cruelty, that is doubtful, as there is no conclusive evidence to show anything other than that Kidder and his detachment were wiped out to the last man.[29]

Custer and his officers concluded that Kidder and his men came to their unhappy fate by missing the trail left by his command as they veered away from the wagon trail and moved southwesterly along the south fork of the Republican five miles beyond the forks. Thinking the trail southward was that of the entire command, they followed it, as Custer believed, and on or about July 2 ran into the large war party that attacked Lieutenant Cooke's wagon train and its escort commanded by Lieutenant Robbins. No one really knows why Kidder and his men chose to follow the southerly track. Perhaps they didn't see the divergence of the two trails, as Custer believed, but with an expert guide like Red Bead, that seems improbable even if they reached it in the night or early morning. They apparently could see the trail they followed, so they would most likely have seen the large trail that left it. If, as Custer said, the wagon trail to Fort Wallace was the heavier, and given that the wagon train and its escort had returned no more than a day and a half prior to the march along the Republican's south fork, in conjunction with the intervening rain Red Bead and Kidder could easily have determined that the heavier trail was that of Custer's command and that he was headed to Fort Wallace. That question will forever remain unanswered. But the ultimate result of the mistake was now known to Custer, and after the horses and mules had grazed, watered, and rested and the burial party had completed its grisly task, he ordered the march resumed.[30]

Leaving the Beaver Creek valley, Custer's column now marched south-southwest by south, following the trail left by his wagon train en route to and from Fort Wallace. South of Beaver Creek the plains were once again level and thickly dotted with prickly pear cactus. After marching approximately ten miles, they reached a series of water holes that they believed

[29] Custer to Weir, August 7, 1867; Custer to Kidder, August 23, 1867; Berthrong, *Southern Cheyennes*, 286–87; Grinnell, *Fighting Cheyennes*, 260–62; Hyde, *Life of George Bent*, 274–75.

[30] Custer to Weir, August 7, 1867; H. Jackson to W. A. Burleigh, September 29, 1867, in Voight, "Death of Lyman S. Kidder," 17–18; G. Custer, *My Life on the Plains*, 190–91.

in winter formed the head of Short Nose Creek, the translated name used by the Indians for the middle fork of Sappa Creek. With sufficient water and good grass in the vicinity Custer put his men into camp, tending to the livestock and preparing their evening meals, after a day's march of twenty-five and a half miles. It had been an eventful and disturbing day, and around their campfires late that afternoon there must have been considerable speculation as to the fate of Lieutenant Kidder and his detachment. Why did they move south toward Fort Wallace instead of along the trail taken by Custer's command, leading to the South Platte? What Indians attacked them, and how many were there? Why had they left the trail and taken refuge in a shallow and vulnerable ravine? How had they died? And there were other perplexing questions. Most of those questions would continue to resonate through history.[31]

On the morning of July 13 they continued on a course south-southwest by south along the wagon train trail. A little less than eight miles brought them to another series of water holes that they called Solomon's Holes and that they believed formed the headwaters of Solomon's Fork. Actually these were a part of the upper reaches of the south fork of Sappa Creek, for the headwaters of the Solomon lay farther east. Three miles beyond they reached yet another cluster of water holes, these being in the bed of a different branch of the south fork of the Sappa. Their course was now ten degrees west of south, and then south to Black Butte Creek (north fork of the Smoky Hill River), which they reached after marching sixteen and three-fourths miles. Though they made no mention of it, during their march south from the south fork of the Sappa to within a few miles north of the Smoky Hill's north fork they were passing through the area where the wagon train was attacked by the Indians during its return trip. But Custer saw neither Cheyennes nor Oglalas. At Black Butte Creek they found good water and good grass and made their crossing, then halted to rest and graze the animals.[32]

A little more than eight miles south of the north fork of the Smoky Hill they crossed the dry bed of Lake Creek, with water standing in pools here and there. Comstock told them that about four miles above their crossing point the stream had flowing water, one of those anomalies of the plains that so perplexed young men from the East. They probably watered their livestock in the pools at Lake Creek, then continued on, now march-

---

[31] Jackson, "March Itinerary," July 12, 1867.
[32] Ibid., July 13, 1867.

ing ten degrees east of south to a large ridge. Then they turned south-southwest and at a little over eight miles from Lake Creek reached the south fork of the Smoky Hill. There they went into camp during the early evening on the river's north bank amid good grass and about a half mile west of Fort Wallace. They had made a day's march of a little more than thirty-three and a half miles. From the time they left Fort Hays on June 1, 1867, they had traveled (according to their odometer reading) nearly seven hundred five miles in forty-three days. And from the time of the expedition's departure from Fort Riley on the morning of March 27 they had been on campaign for 109 days. The men and the livestock were weary to their bones and needed an extended rest before they would be in condition to return to the field to fight Indians. They would stay in camp at Fort Wallace to refit and rehabilitate themselves after their long and exhausting journey, even though their orders were to remain in the field. Their field commander, Lt. Col. George Armstrong Custer, had something else in mind. He was about to embark on a long journey that would bring him to court-martial and disgrace.[33]

---

[33] Ibid.; Davis, "Summer on the Plains," 307.

CHAPTER TWENTY-FIVE

A DASH TO FORT RILEY
AND COURT-MARTIAL

In the summer of 1867 Fort Wallace, like so many of the frontier military posts on the western plains, was a mixture of new permanent buildings, those under construction, temporary buildings, sod or adobe structures, and tents, lending an air of impermanence. The site was on the bluffs overlooking the south fork of the Smoky Hill River about a mile north from the stream. Originally established on October 26, 1865, as Camp Pond Creek, taking its name from the nearby stream and stage station, it was renamed Fort Wallace the next year in honor of Brig. Gen. William H. L. Wallace, killed at the Battle of Shiloh. During its brief life span of less than twenty years the fort would experience within its environs as much or more conflict with the Plains Indians than perhaps any other military post on the Great Plains.[1]

When Custer and his six companies of the Seventh Cavalry reached Fort Wallace late on the evening of July 13, 1867, their horses were in poor condition due to lack of grain and forage and the long, trying marches they had endured since leaving Fort Hays on June 1. The officers generally agreed that the horses were then unfit for hard service. Either that night or the following morning, Custer rode the half mile to the fort to check for further orders from General Hancock and for letters from Libbie. He found neither. Hancock had returned to Fort Wallace from Denver on the afternoon of July 3. With him were Captain Keogh and the men from I Company who composed his escort to Denver and back. But some of the men from I Company, under command of 2nd Lt. Charles C. Cox, continued east as escort for General Hancock when he left a day or two later. After their departure the post had only fifty men in its garrison, and

---

[1] Report on Barracks and Hospitals, 309–12; Oliva, *Fort Wallace*, 29–38, 122.

the remaining cavalry were in bad shape. Keogh wrote to Capt. W. G. Mitchell, adjutant for the Department of the Missouri, on July 16 that his horses were in no better condition than those of the regiment "just come in with General Custer" and without grain would not be fit for any duty. It is clear that there was then little if any grain or forage for the livestock at Fort Wallace and an insufficient supply of horseshoes to refit Custer's cavalry. However, there were enough rations for the men to last until August 15, barring any unusual drain caused by the arrival of additional troops. Arms and ammunition were also in short supply because Fort Wallace was required to provide these to all wagon trains arriving from the east or west that were in need of them.[2]

Although this state of affairs no doubt troubled Custer, it was not from concern for the requirements of Fort Wallace. Requests for resupply had already been made for the post, and before Hancock left, he had promised to see that they were sent. Custer's concern was for the needs of the Seventh Cavalry, and more particularly the part he required as escort for his intended trip eastward. His last orders were to march to Fort Wallace and report to General Hancock. Since Hancock was no longer there, Custer claimed that it was his duty to follow him to Fort Harker or to the nearest telegraph station to report and learn what his new orders were. He told Major Elliott that he would be leaving the post within two days, taking with him an escort of about seventy-six men. Orders for this were issued verbally (probably on July 14) through the adjutant, Myles Moylan, requiring that each company provide a detachment of twelve of its best mounted men, including one noncommissioned officer, to accompany Custer on his march to Fort Harker.[3]

Though Custer had no way of knowing it, General Sherman had arrived at Harker by rail on July 5 and remained until Hancock reached it on July 12 during his return trip from Denver. Sherman was worried about the situation on the Smoky Hill, particularly the area between Forts Harker and Hays, where railroad construction was in full swing along with Indian attacks on the construction crews. A further problem was cholera, which first appeared at Harker on June 28 in troops of the Thirty-eighth Infantry en route to New Mexico and also in an employee of a beef contractor. It soon spread to the garrison and the nearby town of Ellsworth. Following

[2] M. W. Keogh to T. B. Weir, AAAG, July 8, 1867, LS, Fort Wallace, RG 393, NA; M. W. Keogh to W. S. Mitchell, AAAG, July 16, 1867, LS, Fort Wallace, RG 393, NA; Frost, *Court-martial*, 106–107, 131, 182–83; Millbrook, "West Breaks In General Custer," 135; Utley, *Life in Custer's Cavalry*, 81, 85, 95.

[3] Frost, *Court-martial*, 106–107, 114, 199; Utley, *Life in Custer's Cavalry*, 93.

Hancock's arrival, the two men discussed the current situation and how to deal with it. On July 13, before he left Fort Harker, Hancock issued written orders to General Smith, directing him to instruct Custer to operate between the Arkansas and the Platte, using Fort Wallace as his base. He was to draw supplies from Fort Wallace but would find supplies at other forts in the district if his operations made it necessary to visit them. He was to keep his cavalry "constantly employed."[4]

In July 1867, Fort Harker was at the western end of the line of the Union Pacific, E.D., and also of the telegraph system along the Smoky Hill. Fort Wallace lay 212 miles to the west of it by way of the Smoky Hill road. General Smith forwarded Hancock's instructions to Custer on July 16, entrusting them to 2nd Lt. Charles C. Cox, I Company, Seventh Cavalry. Cox had been ordered to escort a slow-moving wagon train from Harker to Fort Wallace during his return from escorting Hancock eastward. There was no way of notifying Custer earlier that new orders had been sent. Even had he known, it is questionable that it would have made any difference in Custer's course of action. He was well aware that his exhausted men and their equally worn horses would require prolonged rest, nourishment, and refitting before they were in condition to return to the field and that would take at least a month. Whether the orders arrived in a day or a month was of little importance, for they could not be acted on in the near term.[5]

Custer's quest for new orders was probably no more than an excuse, a subterfuge permitting him to travel to Fort Harker, Fort Riley, or wherever Libbie was to be reunited with him. From the time he left old Fort Hays on June 1, he had been more concerned about having her with him than in fighting Indians, and in light of his subsequent actions there is no reason to conclude his priorities had changed. He had received no letters from her since he embarked on his scout (though she had written often), and now he was consumed by his desire to have her at his side. Most of the officers of Custer's command believed his true reason for leaving was his need to be with Libbie. Captain Barnitz wrote his own wife, Jennie, to that effect following his return to Fort Wallace. And an employee of the Fort Wallace sutler's store wrote a postscript in a letter to his mother on July 15 that said: "General Custer is going down to Fort Hays after his wife this evening—and has promised to take our mail down—so will send this by him." Capt. Arthur B. Carpenter, Thirty-seventh Infantry, com-

---

[4] *Leavenworth Conservative*, July 7 and August 23, 1867; Frost, *Court-martial*, 106–107, 114, 117–18, 126–28; Millbrook, "West Breaks In General Custer," 131–32.
[5] Frost, *Court-martial*, 128, 131–32, 200–201.

manding the detachment posted at "Fort Downer" (Downer Station), wrote his parents on August 15, 1867, that "he [Custer] came through here about the middle of last month on his way to Reilly, and stopped for dinner." Custer's true reason for making the trip appears to have been no secret at the time. Although neither Major Elliott nor Captain Hamilton considered that even the best of the horses would have recovered sufficiently in two days to undertake such a long and arduous march, Custer gave verbal orders to do just that.[6]

Custer and his escort detachment left Fort Wallace during the late afternoon of July 15, 1867. Accompanying Custer were seventy-six enlisted men and noncommissioned officers, Capt. Louis M. Hamilton, and Lieutenants William W. Cooke and Thomas W. Custer. Hamilton was in command of the escort detachment. Two army ambulances went with them, along with an army supply wagon pulled by six mules. The wagon was carrying rations for the stations on the Smoky Hill stage route that were guarded by troops from Fort Wallace. Because that road had been under almost constant attack or threat of attack by the Cheyennes since midspring, rations were sent out to the troops with any cavalry unit on a mission that could serve as escort. The route of march for Custer's detachment was straight east along the Smoky Hill road to Fort Harker. They would march continuously, with short rest halts lasting about five to ten minutes every hour or so, and six stops for resting men and animals between Fort Wallace and Big Creek Station that would last more than half an hour. For short halts it was their practice to have the troopers wheel their horses front into line and dismount them without unsaddling, then rest standing for the five to ten minutes. For the longer rest stops the horses were unsaddled and grazed, while the men had coffee, ate, and slept a little when they could. A sergeant from Company E was detailed to march at the head of the column to set the gait, the usual cavalry walk of about four and a half miles per hour.[7]

As the column of men and horses moved eastward along the Smoky Hill road and away from Fort Wallace, they first passed Henshaw Springs Station after marching about eight miles. In another eight miles or so they reached the Death Hollow campground at the forks of the Smoky Hill, and six miles beyond that Russell's Springs Station, also called Eaton Sta-

[6] Burkey, *Custer, Come at Once,* 32; Millbrook, "West Breaks In General Custer," 136, 140n106; Utley, *Life in Custer's Cavalry,* 86–88.
[7] Frost, *Court-martial,* 106–11, 117, 121.

tion after Col. Issac E. Eaton.[8] At this station, which they reached some-time between midnight and 1:00 A.M. on July 16, Custer and his men halted for about three-quarters of an hour to allow those with the Fort Wallace supply wagon to distribute rations for the troops stationed there. Beyond Russell's Springs their pace seems to have slowed somewhat, for it took them until nearly daylight to cover the approximately ten miles to Smoky Hill Station. There they halted near the station for their first long rest break. The horses were unsaddled and picketed to graze, while the men made coffee and slept. Meanwhile the supply wagon unloaded the last of the rations it carried, since Smoky Hill Station was as far as it was going. They left it there to return with the next wagon train or cavalry escort that came along.[9]

After resting about two hours, Custer and his escort saddled up and moved on. Beginning at 6:00 A.M. on July 16, they made a thirteen-mile march and reached Monument Station at about 11:00 A.M. They again unsaddled the horses and put them out to graze, remaining for an hour and a half to two hours. Monument Station was one of the most famous and important stations on the trail, in part because of the Indian troubles that compelled the army to maintain a company of cavalry there and designate it as a "fort," and in part because of the unusual rock formations that tow-ered over the plains a mile to the northwest. These formations, composed of the thick chalks of the Niobrara Formation of the late Cretaceous geo-logic age, were carved by the ancestral Smoky Hill River as it flowed through the Niobrara chalk. They stand alone, looming above the surrounding plains as if they were the architectural remnants of some lost civilization. Custer's men must have looked at them with wonder and disbelief.[10]

The men resumed their eastward march at about 1:00 P.M. on July 16 and had progressed only two miles or so beyond the station and cavalry post when they met a wagon train of forage bound for Fort Wallace to resup-ply it. It was one of four large supply trains traveling together with an escort commanded by Capt. Frederick Benteen of H Company, Seventh Cav-alry. Benteen had been on detached duty and was now headed to Fort Wal-lace to rejoin his company. Custer's men stopped the forage train and fed their horses, which had been without forage for some weeks, and took with

---

[8] It was Colonel Eaton who led the construction crew that built the first stations along the route of the Butterfield Overland Despatch.

[9] Frost, *Court-martial*, 110, 117; Lee and Raynesford, *Trails of the Smoky Hill*, 66–68.

[10] Buchanan, *Kansas Geology*, 33; Frost, *Court-martial*, 110, 117; Lee and Raynesford, *Trails of the Smoky Hill*, 66.

them a sufficient amount for two or three added feeds for every horse as well. This was probably carried in one of the two ambulances, the only wagons now with the escort. While they were feeding the animals, Custer would likely have heard any news Benteen could relate, including the fact that Libbie was now at Fort Riley. Continuing on, they passed Carlyle Station in another seven miles, then at sundown halted near Chalk Bluffs Station after marching another nine or so miles. They unsaddled the horses and picketed them to graze, while the men made coffee and got a little rest. This break lasted about an hour and a half to two hours, after which they got back on the trail. From Chalk Bluffs to Grannell Springs Station was about thirteen miles, and it was during this ride that the horses began to break down from exhaustion.[11] When they reached the station, five of the men had horses that could proceed no farther, and both men and horses were left there. The next station was Castle Rock, so-called for another nearby monument of Niobrara chalk about nine miles east of Grannell Springs. There one or two more men and their mounts had to be left behind due to the fatigue of the horses. Custer ordered a halt about two miles east of the Castle Rock Station. It was now the morning of July 17, so they rested there on the open plains for about two hours, with the horses and ambulance mules being grazed and given forage. During this stop two westbound mail coaches came through with a strong escort, and Custer searched the mailbags for letters or orders for himself. He found neither.[12]

Custer's escort had been losing other horses as they marched. Those that broke down on the open plains and could not be taken into a stage station were either shot or abandoned. At first Captain Hamilton ordered them shot after their saddles and equipment were removed, so they would not fall into the hands of the Cheyennes, but after two or three had been killed, it was found that it took too much time. Subsequently they were simply abandoned, and the dismounted men were placed in one of the ambulances and carried down the trail. When the rest stop east of Castle Rock Station ended, Custer called for Sgt. James Connolly. Connolly was in charge of the detail that was watching for spent horses, then picking up their saddles and equipment and taking them along with the dismounted riders to an ambulance. His party normally ranged on either the left or the right flank and at the rear of the column. Custer told Connolly

---

[11] The original given name for this station on the Butterfield Overland Despatch was "Grannell Springs." Later travelers and the military, not knowing this, corrupted it to "Grinnell Springs." See Frost, *Court-martial*, 147; and Lee and Raynesford, *Trails of the Smoky Hill*, 65–66.

[12] Frost, *Court-martial*, 110–12, 117–18, 133, 138, 207; Millbrook, "West Breaks In General Custer," 138.

that Private Young, who had been leading his mare, Fanchon, for him, had remained behind when they passed Castle Rock Station. He ordered Connolly to take six men and a led horse, in case Young's own horse was played out, and go back to Castle Rock to pick up Young and return him and the mare to the column. He told Connolly that they would move a short distance and wait for him to report back. Custer and the rest of the escort then continued on to the east while Connolly's detail went back for Young and the mare. At Castle Rock Station they remounted Young, his own horse being too fatigued to be ridden, and then returned along the stage road, with Young leading Custer's mare.[13]

Sergeant Connolly's detail had reached the place two miles east of Castle Rock Station where the halt had been taken and were about a half mile beyond when suddenly they were attacked by Indians. At first only seven or eight were visible, probably riding up from the river or a canyon or arroyo emptying into it from south of the trail. Later more were seen. In Connolly's opinion there were up to fifty to sixty, although with the constant movement of his detachment and that of the Indians circling their right flank, an accurate count would have been difficult. The warriors were firing at the soldiers, probably with both firearms and bows and arrows, but the rapid movement of the parties made most of their shots go wild. Then the Indians began to crowd closer to the detachment's right flank, causing Custer's mare to become excited and move to the left of the road about three hundred yards, taking Young and his mount with her. Two of the warriors made an effort to cut Young and the mare off from the rest of the detachment, which in turn caused delay while the soldiers moved to prevent it. They fired two shots at the Indians, apparently the only shots fired by the soldiers during the entire engagement, forcing the warriors to wheel off to the right and rear of the detachment. Young had just gotten himself and the mare back on the road when Sergeant Connolly looked back and saw one of his men about four to five hundred yards to the rear. His horse was moving slowly, and the rider appeared very unsteady in his saddle. Shortly he was surrounded by six or seven Indians, a shot was heard, and the man fell from his saddle. At the time the main body of Indians moved in close on the detachment's right flank, nearer the soldiers than the man who had just been shot, making it impossible to go back for him. They continued on at a trot or a lope, but soon another of the men called out to Connolly that he was wounded.[14]

---

[13] Frost, *Court-martial*, 108, 138–40, 144.
[14] Ibid., 139–46.

Sergeant Connolly, who was five to six yards to the trooper's left, rode around to the man's right and asked him where he was wounded. He did not speak but pointed to his hip, where a great deal of blood was beginning to show through his trousers. Connolly rode back around to his left and gave the command for the detachment to halt so they could tie the man to his saddle and take him with them. The two men at the front of the detachment, apparently frightened, rode on rapidly, evidently trying to escape the Indians. This left Connolly with only three men from his detail, including the wounded man and Young, with Custer's mare. Thinking they did not hear his command, Connolly first rode after the other two men, trying to overtake them, but his horse was too fatigued to catch up with them. He fell back and ordered the remaining two fit men, whose horses were in better condition than his, to pursue the two in front and to shoot them down if they did not halt on command. These men were able to catch the fleeing soldiers and force them to halt. Meanwhile the Indians were closing in on Connolly and Private Young, forcing them to leave the wounded man behind and trot after the others. When the two had advanced five to six hundred yards Connolly looked back and could see that the wounded man had either dismounted or fallen from his saddle. The Indians apparently did not see this happen. Connolly and Young caught up with the other four within a half mile or so. By this time most of the Indians had moved back to the rear, where the first man had been killed, leaving perhaps twenty warriors still circling on the detachment's right flank.[15]

The detachment—now down to Sergeant Connolly, four men of the original detail, and Private Young with Custer's mare—continued along the trail, alternately at a trot and a lope. Some of the Indians were still on their right flank, firing occasional shots at them. Connolly and his men expected to find Custer and his escort waiting for them at nearly every ravine or arroyo they passed, but did not catch up with them until reaching Downer Station some seven and a half miles beyond where they were first attacked. The Indians stayed on their flank until they were within a mile and a half from the station and then moved off to the south toward the Smoky Hill. When the detail arrived at Downer Station at about 2:00 P.M., Sergeant Connolly reported the particulars of the attack to Captain Hamilton. Connolly's own horse was wounded, and his entire detachment was demoralized both by their harrowing experience and the loss of two of their number. Custer' and his escort had been at Downer Station

---

[15] Ibid., 140–46.

about half an hour when Connolly and his detachment arrived and Connolly made his report. News of the Indian attack and the loss of two men spread rapidly through the escort personnel and had a demoralizing effect on them all, largely because of the failure to send a strong party back to rescue the wounded soldier and bury the dead man.[16]

Connolly told Hamilton that the attack was made by eighteen Indians, not the fifty to sixty he later related, suggesting that his count of the enemy grew with time. He also reported that one man was wounded and dismounted and that one of the other men thought he had gotten off by himself. On hearing this, Hamilton walked over to Custer, who was sitting in the door of the station about ten to fifteen feet away, and made a report concerning the attack and the loss of life. Since he was so close at the time of Connolly's report, Hamilton felt certain that Custer had heard it all and was aware that one man had been wounded and left dismounted. Hamilton suggested to Custer that the detachment remain at Downer Station until evening, both to rest and to avoid further loss of morale by departing so soon after an Indian attack with casualties taken. Custer seems to have made no direct response either to the report of the attack and the loss of two men or to the suggestion that they remain there until evening. His only reported comment was that "he would have to go along." He issued no orders to send back a party to rescue the wounded man if he was still alive or to find and bury the dead. Shortly after the report, the escort detachment was remounted and continued its march eastward.[17]

Custer and the escort left Downer Station sometime between 2:30 and 3:00 P.M. on July 17. Except for the short halts of five to ten minutes every hour or so, they rode steadily eastward. After a march of ten miles they reached but did not stop at White Rock Station and, after twelve more miles, passed Stormy Hollow Station. They took their next rest stop at about sundown out on the open plains and next to the Smoky Hill River, probably somewhere beyond Stormy Hollow. After that they remounted and rode through the night, passing Lookout Station and reaching Big Creek Station at or near sunup on July 18. It was about twenty miles from Stormy Hollow to Big Creek, and the men and animals were nearing collapse from exhaustion. The men camped a quarter of a mile from the station, watering and picketing their horses to graze, then preparing coffee and a meal for those who wanted it. But most men simply surrendered to

---

[16] Ibid., 107–14, 141–46.
[17] Ibid., 107–14, 142.

sleep. Meanwhile Lieutenant Cooke rode over to the station, one of the meal stops for the stage line, ate breakfast, took a nap, and then set about securing new mules for the ambulances. This chore took him to new Fort Hays, nine miles northeast of Big Creek Station. There he was able to obtain four replacement mules for one of the ambulances from the Quartermaster, leaving behind the spent mules brought from Fort Wallace. The ambulances Custer had with him were probably either the standard Civil War ambulances or Dougherty wagons, each of which was pulled by four mules. Cooke was able to replace the team for only one of the two, undoubtedly leaving the most unfit team behind. When he returned to the detachment's camp at Big Creek Station, they were hitched up, and preparations were made for departure. While at new Fort Hays, Cooke apparently also picked up Libbie's letters to Custer.[18]

Custer' and his escort reached Big Creek Station approximately fifty-five to fifty-seven hours after leaving Fort Wallace, having undertaken a difficult, strenuous, and nearly continuous march with little sleep or food for the men and only a few hours of grazing and rest for the animals. Fort Harker still lay about sixty-seven miles to the east, but the detachment was in no condition to continue without a serious rest stop. Eleven men arriving at Big Creek had been carried in an ambulance, including Sgt. James Connolly, whose own wounded horse had given out five miles west of Lookout Station. At least nine other men had been left with their horses at several of the stage stations during the march, and the escort detachment was now down to forty-five to fifty mounted men. It must have been this that forced Custer to conclude that a halt of at least a day would be necessary if the escort was to reach Fort Harker. Unwilling to endure the delay, he left the detachment under Hamilton's command and pressed on, using the two ambulances. It took Cooke some time to travel the nine to ten miles from Big Creek Station to new Fort Hays, trade out the mule team with the quartermaster, and return. Thus it was not until 1:00 P.M. on July 18 that Custer was able to continue toward Fort Harker. Hamilton was instructed to take the escort detachment on through to Harker as soon as it was sufficiently rested. Accompanying Custer were Lieutenants Cooke and Tom Custer, *Harper's Weekly* correspondent Theodore R. Davis, and at least one enlisted man, presumably as an ambulance driver.[19]

Once on the road the small party of two ambulances moved rapidly east-

---

[18] E. Custer, *Tenting on the Plains*, 701; Eggenhofer, *Wagons, Mules and Men*, 122–23; Frost, *Court-martial*, 110–11, 118–19, 121–23; Millbrook, "West Breaks In General Custer," 136n91.

[19] Frost, *Court-martial*, 118–23, 134, 142–43.

ward, unencumbered by the need to rest broken-down horses and their riders and not restricted to the cavalry walk. They moved steadily, passing the quiet desolation of the abandoned old Fort Hays eight miles east of Big Creek Station and then Walker's Creek Station four miles beyond. Reaching Fossil Creek Station in another ten miles, they may have stopped for a meal and refreshment, since both the stage station and a trading ranch were located there. The next station was Bunker Hill, about ten miles east of Fossil Creek. There Custer's party met 2nd Lt. Charles C. Cox and his detachment from I Company, Seventh Cavalry, escorting another supply train westward to Fort Wallace. His instructions were to deliver the orders from General Hancock, along with a forwarding letter from General Smith, to Custer when he met him, which was originally expected to be at Fort Wallace. It was about 9:00 P.M. on July 18 when Cox met Custer at Bunker Hill where the train he was escorting had camped for the night. He delivered the orders to Custer, and the two men had a brief conversation. Each inquired of the other whether he had encountered any Indians. Cox had not seen any, but Custer said that he had lost two men who had "loitered behind the column and were taken by Indians." He also commented that he had marched from Fort Wallace to Fort Hays in fifty-five hours, including rest stops.[20]

After the conversation ended, Custer and his party continued eastward, passing first Wilson Creek Station and then Buffalo Station in the night and, twelve miles beyond, reaching Fort Harker. By then it was between 2:00 and 2:30 A.M. on July 19. Custer immediately went to the quarters of General Smith and awakened him from a heavy sleep. At that hour of the morning Smith must have been both dulled by sleep and surprised to see the field commander he thought to be at Fort Wallace. Although Custer would later claim that he made a complete report of everything he deemed of importance relating to his operations from June 1 until his arrival at Fort Wallace, along with recommendations for further operations, this appears not to be so. He was not there long enough to have made more than the sketchiest report, and most of what he said concerned his immediate plans. Smith said only that Custer came to his quarters and told him he was leaving for Fort Riley. He did not ask for any specified number of days. Smith made no objection but probably did tell Custer that he must return as soon as possible. Smith then went out to the garrison, where his adjutant, Lieutenant Weir, and another officer were sleeping, and awakened Weir to see

---

[20] Ibid., 126–29, 131–34, 147; Lee and Raynesford, *Trails of the Smoky Hill*, 60–64.

Custer to the train. Weir returned to the commanding officer's quarters with Smith and met Custer. Whatever discussion they had was brief, for Weir then escorted Custer to the train station and saw him off on the 3:00 A.M. train eastbound to Fort Riley and beyond. The train probably arrived at Fort Riley between 6:00 and 7:00 A.M. on July 19.[21]

General Smith assumed that Custer had come to Fort Harker by stagecoach. Had he done so, he would likely have avoided at least in part the difficulties about to befall him. It was during the morning of July 19, as the daily routine at headquarters of the District of the Upper Arkansas resumed, when Smith first learned from his adjutant, Lieutenant Weir, that Custer had marched from Fort Wallace to Fort Hays with a large escort and had traveled from there to Fort Harker with two army ambulances. This both surprised and troubled him because so far as he knew Custer had not come on any army or government business that required his personal appearance but had apparently used military personnel and military vehicles and livestock to speed him on his own personal business. That business, of course, was to see Libbie. Smith and Weir were quite aware that Custer had received his orders from General Hancock, requiring him to be operating aggressively in the area of Fort Wallace, because he had told them of his meeting with Lieutenant Cox and delivery of the orders. He had neither requested nor received any leave from his command through the District of the Upper Arkansas, and Smith and Weir were unaware of leave being granted from any other source, as they surely would have been once he returned to Fort Wallace. Smith was fond of Custer and his wife, but he was also a military officer conscious that a soldier could not be absent from his command without proper leave. Therefore he sent a telegram to Custer that same morning directing him "to return immediately to Fort Wallace and rejoin his command unless he had permission from higher authority to be absent."[22]

Smith's telegram must have been delivered promptly, since Custer responded by telegram the same day, asking if he could wait until the following Monday, July 22. Smith quickly answered that he must return by the first train. In his report to Hancock on July 28, Smith stated that Custer "started by the first train but was delayed with no fault of his until the night of the 21st." The cause of this delay was not stated, and subsequent speculation has centered on the railroad and a possible erratic schedule.

---

[21] G. Custer, *My Life on the Plains*, 213; Frost, *Court-martial*, 119, 128–30, 149–50, 214–15, 218.
[22] Frost, *Court-martial*, 128–30, 150, 226–28; Millbrook, "West Breaks In General Custer," 142–43.

There is no convincing evidence to support a delay, and it was certainly not caused by weather or high water in the lower Smoky Hill or Republican rivers, like that in the early spring. The weather in July was very hot and dry. Railroad crews were still building west toward Fort Hays, albeit with delays resulting from attacks by the Cheyennes. That would not have affected the trains operating daily between Leavenworth and Ellsworth, and clearly the mail, along with construction and other supplies, was moving unimpeded by rail. The answer, though speculative, may lie in Smith's courtly fondness for both Custer and Libbie. When Custer did arrive on Sunday evening, July 21, he was accompanied by Libbie and all of their baggage. He was preparing to move her and their belongings to Fort Wallace to be with him. When her husband arrived without prior notice the morning of July 19 and was ordered back to Fort Harker later the same day, it was probably impossible for Libbie to get all of their baggage packed in sufficient time to make the last train of the day. And although Smith made no mention of either Libbie or her maid, Eliza, referring only to Custer's "family and baggage," it is probable that Eliza was with them, as she nearly always was as a part of the family. When Custer reported to him, Smith immediately placed him under arrest. But because of the presence of a serious outbreak of cholera at the post and his concern for the welfare of Custer's family, Smith sent him back to Fort Riley, where he remained under arrest in his quarters.[23]

Although Smith placed Custer under arrest on July 21, Hancock only heard indirectly of Custer's arrival at Fort Riley and was unaware of any action taken. He instructed his adjutant, W. G. Mitchell, to telegraph Smith on July 22, stating:

> The Major General Commanding directs me to say that he presumes you did not allow Genl. Custer to go to Fort Riley. He should have been arrested as his action was without warrant and highly injurious to the service, especially under the circumstances. The General thinks you should have preferred charges against Genl. Custer giving his instructions to his successor in command but if he has gone back without delay from Fort Harker he leaves the matter in your hands.

Custer, of course, had not returned to Fort Wallace "without delay" and was then under arrest at Fort Riley. In his report of July 28 Smith told Hancock that charges against Custer would be forwarded the following day. This was done. Those charges were, first, absence from his command with-

[23] Frost, *Court-martial*, 204; Millbrook, "West Breaks In General Custer," 142–43.

out leave, since he had proceeded to Fort Harker when he and his command were expected to be actively engaged against the Indians and, second, conduct to the prejudice of good order and military discipline. Under the latter charge, the specifications included overmarching and damaging the horses for a march not on public business, using government ambulances and mules on unauthorized business, and failing to take proper measures to repulse an Indian attack on a detachment of his escort, or for the defense or relief of the detachment, or to take any measures for the recovery of the bodies of those of his command who were reported killed. These charges, which were approved by Hancock, were subsequently supplemented by additional charges preferred by Capt. Robert M. West.[24]

West's allegations also were included in the general charge of "conduct prejudicial to good order and military discipline." The first of four specifications alleged that Custer ordered a party he sent in pursuit of supposed deserters to shoot them down and bring none back alive; the second, that he ordered and caused three enlisted men of his command to be shot down as supposed deserters without trial; the third, that he refused to allow medical attention for the three wounded men; and the fourth, that he caused the death of Pvt. Charles Johnson by the shooting and mortal wounding of the soldier without a trial. Johnson was a member of West's Company K, and his commander was clearly anguished that any of his men should have been dealt with in this summary manner. They had endured repeated long and difficult marches in the blazing heat of a summer on the southern plains and, from the time they first arrived at Fort Hays, were subjected to frequent abusive treatment on Custer's orders.[25]

It has long been suggested that West preferred his charges because he sought revenge for his arrest and a reprimand given him by Custer after arrival at Fort Wallace for "being so drunk as to be unfit for the proper performance of his duty," and because he felt slighted by not being named as commander of the supply train sent to Fort Wallace under Lieutenant Cooke. Actually he was in overall command of the wagon train's escort and charged with scouting Beaver Creek for Cheyennes and Oglalas, a far more important task than oversight of the supply wagons themselves. And although he may have smarted under the reprimand, he and most of the other officers of the regiment had already developed a hearty dislike

[24] Frost, *Court-martial*, 99–100; Millbrook, "West Breaks In General Custer," 142–44; Utley, *Life in Custer's Cavalry*, 91–94.
[25] Frost, *Court-martial*, 100–102; Millbrook, "West Breaks In General Custer," 144; Utley, *Life in Custer's Cavalry*, 92.

and disrespect for Custer as a result of his conduct during the spring and early summer of 1867. There seems to be little reason to suspect that West acted out of motives other than genuine outrage over what he deemed unduly harsh and unlawful actions taken against the deserters. Without question he was a heavy drinker on occasions, as were many of his fellow officers serving with the Indian-fighting army on the lonely western frontier. But he was also acknowledged by his fellow officers to be one of the best company commanders of the regiment. If retaliation or spite was a motive, it was more likely on the part of Custer, who filed his charges against West subsequent to those filed against him.[26]

While Custer and his party were headed east to Fort Harker and ultimately to his disgrace, other events were occurring along the Smoky Hill that would relate to or affect his court-martial. Pvt. Charles Johnson died on July 16 or 17 at Fort Wallace. His death would form the basis for one of the charges made by Captain West. Captain Hamilton and the troopers of Custer's escort remained at Big Creek Station for twenty-four hours to rest the men and horses, then as ordered continued on to Fort Harker and arrived there on July 20. They stayed there for two days, allowing the men good food and rest and feeding, grazing, and rest for the horses. While at Fort Harker twenty more men deserted, probably traveling east along the now little-used part of the Smoky Hill road, supplanted by the railroad east from Harker. The remainder of the detachment, along with Lieutenants Cooke and Custer, returned to Fort Wallace, serving as escort for a slow-moving supply train. Meantime Lieutenant Cox and his men, also escorting a supply train, were inching their way westward, picking up dismounted members of Custer's escort detachment as they went. On July 21 they picked up a man from M Troop at Stormy Hollow Station. and the following day one from Downer Station. They found two men at Castle Rock Station and five at Grannell Springs Station on July 23. All but two of these men had their horses, though most were worn out and unserviceable. Of the seven horses with them, at least five had to be led from the wagons, with only one or two capable of being ridden.[27]

The man wounded by the Indians between Castle Rock and Downer Station was found alive and recovering at Downer but was left there because of his injuries. Captain Carpenter, commanding the infantry company stationed at Fort Downer, reported that after Custer left the station

[26] Frost, *Court-martial*, 86, 89, 91; Millbrook, "West Breaks In General Custer," 147.

[27] Frost, *Court-martial*, 169, 193, 194.

without making any provision to recover the two men presumed dead, he sent out a party of ten soldiers and one wagon to recover them. Moving westward, they found the wounded man first, shot through the leg but not killed. A half mile beyond him they came upon the body of the dead trooper, scalped and stripped of all clothing except his boots. The wounded man told Carpenter that he would probably have died before morning if the party had not arrived to bring him in. Hamilton and Custer's escort detachment, or what was left of it, reached Fort Wallace on August 4 or 5, along with the supply train it had accompanied. With the train were enough horseshoes to reshoe all of the horses of the command. Before the six companies of the Seventh Cavalry left on their next mission on August 12, Major Elliott reported that, of the seventy-six men assigned to Custer's escort, forty-six had returned, two were killed or wounded, six were left behind sick, and twenty had deserted.[28]

The charges made against Custer were sent to General Grant for his review, and on August 27 he ordered a general court-martial to try Custer at Fort Leavenworth on September 17. Fort Leavenworth was selected because it was a large post with better facilities and a larger number of officers available to serve on the court. When it was convened, Custer, acting through his counsel, Capt. Charles C. Parsons, Fourth U.S. Artillery, objected only to Lt. Col. (Bvt. Maj. Gen.) John W. Davidson, now with the new Tenth Cavalry, serving on the court. The objection claimed first that Davidson would be an important witness and, when that was overruled, that he was prejudiced. Davidson himself asked that he be excused so that Custer would be satisfied as to the impartiality of the proceedings. That was done, and the court was sworn. Then Custer was arraigned, and the charges and specifications read to him. To each he entered a plea of not guilty. During the ensuing days, starting on September 17, testimony was elicited from officers, enlisted men, and quartermaster employees who had served with the Seventh Cavalry during the time relevant to the charges, from officers of other units who had witnessed events involved in the charges, and from a stage company employee. Most were first called as witnesses for the prosecution, examined and cross-examined, after which many were recalled as witnesses for the defense. After the last of the witnesses had completed his testimony on October 9, Parsons asked that Custer be given until October 11 to prepare and present his written defense.[29]

[28] Ibid., 135–36, 184, 199; Millbrook, "West Breaks In General Custer," 140, 140n106; Utley, *Life in Custer's Cavalry*, 95.
[29] Frost, *Court-martial*, 86, 92–93, 96–215.

Custer did not take the stand as a witness on his own behalf. Instead he submitted a lengthy unsworn written statement that Parsons read to the court on October 11. By this means Custer avoided having to give testimony under oath and be cross-examined by the prosecution. In essence his statement was a litany of reasons or excuses for his actions, the factual basis for which was undeniable.[30]

When the reading of Custer's written defense was completed, the judge advocate, Capt. (Bvt. Lt. Col.) Robert Chandler, reviewed the written evidence and testimony of witnesses for the court. He carefully pointed out disparities in testimony where they existed, and gave a brief synopsis of the testimony of each important witness and the documentary exhibits for both prosecution and defense. Finally he referred to the tabular statement of deserters admitted into evidence. It showed that, excluding the 20 men who deserted at Fort Harker, 156 men had deserted from the Seventh Cavalry companies under Custer's command between April 18 and July 13, 1867, the time frame beginning with their march north from the Pawnee Fork and ending with their return to Fort Wallace. With that he submitted the matter of Custer's guilt or innocence to the court.[31]

After the close of the proceedings, the court was cleared for deliberations. The members must have been thoroughly convinced by the evidence presented, because that same day, October 11, they returned their verdict. With a few minor modifications as to numbers, names, and government property involved, the verdict was guilty on all charges and specifications. As to the second specification of the first charge, relating to the use of government mules for his conveyance from Fort Hays to Fort Harker on an unauthorized journey for private business, they attached no criminality. Likewise for the third specification of the additional charge, transportation of three wounded deserters for eighteen miles in a government wagon and denying medical attention, the court stripped the language about persistently refusing medical attention, found him guilty of the remaining part, and attached no criminality. The court then sentenced Custer to be suspended from rank and command for one year and to forfeit his pay for that period.[32]

The verdict and sentence were probably as mild as could be expected, considering the nature of the charges and the testimony and findings, but Custer was nevertheless outraged. At the commencement of proceedings,

[30] Ibid., 191, 216–21.
[31] Ibid., 237–45.
[32] Ibid., 245–46.

he had accepted Smith's charges rather calmly. In September Libbie wrote to her cousin, Rebecca Richmond: "Autie made the trip from Fort Wallace on horseback. . . . He took a leave of absence himself, knowing none would be granted him, and Gen'l. Hancock ordered his arrest. . . . When he ran the risk of a court-martial in leaving Wallace he did it expecting the consequences . . . and we are quite determined not to live apart again, even if he leaves the army otherwise so delightful to us." Later, at the conclusion of the trial, she wrote Rebecca on October 13 that "the trial had developed into nothing but a plan of persecution for Autie." During the course of preparing and presenting his defense Custer had clearly convinced himself and his devoted wife of the propriety of all of his actions. But they still held hope that a review of the proceedings would overturn the verdict. On October 14, 1867, a complete transcript of the proceedings was transmitted to the adjutant general in Washington. Custer's hopes were dashed when Gen. Joseph Holt sustained the verdict. As to Smith's charges, he observed that Custer's anxiety to see his wife at Fort Riley overcame "his appreciation of the paramount necessity to obey orders" and that "the excuses he offers for his acts of insubordination are afterthoughts." The sentence pronounced he found "in no sense too severe," especially in view of the finding under the fourth specification of Smith's second charge of his failure to verify the wounding or death of two men from his escort detachment, "though he was officially informed at the time or within less than an hour after." The army was less enthusiastic about the charges made by Captain West, and General Holt reviewed the matter at length. He considered the statistics of desertion from Custer's command and whether that loss placed it in danger of attack by the Indian foe, thereby justifying Custer's action by "an imperative necessity." If it had been an "unwarranted exercise of lawless power," he felt the sentence to be utterly inadequate and that Custer should be immediately tried by a court of competent jurisdiction. He evidently could not go that far, and in the end he upheld the entire verdict and sentence. He remarked, according to Assistant Adjutant General E. D. Townsend, that "the Court, in awarding so lenient a sentence for the offenses of which the accused is found guilty, must have taken into consideration his previous record." From there the matter went to Gen. U. S. Grant for his review. On November 18 General Sherman issued his statement that "the proceedings, finding and sentence in the case of Brevet Major General Custer are approved by General Grant—in which the levity of the sentence, considering the nature of the offenses of Bvt. Major General Custer, if found guilty, is to be remarked on."[33]

Custer was infuriated by the outcome of his trial. Following the initial filing of charges against him and continuing throughout the proceedings, he had undertaken a campaign intended to cast the blame for his own mistakes, misdeeds, and failures on department commander Winfield Scott Hancock, the members of the court, staff officers of the commissary department, Captain West, and others. Commencing on September 9, 1867, he wrote a series of five articles in the form of letters written to the New York publisher of the sportsmen's magazine *Turf, Field, and Farm*, the last being dated December 15, 1867. Weaving game hunting on the plains into the action for the benefit of the sportsmen readers, the installments primarily related Custer's version of the operations of the Hancock expedition from Fort Larned through arrival of the Seventh Cavalry at Fort Hays. In a number of cases they distorted both facts and the timeline. The substance of his articles was to make Custer, thinly veiled as "Nomad," a heroic and capable figure while pointing out the many mistakes of General Hancock in conducting his campaign and causing an Indian war. At the time he blamed Hancock for filing charges against him. Following approval of the verdict, he also wrote a long, rambling letter to the *Sandusky (Ohio) Daily Register* on December 21, 1867, wherein he not only complained of the facts printed in other newspapers reporting on the court-martial but also set forth what he contended were the true facts. There he blamed his conviction on the composition of the court, which included officers of rank inferior to his own (although he had not objected to their being seated at the time), and further that several were members of General Hancock's staff and thus prejudiced against him. He also mentioned one as a member of a commissary who had been censured by him for "corruption in issuing rations." These issues had not been raised before the court was impaneled and sworn or during the proceedings. Custer sent copies of his letter to several other newspapers with wide circulation in New York and elsewhere, engendering a battle of editorials as to his guilt or innocence—none of which served to diminish or commute his sentence.[34]

One might have thought the matter at an end with the venting of Custer's spleen, but it was not to be. Captain West, apparently appalled

---

[33] Ibid., 247; Merington, *Custer Story*, 212–13; Millbrook, "West Breaks In General Custer," 145–47.

[34] Frost, *Court-martial*, 257–60; Millbrook, "West Breaks In General Custer," 146–47; Utley, *Life in Custer's Cavalry*, 54.

at the leniency of Custer's sentence, filed murder charges against Custer and Lieutenant Cooke, the man who had actually fired the shot that resulted in the death of Private Johnson, in a trial court in Leavenworth, Kansas. Warrants for their arrest were issued on January 3, 1868, and the trial began on January 8. Testimony was taken from Captain West, Lieutenant Jackson, Pvt. Clement Willis (one of the deserters from Company K), and Lt. Myles Moylan. The first two officers restated facts already known, and Moylan added only that he did not believe that Custer had denied the wounded men proper medical attention. The most interesting testimony was that of Johnson's fellow deserter, Clement Willis, who said that he was no more than ten steps from Johnson when he saw Cooke shoot him with a revolver. They were in a ravine, he said, when commanded to halt and give up their arms. According to Willis, they complied, then were told to leave. They began to run when the three officers opened fire on them. Johnson was hit in the arm and fell to his knees, begging not to be killed. Lieutenant Cooke then shot him in the head, and after that Johnson asked him to kill him—to finish him off. Willis said that afterward he visited Johnson each day until he died on July 16. Willis's testimony conflicted with that of all other witnesses and was obviously not believed. On January 18 the court discharged both defendants because, the judge said, the charge was not sustained by the evidence.[35]

The court-martial, the findings of guilt, and his sentence never ceased to gall Custer, and with the passage of time he felt increasingly wronged and ever more certain of the propriety of his actions. By the time he wrote his autobiographical *My Life on the Plains*, he had managed to rearrange facts and circumstances to fully exonerate himself—at least in his own mind. To convey his righteous reasons for making the forced march from Fort Wallace to Fort Harker, he rewrote history: Indians were so active that travel on the Smoky Hill route had totally ceased, stages had been taken off the route, and many stage stations abandoned by the employees; no dispatches or mail had been received at Fort Wallace for a considerable time, and the fort was all but under siege. Moreover, the reserve of stores at the post were nearly exhausted and the commander knew of no new supplies being on the way; the bulk of what provisions they did have consisted of rotten bacon and hard bread; and, worst of all, cholera made its appearance and deaths were occurring daily. For this reason, Custer claimed, he selected upward of a hundred men from his command to force

[35] Frost, *Court-martial*, 261–63.

open a way through to Fort Harker, from which point abundant supplies could be escorted back to Fort Wallace under the protection of his men. But none of this was true. The post had an ample supply of rations to last until August 15, according to Captain Keogh, the post commander, and it hadn't been under siege since June. Cholera didn't arrive at Fort Wallace and the Seventh Cavalry companies there until July 22, the day after Custer returned to Fort Harker from Fort Riley with Libbie. Large quantities of supplies were already en route to the post and were passed by Custer and his men. Mail coaches were arriving every week, and Custer passed two of these on his march eastward. The Indians had long since refocused their raiding on railroad construction crews between Forts Harker and Hays. Custer dealt with other charges against him in a like fashion, omitting all reference to his orders to shoot deserters and bring back none alive. Regarding the attack on the detachment sent for his mare, he stated: "Here [near Downer's Station], while stopping to rest our horses for a few minutes, a small party of our men, who had without authority halted some distance behind, came dashing into our midst and reported that twenty-five or thirty Indians had attacked them some five or six miles in rear, and had killed two of their number." Even following his death at Little Big Horn, Custer's widow, Libbie, continued to remold the history of his 1867 campaign in an effort to exonerate him of the charges of which he was convicted.[36]

So ended the last vestige of Hancock's vaunted Expedition for the Plains— not with the Cheyennes and other southern Plains tribes in awe of the army and submissive, but with Custer in disgrace, the army largely ineffective in fighting the Indians, and a full-blown war now raging. Custer's six companies of the Seventh Cavalry from his recent scout were in camp at Fort Wallace, crippled by loss of men through desertion, broken-down horses, and low morale. The Dog Soldier and southern Sutaio Cheyennes, angry and frustrated as their world and their country narrowed before the whites' inexorable advance, fought back with ferocity, hitting railroad construction crews and small army units. For them it was a desperate and frightening time, as they saw their culture and their way of life slipping away from them and the land given to Maheo's people by their Creator being seized by alien invaders who had come from across the Great Waters. It was cataclysmic, an Armageddon for the Tsistsistas. But it had not yet run its course.

---

[36] E. Custer, *Tenting on the Plains*, 695–702; G. Custer, *My Life on the Plains*, 183–87, 203–205, 211; Millbrook, "West Breaks In General Custer," 135, 137.

CHAPTER TWENTY-SIX

A SUMMER OF WAR

Even as Custer was marching north from Fort Hays toward the Platte, attacks were continuing along the Smoky Hill. Gradually they moved eastward, striking stations along the stage line, but more and more focused on the crews constructing the roadbed and tracks of the Union Pacific, E.D. Except for the raid on Colonel Greenwood's survey party on May 18, the Cheyennes had taken no significant action against the railroad, though they had made it apparent that they did not want it in their country and had refused all requests for consent. But the construction made it clear that the whites would build it with or without Cheyenne approval. Behind the surveyors, whose passage was marked only by curious stakes or other markers on the earth, came grading crews with draft animals pulling plows or blades. They tore into the grasses, piling up mounds of dirt and forming a long embankment, flat on the top, that snaked its way from one horizon to the next and impeded the passage of migrating villages, hunting parties, war parties, and the bison and other game animals the Indians depended on. Though they had only a dim understanding of railroads and the part they played in the life of white people, there were two things about them the Indians knew well from observations at the eastern and northern flanks of their country. Steam engines and the cars they pulled frightened and drove away the game from their vicinity, and, worse, they brought more whites to the lands of the People. Many whites traveled beyond, but some stayed and built towns, bringing with them strange animals and terrible diseases for which the Indian peoples had no natural immunity. They established farms and slaughtered the great herds of bison. If the railroads were permitted, in a short time the Indian way of life would be destroyed, and whites would have taken from them all that they held most dear and sacred. It could not be allowed.

The first major attack on the grading crews occurred on June 18, 1867. Robert M. Shoemaker, general superintendent of the Union Pacific, E.D., telegrammed Kansas governor Samuel J. Crawford on June 21 to report that Thomas Parks, one of the principal contractors, and three other men were killed during the attack. General Smith had said that he was giving the railroad workers all the protection he could without more troops, so Shoemaker was asking the governor to provide a regiment of infantry militia "at once." Crawford then wired Secretary of War Edwin Stanton for two thousand stands of cavalry arms and ammunition. On June 24 the governor received another telegram, this one from John D. Perry, president of the railroad. Perry reported that three more men had been killed on June 22 within twenty miles of Fort Harker and that one thousand or more construction workers had been driven in. These were isolated attacks on small parties of men and the claim that a thousand or more workers were driven in is doubtless a gross exaggeration. Nevertheless the news of even a few deaths at the hands of the Indians probably did create great unease and apprehension among the workforce, and that had to be dealt with. Predictably Governor Crawford again bombarded federal officials with demands for action. In a June 24 letter to Stanton he claimed that the line of the railroad west of Fort Harker, the great trails across the plains, and the frontier settlements would all have to be abandoned if "prompt and decisive measures" were not adopted. In a renewal of his earlier demands he offered to raise a sufficient force (at federal expense) to put an end to "frontier depredations."[1]

Secretary Stanton responded quickly to Governor Crawford but ignored his offer to raise volunteer troops. Instead he referred Crawford to General Sherman, who had immediate charge of all military operations against the Indians and the authority to issue supplies, arms, and ammunition. Meanwhile, also on June 24, Robert Shoemaker telegraphed the governor, reporting that on June 22 Colonel Greenwood's survey party had again been attacked west of Monument Station. Later the same day Shoemaker sent a second telegram, this time reporting that two more men were killed near Bunker Hill Station and all workmen were driven off the line. He requested arms and ammunition, failing which their work must be abandoned. Upon receipt of the last message, Crawford telegraphed the commanding officer of Fort Leavenworth on June 24 and asked him

---

[1] Crawford, *Kansas in the Sixties*, 255; Garfield, "Defense of the Kansas Frontier," 331; Snell and Richmond, *Union and Kansas Pacific*, 339–40.

to issue ten thousand rounds of ammunition. He claimed that the Indian attacks had driven back all railroad workers west of Fort Harker. The request was apparently declined, because two days later Crawford telegraphed Stanton, asking him to direct the commanding officer at Fort Leavenworth to turn the arms and ammunition over to the state. This must have worked, for that same day General Hancock directed the commander of the arsenal at Fort Leavenworth to issue ten thousand rounds of .58-caliber cartridges to the State of Kansas. Guns in the possession of the state militia were then called in and one thousand stands packed for immediate shipment for the defense of railroad workers. Soon both arms and ammunition were on their way west, and four wagonloads passed through Junction City on June 25, bound for the employees of Shoemaker, Miller and Company.[2]

Shoemaker was not satisfied. On June 28 he again wired the governor, transmitting a dispatch he had just received, telling that one man had been killed and another badly wounded during an Indian attack on the railroad's construction camp at Wilson's Creek, eighteen miles west of Fort Harker, on the morning of June 27. Shoemaker said that unless his workers received prompt protection, they would all be driven off the road and the white settlers driven out of the country. Later, on July 5, he telegraphed the governor from the end of track to say that he wanted a company of infantry to guard the workers and one of cavalry to patrol the surrounding country. He demanded to know how soon they could be supplied. Shoemaker's many reports, requests, and demands and Crawford's reactions and subsequent actions reflect what must surely have been histrionics to secure complete removal of the Indians. The railroads wanted the Indians gone from the right-of-way, to encourage settlement and profitable commerce. The governor likewise had an agenda that did not include Indians residing in the state, even on reservations. He wanted all of the land for whites. Both railroad workers and settlers were nervous, but the relatively isolated hit-and-run attacks on small parties did not constitute a broad assault on the frontier. Following a visit to Fort Harker to check out conditions for himself, General Sherman wrote to Governor Crawford on July 8, telling him that there were causes other than Indians to explain why the stagecoaches had stopped running and railroad construction was behind schedule. The early June flooding on the Smoky Hill had

---

[2] Crawford, *Kansas in the Sixties*, 256; Garfield, "Defense of the Kansas Frontier," 331–32; Snell and Richmond, *Union and Kansas Pacific*, 340–41.

delayed construction, he said, and the stages stopped "for want of connection and because it was not profitable." He asserted that all posts and the intermediate stations to Denver were safe, wagon trains with light escort were moving, and even single carriers were running from post to post. Sherman also remarked that General Smith had offered sufficient guard for the stage runs, but the stagecoaches still would not go and appeared to be using the state of alarm "to avoid service and claim compensation and damages." He asked Crawford to help calm unnecessary alarm.[3]

Governor Crawford had no intention of calming the situation. On the contrary he did all he could to inflame it. His offer to raise state volunteer troops, something Sherman stoutly opposed, was ultimately referred to Sherman by the secretary of war. Reacting as he had with Governor Hunt of Colorado, Sherman wired Crawford on June 26, accepting a battalion of mounted volunteers, provided that General Smith deemed them necessary. The battalion must consist of six to eight companies to be enrolled for service of not more than four months. On June 27 Smith telegraphed his consent to the governor but withdrew it the following morning because Sherman had changed his mind. This reversal apparently resulted from Sherman's conviction that western governors were not to be trusted. He believed that each wanted the entire army to protect his state's interests and that state volunteers would likely perpetrate massacres on any Indians they found, further inflaming the situation. But Crawford was persistent and immediately sent a telegram to Sherman, stating that reversal of the request for volunteers left frontier settlers, railroad workers, and all others in the western half of the state exposed and "liable to be murdered and scalped at any moment." He told Sherman that he could not move against the Indians with militia but would provide a volunteer force to deal with the situation if Sherman would but call for them. Sherman finally yielded and on July 1 telegraphed Crawford, consenting to the call-up of six to eight companies of volunteers. They were to be at the end of track the following Saturday, and Sherman said he would be there in person.[4]

Crawford lost no time in issuing a proclamation calling for volunteers, probably fearing that Sherman might change his mind again. Dated July 1, 1867, it recited that "Central and Western Kansas has been, and still is, overrun and invaded by bands of hostile Indians, who are indiscriminately

[3] Crawford, *Kansas in the Sixties*, 257; Snell and Richmond, *Union and Kansas Pacific*, 340–41.
[4] Crawford, *Kansas in the Sixties*, 257–58; Garfield, "Defense of the Kansas Frontier," 332; Snell and Richmond, *Union and Kansas Pacific*, 340.

murdering, scalping and mutilating our frontier settlers—travelers on the great western thoroughfares, and the employees on the U.P.R.W., E.D." This was nonsense. The Indians were not invading—they had lived there long before the whites moved in. The truth was that it was the white frontier that was advancing into the Indian country, invading and overrunning the Indian lands. The "great western thoroughfares" and the railroads were crossing the Indian hunting grounds, while the travelers along them were slaughtering their game, felling the meager stands of trees along streams, and disrupting their way of life. It was Crawford's intention to use his volunteers to force the Indians out of the state and onto reservations elsewhere, then settle their country with a new white population. It was this desire that brought the Eighteenth Kansas Volunteer Cavalry into existence.[5]

Organization of the Eighteenth Kansas was not without difficulty. Equipment was not a problem, for General Smith was able to report to Governor Crawford by July 5 that arms and accoutrements had been sent from Fort Leavenworth to Fort Harker for the new regiment and that quartermaster and commissary stores were then arriving. But the authorization was for six to eight companies, with each volunteer to furnish his own horse. Recruiting officers could find enough men, but many were without horses. As Governor Hunt of Colorado did before him, Crawford asked General Sherman if the federal government would provide horses for those who lacked them, and Sherman refused. Crawford then asked if he would accept part of the men unmounted, and Sherman again refused. Infantry were useless in the pursuit of mounted Indians. Crawford finally solved the problem by having the state stand security for notes signed by volunteers for the purchase of their horses, then sending their pay to the creditor until the note was paid. Even by this means, however, only four companies of cavalry could be raised. The Eighteenth Kansas Volunteer Cavalry, consisting of four companies with 358 officers and enlisted men, was mustered into federal service at Fort Harker on July 15, 1867, to serve for four months. During its brief existence the regiment did credible service.[6]

Unfortunately for the Eighteenth Kansas, its members arrived at Fort Harker while cholera was raging at the fort and in nearby Ellsworth. It was said that as many as two hundred soldiers, laborers, and civilians died at

[5] Crawford, *Kansas in the Sixties*, 258–59; Garfield, "Defense of the Kansas Frontier," 332; Snell and Richmond, *Union and Kansas Pacific*, 340–41.

[6] Burgess, "Eighteenth Kansas Volunteer Cavalry," 534–38; Crawford, *Kansas in the Sixties*, 259–60; Garfield, "Defense of the Kansas Frontier," 338–39; Jenness, "Battle of Beaver Creek," 443–44.

the Fort Harker hospital or in the fort's adjacent camps, and another fifty people at Ellsworth. The little town, which had grown to about one thousand people, saw its population drop temporarily to forty as frightened citizens fled to safer climes to avoid infection. The epidemic lasted about three weeks, and during that time every company of the Eighteenth Cavalry lost men to the disease, and more by desertion as panic set in. Company C alone lost thirteen men to cholera and seven by desertion. As a result Maj. Horace L. Moore, commanding the regiment, decided to move away from Fort Harker and take the field as soon as possible. The troops left the post sometime before July 19 and marched southwest to Forts Zarah and Larned. During the evening of the second day of their march, five more men died of cholera and another thirty-six were stricken. On arrival at Fort Larned the sick were placed in the post hospital while the rest of the regiment moved on, turning west and marching up the Pawnee Fork and its north branch. On their second night out from Fort Larned they lost a sergeant to cholera, their last fatality from the disease. They proceeded to scout the country between the Pawnee Fork and Walnut Creek, passing the charred remains of the Cheyenne and Oglala villages destroyed by General Hancock as they did. Farther west they came upon the half-eaten remains of a herd of 250 beef cattle that the Indians had stampeded away from Fort Dodge. The regiment then turned due south, striking the Arkansas River about twenty-five miles west of Fort Dodge and moving east along the river to that post. They remained there only a short time before being ordered north to Fort Hays, where they arrived on August 12.[7]

On July 10, five days before the Eighteenth Kansas Volunteer Cavalry was mustered at Fort Harker and George Custer began his impetuous dash eastward on the Smoky Hill road, General Sherman telegraphed Governor Crawford that a company of cavalry and one of infantry had been assigned to protect the railroad construction crews. The companies referred to were from the Tenth Cavalry and the Thirty-Eighth Infantry, two of the newly formed black regiments. They had just been recruited and were shipped west without having been trained. The cavalry company assigned to Fort Harker, Company F, arrived on June 29 from Fort Leavenworth. So rapidly was this done that the men had not yet been mustered into the service, aptly demonstrating the sense of urgency felt

---

[7] *Kansas Daily Tribune*, 67; Burgess, "Eighteenth Kansas Volunteer Cavalry," 535–36; Garfield, "Defense of the Kansas Frontier," 339; Jenness, "Battle of Beaver Creek," 435–36; Lee and Raynesford, *Trails of the Smoky Hill*, 160; Millbrook, "West Breaks In General Custer," 131; Prowers and Younger, "Cholera on the Plains," 351–93; White, *Hostiles and Horse Soldiers*, 50.

at division and departmental headquarters. Assigned as its first commander was George A. Armes, only a year earlier a newly commissioned second lieutenant reporting for his first assignment at Fort Wallace. It was Armes whom Lyman Kidder had replaced as a second lieutenant with Company M, Second Cavalry, at Fort Sedgwick. Now, having applied for and receiving appointment to the new Tenth Cavalry, Armes was a captain and company commander. On June 29 he put his recruits into a tent camp near the fort that he called Camp Grierson in honor of the regiment's commanding officer, Col. (Bvt. Maj. Gen.) Benjamin F. Grierson. He mustered in his men on June 30 and the next day ordered them out on a scout, looking for Indians seen near Fort Harker. They found only the tracks of unshod horses. But the scouting, which would be their main occupation during July, did give the men a form of on-the-job training, teaching them to ride and providing a sense of discipline and at least some familiarity with the difficulties of soldiering on the vast, treeless plains. They had little training with their weapons, other than oral instructions, since it was at least another twenty years before the army instituted a program of regular practice on a rifle range.[8]

   Armes and his company arrived at Fort Harker on June 29, the day after the first appearance of cholera. The disease had come with several companies of the Thirty-eighth Infantry, marching from Jefferson Barracks near St. Louis to New Mexico under command of Maj. H. C. Merriam. It was confined for several days to troops camping around the post, then finally spread to the garrison and Ellsworth. On the morning of July 3 Captain Armes and F Company were ordered to relieve a railroad construction camp under attack by the Cheyennes several miles west of Fort Harker. His younger brother, William Edward Armes, was visiting him at the time while on a brief vacation before reporting to West Point as a new cadet. Captain Armes left his brother in charge of their camp and the guard detail. When he and his men returned the next day, he was told that his brother had been stricken with cholera shortly after the column left camp in the morning and died that afternoon. Armes was devastated, for he and his brother were very close. After that, cholera began to strike others in the company. In 1867 there was little knowledge of the disease or its causes, and no cure. Men apparently healthy and vigorous at sunup might be dead by sundown. Understandably panic accompanied its appear-

[8] Armes, *Ups and Downs*, 231; Garfield, "Defense of the Kansas Frontier," 335; Nye, *Plains Indian Raiders*, 48, 95–96.

ance, compounding the difficulties faced by military units trying to patrol and protect the frontier and the advancing railroad.[9]

Company F, Tenth Cavalry, was ordered to new Fort Hays on July 21 and arrived there on July 25. At the time, the fort was in the process of construction following its removal from the forks of Big Creek, and nearly all troops, including the garrison, were living in tents. Cholera struck there near the end of the month, and almost every company had two or three deaths each day. Armes moved his men to higher ground in an attempt to avoid the illness. This may have helped somewhat, keeping them away from the more contaminated ground where troops had been living since the move. The Indians were possibly aware of the presence of the disease, which had afflicted them greatly in the past, for they neither raided near the post nor came in for trading or visits so long as it raged. Attacks on railroad construction camps and elsewhere continued, however. While most were small hit-and-run raids intended to run off livestock at the stage stations and construction camps, two of them during this time were of considerable interest to the general public.[10]

The first of these attacks involved the trading caravan of Capt. Francisco Baca, consisting of eighty wagons and ninety armed men, accompanied by the party of Jean Baptiste Lamy, the first bishop of Santa Fe, including ten priests and six nuns. The caravan was returning to Santa Fe after its trading expedition to Missouri and was following the Wet Route of the Santa Fe Trail, intending to travel the Cimarron Route to New Mexico. Curiously, the July 19, 1867, issue of the *New York Herald* reported the capture of the train, the killing of Bishop Lamy and all of the men, and the abduction of the nuns. The story was based on a dispatch of suspect origins from Leavenworth, Kansas. Vivid details of the scalping and mutilation of the men were related, as well as the deplorable fate alleged to have befallen the nuns. None of this was true. An attack did take place at the Cimarron Crossing of the Arkansas three days later, on July 22, at a little after 2:00 in the afternoon of a very hot dry day. It involved a large war party of Cheyennes, including, as was believed, Charlie Bent, the half-blood son of William Bent. This is the same Charlie Bent identified as being present at the fight near Fort Wallace on the Smoky Hill the previous day by those who professed to know him well. The men of the car-

---

[9] Armes, *Ups and Downs*, 231–33; Millbrook, "West Breaks In General Custer," 131; Nye, *Plains Indian Raiders*, 96–98; Prowers and Younger, "Cholera on the Plains," 351–93.

[10] Armes, *Ups and Downs*, 235; Nye, *Plains Indian Raiders*, 98–99; Prowers and Younger, "Cholera on the Plains," 351–93.

avan refused to be drawn away from the wagons, and though the combat continued on and off for about seven hours, the Indians finally left and disappeared into the vastness of the Cimarron desert. No one was injured or killed in the Baca-Lamy parties, and the only casualties they suffered during the trip were ten deaths from cholera, including an eighteen-year-old nun. When word of the false report first reached General Sherman, he wrote a letter of rebuke to the *St. Louis Republican*, which had carried the same story as had the *New York Herald*. He denied the account and admonished journalists against publishing unfounded rumors and unverified reports. Gen. U. S. Grant likewise issued a statement condemning the report and the "wretches who manufacture lying dispatches" in order to inflame public opinion against the Indians, promote a war of extermination, and secure the opening of all western lands to white settlers and speculators.[11]

The second of the more interesting attacks was most unusual. With the coming of the railroad the small settlement of Brookville had been established about fifteen miles west of Salina and twenty miles east of Fort Harker as the interim site of a roundhouse and turntable where engines of the Union Pacific, E.D., could be serviced and repaired. Sometime during the midsummer the Indians, having observed that the iron horse made its journeys to and from that place, decided to destroy the roundhouse and all of the engines in it as a means of keeping them out of their country. The crew of an eastbound train from Fort Harker spotted the approaching war party and warned the workers at the roundhouse as they passed through Brookville. The alarm was given, and the small population, mostly railroad workers and their families, gathered in the roundhouse among the engines, barricading the doors. When the Cheyennes arrived, they began stacking ties against the structure for use in setting it on fire. One of the engines had been under steam outside when word of the danger was received, and it was backed into the roundhouse for protection. There it sat still under steam, facing outward toward Salina. When those inside realized that the Indians intended to burn the building, they decided to run the engine out of the roundhouse and on down the track to summon help. The fireman stoked the boiler, and then the engineer gave it full throttle. The engine burst suddenly through the door, whistle blasting, and headed east to Salina. Its sudden, dramatic appearance,

---

[11] Burkey, *Custer, Come at Once*, 35; Garfield, "Defense of the Kansas Frontier," 337–38; Horgan, *Lamy of Santa Fe*, 340–49.

totally unexpected by the warriors, so unnerved them that they scattered, ran to their horses, and galloped off to the surrounding Smoky Hills.[12]

In late July the Cheyennes made night raids against the infantry soldiers at stage stations on the Smoky Hill route west of Fort Hays, but with little success. Then, early on the afternoon of August 1, twenty-five to thirty warriors attacked a work party from the camp of Campbell and Clinton, contractors preparing the roadbed for the laying of ties and rails. There were seven men in the party working just west of where the railroad would cross the north fork of Big Creek. They had either left their weapons at their camp or laid them beyond easy reach. Six of the men were killed outright, and the seventh was mortally wounded. At least two of the seven were scalped. The warriors then moved farther east, where another construction crew was at work. But when the Indians were close enough to see that these men were well armed, probably alerted by the sounds of the attack to their west, they turned away. While the earlier raid on the railroad workers was occurring, another party of Cheyennes attacked the Big Creek stage station southeast of new Fort Hays. Return fire from the crew and a guard detachment from the Thirty-eighth Infantry killed one attacker and wounded another. The Cheyennes still managed to run off thirty horses and mules and mortally wounded one of the soldiers. Word of the attacks reached new Fort Hays at 2:00 in the afternoon, likely sent by workers at the construction camp and a courier from the stage station. Capt. Henry C. Corbin of the Thirty-eighth Infantry, temporarily commanding, acted promptly, sending Capt. George A. Armes and his F Company of the Tenth Cavalry to the railroad camp of Campbell and Clinton, while he personally led a part of his infantry garrison to Big Creek Station. There Corbin and his mounted infantrymen picked up the trail of the attackers and followed it northward toward the Saline River. But when darkness fell and they lost the trail, Corbin took his men back to Fort Hays, knowing that it would be futile to pursue mounted raiders in the dark.[13]

While Captain Corbin was moving south, George Armes was marching his forty-four men (two officers, including himself, two white scouts, and forty enlisted men) eastward thirteen miles to the site of the attack on the railroad construction workers near the Campbell and Clinton camp on the Big Creek's north fork. When they reached it, they found the six dead men along with the wounded man, William Gould, who died later at the

[12] Lee and Raynesford, *Trails of the Smoky Hill*, 162–63.
[13] Armes, *Ups and Downs*, 236–37; Burkey, *Custer, Come at Once*, 35; Nye, *Plains Indian Raiders*, 99; White, *Hostiles and Horse Soldiers*, 50–51.

Fort Hays hospital. The six dead were buried near where they were found, just south of the railroad roadbed. Armes was told that the raiders had gone up the north fork of Big Creek, and the detachment then followed their trail north. They traveled outbound an estimated eighteen miles but, because of darkness, lost the trail and returned to Campbell and Clinton's camp, reaching it a little after midnight. From there Armes sent six of his men back to new Fort Hays with instructions to bring an additional thirty men and a howitzer. The railroad workers had previously told him there were more Indians than his small company could deal with, and during his march Armes noticed that the Indian trail had broadened. This may have resulted from the first raiding party joining with those from Big Creek Station and their stolen livestock. Armes and the rest of his men remained the night at the camp, awaiting return of the six others with the requested reinforcements.[14]

After waiting for about four hours, Armes evidently concluded that reinforcements were not coming, so at first light he led his men northward once again, this time marching to the Saline River. There were now only thirty-four men, including officers and scouts, as four had been stricken with cholera during the night and had to be left behind. The detachment reached the Saline, due north of the camp, at 8:00 A.M. after a march of about fifteen miles, then turned west along that stream. From there they moved west approximately twelve miles. The valley of the Saline had been cut deep into the plains through millennia, exposing thick limestone bluffs of the Niobrara Chalk Formation that formed the valley walls, pierced at intervals by many dry arroyos and small canyons leading down into the valley from the High Plains above. These provided perfect places of concealment for Indians, and for generations the valley had been a favored camping place for the Cheyennes and Arapahoes. As George Armes and his scouts led his men along the river, at about 9:00 A.M. they were suddenly attacked by a war party riding from one of the side canyons. He estimated that there were about seventy-five warriors, but the number was more likely from thirty to fifty, the size of most such raiding or war parties. After the initial surprise at their unexpected appearance, Armes ordered his troopers to dismount and form a hollow square with the led horses in the center. Some of his men had developed cholera during the morning's ride, and these he assigned to lead the horses. He knew that his

---

[14] Armes, *Ups and Downs*, 236–37; Burkey, *Custer, Come at Once*, 35; Nye, *Plains Indian Raiders*, 99; White, *Hostiles and Horse Soldiers*, 50–51.

inexperienced troopers, without practice in the use of their weapons, would shoot inaccurately while mounted, and only marginally well at a walk.[15]

At first Armes and his company did not retreat. He apparently thought his small force sufficiently strong to keep the circling Indians at bay. Within ten minutes the warriors had completely surrounded the dismounted cavalrymen but remained at a respectful distance—unsure of the marksmanship of their foe. Armes kept his men moving slowly forward at a walk. He hoped to find the camp of the raiding party and recover the livestock run off from Big Creek Station. In the process he might also exact retribution for the killing of the seven railroad workers and the soldier at Big Creek. But as he and his men moved west through the Saline valley, small parties of Cheyennes were building fires up on the bluffs, sending smoke signals to summon nearby bands of raiders or hunters. Soon more mounted warriors appeared, filing along the bluffs and moving down into the valley through the canyons and arroyos. Armes, who from a distance initially thought them to be a herd of buffalo, would later estimate there were 350 to 400 mounted Indians. Clearly that is far more than could have been there, given the number of warriors in the Dog Soldier and southern Sutaio bands, and the fact that the Kiyuksa Oglalas were then well to the northwest on the Republican.[16]

The appearance of additional warriors caused Captain Armes to change his mind about moving farther west or north. Assuming the accuracy of his estimate that they had traveled west twelve miles from the point they intersected the Saline (he had no odometer or other means of measuring distance), Armes and his men were probably approaching the confluence of what he thought was the north fork of the Saline (present Sand Creek) and the south, or main, fork of the stream when they first encountered the Indians. They were moving on foot and could not have gotten far before the Indian reinforcements arrived half an hour later. Then they retreated south in a more or less direct line toward new Fort Hays. The country they traversed was very hilly and broken, making their movement all the more difficult, considering the continuing combat. The warriors circled the slow-moving soldiers as they crossed level or open areas and, when in the rougher country, fired their weapons from behind the protective concealment of rocks, arroyos, ravines, or any other form of cover.

---

[15] Armes, *Ups and Downs*, 236–40; Burkey, *Custer, Come at Once*, 35; Hyde, *Life of George Bent*, 272; Nye, *Plains Indian Raiders*, 100; White, *Hostiles and Horse Soldiers*, 51–52.

[16] Armes, *Ups and Downs*, 236–40; Burkey, *Custer, Come at Once*, 35; Nye, *Plains Indian Raiders*, 100; White, *Hostiles and Horse Soldiers*, 52.

The nervous troopers, experiencing their first combat, were shooting rap-idly and randomly without much effect except to keep the Indians at a distance. From time to time two or more of the bolder warriors would come together and gallop in a circle entirely around the cavalry troopers and occasionally would dash right through their square. Though Armes reported six warriors killed and a number wounded during the fight, the Indians said later that there were no deaths on their side, and minimal casualties on either side that they knew of.[17]

During the course of their retreat Armes was shot in the hip. When his men saw the blood beginning to stain the leg of his uniform, a number of them became unnerved and panicked, firing away all of their ammu-nition aimlessly and then taking refuge in the center of the hollow square. Armes was concerned the Indians would conclude that the soldiers were running out of ammunition and increase the intensity of their attack. To avoid this Armes, 2nd Lt. John A. Bodamer, and the two guides per-suaded the troopers to return to their place in the square, making it appear that they were still able to return fire. They also instructed the other men to hold their fire to a minimum to avoid unnecessary waste of ammuni-tion. Soon the soldiers settled down, and their slow march continued. Meantime Armes was unable to walk or stand and had to be lifted on his horse, although even sitting his saddle was extremely painful. So they con-tinued moving southward, constantly eying their foe and firing at those who came too close to keep them at bay. During the course of the fight six more men came down with cholera and had to be strapped to their saddles in agony in order to be taken back. When they cleared the rougher country around the Saline, probably about halfway back to Fort Hays, the Indians broke off the engagement and disappeared northward into the hills. The troopers were then able to remount their horses and continue their retreat at a faster pace. What would be known as the Battle of the Saline had ended, having lasted about six hours.[18]

During the fight on the Saline, Armes lost one man, Sgt. William Christy, killed in the line of duty, along with two horses killed and three wounded. Only one man, Armes, was wounded. He later reported that the attackers included two white men or half-bloods and that they were led by the Kiowa chief Satanta (Set-tainte). Armes knew little of the Plains

[17] Armes, *Ups and Downs*, 236–40; Burkey, *Custer, Come at Once*, 35; Nye, *Plains Indian Raiders*, 100; White, *Hostiles and Horse Soldiers*, 52.
[18] Armes, *Ups and Downs*, 236–40; Burkey, *Custer, Come at Once*, 35; Nye *Plains Indian Raiders*, 100–101; White, *Hostiles and Horse Soldiers*, 52.

Indians, so this information must have come from the white scouts, Becker
and Brink, who apparently knew little of the Indians either. The Saline
was not in Kiowa country, and the Kiowas were at the time well below
the Arkansas. Moreover they were then engaged in a major raid against
the Navajos, and most of the important chiefs rode with that war party.
Had Satanta been at the fight on the Saline, he would have been easily
recognized by those who knew him, for his customary paint and dress for
battle was crimson, with his shield and horse similarly painted. The identity of the white men or half-bloods (doubtless the latter) with the
Cheyenne raiding party is unknown, though in the succeeding fight on
Prairie Dog Creek, Charlie Bent was said to be among them. A little more
than a week before the fight on the Saline he was reported both on the
Arkansas and in the fight at Fort Wallace, but his alleged appearance at
such disparate locations within a short time frame makes it probable that
he was constantly being misidentified by people who did not know him
(though claiming to), just as were Roman Nose and Satanta.[19]

Armes reported that the Indians were armed with the "improved" version of the Spencer repeating carbine, plus rifles, pistols, and bows and
arrows. However, the warrior Porcupine, a member of Turkey Leg's band
of Óhméséheso Cheyennes, in telling the story of the August 6, 1867,
derailment of a handcar near Plum Creek Station on the Union Pacific
Railroad, stated that the two Spencer carbines found with the handcar
were the first breechloaders they had ever seen. A number of these weapons
were captured from Lieutenant Kidder and his men when they were wiped
out on Beaver Creek, but these likely remained in the hands of the Oglalas.
The Cheyennes thought the new carbines were defective because they
broke open in the middle. If Armes was unable to properly identify the
Indians, their leaders, or their weapons, his judgment in leading his small
force into danger on the Saline seems equally faulty, probably because of
his youth and inexperience. When there were forty-four in his detachment, he was told they were far too few to take on a large war party. Yet
after sending six men back to Fort Hays for reinforcements and losing
four more to cholera, he impetuously moved his remaining thirty-four
men, some of whom subsequently came down with cholera, into the Indian
country. In his report he declared that it was "the greatest wonder in the
world" that he and his men "escaped being massacred." Fortunately for

[19] Armes, *Ups and Downs*, 236–40; Burkey, *Custer, Come at Once*, 35; Nye, *Plains Indian Raiders*, 100–101, 103; White, *Hostiles and Horse Soldiers*, 52.

his men, Armes was brave and cool under fire, and Company F's escape was due in large part to his later good judgment and determination. It was nevertheless a clear victory for the Cheyennes.[20]

When Captain Armes and his troops reached Fort Hays, they found that reinforcements had in fact been sent. Twenty-five mounted infantry-men from the Thirty-eighth Infantry, along with the howitzer, had gone toward the Campbell and Clinton camp. Before reaching it, however, their lieutenant came down with cholera, and they were forced to return. The detachment tried again under the leadership of Sergeant Pittman. Before they could catch up with Armes and his men, they encountered what they estimated to be fifty Indian warriors. They fired three shells from the howitzer, scattering the surprised Cheyennes. Unable to find any sign of Armes and his company, they returned to Fort Hays.[21]

The foray of Captain Armes and Company F to the Saline did not deter further Cheyenne attacks on the railroad construction camps. On the night after his return to Fort Hays a small wagon train and its escort were attacked while camping next to White Rock Station twenty-five miles west of Lookout Station and thirty miles from new Fort Hays. The attack lasted for an hour and a half, and then the war party moved on without casualties on either side. Two days later, August 5, another war party struck a crew of engineers under George F. Wickes, the railroad's chief engi-neer, at Fort Hays Station on the stage line but left when soldiers from the post approached. During the ensuing days a number of men were wounded and many head of livestock were driven off during attacks on railroad construction camps and stage stations along the Smoky Hill. Rail-road construction workers, already nervous from earlier raids, began to come into the fort. Their presence was only partially the result of the raid-ing, however, for they were enticed by the lure of whiskey being sold at the new town of Rome.[22]

Rome seems to have evolved from a tent erected in late May of 1867 by the Lull brothers of Salina, near the place the new railroad would cross the

[20] Armes, *Ups and Downs*, 236–40; Burkey, *Custer, Come at Once*, 35; Grinnell, *Fighting Cheyennes*, 266–67; Nye, *Plains Indian Raiders*, 100–101, 103; Stanley, *My Early Travels*, 154–56; White, *Hostiles and Horse Soldiers*, 52.

[21] Armes, *Ups and Downs*, 236–40; Burkey, *Custer, Come at Once*, 36; Nye, *Plains Indian Raiders*, 101; White, *Hostiles and Horse Soldiers*, 51.

[22] H. C. Corbin to C. McKeever, AAG, August 6, 1867, Fort Hays, LS, T713–RI, NA; H. C. Corbin to T. B. Weir, AAAG, August 7, 1867, Fort Hays, LS, T713–RI, NA; *Kansas Daily Tribune*, August 9, 1867; *Leavenworth Daily Conservative*, August 10, 1867; *Leavenworth Daily Times*, August 8, 1867; White, *Hostiles and Horse Soldiers*, 53.

south fork of Big Creek. Their intention was to satisfy the thirst of the graders just then beginning work on the roadbed in that area. By mid-June, following the removal of Fort Hays to its new site, an incipient town was growing around the Lull brothers' tent. Soon William Rose, who had a contract for grading the roadbed west from Ellsworth, entered into a partnership with William F. (Buffalo Bill) Cody, hired to provide meat for the construction workers, to plat a new town there. They staked out the town and built a general store, the first stone building in Rome. In less than sixty days there were some two hundred tents, dugouts, sod buildings, wooden cabins, and other structures in the town, along with a population of about five hundred. Saloon keeping seems to have been the principal occupation of the citizenry, a curious hodgepodge of soldiers, businessmen, railroad construction workers, gamblers, hunters, con men, cutthroats, and prostitutes. The primary businesses bore such names as "Lone Star," "the Dewdrop Inn," "the Occidental," "the Grader's Retreat," and "the Last Chance," all dealing in (among other things) rotgut whiskey. Although it grew to as many as two thousand people, the "Eternal City," as it was sarcastically called, had only a brief day in the sun. Dr. W. E. Webb, W. F. Wells, Judge Knight, and Phinney Moore, representing a syndicate from St. Louis with ties to the railroad, began a rival town less than a mile east of Rome on the south side of the new roadbed. At the same time, the railroad raised its roadbed at the approach to Big Creek, making a crossing at the site of Rome difficult. Residents of Rome began to move to the new town, and by the 1870s Rome was nothing but scattered ruins.[23]

The attractions of Rome to the graders and other workers building the railroad were irresistible. The combination of heat and high winds of the Kansas summer, fear generated by reports of Indian attacks up and down the line, loneliness, the cholera outbreak, and the solace of drink caused many to abandon their work and flock to Fort Hays and nearby Hays City and Rome. There hundreds of them were lying about hungry, dirty, and drunk, not only delaying progress on the railroad but causing concern for Captain Corbin, who feared another round of cholera. He repeatedly had these men escorted back to their work camps, only to have them return again to the fort or the towns, owing to new reports of Indian attacks. Ultimately Corbin discovered that many of the saloons in Hays City and Rome, and "whiskey ranches" in the vicinity of the fort, were sending run-

---

[23] Beach, "Old Fort Hays," 579n13; "Some Lost Towns of Kansas," 439–40; Lee and Raynesford, *Trails of the Smoky Hill*, 163–65.

ners to the various construction camps and alarming the workers with false reports of Indian attacks, stampeding them back to the post and into the arms of the whiskey peddlers. In desperation he finally ordered the seizure of all of the whiskey in the nearby saloons and whiskey ranches, and at the same time had his men escort the laborers back to their camps. This time they remained.[24]

While the Dog Soldier and southern Sutaio Cheyennes were striving hard to deter railroad construction along the Smoky Hill, on the Platte a new form of railroad harassment was discovered. Turkey Leg took his band of some fifty lodges of Óhméséheso Cheyennes north to the Powder River after the June 14 council with Custer at the forks of the Platte concluded. There they spent their time hunting bison. But when news came that Custer had left the Republican River country and moved south to the Smoky Hill, Turkey Leg again led his people south to camp with the Kiyuksa Oglalas and his friend Pawnee Killer. They reached the Platte west of Plum Creek Station on the Union Pacific Railroad, crossing to the south side and continuing on to the Republican. Meantime, before reaching the Platte, a war party of their young men under the leadership of the warrior Spotted Wolf had moved east, looking for their old enemies the Pawnees. Included in the war party were Wolf Tooth, Porcupine, Red Wolf, Yellow Bull, Big Foot, and Sleeping Rabbit. When they returned and crossed the Platte about four miles west of Plum Creek Station, they halted along the bluffs overlooking the river and the creek to get a better view of the railroad and the installations along it. Plum Creek was a small tributary of the Platte, flowing easterly, nearly parallel to and south of the river, and joining it a little more than fifty miles east of Fort McPherson. There was an old stage station south of the Platte where the Oregon-California Trail crossed Plum Creek, but with the building of the railroad along the river's north side, stage service had been suspended east of the end of track. There was now a new Plum Creek Station on the railroad opposite the old one, and a telegraph line that paralleled the rails. A road next to the tracks accommodated wagon and buggy traffic between the new towns and stations.[25]

---

[24] Corbin to McKeever, August 6, 1867; Corbin to Weir, August 8, 1867; *Junction City Weekly Union*, August 24, 1867; *Kansas Daily Tribune*, August 7 and 22, 1867; *Leavenworth Daily Conservative*, August 10, 1867; *Leavenworth Daily Times*, August 9, 1867; Burkey, *Custer, Come at Once*, 36; White, *Hostiles and Horse Soldiers*, 53.

[25] Grinnell, *Fighting Cheyennes*, 263–66; Grinnell, *Two Great Scouts*, 145; Hyde, *Life of George Bent*, 276–78; Powell, *People of the Sacred Mountain*, 1:488–92; Stands in Timber and Liberty, *Cheyenne Memories*, 173–74; Stanley, *My Early Travels*, 154–56.

From their position on the bluffs overlooking the Platte River and the railroad, on the afternoon of August 6 the members of the Cheyenne war party observed a train coming from the east, growing ever larger as it neared and belching smoke and sparks. Having never seen a train before, one of them commented that it looked like a white man's pipe puffing as he smoked. When it had passed, someone suggested that they should see if they couldn't throw one of those trains from its track and find out what kind of things it carried that would be useful to them. Near dusk they crossed the river and placed a tie they found across the track, built a fire nearby to provide light, then waited to see what would happen. At about 9:00 P.M. they heard a distant rumbling along the tracks to the east. It was a handcar operated by two men and carrying an additional four, a crew sent to repair a telegraph line break west of Plum Creek Station. As the car neared, the Indians rose from their cover and began shooting arrows at the men on the handcar. When they saw the Indians and the fire, the operators began to pump rapidly, trying to get past them as fast as possible. They saw the tie across the track too late. The car slammed into it and was thrown from the track. Each man jumped up and ran, but all were overtaken and killed except one man. William Thompson, an Englishman, was one of the repairmen and, when he ran, was singled out and overtaken by a young warrior who shot him in the arm, clubbed him down, and stabbed him in the neck, then proceeded to scalp him. Though the pain was excruciating, Thompson managed to feign death as he was scalped. When the warrior finished, he left, and as he did, the scalp slipped from where he had secured it to his horse and landed only a few feet from Thompson.[26]

The success realized in overturning the handcar inspired Sleeping Rabbit to suggest that perhaps the same could be done with a whole train. Red Wolf and Porcupine, thinking that a fine idea, secured a few strong levers and, after pulling out some of the spikes, managed to bend a rail up and outward. Then they piled more ties across the tracks beyond and waited to see what would happen. At least an hour and a half passed following the derailing of the handcar before a train approached. All this time William Thompson was lying quietly on the ground where he was attacked, feigning death and enduring terrible pain. He could hear the approaching train and believed he could have stopped it short of the broken rails, but for the presence of the Indians. As it was, there were two

---

[26] Grinnell, *Fighting Cheyennes*, 155–57; Hyde, *Life of George Bent*, 276–78; Powell, *People of the Sacred Mountain*, 1:489–90; Stands in Timber and Liberty, *Cheyenne Memories*, 173–76; Stanley, *My Early Travels*, 155–57.

trains coming from the east, one following the other at a distance of three miles. The first came along at twenty-five miles per hour, hit the broken rail and stack of ties, and was thrown from the tracks. It landed in a ravine about four feet deep with the tender and next five cars coming to rest on top of one another. The effort had succeeded far beyond the Indians' expectations. The warriors gathered at the front of the train, trying to break into the smashed freight cars to see what was in them. As it happened, the first car opened had a shipment of axes, among other things, and with the aid of these the Indians were able to break into all of the remaining cars. They found all kinds of food stuffs and other valuables: sugar, coffee, flour, boxes of tobacco, clothing and shoes, saddles, ribbons, boxes of calicoes and cotton, and other things that amazed them in quantity and kind. When dawn came, the younger members of the party, laughing and clowning as boys will, tied long strips of muslin to the tails of their horses, then dashed about the plains trying to pull off the long trailers floating out behind their friends' horses. But this lasted only a short time before they turned to the more serious duty of loading booty and transporting it south to Turkey Leg's new camp.[27]

While the members of the war party were preoccupied with opening the derailed cars, four men in the caboose managed to escape by running back down the track and halting the following train. It backed up to Elm Creek Station, eighteen miles east of Plum Creek Station, and there telegraphed the news of the train wreck. Meantime William Thompson also made good his escape under cover of darkness, carrying his scalp with him in a bucket of water. He traveled west to Willow Island Station, where he was reached by a rescue party a day or so later and returned to Omaha. There a fruitless attempt was made to reattach his scalp. Word of the train derailment had in the interim been telegraphed to Maj. Frank North, commanding the Pawnee Battalion and responsible for security of the rail line and the construction crews beyond the end of track. North was at the end of track 220 miles west of Plum Creek Station. His nearest company of Pawnees was twelve miles beyond, and these he ordered back. He arranged for a train to be standing by for them, and they boarded when they arrived, immediately setting out for the site of the derailment.[28]

[27] Grinnell, *Fighting Cheyennes*, 263–68; Hyde, *Life of George Bent*, 276–78; Powell, *People of the Sacred Mountain*, 1:490–91; Stands in Timber and Liberty, *Cheyenne Memories*, 173–76; Stanley, *My Early Travels*, 156–58.

[28] Grinnell, *Fighting Cheyennes*, 263–68; Grinnell, *Two Great Scouts*, 145–47; Hyde, *Life of George Bent*, 276–78; Powell, *People of the Sacred Mountain*, 1:491–92; Stands in Timber and Liberty, *Cheyenne Memories*, 173–76; Stanley, *My Early Travels*, 155–61, 163–64.

Meanwhile the Cheyenne war party had reached Turkey Leg's camp, on a tributary of the Republican with Pawnee Killer's Oglalas. When they heard of the derailment and the fine things found in the wreckage, a large party of both Cheyennes and Oglalas was made up—men, women, and children—to move north and retrieve more booty from the smashed cars. They reached the site and were in the process of removing and loading goods when Major North and his Pawnees arrived. The Cheyennes and Oglalas were then south of Plum Creek, and after crossing it, the Pawnees attacked. Armed with new Spencer carbines and pistols, the Pawnees routed their enemy, who were forced to drop much of the captured goods in the process. The reports of what happened during the fight are conflicting. Major North telegraphed his brother Luther that seventeen Cheyennes and Oglalas were killed, but later told George Grinnell that seven were killed. Stanley wrote from Omaha that the number was fifteen. Porcupine told George Grinnell that one old man was killed, while Wolf Tooth told John Stands In Timber that there were no fallen on either side. They all generally agreed that three Cheyennes—a woman, a boy, and a girl—were captured and that the girl subsequently escaped.[29]

After his F Company returned to Fort Hays, Captain Armes was forced to endure a brief confinement to heal his injury. Lieutenant Bodamer took command of the company during this time. The post surgeon, Dr. William F. Buchanan, extracted a rifle ball from Armes's hip on August 2, and he was sitting up two days later. On August 5, despite the doctor's protest, Armes rode in an ambulance to Wickes and Sharp's railroad engineering camp with forty of his men, trying to find and punish the war party that had reportedly killed several immigrants and stolen a great amount of livestock. They found nothing. The next day, he rode along the railroad line to reassure workers he was on watch for Indians, and on August 7 he went on a short scout. He had to stay in camp for the next few days because of his painful wound. During this time a Cheyenne war party attacked Colonel Wickes, the railroad's chief construction engineer, and his fifteen-man infantry escort en route to their camp thirty miles west of the post, driving them back to Fort Hays. But word arrived from Fort Harker that Maj. Horace Moore and his four companies of the Eighteenth Kansas Volunteer Cavalry had been ordered to Fort Hays from Fort Dodge to help protect the railroad line and the workers. In his report of the Battle

[29] Grinnell, *Fighting Cheyennes*, 263–68; Grinnell, *Two Great Scouts*, 145–47; Hyde, *Life of George Bent*, 276–78; Powell, *People of the Sacred Mountain*, 1:491–92; Stands In Timber and Liberty, *Cheyenne Memories*, 173–76; Stanley, *My Early Travels*, 155–61, 163–64.

of the Saline on August 3, Captain Armes expressed his opinion that a large number of hostile Indians were encamped between the Saline and the Solomon, or on the Solomon, and that it would require not less than two to three hundred well-armed and -equipped men to pursue them in broken country. He recommended that such a force be dispatched as soon as possible. The continuing Cheyenne attacks and Armes's report and recommendation evidently persuaded Generals Sherman and Hancock to do just that. Major Moore and his four companies of volunteers were ordered to Fort Hays, arriving there on August 12. The next evening, they were sent in pursuit of the war parties operating all around them, apparently from a village or villages on the Saline or the Solomon.[30]

On the mutual agreement of Major Moore and Captain Armes (now a major by brevet and under army regulations the ranking officer), the force was divided. Moore and Companies A and D of the Eighteenth Kansas were to march northwesterly to the Saline, while Armes with his Company F, Tenth Cavalry, and Companies B and C, Eighteenth Kansas, would march northeast to the river. After scouting the stream carefully, they would move toward each other, joining forces and then determining their next course of action should no Indians be found. Evidently hoping to avoid the intense heat of day and observation by Indian scouts, Armes and his troops left Fort Hays at sundown on August 13, marching northeasterly without halting in an effort to surprise any Indians on the Saline, but found no sign of them. After a rest halt, they continued west along the Saline, meeting Moore and his command at about 4:00 P.M. on August 14. Neither had found recent Indian signs, so they agreed to scout the country farther to the north: Moore to lead his troops northwest to the Solomon and Armes to march with his command northeast to that stream, then turn toward each other and scour the country along the river until they met. They apparently left after dark, each column marching in its own direction. On reaching the Solomon, Armes led his men west, examining the country around the river and its tributaries. Though he and his command moved westward forty miles, they never found Moore. The reason is unclear, Moore claiming that Armes did not take the route he was "ordered" to take, and Armes criticizing Moore for failing to meet him at the specified place. Neither being familiar with the country, likely one or both were lost or at least uncertain of where they were. Moore suggested

---

[30] Armes, *Ups and Downs*, 241–42; Burkey, *Custer, Come at Once*, 36; Nye, *Plains Indian Raiders*, 101; White, *Hostiles and Horse Soldiers*, 53.

that Armes struck the river above his command, but that seems unlikely. Each had white scouts who were presumably competent enough to get their directions straight and to recognize the large trail left by two or three companies of cavalry when they crossed it. Probably both officers were at fault for not jointly preparing a sound plan of action or establishing clear directions.[31]

Failing to find the Moore column after a long search westward along the Solomon, Armes decided to move southwesterly to Monument Station on the Smoky Hill stage road and then scout eastward along the Smoky Hill River. According to Armes, on the night of August 15 his men marched southwesterly for twenty-six miles. After going into camp on the morning of August 16 they hunted buffalo and spent the day drying the meat, hoping to move out in light marching order and surprise the Indians. Armes gave no indication that he knew the whereabouts of any Indians to surprise, but he seems to have been ever certain that they were out there on his line of march. During the day on August 17 they intersected a large Indian trail leading northwest. They followed it to a point near what Armes called Camp Wickes, actually the Wickes and Sharp engineering camp along the future Union Pacific, E.D., right-of-way, some thirty-five miles west of Fort Hays.[32] They appear to have stopped at the camp, perhaps for rest and a meal, before continuing northwest along the Indian trail. On reaching one of the tributaries of the Saline River, they went into camp along its banks about forty-five miles west and north from Fort Hays, calling it McDonald's Camp. By this time the horses needed forage, and rations for the men was running short. Armes tried to find volunteers to ride to the fort for resupply and as many additional men as could be spared, but without success. The memory of soldiers killed while acting as couriers was fresh in the minds of all, so in the end he took three men as escort and went himself, leaving Captain Barker of the Eighteenth Kansas in charge of the camp.[33]

Armes and his escort reached Fort Hays at about 10:00 P.M. on August 17. He ordered four wagons loaded with forage and one with rations and started back at 8:00 the next morning, taking with him twenty-two dis-

[31] H. L. Moore to Governor S. J. Crawford, Fort Hays, Kans., August 31, 1867, Governor's Correspondence, KSHS; Armes, *Ups and Downs*, 242, 245; Burgess, "Eighteenth Kansas Volunteer Cavalry," 536; Nye, *Plains Indian Raiders*, 101–102.

[32] The engineering camp was periodically moved farther west as the work of surveying and staking out the right-of-way progressed. Armes reported the distance as both thirty-five and forty-five miles, but it was then most likely thirty-five miles from Fort Hays.

[33] Armes, *Ups and Downs*, 21–43, 245; Nye, *Plains Indian Raiders*, 102.

mounted cavalrymen to guard the train. While at the post, Armes met Maj. Joel Elliott of the Seventh Cavalry, who had arrived a short time before with his command after scouting eastward from Fort Wallace along the upper reaches of the Saline River. Armes told him of finding the Indian trail and asked for his cooperation to "clean out" the Indians. He thought that Elliott "partly agreed" to start that morning to search for them. Armes, the wagons, and their escort reached their camp on the evening of August 18 and prepared to march the following morning. They were apparently near the confluence of the north and south forks of the Saline, and likely the Indian trail continued northwesterly along the north fork, since Indians usually traveled near a stream unless crossing a divide between watersheds. The difficulty in tracing the succeeding movements of Armes and his command as they marched is compounded by several factors. First, he left no march journal with accompanying sketch maps, so far as known, and in his diary and report gave only occasional references to the direction and mileage traveled. His erratic listing of the number of miles marched each day or night is fragmentary and clearly based on his own estimates that in the main seem inaccurate and excessive. He had no odometer to assist him, as did Custer, and his familiarity with the country north of the Solomon and south of the Republican was probably as limited as that of Major Moore. He almost certainly had a compass, as no army officer on the plains would have intentionally ventured forth without one any more than a sailing captain would have done so at sea.[34]

Having been in the service for less than two months, the Tenth Cavalry troopers Armes led were relatively inexperienced in any of the martial arts. Most of them had never ridden before and at best had marginal skill in the use of their weapons. A forced march like the one Custer undertook to Fort Harker would have been nearly impossible for them and their horses. The Eighteenth Kansas Volunteer Cavalry was probably not much better, despite numbering Civil War veterans among its members, and was without experience in Indian warfare. Moreover the Eighteenth was for the most part mounted on relatively untrained horses owned or purchased by the volunteers. It seems clear that from the time they left the Saline, Armes's command moved slowly and cautiously, mostly at night until reaching the battle site. To protect their horses, they almost certainly followed standard march procedure of moving at a cavalry walk,

---

[34] Armes, *Ups and Downs*, 243, 245; Nye, *Plains Indian Raiders*, 102; Utley, *Life in Custer's Cavalry*, 95–96; White, *Hostiles and Horse Soldiers*, 54.

which periodically alternates the walk with a moderate trot. For those guarding the pack train and the small wagon train and its mule teams, the walk would be the only gait available. Husbanding the strength and wind of the horses would have been foremost in the minds of the troopers to prevent the animals from breaking down from exhaustion, overexertion, and the extreme heat. July and August generally represent the apex of heat during the Kansas summer, and Captain Barnitz wrote his wife on August 13 that "the heat has been fearful at times" and on August 24 that the thermometer was "at 110° in the shade, on the average, between sunrise and sunset." Even the nights were hot, which would mandate regular halts similar to those taken by Custer's escort during his dash to Fort Harker. Therefore none of the marches made by Armes and his men probably averaged more than three miles for every hour marched, and the wagon train less. The hours available for a night march were restricted to the times of dark—that is, from the end of civil twilight, when available light is insufficient for ordinary activity (the sun has dropped six or more degrees below the horizon), until the onset of dawn (morning twilight) when light is again sufficient for observations of or by an enemy.[35]

Captain Armes picked out seventy-five of the best men and horses in his command and led them northwesterly on the morning of August 19, possibly following the line of the Saline's north fork and the Indian trail. At the same time he sent Lt. John W. Price, B Company, Eighteenth Kansas, in charge of the wagon and pack trains (including two ambulances) and the rest of the command, to an unspecified "designated point" on the Solomon River—probably by following in his trace. According to Armes, he and his men marched eighteen miles that day "very cautiously," again making camp on the Saline. Depending on the route and direction of movement this would have left them about ten miles short of the south fork of the Solomon. They resumed their march at 9:00 P.M. on August 19, reaching the Solomon's south fork during the night and making camp on its banks. The camp was evidently located in a small canyon or deep arroyo leading to the river, since Armes wrote that he hid his command "in a deep ravine" during the day so the Indians would not observe it. The command left its concealed camp on the south fork of the Solomon at 6:00 P.M., marched "ten or fifteen miles," and went into camp. Fresh Indian signs were observed during the march. A march of ten to fifteen miles would

---

[35] *Astronomical Almanac*, 2004, A-12; Carter, *Horses, Saddles, and Bridles*, 82–84; Utley, *Life in Custer's Cavalry*, 95–96.

probably have placed them on either Bow Creek or the north fork of the Solomon, although Armes thought it was Beaver Creek. Whichever stream they were on, from their camp they observed a bright light to the east. Capt. George B. Jenness, commanding C Company of the Eighteenth Kansas, volunteered to take a couple of men and investigate the matter. The source of the light was farther than first thought, and they finally reached it near midnight. It turned out to be a burning log at an earlier Indian campsite. Jenness and his companions started back but quickly became disoriented and camped for the night on the open plain.[36]

While Jenness was scouting out the mysterious light, Armes and his command were waiting for their return. When Jenness and his companions failed to return by 2:00 A.M., they were presumed lost to the Indians, and the march resumed until dawn. Because it was dark and their wagons were now with them, their rate of march was significantly slowed, probably averaging about two miles per hour. A four- to five-hour march would have taken them another eight to ten miles northerly, to the vicinity of Prairie Dog Creek. Here they made camp and were eating their breakfast when, at about 9:00 A.M. on August 21, an Indian fired on one of the mounted sentinels guarding the camp. Supposing that more must be near, Armes immediately mounted his men and pushed on to the north, leaving Lieutenant Price and a guard of sixty-five men from the Eighteenth Kansas in charge of the wagons. Price was instructed to move north as rapidly as possible to the Republican River and await further orders. The poor and inaccurate maps of the day and the lack of knowledge of the country by Armes and his personnel, led him to conclude that they were on Beaver Creek and that the Republican lay beyond. They were apparently unaware or uncertain of the location of Prairie Dog Creek or of Sappa Creek, both of which lay between the column and Beaver Creek to the north and northwest. But though disoriented geographically, Armes did have good cause to believe that Indians were near. During their night march the scout Allison J. Pliley, riding ahead to the left of the line of march, saw a number of signal arrows fired to their front. He returned to the column and reported this to Armes, who instructed him to return to his position (not more than one-half mile from the command) and report if he discovered further Indian signs. He was told the command would move due north. During the night, however, the line of march was changed

---

[36] Armes, *Ups and Downs*, 243; Jenness, "Battle of Beaver Creek," 444; White, *Hostiles and Horse Soldiers*, 54.

to the "sharp northwest," which took them to the edge of the valley of the Prairie Dog.[37]

Pliley did return to report later findings to Armes, but because of their change of direction the column passed behind him and he missed their trail. He continued easterly and found the wagon train still in camp, joining them for breakfast soon after Armes and his men had left. Meantime Armes and the rest of the column crossed the stream and continued north across its valley. Then, for reasons not clear, Armes became concerned that Lieutenant Price would follow directly after the cavalry column. He sent Sergeant Carpenter of the Eighteenth Kansas and Sergeant Johnson of F Company, Tenth Cavalry, back to instruct Price to follow the Prairie Dog eight miles downstream before crossing. At about 3:00 P.M., as they were moving north out of the Prairie Dog valley, Armes and his men were struck by what he described as "a war party of several Indians," probably intending to say several hundred. At first Armes sent Capt. Edgar A. Barker with half of the troopers to the left to charge the largest visible band. Before they had moved more than one hundred yards, however, another large party of warriors was seen approaching from the northwest, and Barker and his men were forced back. Armes then dismounted his entire command, placed the horses in a nearby canyon or arroyo, and stationed the men in a large circle around them in a prone position. Captain Barker directed the defense in the rear, where the arroyo opened onto the Prairie Dog valley to the south, while 2nd Lt. Frank M. Stahl, Eighteenth Kansas, was on the front and right, and Lieutenant Bodamer of the Tenth looked after the left. Armes commanded from the center. From this position they withstood repeated charges and harassing fire for several hours until, at about 9:00 P.M., the Indians pulled back and the fighting subsided for the day. During the fighting, the cavalry column suffered eleven men wounded, including First Sergeant Thornton of F Company, whose left leg was broken below the knee. Armes claimed his men inflicted significant casualties on the Indians.[38]

When morning dawned on August 21, Captain Jenness and the two men with him set out to find the main column. The camp they left the previous night was probably on the north fork of the Solomon about eight miles due west of them. Knowing that the column's intended movement was

---

[37] Armes, *Ups and Downs*, 243, 245; Blackburn, "18th Kansas Cavalry," 6; Jenness, "Battle of Beaver Creek," 444; Pliley, "Reminiscences of a Plainsman," March 19, 1931; White, *Hostiles and Horse Soldiers*, 54.

[38] Armes, *Ups and Downs*, 243–46; Nye, *Plains Indian Raiders*, 102–103; Pliley, "Reminiscences of a Plainsman," March 19, 1931; White, *Hostiles and Horse Soldiers*, 54–55.

northerly or northwesterly, they rode in that direction and soon reached the bluffs overlooking the Prairie Dog. From a high point they discovered the camp of the wagon train some three miles farther downstream (northeast) and rode in at a gallop. In the camp they enjoyed a bountiful breakfast and then, joined by the scout Pliley and Pvt. Thomas G. Masterson, who had just arrived with dispatches from Fort Hays, left to find the main command.[39] Meanwhile Lieutenant Price prepared to move out and continue his march. Jenness and the four other men with him rode upstream in search of Armes and his troops and by noon reached the site of their halt and stream crossing. After a brief rest they crossed the shallow waters of the Prairie Dog and proceeded to follow Armes's trail. Shortly they came upon the two sergeants Armes had sent back with orders for Price and the wagon train. They were dismounted and hiking back—a poor idea in the middle of Indian country with abundant signs of hostile warriors all around them. The two men said they had traveled about three miles south from where they left the column. Jenness deemed it unwise to allow them to continue alone and ordered them to follow him northward. They continued for three miles when suddenly they were startled by the war cries of a large party of warriors galloping toward them from a ridge about a half-mile to their west. At almost the same moment, to their great relief, they also saw a party of twenty-two cavalry troopers led by a sergeant, galloping toward them from the direction of Armes and his column. Jenness quickly assumed command, dismounted his men (now swelled to twenty-nine) on Pliley's advice, then formed them in a hollow square with the horses in the center held by every fourth man. They immediately began firing at the oncoming warriors with their seven-shot Spencer carbines.[40]

Soon the Indians formed a complete circle around the Jenness detachment, keeping themselves constantly in motion at the far edge of the effective range of the soldiers' carbines. The warriors were armed with a variety of weapons, some with Springfield or Mississippi rifles, some with shotguns, and most with bows and arrows. Initially they tried to stampede the horses, shaking blankets and lances with streamers and shouting war cries, and this did make the animals uneasy. From time to time individual war-

---

[39] Included in the dispatches were orders for Armes to cease offensive operations and return to Fort Hays in compliance with General Sherman's orders to assume a defensive posture until the Medicine Lodge councils.

[40] Armes, *Ups and Downs*, 245; Blackburn, "18th Kansas Cavalry," 6–7; Jenness, "Battle of Beaver Creek," 444–45; Pliley, "Reminiscences of a Plainsman," March 19, 1931; Powell, *People of the Sacred Mountain*, 1:492; White, *Hostiles and Horse Soldiers*, 55.

riors would wheel their horses inside their circle, rein them in, and discharge their weapons at the slowly moving soldiers. When the cavalrymen were forced to halt for any reason, a number of warriors would dismount, take cover behind prairie dog mounds, buffalo wallows, or clumps of yucca, and pour in a flight of arrows. Several of the men and nearly all of the horses were wounded in this manner. But the constant firing of the Spencer carbines usually kept the Indians at a safe distance. Each cavalryman had about two hundred rounds of ammunition, so there was little immediate danger of running low. On occasion a number of warriors would gather and then make a direct charge at the troopers. In response every second man on the opposite side would rush across to reinforce his comrades, and from a kneeling position they would keep up a constant fire that forced the Indians to retreat. The new phenomenon of the seven-shot repeater puzzled the warriors. Only once did a single Cheyenne, mounted on a splendid white horse and flourishing a pistol, manage to penetrate the soldier's hollow square. He was leading a charge, but his comrades broke before the intense fire from the Spencers. He nevertheless continued, braving the fire and dashing completely through the square unharmed, though at least fifty shots were fired at him.[41]

Jenness continued leading his men northbound along the trail left by Armes and his command. But they were moving slowly, constantly fighting off the repeated Indian attacks, and had gone only about half a mile when Pliley thought he saw an even larger body of Indians ahead of them. They were between Jenness and his men and the main command, so Jenness decided they should return to the creek and find a suitable defensive position where they could erect a breastwork of driftwood. All but four of the horses had been struck by arrows; at least one was killed, and the others were badly wounded. In this condition it was nearly impossible to control them, and the officers decided to give up all but the four unwounded animals. Jenness, recalling the occasion years later claimed the wounded horses were killed to prevent their falling into the hands of the Indians. Pliley, also writing many years later, said that on his advice the horses were released, thereby distracting the Indians and causing a number of them to break their cover in an effort to capture them. This exposed them to the hazard of the soldiers' fire. Captain Barnitz later wrote his wife that Elliott's six companies of the Seventh Cavalry had

---

[41] Blackburn, "18th Kansas Cavalry," 7; Jenness, "Battle of Beaver Creek," 445–46; Powell, *People of the Sacred Mountain*, 1:492–93; White, *Hostiles and Horse Soldiers*, 55–56.

come upon the battlefield and that only one dead horse was observed, thus supporting Pliley's claim. About this time, during their halt, Sergeant Johnson was killed instantly by Indian fire, Private Masterson was mortally wounded, and Cpl. James H. Towell received seven shots that would eventually claim his life. Five of the most seriously wounded men were mounted on the four remaining horses, and the return march to the river began. At the edge of the high ground they entered a deep canyon opening out into the valley, and here they took refuge against the continuing charges from the warriors. Paradoxically the large body of Indians that caused them to turn back later proved to be the old people, women, and children from the nearby Cheyenne village, probably trying to move to a safer location farther west.[42]

The canyon in which Jenness and his men took refuge afforded good protection from the Indian assaults, and the broken ground around it kept the warriors at a distance and allowed the soldiers to get clear shots at those who attempted to move closer. Moreover, in the canyon they found a spring that formed a small stream flowing to the creek beyond. The hot, dry men quickly quenched their thirst and refilled their canteens. By now one man had been killed and fourteen wounded, two mortally. Nine of the wounded were so badly hurt they could not fire a weapon. As the sun began to set in the west, five of the most seriously wounded were again mounted on the horses, and the whole detachment worked its way slowly down through the canyon. Toward its mouth they came upon a stunted growth of cottonwoods and willows where they took refuge until dark. They were well protected, had clear shots at any warrior who approached the rim of the canyon, and after that not another man was wounded. As darkness fell, Pliley and Sergeant Carpenter, scouting down the dry streambed into which the springwater disappeared, found a buffalo trail that led out of the canyon to another small stream that joined the creek beyond. The Indians had withdrawn and the firing ceased, so the nine badly wounded men were placed on the four horses. The horses' hooves were bound with torn-up shirts to muffle the sound as their iron shoes struck the rocks, and movement from the canyon now began. Steep, stony bluffs surrounded them, and the signals of the Indian scouts—the yelp of a coyote or the hoot of an owl—could be heard from time to time. But the soldiers moved unobserved. They silently descended and left the canyon, following the small

---

[42] Blackburn, "18th Kansas Cavalry," 7–8; Jenness, "Battle of Beaver Creek," 446–47; Pliley, "Reminiscences of a Plainsman," March 26, 1931; Utley, *Life in Custer's Cavalry*, 99; White, *Hostiles and Horse Soldiers*, 55–56, 61.

stream to the Prairie Dog. After what seemed five to six miles they reached it, located a shallow crossing point, then selected a canyon in the bluffs on the south bank that they thought defensible if the Indians resumed their attacks the following morning.[43]

Even as Jenness was taking his men to refuge on the south side of Prairie Dog Creek, Captain Armes was leading his command back to the stream through the dark of night, trying to find the wagon train. By now they were running low on ammunition, rations, and forage for their horses. They reached the stream at about 4:00 A.M. on August 22 and halted there to rest until sunrise. As the sun broke the eastern horizon, the command moved out, traveling west (upstream) along the Prairie Dog for two miles. There they found Lieutenants Price and Thomas with the wagon train and the guard. They too were encamped in a small canyon, all safe and unharmed but entirely surrounded by Indians. The warriors were gathered in what Armes described as groups of fifty or more, apparently intent on either starving out their enemy or watching for an opportunity to stampede the stock. After joining Price and his men, Armes learned that Jenness (who he thought had been lost to the Indians when he failed to return) was besieged in another canyon about a mile to the west. Jenness had sent Pliley in search of the wagon train early that morning before the Indians reappeared. He found it soon after, but Price declined to send a detachment to relieve Jenness, on the grounds that there were barely enough men to defend the train. Shortly after that, Armes arrived with the rest of the command, however, and Captain Barker left with a detachment to rescue Jenness and his men. When they reached him after a brief skirmish, they formed a hollow square around the exhausted men and their wounded and escorted them back to the rest of the reunited command.[44]

Sporadic fighting with the Indians continued for most of the day on August 22. At about 4:00 P.M. Armes gathered twenty men, apparently volunteers, then charged the warriors who were sniping at them from the south bank of the creek and drove them back across it. But he had to return to camp quickly when a large body of mounted Indians tried to cut him off from the others. The fighting then subsided for the day, and after dark the command began its retreat to Fort Hays. By the following morning, August 23, the troops were on the south fork of the Solomon. Doubt-

[43] Blackburn, "18th Kansas Cavalry," 8; Jenness, "Battle of Beaver Creek," 446–49; Nye, *Plains Indian Raiders*, 103; Powell, *People of the Sacred Mountain*, 1:494; White, *Hostiles and Horse Soldiers*, 61.

[44] Armes, *Ups and Downs*, 246; Blackburn, "18th Kansas Cavalry," 10; Jenness, "Battle of Beaver Creek," 449–50; Powell, *People of the Sacred Mountain*, 1:494–95; White, *Hostiles and Horse Soldiers*, 61.

less they were surprised to find themselves still surrounded by the Indians, and desultory fighting continued into the afternoon. At 4:00 P.M. a few Indians came toward the troopers' positions, bearing a white flag. Armes sent out a scout named Charlie Cadaro (a half-blood) carrying a white handkerchief on a stick, with instructions to learn what they wanted and to let him know. When they were close enough to recognize him, the Indians called him by name and cursed him, and one of them shot at him with a pistol. That ended the parley. This also seems to have been the close of active combat, and probably after dark the movement back to Fort Hays resumed. The Indians were seen no more, and Armes and his command reached For Hays on the night of August 24. As they approached the post, they passed Major Elliott, leading his six companies of the Seventh Cavalry northward, flags and guidons flying, with his train of supplies and ambulances following in his wake.[45]

So ended what was known as the Battle of Prairie Dog Creek, one of the more interesting but lesser-known fights against the Cheyennes and Oglalas of the southern plains. Though in the main the soldiers fought well, it was nonetheless a clear victory for the Indians. Armes praised his men in his report, including the volunteers, and singled out many for special commendation. His only criticism was against Major Moore, for not joining him on the Solomon, and Major Elliott, for not cooperating with him as he believed they had agreed. Moore was more scathing in his assessment of Armes, believing that he intentionally avoided him in a search for glory for himself and had foolishly divided his forces. Moore, on the other hand, never found any trails—either of Armes or of the Indians—and scouted the region without results. As for Elliott, he appears to have been unaware of the critical comments made by Armes or he likely would have responded. His version of what was discussed and agreed to for "cooperation" with Armes' command would probably have been quite different. Moreover, Elliott had received orders to suspend offensive operations. Captain Barnitz, commanding one of the companies under Elliott, noted in a letter to his wife that at Fort Hays they had found a battalion of Kansas volunteers scouting north of the Saline for a large force of Indians said to be there. His assessment of the volunteers was highly unfavorable, calling them "a set to contemplate with curiosity" and having "no particular business with Indians." Comments critical of Armes and his actions appear

---

[45] Armes, *Ups and Downs*, 244, 246–48; Blackburn, "18th Kansas Cavalry," 10–11; Burkey, *Custer, Come at Once*, 36; Jenness, "Battle of Beaver Creek," 450–51; Nye, *Plains Indian Raiders*, 103; Powell, *People of the Sacred Mountain*, 1:495–96; White, *Hostiles and Horse Soldiers*, 61–64.

to have been largely confined to members of the Eighteenth Kansas Volunteer Cavalry, particularly from Moore and the scout Pliley. This may have represented the usual friction and dislike between the regular military and volunteers, or it may reflect the youth and apparently acerbic personality and temperament of Armes, something that plagued him throughout his career. There were surely good reasons to be critical of nearly all of those involved in the leadership, despite their later self-laudatory writings and criticisms of others.[46]

Armes's report of the engagement on the Prairie Dog indicated that of the 164 men under his command, 32 were wounded and 3 were killed. Corporal Towell had died of his wounds at Fort Hays. Armes reported his belief that no fewer than 50 Indians were killed and another 150 wounded. Between them, Captains Armes and Jenness estimated that approximately 800 to 1,000 warriors were involved in the fight and that they were from the Cheyenne and Kiowa tribes. They and their scouts claimed to have identified Roman Nose, Charlie Bent, and Satanta among the "chiefs" present. It is extremely doubtful that any Kiowas were involved in the fight, and had Satanta been present, he would have been easily identified by his crimson battle colors. It is not unlikely that warriors from the Kiyuksa Oglala band of Lakotas were present, including prominent war leaders such as Pawnee Killer. It is likewise possible that Roman Nose was involved in the fight, and he may have been the brave warrior who dashed through the hollow square of the Jenness detachment unscathed. No one, however, mentioned his magnificent warbonnet with the buffalo horn in the front, so he may not have been there. It is less likely that Charlie Bent was present, since he usually stayed in one of the southern camps and not with the Dog Soldiers.[47]

The estimates of the number of warriors present are far too excessive, given the fighting strength of the Dog Soldier and southern Sutaio Cheyennes and of the Kiyuksa Oglalas combined. No Sicangus (Brulés) were known to be involved, and certainly no more than a handful of Arapahoes. Likewise the number of Indian casualties is unrealistic, almost equaling the total number of warriors these bands of Cheyennes could field. Such wild estimates were not necessarily intentionally inflated but rather resulted from different men counting the same dead and wounded

---

[46] Armes, *Ups and Downs*, 247; Blackburn, "18th Kansas Cavalry," 11–12; Utley, *Life in Custer's Cavalry*, 96, 99; White, *Hostiles and Horse Soldiers*, 63–64.

[47] Armes, *Ups and Downs*, 244, 246–48; Nye, *Plains Indian Raiders*, 103; White, *Hostiles and Horse Soldiers*, 55–56.

and the nearly impossible task of guessing how many constantly moving warriors were present as they appeared, disappeared, and reappeared from behind hills or breaks in the land. Under such circumstances a few would appear to be a great many.

The location of this fight has long been debated and disputed. Both Armes and Jenness thought they were on Beaver Creek, with the Republican the next major stream beyond. Indeed, Jenness referred to it in his later writings as the "Battle of Beaver Creek." But this is clearly in error since neither the reported mileage of their marches and the direction traveled, nor the time factor involved, could possibly have taken them so far. All of the other participants who wrote of the battle placed it on Prairie Dog Creek, which is the most viable candidate given the mileage, time and direction components.[48]

The fight on the Prairie Dog was the last major combat in 1867 with the Indians of the southern plains. The uproar in the East caused by the Hancock expedition and the ensuing Indian war resulted in the passage of an act by Congress on July 20, 1867, creating a peace commission that was to seek an end to the conflict without further bloodshed. Nevertheless it was intended to accomplish the same purpose as the Hancock expedition—the acquisition of the Indian country and removal of the native inhabitants—but through negotiations and voluntary consent. This was something the Indians would never have knowingly submitted to. The commission was to negotiate the nonnegotiable, as it were. But the passage of the act forced General Sherman to accede to the legislative and executive will. He issued orders suspending further offensive operations and confining his troops to protecting the trails and railroad workers from Indian attacks, pending the outcome of the commission's work. There was to be at least an effort, however flawed, to achieve an end to Hancock's War.[49]

---

[48] Blackburn, "18th Kansas Cavalry," 11–12; White, *Hostiles and Horse Soldiers*, 64.
[49] Athearn, *William Tecumseh Sherman*, 174.

CHAPTER TWENTY-SEVEN

THE MEDICINE LODGE
PEACE TREATIES

Winfield Scott Hancock intended to awe the Indians of the southern plains with the power and overwhelming numbers of the United States Army. This, he reasoned, would convince them that resistance was futile and acceptance of the government's terms was their only recourse. He thought that a show of resistance by the Cheyennes, with its inevitable result, might even be desirable. It would provide the other southern tribes with a stern example of the dire consequences of flouting the might of the army. But his flawed and arrogant reasoning failed to take into account the character of his targeted enemy. The Cheyennes were good and honest people, devoted to their families and deeply religious. But they were also of a warrior culture, great hunters and horsemen who loved their country and way of life every bit as much as Hancock loved his. They had no desire to live as white farmers on a reservation or to become Christians. They would surrender neither culture nor country without a fight, and though they could not on their best day field a force of fighting men that was more than a small fraction of that of their opponents, the Fighting Cheyennes would rather make a stand than meekly surrender.

Despite the enormous odds against them in terms of manpower, military weapons, and technology, some factors favored the Cheyennes. They knew their country thoroughly, and their enemy did not; they could ride circles around the best the cavalry had to offer; and they could shoot their arrows more often and with more deadly effect than most soldiers could fire their weapons, some up to ten times in a minute. Then, too, they were defending what was most precious to them—their families, their way of life, their religious beliefs, and their own country. So when Hancock burned the

Cheyenne and Oglala villages on Pawnee Fork on April 19, 1867, the Cheyennes reacted with predictable rage—and they went to war with whites.

Soon eastern newspapers were expressing a sense of uneasiness and apprehension. Critical editorials began to appear. Hancock's much touted expedition had embarked for the plains with high hopes for quick and easy results. Its esteemed leader, the hero who held the line against Pickett's charge on the third day at Gettysburg, seemed certain to produce another grand result in vanquishing the Indians of the southern plains and putting them on reservations. Hancock himself had seen to it that there would be ample advance publicity. Now stories of miscalculations and blundering in dealing with those Indians were appearing, fueled in part by the reports of Indian agents Jesse Leavenworth and Edward Wynkoop that deplored Hancock's actions and predicted war. Peace advocates and eastern humanitarians, concerned about what whites were doing to Indians, began to complain loudly. And as the war erupted and grew in intensity, so did the criticism. It became known as Hancock's War, much to the chagrin of the principal architect, who could sense possible problems for his presidential aspirations. As casualties and costs mounted, concern grew in the halls of government. To bring an end to the conflict, the idea of two large reservations was once again brought up by the Interior Department and the Indian bureau. It was hardly new, but the previous efforts and treaties with the Plains Indians had failed. Referred to as the "concentration policy," it called for one such reservation south of the Arkansas River for the southern Plains tribes, and another north of the Platte for those of the northern plains. With the exception of Indian agents and agency workers, whites would be prohibited from these reserves, supposedly eliminating their constant harassment and the whiskey and other vices they introduced in exchange for the Indians' material goods. Railroads and trails would then be free from Indian attacks, and in time the Indians would be educated, Christianized, "civilized," and turned into yeoman farmers. Naturally this policy did not consider the desires, rights, or needs of the Indians.[1]

The concentration policy ironically found much in common with the ideas espoused by Generals Pope and Sherman, though the latter viewed it from the military perspective of recognizing a hostile Indian from a friendly one, that is, on or off the reservation. And Secretary of Interior Orville H. Browning and Commissioner of Indian Affairs Lewis V. Bogy proposed to accomplish it by peaceful means rather than by force. More-

---

[1] Utley, *Frontier Regulars*, 130–31.

over they were strongly opposed to ignoring existing treaty rights, including the right of the Cheyennes to continue to hunt in the Smoky Hill
country—something most Cheyennes did not believe was even subject to
a treaty. But the coinciding of proposals for defined reservations pleased
Sherman to the point that he did not oppose that of Browning and Bogy.
Lewis Bogy lost his position as Indian commissioner when he failed to
receive Senate confirmation and was succeeded by the former Tennessee
congressman and Methodist minister Nathaniel G. Taylor. Taylor's sense
of piety caused him to embrace and further refine the concept. He made
his proposal to the Senate in a letter of July 12, 1867. It came at a time
when Congress was greatly concerned not only over the failure of the
expensive Hancock expedition to secure the anticipated results but also
by the mounting costs of the continuing conflict attributed to it. In an
address to the Senate on July 16, Sen. John B. Henderson of Missouri,
chairman of the Committee on Indian Affairs, stated: "This war, if it lasts
during the summer and fall, will cost us $100,000,000." He added that
the government was then expending as much as "$125,000 to $250,000"
daily on the war. It was Henderson who introduced legislation for the
creation of a peace commission to pursue Taylor's proposal.[2]

Henderson's bill had the support of eastern and midwestern humanitarians and peace advocates as well as many of the newspapers and those
concerned with the impact of the war on the national budget. It was fiercely
opposed by most westerners, governors of western states like Samuel Crawford, and western newspapers, all of whom feared having either reservations or Indians within their borders. There was contentious debate
between advocates and opponents of the bill, and a number of amendments were proposed. One of these, offered by Kansas senator Edmund
G. Ross (a friend and strong ally of Gov. Samuel Crawford), provided
that if the peace commission failed, the secretary of war was authorized
to accept four thousand volunteers "to conquer a peace," no doubt the
outcome preferred by most westerners. But with his disastrous campaign,
Hancock himself had handed the bill's proponents a strong argument,
recalling for Congress and the public what even Sherman referred to as
"the Chivington process." Moreover, news of his burning of the Cheyenne
and Oglala villages had reached the Lakotas in the north, effectively ruin-
ing the efforts of the peace commission led by General Sully, at that time
meeting with some of the Lakota chiefs at Fort Laramie. An added irony

---

[2] Ibid.; Washburn, *American Indian*, 3:1504.

was the reading in the Senate chambers of General Sherman's June 17 telegram sent from Fort McPherson to Secretary of War Edwin Stanton, wherein he stated that so long as fifty Indians remained between the Platte and the Arkansas they would checkmate three thousand soldiers. "Rather get them out as soon as possible," Sherman wrote, "and it makes little difference whether they be coaxed out by Indian Commissioners or killed." By its own unintended reflection of "the Chivington process," and no doubt to Sherman's dismay, it helped the bill pass. Senate Bill 136, the Henderson Bill, was passed and sent to the president for signature on July 20 and returned with his signature on July 30.[3]

The avowed purpose of the Henderson bill and the peace commission it created was (a) to remove, if possible, the cause of war; (b) to secure as far as practicable the frontier settlements and the safe building of the railroads to the Pacific; and (c) to suggest or inaugurate some plan for the "civilization" of the Indians. It provided for a commission consisting of seven members, four of whom were appointed in the bill itself: Senator Henderson; Commissioner of Indian Affairs N. G. Taylor; Samuel F. Tappan of Boston, humanitarian and head of the military investigation into the Sand Creek Massacre; and John B. Sanborn, a Minnesota lawyer and former major general in the volunteer army during the Civil War. The other three were to be military officers appointed by the president. President Andrew Johnson promptly appointed Alfred H. Terry, commander of the Department of the Dakota;, retired Gen. William S. Harney (former nemesis of the Sicangu Teton Lakotas at the Battle of the Blue Water on September 3, 1855, but now considered sympathetic to the plight of the Indians); and, to his undoubted chagrin, Lt. Gen. William T. Sherman himself. On August 7, 1867, the commissioners—minus Terry and Henderson, who had not yet arrived—met in St. Louis to plan their course of action. They discussed routes of travel, the feeding of the Indians in attendance, procedures for the treaty councils, and other administrative details. Nathaniel Taylor was elected as chairman of the commission. Probably considering the earlier arrival of cold weather to the north, they decided to first treat with the Lakotas during September and then move south to Kansas and meet with the southern Plains tribes during the first full moon of October.[4]

---

[3] W. T. Sherman to E. M. Stanton, June 17, 1867, U.S. Senate, "Indian Hostilities," 121; *Harper's Weekly*, August 3, 1867, 481; Jones, *Treaty of Medicine Lodge*, 17; Leckie, *Military Conquest*, 58; Utley, *Frontier Regulars*, 131–32.

[4] Athearn, *William Tecumseh Sherman*, 171–74; Jones, *Treaty of Medicine Lodge*, 17–21; Utley, *Frontier Regulars*, 132.

While the commission was organizing itself and plotting its future course, General Sherman ordered a halt to offensive operations against hostile Plains Indians until the commission had the opportunity to perform its duty. To General Hancock he telegraphed instructions to place all troops in a defensive mode so the commission's "effort to settle the Indian question peaceably may have a fair chance of success." Hancock sent out orders to implement his instructions. Though not likely his idea, Sherman's command structure was changed as well. The uproar in the East resulting from Hancock's burning of the villages on the Pawnee Fork had focused public attention on the army in an uncomfortable way. Ineptitude and blundering by army commanders was already seen as a prime cause of Indian wars and was recognized as such in the Doolittle Report. The lifeblood of the army was congressional goodwill and appropriations. If an officer came under heavy criticism, it was common practice to transfer him to another command to protect both the army and the officer. In this case it had a double benefit and a dual cause. Philip H. Sheridan, "Little Phil," had been in command of the Fifth Military District (Louisiana and Texas), where his heavy-handed administration of the Reconstruction laws was controversial and ran counter to the president's desires. President Johnson removed him from command on July 31, 1867, and on August 26 assigned Hancock to replace him at the Fifth Military District. On September 12 Sheridan replaced Hancock at the Department of the Missouri.[5]

After their organizational meetings, the commissioners traveled up the Missouri River to interview white citizens of the frontier states and members of various Lakota bands. Moving west by rail, they picked up Senator Henderson at St. Joseph, Missouri, then crossed the river to Fort Leavenworth. There they took testimony from Indian agents, soldiers (including Hancock), and others concerning the Hancock expedition, Indian raiding, inept military officers, thieving Indian agents, and other matters. One of those appearing to testify was Kansas governor Samuel Crawford. A Leavenworth newspaper, commenting on his intended appearance, stated: "The governor will confer with the peace powwowists, but is not known to sympathize with their policy." The testimony completed, the commissioners boarded the riverboat *St. Johns* at nearby Leavenworth to begin their trip upriver. En route they interviewed various groups of Lakotas and at Fort Thompson picked up General Terry.

---

[5] Hutton, *Phil Sheridan and His Army*, 20–27; Jones, *Treaty of Medicine Lodge*, 20; Leckie, *Military Conquest*, 59; Nye, *Plains Indian Raiders*, 105, 105n1.

Finally they worked their way back downriver to Omaha, where they boarded a Union Pacific train bound for North Platte, Nebraska. There they met with a number of Oglala and Sicangu leaders on September 19. The Indians expressed their displeasure with the whites' roads along the Smoky Hill and Powder rivers. These roads were displacing game and interfering with hunting, so the Indians demanded their abandonment. Sherman bluntly informed them that the trails and railroads were there to stay and that they must not interfere with travel on them. During the council, word was received from Fort Laramie, their intended goal, that Red Cloud and the other hostile Lakota leaders would not attend a peace council until the whites first abandoned the Bozeman Trail and the forts along it. Thus the only agreement at North Platte was that the Indians would come again for further talks when the commissioners returned in November. The commissioners moved back to Leavenworth, with hopes that their meeting with the southern Plains tribes would be more fruitful.[6]

When they arrived in Leavenworth, Sherman was recalled by Grant for a leadership conference. At the time, Congress and President Johnson were locked in a struggle that would end in articles of impeachment. Sherman was back in his headquarters in St. Louis by the latter part of September. One of the first matters requiring his attention was attacks against the railroad construction workers along the Smoky Hill route. Robert M. Shoemaker, general superintendent of the railroad, telegraphed Governor Crawford on September 21 informing him that a Cheyenne raiding party had killed one of the principal contractors and three other men on September 19. He was asking again for a full regiment of infantry to guard the working parties. Crawford sent two telegrams to Sherman, describing the situation in the field in dire terms and offering to raise a regiment of volunteers immediately. He exaggerated and embellished his report, claiming the Indians had fired into construction trains, attacked and captured parts of three government trains, attacked most of the work parties along the right-of-way, killed one contractor and eight employees, wounded many more, and committed various other depredations. Sherman responded on September 24, refusing to accept the volunteers and commenting that the railroad should not push its work parties too far out until after the council with the Cheyennes. Crawford, who had no sympathy with the peace commission or its objectives, was no doubt annoyed,

[6] *Leavenworth Daily Conservative*, August 11, 1867; Athearn, *William Tecumseh Sherman*, 175–82; Garfield, "Defense of the Kansas Frontier," 342; Jones, *Treaty of Medicine Lodge*, 21–24.

but Sherman's hands were tied and there the matter stayed. It is possible this represented an effort by Shoemaker and Crawford to scuttle the forthcoming peace talks, which neither wanted. A Mr. Marshall, on the scene at Fort Harker as a representative of the railroad's eastern financiers, wrote from Junction City on September 18 that he had gone to the end of track with the railroad commissioners without problems: "The Indians west of us have been making some trouble lately, but I do not apprehend any trouble with our trains. There have been several attacks made on wagon trains and some stock stolen, and a few men killed, but those things you must expect when you pass over other peoples' grounds." This suggests that the dire reports and predictions of Shoemaker and Crawford were blatantly exaggerated and intended to stir the pot for their own ends.[7]

Aside from their ultimate goal of getting the Indians on reservations and securing peace, the commissioners themselves were not of one mind. Senator Henderson, a scholarly man, believed that the government was violating its treaties with the Plains Indians by promoting construction of western railroads. Moreover, he held that the railroads, stage lines, and telegraph companies all received their franchises with the full knowledge that they faced great dangers when they crossed Indian country, and therefore they should not be seeking protection from the military. Sherman, on the other hand, thought that view impractical. He wrote his brother: "Whether right or wrong, the Roads will be built, and everyone knows that Congress, after granting the charters, and fixing the Routes, cannot now back out and surrender the country to a few bands of roving Indians." Sherman also believed that the granting of permission for construction of railroads, stage lines, and telegraph lines included an implied promise to provide military protection. This was the premise that he worked from in his administration of the Division of the Missouri.[8]

The members of the peace commission gathered again in St. Louis at the end of September. Sherman did not attend because he was once again recalled to Washington. The other members moved to Leavenworth during the first week in October and boarded a train bound for Ellsworth and Fort Harker. Accompanying them was a Kansas delegation, including Governor Crawford and Sen. Edmund G. Ross; nine members of the press corps, with Henry Stanley among them; and a large number of secretaries and aides. As the train clattered westward, there was a great deal

---

[7] Athearn, *William Tecumseh Sherman*, 182–83; Garfield, "Defense of the Kansas Frontier," 341–42; Jones, *Treaty of Medicine Lodge*, 24–25; Snell and Richmond, *Union and Kansas Pacific*, 343.

[8] Athearn, *William Tecumseh Sherman*, 182–83.

of discussion between commissioners and reporters about the troubles with the Indians and the irritants preventing good relations with them. Hancock's burning of the villages on Pawnee Fork was an obvious factor, but there were more fundamental causes of conflict, primarily the entry of whites into the Indian country, the great trails and roads, and now the railroads. Article II of the Treaty of the Little Arkansas provided that the Cheyennes and Arapahoes were "expressly permitted to reside upon and range at pleasure throughout the unsettled portions of that part of the country they claim as originally theirs, which lies between the Arkansas and the Platte Rivers." That included the Smoky Hill country, the heartland of the Dog Soldier and southern Sutaio bands of Cheyennes, none of whom had approved or signed the treaty. Even those Indians who did sign thought this provision prohibited whites from constructing roads, railroads, or further settlements anywhere in it, and they were allowed to believe that was so. As lawyers, Sanborn and Henderson knew the Indians' contentions had merit, especially considering what they were told at the time. Conversations about these and other factors continued until the train arrived at Fort Harker on October 7.[9]

Preparations for the peace council were under way long before the commissioners arrived at the fort. Superintendent Thomas Murphy moved quickly when told to prepare for a council following the first full moon in October. He wrote the two agents, Leavenworth and Wynkoop, telling them of the proposed council and what he wanted them to do. From the army's Quartermaster Department he ordered the large quantity of rations necessary to feed the Indians, as well as the considerable quantity of gifts and supplies required for a large peace council. These were shipped by rail to Fort Harker, then taken by wagon train to Fort Larned for storage until a council ground had been selected and the Indians began arriving. Wynkoop supervised receipt and storage of the supplies from his agency headquarters at Fort Larned. To handle shipment to the council site and distribution to the Indians, Murphy engaged the services of David A. Butterfield. Meanwhile Leavenworth traveled to the mouth of the Little Arkansas River and, using the services of William (Dutch Bill) Griffenstein and James R. Mead, two longtime plainsmen and Indian traders, arranged for runners to be sent to the camps of the tribes with whom the commission intended to meet.[10] They carried with them a written message asking the chiefs of the five south-

[9] Stanley, "British Journalist," 250–51; Jones, *Treaty of Medicine Lodge*, 25–29.
[10] The Little Arkansas River was then the site of the Wichita Indian village and later where the town of Wichita, Kansas, was established.

ern Plains tribes to come to the mouth of the Little Arkansas to talk with Colonel Leavenworth regarding peace proposals.[11]

The first word of a peace council for the Cheyennes was received by Black Kettle, then camping on the north fork of the Red River. Upon receiving the letter, Black Kettle immediately undertook to comply with the request that he attend. He moved his village north to Lake Creek, then set out for the Little Arkansas with George Bent. They found Colonel Leavenworth, Griffenstein, Mead, Jesse Chisholm, and other white men waiting for them, along with the Yamparika Comanche chiefs Ten Bears and Tall Hat and the Kiowa chief Black Eagle. Yellow Horse and two other Arapahoe chiefs arrived the same day. Leavenworth told them all of the peace commission and the proposed peace council. It was old Ten Bears who suggested holding the council at Medicine Lodge Creek.[12]

After this meeting Black Kettle returned to his village to notify his people. Meanwhile George Bent and Griffenstein's Cheyenne wife (known as Cheyenne Jennie) were sent to deliver the message to the various tribes. At the same time, Griffenstein traveled with Jesse Chisholm to Chisholm's trading ranch on the North Canadian River to meet with some of the other Kiowa and Comanche chiefs camped nearby. The message they carried asked the chiefs of the five southern Plains tribes to meet with Superintendent Murphy at Fort Larned and select a place for the great council. Subsequently, many of the chiefs went to the fort and had their talk with Murphy, agreeing that a Medicine Lodge Creek site would be good from the perspective of the Indians. It was in the Kiowa, Comanche, and Plains Apache country, with plenty of water, wood, and good grazing. It was also easily accessible from Fort Larned, but far enough that the Indians would not be nervous about the presence of large numbers of soldiers. Shortly after that meeting Murphy traveled to Medicine Lodge Creek and selected the actual council ground—a wide, level area on the northeast side of the creek, not far from where the Kiowas held their annual Sun Dance. He notified the peace commission of the proposed meeting ground in mid-September, and the commissioners accepted it.[13]

With the council ground determined, Murphy began the process of moving the great stock of foodstuffs and supplies to it. At Medicine Lodge

[11] Hyde, *Life of George Bent*, 278–79; Jones, *Treaty of Medicine Lodge*, 44–45.

[12] Berthrong, *Southern Cheyennes*, 289–93; Grinnell, *Fighting Cheyennes*, 270–73; Hyde, *Life of George Bent*, 278–82; Jones, *Treaty of Medicine Lodge*, 24–25; Powell, *People of the Sacred Mountain*, 1:506–508.

[13] Berthrong, *Southern Cheyennes*, 289–93; Grinnell, *Fighting Cheyennes*, 270–73; Hyde, *Life of George Bent*, 278–82; Jones, *Treaty of Medicine Lodge*, 24–25; Powell, *People of the Sacred Mountain*, 1:506–508.

Creek nearly fourteen hundred Indians were already encamped, mostly Arapahoes and Plains Apaches. These two tribes took it upon themselves to protect the great cache of supplies being accumulated, along with the white personnel and the wagon trains bringing them. From that time on, a steady stream of wagons moved between Fort Larned and the council grounds, bringing the necessary supplies and presents. A constant flow of food to the site was critical in sustaining the tribal encampments until members of the peace commission arrived, for any interruption would likely result in the Indians drifting away to hunt. Large numbers of Indians were arriving daily in response to the invitations sent to their many encampments across the southern plains. Bands of Kiowas and Comanches were soon in camp a few miles downstream from the council grounds, and more were coming every day. There was a solid representation from the major Kiowa bands and from the Penateka (including remnants of the Tenawa and Tanima bands), Nokoni, Kotsoteka, and Yamparika Comanches. Of the Comanches only the Kwahadis of the Staked Plains (Llano Estacado) had either not heard of the council or chose not to attend. Ominously the Cheyennes were the least represented. Only those of Black Kettle's peace faction, with from twenty-five to sixty lodges, were present, located on the southwest side of the stream across from the ration and supply camp established by Murphy and David Butterfield.[14]

Though the Cheyenne presence at the council ground was limited, a very large Cheyenne village lay about fifty miles to the west-southwest on Bluff Creek, a tributary of the Cimarron River. Whites at the time thought it a menacing thing, with rumors abounding that Cheyennes from the village intended to attack the council itself. In fact it had an entirely different purpose. Earlier in the summer, after Hancock's burning of the Pawnee Fork villages and the subsequent drift to war, Stone Forehead, Keeper of the Sacred Arrows, sent a man bearing a sacred pipe and a message to the chiefs and headmen of the Tsistsistas. The message was that the People were to gather at the end of summer, by the Moon-of-Dust-in-the-Face (October), for the renewal of Maahótse, the Sacred Arrows. For the Cheyennes the ceremony of renewal was and still remains the most important of their great sacred ceremonies. It lasts four days and is undertaken on the pledge of a member of the Council of Forty-four or of a warrior during difficult times for the tribe. The purpose is the renewal, purifica-

---

[14] Berthrong, *Southern Cheyennes*, 293–94; Grinnell, *Fighting Cheyennes*, 273; Hyde, *Life of George Bent*, 283; Jones, *Treaty of Medicine Lodge*, 44–45; Nye, *Plains Indian Raiders*, 106–107; Powell, *People of the Sacred Mountain*, 1:509.

tion, and sanctification of the People. At this supreme act of worship, all kindreds and bands of the Cheyennes were expected to be present. By 1867, however, because of the new roads, railroads, military posts, and advancing settlements of the whites, it was nearly impossible for all the northern people to make their way south for even this most compelling of reasons. Still those that could did come. White Head's band of Òhméseheso was now traveling with the Dog Soldiers and southern Sutaio, and possibly Turkey Leg brought his people down from the Republican River country to join them, giving the northern People representation in the spiritual coming together of the Tsistsistas. Though they were aware of a gathering for the great peace council at Medicine Lodge Creek, the Cheyennes could not come nearer to other peoples, white or Indian, until their sacred ceremony was complete.[15]

While Murphy and his men were finishing preparations for the council at Medicine Lodge Creek, back at Fort Harker the commission was leaving for the council grounds. On October 8 they left the fort, crossed the Smoky Hill, and went into camp two miles south of the post to organize their train. There were ten light horse-drawn army ambulances to carry the peace commissioners, their staff, the Kansas delegation, and the newsmen. Moving behind them was a long train of freight wagons, pulled by six-mule teams and carrying treaty goods and supplies. Two companies of the Seventh Cavalry, G and M, led by Captain Barnitz, and the Gatling guns of Battery B, Fourth Artillery, provided their military escort, a total of about two hundred men, commanded by Maj. Joel H. Elliot. They began their march the next morning, following the military road south to Fort Larned and moving into the teeth of the stiff south wind of the southern plains that was to be their constant companion.[16]

The first night, the commissioners stopped along Cow Creek, and by October 10 they were following the old Santa Fe Trail along the Great North Bend of the Arkansas. They camped that night along the river about thirty miles short of Fort Larned. Sometime after dark a messenger rode in from the council ground, sent by Superintendent Murphy to report that General Sherman had telegraphed the commander at Fort Larned to deliver no more food to the Indians until the commissioners arrived. This greatly concerned Murphy, surrounded by some five thousand hungry Indians who might either blame him and his crew or simply leave the site

[15] Berthrong, *Southern Cheyennes*, 52–53, 56–67; Grinnell, *Cheyenne Indians*, 2:211, 285; Hoebel, *Cheyennes*, 6–17; Powell, *People of the Sacred Mountain*, 1:506–509; Powell, *Sweet Medicine*, 2:442–71.

[16] Jones, *Treaty of Medicine Lodge*, 29, 37–40.

to hunt. Sanborn offered to ride to Fort Larned and persuade the post commander to release the rations, and Taylor accepted his offer. He rode all night and was successful in getting another train of provisions on the road the next morning, thus averting a serious problem.[17]

During the afternoon of October 11 the long column of ambulances and wagons reached the intersection of the Wet and Dry routes on the Santa Fe Trail, the latter leading southwesterly to Fort Larned. Most of the column continued south along the Wet Route next to the Arkansas River and crossed the Pawnee Fork near its mouth. Six miles beyond they turned east, left the Santa Fe road, and crossed the river, camping a mile from the crossing. Meanwhile the ambulance carrying Commissioners Harney and Tappan, followed by those of the newsmen, turned southwesterly on the Dry Route and drove to Fort Larned. They were met there by Sanborn and Wynkoop and ushered into a private room at the rear of the sutler's store and saloon. Sanborn offered them liquid refreshments, and they spent a convivial time talking. Shortly thereafter Sanborn led in a delegation of Indians, including Satanta of the Kiowas and Little Raven of the Arapahoes. A friendly "cocktail party" followed at which the Indians were given their fair share of the "fire water." After about an hour Sanborn announced it was time to leave, and the commissioners and reporters returned to their ambulances, while the Indians mounted their horses and accompanied them to the night's encampment.[18]

The first business meeting of the peace commission since leaving Fort Leavenworth was held that night at their camp a mile southeast of the Arkansas. Before coming to the Indian country, the commission had sent a letter to Governor Crawford of Kansas, inviting him to express his views of the peace council—hence the presence of the Kansas delegation. Senator Henderson made a few prefatory remarks, noting the commitments made to the southern Plains tribes in previous treaties and their bearing on the upcoming negotiations. Crawford was impatient and failed to see the relevancy, interrupting Henderson repeatedly. When it was his turn, Crawford presented the commission with his written response—a long, vitriolic letter. In essence it was a litany of complaints and an outline of the history of conflict with the Plains Indians as he saw it, all of which he deemed their fault alone.[19]

---

[17] Ibid., 41–47.
[18] Ibid., 48–54.
[19] Crawford, *Kansas in the Sixties*, 265–72; Jones, *Treaty of Medicine Lodge*, 57–61.

Crawford asserted that all of the Plains tribes had to be removed from the state or else civilization and settlements would end in Kansas. According to him, hundreds of innocent settlers—men, women, and children—had been murdered and scalped, and he wanted all of the perpetrators out of Kansas and all of the lands in the state used exclusively for whites. He even wanted the large Osage Reservation in southeastern Kansas dissolved, the Osages (who he claimed were making war on whites) removed, and their land transferred to the state. Milton Reynolds, editor of the *Lawrence State Journal* and one of the reporters present, wrote that not only were Crawford's charges against the Osages preposterous but the real reason he wanted them removed was that he and Senator Ross were interested in a project to build a railroad to Texas that would cross the Osage Reservation. Success in doing this would bring a fortune to stockholders in the railroad and to those who helped them.[20]

Crawford's diatribe was not well received by the commissioners, especially General Harney, who developed an intense dislike for the governor. While the reactions of the newsmen were varied, a number had the same unfavorable opinion of him and wrote scathing articles for their papers. Nothing came of Crawford's complaints, and the commission refused to stipulate that no more Indian reservations would be established in the state or that troop strengths would be maintained at or above current levels, as Crawford desired.[21]

When the meeting finally broke up, Superintendent Murphy took Taylor and other members of the commission aside to caution them about having too large a military escort when they entered the council grounds and even to suggest having no escort. But the commissioners were unwilling to proceed without military protection, and Murphy's suggestion was not accepted. In fact, before leaving their camp on the morning of October 12, they were joined by Agents Leavenworth and Wynkoop, along with two infantry companies from Fort Larned riding in army ambulances. Also accompanying them were a large number of "camp followers and scavengers," called bummers, a motley crew of civilians claiming various reasons for being there. Mostly they were simply curious and wanting free government rations.[22]

The peace commission camp for the evening of October 12 was to be on

[20] Crawford, *Kansas in the Sixties*, 265–72; Jones, *Treaty of Medicine Lodge*, 57–61.

[21] Jones, *Treaty of Medicine Lodge*, 62–64.

[22] Stanley, "British Journalist," 260; Jones, *Treaty of Medicine Lodge*, 64–66; Stanley, *My Early Travels*, 225.

Rattlesnake Creek, about halfway to the council grounds. During the midafternoon a scout returned to report a large herd of buffalo ahead of the column. Immediately a hunting party of reporters, staff members, orderlies, bummers, and some of the soldier escort rushed out to the peacefully grazing bison and began to shoot them. A few dismounted and cut out tongues or buffalo steaks, but mostly the dead animals were left to rot where they fell. This called down the wrath of Satanta, who complained loudly to General Harney about the foolishness of white men, who killed without need or purpose. As translated for the reporters, he said: "Have the white men become children that they should kill meat and not eat? When the red men kill, they do so that they may live." Harney himself was upset by the senseless slaughter and waste and called for an end to it. Major Elliot was ordered to arrest several of the offenders and return them to the column. With that, the march resumed, and in less than an hour they reached Rattlesnake Creek, where they made camp. That night a small party of horsemen arrived. It was Maj. Gen. C. C. Augur and a number of his aides, come to join the commission. He carried a letter that reported his appointment by presidential order to serve on the commission during the absence of General Sherman.[23]

The following morning the peace delegation broke camp early to begin its last lap to the council grounds. When the column was within a few miles from the site, General Harney ordered the escort to drop back and move to the rear so as not to alarm the Indians. Finally they crossed the last rise and descended into a small natural basin through which wound Medicine Lodge Creek (known to the Indians as the Timber Hill River or Medicine River), about three miles above its junction with Elm Creek.[24] Timber Hill, from which the stream derived one of its Indian names, was farther downstream on the east bank and across from the Sun Dance Lodge, built for the 1866 Kiowa Sun Dance. The commissioners' long column of ambulances, wagons, livestock, and mounted men entered the basin containing the council grounds and the villages of the five southern Plains tribes from its northwest end. In the valley and along the stream banks were scattered stands of trees—mostly cottonwood, elm, and ash, with some persimmon and other scrub trees. Directly ahead of the column as it entered the valley was Murphy and Butterfield's ration camp, and across the river from it the small Cheyenne village of Black Kettle

---

[23] Stanley, "British Journalist," 262–63; Jones, *Treaty of Medicine Lodge*, 66–69; Mayhall, *Kiowas*, 208; Stanley, *My Early Travels*, 228–29.

[24] Today Medicine Lodge Creek is known as the Medicine Lodge River.

and his fellow peace chiefs. According to most estimates, there were about 25 lodges and 150 people in it, though the numbers varied from day to day as families would come and go, especially as the Arrow Renewal ceremony drew closer. Just below the ration camp on the left bank of the stream was the Arapahoe village, at the time largest of all, and beyond it that of the Plains Apaches. According to Stanley and other reporters, there were then 171 Arapahoe lodges and 85 Apache lodges. Across the stream from the latter and below the small Cheyenne village was that of the Comanches, with 100 lodges, and below it on the west bank that of the Kiowas, with 150 lodges. Most of the villages could not be seen in their entirety, but through the trees that lined the creek banks the newly arrived white men could catch glimpses of great numbers of lodges and grazing horse herds on the hills. Apart from the Cheyennes, more members of each of the tribes were arriving daily as additional bands reached the area.[25]

Waiting to meet the commission was a small party of mounted and painted Indians, the most notable being Black Kettle, his tribe's most ardent peace advocate. According to some of the reporters, Black Kettle shocked the commissioners by telling them that the Cheyenne soldier societies might try to attack the council when it convened. But matters soon quieted down, and General Harney went about the task of organizing the commission's camp. The ambulances were drawn up in a hollow square with the tents and campfires inside. The wagon train and the military escort were organized in like fashion farther upstream and at a greater distance from the Indian villages. Strict rules governing entry and exit from the white camps and Indian villages were established, and the routine of camp life began. The next day, October 15, was primarily an opportunity for various tribal leaders to come to the commissioner's camp and have a few informal discussions, while several of the reporters wandered through the Indian villages, observing their daily routines. In the afternoon a tent fly was erected, and a talk held with chiefs from the five tribes in an attempt to establish a time for the grand council. The Kiowas and Comanches wanted to wait for the arrival of the Cheyennes, but Black Kettle pointed out that most of his tribe's members were preparing for the Renewal of the Sacred Arrows, which would take about five days. After further discussions the Kiowas and Comanches agreed to talks in four days, on October 19. To this the Arapahoes and Plains Apaches assented.[26]

---

[25] Stanley, "British Journalist," 261–64; Jones, *Treaty of Medicine Lodge*, 70–75; Mooney, *Calendar History*, 320; Powell, *People of the Sacred Mountain*, 1:511; Stanley, *My Early Travels*, 227–30.
[26] Jones, *Treaty of Medicine Lodge*, 73–83; Powell, *People of the Sacred Mountain*, 1:511.

The initiation of contacts with the Indians highlighted a growing dispute between Senator Henderson and General Harney. Although Henderson had a strong sense of justice and was quite aware of the legal obligations the government had previously undertaken and often failed to live up to, he was impatient and anxious to get on with a treaty. He saw no reason why the Cheyennes should delay. Commissioner Taylor believed in allowing the Indians to do things in their own way and on their own timeline. Harney agreed. He said the most foolhardy thing the commission could do would be to send ultimatums to the Cheyennes. Further, to avoid alarming any of the Indians, who already distrusted whites and particularly the military, he ordered members of the escort party to stay close to their own camp.[27]

At twilight on the evening of October 15 eighty heavily armed warriors chanting in unison rode out of the lengthening shadows to the west, their faces painted and the tails of their horses garlanded with feathers. They paid no attention to the others, whites or Indians, and splashed across the shallow stream at a trot, drew rein, and stopped when only a few yards from General Harney. The chanting ended, and they sat silently for a moment on their horses, the air around them filled with tension. They were Cheyennes, and Harney recognized their leaders as Tall Bull of the Dog Soldiers and White Head of the Óhmésèheso, the latter a man he had known on the northern plains in years past. White Head had with him a statement of his friendliness made out by General Harney in 1858. Harney greeted both with handshakes and backslapping, then led them to his tent while most of the other warriors remained mounted, sitting silently on their horses just outside of the commission circle. The tension continued to hang heavily as the time ticked by. After a while Harney and the two Cheyenne chiefs reappeared with expressions of friendship and handshakes, and the chiefs remounted and led their men back across the stream to Black Kettle's camp, where food provided by the commission awaited them. Later that night they returned to their camp on Bluff Creek. No one ever learned from General Harney the purpose of the visit of the two Cheyenne council chiefs or what was said. But Harney did invite them to return the following evening for hearings the commission intended to hold on the Hancock expedition. They accepted the invitation and did appear.[28]

Among other things, the law creating the peace commission charged it

---

[27] Jones, *Treaty of Medicine Lodge*, 80–83.

[28] Stanley, "British Journalist," 269; Jones, *Treaty of Medicine Lodge*, 84–85; Powell, *People of the Sacred Mountain*, 1:512–13; Stanley, *My Early Travels*, 235–36.

with finding the cause of the war on the plains, and for that purpose they had held hearings at Fort Leavenworth and North Platte, Nebraska. At the council on Medicine Lodge Creek they were particularly interested in determining the accuracy of the information that caused Hancock to take the field in the first place. Much of that information came from Maj. Henry Douglass, commanding Fort Dodge, and was given to Douglass by Fred Jones, one of the post interpreters. To assess this and other matters, the commission began their hearings on October 16, with the first witness being Edward Wynkoop. He testified essentially as he had previously reported to Superintendent Murphy, adding that the stories of Fred Jones about an alliance of southern Plains tribes to make war on whites was a complete fabrication and that the villages on Pawnee Fork were peaceful. General Hancock had been misled from start to finish, he said, and the little girl found in the Cheyenne village was not white but a mentally retarded Cheyenne child who was raped by the soldiers, not tribal members as reported. Wynkoop's testimony was followed by that of Major Douglass, who simply related what he had been told by Fred Jones that he had sent on to General Hancock. After Douglass's testimony the hearing was adjourned until the following day.[29]

Before the hearing on the Hancock expedition resumed the next morning, there was an unexpected period of turmoil and excitement. A rumor spread through the Indian camps that a large column of soldiers was approaching. This caused panic and preparations to flee. But when the great body of mounted men came into sight in the west, their long lances, headdresses, feathers, and blowing hair made it clear the riders were Indians, not soldiers. Tension remained, however, until it was apparent that the riders were additional bands of Comanches coming in for the council, not hostile Cheyennes intending to attack the peacemakers. A little later there was more trouble when Little Raven came to the commission camp to report that the Arapahoe horse herds had been raided, presumably by Pawnees. A war party was organized to pursue the raiders and, to the delight of Little Raven, returned four days later with all of the Arapahoe horses and the fresh scalps of several Kanza Indians killed in the recovery effort. Finally things settled down, and that evening Tall Bull and White Head returned as promised for the continuation of the Hancock hearing. They entered the commission's camp quietly and without escort, prepared to testify.[30]

---

[29] Stanley, "British Journalist," 269–74, 277–78; Jones, *Treaty of Medicine Lodge*, 86–93; Powell, *People of the Sacred Mountain*, 1:513–14; Stanley, *My Early Travels*, 236–43.

[30] Jones, *Treaty of Medicine Lodge*, 93–94; Powell, *People of the Sacred Mountain*, 1:514.

When the proceedings resumed, it was the commissioners' turn to cross-examine Major Douglass. To everyone's surprise, Douglass admitted that Fred Jones was considered untrustworthy by everyone at Fort Dodge, including himself, and that Major Page had refuted everything Jones said. Douglass gave no explanation as to why he forwarded the Jones story to General Hancock while omitting Page's statements in denial of them. Following the conclusion of Douglass's testimony, White Head addressed the commissioners. He told them that ever since Sand Creek, Cheyenne women and children feared having white troops come near their villages, and that is why they fled from Hancock. He claimed that his people were not hostile to whites until their village on Pawnee Fork was burned, and that after they received word of it, they resolved to go to war. White Head also told the commissioners that the little girl found in the Cheyenne village by Hancock's men was a Cheyenne girl and "not in her right mind," that she refused to go with the others and they had to leave her behind. When Sanborn asked if he was certain she was Cheyenne, White Head said that he knew her parents and had watched her grow up "day by day," that she was unharmed when he left the village, and that he was the last to leave. Before more questions could be asked, the meeting was disrupted by a loud and violent altercation in the nearby wagon park, where two teamsters were having a knife fight. By the time order was restored, most of the commissioners had gone to the wagon park, and the Indian witnesses disappeared into the night. This single event put an end to the Hancock hearings. The final report of the peace commission would find that no general war existed on the southern plains prior to General Hancock's entry, that Fred Jones's report was totally false, and that the Hancock expedition was ill-conceived and a cause of the war. The reporters mostly agreed, and even Stanley reversed his position and said that Hancock was misled.[31]

October 19, 1868, was the first day of the grand council. The site was about a mile downstream from the peace commission camp on the northeast bank of Medicine Lodge Creek, just below the Arapahoe village. Across the stream was the small Cheyenne encampment, and below the council site the village of the Plains Apaches. Superintendent Murphy's crew had cleared an area in a grove of cottonwood and elm trees along the creek, removing all brush and a number of trees, and then constructed an arbor twenty feet high in the center of the clearing. Folding tables were placed

[31] Stanley, "British Journalist," 278, 301–302; Jones, *Treaty of Medicine Lodge*, 94–97; Powell, *People of the Sacred Mountain*, 1:514.

at one end for the stenographers who would transcribe the proceedings, with campstools in front of them for the seven commissioners. These were flanked by tables and campstools for the press party. Arranged around the other three sides were several rows of logs on which the chiefs of the five tribes were to be seated. Other Indians or whites would either sit or stand in the shade of the trees beyond the arbor. Those chiefs who would speak for their people were to be seated at the front of their delegation. The Indians began arriving early, and by the time the white commissioners, their staffs, and the correspondents arrived in army ambulances, most were already patiently awaiting them. As the commissioners faced them, the Kiowas were on their left, with Satanta seated on a campstool of his own in front of the other chiefs. Next to the Kiowas were the Comanche chiefs, including Ten Bears and Silver Brooch. To the commissioners' right, Black Kettle and White Head were the only Cheyenne council chiefs present, and behind them sat George Bent, Charlie Bent, and Ed Guerrier as their interpreters.[32] On the right beyond the Cheyennes were the Arapahoe chiefs, led by Little Raven, and on the far right the Plains Apaches.[33]

Each tribe had interpreters of a sort, as did the commissioners. And herein lay one of the many great problems involved in whites and Indians attempting to understand each other's communications and intentions. The cultural abyss was huge, but compounding it was the inability to accurately convey meanings, because the signification of the language and words of one culture did not translate well into that of the other, even with the most sincere and objective effort. The finest and best-intentioned white interpreters heard and spoke through a thick veil of misunderstanding stemming from cultural differences, and it was no different for the Indians. Logically the best interpreters would have been the mixed-bloods, hearing since infancy the thoughts and expressions of both parents uttered in their native tongues. But even then it was not possible to give expression to words of one language for which there was no real equivalent in the other. Also the lack of common cultural concepts such as governmental sovereignty, private ownership of real property, outside restrictions on personal freedom, and similar European values and ideas made the task of adequately communicating intentions for a treaty insurmountable. Adding to this problem, few of the white interpreters used by the army, the Indian bureau, or other whites were very well qualified.[34]

---

[32] White Head's name was translated as "Gray Head," and so he was known to the whites present.
[33] Jones, *Treaty of Medicine Lodge*, 110–11.
[34] Ibid., 104–105.

Translating for the Comanches, whose Shoshonean language was that used for trade on the southern plains, was Phillip McCusker, a frontiersman and one of the few whites married to a Comanche woman. He was not raised in the Indian culture and thus faced the common problem of all whites in communicating meanings. The Kiowas had no interpreter who could translate from English and instead relied on Bä'o (Cat) to translate from McCusker's Comanche words. This undoubtedly further ensured that those words would be misunderstood. The Kiowa-Apaches, who camped with and constituted a part of the Kiowa tribal circle, spoke an Athapascan language that was so altered by long years of separation from other Athapascan-speaking peoples, and an almost equally long period of association with the Kiowa tribe, that they could not be understood by any of the other tribes. With no interpreter of their own to translate from English, they probably relied on a tribal member who could understand Kiowa to translate Cat's rendition of McCusker's Comanche. There was also no interpreter for the other Plains Apaches. These people spoke an understandable Apache dialect, and according to one of the correspondents present, their speeches were translated into Arapahoe by an Apache-speaking member of the Arapahoe tribe, then translated into English by the Arapahoe interpreter. Though it is often assumed these people were the same as the Kiowa-Apaches, most were of a different origin, possibly the consolidated remnants of earlier Apache bands roaming the plains, including Mescaleros, Jicarillas, Lipans, Conejeros, Palomas, Padoucas, and others. All Kiowa-Apaches were Plains Apaches, in the broad sense, but not all nor even most Plains Apaches were Kiowa-Apaches. Eighty-five lodges of Plains Apaches were camping separately at the Medicine Lodge Council, or about 510 people. James Mooney stated that there were probably never, at any time, much more than 350 Kiowa-Apaches. Translating for the Arapahoes was Margaret Adams, daughter of French-Canadian trader John Poisal and an Arapahoe woman, and widow of Thomas Fitzpatrick (Broken Hand), her first husband. For the Cheyennes there were George Bent, Charlie Bent, and Ed Guerrier, while John S. Smith translated Cheyenne speeches for the whites.[35]

A little after 10:00 A.M. Commissioner Taylor announced that Senator Henderson would speak for the government as soon as he arrived. White Head took the opportunity to advise that the Cheyennes would have noth-

[35] Haley, *Apaches*, 10, 13n; Jones, *Treaty of Medicine Lodge*, 105–108; Mayhall, *Kiowas*, 166; Mooney, *Calendar History*, 246–53, 321; Terrell, *Plains Apaches*, 15–23.

ing to say until the Arrow Renewal ceremony was completed and the other chiefs arrived from the Cimarron (Bluff Creek) village. Black Kettle said nothing, and probably with good reason. After the Hancock hearings concluded the previous evening, White Head and Tall Bull had gone to his camp and summoned him to the village on Bluff Creek to explain what he thought might be gained by trying to make peace with the *veho*.[36] If he failed to appear, Tall Bull told him, Dog Soldier warriors would kill all of his horses. By now Black Kettle, though a council chief and a member of the Council of Forty-four, had little influence in the tribe outside of his own followers. Senator Henderson arrived while White Head was still talking, and when the Óhméséheso chief took his seat, the senator began to speak. Dispensing with pleasantries, he first called attention to the treaties made in 1865 at the mouth of the Little Arkansas, asserting that the Indians had violated them, killing and kidnapping whites, obstructing free travel on the great roads, and interfering with construction of the railroad along the Smoky Hill. This, he said, disappointed the Great Father, who had sent the commission to learn who was responsible and the reason for their acts. Then he asked if the Indians had been mistreated by soldiers or agents, saying that the peace commission had come to correct any wrongs done to them. Henderson talked at length about the purposes of the commission and of the government's desire to provide homes and education for the Indians and give them arable land, cattle, farm equipment, schools, hospitals, churches, barns, and "all of the comforts of civilization." When he finished and invited response from the chiefs, it was Satanta who rose to answer first for the southern Plains tribes.[37]

In his speech Satanta first denied that the Kiowas or Comanches had been making war on whites. That he attributed to the Cheyennes. He then told the commissioners that the Kiowas and Comanches claimed all of the land south of the Arkansas and had no desire to give any of it away. After that, he spent a good deal of time discussing the homes, farms, hospitals, and churches that Henderson had mentioned, stating that he disapproved of them and his people did not want them. They loved the open plains and the buffalo, free of white structures and farms. When he finished, he was followed by old Ten Bears of the Yamparika Comanches

---

[36] The term *veho* means "spider." The spider was considered a creature of unique powers, and Cheyennes applied the term to whites, whose inventions so amazed them. It also carried with it the connotation of a trickster, the mind of whites being deceitful and intent upon tricking the Cheyennes and destroying their way of life. See Powell, *Sweet Medicine*, 1:299–300.

[37] Jones, *Treaty of Medicine Lodge*, 112–13; Stanley, *My Early Travels*, 244–47.

and then Silver Brooch of the Penateka Comanches. When Silver Brooch sat down, it was the turn of Gúaũtekánce (Poor Bear) of the Kiowa Apaches. The speeches of all of these men were filled with a sadness and pathos reflecting their prior experience with whites and the growing desperation they felt as the white world crowded in around them. When Poor Bear finished his speech in midafternoon, the commissioners adjourned the meeting until 10:00 A.M. the following day. They returned to their camp in ambulances and spent the rest of the day discussing the morning's events, preparing a final draft of a Kiowa-Comanche treaty, and making their next day's plans. Before evening on October 19 the commissioners finished work on the treaty they intended to present, probably using the treaties made at the Little Arkansas as their model. There were significant differences in some provisions. The Indians would be required to actually live on their reservation and must actively farm the land there to be eligible for treaty benefits. They would surrender their right to live or camp on former tribal lands outside of the reservation. So long as bison remained in sufficient numbers to justify hunting, they would be allowed to hunt in any unsettled country south of the Arkansas River in Kansas.[38]

After dark on October 19, word came that there were Indians out on the plains who were not of the five treaty tribes. Shortly after, about twenty Osage warriors came in to the commissioners' camp. They were comparatively tall men, though not as tall as the Cheyennes. They wished to see what was happening, to meet the commissioners, and to be fed, since they were tired and worn from their long journey. They ate just outside of the ring of commissioners' ambulances, then disappeared silently into the night and were not seen again by the whites. When morning came on October 20, the commissioners prepared themselves for the questions they were sure would be raised when the treaty provisions were read. But when they arrived at the council arbor at the appointed time, the Indians were not there. They finally appeared shortly before noon, some still drunk and many suffering hangovers from a night of drinking. General Harney believed this was the result of the Osages being present to trade whiskey for horses. Fortunately the chiefs were not under the influence, or so it was reported, and therefore the proceedings were opened by Commissioner Taylor.[39]

Ten Bears spoke first. He said the Comanches wanted nothing to do with reservations, barns, hospitals, or any of the other things the whites

[38] Stanley, "British Journalist," 281–84; Jones, *Treaty of Medicine Lodge*, 113–18; Mooney, *Calendar History*, 251.

[39] Stanley, "British Journalist," 284–85; Jones, *Treaty of Medicine Lodge*, 119–23.

wanted to give them. What they did want was to be left alone to roam the plains and hunt bison as they had always done. And he added that it was the whites who first broke the promises of the previous treaties. It was a poignant and touching speech, and his words were greeted by loud shouts of approval from the other Indians.[40]

After an added statement by Satanta, Senator Henderson stood and began his reply. He told the Indians the buffalo would not last forever and even then were becoming fewer. Before the white settlers took all of the good land, Henderson said, the commissioners wished to set aside a part of it for the exclusive use of the five tribes. There they would build a house (agency warehouse) to hold the goods that would be provided for them and where they could go to be fed and clothed. With that he outlined the terms of the treaty as it had been written—or so it was said. In substance it called for the Kiowas and Comanches to be placed on an island of land a tiny fraction the size of their own country, to adopt a farming way of life, and to surrender their ancient culture. For this and small annuities for a period of some years they would give their country to the white government—thousands of square miles in exchange for a tribal home of three million acres of the country that was already theirs. Further, Henderson phrased his explanation to conceal the real goal of the treaty, making a reservation sound more like a base of operations: "We do not ask you to cease hunting the buffalo. You may roam over the broad plains south of the Arkansas river and hunt the buffalo as you have done in years past, but you must have a place you can call your own. . . . We propose to make that home on the Red River and around the Wichita mountains, and we have prepared papers for that purpose. Tomorrow . . . we want your chiefs and headmen to meet us at our camp and sign the papers." However well intended from the perspective of the white commissioners, the proposed treaty had serious flaws and shortcomings as a tool to "civilize" the Indians. It aimed to make some of the greatest horsemen and horse breeders on earth into tillers of the soil on the marginal semiarid lands of the southern plains. And it was meant to convert proud, free nomads into meek, submissive agronomists within a matter of a few years.[41]

When Henderson finished, he asked if anyone had any comments on the treaty provisions. There is considerable doubt about how much of his

---

[40] Stanley, "British Journalist," 285–86; Jones, *Treaty of Medicine Lodge*, 122–26; Powell, *People of the Sacred Mountain*, 1:517–18.

[41] Stanley, "British Journalist," 286–87; Jones, *Treaty of Medicine Lodge*, 127; Powell, *People of the Sacred Mountain*, 1:518–19.

speech and explanation was translated properly or understood. Following a long silence, Satanta stood and spoke briefly: "I ask the Commission to tell the Great Father what I have to say. When the buffalo leave the country, we will let him know. By that time we will be ready to live in houses." There being no other speakers, Taylor adjourned the meeting, telling the Indians to return to the council arbor the next morning to sign the treaty. At 9:00 A.M. on October 21, 1867, they did so, with nine of their chiefs signing for the Kiowas and ten for the Comanches. At that time they believed they retained the right to go anywhere they wanted in their old country to hunt, which to their way of thinking also meant to live. Whether they understood that whites would soon settle in those lands is doubtful. Certainly Stanley and others, including Joel Elliott, were convinced that the treaty was never fully read or explained to the Kiowa and Comanche chiefs and that only pleasing extracts had been read.[42]

Once the treaty was signed by the assenting chiefs placing their marks on it, the commissioners led the Indians to the wagon park where Murphy and Leavenworth were preparing to distribute the 1867 Kiowa and Comanche annuities owing under the Treaty of the Little Arkansas. As they left, the commissioners told the Indians that the Medicine Lodge presents would be distributed to them the next day. A little before dark it began to rain, the drops driven slantwise by a high wind as they spattered against the tents. While the commissioners and the reporters were settling into their evening tasks, a sentry approached General Harney with news that a small party of Cheyennes had appeared, wanting to see the commissioners. Harney went out to greet them at once. They were tall, powerfully built men who had ridden through the day and into the night, coming from their village on Bluff Creek near fifty miles away. Now they sat silently on their horses just outside the ambulance enclosure, waiting for an invitation to come in for a talk. They had first gone to Black Kettle's camp to bring him with them. Included were Little Robe, a council chief; Gray Beard of the southern Sutaio, representing his father-in-law, Black Shinn; Minimic (Eagle's Head), a headman of the Bowstring military society; and of course Black Kettle.[43]

General Harney led the Cheyenne delegation into a commission tent and summoned the other commissioners and John Smith to translate for

---
[42] Stanley, "British Journalist," 286–89; Jones, *Treaty of Medicine Lodge*, 127–35; Powell *of the Sacred Mountain*, 1:319–20.

[43] Stanley, "British Journalist," 288–90; Jones, *Treaty of Medicine Lodge*, 135–37; Powell, *People of the Sacred Mountain*, 1:520–21.

them. Smith first told the commissioners that the Cheyennes had not had an opportunity to talk with Black Kettle and wanted a brief discussion with him. This was permitted, and those present, including reporters, noted that Black Kettle was highly nervous and finally quite agitated. This was likely because of his failure to attend the Renewal of the Sacred Arrows, something required of all Cheyennes. He had been warned and knew the penalty for failure. When the discussion was completed, Little Robe addressed the commissioners, speaking for the Cheyennes. The Cheyennes, he said, would like the other tribes to remain until they had completed their Arrow Renewal ceremony, since they had important things to say that they wanted all to hear. After a discussion, it was pointed out to the Cheyennes that the Kiowa and Comanche presents would be distributed the next day, and while they could and would request that those tribes remain, they had no way of forcing them to. Little Robe told them his tribe was now in the midst of the Renewal of the Sacred Arrows, that no one was allowed to leave until it was completed, and that it would be another four or five days before his people could come. Commissioner Taylor and generals Harney and Augur were in favor of granting the extra time, but Senator Henderson, impatient to get home, was opposed. He saw no reason why the Cheyennes could not cut short their religious observances for the council. Both Augur and Harney assured him that this was something the highly religious Cheyennes could not do and that they were far truer to their beliefs than were most whites. In the end Taylor told Little Robe that the commissioners would wait four more days but would then have to leave. Little Robe said that the ceremony should be finished by then and that they looked forward to meeting with the peace commission. With that the Cheyennes rode off into the night.[44]

After the Cheyennes' departure, Superintendent Murphy delivered two messages to the commissioners. The Arapahoes, according to Little Raven, desired to make a peace separately from their old friends and allies the Cheyennes, whose hostility to whites entering their country, they said, had brought them nothing but grief. The other message was from the Plains Apaches, who wished to be confederated with the Kiowas and Comanches, their traditional allies, and to share their reservation. Taylor directed Henderson and Sanborn to draw up a treaty document for the Apaches as an appendix to the Kiowa-Comanche treaty. But to Little Raven the com-

[44] Stanley, "British Journalist," 289–91; Jones, *Treaty of Medicine Lodge*, 137–41; Powell, *People of the Sacred Mountain*, 1:521–23.

missioners gave no response—-they didn't want a separate reservation for the Arapahoes and the Cheyennes, a mistake that has had an adverse effect on both tribes to the present day. The following morning, October 22, the Kiowa and Comanche presents for the Medicine Lodge treaty were distributed to them. While that was occurring the treaty with the Plains Apaches was read to their chiefs and explained to the extent possible, considering the great language barrier. They were given two days to consider it. The Kiowas and Comanches in the interim agreed to remain as long as did the commissioners while awaiting arrival of the Cheyennes. After that, the great encampment settled into a routine of a daily intermingling of peoples, with Indians and whites satisfying their curiosity about each other by visiting their respective camps. On October 25 the treaty with the Plains Apaches was signed. Even before that was done the Kansas delegation left, to the sorrow of none of those remaining. Both in their actions and talks with the commissioners, and in their subsequent press releases concerning the treaties, Governor Crawford and Senator Ross amply demonstrated their ignorance and prejudice against the Native peoples.[45]

A meeting at the council arbor was held on the morning of Saturday, October 26, to determine whether the commissioners and the other Indians should continue to wait for the Cheyennes, who were already one day late. Black Kettle told them that the Arrow Renewal ceremony would take two more days, so the commissioners decided to wait until the following Monday. To this the Kiowas, Comanches, Plains Apaches, and Arapahoes grudgingly agreed, despite their anxiety to move on to their winter camps. That evening the Arapahoe chief Little Raven appeared at the commissioners' camp to warn that the Cheyennes might attack them at any time. This caused concern for all except General Harney, who expressed his trust in the Cheyennes. Little Raven had hardly finished his warning when Little Robe of the Cheyennes rode into the camp. He said that his people would be riding in the next morning and that many of the warriors would be firing their weapons into the air as an expression of joy at being able to meet with the representatives of the government. Little Robe was concerned that the soldier guards would become excited, thinking it was an attack on the peace camp. Many among the whites were concerned at the thought of a large body of Cheyenne warriors riding into their camp with weapons in hand, and Little Robe therefore visited with each of the

---

[45] Stanley, "British Journalist," 291–97; Jones, *Treaty of Medicine Lodge*, 141–55; Powell, *People of the Sacred Mountain*, 1:523–24.

commissioners to reassure them of the peaceful intentions of his people. After that he had a brief meeting with Wynkoop. It apparently did not go well, since he became very angry and left, refusing to shake the agent's hand or to accept tobacco from him. Then he rode off into the night.[46]

Sunday morning, October 27, dawned bright and clear, heralding a day that would prove the most thrilling and dramatic of all at the Medicine Lodge councils. A number of whites, mostly newsmen but including Phillip McCusker, David Butterfield, and a few others, decided to go on a sightseeing tour downstream. Their intention was to inspect the great Medicine Lodge built by the Kiowas for their 1866 Sun Dance and still standing. They rode cautiously along the stream's southwest bank, past the vast encampments of Comanches and Kiowas, probably knowing this would not be acceptable to the Indians. Finally they came to the site of the lodge, about twelve miles downstream from the commissioners' camp. Curiosity overcame good judgment, and they proceeded to strip away as souvenirs many of the sacred objects left in the lodge as an offering to the Supreme Being. When they were finished, they began to nervously work their way back upstream, keeping the lowest possible profile so as not to be noticed by the Kiowas or Comanches. They had reached a point nearly opposite the southwest corner of the Arapahoe village when suddenly they heard firing ahead. Someone in the group shouted, "Cheyennes!"[47]

It was at about 10:00 in the morning when Indian scouts first rode into the great encampment to announce that the Cheyennes were coming. Because of the many rumors that the Cheyennes would attack the commissioners' camp and possibly the camps of other tribes, alarms were sounded in all of them. Criers went through the tribal villages, calling for the men to get their weapons and for the women, children, and elderly to return to their lodges. Everywhere people were running in different directions. At the commissioners' camp there was a sense of near panic. The Indians roaming through disappeared, while the remaining news correspondents, who had been relaxing in the warm sun outside their tents—playing cards, reading, or speculating on whether or not the Cheyennes would ever come—quickly retrieved their weapons and listened anxiously for word from the commissioners. The commissioners themselves engaged in a debate as to whether they should remain in their camp or move as a body down to the river to greet the Cheyennes as General Harney desired. Harney finally con-

---

[46] Stanley, "British Journalist," 299; Jones, *Treaty of Medicine Lodge*, 159–60; Powell, *People of the Sacred Mountain*, 1:524.

[47] Stanley, "British Journalist," 308–310; Jones, *Treaty of Medicine Lodge*, 160–62.

vinced the others that a show of confidence was important. Others in the camp, including the teamsters, climbed to the top of the ambulances and wagons to see the anticipated arrival of the storied warriors of the Fighting Cheyennes. In the camp of the military escort, preparations were made for a defense, and everywhere the sentries were on the alert at their posts.[48]

Medicine Lodge Creek (or River) rises on the High Plains of present Kiowa County, Kansas, but most of its sojourn southeasterly in Kansas is through the Red Hills physiographic region. Here Permian Age red shale beds were capped by beds of light gray gypsum and dolomite rock and then exposed by erosion. This created a ruggedly beautiful area of buttes and mesas, lending a desertlike aspect to the scene. The water from the springs and streams that flow through this region contains calcium and magnesium sulfates (Epsom salt) along with other natural salts dissolved from the gypsum and dolomite beds. The Indians, who used these waters to draw infection from wounds and promote healing, referred to the country as the Medicine Hills and to the major stream as the Medicine River or Timber Hill River. The most dramatic of the buttes and mesas lie to the southwest of Medicine Lodge River, and it was through these that the Cheyennes were coming as they rode easterly from their Bluff Creek village. An hour passed between the time word was received that they were on their way and there was visible evidence of their approach. To the southwest of the commissioners' camp, from a canyon between some of the buttes and mesas, a cloud of sand rising in spiral columns was seen. The cloud seemed to whirl closer but was still at a distance. Later several dark masses appeared to surge forward from under the cloud, only to disappear again behind intervening hills and trees.[49]

A large number of Arapahoe warriors were gathered on a hill near the commissioners' camp, with Little Raven in front, likely expecting the attack he predicted. Beyond them on another hill the fighting men of the Kiowas and Comanches sat silently on their horses, their chiefs or war leaders in front, watching the slow approach of the Cheyennes. All present waited to see what the next few minutes would bring. From the swirl of dust and sand rising beyond the river, there gradually came a drumming sound—the hoofbeats of hundreds of horses. Closer and ever louder came the sound, until it seemed like the thunder of an approaching storm.

[48] Stanley, "British Journalist," 304–305; Jones, *Treaty of Medicine Lodge*, 164–65; Powell, *People of the Sacred Mountain*, 1:524–25.

[49] Stanley, "British Journalist," 305; Buchanan, *Kansas Geology*, 21–22; Jones, *Treaty of Medicine Lodge*, 165; Powell, *People of the Sacred Mountain*, 1:524–25.

Then came the eerie sound of chanting rising above the hoofbeats. Suddenly to their right the great column of Cheyenne warriors appeared as they topped the last ridge overlooking Medicine Lodge Creek. A number of council chiefs rode in the lead, followed by the members of the five military societies riding together with their brothers. Bringing up the rear were the Dog Soldiers, the watchdogs of the People. To the white observers it seemed as though they were organized in five separate columns of about one hundred men each, riding abreast. On they came, then at some unseen and unheard command the entire column turned and became five ranks riding parallel with the river at a double trot. It was a stunning sight, with the war lances, coupsticks, warbonnets, and feathers fluttering and twirling in the wind creating a kaleidoscope of color. The faces of the warriors were painted in a variety of brilliant hues, and they wore their finest garments, embroidered with rich quillwork and beadwork. The bravest among them wore scalp shirts, and their leggings were trimmed with hair. The bright midday sun glinted off of the silver disks attached to scalp locks, as well as the blades of lances and the barrels of firearms. The whole scene was, wrote Stanley, "exciting in the extreme."[50]

As their column turned parallel to the stream, Black Kettle raced his horse across it, covered with foam, and came to a halt in front of the commissioners. He warned that his people were coming and would be firing their weapons, but that it was in celebration and there was no need for concern. When the long ranks of Cheyenne warriors came parallel with the commissioners' camp, bugles sounded and they came to a sudden halt, turned and faced the commissioners across the stream, five ranks deep. For a moment they stood silently, their warhorses prancing as if eager for action. It was a spectacle that few white men had ever seen—or lived to tell about. The tall, muscular warriors were sitting their warhorses, their medicine shields on their left arms and long lances held in their right hands, and their painted faces looking directly across at the commissioners. The warm noonday breeze rippled through the mass of feathers adorning the men, their weapons, and their horses. Then, from somewhere deep within the body of Cheyenne warriors a bugle sounded, there was a great shout, and some men began to sing a song of praise, while from the throats of others there arose a great warbling cry. At some unseen signal the first rank suddenly surged forward, the horses leaping into the shallow waters of the

[50] Stanley, "British Journalist," 305–307; Jones, *Treaty of Medicine Lodge*, 165–66; Powell, *People of the Sacred Mountain*, 1:524–25.

river and throwing up a great white spray. As they did this, many of the warriors began to fire pistols into the air. When they moved farther into the stream, the second rank followed, then the third and the fourth, and finally the fifth. When the first rank reached the northeast riverbank, the men turned to their left flank, whipping their horses into a fast trot, and moved rapidly toward the commissioners at an oblique angle. The following ranks did the same, maintaining perfect order and discipline. It was a display of superb horsemanship that even the Comanches, the greatest horsemen of the southern plains, could appreciate and admire.[51]

For a few tense moments it appeared as if the oncoming Cheyennes would ride right over the white men and their encampment. But once again, at some unseen and unheard signal, the chiefs and warriors reined in their horses so hard that they came to a squatting halt and their riders slid effortlessly from their backs. They stopped not more than twenty yards from General Harney, who neither flinched nor moved. The firing of weapons, the singing, and the shouts and cries ended at almost the same time, and the chiefs moved forward, broad smiles on their faces, and began to shake hands with the commissioners. The tension that had built among all in the peace camp was broken, and good cheer returned. The hand shaking was interrupted momentarily by the sudden return of the sightseeing party from the Kiowa Medicine Lodge. Fearing that the Cheyennes were attacking the commissioners' camp, they had thrown their pilfered souvenirs into the creek and ridden pell-mell to what they thought would be the relative safety of the camp. But their arrival was only a brief distraction, after which the commissioners led the chiefs and headmen to one of the commission tents. There they offered their guests coffee and tobacco. As they sat drinking and smoking, Little Robe (as translated by John Smith) said that a number of men from the Kanza tribe had been shadowing their horse herds as they moved east. The Cheyennes were concerned for their animals and could not stay long to talk, and therefore another meeting was arranged for later that afternoon. Then, after thanking the commissioners for their hospitality, the chiefs moved back to their waiting warriors and with a flourish of their lances and pistols charged back across Medicine Lodge Creek to the new camp being erected next to that of Black Kettle.[52]

---

[51] Stanley, "British Journalist," 306; Jones, *Treaty of Medicine Lodge*, 165–66; Powell, *People of the Sacred Mountain*, 1:525.

[52] Stanley, "British Journalist," 306–307; Jones, *Treaty of Medicine Lodge*, 166–67; Powell, *People of the Sacred Mountain*, 1:525–26.

There followed a great deal of discussion between the commissioners and reporters concerning what they had seen during the preceding hours. All of those present were mightily impressed by the Cheyennes' display of horsemanship and discipline and especially the appearance of the warriors. They were well-built men, taller than the other Plains Indians and, indeed, apparently taller than the average white man of that era. Equally noted were their good looks, for the Cheyennes were almost universally considered to be the handsomest Indians on the plains by those who knew them. Moreover they were high-spirited and sensitive, a people who bore themselves with a justifiable dignity and pride. Most agreed that there was good reason for those intruding on their lands to fear the Cheyenne fighting men when they were hostile. Near dusk a number of the Cheyenne council chiefs and headmen appeared at the commissioners' camp for the promised meeting, spending about an hour in friendly conversation with the commissioners. It was agreed that they would be at the council arbor at 10:00 the next morning for their grand peace council. With that they returned to their camp. Later a young Cheyenne woman appeared, bringing with her a horse that she wished to give to General Harney. She had just given birth to a son and, in celebration and in accordance with Cheyenne custom, was making gifts. Harney, a favorite of the Cheyennes, accepted the horse gratefully.[53]

On the morning of October 28 the Cheyenne council chiefs arrived promptly at 10:00, but for a time stood talking among themselves before taking their places in the arbor. The Cheyennes sat on one side and the Arapahoes on the other, while the Kiowas, Comanches, and Plains Apaches, as observers, sat beyond. Senator Henderson spoke first, telling the assemblage that the Great Father was unhappy that the Cheyennes warriors had broken the peace made at the Little Arkansas but was now aware that much of the fault lay with bad whites. They had misled General Hancock, and that had caused him to burn the villages on the Pawnee Fork. He then turned to the matter of the treaty, commenting that the buffalo were fast disappearing, but that so long as they remained in numbers sufficient to justify the chase, the Cheyennes and Arapahoes would be allowed to hunt as permitted by the Treaty of the Little Arkansas. That treaty specifically allowed the Cheyennes to hunt in all of the unsettled portions of their country between the Platte and Arkansas so long as bison

---

[53] Stanley, "British Journalist," 307; Jones, *Treaty of Medicine Lodge*, 167–69; Powell, *People of the Sacred Mountain*, 1:526.

and other game remained in sufficient numbers. The Indians thought that also meant whites were prohibited from further settlement in their country. The terms of the treaty were substantially the same as those in the Kiowa and Comanche treaty except for the reservation. The Cheyenne and Arapahoe reservation would be that provided for them in the Little Arkansas treaty, as amended by the Senate—that is, the lands bounded on the south and west by the Cimarron River, on the east by the Arkansas River, and on the north by the southern boundary of Kansas. Senator Henderson said that the Cheyennes and Arapahoes must select a rich piece of land for a reservation before whites settled it, although the commissioners had already made that selection and written it into the treaty prepared for the council. It was anything but a "rich piece of land," but Henderson told the Cheyennes the government would provide them with livestock and farm implements so they could sustain themselves on it.[54]

After Henderson's speech the Indians were invited to respond. The Cheyennes deferred to Little Raven, saying the Arapahoes had been waiting a long time. Little Raven began his speech by stating that the Cheyennes were like his own flesh, that he and his people had always loved them, and they would remain friends forever. No one mentioned that two days earlier Little Raven was warning the commissioners of a possible Cheyenne attack on their camp. He went on to say the Arapahoes would like to have their own reservation and that it should be near Fort Lyon. When he finished, the spokesman for the Cheyennes arose to speak. He was Buffalo Chief, described as tall, handsome, and warlike-looking, with his hair in two long braids hanging on either side of his face and, like most Cheyennes, wearing feathers at the back of his head.[55] He first inquired of Henderson if it was true that the Great Father had sent the commissioners to make peace with them. When assured it was true, he seemed pleased and began his speech. It was simple and straight to the point, in the Cheyenne manner. After stating that he would then take the commission by the hand, he said:

> You spoke about the railroads, well, we will hold it together. We will both have a right in it. I believe you were sent by the Great Father to make peace with us. We sprung from the prairie, we live by it, we prefer to do so, and, as

---

[54] Stanley, "British Journalist," 310–13; Jones, *Treaty of Medicine Lodge*, 170–71; Powell, *People of the Sacred Mountain*, 1:526–27.

[55] The identity of this Buffalo Chief has never been satisfactorily established. He may have been a new council chief appointed after the Sand Creek Massacre. See Powell, *People of the Sacred Mountain*, 1:528n, 657n32.

yet, we do not want the blessings of civilization. We do not claim this country south of the Arkansas, but that country between the Arkansas and the Platte is ours. We are willing, when we desire to live as you do, to take your advice about that, but until then we will take our chances. It were well that those on the Arkansas road were out of the country, that we might roam over the country as formerly; the bones of our forefathers may rest then. You think that you are doing a great deal for us by giving these presents to us, but we prefer to live as formerly. If you gave us all the goods you could give, yet we would prefer our own life. You give us presents and then take our lands; that produces war. I introduce to your notice Colonel David Butterfield. I want him for our trader. He is a good man. I have said all.

With that, Buffalo Chief sat down. The commissioners waited in silence for another Cheyenne to speak, until finally it dawned on them that Buffalo Chief was their only speaker and that he had said all they wanted said.[56]

The commissioners sat stunned when they realized that the Cheyennes had told them they would give up neither their country nor their way of life. They would tolerate the railroad to achieve peace, but nothing more. The commissioners began to whisper among themselves as they saw their chance for a treaty with the Cheyennes slipping away. While they talked, Little Raven again stood up and began to add to his previous list of requests. But the commissioners were preoccupied with what Buffalo Chief had said and paid Little Raven no heed. He soldiered on with his list of wants, seemingly unaware that he had no chance of realizing any of them. Meanwhile the commissioners concluded that the Cheyennes would not accept the treaty as drawn and were considering an adjournment to draft amendments that would hopefully make it more palatable to them. As they debated, Little Man, a Cheyenne headman or war leader, stood to harangue the commissioners with accusations that the Kiowas and Comanches had been spreading lies about the Cheyennes, accusing them of plotting an attack against the commissioners' camp. He made no mention of the Arapahoes, whose chief Little Raven had actually made those accusations. The Kiowas and Comanches sat placid and unconcerned, probably because Little Man's speech was not translated for them and they could not understand a word he said. The commissioners continued their own debate, with Senator Henderson strongly opposing an adjournment. He believed he could get the treaty signed that day, and after a time the interpreters were called to him and he led them away to

---

[56] Stanley, "British Journalist," 314–15; Jones, *Treaty of Medicine Lodge*, 172–73; Powell, *People of the Sacred Mountain*, 1:528–29.

a point beyond the hearing of the other commissioners, the reporters, or anyone else. Then a number of the Cheyenne council chiefs, including Buffalo Chief, were summoned to join them.[57]

The private conversations with Henderson took some time. There was animated discussion between Henderson, interpreters John Smith and George Bent, and the participating chiefs. Finally those watching could see Buffalo Chief taking Henderson's hand and holding it as he spoke. When at last they returned to the arbor, the Cheyenne chiefs were smiling and Henderson was relieved. The senator told the others that he promised the Cheyennes they need not go to a reservation right away but could continue to live and hunt in their own country for so long as there were buffalo in numbers sufficient to sustain them and as provided by the Treaty of the Little Arkansas. Having neither authorized nor signed that treaty, most chiefs did not know what that meant, and those that had signed thought it prevented whites from making further settlements in their country. But the U.S. government considered its written language binding on them, prohibiting them from approaching closer than ten miles to any road, trail, railroad, or white settlement. How the Cheyennes could possibly hunt and camp in their country without crossing the lines of travel that were extending ever farther into it was never explained. The Indians would be expected to move to the new reservation in the Indian Territory when the buffalo were gone, and Henderson assured the commissioners and reporters that would be shortly. Few Cheyennes could imagine an end to the great beasts that held a sacred place in their culture and sustained their life. They thought that the old ways could continue and that the westward thrust of whites into their domain would be halted. They could anticipate neither that whites would soon begin to hunt bison to near extinction, nor that white settlement would continue and increase despite what they believed they had agreed to.[58]

With his promises, Senator Henderson convinced many of the Cheyennes present that the treaty should be accepted to secure peace. They clearly believed they would be allowed to continue their traditional life in their old country for the foreseeable future and that whites would move no farther into it. They would tolerate the existing roads and the railroads now moving westward in exchange for peace. When the bison

[57] Stanley, "British Journalist," 315–16; Jones, *Treaty of Medicine Lodge*, 174–76; Powell, *People of the Sacred Mountain*, 1:529–30.

[58] Stanley, "British Journalist," 318–19; Jones, *Treaty of Medicine Lodge*, 176–77; Powell, *People of the Sacred Mountain*, 1:530.

were gone, they would accept the *veho*'s advice in realizing the "blessings of civilization," but not before. The other commissioners, meantime, were discussing at least a brief adjournment in order to revise the treaty in line with Henderson's promises. To this Henderson said, "It's no time for bickering." The treaty was brought forth as originally drafted and was signed by the commissioners, after which eight Arapahoe chiefs signed. But when it was the Cheyennes' turn, it was discovered that they had all left. There were tense moments as John Smith, interpreter for the commissioners, was sent to tell them that no treaty presents would be distributed until they made their mark on the treaty document. Written documents of any kind were not a part of their culture, having no system of writing, and an oral agreement or promise was sufficient for them. They had no way of reading or understanding the written treaty themselves, and unlike the one with the Kiowas and Comanches, who heard at least favorable clauses read to them, the treaty was apparently never read aloud and translated for the Cheyennes and Arapahoes. To them the treaty was only what they had said and what Henderson had promised.

With reluctance tempered by a sense of relief at the promise of peace, they returned to the arbor, and ten Cheyennes made their mark on the document, relying on the white men's statements about what it said. A large number of council chiefs refused to sign, however, and there were more tense moments while John Smith, at Superintendent Murphy's insistence, tried to persuade Bull Bear, White Horse, and Little Robe to sign. Murphy was especially concerned that the Dog Soldier chiefs sign and consider themselves bound. But even when told the Great Father would be greatly disappointed if they did not sign, they still refused, being unconcerned about the Great Father's disappointment. Finally the commissioners asked Smith and George Bent to convince them. After a heated argument, the substance of which was never revealed, they reluctantly made their marks, Bull Bear angrily pressing down so hard that the pen penetrated the paper.[59]

There is no question that the Cheyenne council chiefs who signed, twelve in number, believed they were retaining their country through the Medicine Lodge treaty. As they made their mark, both Bull Bear and Buffalo Chief declared, "We will hold that country between the Arkansas and Platte together. We will not give it up yet, as long as the buffalo and elk are roaming through the country." Thirteen Cheyennes made their

---

[59] Stanley, "British Journalist," 317–19; Hoig, *John Simpson Smith*, 189–90; Jones, *Treaty of Medicine Lodge*, 176–78; Powell, *People of the Sacred Mountain*, 1:530–31.

mark at the request of the commissioners, but one of these, Heap of Birds (Many Magpies), was a headman of the southern Sutaio, not a council chief. Perhaps more important were those council chiefs who refused to sign, including Black Shin (one of the two council chiefs of the southern Sutaio), his son-in-law Gray Beard, Old Little Wolf, Sand Hill, Black White Man, and Seven Bulls. Tangle Hair, one of the Dog Soldier headmen, also refused to sign when requested. The aged Bull Chip, the other council chief of the southern Sutaio, did not sign either, but it is uncertain that he was still living at the time. Most important of those not signing was Stone Forehead, Keeper of the Sacred Arrows, who was not present, having remained at the Bluff Creek village. His presence with Maahótse, the Sacred Arrows, was an indispensable ingredient for any valid treaty that would affect how and where the Cheyennes lived, for without his blessing and approval it was worthless. Stone Forehead was unwilling to countenance any treaty or agreement that would surrender the country of the Tsistsistas. Neither the commissioners nor any of those representing the Indian bureau knew that, of course, nor had any ever inquired as to what was necessary for the Cheyennes to make a treaty or who could sign. From the perspective of the Cheyennes, they had merely agreed to make peace with the whites and to tolerate the roads and railroads. What they did not know was what the other provisions of the treaty document contained or that Senator Henderson's promise was not a part of the treaty.[60]

After the signing of the treaty with the Cheyennes and Arapahoes, the treaty presents were distributed to those tribal members in attendance. Superintendent Murphy estimated that about two thousand Cheyennes were there for the distribution, but this seems inflated, considering that most chiefs and their people still remained at the Bluff Creek village with the Arrow Keeper. When the distribution was finished, the proceedings were complete, and everyone departed early the next day. The commissioners, their staff members, the reporters, and all of the other whites returned to Fort Harker via Fort Larned, and from Harker took the train eastward. The Cheyennes and Arapahoes dispersed to their winter camps, some on the Arkansas, some on Pawnee Fork, and the Dog Solders and southern Sutaio, along with White Head's Óhméséheso, to the Solomon River country. All of them thought a lasting peace had been made, except a few of the

[60] Henry M. Stanley, in *Kansas Weekly Tribune*, November 11, 1867; Stanley, "British Journalist," 316; Jones, *Treaty of Medicine Lodge*, 177–78; Powell, *People of the Sacred Mountain*, 1:530–31.

military men and reporters. After the treaty was signed, Captain Barnitz wrote in his journal:

> After the council the Cheyennes were with great difficulty persuaded to sign the treaty. They were superstitious in regard to touching the pen, or perhaps supposed that by doing so they would be "signing away their rights"—which is doubtless the true state of affairs, as they have no idea that they are giving up, or that they have ever given up the country which they claim as their own, the country north of the Arkansas. The treaty all amounts to nothing, and we will certainly have another war sooner or later with the Cheyennes, at least, and probably with the other Indians, in consequence of misunderstanding of the terms of present and previous treaties.

His words were insightful and prophetic.[61]

Thus ended Hancock's War, or so the white men would claim and believe. But they were of course wrong.

---

[61] Stanley, "British Journalist," 319–20; Jones, *Treaty of Medicine Lodge*, 178–80, 188–91; Powell, *People of the Sacred Mountain*, 1:531; Utley, *Life in Custer's Cavalry*, 115.

Epilogue

Sweet Medicine, the great Prophet of the Tsistsistas, had warned long ago that their way of life and the People themselves would someday be threatened with destruction by a pale-faced race coming from the east. It was happening now, and the invaders came in numbers that the People could not imagine. Daily the enemies made inroads into the Cheyenne country. They slaughtered the great herds of bison and other game the People depended on, and they crisscrossed the land with roads and railroads that, like great tentacles, extended ever farther westward. In the wake of the roads came the white settlements and gradually the People's land was seized and occupied by the intruders. For a time the Cheyennes still dreamed that their country, bounded by far horizons and capped by a brilliant blue sky, was wide enough that the whites might be satisfied with its eastern and western fringes, leaving to them the plains between. For a time they thought the pipe of peace they had smoked at Medicine Lodge Creek might bring an end to war, an end to further incursions by white settlers, and an end to the ceaseless slaughter of the buffalo. Yet many did not trust white promises—so often and so easily made, and as often broken. They feared their smile and ready pledge of peace. The whites had already taken much of their land, leaving them an ever- smaller portion. Tomorrow, the Cheyennes feared, they would take even that. So it was that Stone Forehead, the Arrow Keeper, and most members of the Council of Forty-four would not go to Medicine Lodge Creek and would not consent to any treaty that might compromise their country or way of life.

As the different bands of the five southern Plains tribes rode away from the council grounds on Medicine Lodge Creek, they must have felt a variety of emotions. For some there may have been hope; for others, despair. They neither knew nor understood the words written into the documents prepared by Senator Henderson and John Sanborn. Most probably realized that the whites hoped the tribes would someday, after the bison were gone, abandon their nomadic hunting ways and settle down to live as whites did in fixed houses. But they could not foresee this happening within the lifetimes of even their grandchildren. The reservation described in the Cheyenne and Arapahoe treaty, as told to them, would be in lands south of the Arkansas. It was a country unfamiliar to most of them, with bitter, brackish water and little game. They had no intention of going there and would remain in their own homeland, for surely the great herds of buffalo would remain into a distant future. The whites said they would not disturb them if there was game to hunt, and they believed that whites were prohibited from settling in their country for so long as that was so. This was what they believed. But in fact the whites had no intention of allowing the Cheyennes and Arapahoes to keep their country.

The Treaty

The document the peace commissioners signed and to which twelve Cheyenne council chiefs impressed their mark on October 28, 1867, was meant to bring peace. But it contained a variety of provisions, couched in legal and diplomatic terminology, that either were not read to the Cheyennes or were not properly explained to them and that they would not have comprehended if they had been. It was language intended to strip them of their country, remove them from it, give it to white settlers, and "concentrate" the Cheyennes on a reservation far away, where whites believed that their culture and way of life would not survive. In part the incomprehensibility was probably calculated by the government, eager to acquire a paper purporting to transfer ownership of the land to it. But in part it was the natural result of the gulf in cultures. To the southern bands of Cheyennes, their "permanent home," as Senator Henderson referred to it, was the country between the Platte and Arkansas rivers, not a specific part of it or any other place. Even when the white commissioners attempted to explain what they wanted of the tribe, their words could not convey the meanings they wished to impart. There was also the intention to mislead. The commissioners had to know that most Indians could not comprehend that the buffalo would cease to roam the plains in numbers sufficient to sustain their lives within the foreseeable future. This helped Senator Henderson induce some of the chiefs to make their marks on the treaty document.

The treaty as executed did not contain Senator Henderson's promises. Nothing was written into the document then or later that permitted the Cheyennes and Arapahoes to continue hunting in their own country. Henderson made no effort to conceal his promise to the Cheyennes and in fact specifically mentioned it in his written abstract of the treaty distributed to members of the press. All of the correspondents present mentioned it in their newspaper articles. After General Sherman approved the treaty (he was still the dominant member of the peace commission), he published his General Order No. 10, in which he specifically referred to the right of the Cheyennes and Arapahoes to hunt in their traditional homelands between the Arkansas and the Platte.[1]

Though not kept secret from those who were there, the fact remains that the promise was never placed in the written treaty, it was not included in the peace commission minutes, and when the Senate finally ratified the treaty, it was not there. Once again the Indians had been told one thing, but their treaty said quite another. In fact the Cheyenne and Arapahoe treaty gave them the right to hunt only in unsettled lands south of the Arkansas—lands included in the reservation granted them in the Treaty of the Little Arkansas prior to its unilateral amendment by the Senate. Even then there were restrictions—hunting must be with the written permission of their agent, and they must not come within ten miles of a military post or a public road. This was nearly impossible, given that the Indians might at any time be many miles from their agent and that none knew what "ten miles" meant. Nor could they move any distance without coming to and crossing roads or trails.[2]

Besides the omission from the written document of the rights orally promised to the Cheyennes and Arapahoes, other items were included that they either were not told of or did not understand. By its terms they specifically surrendered to the government the lands they told the commissioners they would not give up; they agreed to remove to a reservation where they orally said they would not go; they agreed to accept instruction, tools, and seeds for farming (something totally alien to their way of life) and to send their children to schools to be educated in English; and they agreed to surrender tribal members for trial in white courts for violations of laws they knew nothing of and to no longer oppose the construction of roads and railroads in their country. And there were other

---

[1] Jones, *Treaty of Medicine Lodge*, 180–82, 191–92.
[2] Ibid., 182.

provisions they did not understand and about which they were not informed. Equally important were verbal promises, apart from the promised hunting rights, that had not been included in the treaty document. Senator Henderson told them that the reservation was a place where they could go to their agent and receive issues of food and clothing when hunting was poor. But nowhere in the treaty did the government commit to feeding tribal members.[3]

There were many other deficiencies in the Medicine Lodge treaties that militated against their achieving the lasting peace they proclaimed. Although the Cheyenne treaty recited that it was made on behalf of the Cheyenne and Arapahoe tribes by "their chiefs and head-men duly authorized and empowered to act for the body of the people of said tribes," in fact no effort was ever made to determine if this was true. And it was not. Of the forty-four Cheyenne council chiefs, only twelve gave their assent, and those thought they were simply committing themselves to peace. To them a reservation was a place they might go only after the buffalo were gone. Moreover, Stone Forehead, Keeper of the Sacred Arrows and the indispensable party to any valid treaty, was not present and neither approved nor signed the treaty. Ironically, having accepted the marks of only twelve of the forty-four council chiefs to make a treaty on behalf of the entire tribe, the government inserted as Article 12 a provision that no future cessions of tribal reservation lands could be made unless "signed by at least three-fourths of all the adult male Indians occupying or interested in the same," an entirely different standard from that used for the treaty. Following the General Allotment Act of 1887, known as the Dawes Act, which specified that the Indians were to assume individual land ownership and citizenship, the government arranged for a land cession agreement on October 13, 1890, that sold to itself most of the Cheyenne and Arapahoe reservation for $1.5 million. Families would retain 160 acres each, but they and their tribes would surrender all rights to any other lands they had ever owned or claimed. When most traditional males of the two tribes refused to sign, the then agent, Charles F. Ashly, used the signatures (marks) of forty-two minors and one hundred women to accomplish the government's purpose.[4]

The problems stemming from the Medicine Lodge treaties were not confined to the differences between the written provisions of the documents and the actual oral agreements of the parties. By its terms the government's

---

[3] Ibid., 181–83.
[4] Berthrong, *Cheyenne and Arapaho Ordeal*, 167; Kappler, *Indian Affairs*, 2:988.

obligations were to begin immediately, but a parsimonious Congress ignored the pleas of the peace commissioners and the Indian bureau. The commissioners submitted their report to the president on January 7, 1868, but the House and the Senate differed on the financial provisions of the treaties. The Senate did not ratify them until July 25, 1868, and they were not proclaimed as valid treaties binding on the United States until the following August 19. Meantime no provisions were made to establish the reservations supposedly agreed to, and no provisions to feed the Indians. The Cheyennes and Arapahoes remained on the plains. Some were in villages along the Cimarron and Bluff Creek, while the Dog Soldiers and southern Sutaio were in their own country between the Pawnee Fork and Solomon's Fork. As the winter of 1867–68 slipped by, railroad construction continued westward along the Smoky Hill. On October 30, 1867, two days after the Cheyenne and Arapahoe treaty was signed to the government's satisfaction at Medicine Lodge Creek, it reached milepost 300, well beyond Fort Hays and the new Hays City. By December 12, 1867, track had been laid to milepost 330, and by May 16, 1868, it was eighty-five miles west of Hays. And as the railroad moved west, so did new settlements that sprang up along its tracks or spread along the very streams the Indians camped on. It was not the railroad itself that would scuttle the tenuous peace, because Buffalo Chief had said his people would live with it. Instead it was the influx of large numbers of settlers that followed in its wake—the taking of the land, the building of towns, and the ensuing slaughter of the buffalo.[5]

THE WAR

The winter of 1867–68 passed peacefully enough, but the seeds for continued war were not far below the surface. On November 21, 1867, a small mixed hunting party of Cheyennes and Arapahoes ran into a well-armed party of Kanza Indians along the Arkansas River about twenty-five miles east of Fort Zarah. During the ensuing combat the rifles of the Kanzas killed five of their enemy and seriously wounded seven others. In the tradition of the Plains Indians this called for revenge in kind. The Cheyennes made plans to raid the Kanza reservation outside of Council Grove the next spring. Meantime other factors were at work to heighten prospects

---

[5] Greene, *Washita*, 38; Kappler, *Indian Affairs*, 2:984; Leckie, *Military Conquest*, 64; Powell, *People of the Sacred Mountain*, 1:532–34; Snell and Richmond, *Union and Kansas Pacific*, 344–45; Utley, *Frontier Regulars*, 133–34, 136.

for renewed warfare. Unscrupulous whites continued trading whiskey for buffalo robes. Surveyors began to appear along the Arkansas, presaging a new road or railroad. More and more whites began crowding into Cheyenne country, spreading their settlements up the valleys of the lower Smoky Hill, Saline, and Solomon rivers and tributaries in open violation, as the Cheyennes saw it, of the recent peace treaty. And the government did nothing to provide the food, arms, and ammunition for hunting promised them at Medicine Lodge.[6]

There was an undercurrent of restlessness among the people as a war party was made up to raid the Kanza reservation outside of Council Grove. The war party, led by Little Robe as pipe bearer and including Tall Bull and Old Whirlwind, left their village on the Pawnee Fork late in May and moved east, following the Santa Fe Trail. They rode boldly through the Main Street of Council Grove, and though they frightened the population, they made no effort to harm them. There followed an inconclusive three- to four-hour engagement with the Kanzas in which the Cheyennes gave a dazzling display of horsemanship, but neither side suffered serious casualties. As dark approached, Little Robe called an end to the attack and led his warriors westward back to their village on the Pawnee Fork. The only losses incurred by whites were eleven head of cattle and some poultry taken by the warriors for food when they found there was no longer any game in the area that they could hunt. After returning to their own country, Little Robe apologized to Colonel Wynkoop for taking the livestock and offered to pay for the slaughtered animals from the tribe's annuities. But his effort was to no avail.[7]

The government viewed the Cheyenne incursion into an area of white settlements to be a violation of their peace treaty. Commissioner Taylor, on instructions from the secretary of the interior, directed that the arms and ammunition intended for delivery to the Cheyennes be withheld until they satisfied the government that they intended to keep their treaty pledges in good faith. The Cheyennes, of course, were unaware of any agreement that prohibited them from fighting back against an Indian enemy. When Wynkoop told them that they would not be receiving their promised arms and ammunition, they refused to accept any of their annuities. They told him that they feared "their white brothers were pulling

---

[6] Berthrong, *Southern Cheyennes*, 299–300; Powell, *People of the Sacred Mountain*, 1:532–33.

[7] Berthrong, *Southern Cheyennes*, 303–304; Leckie, *Military Conquest*, 64, 68–69; Powell, *People of the Sacred Mountain*, 1:534–67; Utley, *Frontier Regulars*, 138.

away from them the hand they had given them at Medicine Lodge Creek," but that they would wait with patience for the Great Father to relent and let them have their arms and ammunition. In a July 20, 1868, letter to Superintendent Thomas Murphy, Wynkoop urged that the issue of arms and ammunition be made, stressing its importance in keeping the peace. He also reported that whites had been treating the Cheyennes badly since the treaty, by firing on them and otherwise mistreated them, but that in no instance had they retaliated.[8]

Wynkoop's remonstrance convinced Taylor that the arms and ammunition should be issued for the sake of peace. On July 23 he directed Superintendent Murphy to exercise his discretion to do so if it was necessary to preserve peace and if "no evil will result." Taylor telegraphed these instructions to Wynkoop via Fort Harker the same day. Murphy subsequently reported the issuance of a small amount of arms and ammunition to the Arapahoes and Plains Apaches at Fort Larned on August 1. On August 9, Wynkoop delivered Cheyenne annuities, including arms and ammunition, to those present at Fort Larned, reporting that they were well pleased and that he anticipated no trouble from them that season. What neither Wynkoop, Murphy, nor Taylor knew was that on August 2, believing their goods withheld, a war party of some two hundred young men along with twenty Oglalas and four Arapahoes, had left the Dog Soldier village on the north fork of Walnut Creek. Their intention was to strike their ancient enemies the Pawnees in the Platte River country. But as they moved northward, on August 10 they came to the westernmost of the new white settlements then spreading into their country along the Saline and Solomon rivers and tributaries in what are now Lincoln, Mitchell, Cloud, Ottawa, and Jewell counties in north-central Kansas.[9]

No one knows just how the conflict began. It was not the original intention of those in the war party. But a sudden awareness of the new settlements, irritation over the arms ban, mutual suspicions of both Indians and white settlers, and possibly provocation by some of the whites who fired on them ignited a storm of anger that unleashed itself against the settlers. At first a great majority of the warriors were opposed to any conflict, but when they could not control those who instigated the first actions, the rest (except a small party that continued north to the Pawnee country) joined

[8] *Annual Report of the Commissioner of Indian Affairs, 1868*, 66–68; Berthrong, *Southern Cheyennes*, 304–305; Powell, *People of the Sacred Mountain*, 1:568–69.

[9] *Annual Report of the Commissioner of Indian Affairs, 1868*, 67–70; Berthrong, *Southern Cheyennes*, 305–308; Powell, *People of the Sacred Mountain*, 1:568–69; Utley, *Frontier Regulars*, 138–39.

in a violent attack on the small settlements and isolated cabins. Between August 10 and 12 they looted and burned cabins, raped five women and killed fifteen men, ran off livestock, and stampeded eastward many of the settlers who had ventured the farthest into Cheyenne country. Then they returned to their villages.[10]

Word of the raids rippled through the frontier and made its way east. Indignation and anger flared among the general population, in the halls of government, in the army, and even in the Indian bureau. By their way of thinking the Medicine Lodge treaty with the Cheyennes, ratified barely two weeks earlier by the Senate and yet to be proclaimed, had already been breached by the Indians. It had been trumpeted as a fair and generous agreement with the enemy tribe, a humane and noble effort to bring peace and civilization to a barbarous people who wantonly slaughtered and scalped innocent white settlers. Never mind that it was those same whites who forced their way into the country that had belonged to the Indians for millennia; never mind that the written treaty document did not state the actual agreement with the Cheyennes; and never mind that the whites were violating the terms the Indians who signed thought had been agreed to. It would be the whites' version of the facts that they, as the ultimate victor, would write into their history.[11]

And so Hancock's War, which had been dampened to smoldering embers by the coming of the season of cold and by a forlorn hope of a peace with whites that would leave the Cheyennes alone in their own country, flared back into life with a renewed vigor. General Sherman reacted swiftly. From a grudging approval of the peace commission's work, he reverted to his long-held view that force was the only solution to the Indian "problem." On October 7, 1868, the peace commission convened for the last time in Chicago. Only Senator Henderson was absent. For two days there followed a heated struggle between Taylor and Tappan on one hand and Sherman on the other. However, with Augur, Harney, and Terry squarely behind him, Sherman won every vote. A series of resolutions were adopted, calling for a unilateral abrogation of the provisions of all of the Medicine Lodge treaties that allowed the Indians to hunt off of their reservations and for the use of the military to force the Indians onto them. The resolutions also called for the government to cease recognizing Indian

---

[10] Berthrong, *Southern Cheyennes*, 308; Greene, *Washita*, 49–50; Leckie, *Military Conquest*, 71–73; Powell, *People of the Sacred Mountain*, 1:568–71; Utley, *Frontier Regulars*, 138.

[11] Greene, *Washita*, 51–54; Leckie, *Military Conquest*, 73; Powell, *People of the Sacred Mountain*, 1:569–71; Utley, *Frontier Regulars*, 143–44.

tribes as "domestic dependent nations," to end treaty making with them, and to hold each tribal member individually subject to federal laws (that they were neither aware of nor understood), so far as allowable under existing treaties. Lastly, they recommended that the Office of Indian Affairs be transferred back to the War Department. Then the peace commission adjourned, never to meet again.[12]

The government, holding the Medicine Lodge treaties valid and binding on the tribes, viewed the raiding by the Cheyennes as a breach of their treaty promises. From the Cheyennes' perspective, however, the matter of treaty violations had quite a different cast. Yesterday they had enjoyed their own country. Then the whites came, forcing their roads across it, killing the game, and finally wanting the land itself. Some had put their mark on the papers that they were told meant peace. Today they found to their surprise that the white men were claiming all of the Cheyenne country as their own, asserting that the Cheyennes had by the treaty voluntarily given it to them and had agreed to remove to a small reservation away from their homeland, where they would be taught to live as whites did.

Bewildered, the Cheyennes groped for the light, beseeching Maheo to guide them through this dark time. They found once again that words were split from deeds by the forked tongue of whites. And they sensed the end of their ancient ways as they watched the whites' plows tearing at Mother Earth, the ceaseless slaughter of the bison, and the violation and destruction of the places of their dead. Some counseled submission to the irresistible power and numbers of the white enemy. Still, they were a proud warrior people, and some among them, recognizing that an end to their sacred way of life was looming, argued that it was better to resist and die fighting, their battle wounds in front, than to become helpless wards of the *veho*.

The raids that began along the Saline and Solomon expanded through the late summer and early fall of 1868, with attacks on traffic along the Santa Fe and Smoky Hill roads as well as the railroad. Their starving condition, frustration with what they saw as white deception and lies, the influx of aggressive settlers, the mindless slaughter of the bison, the tendency of whites to randomly shoot at them from railroad cars, water tanks, cabins, and wagon trains as they approached, and other factors all combined to fuel their rage. Military officers saw it differently. They knew of nothing that the army, the settlers, the railroad, or the travelers along the great trails

---

[12] Utley, *Frontier Regulars*, 138–39.

had done to provoke Indian attacks. General Sheridan, now commanding the Department of the Missouri, with Sherman's full approval planned a strategy to pressure the Indians as much as possible during the fall and then, as winter came and the various bands went into their winter camps, to strike them hard. The long-held army view that an entire tribe should be deemed responsible and punished for the perceived crimes of any of its members came once more to the fore. Sherman and Sheridan determined that all Cheyennes and Arapahoes should be driven south onto their reservation by force and that any who refused should be pursued and killed. The doctrine of "total war," so ruthlessly applied by Sheridan in the Shenandoah Valley of Virginia, was to be visited upon the Cheyennes with unrelenting vigor until they were incapable of further resistance.[13]

So began the long campaign that would eventually end freedom for the southern bands of Cheyennes and Arapahoes. It started slowly but quickly gained momentum. First came the clash with Forsyth's scouts on the Arickaree Fork of the Republican, known variously as the Battle of the Arickaree or the Battle of Beecher's Island. Though the event was glorified by the press because most of the little force survived, in truth the Indians had the better of it. Except for the loss of the great Cheyenne warrior Roman Nose, the Indians considered it a minor affair. At about the same time, Lt. Col. (Bvt. Brig. Gen.) Alfred Sully led eight companies of the Seventh Cavalry and one of the Third Infantry south of the Arkansas to attack villages of Cheyennes and Arapahoes encamped on Crooked Creek and the Cimarron River, whose warriors were thought to be responsible for raids on traffic along the Santa Fe Trail. The Indians responded by attacking Sully's column on the Cimarron. Though he followed them south through the sand hills to Wolf Creek, sparring with Indians along the way, he called an end to the pursuit on September 14 and returned to Fort Dodge, his expedition a failure.[14]

On October 1, Maj. (Bvt. Col.) William B. Royall and seven companies of the Fifth Cavalry marched west from Fort Harker to Fort Hays and from there northwest to scout the region of Beaver Creek. They camped on Prairie Dog Creek, while two detachments of three companies each were sent to scout Beaver Creek and the Republican. Neither found any

[13] Berthrong, *Southern Cheyennes*, 307–10; Greene, *Washita*, 51–60; Leckie, *Military Conquest*, 72–75; Powell, *People of the Sacred Mountain*, 1:571–72; Utley, *Frontier Regulars*, 143–47.
[14] Berthrong, *Southern Cheyennes*, 310–14, 318–20; Grinnell, *Fighting Cheyennes*, 378–92; Hyde, *Life of George Bent*, 293, 298–309; Leckie, *Military Conquest*, 75–83; Powell, *People of the Sacred Mountain*, 1:573–82, 588–90; Utley, *Frontier Regulars*, 147–48; White, *Hostiles and Horse Soldiers*, 70–84.

Indians, but on October 14, before their return, Tall Bull's Dog Soldiers found Royall and the remaining company in their camp on the Prairie Dog and attacked them, killing two troopers and running off twenty-six cavalry horses. When the two detachments returned, Royall led his column in a futile pursuit. Finally, with the Indians nowhere to be found, the troops turned south and marched to the railway line at the new Buffalo Park Station. Meantime the regimental commander, Maj. (Bvt. Maj. Gen.) Eugene A. Carr, with an escort of two companies of the Tenth Cavalry commanded by Capt. (Bvt. Lt. Col.) Louis H. Carpenter, marched northeast from Fort Wallace to Beaver Creek in search of Royall and his men. On October 17 a large Cheyenne war party attacked them. There followed a classic little fight in which the Cheyennes tested the powers claimed by an Óhméséheso warrior named Wolf Man, who was said to possess the ability to protect those he chose from bullets. The Spencer carbines proved him wrong, causing the death of two of his five volunteers. The disappointed Cheyennes departed, and Carr and his escort returned to Fort Wallace.[15]

Sheridan's fall campaign proved a humiliating failure in terms of success in battle. It did, however, keep the Indians on the move and unable to hunt, thus limiting their winter food supply. And when winter came, Sheridan's luck changed. Early on the morning of November 27, Custer, returned to active duty at the request of Sheridan and again acting as field commander of the Seventh Cavalry, led his men in a surprise attack against the sleeping village of Black Kettle's Southern Eaters band of peaceful Cheyennes. The attack was in keeping with the policy approved by Sherman and Sheridan that the entire tribe was to be held responsible and punished for the raids and "crimes" of any war parties. It resulted in the death of between 29 and 38 Indians, including council chiefs Little Rock and Black Kettle, Black Kettle's wife, and 12 other men (two of them Arapahoes), 11 or 12 other women (two of them Lakotas), and the rest children. Perhaps twice as many were wounded. Custer originally claimed 103 warriors killed and 53 women and children captured. He later revised those figures upward to 140 "warriors" killed and estimated the total of those killed, wounded, and missing at close to 300—more than were in the camp.[16]

Although the army would refer to the attack as the Battle of the Washita, it was not a battle in the conventional sense of two opposing forces of

[15] Berthrong, *Southern Cheyennes*, 314–16; Grinnell, *Fighting Cheyennes*, 293–97; Hyde, *Life of George Bent*, 309–11; Leckie, *Military Conquest*, 83–86; Powell, *People of the Sacred Mountain*, 1:583–87; Utley, *Frontier Regulars*, 148–49.
[16] Greene, *Washita*, 116–38, 188–91.

armed combatants engaging in a prolonged struggle. Rather it was an offensive strike against a sleeping village containing a large number of noncombatant women, children, and elderly. Little or no effort was made to distinguish between genders or age during the initial attack, often difficult in the heat of battle. When active combat ended, all wounded males were deliberately and summarily executed by the soldiers. Of the approximately 875 Cheyenne horses captured, most were slaughtered on Custer's order. Except for the taking of the 53 women and children as captives, it came perilously close to being a massacre in the manner of Sand Creek but nonetheless was within the scope of Custer's orders to destroy Cheyenne villages and horses, kill all warriors, and take captive all women and children. On the army side, Maj. Joel Elliott, Capt. Louis M. Hamilton, and eighteen enlisted men were killed during the fight, while Capt. Albert Barnitz, 1st Lt. Tom Custer, and 2nd Lt. T. J. March were wounded, along with twelve enlisted men. Two of the injured enlisted men subsequently died of their wounds.[17]

Sheridan continued applying pressure on all Indians of the southern plains for the remainder of the winter of 1868–69. Columns of cavalry were kept on the prowl, seeking the camps of Indians away from their assigned reservations, even though this was expressly permitted by the Medicine Lodge treaties. Sherman and Sheridan simply ignored those provisions, but by enforcing the remainder, they intended to achieve confinement of the Indians. On Christmas Day 1868, Maj. (Bvt. Lt. Col.) Andrew Evans and his Third Cavalry troopers stumbled on the village of Horse Back's Nokoni Comanches at Soldier Spring, on the north fork of the Red River. The Indians were dispersed with howitzer fire, and then their lodges and the contents were burned. Fear and starvation soon forced most of the Kiowas and Comanches still off of the reservation to surrender. In March of 1869 Custer led nine companies of the Seventh Cavalry and the Nineteenth Kansas Volunteer Cavalry in search of any Cheyennes south of the Arkansas, although that was where they were allowed to hunt by the written terms of the Medicine Lodge treaty. On March 15 he found two villages on Sweetwater Creek near the present Texas-Oklahoma border. Altogether more than half of the living council chiefs of the Cheyenne tribe were in the two camps. The Dog Soldiers, southern Sutaio, and White Head's band of Óhmésêheso were then on a tributary of the Republican.[18]

[17] Ibid., 188–91.
[18] Hyde, *Life of George Bent*, 339–40; Powell, *People of the Sacred Mountain*, 2:706–707, 722.

Because two white women were said to be prisoners in the village, Custer did not immediately attack, as he had at the Washita, but instead accepted an invitation to council with the Cheyenne chiefs. He was taken to the great ceremonial lodge of the Arrow Keeper, Stone Forehead, and met with fifteen council chiefs and Stone Forehead himself. There, in the presence of the Maahótse—the Sacred Arrows—Custer was invited to smoke the sacred pipe, and there he proclaimed his peaceful intentions. After the pipe was smoked out, Stone Forehead loosened the ashes in the catlinite bowl, lightly sprinkled them on Custer's boot, and prayed to Maheo that if Custer ever lied to or deceived the Tsistsistas again, he and all of the men with him would die. Later the chiefs rode to the cavalry camp to council with Custer, who then tried to seize all of them and Stone Forehead as hostages to secure the release of the two white women and removal of the Cheyenne villages to the vicinity of Camp Supply. All except four men, including two council chiefs (Lean Face and Curly Hair of the Poor People band), escaped. But to gain the release of the two chiefs and the warrior Fat Bear (all three of whom Custer threatened to hang if his demands were not met), the Cheyennes were forced to agree to give up the two white women and to surrender at Camp Supply when spring came and their horses regained their strength. Custer refused to release his hostages after the two white women were delivered and the surrender was promised, keeping them instead to ensure that the Cheyennes surrendered. This breach of promise caused the people to flee, taking their horse herds, lodge covers, and most possessions but leaving the lodge poles standing, some household possessions and equipment, and a few worn-out horses. Custer put the lodge poles and possessions to the torch, just as he had done at the Washita and Hancock had done on the Pawnee Fork. Then he led his column back to Camp Supply, where they found that, following Grant's election as president, Sherman was appointed to succeed him as General of the Army and Sheridan became commander of the Division of the Missouri. Operations were terminated, and Custer and his men returned to Fort Hays via Fort Dodge, taking their Cheyenne prisoners with them.[19]

When spring came in 1869, most southern bands of Cheyennes were camping in the country between the South Canadian River and the Washita, hunting and trying to restore their losses. The Dog Soldiers and southern Sutaio had moved to Beaver Creek to hunt. Stone Forehead sent runners to each of the bands, summoning them to a council of the southern chiefs

---

[19] Greene, *Washita*, 180–81; Powell, *People of the Sacred Mountain*, 2:708–17.

516   EPILOGUE

to be held on the Washita in early May, at which their future course of action was to be decided. The council did not go well, resulting in a split in the leadership. Little Robe and some of the others favored surrendering their country to find the peace and freedom from attack they yearned for. Others, especially the Dog Soldiers and Sutaio, refused to consider giving up their freedom and the right to remain in their own country. They returned north to Beaver Creek in great anger and once again set up their village on its banks. But hardly were they there when trouble came.[20]

Maj. Eugene Carr led his Fifth Cavalry troopers north from Fort Wallace, looking for signs of Cheyenne or Arapahoe villages not on the treaty reservation. In mid-May they found the trail of the village and began pursuit. A small hunting party alerted the Cheyennes to the approach of the soldiers, and they were able to escape. But a number of frightened women fled in panic, leaving their lodges and possessions behind. Carr burned the lot, causing great anger and resentment among the Dog Soldiers and Sutaio. They took vengeance by unleashing a series of violent attacks on white settlements in north-central Kansas and indeed across the width of their country. From late May through early July they struck hard, derailing a train on the Kansas Pacific Railroad, destroying wagon trains, burning cabins, killing male settlers and raping their women. Custer led the Seventh Cavalry in search of them, but without success.[21]

Major Carr and the Fifth Cavalry had refitted at Fort McPherson and now returned south, looking for the raiders. This time they were reinforced by three well-armed companies of the Pawnee Battalion, led by Maj. Frank North and his brother, Luther. For several weeks the raids continued, with neither Carr nor Custer able to find the Cheyennes. In early July the Dog Soldiers, southern Sutaio, Two Strike's Sicangu, and Whistler's Oglalas were camping on Cherry Creek a few miles from where it flows into the South Fork of the Republican. Carr put his men and the Pawnees into camp at the mouth of that stream, unaware of the proximity of their quarry. Scouts from the villages discovered the soldier camp, and minor skirmishes followed on July 5 and July 8. Because of the closeness of their enemy, the Cheyenne and Lakota chiefs decided it was time to move north to safety, where, they hoped, they might be free to live their traditional roaming life. They broke camp and, after crossing the Arickaree Fork, the North Fork,

[20] Powell, *People of the Sacred Mountain*, 2:723–25.

[21] Berthrong, *Southern Cheyennes*, 340; Leckie, *Military Conquest*, 128; Powell, *People of the Sacred Mountain*, 2:725. The name of the railroad was changed to Kansas Pacific by Congress on March 3, 1869; Snell and Richmond, *Union and Kansas Pacific*, 347.

and finally Frenchman's Fork of the Republican, made camp at the springs flowing from White Butte (Summit Springs) to the South Platte. Here Tall Bull made a fatal mistake. With his people and their horses tired from their long and rapid journey, he decided to let them rest for two days. His warriors had set fires along their back trail to obliterate any trace of their passage, and they felt secure from detection despite reports from a Lakota war party that soldiers were on their trail. Made nervous by the report, the Sicangus and Oglalas, along with some Cheyennes, moved on across the South Platte for safety.[22]

Carr's Pawnee scouts spotted the Cheyennes and Lakotas crossing Frenchman's Fork and quickly reported it, resulting in a forced march in pursuit. Tall Bull had scouts out watching their back trail to the south, but Carr and his troops moved around them on the north undetected, prepared to strike from the northwest. Carr organized his men in two ranks of three parallel columns, double file, with the Pawnees on their left. The charge was sounded, and the cavalry and Pawnee scouts swept southeast toward the village. The only effective warning of the impending attack was that given by a brave fifteen-year-old Cheyenne boy who was herding horses. When he saw the Pawnees coming, he gathered up the herd and drove them at a gallop to the village to provide his people a means of escape. He was later killed trying to defend them. Everywhere there was chaos as the soldiers and Pawnees charged through and around the village. Escape lay only to the south, and there the women and children fled, protected by the fighting men as best they could. Almost totally surprised, the Cheyennes nevertheless managed a stout defense. Although the village was captured and fifty-two of its occupants killed, including many women and children, most escaped out onto the plains.[23]

The great chief Tall Bull, heartsick at the disaster his misjudgment had brought to his people, led those on foot to a ravine for protection—mostly the aged, women, and children, including two of his own wives. He stabbed his horse in the foot to signify that he would die there and was found shot through the head when the fighting ended. Other brave men died that day doing what they could to protect their people. It was a devastating blow, and Cheyenne tradition holds that it was the Pawnee scouts who were most responsible. Despite their losses, the Dog Soldiers and Sutaio were not destroyed. They came together again on the Republican and slowly began

---

[22] Powell, *People of the Sacred Mountain*, 2:728–34.

[23] Berthrong, *Southern Cheyennes*, 342–44; Grinnell, *Fighting Cheyennes*, 311–18; Powell, *People of the Sacred Mountain*, 2:28–34; Utley, *Frontier Regulars*, 311.

to replace the lost lodges and possessions that Carr's men had burned. Though they lost many horses, they still had the larger part of their herds. But what they no longer did have was the cohesive and adamant will to resist the taking of their country. They spent the rest of July and most of August along various branches of the Republican. Then, in August, Major Royall returned south with the Fifth Cavalry, and they were once again forced to stay on the move. Finally they split up on the South Fork of the Republican, Bull Bear leading his band of Dog Soldiers, along with Black Shin's southern Sutaio, southeast to rejoin the other southern bands. With them went twenty-two lodges of Tall Bull's people. White Horse and his Dog Soldiers rode north to the country of the northern bands, where they hoped to resume the old life. But the cold winters there and homesickness for their old country and relatives finally overcame their determination, and the following spring most returned south to begin a new life.[24]

While the winter campaign did much to force the southern bands of Cheyennes out of their country and onto the reservation, more than any other factor it was the surprise attack on the Dog Soldier camp at Summit Springs that truly ended Hancock's War. Without the resolve, the fighting spirit, and the leadership of the fierce Dog Soldiers, the cause of the People was irretrievably wounded. More fighting lay ahead in what would be known to whites as the Red River War, and to the Indians the War to Save the Buffalo. But for the Cheyennes and the other tribes of the southern plains, their freedom to live the old life in their own country was gone.

Soldiers and Warriors

Destiny takes strange turns in directing the lives of humans, and it did no less for those who played the most conspicuous parts in Hancock's War. Winfield Scott Hancock, whose decisions and judgment (or lack thereof), were responsible for igniting the fires of war on the southern plains, left it behind for other, more sedentary duties. Following a sometimes tumultuous period administering the Reconstruction laws in New Orleans, where he became identified with the white cause and the Democratic Party, he was transferred back to the Division of the Missouri by newly elected President Grant and became commander of the Department of the Dakota under General Sheridan. On the death of General Meade, the army's senior major general, he succeeded as commander of the Division of the

---

[24] Berthrong, *Southern Cheyennes*, 342–44; Grinnell, *Fighting Cheyennes*, 311–18; Powell, *People of the Sacred Mountain*, 2:728–35; Utley, *Frontier Regulars*, 157.

Atlantic, where he remained for the rest of his life. His tries for the Democratic nomination for president failed until 1880, when he narrowly lost the general election to James A. Garfield. He remained a dedicated soldier until his death on February 8, 1886. He never conceded any mistakes or lapses of judgment in his dealings with the Indians, and vigorously defended his actions through his reports, correspondence, and articles. Despite his failures on the western frontier, he was considered a good, generous, and warmhearted man by family and friends and during most of his life served his country faithfully to the best of his ability.

Of the other officers serving under Hancock in 1867, Gen. A. J. Smith remained as the Seventh Cavalry regimental colonel until May 6, 1869, when he resigned his commission and was appointed as postmaster of St. Louis, Missouri, by President Grant. He was succeeded as colonel of the regiment by Samuel D. Sturgis. Smith died on January 30, 1897. After leaving the Hancock expedition, Maj. Alfred Gibbs, the senior major of the Seventh Cavalry, spent most of his remaining career in commanding first Fort Riley and then Fort Hays, where he remained until October 1868. He then returned to Fort Leavenworth due to ill health and died there on December 26, 1868. His successor was Maj. (Bvt. Col.) Marcus Reno. For the ambitious and reckless George Armstrong Custer, who acted as field commander of the Seventh Cavalry during most of the period from 1867 until June 26, 1876, the Hancock expedition had provided his first experience in Indian warfare. Because the Indians had eluded and humiliated him, that experience apparently resulted in his determination never to allow their escape again. Thereafter he divided his forces to attack from different directions and thwart any attempt to flee. Except for Maj. Joel Elliott's detachment, that tactic worked at the Washita during his surprise attack on Black Kettle's sleeping village. But on June 26, 1876, it proved to be a terrible mistake for Custer, and he led 215 of his officers and men to their death at the Little Big Horn, fulfilling Stone Forehead's prophecy. Ironically, from failure and disgrace during the Hancock expedition, he was vaulted to prominence as the country's most celebrated Indian fighter, based on his actions at the Washita and later at the Little Big Horn, his only two significant Indian fights. Maj. Joel Elliott and Capt. Louis M. Hamilton both fell at the Washita, bringing an end to promising careers and, in Elliott's case, generating further controversy concerning Custer's judgment. Medicine Bill Comstock, the able army scout, was killed on the Smoky Hill by Cheyennes on August 16, 1868.

Jesse Leavenworth and Edward W. Wynkoop, the Indian agents involved with the Hancock expedition, both resigned within a year of the Medicine Lodge treaties. Wynkoop submitted his resignation after a dispute with Superintendent Murphy over the culpability of all Cheyennes for the actions of the war party that initiated the 1868 raiding. Both Wynkoop and Leavenworth returned to their eastern homes to pursue other careers, but Wynkoop never ceased defending his charges or condemning Custer's actions at the Washita. Following the election of President Grant, a new peace policy was initiated, calling for the appointment of agents designated by several religious bodies—for the Cheyennes it was the Quakers. No longer were treaties sought, and on August 10, 1869, President Grant signed an executive order creating a new reservation for the Cheyennes and the Arapahoes. Although clearly not where they wanted to be—in their old country—it was more to their liking than that created by the Medicine Lodge treaty. It was bounded on the north by the so-called Cherokee Outlet, on the east by the Cimarron River and the ninety-eighth meridian, on the south by the Comanche-Kiowa reservation, and on the west by the one-hundredth meridian—the western border of the Indian Territory south of the Cherokee Outlet. Here the Quakers tried, largely unsuccessfully, to educate Cheyenne children in English, to change the Indian culture from that of nomadic hunters to sedentary farmers, and to convert the Cheyennes to Christianity.

The most notable Cheyenne council chiefs and war leaders met varied fates. Roman Nose, the great Óhméséheso warrior, was killed while heroically leading a charge at the fight on the Arickaree in 1868, despite knowing his protective medicine was breached. The Dog Soldier chief Tall Bull died at Summit Springs the next year. Bull Bear and White Horse of the Dog Soldiers, Black Shin of the southern Sutaio, and Little Robe, the former Dog Soldier council chief, died peaceful deaths. Lean Face, the eighty-year-old council chief taken prisoner by Custer early in 1869, was killed by soldier guards at Fort Hays who thought he was trying to escape, but he thought they had come to kill him and the other two male prisoners. Gray Beard, who succeeded his father-in-law, Black Shin, as a council chief of the southern Sutaio, was shot and killed when he attempted to escape while being taken to the prison at Fort Marion, Florida, after the Red River War. For all of the Indians their confinement on the reservation was to be a time of tragedy, death, poverty, and despair. They suffer the effects of these terrible times to the present day.

Conclusion

Hancock's War ended with the Cheyennes and Arapahoes forced from their country and onto the reservation. It was the objective Hancock himself had intended to accomplish by "awing" the southern Plains tribes with the size and power of his expedition. Although he was not adverse to giving the Cheyennes a sound thrashing as an object lesson for themselves and the other tribes, he never considered that a long and difficult war would follow. His actions at the villages on the Pawnee Fork clearly triggered the conflict that began in 1867 and ended in late 1869. The Indians themselves credited him with it. But in a larger sense Hancock was merely the one who threw the first stone. If not him, it would have been someone else. The fundamental cause of war was the continuing entry of aggressive whites into the lands of the Plains Indians, the building of the railroads and wagon roads, the advancing line of white settlements, the taking of the land, the slaughter of the bison and other game, and other actions that led to the destruction of the Plains Indian way of life.

It was popular during the era of the western frontier to claim that the Indians freely transferred their lands to the government by treaty in exchange for liberal benefits in the form of food, clothing, shelter, and education in how to achieve the blessings of civilization. This view, to a degree, has persisted into the twenty-first century. But it was never true. If one considers the relative negotiating power of the parties to Indian treaties, it is clear that there was always a grossly unequal exchange of value brought about by whites, using their superior coercive bargaining position. In exchange for the promise of peace and freedom from white harassment, along with temporary support and supposed "education," Indians were expected to surrender their country, culture, and religion and move to generally unfamiliar locations where they could be trained to live as whites. The treaties themselves were almost universally achieved by force, aided by considerable fraud and misrepresentation perpetrated on a people who could neither read, write, nor understand the English language and who never intended to give away their country. And when the Indians failed to perform the literal terms of treaties they did not understand, it was they who were blamed and then subjected to military action to force their compliance. Adding insult to injury, unscrupulous whites devised ways of securing the treaty goods and annuities for themselves by fraudulent claims against them for alleged losses, trading whiskey for the goods and possessions of a despairing people, and other equally larcenous means.

If there is any clear conclusion to be drawn from the events leading to and stemming from Hancock's War, it is that the European immigrants who created our great democracy did so at the expense of and without regard to the rights of the Native peoples. It should be recognized by later generations that the lands of the Cheyennes, Arapahoes, and other Indian tribes were acquired not by valid treaties but rather through conquest by force of arms and deceit. Despite that conquest, however, they were and remain the only true native Americans. They fought and died for their country, and they lost. More remarkably, they continue to fight and die for the nation that subjugated them and are among its most faithful citizens. In the long run, perhaps, the Indians could justifiably say of whites that they truly kept only one of the promises made to them: they said they would take their country—and they did. It was the end of the dream.

Our lives are in the hands of the Creator. We are determined to defend our lands, and if it be His will, we wish to leave our bones upon them.

Tecumseh, Shawnee chief

You might as well expect the rivers to run backward as that any man who was born free should be contented to be penned up and denied liberty to go where he pleases.

Chief Joseph, Nez Percé

What treaty that the whites have kept has the red man broken? Not one. What treaty that the white man ever made with us have they kept? Not one. When I was a boy the Sioux owned the world; the sun rose and set on their land; they sent ten thousand men to battle. Where are the warriors today? Who slew them? Where are our lands? Who owns them?

Sitting Bull

Bibliography

Government Documents

U.S. Congress. House. "Difficulties with the Indian Tribes." House Ex. Doc. 240, 41 Cong., 2 Sess., vol. 7, 1870 (Serial 1418).

———. "Protection across the Continent." House Ex. Doc. 23, 39 Cong., 2 Sess., vol. 6, 1866 (Serial 1288).

U.S. Congress. Senate. "Condition of the Indian Tribes." Senate Report 156, 39 Cong., 2 Sess., 1867 (Serial 1279).

———. "Expeditions against the Indians." Senate Ex. Doc. 7, 40 Cong., 1 Sess., 1867 (Serial 1308).

———. "Fort Phil Kearny Massacre." Senate Ex. Doc. 16, 39 Cong., 2 Sess., 1867 (Serial 1277).

———. "Indian Hostilities." Senate Ex. Doc. 13, 40 Cong., 1 Sess., 1867 (Serial 1308).

U.S. Department of Agriculture, Soil Conservation Service. Soil surveys for the following Kansas counties: Barton, Dickenson, Edwards, Ellis, Ellsworth, Geary, Gove, Logan, Ness, Pawnee, Riley, Rush, Saline, Sherman, Trego, and Wallace.

U.S. Department of the Interior. *Annual Report of the Commissioner of Indian Affairs, 1867.* House Ex. Doc. 1, 40 Cong., 2 Sess., vol. 2 (Serial 1326).

———. *Annual Report of the Commissioner of Indian Affairs, 1868.* House Ex. Doc. 1, 40 Cong., 3 Sess., vol. 2 (Serial 1366).

———. "Indian Peace Commission Report to President Andrew Johnson, January 7, 1868." In *Annual Report of the Commissioner of Indian Affairs, 1868*, House Ex. Doc. 1, 40 Cong., 3 Sess., vol. 2 (Serial 1366).

———. Office of Indian Affairs. Letters Received, Record Group 95, NA.

———. Upper Arkansas Agency. Letters Sent, Record Group 95, NA.

U.S. Department of War. *Annual Report of the Secretary of War, 1867.* House Ex. Doc. 1, 40 Cong., 2 Sess., vol. 2, parts 1 and 2 (Serial 1324 and 1325).

———. *Annual Report of the Secretary of War, 1868.* House Ex. Doc. 1, 40 Cong., 3 Sess., vol. 3 (Serial 1367).

———. Office of the Adjutant General. Letters Received (1866, 1867), Record Group 94, NA.

———. Office of the Secretary of War. Letters Received (1865–69), Record Group 107, NA.

———. Office of the Secretary of War. Telegrams Received (1866–67), Record Group 107, NA.

———. U.S. Army Continental Commands (1821–1920), Record Group 393, NA.
    Division of the Mississippi. Letters Sent (1865–66, 1867).
    Division of the Missouri. Letters Received (1867) and Letters Sent (1867).
    Division of the Missouri, Department of the Missouri. Letters Received (1866, 1867) and Letters Sent (1866, 1867).
        ———. District of the Upper Arkansas. Letters Received (1867) and Letters Sent (1866, 1867).
        ———. Fort Hays, Kans. Letters Sent (1867).
        ———. Fort Wallace, Kans. Letters Sent (1867) and Post Returns (March 1866–December 1873).
        ———. Records of U.S. Army Mobile Units, Seventh Cavalry (1867–68).
    Division of the Missouri, Department of the Platte. Letters Received (1867).
U.S. Statutes at Large, vol. 7.

BOOKS

Armes, George A. *Ups and Downs of an Army Officer*. Washington, D.C.: privately published, 1900.

Astronomical Almanac. Washington, D.C.: U.S. Government Printing Office, 2004.

Athearn, Robert G. *William Tecumseh Sherman and the Settlement of the West*. Norman: University of Oklahoma Press, 1956.

Baldwin, Alice. *An Army Wife on the Frontier*. Salt Lake City: University of Utah Library, 1975.

Barnard, Sandy, ed. *Ten Years with Custer: A 7th Cavalryman's Memoirs*. Fort Collins, Colo.: Citizen Printing, 2001.

Bass, Althea. *The Arapaho Way*. New York: Charles N. Potter, 1966.

Bell, William A. *New Tracks in North America*. London: Chapman and Hall, 1870; New York: Scribner, Wellford and Co., 1870; reprint, Albuquerque, NM: Horn and Wallace, 1965.

Berthrong, Donald J. *The Cheyenne and Arapaho Ordeal*. Norman: University of Oklahoma Press, 1976.

———. *The Southern Cheyennes*. Norman: University of Oklahoma Press, 1963.

Boniface, 1st Lt. John J. *The Cavalry Horse and His Pack*. Kansas City, Mo.: Hudson-Kimberly Publishing Co., 1903; reprint, Minneapolis: C&K Publishing Co., 1977.

Buchanan, Rex, ed. *Kansas Geology*. Lawrence: University of Kansas Press, 1984.

Buchanan, Rex, and James R. McCauley. *Roadside Kansas*. Lawrence: University Press of Kansas, 1987.

Burkey, Blaine. *Custer, Come at Once*. Hays, Kans.: Thomas Moore Prep., 1976.

———. *Wild Bill Hickok: The Law in Hays City*. Hays, Kans.: Ellis County Historical Society, 1996.

Carley, Kenneth. *The Dakota War of 1862*. St. Paul: Minnesota Historical Society, 1961, 1976.

Carrington, Margaret I. *Absaraka, Home of the Crows*. Philadelphia: J. P. Lippincott, 1868.

Carter, William H. *Horses, Saddles and Bridles*. Santa Monica, Calif.: Quail Ranch Books, 1982.

Chalfant, William Y. *Dangerous Passage: The Santa Fe Trail and the Mexican War*. Norman: University of Oklahoma Press, 1994.

Chandler, Melbourne C. *Of GarryOwen in Glory: The History of the Seventh United States Cavalry*. Annandale, Va.: Turnpike Press, 1960.

Crawford, Samuel J. *Kansas in the Sixties*. Chicago: A. C. McClurg and Co., 1911.

Custer, Elizabeth B. *Tenting on the Plains*. New York: Charles L. Webster and Co., 1889.

Custer, George A. *My Life on the Plains*. New York: Sheldon and Company, 1874; New York: Citadel Press, 1962.

Custer, George A., et al. *Wild Life on the Plains and Horrors of Indian Warfare*. St. Louis: Continental Publishing Co., 1891; reprint, New York: Arno Press, and the New York Times, 1969.

Davidson, Homer K. *Black Jack Davidson, a Cavalry Commander on the Western Frontier*. Glendale, Calif.: Arthur H. Clark, 1974.

Dippie, Brian W., ed. *Nomad: George A. Custer in Turf, Field and Stream*. Austin: University of Texas Press, 1980.

Dobak, William A. *Fort Riley and Its Neighbors*. Norman: University of Oklahoma Press, 1998.

Dorsey, George A. *The Cheyenne*. Chicago: Field Columbian Museum, 1905; reprint, Fairfield, Wash.: Ye Galleon, 1975.

Eggenhofer, Nick. *Wagons, Mules and Men*. New York: Hastings House, 1961.

English-Cheyenne Student Dictionary. Lame Deer, Mont.: Language Research Department of the Northern Cheyenne, 1976.

Frost, Lawrence A. *The Court-martial of General George Armstrong Custer*. Norman: University of Oklahoma Press, 1968.

Gaeddert, G. Raymond. *The Birth of Kansas*. Lawrence: University of Kansas Press, 1940.

Gard, Wayne. *The Chisholm Trail*. Norman: University of Oklahoma Press, 1954.

Greene, Jerome A. *Washita: The U.S. Army and the Southern Cheyennes, 1867-1869*. Norman: University of Oklahoma Press, 2004.

Grinnell, George Bird. *The Cheyennes Indians: Their History and Way of Life*. 2 vols. New York: Cooper Square, 1962.

———. *The Fighting Cheyennes*. Norman: University of Oklahoma Press, 1956.

———. *Two Great Scouts and Their Pawnee Battalion*. Glendale, Calif.: Arthur H. Clark, 1928; reprint, Lincoln: University of Nebraska Press, 1973.

Hafen, LeRoy R. *Broken Hand*. Denver: Old West Publishing Co., 1931; reprint, Lincoln: University of Nebraska Press, 1981.

Hafen, LeRoy R., and Marion Young. *Fort Laramie and the Pageant of the West.* Glendale, Calif.: Arthur H. Clark, 1938; Fort Laramie Historical Association ed., Lincoln: University of Nebraska Press, 1984.

Haley, James L. *Apaches: A History and Cultural Portrait.* Garden City, N.Y.: Doubleday, 1981; reprint, Norman: University of Oklahoma Press, 1997.

Heitman, Francis B. *Historical Register and Dictionary of the United States Army, 1789–1903.* 2 vols. Washington, D.C.: U.S. Printing Office, 1903; reprint, Urbana: University of Illinois Press, 1965.

Hoebel, E. Adamson. *The Cheyennes.* New York: Holt, Rinehart and Winston, 1960.

Hoig, Stan. *The Sand Creek Massacre.* Norman: University of Oklahoma Press, 1961.

————. *The Western Odyssey of John Simpson Smith.* Glendale, Calif.: Arthur H. Clark, 1974.

Hollibaugh, E. F. *Biographical History of Cloud County, Kansas.* Privately published, 1903.

Horgan, Paul. *Lamy of Santa Fe.* New York: Farrar, Straus and Giroux, 1975.

Hutton, Paul Andrew. *Phil Sheridan and His Army.* Lincoln: University of Nebraska Press, 1985.

Hyde, George E. *Life of George Bent.* Edited by Savoie Lottinville. Norman: University of Oklahoma Press, 1968.

Inman, Henry. *The Old Santa Fe Trail.* New York: Macmillan, 1898.

Johnson, Randy, and Nancy P. Allan. *Find Custer! The Kidder Tragedy.* Privately published, 1988.

Jones, Douglas C. *The Treaty of Medicine Lodge.* Norman: University of Oklahoma Press, 1966.

Jordan, David M. *Winfield Scott Hancock: A Soldier's Life.* Bloomington: Indiana University Press, 1988.

Kansas Constitutional Convention. *Proceedings.* Reprint, Topeka: Kansas State Printer, 1920.

Kappler, Charles J., comp. and ed. *Indian Affairs: Laws and Treaties.* 2 vols. Washington, D.C.: U.S. Government Printing Office, 1904.

Kennedy, W. J. D., ed. *On the Plains with Custer and Hancock: The Journal of Isaac Coates, Army Surgeon.* Boulder, Colo.: Johnson Books, 1997.

Killoren, John J. *"Come, Blackrobe": DeSmet and the Indian Tragedy.* Norman: University of Oklahoma Press, 1994.

Knight, Oliver. *Following the Indian Wars.* Norman: University of Oklahoma Press, 1960.

Kraenzel, Carl Frederick. *The Great Plains in Transition.* Norman: University of Oklahoma Press, 1955.

Leckie, William H. *The Military Conquest of the Southern Plains.* Norman: University of Oklahoma Press, 1963.

Lee, Wayne C., and Howard C. Raynesford. *Trails of the Smoky Hill.* Caldwell, Idaho: Caxton Printers, 1980.

Llewellyn, Karl N., and E. Adamson Hoebel. *The Cheyenne Way.* Norman: University of Oklahoma Press, 1941.

Lowe, Percival G. *Five Years a Dragoon.* Norman: University of Oklahoma Press, 1965.

Mayhall, Mildred P. *The Kiowas.* Norman: University of Oklahoma Press, 1962.

McCoy, Joseph H. *Historic Sketches of the Cattle Trade in the West and Southwest.* Kansas City, Mo.: Ramsey, Millet and Hudson, 1874.

Mead, James R. *Trading and Hunting on the Great Plains.* Edited by Schuyler Jones. Norman: University of Oklahoma Press, 1986.

Merington, Marguerite. *The Custer Story.* New York: Devin-Adair, 1950; reprint, Lincoln: University of Nebraska Press, 1987.

Merriam, Daniel F. *The Geologic History of Kansas.* State Geological Survey of Kansas Bulletin 162. Lawrence: University of Kansas Publications, 1975.

Mooney, James. *Calendar History of the Kiowa Indians.* Washington, D.C.: Smithsonian Institution Press, 1898; reprint, 1979.

Nadeau, Remi. *Fort Laramie and the Sioux.* Englewood Cliffs, N.J.: Prentice-Hall, 1967; Lincoln: University of Nebraska Press, 1982.

Nichols, Roger L. *General Henry Atkinson: A Western Military Career.* Norman: University of Oklahoma Press, 1965.

Nye, Wilbur Sturtevant. *Plains Indian Raiders.* Norman: University of Oklahoma Press, 1968.

Oliva, Leo E. *Fort Dodge: Sentry of the Western Plains.* Topeka: Kansas State Historical Society, 1998.

————. *Fort Harker: Defending the Journey West.* Topeka: Kansas State Historical Society, 2000.

————. *Fort Hays: Keeping Peace on the Plains.* Topeka: Kansas State Historical Society, 1980; rev. ed., 1996.

————. *Fort Larned: Guardian of the Santa Fe Trail.* Topeka: Kansas State Historical Society, 1982; rev. ed., 1997.

————. *Fort Wallace: Sentinel on the Smoky Hill Trail.* Topeka: Kansas State Historical Society, 1998.

————. *Soldiers on the Santa Fe Trail.* Norman: University of Oklahoma Press, 1967.

Page, Thomas. *Legislative Apportionment in Kansas.* Lawrence: University of Kansas, 1952.

Powell, Peter J. *People of the Sacred Mountain.* 2 vols. San Francisco: Harper and Row, 1981.

————. *Sweet Medicine.* 2 vols. Norman: University of Oklahoma Press, 1969.

Prairie and Range Plants. Hays, Kans.: Fort Hays State University, 1989.

Pride, W. F. *The History of Fort Riley.* Fort Riley, Kans.: privately published, 1926.

Reedstrom, E. Lisle. *Custer's 7th Cavalry: From Fort Riley to the Little Big Horn.* New York: Sterling, 1992.

Rosa, Joseph G. *They Called Him Wild Bill.* Norman: University of Oklahoma Press, 1964; 2nd ed., 1974.

Rydjord, John. *Indian Place Names.* Norman: University of Oklahoma Press, 1968.

————. *Kansas Place Names*. Norman: University of Oklahoma Press, 1972.

Schultz, Duane. *Month of the Freezing Moon*. New York: St. Martin's Press, 1990.

Simmons, Marc, and Hal Jackson. *Following the Santa Fe Trail*. Santa Fe, NM: Ancient City Press, 1984, 2001.

Stands in Timber, John, and Margot Liberty. *Cheyenne Memories*. New Haven: Yale University Press, 1967.

Stanley, Henry M. *My Early Travels and Adventures in America*. Lincoln: Bison Books, University of Nebraska Press, 1982. Originally published as *My Early Travels in America and Asia*, vol. 1 (London: S. Low, Marston, 1895).

Strate, David K. *Sentinel on the Cimarron*. Dodger City, Kans.: Cultural Heritage and Arts Center, 1970.

Terrell, John Upton. *The Plains Apaches*. New York: Thomas Y. Crowell, 1975.

Thomas, Clayton L., ed. *Taber's Cyclopedic Medical Dictionary*. 16th ed. Philadelphia: F. A. Davis, 1989.

Trenholm, Virginia Cole. *The Arapahoes*. Norman: University of Oklahoma Press, 1970.

Utley, Robert M. *Cavalier in Buckskin*. Norman: University of Oklahoma Press, 1988; rev. ed., 2001.

————. *Frontier Regulars: The United States Army and the Indians, 1866–1891*. New York: Macmillan, 1973.

————. *Frontiersmen in Blue: The United States Army and the Indians, 1848–1865*. New York: Macmillan, 1967.

————. *The Indian Frontier of the American West, 1846–1890*. Albuquerque: University of New Mexico Press, 1984.

————, ed. *Life in Custer's Cavalry: Diaries and Letters of Albert and Jennie Barnitz, 1867–1868*. New Haven: Yale University Press, 1977.

Walton, George. *Sentinel of the Plains: Fort Leavenworth and the American West*. Englewood Cliffs, N.J.: Prentice-Hall, 1973.

U.S. Department of War, Surgeon General's Office. *Report on Barracks and Hospitals, December 5, 1870*. Circular 4. Reprint, New York: Sol Lewis, 1974.

Washburn, Wilcomb E. *The American Indian and the United States: A Documentary History*. 4 vols. New York: Random House, 1973; reprint, Westport, Conn.: Greenwood Press, 1979.

White, Lonnie J. *Hostiles and Horse Soldiers*. Boulder, Colo.: Pruett, 1972.

Williams, Dallas. *Fort Sedgwick, Colorado Territory*. Sedgwick, Colo.: F.S.R. Trust, 1993.

Wooster, Robert. *The Military and the United States Indian Policy, 1865–1903*. New Haven: Yale University Press, 1988; reprint, Lincoln: University of Nebraska Press, 1995.

Worcester, Donald E., ed. *Forked Tongues and Broken Treaties*. Caldwell, Idaho: Caxton Printers, 1975.

Wright, Robert M. *Dodge City, The Cowboy Capital, and the Great Southwest*. Wichita, Kans.: Wichita Eagle Press, 1913.

Wynkoop, Edward W. *The Tall Chief: The Unfinished Autobiography of Edward W. Wynkoop, 1856–1866.* Edited by Christopher B. Gerboth. Colorado Historical Society Monograph 9. Denver, 1993.

ARTICLES, LETTERS, AFFIDAVITS, AND MANUSCRIPTS

Barry, Louise. "The Ranch at Cimarron Crossing." *Kansas Historical Quarterly* 39, no. 3 (1973): 345–66.

———. "The Ranch at Cow Creek Crossing." *Kansas Historical Quarterly* 38, no. 4 (1972): 416–44.

———. "The Ranch at Little Arkansas Crossing." *Kansas Historical Quarterly* 38, no. 3 (1972): 287–94.

———. "The Ranch at Walnut Creek Crossing." *Kansas Historical Quarterly* 37, no. 2 (1971): 121–47.

Beach, James H. "Old Fort Hays." Kansas Historical Collections 11 (1909–10): 571–81.

Betts, John H. Deposition of August 24, 1867. In *Wells Fargo and Co. v. United States et al.*, U.S. Court of Claims, 10110, 10032, and 10572.

Blackburn, Forrest R. "The 18th Kansas Cavalry and the Indian War." *Trail Guide: The Kansas City Posse of the Westerners* 9, no. 1 (1964): 6.

Burgess, Henderson Lafayette. "The Eighteenth Kansas Volunteer Cavalry." Kansas Historical Collections 13 (1913–14): 534–38.

Chalfant, William Y. "In Search of Pretty Encampment." *Wagon Tracks* (Santa Fe Trail Association) 6, no. 3 (1992): 12–15.

Clapsaddle, David. "The Wet and Dry Routes of the Santa Fe Trail." *Kansas History* 15, no. 2 (1992): 98–115.

Davis, Theodore R. "A Summer on the Plains." *Harper's New Monthly Magazine* 36 (December 1867–May 1868): 292–307.

———. "With Generals in Their Camp Homes: General George A. Custer." Kansas State Historical Society, Manuscripts Department, Collection M20, Theodore R. Davis file.

Garfield, Marvin. "Defense of the Kansas Frontier, 1866–1867." *Kansas Historical Quarterly* 1, no. 4 (1932): 326–44.

Grant, Ulysses S. U.S. Grant Papers. Library of Congress, Washington, D.C.

Gray, John S. "Will Comstock, Scout: The Natty Bumppo of Kansas." *Montana, the Magazine of Western History* 20, no. 3 (1970): 2–15.

Hunnius, Ado. Sketches of Fort Zarah in 1867. Manuscript Division, Hunnius Collection. Kansas State Historical Society.

Jenness, George B. "The Battle of Beaver Creek." Kansas Historical Collections 9 (1905–1906): 443–52.

Keogh, Myles, to Myles Moylan, May 13, 1867, Fort Wallace, Kans. Ayers Collection (228/843), Newberry Library, Chicago.

Mead, James R. "The Saline River Country in 1859." Kansas Historical Collections 9 (1905–1906): 8–19.

Millbrook, Minnie Dubbs. "Custer's First Scout in the West." *Kansas Historical Quarterly* 39, no. 1 (1973): 75–95.

———. "The West Breaks In General Custer." *Kansas Historical Quarterly* 36, no. 2 (1970): 113–48.

Montgomery, Mrs. Frank C. "Fort Wallace." Kansas Historical Collections 17 (1926–28): 189–283.

Moore, Horace L., to Gov. Samuel Crawford, August 31, 1867, Governor's Correspondence, Kansas State Historical Society, Topeka.

Pliley, Allison J. "Reminiscences of a Plainsman." *Olathe Mirror*, March 19 and 26, 1931.

Powell, Peter J. Letters to W. Y. Chalfant, June 9, 2004, and July 11, 2005.

Prowers, Ramon, and Gene Younger. "Cholera on the Plains: The Epidemic of 1867 in Kansas." *Kansas Historical Quarterly* 37, no. 4 (1971): 351–93.

Sherman, William T. William T. Sherman Papers. Library of Congress, Washington, D.C.

Shortridge, James R. "The 'Missing' Railroad Towns along the Union Pacific and the Santa Fe Lines in Kansas." *Kansas History* 26, no. 3 (2003): 187–205.

Snell, Joseph W., and Robert W. Richmond. "When the Union and Kansas Pacific Built through Kansas." *Kansas Historical Quarterly* 38, part 1, no. 3 (1966): 161–86, and part 2, no. 3 (1966): 334–52.

"Some Lost Towns of Kansas." Kansas Historical Collections 12 (1911–12): 426–90.

Stanley, Henry M. "A British Journalist Reports the Medicine Lodge Peace Councils of 1867." *Kansas Historical Quarterly* 33, no. 3 (1967): 249–320.

Swan, Nate. Deposition of, September 7, 1867, in *Wells-Fargo and Co. v. United States et al.*, 10110, 10032, 10573.

Tisdale, Henry. "Travel by Stage in the Early Days." Kansas Historical Collections 7 (1901–1902): 459–64.

Voight, Barton R. "The Death of Lyman S. Kidder." *South Dakota History* 6, no. 1 (1975): 1–32.

Maps

Bryan, Francis T. "Reconnaissance of a Road from Fort Riley to Bridger's Pass, June 1856–Mar. 1857." NA, RG 77, Roads, 144.

———. "Reconnaissance of a Road from Fort Riley to the Big Timbers, July–Sept. 1855." NA, RG 77, Roads, 139.

Cooke, Philip St. George. "Map of the Santa Fe Trace from Independence to the Crossing of the Arkansas (with part of the Military Road from Fort Leavenworth, West Missouri), 1843." NA, RG 77, Q 17.

Freyhold, E. "Map Exhibiting the Lines of March Passed Over by the Troops of the United States during the year ending June 30, 1858, Nov. 1858." NA, RG 77, Civil Works Map File, US-481.

Jackson, Henry. "Map of Indian Territory, with parts of neighboring states and territories, Sept. 1869." NA, RG 77, Q 148.

Merrill, William E. "Map of Kansas, with parts of neighboring states and territories, Sept. 1869." NA, RG 77, Q 140.

U.S. Army. "Kansas Military Map." 2nd ed., with corrections by Lt. Henry Jackson, Seventh Cavalry, Acting Chief Engineer, Department of the Missouri, Oct. 1868. NA, RG 77.

U.S. Department of War, Engineer Bureau. "Section of the Map of the States of Kansas and Texas and Indian Territory, with Parts of the Territories of Colorado and New Mexico, 1867." Plate 119, Atlas to Accompany the Official Records of the Union and Confederate Armies, 1861–65. NA, RG 77.

U.S. Geological Survey. USGA 1:100,000 Scale Metric Topographic Maps, 30 × 60 Minute Quadrangle. Colorado: Bonny Reservoir, Fort Morgan, Julesburg, Last Chance, Sterling, and Wray. Kansas: Goodland, Hays, Healy, Norton, Plainville, St. Francis, and. Sharon Springs.

——. USGA 1:250,000 Scale Metric Topographic Maps. Colorado: Sterling, NK 13-12; and Limon, NJ 13-3. Kansas: Goodland, NJ 14-1; Beloit, NJ 14-2; Scott City, NJ 14-4; and Great Bend, NJ 14-5. Nebraska: North Platte, NK 14-7; McCook, NK 14-10; and Grand Island, NK 14-11.

——. USGA 1:500,000 Scale Metric Topographic Maps. State of Colorado, State of Kansas, and State of Nebraska.

U.S. Office of Indian Affairs. "Map of Nebraska and Northern Kansas." N.d. NA, RG 75, Map 396.

NEWSPAPERS AND PERIODICALS

Army and Navy Journal (Washington, D.C.), April 6, 1867.

Frank Leslie's Illustrated Newspaper (New York), May 11, 1867.

Harper's Weekly (New York), May 11 and 25, June 8 and 29, July 6, and August 3, 17, 24, 1867.

Junction City Weekly Union (Junction City, Kans.), April 18 and 27, May 2, June 1, and August 3 and 24, 1867.

Kansas Daily Tribune (Lawrence), August 4, 7, 9, 13, and 22 and November 11, 1867.

Leavenworth Daily Conservative (Leavenworth, Kans.), July 7 and August 10, 11, and 23, 1867.

Leavenworth Daily Times (Leavenworth, Kans.), August 8 and 9, 1867.

Missouri Republican (St. Louis), October 24, 26, and 29 and November 9, 21, 23, and 30, 1867.

Olathe Mirror (Olathe, Kans.), March 19 and 26, 1931.

Rocky Mountain News (Denver), April 20, 1967.

INDEX

CPSIA information can be obtained at www.ICGtesting.com
Printed in the USA
LVOW10s0035230414

382836LV00001B/1/P